Communicating in Small Groups

Principles and Practices

Twelfth Edition

Steven A. Beebe
Texas State University

John T. Masterson
Texas Lutheran University

Portfolio Manager: *Priya Christopher*
Portfolio Manager Assistant: *Anna Austin*
Product Marketer: *Christopher Brown*
Content Developer: *Elisa Rogers*
Art/Designer: *SPi Global*
Digital Studio Course Producer: *Amanda A. Smith*
Full-Service Project Manager: *Bhanuprakash Sherla, SPi Global*
Compositor: *SPi Global*
Printer/Binder: *LSC Communications, Inc.*
Cover Printer: *LSC Communications, Inc.*
Cover Design: *Lumina Datamatics, Inc*
Cover Art: *Rawpixel.com/Shutterstock*

Acknowledgments of third party content appear on pages 283–286, which constitute an extension of this copyright page.

Library of Congress Cataloging-in-Publication Data
Names: Beebe, Steven A., 1950- author. | Masterson, John, author.
Title: Communicating in small groups : principles and practices / Steven A. Beebe, Texas State University, John T. Masterson, Texas Lutheran University.
Description: Twelfth edition. | Hoboken, NJ : Pearson, [2020] | Includes bibliographical references and index. | Identifiers: LCCN 2019024281 | ISBN 9780135712160 (Rental Edition) | ISBN 0135712165 (Rental Edition) | ISBN 9780134636931 (Loose-Leaf Edition) | ISBN 0134636937 (Loose-Leaf- Edition) | ISBN 9780134636900 (Instructor's Review Copy) | ISBN 0134636902 (Instructor's Review Copy) | ISBN 9780134636177 (Revel Access Code Card) | ISBN 0134636171 (Revel Access Code Card) | ISBN 9780135712221 (Revel Combo Card) | ISBN 013571222X (Revel Combo Card)
Subjects: LCSH: Small groups. | Communication in small groups. | Group relations training.
Classification: LCC HM736 .B43 2020 | DDC 302.3/4--dc23
LC record available at https://lccn.loc.gov/2019024281

2 2019

Revel Access Code Card
ISBN-10: 0-13-463617-1
ISBN-13: 978-0-13-463617-7

Revel Combo Card
ISBN-10: 0-13-571222-X
ISBN-13: 978-0-13-571222-1

Rental Edition
ISBN-10: 0-13-571216-5
ISBN-13: 978-0-13-571216-0

Loose-Leaf Edition
ISBN-10: 0-13-463693-7
ISBN-13: 978-0-13-463693-1

Instructor's Review Copy
ISBN-10: 0-13-463690-2
ISBN-13: 978-0-13-463690-0

Dedicated to
Sue and Nancy

Brief Contents

Contents

Preface

From our first edition to this, our twelfth edition, our goal in writing this book has remained the same: to write a book that students find interesting and practical, and that instructors find clear and comprehensive. We are pleased that the previous 11 editions continue to be praised and widely used by both teachers and students and that our text remains a market leader.

We have written the twelfth edition of *Communicating in Small Groups: Principles and Practices* to serve as the primary text for a college-level course that focuses on group communication. We continue to seek a balanced approach to presenting the latest small group principles informed by classic and contemporary research, while also identifying practical practices that bring those principles to life.

New to the Twelfth Edition

In this new edition, we have thoroughly updated the research that anchors the principles and skills we present, incorporated new pedagogical features to enhance student learning, and added new applications of technology to enhance engagement collaboration. Here's an overview of what's new.

REVEL LEARNING PLATFORM We are excited to offer instructors and students a Revel version of *Communicating in Small Groups: Principles and Practices.* Revel provides students with interactive demonstrations, simulations, and video examples that help bring the topics covered in small group communication courses to life. It embeds these learning tools in a format that presents the text in new and visually engaging ways. Students will also benefit from Revel's abundant opportunities for testing their knowledge and applying it to real-world scenarios.

EXPANDED EMPHASIS ON VIRTUAL COLLABORATION From the first page of Chapter 1 through the appendices, we have added new research-based information about the role that technology plays in facilitating collaboration in contemporary society. Students who have used technological tools all their lives are becoming increasingly more sophisticated about the use of technology. In this twelfth edition, we have revised our coverage of technology and the use of new media, including the use of avatars and artificial intelligence, to reflect students' existing knowledge about technology while also building on it.

UPDATED EMPHASIS ON GROUP COMMUNICATION SKILLS Students take a course in group communication not only to improve their knowledge, but also to become more skilled communicators. How to develop a discussion plan, create an agenda, facilitate a meeting, manage conflict, make efficient and effective decisions, lead others, and collaboratively solve problems are just a few of the skill sets that are presented. To help students bolster their communication competence, we have expanded our application of specific group communication skills throughout the book. In addition, we've added new examples and research applications to ensure that students can increase their group communication skill.

EXPANDED AND UPDATED LEARNING OUTCOMES To help students learn, review, and master the chapter content, we have significantly expanded the number of learning outcomes included in each chapter. These learning outcomes directly correspond to specific chapter headings and sections. Students can easily confirm their mastery of each section of the material by reviewing the chapter objectives.

STREAMLINED CHAPTER CONTENT Sometimes less is more. To help students quickly grasp ideas and information, we have looked for ways to condense the text's content by using bullets, new subheads, and streamlined prose to assist students' mastery of the material.

UPDATED DISCUSSION OF CONTEMPORARY GROUP COMMUNICATION RESEARCH As we have for more than 35 years, we've done our best to find the latest research about small group communication and add it to our already comprehensive digest of small group communication research applications. Each chapter includes new and updated references to the latest applications of and insights into communicating in small groups.

AND MUCH, MUCH MORE Each chapter includes new examples, illustrations, cartoons, and updated pedagogy to make *Communicating in Small Groups: Principles and Practices* the best learning tool possible. We've made a special effort to streamline our coverage of content to make room for new research and additional pedagogical features so as not to add to the book's overall length.

Content Highlights

Here's a brief summary highlighting several specific changes we've made to the twelfth edition:

Chapter 1: Introducing Group Principles and Practices

- New research conclusions about the impact of social media on group collaboration
- New examples related to virtual collaboration
- New research about the importance of communication to developing effective teams
- Streamlined discussion of the advantages and disadvantages of groups
- Updated coverage of virtual collaboration

Chapter 2: Understanding Small Group Communication Theory

- New, more contemporary case studies
- Streamlined discussion of theory and theory building
- Expanded discussion of communication and technology
- Updated research base and new examples relevant to nontraditional students

Chapter 3: Facilitating Group Development

- Enhanced discussion of technology as it affects group formation
- Updated research base, especially as it relates to virtual groups and culture
- New research on the effects of homogeneity and diversity in group composition
- New research on culture and group formation

Chapter 4: Preparing to Collaborate

- Streamlined coverage of how to develop a discussion plan
- New information about how to gather and analyze information
- New and updated coverage of how to develop a meeting agenda
- New research conclusions about how information is shared during group discussion
- Updated discussion of virtual collaboration

Chapter 5: Relating to Others in Groups

- Expanded treatment of gender, culture, and sexual orientation
- Streamlined discussions throughout for easier student access to key points
- New research on workplace incivility and productivity
- New research and discussion of trust in face-to-face and virtual teams
- Enhanced discussion of technology throughout

Chapter 6: Improving Group Climate

- Updated, more contemporary examples
- New research about cohesiveness in virtual teams
- Streamlined discussion of defensive and supportive communication
- New research and research-based recommendations about building cohesiveness in virtual teams
- Amplified discussion of technology and group climate

Chapter 7: Enhancing Communication Skills in Groups

- Chapter streamlined for easier student access
- Research base updated throughout
- New, more contemporary examples for nontraditional students
- New research and discussion of critical-listening and task-listening styles

Chapter 8: Managing Conflict

- Updated coverage of the role of culture in managing conflict
- New discussion and research about relational conflict in groups
- Streamlined coverage of conflict management styles
- Updated discussion of virtual collaboration and conflict management
- New research about strategies for developing consensus

Chapter 9: Leading Groups

- New, more contemporary examples
- Revised discussion of the Minnesota Studies
- New research on transformational cultures in virtual teams

- New research on leadership and gender
- New research and discussion of shared leadership

Chapter 10: Making Decisions and Solving Problems

- New research about information sharing and group decision making
- Updated coverage of the "risky shift" phenomenon during both virtual and non virtual group discussion
- New research about artificial intelligence and group decision making
- New research about virtual collaboration and group problem solving
- Updated coverage of diversity and group problem solving

Chapter 11: Using Problem-Solving Techniques

- New references to the group development phases—forming, storming, norming, and performing
- New research about strategies and techniques for solving problems
- New applications of research about virtual collaboration and group problem solving
- Streamlined coverage of question-oriented approaches to group problem solving
- Moved Competent Group Communicator assessment instrument to the appendices

Chapter 12: Enhancing Creativity in Groups

- New research about the relationships among intuition, creativity, and group decision making
- New research about the importance of being open and receptive to ideas and group creativity
- New research conclusions about the value of providing ample time for group brainstorming
- New research about strategies for developing a climate of trust and enhanced group creativity
- New research conclusions about the role of avatars in enhancing group creativity

Appendices

- Appendix A, which highlights the principles and practices of effective meetings, has been thoroughly updated.
- Appendix B has been expanded to include current strategies for delivering group presentations.
- The Competent Group Communicator assessment form has been moved to a new Appendix C focusing on assessing small group problem-solving competencies.

Balanced Coverage: Principles and Practices

Communicating in Small Groups: Principles and Practices provides a carefully crafted integration of both principles and practices that provide a strong theoretical scaffolding for the practical "how to" skills needed for communicating in small groups. Theory without application can leave students understanding group principles but not knowing how to enhance their own performance. Conversely, presenting lists of techniques without providing an understanding of the principles that inform their skill would result in a laundry list of do's and don'ts without insight as to when to apply those skills. The balanced tension between theory and application, structure and interaction, and task and process is evident in all communication study, but especially in the dynamic context of a small group. We believe that emphasizing theory without helping students apply principles can result in highly informed, yet under-skilled group members. While our students often clamor for techniques to enhance their skills, such approaches alone do not give students the underlying principles they need to inform their newfound applications.

When we summarize research conclusions, we hear our students' voices echoing in our heads, asking, "So what?" In response to those queries, we ask ourselves how the research conclusions we cite can enhance the quality of collaboration. We seek to provide principles and practices of small group communication that make a real difference in our students' lives.

Both of us abhor boring meetings that seem adrift and pointless. Consequently, we draw upon our 80 years of combined university administrative and teaching experience as we sift through the latest research to keep our focus on application while anchoring our prescriptions in principled theory. Our goal is to provide a comprehensive, yet laser-focused compendium of the latest thinking about group and team communication.

Popular Features We've Retained

A hallmark of this book, according to educators and students, is our get-to-the-point writing style coupled with our comprehensive distillation of contemporary and classic group communication research. We continue to receive praise for the clear applications of the research we describe. We've done our best to keep the features that instructors and students like best about our book: its lively, engaging writing style; references to the most recent research; and emphasis on not overwhelming readers with unnecessary rambling narratives. As we have in previous editions, we've revised and updated all of our pedagogical features, including chapter objectives, discussion questions, and chapter activities. Case studies and a renewed emphasis on virtual collaboration are continuing features in this new edition.

Revel™

Educational technology designed for the way today's students read, think, and learn

When students are engaged deeply, they learn more effectively and perform better in their courses. This simple fact inspired the creation of Revel: an immersive learning experience designed for the way today's students read, think, and learn. Built in collaboration with educators and students nationwide, Revel is the newest, fully digital way to deliver respected Pearson content.

Revel enlivens course content with media interactives and assessments—integrated directly within the authors' narrative—that provide opportunities for students to read about and practice course material in tandem. This immersive educational technology boosts student engagement, which leads to better understanding of concepts and improved performance throughout the course.

Learn more about Revel: www.pearsonhighered.com/revel

Supplemental Resources for Instructors

The following resources are available for instructors. These can be downloaded at http://www.pearsonhighered.com/irc. Login required.

INSTRUCTOR'S MANUAL AND TEST BANK The Instructor's Manual portion of the IM/TB includes the following resources: sample syllabi for structuring the course; an outline and summary for each chapter that includes the major ideas covered; chapter objectives; discussion questions; and experiential activities. The Test Bank portion of the IM/TB contains multiple-choice, true/false, and essay questions, all of which are organized by chapter.

PEARSON MYTEST COMPUTERIZED TEST BANK The twelfth edition Test Bank comes with Pearson MyTest, a powerful assessment-generation program that helps instructors easily create and print quizzes and exams. You can do this online, allowing flexibility and the ability to efficiently manage assessments at any time. You can easily access existing questions and edit, create, and store questions using the simple drag-and-drop and Word-like controls. Each question comes with information on its level of difficulty and is also mapped to the appropriate learning objective. For more information, go to www.pearsonhighered.com/mytest.

POWERPOINT PRESENTATION The PowerPoint presentation that accompanies *Communicating in Small Groups* includes ADA-compliant lecture slides based on key concepts in the text and can be easily customized for your classroom.

Acknowledgments

More than four decades ago, we met as new college professors sharing an office at the University of Miami. Today, we live only miles apart in different Texas communities and remain united by a common bond of friendship that has grown stronger over the years. Our collaboration as friends continues to make this book a labor of love. This book is a partnership not only between us as authors, but also with a support team of scholars, editors, colleagues, reviewers, students, and family members.

We are grateful to those who have reviewed this edition of our book to help make this a more useful instructional resource. Specifically, we thank Traci Letcher, University of Kentucky; James Luhrey, Mercyhurst University; Terri Lynne Johnson, Cleveland State University; Yeprem P. Davoodian, Los Angeles Pierce College; Brandy Stamper, UNC Charlotte; Deena Godwin, Clark College; Stephen DiDomenico, State University of New York Plattsburgh; Scott McAfee, College of the Canyons; Raymond Ozley, University of Montevallo; Suzanne Atkin, Portland State University; and Rod Carveth, Morgan State University.

We continue to be thankful for the talented editorial staff at Pearson. We are especially grateful to our talented editor, Priya Christopher, for her guidance and keen attention to detail along with the wealth of ideas provided by our content developer Elisa Rogers. We also thank Bhanuprakash Sherla for his expert assistance in skillfully keeping us on track and managing the logistics of preparing this new edition. We will always be grateful for the invaluable support of our long-time editor, publisher, and friend, Karon Bowers.

Steve thanks his colleagues and students at Texas State University for their encouragement and support. Casey Chilton, Mike Cornett, and Sue Stewart are gifted teachers who offer advice, encouragement, and friendship. We especially thank Kosta Tovstiadi, who provided expert assistance in helping to gather research for this new edition; we appreciate his ongoing friendship and expertise. We also acknowledge Dennis and Laurie Romig of Side by Side Consulting, for their rich knowledge and practical insight about groups and teams that they have shared with us for many years. Sue Hall, Bob Hanna, and Chelsea Stockton are talented administrative assistants at Texas State and are invaluable colleagues who provide ongoing structure and interaction to maintain Steve's productivity.

John thanks his friends, colleagues, and students at Texas Lutheran University, who have taught, challenged, and inspired him.

Finally, as in our previous editions, we offer our appreciation and thanks to our families, who continue to teach us about the value of teamwork and collaboration. Our sons are taking their place in the world, and our spouses continue to be equal partners in all we do. John's sons, John III and Noah, are older than we both were when we began the first edition of this book. John III and Noah continue to make their dad smile with pride at their successes. Nancy Masterson continues, as always, as John's greatest love, best friend, and most respected critic.

Steve's sons, Mark and Matt, are now also older than their dad when he started this project. Matt and his wife Kara, both educators, teach us the power of supportive collaboration and teamwork. Steve's granddaughter, Mary, offers lessons of creativity, joy, and love. Mark and his wife Amanda continue to teach the importance of endurance and ever-present power of renewal, even when life presents ongoing challenges. Susan Beebe has been an integral part of the author team in this and every previous edition for 40 years. She continues to be Steve's personal Grammar Queen, life's love, and best friend.

Steven A. Beebe, San Marcos, Texas
John T. Masterson, Seguin, Texas

About the Authors

Steven A. Beebe

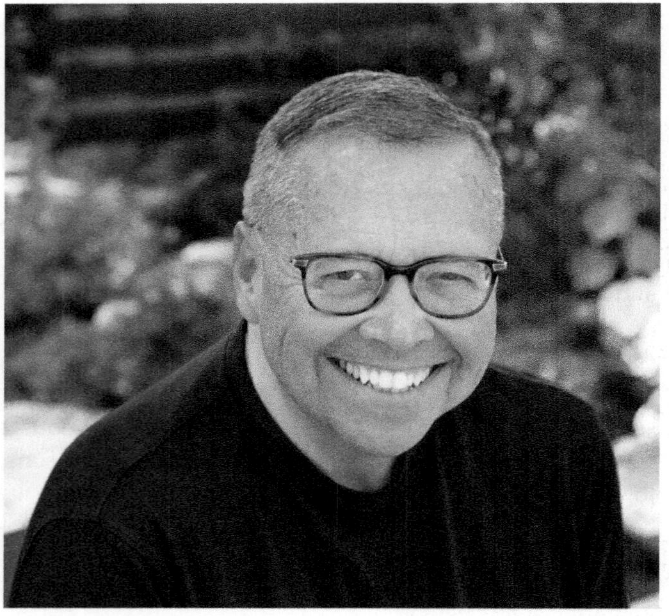

© Lancia E. Smith

Steven A. Beebe is Regents' and University Distinguished Professor *Emeritus* of Communication Studies at Texas State University. He served as chair of his department at Texas State for 28 years and concurrently as associate dean of the college of Fine Arts and Communication for 25 years. Before joining Texas State University, he was on the faculty of the University of Miami (Florida) for 10 years.

Professor Beebe is author and co-author of 12 books (with most books in multiple editions) that have been used at hundreds of universities throughout the world. He has also authored or co-authored more than 60 articles and book chapters and 150 professional papers with an emphasis on communication skill development.

Dr. Beebe has been a Visiting Scholar at both Oxford University and Cambridge University, and has given lectures and conference presentations internationally. During his 15 visits to Russia, he helped to establish the first communication studies programs in that country.

Dr. Beebe served as president of the National Communication Association and has received his university's top research and service awards; he was recently named a Piper Professor for the State of Texas. The National Speaker's Association has named him Outstanding Communication Professor in America.

He enjoys traveling, reading, researching and writing about C. S. Lewis, and playing the piano, and is a struggling cellist.

John T. Masterson

John T. Masterson is Executive Vice President and Provost *Emeritus* of Texas Lutheran University. He taught communication courses for more than 30 years and has presented or published dozens of papers and articles as well as books co-authored with Steven A. Beebe. He has been the recipient of numerous awards and honors for his teaching, scholarship, and service.

Prior to his move to Texas, Dr. Masterson served the University of Miami (Florida) for 22 years as professor of communication, associate dean of the School of Communication, dean of the Graduate School of International Studies, and vice provost for Undergraduate Affairs.

In his spare time, Dr. Masterson plays guitar and sings with the band Tin Roof Texas. Whenever possible, he and his wife Nancy take long road trips on their Harley Davidson motorcycle.

Chapter 1

Introducing Group Principles and Practices

"Working together works."

—Rob Gilbert

Learning Objectives

1.1 Define small group communication

1.2 Evaluate teams for effective practices

1.3 Identify the advantages and disadvantages of participating in small groups

1.4 Compare primary and secondary groups

1.5 Use methods to make virtual group meetings effective

1.6 Describe competencies of small group communication

Human beings collaborate. We are raised in family groups. We are educated and entertained in groups, and we work and worship in groups. We feel the need to establish collaborative relationships with others.

Regardless of your career choice, you will spend a considerable part of your work life collaborating with others in groups and teams. One survey of *Fortune* 500 companies found that 81 percent use team-based approaches to organize the work that needs to be done.[1] In addition, 77 percent use temporary teams and work groups when new projects develop.[2] The typical manager spends one fourth of the workweek in group meetings. In fact, the higher you rise in position and leadership authority, the more time you'll spend in meetings. Top-level leaders spend up to two-thirds of their time—an average of three days a week—in meetings or preparing for meetings.[3]

Not only will you spend time working with others in groups and teams, but you'll also find that the ability to collaborate with others is among the highest-valued skills in the workplace.[4]

Not all of our collaborations are face to face. In the twenty-first century, our collaboration has dramatically increased because of our use of technology. We are "hyper-connected."[5] Computer power that once needed a room-size space now fits in our pocket. We not only *GoToMeetings* online (thanks to *GoToMeeting* software) and *Zoom*, but because of "iCommunication" devices (iPhone, iPad,), numerous apps, Skype, Facebook, Twitter, LinkedIn, and ultra-high-speed/big-data/cloud-computing methods, we are connected to virtual groups and teams nearly all of our waking moments. Social networking platforms that include a mix of text messaging, blogs, video, and a host of other social media applications are not only taking the place of e-mail, but also making it likely that you will communicate in virtual groups more often than in face-to-face groups.[6] Collaboration, whether in person or using various forms of electronic media, is a daily element of our work, family, and social lives.[7] Applications of artificial intelligence (AI) and electronic collaboration are increasing. According to research firm McKinsey Global Institute, almost $40 billion was invested in AI research in 2016, and that investment continues to grow each year.[8]

Yet despite our constant collaboration whether in person or using technology, we sometimes (even often) have difficulty working collectively. Collaboration is hard. Because working collaboratively is challenging, we sometimes try to make collaboration less stressful. One study found that taking pain medication before a meeting makes attending the meeting more pleasant.[9] But rather than taking a pill, we want you to be successful because you have collaboration skills and the knowledge needed to be effective. Good communication skills help make collaboration more satisfying and effective.

Despite the widespread nature of working in groups, some people hate collaborating. Communication researcher Susan Sorenson coined the term **grouphate** to describe the dread and repulsion many people have about working in groups, teams, or attending meetings.[10] But we have good news: Grouphate diminishes when people receive training and instruction about working in groups. The purpose of this text, therefore, is to help you learn communication principles and become skilled in the practices that make working in groups productive and enjoyable.

Communication is the central focus of this text. Communication makes it possible for groups and teams to exist and function. If you use the text as a tool to help you learn to communicate in groups, you will distinguish yourself as a highly valued group member.

1.1: Communicating in Small Groups

OBJECTIVE: Define small group communication

Consider these situations:

- After the stock market plunges 1000 points in a week, the U.S. president appoints a high-level task force of economists to identify the causes of the market collapse.
- During a bid by the social networking site Connect.com to merge with a rival company, Relate.com, the chair of the board of Connect.com calls the board together to consider the virtues and pitfalls of the possible merger.
- To prepare for the final exam in your group communication class, you and several class members develop a webpage to share information and occasionally hold a video conference with other classmates to study and review for the test.

Each of these three examples involves a group of people meeting and communicating for a specific purpose. As group members communicate with one another, they are communicating transactively: They are simultaneously responding to one another and expressing ideas, information, and opinions. Although the purposes of the groups in these three scenarios are quite different, the groups have something in common—something that distinguishes them from a cluster of people waiting for a bus or riding in an elevator, for example. Just what is that "something"? What are the characteristics that make a group a group? We define **small group communication** as *communication among a small group of people who share a common purpose, who feel a sense of belonging to the group, and who exert influence on one another.* Let's explore this definition in more detail.

By the end of this module, you will be able to:

1.1.1 **Describe the process of communication**

1.1.2 **Describe the characteristics of a small group**

1.1.3 **Identify the characteristic of meeting with a common purpose as an essential element of small group communication**

1.1.4 **Identify the characteristic of feeling a sense of belonging to a group as an essential element of small group communication**

1.1.5 **Identify the characteristic of exerting influence on others as an essential element of small group communication**

1.1.1: Communication

OBJECTIVE: Describe the process of communication

Reduced to its essence, **communication** is the process of acting on information.[11] Someone does or says something, and there is a response from someone else in the form of an action, a word, or a thought. Merely presenting information to others does not mean there is communication: Information is not communication. "But I told you what I wanted!" "I put it in the memo. Why didn't you do what I asked?" "It's in the syllabus." Such expressions of exasperation assume that if you send a message, someone will receive it. However, communication does not operate in a linear, input–output process. What you send is rarely what others understand. **Human communication** is the process of making sense out of the world and sharing that sense with others by creating meaning through the use of verbal and nonverbal messages.[12]

Communication Process

Communication Is about Making Sense—We make sense out of what we experience when we interpret what we see, hear, touch, smell, and taste. Typically, in a small group, multiple people are sending multiple messages, often at the same time. To make sense of the myriad messages we experience, we look for patterns or structure; we relate what happens to us at any given moment to something we've experienced in the past through the lens of our culture.[13]

Communication Is about Sharing Sense—We share what we experience by expressing it to others and to ourselves. We use words as well as nonverbal cues (such as gestures, facial expressions, clothing, and music) to convey our thoughts and feelings to others.

Communication Is about Creating Meaning—Meaning is created in the hearts and minds of both the message source and the message receiver. We don't send meaning; we create it based on our experiences, background, and culture.

Communication Is about Verbal and Nonverbal Messages—Words and nonverbal behaviors are symbols that we use to communicate and derive meaning that makes sense to us. A **symbol** is something that represents a thought, concept, object, or experience. The words on this page are symbols that you are using to derive meaning that makes sense to you. Nonverbal symbols such as our use of gestures, posture, tone of voice, clothing, and jewelry primarily communicate emotions—our feelings of joy or sadness, our likes and dislikes, or whether we're interested or uninterested in others.

Communication Is Transactional—Live, in-person, human communication, as well as communicating virtually via video channels, is **transactional,** meaning that when we communicate, we send and receive messages simultaneously. As you talk to someone, you respond to that person's verbal and nonverbal messages, even while you speak. In the context of a small group, even if you remain silent or nod off to sleep, your nonverbal behavior provides information to others about your emotions and interest, or lack of interest. The transactive nature of communication suggests that you cannot avoid communicating. Ultimately, people judge you by your behavior, not by your intent. And since you behave in some way (even when you're asleep), there is the potential for someone to make sense out of your behavior.

Communication Includes Several Elements—Key elements of communication include the source, message, receiver, and channel. The **source** of the message is the originator of the ideas and feelings expressed. The **message** is the information being communicated. The **receiver** of the message is the person or persons who interpret the message. The **channel** is the means by which the message is expressed to the receiver. **Noise** is anything that interferes with a message being interpreted by the receiver as intended by the source. **Feedback** is the response to a message. **Context** includes the physical and psychological environment for communication.

Communication May Be Mediated—Do groups need to communicate face to face to be considered a group? More and more small group meetings occur in a **mediated setting**—a setting in which the channel of communication is a phone line, fiber-optic cable, wireless signal, the Internet, or other means of sending messages to others; the interaction is not face to face. In the twenty-first century, it has become increasingly easy and efficient to collaborate using the Internet, and other technological means of communicating. So, yes: A group can be a group even without meeting face to face.[14]

Mediated Communication Can Enhance Group Communication—In the past four decades, we have learned more about how mediated communication can enhance group communication. For example, evidence shows that some groups linked together only by e-mail or a computer network can generate more and better ideas than groups that meet face to face.[15] Unfortunately, such communication may be hindered by sluggish feedback or delayed replies, which are not problems when we collaborate in person. Also, although more ideas may be generated in a mediated meeting, complex problems and relationship issues are better handled in person than on the Internet or through another mediated network.[16] In most cases, in-person communication affords the best opportunity to clarify meaning and resolve uncertainty and misunderstanding. We will discuss the use of technology in groups and teams in a section in this chapter and throughout the text in a special feature called Virtual Collaboration.

Communication Is Essential for Effective Group Outcome—Does the quality of communication really affect what a group accomplishes? Because this is a book about group communication, you won't be surprised that our answer is *yes*—whether communicating in person or virtually.[17] Researchers have debated, however, the precise role of communication in contributing to a group's success.[18] Success depends on a variety of factors besides communication, such as the personality of the group members, how motivated the members are to contribute, how much information members have, and the innate talent group members have for collaboration. Nevertheless, several researchers have found that the way group members communicate with each other is crucial in determining what happens when people collaborate.[19] Research investigating the importance of small group communication in a variety of situations continues to increase.

1.1.2: A Small Group of People

OBJECTIVE: Describe the characteristics of a small group

A group includes at least three people; two people are a **dyad**. The addition of a third person immediately adds complexity and an element of uncertainty to the transactive communication process.

If at least three people are required for a **small group**, what is the maximum number of members a group may have and still be considered small? Scholars do not agree on a specific number. However, having more than 12 people (some say 13, others say 20) in a group significantly decreases individual members' interaction. Research documents that larger groups just aren't as effective as smaller groups.[20] The larger the group, the less influence each individual has on the group and the more likely it is that subgroups will develop.[21] With 20 or more people, the communication more closely resembles a public-speaking situation when one person addresses an audience, providing less opportunity for all members to participate freely. The larger the group, the more likely it is that some group members will become passive rather than actively involved in the discussion.

1.1.3: Meeting with a Common Purpose

OBJECTIVE: Identify the characteristic of meeting with a common purpose as an essential element of small group communication

Why do small groups convene? The president's economic task force, the Relate.com company executives' group, and your communication study group have one thing in common: Their members have a specific purpose for meeting. They share a concern for the objectives of the group. Although a group of people waiting for a bus or riding in an elevator may share the goal of transportation, they do not have a collective goal. Their individual destinations are different. Their primary concerns are for themselves, not for others. As soon as their individual goals are realized, they leave the bus or elevator. In contrast, a goal keeps a committee or discussion group together until that goal is realized. Many groups fail to remain together because they never identify their common purpose. While participants in small groups may have somewhat different motives for their membership, a common purpose cements the group together.

1.1.4: Feeling a Sense of Belonging

OBJECTIVE: Identify the characteristic of feeling a sense of belonging to a group as an essential element of small group communication

Not only do group members need a mutual concern to unite them, but they also need to feel they belong to the group. Commuters waiting for a bus probably do not perceive themselves to be part of a collective effort. Members of a small group, however, need to have a sense of identity with the group; they should be able to feel it is their group.[22] Members of a small group are aware that a group exists and that they are members of the group to work for the common goals of the group.[23]

1.1.5: Exerting Influence

OBJECTIVE: Identify the characteristic of exerting influence on others as an essential element of small group communication

Each member of a small group, in one way or another, potentially influences others. Even if a group member sits in stony silence while other group members actively verbalize opinions and ideas, the silence of that one member may be interpreted as agreement by another member. Nonverbal messages have a powerful influence on a group's climate.

At its essence, the process of influencing others defines leadership. To some degree, each member of a small group exerts some leadership in the group because of his or her potential to influence others.[24] Although some groups have an elected or appointed leader, most group members have some opportunity to share in how the work gets done and how group members relate to each other. Thus, if we define the role of leader rather broadly, each group member has an opportunity to fill the role of leader by offering contributions and suggestions. Regardless of its size, a group achieves optimal success when each person accepts some responsibility for influencing and leading others.

To some degree, each team member is a leader because of his or her potential to influence other members, and to accept a share in the responsibility of influencing the team.

WRITING PROMPT

Studying Small Group Communication

As you begin your study of small group communication, identify several specific objectives of your study. Consider these questions: What would you like to learn about small groups? Which specific communication skills would you like to improve? How would you like the meetings you attend to be improved?

The response entered here will appear in the performance dashboard and can be viewed by your instructor.

Submit

1.2: Communicating in Teams

OBJECTIVE: Evaluate teams for effective practices

"Go, team!" You can hear this chant at most sports events. Whether playing in a touch football game or in the Super Bowl, members of sports teams are rewarded for working together. Corporate America has also learned that working in teams can enhance productivity, efficiency, worker satisfaction, and corporate profits. Regardless of whether its members play football or construct webpages, a **team** is a coordinated group of individuals organized to work together to achieve a specific, common goal. Teamwork is increasingly emphasized as a way to accomplish tasks and projects because teamwork works.[25] An effectively functioning team gets results.[26] Research clearly documents the increased use of teams in corporate America during the past two decades, especially in larger, more complex organizations.[27]

Because we have clearly defined small group communication, you may be wondering, "What's the difference between a group and a team?" Often people use the terms "group" and "team" interchangeably. But are they different concepts, or is there merely a semantic difference between a group and a team? Our view is that teams are often more highly structured than typical small groups. Teams have more clearly defined roles, rules, goals, and procedures. All teams are small groups, but not all groups operate as a team. The terms are not interchangeable.

Four Attributes That Define Teams

Highly effective teams usually have at least four attributes that give the term *team* distinct meaning.

Teams Develop Clear, Well-Defined Goals—Team goals are clear, specific, and measurable. They are also more ambitious than the goals that could be achieved by any individuals on the team. Teams that develop and use clear goals have been found to perform better than groups without clear-cut goals.[28] A sports team knows that the goal is to win the game. An advertising team's goal is to sell the most product. Teams develop a clear goal so that the members know when they've achieved it.

Teams Develop Clearly Defined Roles, Duties, and Responsibilities—People who belong to a team usually have a clear sense of their particular role or function on the team. As on a sports team, each team member understands how his or her job or responsibility helps the team achieve the goal. The roles and responsibilities of team members are explicitly discussed.[29] If one member is absent, other members know what needs to be done to accomplish that person's responsibilities. Sometimes team members may be trained to take on several roles just in case a member is absent; this is called **cross-functional team-role training**. Team members' understanding of other members' responsibilities helps the team to work more effectively.[30] In a group, the participants may perform specific roles and duties; by comparison, on a team, greater care must be devoted to explicitly ensuring that the individual roles and responsibilities are clear and linked to a common goal or outcome. In fact, the key challenge in team development is to teach individuals who are used to performing individual tasks how to work together.

Teams Have Clearly Defined Rules and Expectations—Teams develop specific operating systems to help them function well. A **rule** is a prescription for acceptable behavior. For example, a team may establish as a rule that all meetings will start and end on time. Another rule may be that if a team member is absent from a meeting, the absent member will contact the meeting leader after the meeting to get an update. Although expectations develop in groups, in a team those expectations, rules, and procedures are often overtly stated or written down. Team members know what the rules are and how those rules benefit the entire team.

Teams Are Coordinated and Collaborative—Team members discuss how to collaborate and work together. Sports teams spend many hours practicing how to anticipate the moves of other team members so that, as in an intricate dance, all team members are moving to the same beat. Team members develop interdependent relationships: What happens to one affects everyone on the team. Of course, team members may be given individual assignments, but those assignments are clearly coordinated with other members' duties so that all members are working together. Today, it is increasingly likely that team members will belong to several teams and will need to clarify the roles they assume in multiple teams simultaneously.[31] Coordination and collaboration are the hallmark methods of a team.[32] Research shows that when teams are trained to coordinate and adapt their communication with one another, they have greater success than teams not trained to coordinate their communication.[33] Although groups work together, they may accomplish their goal with less collaboration and coordination.

Even though we've made distinctions between groups and teams, we are not saying they are dramatically different entities. Think of these two concepts as existing on a continuum: Some gatherings will have more elements of a group, whereas others will be closer to our description of a team.

Business and nonprofit organizations tend to use the term "team" rather than "group" to identify individuals who work together to achieve a common task. Corporate training departments often spend much time and money to train their employees to be better team members covering communication principles and practices such as: problem solving, decision making, listening, and conflict management. In addition to using communication skills, team members set goals, evaluate the quality of their work, and establish team operating procedures.[34] Research has found that people who have been trained to work together in a team are, in fact, better team members.[35] So the news is good: There is evidence that learning principles and practices of group and team communication can enhance your performance.

Review

Comparing Groups and Teams

All teams are small groups. Thus, when we refer to a team, we will also be referring to a small group. Likewise, the principles and practices of effective small group communication also apply to teams.

	Groups	Teams
Goals	Goals may be discussed in general terms.	Clear, elevating goals drive all aspects of team accomplishment.
Roles and responsibilities	Roles and responsibilities may be discussed but are not always explicitly defined or developed.	Roles and responsibilities are explicitly developed and discussed.
Rules	Rules and expectations are often not formally developed and evolve according to the group's needs.	Rules and operating procedures are clearly discussed and developed to help the team work together.
Methods	Group members interact, and work may be divided among group members.	Team members collaborate and explicitly discuss how to coordinate their efforts and work together. Teams work together interdependently.

By the end of this module, you will be able to:

1.2.1 **Describe an effective team at work**

1.2.2 **Identify effective teammates by their actions**

1.2.3 **Characterize behaviors of effective team members**

1.2.1: Characteristics of an Effective Team

OBJECTIVE: Describe an effective team at work

A number of researchers have studied ways to make teams function better.[36] One study found that team members need work schedules compatible with those of their colleagues, adequate resources to obtain the information needed to do the work, leadership skills, and help from the organization to get the job done.[37] Another study concluded that it's not how smart team members are, but rather how well they communicate that improves teamwork.[38] Researchers who speculate about the ideal team characteristics of those astronauts who may one day travel to Mars suggest that an effective team of space travelers needs to be flexible and adapt to changing conditions, embrace the shift from individual to collective tasks, and recognize that the nature and function of team characteristics is a "moving target."[39]

Ideal Team Characteristics

Using studies of several real-life teams (such as NASA, McDonald's, and sports teams), Carl Larson and Frank LaFasto identified eight classic hallmarks of an effective team. The more of these characteristics a team has, the more likely it is that the team will be effective.[40]

A Clear, Elevating Goal—Having a common, well-defined goal is the single most important attribute of an effective team.[41] But having a goal is not enough; the goal should be elevating and important—it should excite team members and motivate them to make sacrifices for the good of the team. Sports teams use the elevating goal of winning the game or the championship. Corporate teams also need an exciting goal that all team members believe is important.

A Results-Driven Structure—To be results-driven is to have an efficient, organized, and structured method of achieving team outcomes.[42] Team structure is the way in which a team is organized to process information so as to ensure that enough time is spent on the task to achieve the goal.[43] Explicit statements of who reports to whom and who does what are key elements of team structure. It is useful, therefore, for teams to develop a clear sense of the roles and responsibilities of each team member. A team needs individuals who perform task roles (getting the job done) and individuals who perform maintenance roles (managing the team process) to accomplish the task.[44] A structure that is not results-driven—one that tolerates ineffective meetings, off-task talk, busywork, and "administrivia"—always detracts from team effectiveness.

Competent Team Members—Team members need to know not only *what* their assignment is, but also *how* to perform their job.[45] Team members need to be trained and educated so they know what to do and when to do it. Without adequate training in both teamwork skills and job skills, the team will likely flounder.[46]

Unified Commitment—The motto of the Thre Musketeers—"all for one and one for all"—serves as an accurate statement of the attitude team members should have when working together to achieve a clear, elevating goal. Team members need to feel united by their commitment and dedication to achieve the task.

A Collaborative Climate—Effective teams foster a positive group climate and the skills and principles needed to achieve their goal. Effective teams operate in a climate of support rather than defensiveness.[47] Team members should confirm one another, support one another, and listen to one another as they perform their work.

Standards of Excellence—A team is more likely to achieve its potential if it establishes high standards and believes it can achieve its goals.[48] Goals that cause the team to stretch a bit can serve to galvanize a team into action. Unobtainable or unrealistic goals, however, can result in team frustration. If the entire team is involved in setting goals, the team members are more likely to feel a sense of ownership of the standards they have established.

Does having high standards really have an impact on what a team can produce? If you've ever heard a Steinway piano—the gold standard of pianos—then you've benefited from the high standards of teamwork. Einrich Englehard Steinwege emigrated from Germany to New York in 1850, changed his name to Henry Steinway, and with four of his sons started his own piano company. Since 1853, each piano has been made by a team of workers with exacting standards. Steinway pianos have remained the most desired piano among concert pianists for more than 100 years. Steinway pianos are found in 95 percent of all concert halls in the world because of the unflinching high standards of each piano-making team. Having high standards of excellence is an important element in a team that endures.[49]

External Support and Recognition—Teams in any organization do not operate in isolation: They need support from outside the team to help acquire the information and materials needed to do the job. Perhaps that's why evidence suggests that teams who have a broad social network of colleagues and friends perform better than teams who lack a well-developed social network.[50] Team members also need to be recognized and rewarded for their efforts by others outside the team.[51] Positive, reinforcing feedback enhances team performance and feelings of team importance.[52] Evidence suggests that less positive support from others discourages some team members from giving their full effort; negative feedback causes more group members to withhold their full effort.[53] Most coaches acknowledge the "home-field advantage" that flows from the enthusiastic support and accolades of team followers. Corporate teams, too, need external support and recognition to help them function at maximum effectiveness.

Principled Leadership—Teams need effective leaders. This is not to say that a team requires an authoritarian leader to dictate who should do what. On the contrary, teams usually function more effectively when they adopt shared approaches to leadership. In the most effective teams, leadership responsibilities are spread throughout the team.

1.2.2: Characteristics of Effective Team Members

OBJECTIVE: Identify effective teammates by their actions

Whether you are selecting team members to win a game or to work with you on a class project, you should look for certain characteristics when picking effective team members.[54]

- **Experienced** team members are practical in managing the problems and issues they face; they've "been there, done that."
- **Skilled problem-solvers** effectively identify and solve problems. Being indecisive, dithering, and shying away from team problems have negative impacts on team success.

- **Open to new ideas** is a basic ingredient for team success; having team members who are straightforward and willing to appropriately discuss delicate issues is a predictor of team success.
- **Supportive** team members listen to others, are willing to pitch in and accomplish the job, and have an optimistic outlook about team success.[55] Supportive team members talk with group members outside formal group meetings; they develop a positive relationship with group members that is not solely based on accomplishing the task.[56] Unsupportive members try to control team members and focus on their individual interests rather than on team interests.
- **Positive** team members are encouraging, motivated, patient, enthusiastic, friendly, and well liked.[57] By contrast, being competitive, argumentative, negative, and impatient are perceived as hindrances to team success. Effective team members believe they have the skills and resources necessary to accomplish their task.[58] Team members who think they will be less effective are, in fact, less effective.[59] By contrast, team members who are more effective think they will have more positive results because of the self-perceived quality of the team.[60]
- **Action-oriented** team members focus on "strategic doing" as well as on "strategic thinking" and are vital for team success. Procrastinating and being slow to take action reduce team effectiveness.[61]
- **Adaptive** team members learn from both their successes and their failures.[62] They see which results they get and then adapt their behavior accordingly. Ineffective teams don't learn from their mistakes and don't try new things; they keep making the same mistakes over and over again. One of the important characteristics that individual team members need to have is the ability to learn and adapt their behavior so that they can adjust to new circumstances.[63]

1.2.3: Strategies for Becoming an Effective Team Member

OBJECTIVE: Characterize behaviors of effective team members

It's one thing to know what effective team members should do to be effective, such as being supportive, understanding the problem-solving process, and having a positive personal style. It's even more important, though, to actually putting those principles into practice. The research is clear that team members who receive team training in how to perform specific skills to enhance team performance are more effective.[64]

Group communication researcher Jessica Thompson discovered that the following behaviors can enhance your perception of competence when you work with other team members:[65]

- **Be there** and spend time together with other team members. Team members who don't spend as much time interacting with one another aren't perceived as competent.
- **Talk about the importance of trusting one another.** Make trust a specific expectation for all team members by verbalizing the importance of developing trust.
- **Talk about the task** you are undertaking as a team. Rather than just quietly doing the work, explicitly talk about what the team is doing to accomplish the team goal.
- **Be clear** with the meanings of words and phrases by defining words that may be unfamiliar to other team members. Also, avoid using unfamiliar acronyms (abbreviations for phrases, such as "PDC" for Personnel and Discipline Committee), unless such phrases are common knowledge to all team members.
- **Listen** to one another and observe and reflect upon what team members see and hear.
- **Talk "backstage."** Talk with group members outside formal group meetings; develop a relationship with group members that is not solely based on being task oriented.
- **Laugh** and have fun together. Use appropriate humor and share jokes with one another.

What are the behaviors that might hurt the perception of a team member's competence?

According to the same researcher, here's a list of what not to do:

- **Don't be negative** or question the expertise of other group members.
- **Don't use mean humor**—that is, negative humor (a joke at someone's expense) or sarcasm.
- **Don't verbally express your boredom** by telling other team members that you are bored.
- **Don't grab credit** by jockeying for a position of power and trying to gain personal credit for the work you do (and even don't do).

Enacting this simple list of dos and don'ts won't ensure that you'll be a competent team member, but research suggests that these behaviors can contribute to an overall perception of competence. In addition to these specific strategies, make sure your team also exemplifies the characteristics of an effective team and team members. If others perceive you as competent, you are more likely to behave in ways that enhance competent behavior.

1.3: Communicating Collaboratively in Groups: Advantages and Disadvantages

OBJECTIVE: Identify the advantages and disadvantages of participating in small groups

There is no question about it: You will definitely find yourself working in groups and teams. Collaborative projects are becoming the mainstay method of accomplishing work in all organizations. Students from kindergarten through graduate school are frequently called on to work on group projects.

How do you feel about working in groups and teams? Maybe you dread attending group meetings. Perhaps you agree with the observation that a committee is a group that keeps minutes but wastes hours. You may believe that groups bumble and stumble along until they reach some sort of compromise—a compromise with which no one is pleased. "To be effective," said one observer, "a committee should be made up of three people. But to get anything done, one member should be sick and another absent."

By understanding both the advantages and the potential pitfalls of working collaboratively, you can form more realistic expectations while capitalizing on the virtues of group work and minimizing the obstacles to success.[66] First, we'll identify advantages of group collaboration; then we'll present potential disadvantages.

By the end of this module, you will be able to:

- **1.3.1** **Describe the advantages of group work**
- **1.3.2** **Explain how to overcome the disadvantages of working in small groups**
- **1.3.3** **Determine when group work is unnecessary**

1.3.1: Advantages of Working in Groups

OBJECTIVE: Describe the advantages of group work

Collaboration has benefits. Working in groups and teams has many advantages over working alone. Working collaboratively results in more information, enhanced creative problem solving, greater comprehension, enhanced satisfaction, and enhanced self-understanding.

MORE INFORMATION On the TV game show *Who Wants to Be a Millionaire?* contestants who phone a friend get the right answer to the question 65 percent of the time. But if the contestant asks the audience for help, they get the right answer 91 percent of the time.[67] As this example suggests, there's wisdom in groups and teams. Because of the variety of backgrounds and experiences that individuals bring to a group, the group as a whole has more information and ideas from which to seek solutions to a problem than one person would have alone.[68] Because they have access to more information and ideas, groups usually outperform individual performance—that's why it's important to study how we communicate in small groups.[69] Research clearly documents that a group whose members have diverse backgrounds, including ethnic diversity, comes up with better-quality ideas.[70] With more information available, the group is more likely to discuss all sides of an issue and to arrive at a better solution.[71] The key, of course, is whether group members share what they know. When group members do share information, the group outcome is better than when they don't share what they know with other group members.[72] Although group members tend to start out by discussing what they already know, groups still have the advantage of having greater potential information to share with other group members.[73]

ENHANCED CREATIVE PROBLEM SOLVING Research on groups generally supports the maxim that "two heads are better than one" when it comes to solving problems.[74] Groups usually make better decisions than individuals working alone, because groups have more approaches to or methods of solving a specific problem. A group of people with various backgrounds, experiences, and resources can more creatively consider ways to solve a problem than one person can.

GREATER COMPREHENSION Working in groups and teams fosters improved learning and comprehension, because you are actively involved rather than passive. Imagine that your history professor announces that the final exam will be comprehensive. History is not your best subject, and you realize you need help to prepare for the exam. What do you do? You may form a study group with other classmates. Your decision to study with a group of people is wise; education theorists claim that when you take an active role in the learning process, your comprehension of information is improved. If you studied for the exam by yourself, you would not have the benefit of asking and answering questions of other study group members. By discussing a subject with a group, you learn more and improve your comprehension of the subject.

ENHANCED SATISFACTION Group problem solving provides an opportunity for group members to participate in making decisions and achieving the group goal. Individuals who help solve problems in a group are more committed to the solution and better satisfied with their participation in the group than if they weren't involved in the discussion.

ENHANCED SELF-UNDERSTANDING Working in groups helps you gain a more accurate picture of how others see you. The feedback you receive helps you recognize personal characteristics that you may be unaware of but that others perceive. By becoming sensitive to feedback, you can understand yourself better (or at least better understand how others perceive you) than you would if you worked alone. Group interaction and feedback can be useful in helping you examine your interpersonal behavior and in deciding whether you want to change your communication style.[75]

Why do these advantages occur? One explanation is **social facilitation**[76]—that is, the tendency for people to work harder simply because other people are present.[77] Why does this happen? Some researchers suggest that the increased effort may occur because people need and expect positive evaluations from others; some people want to be liked and they work harder when others are around so that they gain more positive feedback. Social facilitation seems to occur with greater consistency if the group task is simple rather than complex.

1.3.2: Disadvantages of Working in Groups

OBJECTIVE: Explain how to overcome the disadvantages of working in small groups

Although working in small groups and teams can produce positive results, problems sometimes occur when people congregate. Consider some of the disadvantages of working in groups.

Common Problems in Group Work and How to Fix Them

Pressure to Conform—Most people dislike conflict; they generally try to avoid it. Some avoid conflict because they believe that in an effective group, members readily reach agreement. But this tendency to avoid controversy in relationships can affect the quality of a group decision. What is wrong with group members reaching agreement? Nothing, unless they are agreeing to conform to the majority opinion or even to the leader's opinion just to avoid conflict. Social psychologist Irving Janis calls this phenomenon **groupthink**—when groups agree primarily to avoid conflict.[78] Speaking up to avoid groupthink is a good thing to do: Research has found that a well-spoken minority opinion can sway a group outcome.[79]

Solutions: Encourage critical, independent thinking. Be sensitive to status differences that may affect decision making. Invite someone from outside the group to evaluate the group's decision-making process. Assign a group member the role of devil's advocate.

Individual Domination—In some groups, it seems as if one person must run the show. That member wants to make the decisions and insists that his or her position on the issue is the best one. "Well," you might say, "if this person wants to do all the work, that's fine with me. It sure will be a lot easier for me." Yes, if you permit a member or two to dominate the group, you may do less work yourself—but you also forfeit the greater fund of knowledge and more creative approaches that come with full participation. Other members may not feel satisfied because they feel alienated from the decision making.

Solutions: Try to use the domineering member's enthusiasm to the group's advantage. If an individual tries to monopolize the discussion, other group members should channel that interest more constructively. The talkative member, for example, could be given a special research assignment. Of course, if the domineering member continues to monopolize the discussion, other members may have to confront that person and suggest that others be given an opportunity to present their views.

Uneven Work Distribution—When working in groups, individuals may be tempted to rely too much on others rather than pitch in and help. In the problem known as **social loafing**, some group members hold back on their contributions (loaf), assuming others will do the work.[80] They can get away with this behavior because in a group or team, no one will be able to pin the lack of work on a single group member. There is less accountability for who does what.[81] Working together distributes the responsibility of accomplishing a task among all members, which should be an advantage of group work. However, when some members allow others to carry the workload, problems can develop. Just because you are part of a group, it does not mean that you can get lost in the crowd: Your input is needed. Do not abdicate your responsibility to another group member.[82] There's also evidence that people are more likely to hang back and let others do the work if they simply don't like to work in groups or don't really care what others think of them.[83]

Solutions: Encourage less-talkative group members to contribute to the discussion. Make sure each person knows the goals and objectives of the group. Encourage each member to attend every meeting. Poor attendance at group meetings is a sure sign that members are falling into the "Let someone else do it" syndrome. See that each person knows and fulfills his or her specific responsibilities to the group.

Time—One of the major frustrations about group work is the time it takes to accomplish tasks. Not only does a group have to find a time and place where everyone can meet (sometimes a serious problem in itself), but a group simply requires more time to talk and listen, define, analyze, research, and solve problems than do individuals working alone. And time is money! One researcher estimates that one 2-hour meeting attended by 20 executives would cost the equivalent of a week's salary for one of them.[84] Still, talking and listening in a group usually results in a better solution.

Solutions: Budget more time to work on problems and issues collaboratively than you would individually. To minimize the time expenditure, make sure you have a clear goal and that all group members have the same goal in mind as they participate in the group deliberations. Use a well-developed agenda to keep group members focused on the issues at hand. Time is wasted when groups get off-task and pursue individual rather than group goals. Use good facilitation skills to summarize the group's progress, keep the group on-task, and ensure that the group's relational needs are addressed.

Review

Advantages and Disadvantages of Communicating Collaboratively

Advantages	Disadvantages
Groups have more information.	Group members may pressure others to conform.
Groups are often more creative problem solvers.	Groups could be dominated by one person.
Group work improves learning.	Group members may rely too much on others and not do their part.
Group members are more satisfied if they participate in the process.	Group work takes more time than working individually.
Group members learn about themselves.	

1.3.3: When Not to Collaborate

OBJECTIVE: Determine when group work is unnecessary

Although we've noted significant advantages to working in groups and teams, our discussion of the disadvantages of groups and teams suggests there may be situations when it's best *not* to collaborate. What situations call for individual work? Read on.

WHEN THERE IS LIMITED TIME If a decision must be made quickly, it may sometimes be better to delegate the decision to an expert. In the heat of battle, commanders usually do not call for a committee meeting of all their troops to decide when to strike. True, the troops may be better satisfied with a decision that they have participated in making, but the obvious need for a quick decision overrides any advantages that may be gained from meeting as a group.

WHEN AN EXPERT HAS THE ANSWER If you want to know what it's like to be president of a university, you don't need to form a committee to answer that question: You should just ask some university presidents what they do. Or, if you want to know mathematical formulas, scientific theories, or other information that an expert could readily tell you, go ask the expert rather than forming a fact-finding committee. Creating a group to gather information that an expert already knows wastes time.

WHEN THE INFORMATION NEEDED IS READILY AVAILABLE In this information age, a wealth of information is available with a click of a mouse. It may not be necessary to form a committee to chase after information that already exists. It may be helpful to put together a group or team if the information needed is extensive and several people are needed to conduct an exhaustive search. But if names, facts, dates, or other pieces of information can be quickly found on the Internet, use those methods rather than making a simple task more complex by forming a group to get the information.[85]

WHEN CONFLICT IS UNMANAGEABLE Although both of your authors are optimists, sometimes bringing people together for discussion and dialogue is premature. When conflict clearly may explode into something worse, it may be best to first try other communication formats before putting warring parties in a group to discuss the contentious issue. What may be needed instead of group discussion is more structured communication, such as mediation or negotiation with a leader or facilitator. Or, if group members have discussed an issue and just can't reach a decision, they may decide to let someone else make the decision for them. The judicial system is used when people can't or won't work things out in a rational, logical discussion.

But you shouldn't avoid forming or participating in groups just because of conflict. Conflict is almost always present in groups; disagreements can challenge a group to develop a better solution. Even so, if the conflict is intractable, another method of making the decision may be best.

Be aware that collectivistic cultures value group or team achievement more than individual achievement. Many people from Asian countries such as Japan, China, and Taiwan typically value collaboration and collective achievement more than do some people from individualistic cultures. Venezuela, Colombia, and Pakistan are other countries in which people score high on a collective approach to work methods.[86] In collectivistic cultures, *we* is more important than *me*. Collectivistic cultures usually think of a group as the primary unit in society, whereas individualistic cultures think about the individual.[87]

As you might guess, people from individualistic cultures tend to find it more challenging to collaborate in group projects than do people from collectivistic cultures.

The advantages of communicating in groups and teams are less likely to be realized if individualistic assumptions consistently trump collectivistic assumptions.

Individualism and Collectivism in Small Groups[88]

Individualistic Assumptions	Collectivistic Assumptions
The most effective decisions are made by individuals.	The most effective decisions are made by teams.
Planning should be centralized and done by the leaders.	Planning is best done by all concerned.
Individuals should be rewarded.	Groups or teams should be rewarded.
Individuals work primarily for themselves.	Individuals work primarily for the team.
Healthy competition between colleagues is more important than teamwork.	Teamwork is more important than competition.
Meetings are mainly for sharing information with individuals.	Meetings are mainly for making group or team decisions.
To get something accomplished, you should work with individuals.	To get something accomplished, you should work with the whole group or team.
A key objective in group meetings is to advance your own ideas.	A key objective in group meetings is to reach consensus or agreement.
Team meetings should be controlled by the leader or chair.	Team meetings should be a place for all team members to bring up what they want.
Group or team meetings are often a waste of time.	Group or team meetings are the best way to achieve a goal.

© Harry Bliss/The New Yorker Collection/The Cartoon Bank

Review

Group Collaboration

Knowing when to collaborate (and when not to collaborate) will maximize the efficacy of individuals as well as groups.

WRITING PROMPT

What Type of Collaboration Is Appropriate?

Review the following scenarios and identify whether each one requires a group, requires a team, or doesn't require collaboration.

Scenario 1: Several of your friends have decided to meet once a month to form a book club.

Scenario 2: You are working with several people who are trying to get your good friend elected to the local school board.

Scenario 3: You are working with members of your local library to obtain financial sponsors for the community book drive to raise money for the library.

Scenario 4: You want to identify the number of people who do not wear seatbelts in your state.

▶ The response entered here will appear in the performance dashboard and can be viewed by your instructor.

Submit

1.4: Communicating in Different Types of Groups

OBJECTIVE: Compare primary and secondary groups

There are two broad categories of groups—primary and secondary. Within these broad types, groups can be categorized according to their purpose and function. To give you an idea of the multiple types of groups to which you belong, we'll define these two broad types and then note specific functions within each type.

By the end of this module, you will be able to:

1.4.1 **Explain how primary groups fulfill their purpose**

1.4.2 **Characterize secondary groups**

1.4.1: Primary Groups

OBJECTIVE: Explain how primary groups fulfill their purpose

A **primary group** is a group whose main purpose is to give people a way to fulfill their need to associate with others. It is primary in the sense that the group meets the primary human need to relate to others. The main function of such a group is to perpetuate the group so that members can continue to enjoy one another's company. Primary groups typically do not meet regularly to solve problems or make decisions, although they sometimes do both of those things.

FAMILY GROUPS Your family is the most fundamental of all primary groups. In his poem "The Death of the Hired Man," Robert Frost mused, "Home is the place where, when you have to go there/They have to take you in." Family communication usually does not follow a structured agenda; family conversation is informal and flows naturally from the context and content emerging from the family's experiences. Although family groups do accomplish things together, at the core of a family group is the association of simply being a family.

SOCIAL GROUPS In addition to family groups, you may have groups of friends who interact over an extended period of time. These groups also exist to meet the primary human need for fellowship and human interaction. As in a family group, conversation in social groups, such as your various groups of friends, is informal and typically does not have a preplanned agenda. You associate with one another for the joy of community—to fulfill the basic human need to be social. Our focus in this text is less on primary groups and more on secondary groups, which accomplish specific tasks such as problem solving, decision making, and learning.

1.4.2: Secondary Groups

OBJECTIVE: Characterize secondary groups

Secondary groups exist to accomplish a task or achieve a goal. Most of the groups you belong to at work or school are secondary groups. You are not involved in a committee or a class group assignment just for fun or to meet your social need for belonging (even though you may enjoy the group and make friends with other group members). Instead, the main reason you join secondary groups is to get something done.[89]

Types of Secondary Groups

There are several kinds of secondary groups to which you may belong at some point in your life.[90]

Problem-Solving Groups—A **problem-solving group** exists to overcome some unsatisfactory situation or obstacles to achieving a goal. Many, if not most, groups in business and industry are problem-solving groups. The most common problem that any organization faces (whether it's a for-profit business or a nonprofit organization) is finding a way to make more money.

Decision-Making Groups—The task of a **decision-making group** is to make a choice from among several alternatives. The group must identify what the possible choices are, discuss the consequences of the choices, and then select the alternative that best meets a need or achieves the goal of the group or parent organization. A committee that screens applicants for a job has the task of making a decision. The group must select one person from among the many candidates who apply.

Decision making is usually a part of the problem-solving process. Groups that have a problem to solve usually must identify several possible solutions and decide on the one that best resolves the problem. Although all group problem solving involves making decisions, not all group decision making solves a problem.

Study Groups—As a student, you are no doubt familiar with **study groups**. The main goal of these groups is to gather information and learn new ideas. We have already noted that one advantage of participating in a group is that you learn by being involved in a discussion. A study group also has the advantage of having access to more information and a wider variety of ideas through the contributions of different individuals.

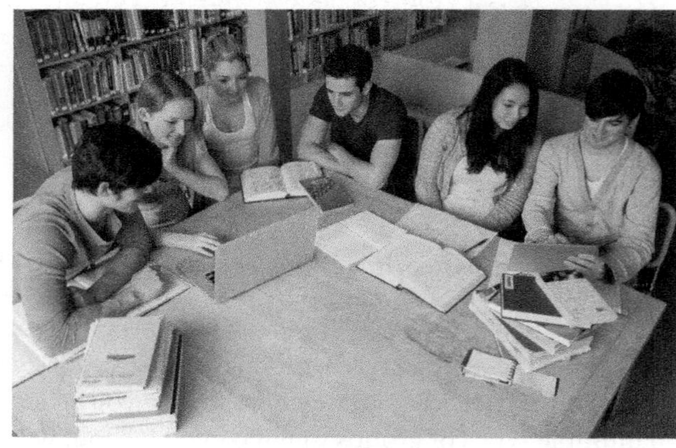

Therapy Groups—A **therapy group**, also called an encounter group, support group, or T-group, helps group members work on personal problems or provides encouragement and support to help manage stress. Such groups are led by professionals who are trained to help members overcome, or at least manage, individual problems in a group setting. Group therapy takes advantage of the self-understanding that members gain as they communicate with one another. Members also learn how they are perceived by others. Groups such as WW (formerly known as Weight Watchers) and Alcoholics Anonymous also provide positive reinforcement when members have achieved their goals. By experiencing therapy with others, members take advantage of the greater knowledge and information available to the group.

Committees—A **committee** is a group of people who are elected or appointed for a specific task. Some committees are formed to solve problems; others are appointed to make a decision or simply to gather information so that another group, team, or committee can make a decision. A committee may be either a **standing committee**, which remains active for an extended time period, or an **ad hoc committee**, which disbands when its special task has been completed. Like many other people, you may react negatively to serving on a committee. Committee work is often regarded as time consuming, tedious, and ineffective. Perhaps you have heard that "a committee is a way of postponing a decision" or "a committee is a group of people who individually can do nothing and who collectively decide nothing can be done." Although frustration with committees is commonplace, you are not doomed to have a negative experience when working with others on a committee.

Focus Groups—A **focus group** is a small group of people who are asked to focus on a particular topic or issue so that others can better understand the group's responses to the topic or issue presented. One person usually serves as moderator, and this person asks open-ended questions and then simply listens to the responses of the group members. Many advertising agencies show new advertising campaigns to focus groups and then listen to the responses of the group members to assess the impact or effectiveness of the campaign.

WRITING PROMPT

Primary and Secondary Groups

Identify examples of primary and secondary groups with which you interact. What are the functions or goals of the secondary groups to which you belong?

▶ The response entered here will appear in the performance dashboard and can be viewed by your instructor.

Submit

1.5: Communicating in Virtual Groups

OBJECTIVE: **Use methods to make virtual group meetings effective**

With today's technological advances, people can work together even when they are in different physical locations.[91] In **virtual small group communication**, three or more people collaborate from different physical locations, perform interdependent tasks, have shared responsibility for the outcome of the work, and rely on some form of technology to communicate with one another.[92] Although technology seems to be a pervasive and revolutionary fact of life—in both our personal and our professional lives—communication researchers predict that technology will play an even larger role in how we collaborate with one another in the future.[93] Evidence suggests that although virtual groups can usually perform just as effectively as face-to-face groups, we don't always enjoy the work as much as we do when we are collaborating live and in person.[94] Research also suggests that virtual groups need special support in place to help them manage individual differences and operate at peak effectiveness.[95]

By the end of this module, you will be able to:

1.5.1 **Compare virtual and non-virtual collaboration**

1.5.2 **Apply theories to virtual groups**

1.5.3 **Determine methods to make virtual group meetings beneficial for the participants**

1.5.1: Differences between Virtual and Non-virtual Collaboration

OBJECTIVE: **Compare virtual and non-virtual collaboration**

Although virtual and non-virtual collaboration reflects elements common to all group collaboration, there are clear distinctions.

Virtual versus Non-virtual Collaboration

How does virtual group collaboration differ from live, face-to-face meetings?

Time—Virtual collaboration with others can occur in four conditions: (1) same time/same place; (2) same time/different place; (3) different time/same place; and (4) different time/different place.[96]

An **asynchronous message** is not read, heard, or seen at the same time you send the message; that is, there is a time delay between when you send and receive a message. Examples are sending a text message to someone who is not monitoring Facebook and leaving a voice message.

Synchronous messages occur instantly and simultaneously, with no time delay between sending and receiving a message. The more synchronous our interaction, the more similar it is to face-to-face interactions. The more a technology resembles a face-to-face conversation, the more social presence there is. A live video conference is an example.

Social presence is the feeling we have when we act and think as if we're involved in an unmediated, face-to-face conversation. Even in face-to-face interactions, sound takes time to travel, but that "delay" is really imperceptible. When we send text messages back and forth or instant-message with a group of people, we create a shared sense of social or psychological presence with our collaborators.

Varying Degrees of Anonymity—Maybe you've seen the now-classic cartoon of a dog sitting at a computer, speaking the tagline "On the Internet, nobody knows you're a dog." Being able to contribute to a group and knowing that other group members may not know who you are can be liberating and make you feel freer to share ideas with others. Anonymity may lead you to say things that are bolder, more honest, or even more outrageous than if your collaborators knew who you were. At the same time, it may also be easier for a group member not to contribute to the conversation because there is no accountability for who says what.

Potential for Deception—Anonymity may tempt you and other group members to say things that aren't true. With many forms of virtual communication (such as text messages), when you can't see or hear others, it's easier to lie. A survey of college students found that 40 percent had lied on the Internet: 15 percent lied about their age, 8 percent about their weight, 6 percent about their appearance, 6 percent about their marital status, and 3 percent about what sex they were.[97] Another study found that almost 90 percent of people have been less than truthful about their appearance when online at one time or another.[98]

Nonverbal Messages—Words and graphics become more important when you are collaborating virtually rather than face-to-face because when texting or e-mailing, you must rely solely on them to carry nonverbal cues. Of course, a YouTube video does include nonverbal messages—but even on YouTube some cues may be limited, such as the surrounding context and reactions from others.

Some researchers have found that trust takes longer to develop in virtual forms of communication because team members can't see one another. Since visual cues provide confirmation of verbal messages, without seeing other members, trust may emerge only slowly.[99]

For example, some basic ways to add emotion to text messages include CAPITALIZING THE MESSAGE (which is considered "yelling"), making letters bold, inserting graphics, and using emoticons or emojis. In face-to-face communication, we laugh, smile, or frown in direct response to what others are saying. We use emoticons/emojis to provide the same kind of emotional punctuation in our written message.[100] Also, the ability to tease or make sarcastic remarks is limited when using text messages. Because the written message lacks a tone of voice, emoticons help provide information about the intended emotional tone. You can also write out an accompanying interpretation—for example, "What a kook you are! (just kidding)"—to compensate for the limits of emotional cues.

Written Messages—Reliance on the written word also affects virtual collaborations. One online scholar suggests that a person's typing ability and writing skills affect the quality of any relationship that is developed.[101] Not everyone has the ability to encode thoughts quickly and accurately into written words. Writing skills affect your ability to express yourself online, and how others perceive you. Your written messages provide cues to others about your personality, skills, sense of humor, and even your values.

Distance—Although we certainly can collaborate virtually with people who live and work in the same building, there is typically greater physical distance between people who are communicating virtually. When using the Internet or a cell phone, we can just as easily send a text or video message to someone on the other side of the globe as we can to someone on the other side of the room.

1.5.2: Virtual Group Theories

OBJECTIVE: Apply theories to virtual groups

Three theories have been developed that further explain and predict how we use electronic meeting systems. The role of nonverbal messages is an integral part of each of these theories. Understanding the various theoretical approaches can help you better fulfill the role and function of the virtual groups in which you participate.

CUES-FILTERED-OUT THEORY One early theory of communication via the Internet was the **cues-filtered-out theory**. This theory suggests that emotional expression is severely restricted when we communicate using only text messages; the nonverbal cues such as facial expression, gestures, and tone of voice are filtered out. The assumption was that text messages were best used for brief, task-oriented messages such as sharing information or asking questions; they were assumed to be less effective in helping people establish meaningful relationships or in solving more complex problems.[102] This theory also suggests that because of the lack of nonverbal cues and other social information, we are less likely to use text-based electronic messages to manage relationships. Although using Facebook may include photos, videos, and ample personal information, it's still not as rich as a face-to-face conversation.

MEDIA RICHNESS THEORY Another theory helps us predict which form of media we would use, depending on the richness required to convey messages, especially emotional and relational ones. **Media richness theory** suggests that the richness of a communication channel is based on four criteria:

1. The amount of feedback that the communicators can receive
2. The number of cues that the channel can convey and that can be interpreted by a receiver
3. The variety of language that communicators use
4. The potential for expressing emotions and feelings[103]

Using these four criteria, researchers have developed a continuum of communication channels, from "communication rich" to "communication lean." As illustrated in Figure 1-1,[104] face-to-face conversation is the most media rich, and simply posting an announcement or a flyer is the most media lean.

Some evidence indicates that those wishing to communicate a negative message, such as ending a relationship, may select a less-rich communication message: They may be more likely to send a letter or an e-mail rather than share the bad news face to face.[105] Similarly, people usually want to share good news in person, where they can enjoy the positive reaction. Both the cues-filtered-out theory and the media richness theory suggest that the

Figure 1-1 A Continuum of Media-Rich to Media-Lean Message Sources

A Continuum of Media-Rich to Media-Lean Message Sources	
Face-to-face, one-on-one discussion	Media rich
Face-to-face group meetings	↑
Video-conference	
Telephone conversation	
Computer conference (interactive e-mail)	
Voice mail	
Noninteractive e-mail	
Fax	
Personal letter	
Impersonal memo	↓
Posted flyer or announcement	Media Lean

restriction of nonverbal cues, which provide information about the nature of the relationship, hampers the quality of relationships that can be established virtually. A newer perspective, however, suggests that eventually we may be able to discern relational information when collaborating virtually.

SOCIAL INFORMATION-PROCESSING THEORY **Social information-processing theory** suggests that we can communicate relational and emotional messages via the Internet, but it may take longer to express messages that are typically communicated using facial expressions and tone of voice. A key difference between face-to-face and computer-mediated communication is the rate at which information reaches you. During a live, in-person conversation, you process a lot of information quickly—the words you hear as well as the many nonverbal cues you see (facial expression, gestures, and body posture) and hear (tone of voice and the use of pauses). During text-only interactions, less information is available to process (no audio cues or visual nonverbal expressions), so it takes a bit longer for the relationship to develop—but it does develop as you learn more about your e-mail partner's likes, dislikes, and feelings.

Social information-processing theory also suggests that if you expect to communicate with your electronic communication partner again, you are likely to pay more attention to the relationship cues—expressions of emotions that are communicated either directly (such as someone writing, "I'm feeling bored in this meeting today") or indirectly (such as when you write a long e-mail message and your e-mail collaborator writes back only a sentence, suggesting he or she may not want to spend much time "talking" today).

A study by Lisa Tidwell and Joseph Walther extended the application of social information-processing theory. They investigated the effects on computer-mediated communication on how much information people reveal about themselves, how quickly they reveal it, and the overall impressions people get of one another. In comparing computer-mediated exchanges with face-to-face conversations, Tidwell and Walther found that people in computer-mediated "conversations" asked more direct questions, which resulted in people revealing more, not less, information about themselves when online.[106]

If you expect to communicate with your electronic partner again, evidence also suggests that you will pay more attention to the relationship cues that develop. In one study, Joseph Walther and Judee Burgoon found that the development of relationships between people who meet face to face differed little from those between people who had computer-mediated interactions.[107] In fact, they found that many computer-mediated groups actually developed more satisfying relationships compared to the face-to-face groups.

WRITING PROMPT

How to Prepare for a Virtual Team Meeting

Based on the discussion of best practices for organizing a virtual team meeting, what are specific strategies for preparing a team for their first virtual meeting?

The response entered here will appear in the performance dashboard and can be viewed by your instructor.

Submit

1.5.3: Strategies for Participating in Virtual Groups

OBJECTIVE: Determine methods to make virtual group meetings beneficial for the participants

It's one thing to understand how virtual group collaboration is different from collaborating face to face, and to understand different theoretical approaches to virtual collaboration. On a practical level, it will help you to know the dos and don'ts of collaborating virtually.

PARTICIPATING IN VIRTUAL GROUPS Two researchers recommend the following best practices, which can enhance virtual team success:[108]

- **Start early.** It takes longer to develop relationships when participating in virtual teams.
- **Communicate often.** The messages need not be lengthy, but more frequent message exchanges let other group members know you're still involved and connected.[109]
- **Multitask skillfully.** Teams can work on more than one task at a time by dividing and conquering the work. It's okay to make assignments and have different team members working on different parts of the project all at the same time.
- **Respond to others' messages.** Overtly acknowledge that you have read another person's message.
- **Use technology skillfully.** Effectively use the tools and technology for collaborating virtually. If you don't know how to use the technology, ask for help.[110]
- **Be clear.** People can't guess what you're thinking because they may not be able to see you, so spell out what you think and feel when writing e-mail or text messages.
- **Be flexible.** Sometimes virtual group members need a quick response; at other times they may need more detailed information that will take longer to develop. When sending a message to the group, consider the needs of group members for information.[111]
- **Set deadlines.** Team members should be given clear, specific due dates, and they should report whether they are meeting them.

LEADING VIRTUAL GROUPS If you are in a leadership role and are encouraging others to collaborate virtually, you can take several steps to support a virtual group. Specifically, the following types of assistance seem to help virtual teams function best:[112]

- **Provide the right resources.** Teams need adequate resources, such as the right people, adequate time to do the work, and enough money to buy what they need to get the job done.
- **Provide technology training.** Team members should be appropriately trained in using the technology to stay connected.
- **Provide good tech support.** Make sure team members aren't slowed down by ineffective technology. It's important that team members have someone who can help them use the technology effectively—especially when the technology doesn't work or breaks down.
- **Openly reward and compliment team members.** Make sure team members feel valued.
- **Ensure effective communication skill.** Team members should have appropriate training in communication skills, technical skills, customer service skills, and in how to collaborate from remote locations.

In practice, working in a virtual group may reveal several underlying challenges that need to be managed, as illustrated in the following case study.

To help you determine whether your group is using the best practices for communicating in a virtual group, use the assessment instrument in the following Virtual Collaboration sidebar.

CASE STUDY

The Battle over Working as a Virtual Group

It seemed simple enough. Their history professor had divided the class into groups of five or six people to present an oral report to the class about the Civil War. Each group had an assigned topic. Although some class time was devoted to the project, the professor assumed that the groups would also spend out-of-class time to collaborate on the report. The problem was that the members of the group assigned to cover the Battle of Appomattox all had part-time jobs, two members had busy lives as parents, and another member commuted to campus an hour away. After comparing their schedules, it was obvious they would have difficulty finding a time when they could all get together.

The group members decided that rather than meeting face to face, they would connect outside class via the Internet. Although the professor wanted them to meet in person, the group just didn't see how that was possible. So they exchanged e-mail addresses and phone numbers, established a collaborative Google Docs space, and agreed to share information virtually. They found, however, that it was tricky to make much progress. A couple of the group members weren't clear about the goal of the assignment and just waited for others to start sharing information to see what the group project was all about. Because of a heavy workload, another member just didn't have time to devote to the project and didn't seem very committed to the group. Two members started sharing their research findings with the entire group—but when they realized they were the only two doing the work, they stopped volunteering to share their information with the group and shared their work just with each other. One of the top-performing group members started criticizing the group members who weren't doing their fair share of the work. The criticism didn't do much for the group's climate. Soon members were spending more time complaining about their colleagues than they were working on the project.

At the midway point, the group wasn't making much progress. Something needed to be done to get the group back on track or they were going to present an oral report that would not only be embarrassingly bad, but also significantly lower their course grades. The professor scheduled one more in-class meeting and announced that the rest of the time the groups would have to meet on their own. The Battle of Appomattox group sensed disaster looming. Mistrust and inaction on the project were increasing.

WRITING PROMPT

Question for Analysis—The Battle over Working as a Virtual Group

Identify the key problems this group is having. What should they focus on when they have their in-class meeting? What could they do differently to function as a more effective team? Provide specific recommendations to get the group back on track.

The response entered here will appear in the performance dashboard and can be viewed by your instructor.

Submit

Virtual Collaboration

Assessing Virtual Group Practice

Survey: Assessing Virtual Group Practice

Use the following assessment instrument to help you determine whether a virtual group you belong to is operating at peak efficiency.[113]

1 = Always;
2 = Sometimes;
3 = Never;
N/A = Not Applicable.

1. Our group meets face to face, especially early in our group's history, to establish procedures and rules that structure how we will interact virtually.	1	2	3	N/A
2. Our group sends frequent messages to the entire group.	1	2	3	N/A
3. Our group sends frequent messages to individual group members.	1	2	3	N/A
4. Our group has divided the overall task into smaller tasks.	1	2	3	N/A
5. Our group has assigned group members to specific tasks linked to achieving the group's goal.	1	2	3	N/A
6. Our group acknowledges receiving electronic messages from one another.	1	2	3	N/A
7. Our group develops clear, brief messages that are usually understood by other group members.	1	2	3	N/A
8. Our group sets deadlines.	1	2	3	N/A
9. Our group meets deadlines.	1	2	3	N/A
10. Our group members understand and appropriately use technology to help us stay connected.	1	2	3	N/A

Summary

The lower the score (out of a possible 30 points), the more likely it is that your virtual group is collaborating well. If you answered "never" (a high score of 3 points) to a statement, consider the following suggestions:

High-Score Feedback for Question 1: Start early and meet face-to-face if/when possible. It takes longer to develop relationships when participating in virtual teams.

High-Score Feedback for Question 2: The messages to the entire team need not be lengthy, but more frequent message exchanges let other group members know you're still involved and connected.

High-Score Feedback for Question 3: The messages to individual team members need not be lengthy, but more frequent message exchanges let other group members know you're still involved and connected.

High-Score Feedback for Question 4: Your group can work on more than one task at a time by dividing and conquering the work.

High-Score Feedback for Question 5: Your group can make assignments and have different team members working on different parts of the project at the same time.

High-Score Feedback for Question 6: Overtly acknowledge that you have read another person's message.

High-Score Feedback for Question 7: Be clear. People can't guess what you're thinking because they may not be able to see you, so spell out what you think and feel when writing e-mail or text messages.

High-Score Feedback for Question 8: Team members should be given clear, specific due dates.

High-Score Feedback for Question 9: Have team members report whether they are meeting their deadlines.

High-Score Feedback for Question 10: Effectively use the tools and technology for collaborating virtually. If you don't know how to use the technology, ask for help.

1.6: Communicating Competently in Small Groups

OBJECTIVE: Describe competencies of small group communication

A number of principles and skills can enhance your competence as a member of a small group. You may be wondering, "Precisely what does a competent communicator do?" A **competent group communicator** is a person who is able to interact appropriately and effectively with others in small groups and teams. Communication researcher Michael Mayer found that the two most important behaviors of group members were (1) fully participating in the discussion, especially when analyzing a problem, and (2) offering encouraging, supportive comments to others.[114] Stated succinctly: Participate and be nice.

Researchers who have studied how to enhance communication competence suggest that three elements are involved in becoming a truly competent communicator:

1. You must be motivated.
2. You must have appropriate knowledge.
3. You must have the skill to act appropriately.[115]

Motivation is an internal drive to achieve a goal. To be motivated means you have a strong desire to do your best, even during inevitable periods of fatigue and frustration. If you are motivated to become a competent small group communicator, you probably have an understanding of the benefits or advantages of working with others in groups.

Knowledge is the information you need to do competently what needs to be done. One key purpose of this text is to give you knowledge that can help you become a more competent communicator in groups, on teams, and during the many meetings you will undoubtedly attend in the future.

A **skill** is an effective behavior that can be repeated when appropriate. Just having the desire to be effective (motivation) or being able to rattle off lists of principles and theories (knowledge) doesn't ensure that you will be competent; you have to have the skill to put the principles into practice. The subtitle of this text—*Principles and Practices*—emphasizes the importance of being able to translate into action what you know and think.

Research supports the commonsense conclusion that practicing group communication skills, especially when you practice the skills in a group or team setting, enhances your group performance.[116]

WRITING PROMPT

Elements of Communication Competence

Reflect on a group or team to which you belong. Write a brief description of your motivation (Why participate in the group?), knowledge (What information do you have that helps the group?), and skill (What specific skills will help the group?) in achieving the goals of the group or team.

The response entered here will appear in the performance dashboard and can be viewed by your instructor.

Submit

By the end of this module, you will be able to:

1.6.1 **Describe two problem-oriented, three solution-oriented, two discussion-management, and two relational group problem-solving competencies**

1.6.2 **Identify attributes of ethical small group communication**

1.6.1: Nine Core Competencies of Group Communication

OBJECTIVE: Describe two problem-oriented, three solution-oriented, two discussion-management, and two relational group problem-solving competencies

Although we've described the personal qualities of competent group or team members, you may still be wondering, "What specifically do effective group members do?" Following is an overview of some of the competencies that are essential for members of problem-solving groups. It's important to emphasize that this overview targets problem-solving discussions. To solve a problem or to achieve a goal, you must seek to overcome an obstacle. There is more communication research about how to solve problems and make effective decisions in small groups and teams than on any other topic.

These nine competencies were identified after examining several bodies of research and consulting with several instructors of small group communication.[117] They are grouped into four categories.

PROBLEM-ORIENTED COMPETENCIES

- **Define the problem.** Effective group members clearly and appropriately define or describe the problem to be solved and the obstacles to be overcome. Ineffective group members either define the problem inaccurately or make little or no attempt to clarify the problem or issues confronting the group.

- **Analyze the problem.** Effective group members offer statements that clearly and appropriately examine the causes, history, symptoms, and significance of the problem to be solved. Ineffective members either don't analyze the problem or they do so inaccurately or inappropriately.

SOLUTION-ORIENTED COMPETENCIES

- **Identify criteria.** Effective group members offer clear and appropriate comments that identify the goal that the group is attempting to achieve or identify specific criteria (or standards) for an acceptable solution or outcome for the problem facing the group. Ineffective group members don't clarify the goal or establish criteria for solving the problem. Ineffective groups aren't sure what they are looking for in a solution or outcome.
- **Generate solutions.** Effective group members offer several possible solutions or strategies to overcome obstacles or decision options regarding the issues confronting the group. Ineffective group members offer fewer solutions, or they rush to make a decision without considering other options or before defining and analyzing the problem.
- **Evaluate solutions.** Effective group members systematically evaluate the pros and cons of the solutions that are proposed. Ineffective group members examine neither the positive and negative consequences nor the benefits and potential costs of a solution or decision.

DISCUSSION-MANAGEMENT COMPETENCIES

- **Maintain task focus.** Effective group members stay on track and keep their focus on the task at hand. Although almost every group wanders off track from time to time, the most effective groups are mindful of their goal and sensitive to completing the work before them. Effective group members also summarize what the group is discussing to keep the group oriented. Ineffective group members have difficulty staying on track and frequently digress from the issues at hand. They also seldom summarize what the group has done, which means that group members aren't quite sure what they are accomplishing.
- **Manage interaction.** Effective group members don't monopolize the conversation; rather, they actively look for ways to draw quieter members into the discussion. Neither are they too quiet; they contribute their fair share of information and look for ways to keep the discussion from becoming a series of monologues; they encourage on-task, supportive dialogue. Ineffective group members either rarely contribute to the discussion or monopolize the discussion by talking too much. They also make little effort to draw others into the conversation and are not sensitive to the need for balanced interaction among group members.

RELATIONAL COMPETENCIES

- **Manage conflict.** Conflict occurs in the best of groups. Effective group members are sensitive to differences of opinion and personal conflict, and they actively seek to manage the conflict by focusing on issues, information, and evidence rather than on personalities. Ineffective group members deal with conflict by making it personal; they are insensitive to the feelings of others and generally focus on personalities at the expense of issues.
- **Maintain a positive climate.** Effective group members look for opportunities to support and encourage other group members.[118] Although they may not agree with all comments made, they actively seek ways to improve the climate and maintain positive relationships with other group members through both verbal and nonverbal expressions of support. Ineffective group members do just the opposite: They are critical of others, and their frowning faces and strident voices nonverbally cast a gloomy pall over the group. Ineffective members rarely use appropriate humor to lessen any tension between members.

Communicating effectively in small groups and teams involves a variety of competencies. Even as we present these nine competencies, we are not suggesting that they are the only things you need to learn. Instead, they represent a practical beginning to learning the essentials of communicating in small group problem solving and decision making.

© Jim Sizemore/www.cartoonstock.com

Your Small Group Communication Competencies

Based on the description of the nine core small group competencies, rate your skill in using these competencies in a group or a team on a scale from 1 (low) to 10 (high).

Core Competencies	Your Rating
Define the problem	
Analyze the problem	
Identify criteria	
Generate solutions	
Evaluate solutions	
Maintain task force	
Manage interaction	
Manage conflict	
Maintain a positive climate	

Summary: In which core competencies did you score the highest? The lowest? Identify the competencies where you have the most room for improvement, and review the above descriptions of the competencies to note how you can become a more effective group member in these areas. At the end of the course, take this survey again and compare the results with your earlier results. Which areas show improvement?

1.6.2: Ethically Communicating in Small Groups

OBJECTIVE: Identify attributes of ethical small group communication.

Each of the nine group communication competencies is founded on the assumption that to be a competent communicator, you must be an ethical communicator. **Ethics** are the beliefs, values, and moral principles by which we determine what is right and what is wrong. Ethical principles are the basis for many of the decisions we make in our personal and professional lives. Among the attributes of an ethical small group communicator are listening to others, using evidence to support key ideas, sharing information honestly and truthfully, and doing an appropriate share of the work to contribute to the group goal. Throughout this text we will be spotlighting the importance of being an ethical group communicator in a feature we call Ethical Collaboration Each one poses an ethical question or dilemma and then invites you to consider the most ethical course of action to take. The first one immediately appears in the following section.

In the classic book *All I Really Need to Know I Learned in Kindergarten*, Robert Fulghum suggested that while he was in kindergarten he mastered the basics of getting along with others and accomplishing tasks effectively. This text is designed to add to what you learned in kindergarten and later, so you can become a valued member of the groups to which you belong.

Ethical Collaboration

Is It Okay to Borrow Research?

Your underlying ethical principles are like your computer's operating system, which is always on when you are working with other programs on your computer. How you interact with others is based on your underlying assumptions and beliefs about appropriate and inappropriate ways to treat others.

Suppose you found yourself in the following situation. Your group communication instructor has assigned all students to small groups to work on a semester-long group project. One member of your group has a friend who took the course last semester with a different instructor. He suggests that your group select the same discussion topic that his friend had so that the group could benefit from the research already gathered by his friend's group. Your group can also do some original research to build on the previous group's research, but you will rely heavily on the information already collected.

WRITING PROMPT

Original versus Borrowed Research

Consider the preceding scenario. Is it ethical to use the work of another group in this situation? Are there any conditions that would make it more ethical to use the work of the previous group? Even if the group you're in gathers additional research, is it appropriate to "borrow" heavily from the work already completed by others, especially if the goal is to learn how to conduct original research?

The response entered here will appear in the performance dashboard and can be viewed by your instructor.

Submit

Summary: Group Principles and Practices

1.1: Communicating in Small Groups

- Small group communication is communication among a small group of people who share a common purpose, who feel a sense of belonging to the group, and who exert influence on one another.
- The nine group communication competencies are define the problem, analyze the problem, identify criteria, generate solutions, evaluate solutions, maintain task focus, manage interaction, manage conflict, and maintain climate.

1.2: Communicating in Teams

- A team is a coordinated group of individuals organized to work together so as to achieve a specific, common goal.
- The key elements that make a team effective are a clear, elevating goal; a results-driven structure; competent team members; unified commitment; a collaborative climate; standards of excellence; external support and recognition; and principled leadership.
- Effective team members are experienced, skilled problem-solvers, who are open to new ideas, supportive, positive, action oriented, and adaptive.
- Teams differ in important ways from groups. In a group, goals may be general, roles and responsibilities are not always explicitly defined, rules and expectations often develop informally and evolve according to the group's needs, group members interact, and work may be divided among group members. By contrast, teams have a clear, elevating goal that drives all aspects of team accomplishment; roles and responsibilities are explicitly developed; rules and operating procedures are clearly developed; team members collaborate and discuss how to coordinate their efforts; and teams work together interdependently.

1.3: Communicating Collaboratively in Groups: Advantages and Disadvantages

- Working in groups has the following advantages: more information, more creative problem solving, improved learning, more satisfied members, members' ability to learn about themselves.
- Working in groups has some disadvantages, too: Members may pressure others to conform, the group could be dominated by one person, members may rely on others and not do their part, and group work takes more time than individual work.

1.4: Communicating in Different Types of Groups

- Primary groups include family groups and social groups, a group whose main purpose is to give people a way to fulfill their need to associate with others.
- Secondary groups exist to accomplish a task or achieve a goal.

1.5: Communicating in Virtual Groups

- Virtual small group communication consists of three or more people who collaborate from different physical locations, perform interdependent tasks, have shared responsibility for the outcome of the work, and rely on some form of technology to communicate with one another.
- Methods of virtual collaboration include the telephone, e-mail, video, and the use of electronic meeting systems.

1.6: Communicating Competently in Small Groups

- Problem-oriented competencies include defining and analyzing the problem.
- Solution-oriented competencies include identifying criteria, generating solutions, and evaluating solutions.
- Discussion-management competencies include maintaining task focus and managing interactions.
- Relational competencies include managing conflict and maintaining a positive climate.

Chapter 2

Understanding Small Group Communication Theory

"To despise theory is to have the excessively vain pretension to do without knowing what one does, and to speak without knowing what one says."
—Bernard le Bovier de Fontenelle

Learning Objectives

2.1 Explain how people use theory to make sense of themselves and the world

2.2 Create a systemic explanation using theory

2.3 Relate theory to the sense-making function of small group communication

2.4 Differentiate between major theories of group communication

2.5 Apply theory to group communication

We encounter theories every day. Evolution, climate change, the "Big Bang"—all of these may be discussed and evaluated in classrooms, in our daily conversations, in newscasts, and in political debates. When we view crime dramas, fictitious detectives develop theories of crimes as we follow along and try to predict outcomes. But few of us take the time to think about what theories actually do for us. Where do they come from? How are they built? What are they good for?

Many of today's students are interested in relevant, practical knowledge, and sometimes they assume that theory is neither relevant nor practical. In truth, theory is very practical. Theorizing helps to explain or predict the events in people's lives; it is a very basic form of human activity.[1]

People theorize on a rudimentary level when they reflect on the past and make decisions based on these reflections. **Theory** is a set of interrelated facts, observations, and ideas that explains or predicts something. Theory, then, has two basic functions: to explain and to predict.

By the end of this module, you will be able to:

2.1.1 **Outline the process of forming a theory as it relates to self-concept**

2.1.2 **Relate theory to group communication**

2.1: The Nature of Theory and the Theory-Building Process

OBJECTIVE: Explain how people use theory to make sense of themselves and the world

Theories are useful in our everyday lives. Suppose, for example, that you do your weekly grocery shopping every Thursday after your late-afternoon class. When you arrive at the store, you are pleased to see that several checkout lanes are open, with no one waiting at any of them. You say, "I'll be out of here soon." You proceed up one aisle and down the next. To your dismay, you notice that each time you pass the checkout lanes, the lines have grown a bit longer. By the time you fill your cart, at least six people are waiting in each lane. You now have a 20-minute wait at the checkout.

If the situation just described were to occur once, you would probably curse your luck or chalk it up to fate. But if you find that the same events occur each time you visit the market, you might begin to see a consistency in your observations that goes beyond luck or fate. In noticing this consistency, you have taken the first step in building a theory: You have observed a phenomenon. In other words, you have witnessed a repeated pattern of events for which you believe there must be some explanation. So you ponder the situation. In your mind you organize all the facts available to you: the time of your arrival, the condition of the checkout lanes when you enter the store each time, and the length of the lines when you complete your shopping. You discover that you arrive at the store at approximately 4:45 each afternoon and reach the checkout lanes about 25 minutes later. You conclude that between the time you arrive and the time you depart, thousands of workers head for home, some of them stopping off at the store on the way. Voilà—you have a theory. You have organized your information to explain the phenomenon.

Assuming that your theory is accurate, it is now very useful for you. Having explained the phenomenon, you may now reasonably predict that under the same set of circumstances, the phenomenon will recur. In other words, if you continue to do your weekly shopping after your late afternoon class on Thursday, you will repeatedly be faced with long checkout lines. Given this knowledge, you can adapt your behavior accordingly, perhaps by doing your shopping earlier or later in the day.

2.1.1: Theory and Self-Concept

OBJECTIVE: Outline the process of forming a theory as it relates to self-concept

On a more personal level, your theory about yourself—your **self-concept**—influences the choices you make throughout the day. Your self-concept emerges as a consequence of your interactions with others, starting with your caregivers from childhood. You behave, others respond to you, and you observe their responses. You formulate your self-concept based on the reflected appraisals of others. You tend to behave consistently (predictably) with your self-concept. In essence, this self-concept, or "self-theory," serves to explain you to yourself, thereby allowing you to predict your behavior and to successfully select realistic goals. This is theory at its most personal and pervasive.

2.1.2: Theory and Group Communication

OBJECTIVE: Relate theory to group communication

Theory building is a common, natural process. You notice consistencies in your experience and examine relationships among the consistencies. You then build an explanation of the phenomenon that allows you to predict future events and, in some cases, to exercise some control over situations. Some theories, of course, are very elaborate and formal, but even in these cases the fundamental features of explanation and prediction can be seen. George Kelly's definition of theory refers to these features:

> A theory may be considered as a way of binding together a multitude of facts so that one may comprehend them all at once. When the theory enables us to make reasonably precise predictions, one may call it scientific.[2]

Theory is crucial to the study of group communication. The explanatory power of good theory helps make sense of the processes involved when people interact with others in a group. The predictive precision of theory allows people to anticipate probable outcomes of various types of communicative behavior in the group. Armed with this type of knowledge, people can adjust their own communicative behavior to help make group work more effective and rewarding.

WRITING PROMPT

Informal Theories

Make a list of informal theories you have about an ordinary day (Professor X is boring, I'm afraid of speaking in class, and so on). On what basis did you formulate these theories? How do they affect your behavior? What might cause you to alter them? Write a brief response addressing these questions.

The response entered here will appear in the performance dashboard and can be viewed by your instructor.

Submit

2.2: Theory as a Practical Approach to Group Communication

OBJECTIVE: Create a systemic explanation using theory

Theory, both formal and informal, helps us make intelligent decisions about how to conduct ourselves. Working in small groups is no exception. Everyone brings a set of theories to small group meetings—theories about oneself (self-concept), about other group members, and about groups in general. While participating in the group, we regulate our behavior according to these theories. We behave in ways consistent with our self-concepts. We relate to others in the group according to our previous impressions (theories) of them. If we believe (theorize) that groups are essentially ineffectual—that "a camel is a horse designed by committee" or that "if you really want something done, do it yourself"—then we probably will act accordingly and reinforce that belief. Conversely, if we come to the group having learned that groups are capable of working effectively, we will behave very differently and contribute much more to the group's effectiveness.

By the end of this module, you will be able to:

2.2.1 **Explain how theory helps a group determine its needs**

2.2.2 **Describe how a theory helps a group achieve its goals**

2.2.1: Explanatory Function

OBJECTIVE: Explain how theory helps a group determine its needs

To be practical, theories of small group communication must suggest ways in which participants can make group discussion more efficient and rewarding. The **explanatory function** of theory is important in this regard. If we understand why some groups are effective whereas others are not, or why certain styles of leadership are appropriate in some situations but not in others, then we are better prepared to diagnose the needs of our own groups. The explanatory function of theory leads us to understand group dynamics. Understanding is the first critical step in improving group process.

We commonly use theories to explain and predict. When are the best times to shop if we wish to avoid long lines? Understanding is the first critical step.

2.2.2: Predictive Function

OBJECTIVE: Describe how a theory helps a group achieve its goals

In medicine, a diagnosis is not helpful unless it suggests a course of treatment. Nevertheless, diagnosis—explanation—is a necessary first step. Understanding the process suggests ways of improving the process; therein lies the usefulness of the **predictive function** of theory. By understanding a specific group and group communication in general, and by being aware of possible alternative behaviors, you can use theory to select behaviors that will help you achieve the goal of your group. In other words, if you can reasonably predict that certain outcomes will follow certain types of communication, you can regulate your behavior to achieve the most desirable results. For example, predictions about time—such as how much time a task will take—that are made through group discussion tend to be more optimistic than predictions made by individuals in the group, probably because of the assumption that "many hands make light work." This tendency may lead to unrealistic time estimates and failure to meet deadlines. If you are a leader or a member of a group or team facing such a situation, knowledge of this tendency can help you to moderate its effect by alerting the group and suggesting that you collectively allocate a little more time for the project at hand.[3]

Some theories presented in this book explain group and team phenomena. These theories are referred to as **process theories**. Other theories, called **method theories**, take a prescriptive approach to small group communication. These how-to theories are particularly useful in establishing formats for solving problems and resolving conflicts in a group. Both types of theories add to the knowledge and skills that can make you a more effective communicator. Central to your effectiveness as a communicator is the ability to use words.

WRITING PROMPT

Theory Building

You have seen how various theories can be applied to ordinary, practical activities. Choose another everyday phenomenon and then build a systematic explanation. Explain which predictions you can make based on your theory.

The response entered here will appear in the performance dashboard and can be viewed by your instructor.

Submit

2.3: Communication as Sense-Making in Small Groups

OBJECTIVE: Relate theory to the sense-making function of small group communication

Communication is the vehicle that allows a group to move toward its goals, and words are the primary tools of communication. A verbal description of a planned new product at a company's board meeting creates a vision of that product for board members. Presented effectively, the description may result in new or changed attitudes and behaviors; the idea may be adopted. Words have the power to create new realities and to change attitudes; they are immensely beneficial tools. Although this may seem obvious, language often goes unnoticed. We spend so much of each day speaking, listening, reading, and writing that language seems simple to us. In truth, it is not. Through language, we unravel the enormous complexity that characterizes our world. With language, we build the theories that explain the world to ourselves and others.

Human communication is a transactive process by which we make sense out of the world and share that sense with others. Communication organizes and makes sense out of all the sights, sounds, odors, tastes, and sensations we perceive within our environment. As communication scholar Dean Barnlund states, "Communication occurs any time meaning is assigned to an internal or external stimulus."[4] Thus, when people arrive at a meeting room and begin to shiver, the sensation brings to their minds the word "cold." Within themselves, or on an ***intrapersonal level***, they have reduced uncertainty about the nature of an experience: The room is too cold. Giving verbal expression to an experience organizes and clarifies that experience.

"Where are you going with this, Wingate?"

At the ***interpersonal level*** of communication, the sense-making process is even more clearly evident. As you get to know someone, you progressively discover what makes that person unique. By developing an explanation of the person's behavior, you can predict how he or she is likely to respond to future communication and events. You base your predictions on what you know about the person's beliefs, attitudes, values, and personality. In essence, you build a theory that allows you to explain another person's behavior, to predict that person's future responses, and to control your own communicative behavior accordingly. Theories help people make sense of others.

By the end of this module, you will be able to:

2.3.1 Identify the six personas involved in one-on-one communication

2.3.2 Describe the complexity involved in group relationships

2.3.1: The Complexity of Getting to Know Someone

OBJECTIVE: Identify the six personas involved in one-on-one communication

Getting to know someone is a process of progressively reducing uncertainty—and a lot of uncertainty exists, especially at the outset of working with others in groups and teams. Think back to your first day at college or to your first day in group communication class. You were probably surrounded by many unfamiliar faces. At times such as these, you may feel tentative or uncertain and think, "What am I doing here?" and "Who are all of these other people?" In the cafeteria line, you encounter a person you find attractive. You say, "Hi! Are you new? What do you think of school so far?" This kind of engagement takes some courage because you don't know what kind of response you will get. So you hesitate. You make small talk and look for signs in the other person's behavior that might indicate whether that person desires further communication. You communicate, observe the response, and base your subsequent communication on your interpretation of that response. This is a complex process, particularly because both you and the other person must communicate, observe, respond, and interpret simultaneously!

The complexity of the process creates uncertainty—a sense of not being able to predict what will happen in the future. The presence of other people always creates uncertainty because you don't know for sure what they will do or say. Many communication theorists have noted that whenever an individual communicates with another person, at least six people are involved:

1. Who you think you are
2. Who you think the other person is
3. Who you think the other person thinks you are
4. Who the other person thinks he or she is
5. Who the other person thinks you are
6. Who the other person thinks you think he or she is

All six of these people influence and are influenced by the communication—a very complex matter indeed.

WRITING PROMPT

Six-Person Conversation

Think of a recent, memorable conversation you had with another person. Briefly describe the conversation and explain who the "six people" were in this conversation.

The response entered here will appear in the performance dashboard and can be viewed by your instructor.

Submit

2.3.2: The Complexity of Small Group Relationships

OBJECTIVE: Describe the complexity involved in group relationships

Complexity increases dramatically with group size, even when one relationship involves two, not six, people. When eight people interact, literally thousands of factors influence communication and are influenced by it—factors such as "who I think Ted thinks Rosa thinks Amit is" or "who I think Lourdes thinks Tom thinks I am."

Adding to the complexity are group members' thoughts and beliefs about the group itself. For example, considerable research has shown that athletic teams' beliefs about their own ability to perform have a clear effect on actual team outcomes. When researchers artificially manipulate feedback about a team's performance by inaccurately reporting exceedingly high or low baseline performance, such feedback affects subsequent team performance. Beliefs about the group itself—even when inaccurate—serve to explain, predict, and influence behaviors.[5]

Furthermore, when facing a problem or decision, humans have the unique ability to envision scenarios and eventualities in a variety of ways. Decisions are complex tasks that are not always welcomed by group members, who may view the uncertainty of decision making with apprehension and anticipation of regret.[6] All of these dynamics add to the complexity of small group communication.

Complexity increases with group size.

WRITING PROMPT

Complexity and Diversity in Groups

Complexity increases with group size, but also with the diversity of group members' beliefs and experiences. Examine the photograph above. Which factors do you observe that may add to the complexity of the group's interactions? Imagine a story line that explains what is happening in the picture. Which additional factors can you imagine that might influence the interactions among group members? Based on these factors, what do you think will be likely positive or negative outcomes for the group? Why?

The response entered here will appear in the performance dashboard and can be viewed by your instructor.

Submit

2.4: Theoretical Perspectives for the Study of Group Communication

OBJECTIVE: Differentiate between major theories of group communication

Small group communication theory attempts to explain and predict group and team phenomena. Given the complexity of the process and the number of variables that affect small group communication, no single theory can possibly account for all the variables involved, nor can one theory systematically relate the variables to one another. Therefore, a number of approaches to group communication theory have emerged in recent years. Each seeks to explain and predict group behavior while focusing on different facets of the group process. We will briefly introduce five broad theoretical perspectives that provide fairly holistic approaches:

1. Systems theory
2. Social exchange theory
3. Symbolic convergence theory
4. Structuration theory
5. Functional theory

By the end of this module, you will be able to:

2.4.1 **Describe the elements of systems theory**
2.4.2 **Outline a social exchange according to social exchange theory**
2.4.3 **Apply symbolic convergence theory to group interaction**
2.4.4 **Explain how structuration theory applies to groups**
2.4.5 **Identify functional group relationships that lead to better problem solving**

2.4.1: Systems Theory

OBJECTIVE: Describe the elements of systems theory

Perhaps the most prevalent approach to small group communication is **systems theory**. This theory is popular because it is flexible enough to encompass the vast array of variables that influence group and team interaction.

One way to approach the concept of a system is to think of your own body. The various organs make up systems (digestive, nervous, circulatory) that, in turn, make up the larger system (your body). Each organ depends on the proper functioning of other organs, because a change in one part of the system causes changes in the rest of the system. Furthermore, the physiological system cannot be isolated from the environment that surrounds it; to maintain the proper functioning of your physiological systems, you must adjust to changes outside your body. A decrease in oxygen at a higher elevation will cause you to breathe more rapidly, a rise in temperature will make you perspire, and so forth. In other words, your body is an open **system** composed of interdependent elements. It receives input from the environment (food, air, water), processes that input (digestion and oxygenation), and produces an output (writing poetry, designing a webpage, cooking a fabulous dinner). In addition to receiving input, processing input, and producing output, a small group system exhibits the properties of synergy, entropy, and equifinality.

Elements of Systems Theory

Openness to Environment—Groups do not operate in isolation, but rather are affected continually by interactions with the environment. New members may join and existing members may leave; demands from other organizations may alter a group's goals. Even the climate can affect the group's ability to work. For instance, a snowstorm may force cancellation of a meeting or a beautiful day outside can cause minds in a meeting room to drift.

Interdependence—The components of the group process are interrelated, meaning that a change in one component can alter the relationships among all other components. A shift in cohesiveness or composition can change the group's productivity level.[7] The loss of a group member or the addition of a new member may cause a change that ripples throughout the system. **Interdependence** in a small group makes the study of small group communication both fascinating and difficult: None of the variables involved may be understood properly in isolation.[8]

Input Variables—Input variables in the small group system include group members and group resources, such as funds, tools, knowledge, purposes, relationships to other groups or organizations, and the physical environment.[9]

Process Variables—Process variables relate to the procedures that the group follows to reach its goals. Many of these variables are represented in Figure 2-1.

Output Variables—Output variables—the outcomes of the group process—range from solutions and decisions to personal growth and satisfaction.

Synergy—Just as you are more than a composite of your various parts, so groups are more than the sum of their elements. **Synergy** is present when the whole is greater than the sum of its parts. When individuals form groups, they create something—the group—that didn't exist before; the group is more than the individuals who compose it. In turn, the performance of the group is often superior to the performance of the individuals within it.[10]

Entropy—The measure of randomness or chaos in a system is called **entropy**. Systems tend to decay (their entropy increases) if not balanced by some countervailing force. For example, interpersonal relationships separated by distance tend to cool rapidly, unless maintained actively through visits, text messages, phone calls, and other social media. So, too, groups and teams experience entropy when they don't meet together regularly.

Equifinality—The principle of **equifinality** states that a system's final state may be reached by multiple paths and from different initial states; there is more than one way to reach the goal. This is an inherent characteristic of open systems. Even systems (or groups and teams) that share the same initial conditions can reach very different end states.

Although systems theory does not fully explain small group phenomena, it serves as a useful organizational strategy. It also reminds us that a full understanding of group communication involves the broader contexts or environments in which groups operate.

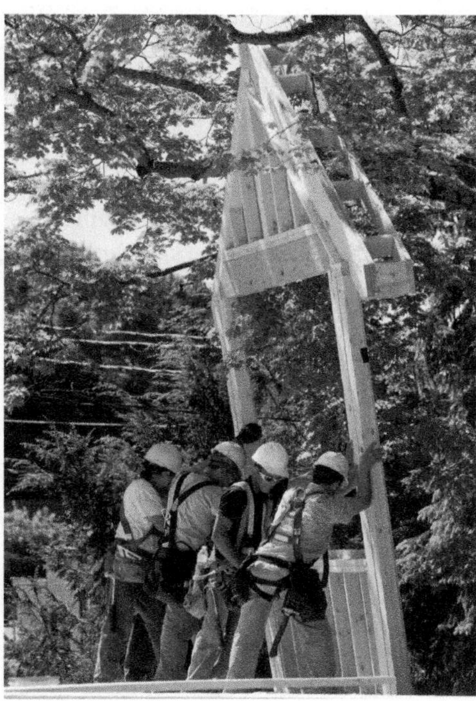

Small groups can be viewed as open systems encompassing different interdependent variables. Which input and output variables might there be for the group in this photograph?

2.4.2: Social Exchange Theory

OBJECTIVE: Outline a social exchange according to social exchange theory

Social exchange theory explains human behavior in terms of their rewards and costs, and their profits and losses. Rewards are pleasurable outcomes associated with particular behaviors; costs include such things as mental effort, anxiety, or even embarrassment.[11] Profit equals rewards minus costs; as long as rewards exceed costs, a relationship remains attractive.

Rewards and costs can take many forms in a group. For example, groups can provide rewards such as fellowship, job satisfaction, achievement, status, and meeting personal needs and goals. At the same time, group work takes time and effort and may be frustrating—all forms of costs. In one community theater group, participants identified meeting people and the opportunity to perform as the primary rewards, while they saw disorganization, lack of coordination, and time issues as costs.[12] Social exchange theory predicts that as long as rewards exceed costs—that is, as long as group membership is "profitable"—group membership will continue to be attractive. Small group variables such as cohesiveness and productivity are directly related to how rewarding the group experience is to its members. As with all theories discussed in this book, social exchange theory has its limitations. For example, it does not account for the effects of gender and power relationships in groups.[13]

The basics of social exchange theory are useful in their descriptiveness. Keep them in mind as you read the remaining chapters and as you observe working groups.

WRITING PROMPT

Costs and Rewards of Interpersonal Relationships

Choose one interpersonal relationship that is important to you. Identify the rewards and costs associated with this relationship. Does this help explain why you are attracted (or not) to this person?

▶ The response entered here will appear in the performance dashboard and can be viewed by your instructor.

Submit

2.4.3: Symbolic Convergence Theory

OBJECTIVE: Apply symbolic convergence theory to group interaction

Symbolic convergence theory describes how groups' identities develop through shared fantasies. If you consider your closest interpersonal relationships, you can probably remember a point at which each relationship took on a life of its own. For example, when you and an acquaintance become friends, the relationship takes on an identity based on your experiences together and your shared stories and visions of those experiences. Perhaps you develop "inside," or private, jokes that have meaning only for the two of you.

Groups take on this kind of shared personality as well. The **symbolic convergence theory** of communication explains how certain types of communication shape a group's identity and culture, which in turn influences other dynamics such as norms, roles, and decision making. Over time, groups develop a collective consciousness replete with shared emotions, motives, and meanings.[14]

FANTASY This sort of group consciousness evolves as group members share group fantasies or stories. Within this theory, the term **fantasy** does not have its usual meaning—something not grounded in reality. Rather, it refers to the creative and imaginative shared interpretation of events that fulfills a group's need to make sense of its experience and to anticipate its future.[15] A fantasy is usually introduced as a story that captures the imagination of the group and momentarily takes the group away from the specific issue under discussion. A group fantasy usually deals with real-life people and situations.

In groups, as in almost all forms of human endeavor, we can discern two levels of reality: (1) what actually happens and (2) our interpretations and beliefs about what happens. What remains in our memories and what guides our subsequent behavior is the latter. As an example, suppose you are in a group discussing how to reduce cheating and other forms of academic dishonesty. A group member says, "Hey, did anyone see the *Tonight Show* last night? They had a guy who won the national lying championship. He was so funny. He talked his way into getting photographed with the president of the United States." Another group member chimes in: "Yeah, I saw that. I had an uncle who used to tell whoppers. He once convinced my aunt that he had won a million dollars in the lottery." Yet another group member says, "My brother always plays practical jokes on my mom." Before you know it, the pace of conversation quickens and other group members tell stories about people who love to play practical jokes. A **fantasy theme** consists of the common or related content of the stories the group tells. The fantasy of one group member leads to a **fantasy chain**—a string of connected stories that revolve around a common theme. These fantasy chains help the group develop a shared sense of identity, just as the unique stories and experiences you have with a close friend give your relationship a unique identity. Usually a fantasy chain includes all the elements you would find in any well-told story: conflict, heroes, villains, and a plot that shapes the story.

By being mindful of the fantasies or stories that develop in a group, you can gain insight into what the group values. Some seemingly "off-task" behavior, such as talking about TV programs, movies, or events seemingly unrelated to the group's agenda, can actually be beneficial in giving the group a sense of identity. Noting the common themes of the group's fantasy (such as who the villains are in the stories or who wins or loses in the story) can also give you insight into a group's values and culture. In addition, fantasies may be a way for groups to deal with sensitive issues in an indirect way.

CASE STUDY

How Do You Keep a Group on Task?

You have been appointed to a task force whose purpose is to recommend ways to better integrate students who take mostly online courses with students who commute to the campus as well as resident students. The dean of students is concerned with the dropout rate and hopes that your group will offer positive suggestions that can enhance the college experience for all students.

The committee is composed mostly of juniors and seniors. The dean thinks they have been around long enough to "know the ropes." A majority of group members are traditional undergraduates who live in residence halls. One is a single mother who takes her classes online. As president-elect of next year's sophomore class, you are the youngest of the six committee members. You are also one of the few commuter students on the committee. The chairperson is a graduating senior and an assistant in the residence halls.

You arrive at the first meeting ready to work. You are excited about being a part of a decision-making process that will have a real impact on students' lives. To your dismay, the other members of the group seem to disregard their assignment and spend the meeting discussing the prospects for the basketball team, hardly mentioning the task at hand. You leave the meeting confused but hopeful that the next meeting will be more fruitful. You resolve to take a more active role and to try to steer the next meeting more toward the committee's task.

At the second meeting, you suggest that the committee discuss the assigned problem. Members concur at first, but then make jokes about the futility of retention programs and the administration's propensity to look for new ways to collect more tuition from students. When the chairperson makes no effort to keep the group on track, you feel overwhelmed and bewildered. You know that the dean expects a report within a month.

Questions for Analysis: How Do You Keep a Group on Task?

1. Analyze the situation in this scenario. What are the important components? Differences in status among group members? Other differences? Time constraints? The group's task? What else? How many can you identify? Which of these factors do you think will help you explain the situation, make predictions, and choose the most effective course of action?
2. Use the variables you identified to write a one-paragraph explanation of the situation.
3. Review Section 2.4.2 on social exchange theory. Which costs and rewards (real or potential) can you identify in this situation that might influence participants' behaviors?
4. Consider this group as a system: How would a change in one part of the system affect the other components? For instance, if the dean gives the group three additional months to complete the work, what is likely to happen?
5. If you were really in this situation, what would you do?

By describing how people in groups come to share a common social reality, symbolic convergence theory explains how groups make decisions and make sense of the decision-making process.[16] It points out that groups, like individuals, have unique "personalities," cultures, or identities built on shared symbolic representations related to the group; these cultures evolve through the adoption of fantasy themes or group stories. Just as we try to understand someone's behavior by taking into account "what sort of person he or she is," we must do the same for groups. Reflecting on the stories a group tells, which may seem off the topic, can give you insight into a group's personality, culture, values, and identity.

2.4.4: Structuration Theory

OBJECTIVE: Explain how structuration theory applies to groups

Anthony Giddens offers another contemporary theoretical approach to help us understand how people behave in small groups.[17] This approach has been further advanced by communication researcher Marshall Scott Poole and his colleagues.[18] **Structuration theory** provides a general framework that explains how people structure their groups by making active use of rules and resources. The theory focuses attention on individuals' *behaviors* in groups rather than on the dynamics of groups per se. This process theory is especially useful for explaining change within groups and organizational systems.[19]

Structuration theory involves two key concepts: *systems* and **rules**. "Don't talk while others are talking" and "Don't leave the meeting until the boss says everyone is dismissed" are examples of rules. These rules determine how the group structures itself and performs tasks, and how group members talk to one another.

Every group develops its own set of rules and resources that structure individuals' behaviors within the group. Note the two groups pictured here. How might their rules and resources be different from each other?

Structuration theory suggests that when we join a new group, we use rules we learned in other groups to structure our behavior. For example, when you walked into your first college class, you probably drew on your experiences as a high school student to know how to act. But groups also create their own rules and resources to determine what is appropriate and inappropriate. Over time, you learned that a college class is similar to, but not exactly like, a high school class. You also discovered that different classes have different rules or structure: Some classes have informal rules, whereas others have more formal ones. One teacher may deduct points for being absent; another teacher may not take roll at all. How communication rules are organized is based on factors both internal and external to the group. Structuration theory helps explain why and how groups develop the rules and behavior patterns they adopt. It can be especially useful for understanding group communication within broader organizational cultures,[20] such as how a group of jurors in a trial draws on rules each juror has observed from other juries and from dramatic depictions of jury deliberations.[21]

Skilled Collaboration

Structuration and the Exercise of Free Will

Concepts and theories are useful because they allow us to explain and predict group phenomena and thus give us a measure of control—over our own actions and, to an extent, over group processes and outcomes.

Structuration theory reminds us that groups are not simply the products of external factors: They are composed of individual human beings who think and act and who can intentionally change the course of the group. Forces such as status differences, norms, stress levels, and leadership styles are not absolute, but rather are mediated by the ways group members choose to react to them. This should be obvious, but it's an important point to emphasize. Armed with an understanding of these forces (provided by theories), you can use available rules and resources more effectively to achieve your goals and those of the group.

The usefulness of any theory lies in its real-life application. Structuration theory deals with the power of each individual group member to change the behavior of a group by applying rules and resources during interactions. Every action in a group structures subsequent actions. Consider the following:

- Whenever you act, you are making choices—exercising your free will in a way that has consequences for, and that structures, subsequent group interactions.
- Our choices are somewhat constrained by external forces, existing group structures, and other members' behaviors. Try to be more aware of the choices—and constraints—before you.
- Members of distributed, virtual groups are much less likely to accept personal responsibility when the group is not going well; that is, we are much more likely to blame others for dysfunction in virtual groups than in face-to-face groups.[22] Recognizing this tendency can help you structure such groups so as to attain better outcomes.
- Work to identify the rules that are governing group members' behaviors. Are these rules contributing to the group's work, or are they perhaps impeding it? You can call attention to dysfunctional rules and help the group change them. You can sometimes change rules by violating them.
- Ask yourself which resources are available to you and to the rest of the group. Do you have particular knowledge or skills that are useful? Do others in the group have resources that you can help them tap into? Subtly bending group rules, sharing resources, and encouraging others to do the same are all ways to affect group processes and outcomes.

Rules and resources in interaction provide the structures that define your group's system. These systems change over time—sometimes suddenly—through the choices that individual group members make. This text and the course you're taking are designed to arm you with an ever-greater understanding of the rules and resources available to you in group interaction.

2.4.5: Functional Theory

OBJECTIVE: Identify functional group relationships that lead to better problem solving

Much of this course aims to help you identify and enact behaviors that will help your groups reach their intended goals. The term **function** refers to the effect or consequence of a given behavior within a group system. For example, communication can help a group make decisions or manage conflict. Communication has an effect on the group; it has a function. Theories that concern themselves with group functions seek to identify and explain behaviors that help or allow a group to achieve its goals. Functional relationships exist within a group when an outcome occurs as a consequence of a specific behavior, which in turn was intended to produce the consequence.[23]

Three Propositions

The functional theory developed by Dennis Gouran and Randy Hirokawa advances three propositions. These researchers suggest that effective group problem solving and decision making are most likely to occur under these propositions.[24]

Satisfy Task Requirements—Group members attempt to satisfy task requirements (including understanding the issue to be resolved, the characteristics of acceptable solutions, and the realistic alternatives; examining the alternatives; and selecting the alternative most likely to satisfy the requirements of the problem).

Overcome Constraints—Group members use communication to overcome constraints such as stress from deadlines, interpersonal conflicts, or self-serving interactions.

Review Decisions—Group members take the time to review the process through which they arrived at choices and, if necessary, reconsider their choice.

Functional theories provide the basis for how communication in groups promotes appropriate consequences—sound reasoning, critical thinking, the prevention of errors, and the building of productive relationships among group members.[25]

Review

Theoretical Perspectives for the Study of Small Group Communication

- Systems theory: The small group is an open system of interdependent elements, employing input variables and process variables to yield output.
- Social exchange theory: Groups remain attractive to their members so long as the rewards of group membership exceed the costs.
- Symbolic convergence theory: Group members develop a group consciousness and identity through the sharing of fantasies or stories, which are often chained together and share a common theme.
- Structuration theory: People use rules and resources to structure social interactions.
- Functional theory: Communication in groups promotes sound reasoning, prevents errors, and builds productive relationships among members.

2.5: A Model of Small Group Communication

OBJECTIVE: **Apply theory to group communication**

A model that takes into account all the possible sender, receiver, and message variables in a small group would be hopelessly complicated. Moreover, a complete systems model of group and team communication would necessarily include psychological forces as well as communication variables.[26] No model is ever complete. Consequently, the model we offer is less than comprehensive but suggests the main features and relationships critical to understanding small group communication.

By the end of this module, you will be able to:

2.5.1 Describe the elements of a communication model

2.5.2 Explain how to use theories to their best advantage when thinking about groups

2.5.1: Parts of a Descriptive Model

OBJECTIVE: **Describe the elements of a communication model**

Figure 2-1 presents a descriptive model that includes important features of a group process and suggests relationships among those features. In this framework, small group communication comprises a constellation of variables, each related to every other. Communication establishes and maintains the relationships among these essential variables. This model thus reflects a systems approach to group and team communication.

Variables of the Descriptive Model

This model identifies the components of a group process that are central, critical considerations for effective group communication.

Communication—Human communication is how you make sense out of the world and share that sense with others. Communication is what people say, how they say it, and to whom they say it. This process is the primary focus of study in small group communication research.

Leadership—Behavior that exerts influence on the group is called **leadership**.

Goals—All groups have **goals**. For example, the group goal may be to provide therapy for members, to complete some designated task, or simply to have a good time. Individual group members also have goals. Often individual goals complement the group goal, but not always. Effective teamwork requires shared, clear, specific goals.[27]

Norms—A **norm** is a standard that establishes which behaviors are normally permitted or encouraged within the group and which are forbidden or discouraged. Every group—from your family to the president's cabinet—develops and maintains norms. Some norms are formal, such as a rule about when a group must use parliamentary procedure. Formal, explicitly stated norms are rules that prescribe how group members should behave. Other norms are informal, such as the fact that your study group always meets 15 minutes late. Norms guide and direct behavior in groups, and can also be viewed as characteristics of a group that differentiate it from all other groups.[28]

Figure 2-1 Constellation of Variables in Small Group Communication

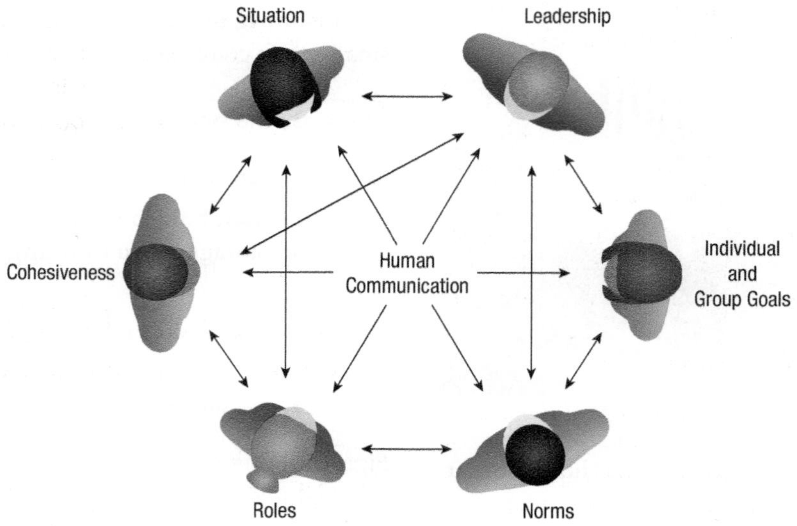

Roles—The sets of expectations people hold for themselves and for others in a given context are **roles**. People play different roles in different groups. Researchers have identified several roles that need to be filled for a small group to reach its maximum levels of satisfaction and productivity.

Cohesiveness—Feelings of loyalty help unite the group. **Cohesiveness** is the degree of attraction that group members feel toward one another and toward the group.

Situation—The **situation**, or context in which group communication occurs, is of paramount importance. The task is significant, but many other important situational variables also influence the group's functioning, such as the group's size, the physical arrangement of group members, the location or setting, the group's purpose, and even the amount of stress placed on the group by time constraints or other internal or external pressures.

The combined effect of these variables results in group outcomes—that is, what the group or team accomplishes. Group and team outcomes may include solving problems, making decisions, feeling satisfied, reaching agreement, or even making money. Small group communication theories seek to explain the relationships among these and other variables and to make predictions about group outcomes. These theories help explain most of the complexity and uncertainty that surface at every level of group and team interaction. A good theoretical understanding of small groups, coupled with an expanded repertoire of communicative behavior, is the recipe for developing group communication competence—the objective of this course.

Virtual Collaboration

Modes of Communication

Face-to-face communication is "media rich" because it involves numerous modes of communication. A mode is the particular way or means through which communication is expressed. In face-to-face communication, the modes correspond to our senses. Thus, the message "I'm so glad to see you" is reinforced when accompanied with a smile and a hug. Modal contradiction occurs when modes conflict, as when a person smirks and continues staring into her cell phone while saying without enthusiasm, "I'm so glad to see you."

Generally speaking, modal reinforcement is desirable; adding modalities strengthens the message. But modal contradiction can also be used to subtly affect the intended message. It is, after all, the mother of sarcasm.

In virtual communication, the nonverbal cues that come so naturally through our senses are largely absent. Even so, the principles of modal reinforcement and contradiction still apply. Some researchers have argued that the goal of communication technology should be to maximize media richness for a particular task by using redundant or complementary modalities.[29] Today's technology offers visual and auditory possibilities for communication that were not present even a few years ago. The goal in virtual communication is to approximate face-to-face interaction as closely as possible.

How can you best match your text-based or audiovisual modality to the communication occurring in virtual teams? The best way to develop this skill is to be conversant with the communication modalities available to you, and then to consider your intended message from your target receivers' point of view. Which combinations of modalities will best strengthen your message without providing so much media richness as to be distracting?

2.5.2: Tips for Using Theory

OBJECTIVE: Explain how to use theories to their best advantage when thinking about groups

The theories presented in this chapter will be useful to you to the degree that you learn and internalize them. Therefore, the first step in turning theory into practice is to really learn the theories. Study them to the point that you can teach them to another person without using notes. Once you have internalized this information, the theories become a part of you, a resource you can draw on throughout your life.

Here are some tips for using each theory:

- Systems theory gives you broad perspective. Learn to think about your groups holistically. Every group comprises interdependent parts that affect one another while responding to and shaping the environment.
- Social exchange theory focuses on the costs and rewards associated with group membership. Do a simple cost–benefit analysis of your group and then work to minimize costs and maximize rewards for greater group satisfaction and productivity.
- Symbolic convergence theory alerts us to the importance of group "personality." Be mindful of the "fantasies" or stories that circulate within the group and that may give you insight into the group's values and ways of dealing with sensitive issues.
- Structuration theory focuses on group rules and resources. Identifying and understanding these rules and resources will strengthen your influence within your groups.
- Functional theories focus on behaviors that help the group move toward its goals. Effective group communication involves specific competencies that help groups achieve their goals. Learn these competencies well and work to improve your group communication skills.

Our general model of small group interaction includes seven variables: communication, leadership, goals, norms, roles, cohesiveness, and situation. Use these categories to help structure your thinking about groups.

As you continue reading, seek ways to apply what you're learning. The practicality of theories is measured only by how we can use them to be more effective group leaders, members, and scholars.

Summary: Understanding Small Group Communication Theory

2.1: The Nature of Theory and the Theory-Building Process

- Theory building, like communication, is a process for organizing and understanding.
- We begin by noticing consistencies in our experiences, examining relationships among those consistencies, and then building explanations. Based on our explanations, and given a similar situation, we can make predictions about events.

2.2: Theory as a Practice Approach to Group Communication

- Theories are conceptual tools for understanding and decision making.
- The explanatory power of good theory helps us make sense of the processes involved when people interact with others in a group.
- The predictive precision of theory allows people to anticipate probable outcomes of various types of communicative behavior in the group.
- Armed with this type of knowledge, people can adjust their own communicative behavior to help make group work more effective and rewarding.

2.3: Communication as Sense-Making in Small Groups

- Communication organizes and makes sense out of all the sights, sounds, smells, tastes, and sensations in our environment.
- At the interpersonal level, we use communication to make sense of—to explain and predict—other people's behavior.
- Uncertainty and complexity increase as group size increases, making effective communication essential to group success.

2.4: Theoretical Perspectives for the Study of Group Communication

- Theories explain consistencies in communicative behavior that researchers have observed within small groups.
- Five theories are especially important in regard to small group communication: systems theory, social exchange theory, symbolic convergence theory, structuration theory, and functional theory. Each of these theories provides a particular vocabulary and set of conceptual tools for understanding small group dynamics.

2.5: A Model of Small Group Communication

- The model depicts small group communication as a constellation of variables, each related to every other.
- Communication establishes and maintains the relationships among these essential variables.
- The other variables are leadership, goals, norms, roles, cohesiveness, and situation.

SHARED WRITING

Self-Concepts and Ethical Principles

Ethical principles help people decide what's right or wrong. These theoretical constructs help people explain situations in which they find themselves, predict possible outcomes from a set of potential actions, and control their behavior to achieve desired effects. Sometimes people are unaware of their own ethical principles until they are confronted with specific situations that require ethical judgments.

Imagine you and your three roommates see an advertisement for a $1500 ultra-high-definition, big-screen television. You currently have a small, low-resolution TV in your apartment, and on your limited budgets, you can't really afford a new one. The ad says you may try out the TV in your home for six months with no obligation to buy. If you are not completely satisfied, you can return the set with no questions asked. If you decide to keep the set, you will begin making monthly payments at that time. Will you try out the TV, knowing that there is no way you can keep it longer than six months? Or will you pass on the offer?

You may think there is clearly a right answer, but others may hold the opposite view and see it just as clearly. Our theories of ourselves (self-concepts) include ethical beliefs and principles.

In this situation, what would you do, and why? Can you identify the ethical principle that explains your decision in this case? Write a short response that your classmates will read. Be sure to include specifics in your discussion.

▶ A minimum number of characters is required to post and earn points. After posting, your response can be viewed by your class and instructor, and you can participate in the class discussion.

Post

Chapter 3

Facilitating Group Development

"Coming together is a beginning; keeping together is progress; working together is success."

—Henry Ford, Sr.

Learning Objectives

3.1 Relate interpersonal needs to group communication

3.2 Analyze the ways in which people develop and commit to common goals

3.3 Analyze attraction between people and groups

3.4 Evaluate how cultural norms influence group interaction

3.5 Analyze the process of group development

Like individual people, groups and teams are born, grow, change, move through predictable stages of life, and die. They require nurturing and sometimes get sick. When this happens, they need diagnosis and treatment. Their health relies on keeping various systems and subsystems in balance.

This chapter is about group formation and development. Formation is more than a one-time event. While there is often an identifiable moment in which groups come into being, they are continually engaged in a process of reinvention as they develop over time. What brings people together in groups? Group formation—and development over time—involves an interplay of needs, goals, attraction, and communication. A competent group communicator recognizes these dynamics and works to keep them in balance.

3.1: Interpersonal Needs

OBJECTIVE: Relate interpersonal needs to group communication

For all people, the formation of groups—from families to teams to corporate boards—is part of a biological imperative that is simply inherent to the human species; we humans are social animals by nature.[1] Some common dynamics affect all groups. We are born into family groups and assigned or elected to other groups and committees. But we also actively choose many of our affiliations. Individuals differ in their motivation for joining a group as well as in their commitment and contribution to it. The reasons why people join groups can be organized into five broad categories:

1. Interpersonal needs
2. Individual goals
3. Group and team goals
4. Interpersonal attraction
5. Group attraction

Theories developed by Abraham Maslow and William Schutz focus on interpersonal needs as the basis for attraction.

By the end of this module, you will be able to:

3.1.1 Outline Maslow's hierarchy

3.1.2 Describe the cyclical nature of groups according to Schutz

3.1.1: Maslow's Theory

OBJECTIVE: Outline Maslow's hierarchy

Abraham Maslow asserted that all humans have basic needs that can be arranged in a hierarchy. According to Maslow, people do not concern themselves with higher-level needs in this hierarchy until their lower-level needs are satisfied.[2] Figure 3-1 illustrates how interpersonal needs form a hierarchy.

Figure 3-1 Hierarchy of Interpersonal Needs[3]

1. *Physiological needs* are the first level of needs, found at the bottom of the hierarchy. We have physiological needs for air, water, and food.
2. *Safety needs* relate to one's security and protection. Maslow called the first two levels of the hierarchy "survival needs"—reflecting the fact that satisfaction of these needs is necessary for basic human existence. During childhood years, the family satisfies these needs.

Psychological needs follow after survival needs are fulfilled. These higher-level needs—the need to belong, the need for esteem, and the need for self-actualization—then become more important. Psychological needs may affect people's group memberships throughout their lives.

3. *Belongingness need* is the need for people to feel that they are a part of some group. Families provide a sense of belonging for children, but as children get older they begin to look outside the family to satisfy this need. Peer groups gain special importance during adolescence. At that time, people's need for affiliation is at its strongest.
4. *Esteem need* arises after people have developed a sense of belonging; they then crave respect or esteem. Individuals need to feel not only that they are accepted but also that they are considered worthwhile and valued by others. When we are promoted, recognized, congratulated, thanked, and given awards, our esteem needs are addressed.
5. *Self-actualization need* is different from the other four needs. Maslow termed the other four needs "deficiency needs" because individuals subconsciously perceive these needs as inner voids, which they fill by drawing on the resources of other people. In contrast, Maslow identified the need for self-actualization as a "being need." This need motivates people to try to fulfill their potential and live life to its fullest. Self-actualized individuals are ready to function as autonomous beings, operating independently in quest of their own full potential. They no longer need groups

to take care of their deficiencies; instead, they need groups in which to find and express their wholeness. Participation in service-oriented groups such as Habitat for Humanity may fulfill self-actualization needs in many people.

Although the self-actualization need level is perhaps the most difficult to grasp conceptually, Maslow's hierarchy is consistent: People need groups to satisfy interpersonal needs. The higher we move up Maslow's hierarchy, the more important communication becomes in need satisfaction.[4]

3.1.2: Schutz's Theory

OBJECTIVE: Describe the cyclical nature of groups according to Schutz

William Schutz suggested that three basic human needs influence individuals as they form and interact in groups: the need for *inclusion*, the need for *control*, and the need for *affection*.[5] Individuals' needs vary, but groups often provide settings in which such needs can be satisfied.

- **Inclusion**. Just as Maslow postulated a belongingness need, Schutz said people join groups to fulfill their need for inclusion. We need to be recognized as unique individuals and to feel understood. When someone tries to understand you, the implication is that you are worth their time and effort. In this respect, Schutz's inclusion need is also related to Maslow's esteem need.
- **Control**. People need control to gain status and power. We need to have some control over ourselves and others, and sometimes we need to give others some control over us, such as when we seek guidance and direction. There is wide variation in individuals' control needs. Such needs are often observed as bossiness or, conversely, submissiveness.
- **Affection**. The need for affection drives people to give and receive emotional warmth and closeness. Some people are natural caregivers and exercise their need to nurture others in groups. Others (and sometimes the same people) need to feel the acceptance, warmth, and love that groups can provide.

In a broad sense, groups are more than collections of people with common goals: They are arenas in which individual needs are satisfied or frustrated. Schutz asserted that people's needs for inclusion, control, and affection influence group development throughout the life of the group. In the initial stages of group formation, communication is aimed primarily toward fulfilling members' inclusion needs. Group members are friendly but cautious as they try to evaluate one another and gain acceptance by other members. As the group develops, control needs become more evident; members contest issues and vie for leadership. Schutz observed that as conflicts resolve, people turn toward affection needs. Members characteristically express positive feelings in this phase. The progression is cyclical.

REPEATING CYCLES OF GROUP DEVELOPMENT From Schutz's perspective, the process of group formation is not limited to the initial coming together of group members. Rather, formation patterns repeat themselves as the group develops over time. Group decision making involves a series of smaller decisions that are reached on the way toward achieving the group's primary goal. For example, a group of engineers planning to construct a bridge must decide whether it will engage in virtual and/or face-to-face meetings, choose locations for and frequency of the group's meetings, and agree on the design and materials for the bridge. A group progresses through developmental phases throughout its life, and this cyclical pattern of formation and reformation occurs whenever the group approaches a new meeting and a new decision. If this process could be visualized, it might look something like a large jellyfish moving through the water. The jellyfish floats in the water in a relatively aimless way until it needs to move forward. Then it organizes itself, contracts, and propels itself through the water, after which its movements again become less organized. A group progresses through a similar series of contractions until it reaches its ultimate goal.

In essence, every group is defined (in part) by a common purpose, and that purpose contains several smaller goals. As a group reaches each of these goals, it momentarily loses a bit of its definition until a new goal replaces the old one. As people accomplish each new goal, they begin a new cycle of inclusion, control, and affection behaviors. The example on the next page illustrates this point.

In this example you can see the end of one cycle and the beginning of the next. Members express positive feelings about the group and its accomplishments, then pause in their conversation before regrouping to attack a new facet of their problem. The sense of cohesiveness peaks during the affection phase and then falls off, only to build anew around the next task. Like the jellyfish, which organizes its efforts around its task of propulsion, the small group does not end up back where it started; instead, the whole process moves forward. In this sense, the phases aren't purely cyclical: Certain types of communicative behaviors recur, but each time the whole process progresses. As an analogy, you can think of human communication as being like a helix.[6] A helix is both linear and circular; it turns in on itself and yet always moves forward. Seen in this light, group formation does not cease but pulses throughout the life of the group.

Review

Schutz's Theory

Individuals join groups in part to satisfy three needs:

- Inclusion: They want to be recognized and feel included. They also have needs to share and want to include others in their activities.
- Control: People have varying needs to control or to be controlled that groups can satisfy.
- Affection: Individuals satisfy their affection needs through giving and receiving emotional support in groups.

Groups pass through observable, cyclical phases of these needs.

WRITING PROMPT

Motivations Based on Need

Consider your own interpersonal needs. What motivates you? In Schutz's scheme, how would you evaluate your level of need to receive or express inclusion, control, or affection? What does this reveal to you about your participation in groups?

The response entered here will appear in the performance dashboard and can be viewed by your instructor.

Submit

3.2: Goals and Mutuality

OBJECTIVE: Analyze the ways in which people develop and commit to common goals

Theories of psychological and interpersonal needs explain some of the bases for group development. So, too, do individual goals. Goals have a more tangible and obvious effect on your selection of group memberships. What do you want out of life? Happiness? Status? Power? Money? Fame? Recreation? Education? Personal growth? In other words, what goals do you have that exist apart from any particular group membership?

"Somewhere along the line, our sewing circle took a strange turn."

By the end of this module, you will be able to:

- 3.2.1 **Explain how individual goals motivate action**
- 3.2.2 **Differentiate group goals from individual goals**
- 3.2.3 **Analyze the ways that groups balance individual and group commitment**

3.2.1: Individual Goals

OBJECTIVE: Explain how individual goals motivate action

Individual goals are instrumental in determining the groups that people join. If people enjoy arranging flowers and wish to improve their skills, they may join garden clubs. If they desire status and power, they may seek membership in elite social or professional groups. Sometimes the prestige associated with a particular group is enough to make membership attractive. Whatever their individual goals may be, people bring those goals with them when they join groups.

Sometimes individual goals are group-centric; that is, an individual's goal may be significant for the group's or team's success. Consider, for example, a basketball player with the goal of helping her team be successful in any way possible. Her behavior on the court will be different—and more helpful—than that of the player whose individual goal is to score as many points as possible, which may negatively affect her defensive play or her tendency to pass the ball to a teammate.[7] When individual and group goals coincide, greater productivity often follows.

WRITING PROMPT

Individual Goals and Team Success

Consider the performance of an athletic team and some possible individual goals that the players bring to it. How would you rank the following individual goals as they relate to the team's success, with number 1 representing the most valuable, and so on: status, power, fame, happiness, money, success, education, and friendship. Why is your number-one ranking the most important?

▶ The response entered here will appear in the performance dashboard and can be viewed by your instructor.

Submit

3.2.2: Group Goals

OBJECTIVE: Differentiate group goals from individual goals

Group goals are identifiable future achievements that transcend the group members' individual goals. This is the paradox of group membership: We often join groups to meet personal goals, which must then be made secondary, in part, for the group to succeed. But there's a payoff: In the workplace, group or team goal achievement is related to greater group attraction, individual satisfaction, and employee job satisfaction.[8]

When personal goals conflict with group goals, the results can be counterproductive. Especially when high levels of commitment are required, groups should question their participants' **mutuality of concern**—the degree to which members share the same level of commitment to the group or team—during the early stages of group formation.[9]

Individual Goals and Their Implications for the Group

Dave—Dave is a senior in college majoring in economics. He is a driven student who wants to get his MBA and work in an investment firm. To get into the best business school he can, Dave is building up his résumé by participating in an internship, working as a store manager, and collaborating with other business students to implement marketing strategies to increase sales of the college's sports team merchandise. He has little time to devote to the group but wants credit for participating. Recently he has noticed that the group no longer asks him to perform contributory tasks, which is somewhat a relief because he would not have time for them anyway. However, Dave knows he must stay in the group to include it on his résumé.

Amit—Amit loves his college and felt honored to be asked by the Development Office to participate in the annual fundraising campaign. Arriving at the designated location, he was delighted to see some of the most active and visible student leaders on the campus had been recruited as well. Membership in this group made Amit feel proud. As they made phone calls, mostly to alumni/ae of the college, they discovered the wonderful loyalty that graduates felt for the school. Between calls, Amit and the other group members shared stories and bonded with one another and felt closer than ever to their future alma mater.

Paul—Paul loves to hike and has come to appreciate well-maintained trails, recognizing their benefits to people as well as the surrounding environment. Wanting to help others enjoy trails as much as he does, he joined a volunteer trail-building organization that maintains trails throughout the area. Working side by side with his fellow members, he has developed friendships and learned new skills. Upon completing each job, Paul feels satisfied that the team has created something of value that people will use for years to come. He also feels proud of the role he has played and the skills he has developed in the process.

Robert—Ever since they were first-year students, Robert has been unable to get Dulce off his mind. To him, Dulce is the most beautiful woman in the world. Unfortunately, despite his multiple attempts to engage her in conversation and invitations to go for coffee, she has expressed no interest in Robert. In fact, she appears to be avoiding him. He is resorting to increasingly desperate measures to gain her attention. Learning that Dulce is passionate about Habitat for Humanity's mission to build affordable housing for low-income families, Robert has joined the student chapter, even though he has no interest or skill in building houses. At the meetings, all he can think about is Dulce.

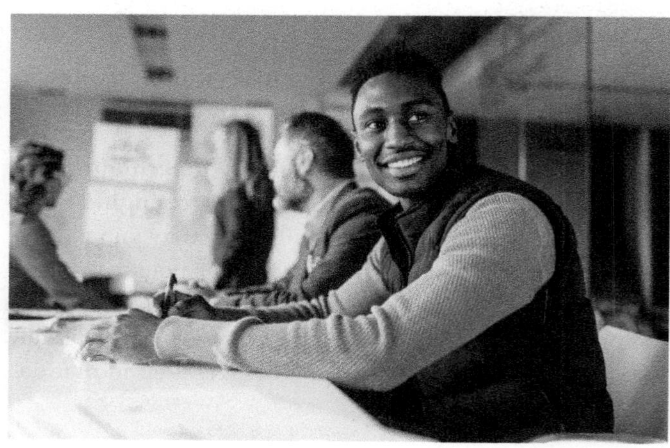

3.2.3: Establishing Mutuality of Concern

OBJECTIVE: Analyze the ways that groups balance individual and group commitment

When people join groups, they often assume that other group members share their commitment to the group's task. In reality, each person brings a different perspective to a group. Some group members are invariably more conscientious than others. Studies have shown that the more dissimilar team members are in this respect, the less satisfied they are likely to be with their team.[10] Conversely, strong conscientiousness within a group is strongly related to group performance.[11]

COMMITMENT People bring different levels of commitment to groups. Suppose you have been appointed to a student-government group whose task is to recommend whether your college should institute a plus/minus grading system or continue with a traditional *A, B, C, D* grading policy. If you are a first- or second-year student, this policy change could have a direct effect on your grade-point average over your four years in college. If you are a graduating senior, this policy change would have little or no effect on you. Hence, the level of concern over the problem can vary from member to member of the group. Those students affected directly by the problem will probably become more active in the group than those who are not.

CONCERN FOR TASK The degree to which members are concerned with the group's task should be clarified at the outset. All group members should clearly state their personal commitment, needs, and goals regarding the topic area. Clarifying mutuality of concern can resolve much misunderstanding and avoid needless conflict.

People often form groups simply because they enjoy the same activities. What groups do you belong to for this reason?

INDIVIDUAL NEEDS AND GOALS Although individual needs and goals may bring a group together in the first place, they can also break a group apart. The success or failure of a group depends, in part, on the degree to which members adopt its goal as their own. Unsatisfied or unclarified individual needs and goals can become hidden agendas—private goals toward which individuals work while seeming to work toward the group goal. Such hidden agendas can prove extremely disruptive to the group. Establishing mutuality of concern can help reduce this negative influence.

Skilled Collaboration

Mutuality of Concern

Individual needs and goals can bring a group together, but they can also break a group apart. For groups to succeed, the collective goal should transcend the goals of individual group members. Groups should clarify the degrees to which members are concerned with the group's task at the outset. Establishing realistic expectations among group members will help minimize misunderstandings and conflict.

Real-Life Applications

Communication scholar Michael Kramer studied a community theater group to see how its members managed multiple group roles. A community theater is a good example of a group that sometimes requires extraordinary commitments of time and effort over a limited period of time. Members had to make their participation in the theater group a priority over their membership in other groups until the production ended, after which they could again devote time and effort to their other commitments.

Members of the theater group managed conflicts among their several group memberships in three ways. First, they auditioned for productions only if they thought conflicts would be minimal. Second, they negotiated conflicts (such as being required to attend regular meetings of other groups) in advance, so the theater group could allow for such time conflicts in its planning. Third, they informed members of their other groups of their temporary conflicts.[12] These strategies translate well to many types of groups and contexts. Consider the following ways to demonstrate mutuality of concern:

- Avoid putting yourself in group situations if you don't have the time, energy, or interest to commit and do a good job.

- When you have conflicts and other interests that will compete for your time and attention, be "up front" with your group: Explain your situation and work to find acceptable solutions.
- When you accept new positions or assignments, explain the new demands on your time to members of groups you're already a part of; in other words, renegotiate your level of commitment.

Also, as you consider joining new groups and teams, keep the following practical questions in mind:

- How does participating in the group relate to your overall goals and objectives?
- What will you have to give up if you participate in this group?
- How will your new group affect your existing obligations to your employer, colleagues, friends, or family members?

TECHNOLOGY AND MUTUALITY OF CONCERN Another variable in establishing mutuality of concern is the introduction of technology—the key means of communication in virtual teams. While virtual teams have the advantage of crossing time and space, they are often vulnerable to **social loafing**, the tendency for people to hold back from contributing (to loaf) in a group because they assume someone else will do the work. Social loafing is more prominent in virtual groups than in face-to-face groups because the technology-supported environment makes such behavior easier to engage in. Combatting social loafing is a matter of fostering cognitive engagement.[13] In any given situation, the interaction of individual and group needs will cause one of four possible outcomes:

1. Individual and group needs may be so diverse that they interfere with each other, with no positive effects accruing either to individuals within the group or to the group as a whole.
2. Group interaction may result in the realization of group goals, while individual needs go unmet.
3. One or more group members may have their needs met, to the detriment or destruction of the group.
4. Individual and group needs may blend so completely that the needs realized by the group as a whole are the same needs individuals wish to realize.[14] In the ideal, fully integrated group, this fourth alternative is realized. Mutuality of concern can merge individual and group needs and goals.

Ethical Collaboration

Personal Goals versus Group Goals

We often join groups to satisfy personal needs or to accomplish personal goals. But is it ethical to join groups to promote personal objectives? Is it selfish?

Imagine that you are part of an important team preparing to launch a new project. Each team member knows that the project will involve hard, time-consuming work, but if it succeeds, it will bring great benefits to your organization. A position opens up on your team because one of the members moves away. On several occasions, one of your best friends has indicated that if a position on the team ever became available, she would like to be considered. You know that your friend is intelligent and capable and could make a contribution to the team's efforts if she would truly commit to it. The problem is that you know your friend has already spread herself too thin. She is ambitious and has already accepted leadership positions in several organizations, as she builds her résumé while applying to prestigious graduate schools. She says that appointment to your team would mean a lot to her and could make the difference in her graduate school acceptance.

WRITING PROMPT

Help Your Friend or Protect the Group?

Would you recommend your friend for an appointment to the team? Why or why not?

▶ The response entered here will appear in the performance dashboard and can be viewed by your instructor.

Submit

3.3: Attraction

OBJECTIVE: Analyze attraction between people and groups

Why do you like who you like? Why are you drawn to certain people but not to others? Often people are attracted not to groups but to the people in the groups.

By the end of this module, you will be able to:

3.3.1 **Identify elements that draw individuals together**

3.3.2 **Explain how individuals can become attracted to a group**

3.3.1: Interpersonal Attraction

OBJECTIVE: Identify elements that draw individuals together

Often people are attracted not to groups but to the people in the groups. Of the many factors that influence interpersonal attraction, four are especially significant.

Factors Influencing Interpersonal Attraction

Similarity—One of the strongest influences in interpersonal attraction is **similarity**. Remember your first day on campus—that feeling of being new and alone? In looking for a friend, did you seek out someone whom you perceived to be very different from you? Most likely not. As the principle of similarity in interpersonal attraction suggests, you probably looked for someone who appeared to be in the same situation—another lonely newcomer, or perhaps someone dressed as you were.

Who are your closest friends? Do you share many of the same attitudes, beliefs, and values? Do you enjoy the same activities? People are often attracted to those individuals whom they consider to be like them. A probable explanation for such attraction is that similar backgrounds, beliefs, attitudes, and values make it easier to understand one another—and we all like to feel that others understand us. The converse of the similarity factor may also be true: People may be repelled by those whose attitudes differ from theirs.[15]

One danger of the similarity factor in group formation is that our tendency to be attracted to people like ourselves may result in a group that is too homogeneous to approach a complex task effectively. Research on classroom groups found that by a two-to-one margin, students reported their worst experiences occurred in groups they had formed themselves. Their best experiences were most likely to occur in groups to which professors had assigned them.[16]

Complementarity—In reading the description of similarity, some of you probably shook your heads and said, "No, that's not the way it is at all. My best friend and I are about as similar as an orchid and a fire hydrant!" While birds of a feather may flock together, it is also true that opposites attract. Some interpersonal relationships are based primarily on similarity, whereas others are based on **complementarity**.[17] At times people may be attracted to others who exhibit qualities that they lack but that they admire, as when a socially anxious person is attracted to a smiling, welcoming, outgoing group of strangers at a party.[18] Consider Schutz's theory of interpersonal needs, discussed earlier. According to this theory, a person who has a high need to control, for example, would be most compatible with a person who has a high need to be controlled. The same would be true of the needs to express and to receive affection as well as the needs to feel included and to include others. These are complementary needs rather than similar needs.

Proximity, Contact, and Interaction—You tend to be attracted to people who are physically close to you, who live or work with you, and whom you see or communicate with often. If you know that you have to live or work close to another person, you may ignore that person's less desirable traits in an effort to minimize potential conflict. Furthermore, proximity, contact, and interaction breed familiarity, and familiarity has a positive influence on interpersonal attraction.[19] Interaction with another person helps you get to know that person, and through this process the two of you may discover similarities and ways in which you can satisfy each other's interpersonal needs. So, the actual physical distance between people does not influence attraction, but the interpersonal possibilities illuminated by proximity, contact, and interaction do.

Physical Attractiveness—At least in the initial stages of interpersonal attraction, physical attractiveness influences people. Research has shown that even the shapes of faces can be influential.[20] If a person is physically beautiful, others tend to want to affiliate with him or her.[21] However, evidence indicates that this factor diminishes in importance over time, and that—at least in North American cultures—physical beauty is more important to males than to females.[22]

In sum, people seem to be attracted to others who are similar to them and thus likely to understand them, who can fulfill their needs and complement their personalities, who are familiar to them because of repeated contact, and who are physically appealing. Those qualities in group members constitute a powerful influence on people's selection of groups.

3.3.2: Group Attraction

OBJECTIVE: Explain how individuals can become attracted to a group

Although individuals may be attracted to a group because of the members who compose it, they may also be attracted to the group itself. Such attraction usually focuses on the group's activities or goals, or simply on the desirability of group membership.

GROUP ACTIVITIES Although research is not extensive in this area, it seems fairly clear that people who are interested in the same activities tend to form groups.[23] People who enjoy intellectual pursuits may join literary discussion groups. Those who enjoy playing soccer join soccer teams.

Review

Factors in Interpersonal and Group Attraction

Factors in Interpersonal Attraction

Factors	Definition	Comments
Similarity	The degree to which two people are alike	You tend to like people who resemble you in their thinking and experiences; they are more likely than most other people to understand you.
Complementarity	The degree to which two people are compatibly different from each other	You tend to be attracted to people who possess qualities that you admire but do not yourself possess.
Proximity, contact, and interaction	The actual, physical availability of other people	Interacting with others reveals their similar and complementary traits and, therefore, enhances their attractiveness to you.
Physical attractiveness	Physical beauty or handsomeness	Physical attractiveness is especially important in the early stages of a relationship, though it becomes less important after you get to know someone.

Factors in Group Attraction

Factors	Comments
Group activities	People interested in the same activities tend to group together; for some people, the structure and human contact of group activities may themselves provide rewards.
Group goals	People interested in particular goals join groups dedicated to those goals; civic groups, parent/teacher organizations, and environmental groups are examples.
Group membership	Some people seek the rewards of membership itself; group membership is often seen as having prestige or status.

Beyond these obvious examples, people may be attracted to the activities of a group in a more general sense. Some may join groups simply because they enjoy going to regular meetings and joining in group discussions, regardless of the group's specific aims or goals. The structure and human contact provided by groups are potentially rewarding in and of themselves.

GROUP GOALS A group's goal is another factor that may attract people to the group. If, for example, they believe in preserving and protecting the natural environment, they may join the Nature Conservancy, the Sierra Club, the Audubon Society, or another organization that professes a similar goal.

GROUP MEMBERSHIP Sometimes it is not a group's members, activities, or goals that attract people, but rather membership itself. Potential members may perceive that membership in an exclusive club or honor society will bring them prestige, acceptance, or professional benefits outside the group. For example, company officials may expect a young executive to belong to some civic group because such memberships provide good public relations for the firm.

The need for affiliation—Maslow's belongingness need and Schutz's inclusion need—is basic to human nature and can make group membership attractive. Group membership also fulfills our needs for achievement and identity.[24] Indeed, a substantial body of research indicates that the satisfaction provided by group membership is important to our happiness.[25]

3.4: Culture and Group Development

OBJECTIVE: Evaluate how cultural norms influence group interaction

One increasingly common source of diversity in our global community is interaction among people from different cultural backgrounds. **Culture** is a learned system of knowledge, behavior, attitudes, beliefs, values, and norms that is shared by a group of people.[26] We often think of cultural differences as existing between national, ethnic or religious groups, but they can also exist between families, organizations, or even different parts of the same country or state. Not surprisingly, when individuals of different cultures interact, their differences can affect a group's development: Cultural differences affect the way we relate to others.

These differing cultures, as well as individual differences, can contribute to a kind of tension in the group that communication scholars describe as "the product of two ideas being equally valid when considered alone, but contradictory when paired."[27] They give the following pairs of statements as examples:

I need to behave consistently in a group.

I need to adapt my behavior to changes in the group situation.

It is important to fit in with and be like other group members, even when doing so goes against my personal beliefs.

It is important to maintain my individuality when I am in a group.

Good group members defer their own needs to the larger needs of the group.

Good group members act independently within the group and pursue their personal agendas.[28]

While it may be tempting to make stereotypical inferences about all people within a given culture based on some of the research findings, communication scholars caution against making broad, sweeping generalizations about a specific culture.[29] Research has found significant variations in nonverbal behavior within cultures, indicating that individual members of a culture may differ in important ways from their fellow group members. Our discussion intends simply to document the existence of cultural differences and to warn that such differences may hamper effective communication in small groups if they are not recognized and accommodated.

No list of simple suggestions or techniques will help you manage all possible cultural differences that you may encounter in groups. However, a basic principle can help: When interacting with people from a culture other than your own, note differences you think may be culture based and adapt accordingly. Become "other-oriented." We are not suggesting that you abandon your cultural norms, traditions, and expectations—only that you become more flexible, thereby minimizing the communication distortion that cultural differences may cause. If you think you have offended someone or acted inappropriately, you can ask the other person if you have, and if so, find out what exactly you did wrong.[30] Being aware of and responding to cultural differences in small groups can enhance your ability to interact with others.

By the end of this module, you will be able to:

3.4.1 **Explain challenges associated with cultural differences in individualism**

3.4.2 **Differentiate methods of expression between high- and low-context cultures**

3.4.3 **Describe group dynamics in high- and low-contact cultures**

3.4.4 **Compare homogenous and diverse groups**

3.4.1: Individualism and Collectivism

OBJECTIVE: Explain challenges associated with cultural differences in individualism

Groups often have difficulty establishing norms and roles because of cultural variations in individualism among group members. In some cultures (such as among Americans), individual autonomy and initiative are valued; in others (Japanese culture, for instance), collective well-being takes precedence over individual achievement. As a consequence, people from collectivist cultures are more likely to view assertive individualists as self-centered, while individualists may interpret their collectivist counterparts as weak. Collectivists are more likely to conform to group norms and to value group decisions highly.[31] However, we caution against overgeneralization. Although different cultures clearly foster different orientations, ample evidence also indicates that there are vast differences among people *within* any culture. Thus, it is nearly impossible to predict with certainty that a person will embrace an individualist or a collectivist orientation based on that person's culture alone.[32]

Although differences in individualism always exist in groups, these differences can be extreme if group members are culturally diverse. Extreme differences can result in low group satisfaction and difficulty establishing mutuality of concern. Again, if group members are aware of cultural differences and adapt their communication accordingly, this can help improve group interactions.

3.4.2: High-Context and Low-Context Cultures

OBJECTIVE: Differentiate methods of expression between high- and low-context cultures

In some cultures, the surrounding context of an interaction or the unspoken, nonverbal message plays a greater role than it does in other cultures.[33] A **high-context culture** is one that places more emphasis on nonverbal communication. In such a culture, the physical environment is important in helping communicators interpret the message. The environment, the situation, and the communicator's mood are especially significant in decoding messages. A **low-context culture** places more emphasis on verbal expression. Figure 3-2 shows cultures arranged along a continuum from high to low context.

In a small group, high- or low-context orientation can play a role in the amount of time a person talks and his or her sensitivity in responding to unspoken dynamics of a group's climate.

Figure 3-2 Where Different Cultures Fall on the Context Scale

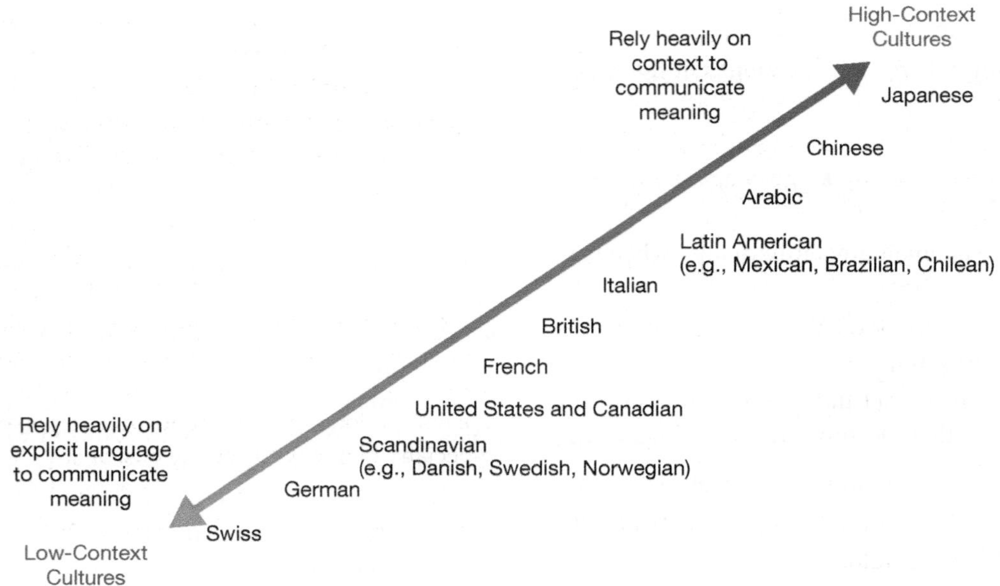

Characteristics of High-Context and Low-Context Cultures[34]

Factors	High-Context Cultures	Low-Context Cultures
Physical environment/ situation/ communicator's mood	More sensitive to nonverbal cues	Less sensitive to nonverbal cues
	More skilled in interpreting nonverbal information	Les skilled in interpreting nonverbal information
	May find those from low-context cultures less credible or trustworthy	
Verbal expression	Use fewer words to express themselves More indirect communication; rely more on implicit cues	Place greater emphasis on speech; talk more More likely to make explicit requests for information by saying, "Talk to me," "Give it to me straight," or "Tell it like it is."

3.4.3: High-Contact and Low-Contact Cultures

OBJECTIVE: Describe group dynamics in high- and low-contact cultures

In some cultures, people are more comfortable being touched or being physically close to others; these are said to be **high-contact cultures**. In contrast, individuals from **low-contact cultures** tend to prefer more personal space, typically make less eye contact with others, and are much more uncomfortable with being touched or approached by others.[35]

Whether group members are from high- or low-contact cultures can affect preferred seating arrangements and other aspects of small group ecology. For example, people from some cultural groups, such as the Chinese, prefer sitting side by side rather than directly across from one another.[36] Fathi Yousef and Nancy Briggs found that in Middle Eastern countries it is appropriate to stand close enough to someone to smell their breath.[37] North Americans usually prefer more space around them than do Latin Americans, Arabs, and Greeks.[38] Cultural differences can also be found among ethnic groups within the same country.

Characteristics of High-Contact and Low-Contact Cultures

People from high-contact cultures are more comfortable with less personal space.

Reaction to touching is an important difference between high- and low-contact cultures.

People from low-contact cultures are more comfortable keeping others "at arm's length."

3.4.4: Homogeneity and Diversity

OBJECTIVE: Compare homogenous and diverse groups

Dynamic tension arises when individual goals and group goals conflict. Each of us seeks to be independent and autonomous, while depending on the groups to which we belong. We need to influence and control others, as well as to be influenced and controlled by others. Even in the most homogeneous groups, varying levels of these needs coupled with differing views of the group and its goals can make for an interesting time and a fascinating field for study.

As we join or are assigned to groups, we are likely to find that those groups are characterized by increasing diversity. Research showing that women represent 47 percent and minorities 32 percent of the workforce in the United States is one indication of this trend.[39] Diversity can both enhance and disrupt group productivity.[40]

Comparison of Homogenous and Diverse Groups

Composition: Homogeneous or Diverse?—Are groups that are more homogeneous in terms of race, gender, culture, and general ability more effective or less effective than more diverse groups? Which should we choose? Perhaps not surprisingly, both more and less diverse groups have their own advantages and disadvantages. Evidence suggests that over time diverse groups can be more effective because their members have more potential for problem solving owing to their broader set of skills and approaches to problems. For example, in groups where high levels of difficult cognition are required, diversity in educational specialization and age contribute positively to team identification and team performance.[41] However, evidence also shows that differences in age and nationality often contribute to personality clashes, especially in newly formed teams. Such groups tend to fare better if they acknowledge their diversity at the outset and create a supportive climate tolerant of diverse opinions and personalities.[42]

The effectiveness of a multicultural team depends, in part, on the diversity climate within the group—whether and how diversity is embraced as a positive group norm.[43] It is helpful for highly diverse groups to focus most sharply on the group's task in the early stages of the group's development.[44]

Is One Better Than the Other?—When comparing homogeneous work groups with diverse work groups, researchers find that diverse work groups often have more trouble initially, but over time they become more productive than homogeneous groups. This outcome makes sense. We are more comfortable with people whom we think are similar to us. This makes for easier interactions in the initial stages of group formation. With a little effort, though, diverse groups can find the common ground needed to make their interactions work more smoothly; their diversity often produces more flexibility, more options, and more ways of looking at a problem.[45] Diversity in groups is clearly associated with positive outcomes for groups, particularly with task-oriented or productivity outcomes.[46]

3.5: Group Formation over Time

OBJECTIVE: Analyze the process of group development

The process of group development is a progressive movement along a continuum ranging from a loose aggregate of people to a high-functioning team. This transformation from nongroup to group encompasses factors such as identification with the group, interrelationship, coordination among

Virtual Collaboration

Cultural Considerations

When forming a group, remember that people from different cultures often have differing views and preferences when it comes to using virtual technologies. You may encounter some of the following attitudes about technology based on five cultural factors.[47]

Cultural Factor	Technological Considerations
Power difference	People from cultures with substantial differences in power and status may more freely use technologies that are asynchronous and allow anonymous input. These cultures sometimes use technology to indicate status differences between team members.
Uncertainty avoidance	People from cultures uncomfortable with uncertainty may be slower to adopt technology. They may also prefer technology that produces more permanent records of discussions and decisions.
Individualism–collectivism	People from highly collectivistic cultures (those that value group and team achievement over individual success) may prefer face-to-face interactions.
Masculinity–femininity	People from cultures with a more "feminine" orientation (concerned with nurturing, cooperation, and sharing), in contrast to a more "masculine" orientation (concerned with earning visible success and possessions), may be more prone to use technology in a nurturing way, especially during team startups. They may also prefer face-to-face meetings to virtual meetings.
Context	People from cultures in which the context of a message is highly important may prefer more information-rich technologies as well as those that offer social presence (synchronous, real-time communication). They may resist using technologies with low social presence to communicate with people whom they have never met. People from cultures in which the context of a message is less important may prefer more asynchronous communications.

Despite cultural differences, several commonalities also exist. If you are the leader of a virtual group, four tactics will enhance team members' identification with the team: catering to the individual (asserting team members' individuality and their rights to different opinions), giving positive feedback, pointing out common goals, and talking up team activities and face-to-face interactions.[48]

group members, and orientation to group goals.[49] Group diversity and intercultural differences make it important to recognize, understand, and adapt to differences from the beginning of a group's formation.

Once a group forms, it continues to grow and develop. Many researchers observe that group development follows fairly predictable stages.

By the end of this module, you will be able to:

3.5.1 Outline the four stages of group development

3.5.2 Explain how individuals staying or leaving influences the character of a group

3.5.3 Relate trust to group communication

3.5.1: Four Developmental Stages of Group Formation

OBJECTIVE: Outline the four stages of group development

Perhaps the best-known scheme for the stages of group formation was advanced by Bruce Tuckman, as illustrated in Figure 3-3.[50]

Although not all groups neatly cycle through these stages, you will probably be able to detect forming, storming, norming, and performing behaviors in many of the groups and teams in which you participate.

Figure 3-3 Four Stages of Group Formation

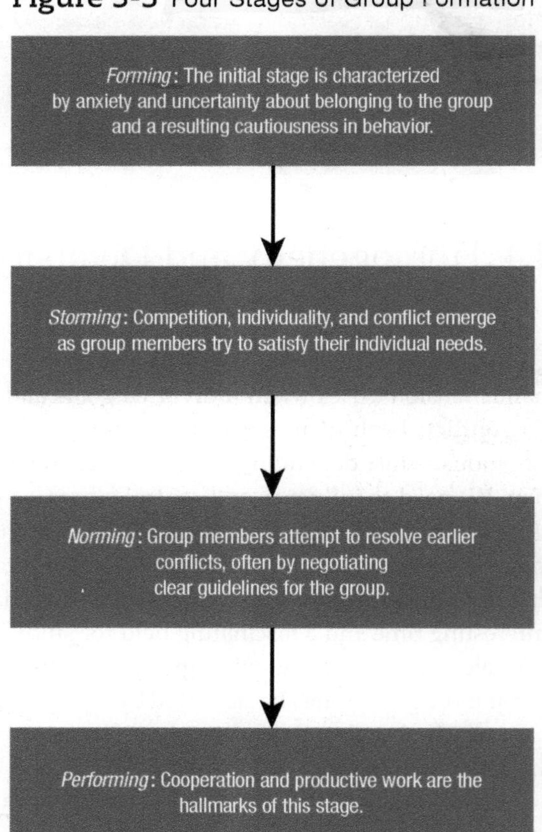

Forming: The initial stage is characterized by anxiety and uncertainty about belonging to the group and a resulting cautiousness in behavior.
Storming: Competition, individuality, and conflict emerge as group members try to satisfy their individual needs.
Norming: Group members attempt to resolve earlier conflicts, often by negotiating clear guidelines for the group.
Performing: Cooperation and productive work are the hallmarks of this stage.

Remember these stages as you progress through this course. Developmental changes in the life of a group relate to many important group dynamics, including conflict management and leadership.

3.5.2: Old Members/New Members

OBJECTIVE: Explain how individuals staying or leaving influences the character of a group

Groups change over time, and sometimes group members leave and are replaced by new members. Socializing these new members to their new group is important. Over time, groups develop a "personality" of their own. Group or team members become oriented to one another, they set patterns of behavior and group norms, and they develop a shared collective experience—their own fantasy chains, rules, and systems. But what happens when a newcomer joins the team? Changes in membership alter the group's dynamics, sometimes profoundly. Continuing success depends on how well the new member adapts to particular group dynamics (is socialized) and how well the group adapts to the characteristics, abilities, and skills of the new member.

Membership Turnover in a Group

Before: Groups have their own cast of characters and develop a group personality. Interaction patterns become predictable. Levels of uncertainty and tension are low; comfort and performance are high.

After: When the constituency of the group changes, the group must go back through stages of formation. With new members, uncertainty increases. Primary tension—Who are these people?—returns to the group. While the reconstituted group will be similar to the original group in many ways, a change in the group's personality is inevitable.

3.5.3: Developing Trust Takes Time

OBJECTIVE: Relate trust to group communication

As group membership changes, groups will begin to include members experiencing different membership phases. One key issue that arises in such groups is trust. Mutual trust takes time to build among newer and more established group members, as new members may not yet be fully accepted by the veteran members.[51] When new members join a group, the group re-forms and will likely repeat the "forming" and "storming" phases of development to some degree.

Successfully socializing a new group or team member depends largely on expectations: the newcomer's expectations of his or her own performance as well as the group's expectations of the newcomer. The degree to which these expectations are compatible is the primary determinant of a successful transition. Just as a group should spend time establishing mutuality of concern at the beginning of its life, so it should revisit these considerations when group membership changes.

SOCIALIZING NEW MEMBERS In many respects, the group is new each time its membership changes. This re-formation presents its own stages of development. The socialization of a newcomer actually begins with a period of anticipation prior to the first meeting at which the newcomer is present, in which the group formulates initial expectations. These expectations are modified or reinforced very quickly during the initial face-to-face encounter among team members. In the final phase of socialization, adjustment, newcomer and team members adjust to one another and team performance stabilizes.[52]

POSITIVE EXPECTATIONS Positive team expectations for a new member enhance the probability of a successful outcome. Likewise, viewing changing team membership as beneficial will enhance the probability of a good outcome. Successful integration of new members is especially important in teams in which members have specialized roles and are highly interdependent.[53]

CASE STUDY

How Do You Manage Conflicting Needs and Goals?

The town of Boysenberry has recently built a new city park. The city council has appointed a team of volunteers to recommend to the city a landscaping plan for the new park. One section of the park in particular (the Boysenberry Preserve), has been designated as green space, with no recreational facilities other than walking paths.

The team comprises the following members:

Latasha Greene is the task force chair and the president of her Master Gardeners chapter. The rose garden at her home is the envy of her neighborhood.

Thurman Jester is a local realtor. People refer to his "sales" personality. Naturally gregarious, Thurman is also a champion of "curb appeal." He is hoping the Boysenberry Preserve will be a place of great natural color and beauty that will attract new residents (and clients) to the community.

Ahmed Hijazi has moved to Boysenberry from Seattle, where he became familiar with the concept of community gardens. Fresh vegetables, available to the community in such gardens, provide not only nutrition but also economic support to people of modest means. The park is located in a low-income area.

Roberto Cisneros has tried—and failed—on three occasions to be elected to local office. He is excited about the publicity he can draw to himself through this committee's work. He is preparing to run again for a council seat. Roberto has a high need for control.

Molly Milkweed has recently become concerned that the dwindling natural habitat is decimating the migrating population of monarch butterflies. She reasons that humans have been the cause of habitat loss, so the least we can do is to replace it when we can. Molly has high affection needs.

Jack Franke is the director of the township parks department; his grounds crew will have responsibility for installing, watering, and maintaining the new Boysenberry Preserve. He is very aware that plants and shrubs that are native to the area will require the least effort to maintain.

Questions for Analysis: How Do You Manage Conflicting Needs and Goals?

1. Analyze the situation in this scenario. Where are the most likely sources of conflict?
2. The assigned group goal is to develop a landscaping plan for Boysenberry Preserve. Can you identify the real or possible individual goals of the group members? What potential conflicts do you see?
3. What issues do you see arising in a discussion of mutuality of concern?
4. Some research suggests that a conflict between individual and group goals can actually be positive when deviance from group norms causes the group to examine its goals more closely. Do you see any potentially positive effects within the tension among conflicting goals?
5. If you were a member of this group, what suggestions would you make at your first meeting?

DYNAMIC INTERRELATEDNESS The dynamic interrelatedness of all the variables that affect small group processes makes the study of small group communication challenging and exciting. As you continue through the rest of this course, it is important that you retain what you have previously learned. Only when you have fit all the puzzle pieces together will you see a clear picture of small group communication.

This chapter highlights one part of the puzzle: the needs and goals that motivate people to join groups and that influence their behavior within those groups. In the initial stages of group development, the level of uncertainty—about the group, about its goals, and about each member's place in it—is at its peak. How you communicate at this sensitive stage of group development provides the basis for future interaction.

Summary: Facilitating Group Development

3.1: Interpersonal Needs

- People join groups to satisfy interpersonal needs and to pursue individual and group goals. Sometimes people are assigned or elected to groups.
- Maslow's hierarchy of needs includes physiological, safety, belongingness, esteem, and self-actualization needs. Schutz's theory proposes inclusion, control, and affection as primary human needs.
- Groups pass through observable, cyclical phases.

3.2: Goals and Mutuality

- Individuals often join groups that they believe will help them advance toward their personal goals. Sometimes the group's goals themselves attract members. Conflict between individual goals and group goals can be counterproductive.
- All members of a group may not be equally committed to the group or its task. For this reason, it is important to take time early in the life of the group to clarify each member's level of commitment and ability to devote time to the task.

3.3: Attraction

- The four main factors affecting interpersonal attraction are similarity, complementarity, proximity/contact/interaction, and physical attractiveness.
- Three factors that affect group attraction are group activities, group goals, and group membership.

3.4: Culture and Group Development

- Diversity within a group in terms of culture, gender, race, and experience is a strength because of the multiple perspectives brought to the group. These differences can be obstacles as well.
- When interacting with people from a culture other than your own, note differences you think may be culture based and adapt accordingly. Become other-oriented.

3.5: Group Formation over Time

- The phases of group development are forming, storming, norming, and performing.

SHARED WRITING

Why Do You Like Who You Like?

Consider the multiple factors affecting interpersonal and group attraction. Reflect on your current friendships and the groups to which you belong. Which factors are most important to you personally? Why are they the most important? Write a short response that your classmates will read. Be sure to include specifics in your discussion.

A minimum number of characters is required to post and earn points. After posting, your response can be viewed by your class and instructor, and you can participate in the class discussion.

Chapter 4
Preparing to Collaborate

"If I had an hour to solve a problem I'd spend 55 minutes thinking about the problem and 5 minutes thinking about solution."
—Albert Einstein

Learning Objectives

4.1 Apply preparation strategies for group discussion

4.2 Determine appropriate questions for group discussion

4.3 Support an argument using a logical reasoning method

4.4 Analyze the ways evidence is used in group discussions

Have you ever spent an hour or two at a group or team meeting, only to find out no one was ready to make a meaningful, informed contribution? Many wasted meetings boil down to the fact that group members just haven't done their homework. GIGO is the acronym that computer programmers use for the expression "Garbage in, garbage out." If you put poor information (garbage) into a computer program, you get poor results as output. It works the same way in group discussions.[1] To achieve a high-quality decision, a group needs quality information gleaned from research as well as effective reasoning and critical-thinking skills.[2]

In this chapter, we will examine the processes by which groups accomplish their work and achieve their goals, how to prepare effectively for a group discussion, and how to use research and critical-thinking skills to enhance the quality of the work accomplished by group members.

The Greek philosopher Socrates believed that the primary goal of dialogue and discussion was the search for truth. Today, group discussion continues to be a trusted method of seeking answers to tough questions. Our legal system is based on the idea that a jury of adults, after hearing evidence and using their best critical-thinking and analysis skills, should be able to decide whether someone is guilty of a crime. In corporations, teams and task forces hammer out key decisions. Regardless of a group's composition, goal, or context, its discussion will be more productive if the group members have prepared for it, and if they know how to critically evaluate information that has been used to reach reasoned conclusions.[3]

4.1: How to Develop a Discussion Plan

OBJECTIVE: Apply preparation strategies for group discussion

Imagine the instructor in your group communication class has assigned you to a group or committee so that you can make a recommendation, solve a problem, or make a decision. What should you do first? How would you develop a plan to accomplish your work? What should you avoid doing? It's all too tempting for members to jump in with both feet and start deciding what to do without adequate research or preparation. Suggesting solutions or making final recommendations at your first meeting, however, is a bad idea.

The most effective groups develop a plan for accomplishing their goal. Groups are more likely to deliberate effectively if group members clarify their goals, use good discussion skills, and are motivated to do a good job.[4] Effective groups prepare for discussion.[5]

By the end of this module, you will be able to:

- **4.1.1 Implement effective ways of beginning group collaboration**
- **4.1.2 Identify group goals**
- **4.1.3 Determine the planning method for group projects**
- **4.1.4 Write a group agenda**
- **4.1.5 Describe group information-sharing strategies**
- **4.1.6 Compare presentation formats**

4.1.1: Get Acquainted with Your Group Members

OBJECTIVE: Implement effective ways of beginning group collaboration

"Let's get down to business," "Get to the point," and "What are we supposed to do?" are typical statements heard at first group meetings. However, it's important to take a few minutes to get better acquainted with group members before focusing on the task, especially if you are just getting started or if new members are joining the group.[6] Teamwork research consistently indicates that getting to know one another helps groups develop appropriate roles and responsibilities.[7] In fact, often the most serious problems that group and team members encounter are not caused by task issues, but rather by relationship issues. Taking time to establish good working relationships and trust can help a group or team be more productive in the long run.[8]

SHARE EXPERTISE Do more than just announce your name when introducing yourself to the group.[9] Perhaps you can provide information about how much experience you have with the topic, or, if no specific task has been identified or assigned, you can talk about your previous experience in working on group projects. Identify what you have in common with other members as well as the unique, individual talents and skills you have.[10] Some groups appoint someone to help facilitate their discussion, but most groups figure out the best way to get started on their own. Self-managing groups can be quite effective, especially when managing routine tasks such as figuring out when and where to meet.[11]

SHARE PERSONAL INFORMATION Sharing personal information, such as your interests, as well as individual expertise can establish a climate of cooperation and help the group decide who should do what.[12] Research suggests that it's important to encourage all members to participate early in the group's history. In fact, communication researcher Joseph Bonito found that groups that had higher rates of participation within the first minute of their discussion had higher-quality discussion during the entire meeting.[13] His findings suggest that sharing both personal information as well as participating early in the discussion can help enhance group success.

SHARE PATIENTLY Avoid the temptation to make quick decisions about accomplishing the task. Be patient; don't try to accomplish too much too quickly. Some groups encounter a "speed trap" when group members focus too much on speed and not enough on quality.[14] An overemphasis on making fast decisions traps a group in a spiral of emphasizing speed and efficiency over high-quality decision making. Since norms are established early in the group's history, make sure speedy decision making doesn't become the group's goal.

SHARE VIRTUAL COMMUNICATION STRATEGIES With the prevalence of social media, text messages, e-mail, and other apps that help you connect to others, it's important to develop a way to communicate with group members when you are not meeting face to face. Sharing phone numbers or e-mail addresses, or ensuring that group members can share information via software such as Google Drive, provides a way to facilitate sharing information and ideas as well as a mechanism for scheduling future meetings.

Virtual Collaboration

Sharing Information

When working on a group or team project, it may be useful to share your initial research findings electronically via e-mail, a group Facebook page, or other electronic means. Evidence suggests that when virtual groups collaborate only electronically, group members usually have access to more information.[15] In addition, although face-to-face group meetings result in more information sharing initially, over the long term, exchanging information via e-mail may ensure that more information is shared and that all members of the group receive the information.

When collaborating in virtual groups consider the following strategies to facilitate sharing information:

- Develop a group listserv or website, or use other strategies to text all group members so that everyone can share information simultaneously.
- For an extensive group project, consider developing a group webpage, use Facebook, or use other collaborative apps such as Google Drive to develop a common virtual space where group members can "meet."
- Consider assigning roles to different members for maintaining the website, such as posting minutes of previous meetings, serving as the webmaster of the site, and keeping track of whether projects are completed on time.
- Periodically ask virtual group members if they have information to share with all group members.

4.1.2: Clarify the Goals of the Group

OBJECTIVE: Identify group goals

Once you've completed introductions, make sure you know the group's purpose, goal, and assignment.[16] As the group begins focusing on the goal, a key question to ask is, "When do you know you're finished with your task?" Visualize what the completed project will look like. For example, is the goal to produce a written report, or is it to deliver an oral presentation in which you will make recommendations?

IDENTIFY THE TASK Most work-group goals boil down to one of three tasks:

1. Generating ideas, information, or options.
2. Making a choice, often about how to solve a larger problem.
3. Putting an idea into action.

Your team may be involved in only one of these tasks, or it may tackle all three. Whatever the group goal, it should be expressed in the form of a question that the group will discuss. We suggest that you formulate a discussion question as either a fact (something did or did not happen), a prediction (something will happen), a value (something is better or worse than something else), or a policy (something should be done). Consider writing your question or group goal on a chalkboard or flipchart for all team members to see.

STAY FOCUSED ON THE GOAL When the group starts to wobble or get off track, point group members back to the central reason for the discussion—to achieve the goal of the group. Having a clear, elevating goal is one of the essential requirements for an effective team. Leadership expert Stephen Covey suggests that to be successful you should "begin with the end in mind."[17] Visualize your success.[18]

If you find that your group is not achieving its goals or that you're just not making the progress you expect, the reasons may be because team members:

- Have an unclear vision of what the group wants to accomplish.
- Need help clarifying their roles.
- Are unclear about the process of how work gets done.
- Aren't getting along.[19]

Taking time to establish clear goals can help group members have a clearer vision, understand their individual roles, develop a work plan, and address the uncertainty that is present when the group first convenes.[20]

Identifying Group Goals

Choose the correct answer from among the four options provided.

Question	The Planning and Zoning Committee of your city is meeting to determine whether a new master planning policy is needed due to significant population growth. Some members of the committee want to protect the environment. Other members want to make sure the business interests of the community are met. Still other group members want to maintain the beauty of the architecture of the community. What would be a useful strategy for developing a clear goal?
Option 1	The group should carefully review the evidence and the opinions of group members while considering the issue of population growth, and then rank-order the possible goals to develop a consensus about what the highest priorities of the group should be.
Option 2	The group should not worry about developing a specific priority because all goals are of equal value. Trying to rank the importance of these admirable goals would limit the group.
Option 3	The group should brainstorm a longer list of goals and objectives and include all of the goals into a single comprehensive goal statement.
Option 4	The group should reject the ideas and opinions of group members who hold a minority opinion. The group should take a quick vote to determine the best goal to select.
Correct Answer Feedback	Option 1: When group members disagree about the primary goal or priority of the group, it is important to take time to explore differences, share information and opinions, and then discuss the merits of the most appropriate goal or goals for the group.

4.1.3: Plan How to Gather Information and Analyze Issues

OBJECTIVE: Determine the planning method for group projects

Once you develop your discussion question and clarify your goal, you need to collect information and research conclusions to help answer your question.

Gather Information and Analyze Issues

Be Realistic—Don't try to accomplish too much in a short amount of time.[21] It usually takes more—rather than less—time to accomplish group tasks than group members realize.[22] Preparing a step-by-step plan that involves all group members will help your group work effectively and create a realistic timetable for accomplishing the goal.[23] However, although planning is important, research also suggests that it is beneficial to adjust your plans as your group continues its work.[24] Have a plan, but give yourself permission to react and respond to what you discover as you make decisions or solve a problem.

Review What You Already Know—Before you start surfing the Internet for information, find out what information your group already has related to the topic and issues.[25] Consider using social media or online space to pool the information you already have. One of the most important things you can do early in a group's history is to identify who in your group has special skills or is an expert on the topic you're discussing.[26] Invite those members to contribute to the group's conversation.[27]

Identify What You Don't Know—After assessing your group's knowledge, figure out what you don't know. Ask, "What do we need to know that we don't know now?" Then develop a strategy to gather the information you need. Groups that

identify knowledge gaps do a better job of managing conflict and are overall more effective in achieving their goal.[28]

Coordinate the Work—Begin to "divide and conquer." Assign members—or ask for volunteers—to begin researching the topic. Coordinate your group's research efforts rather than having group members scatter and then plunge into the research process. Without coordination, you

may needlessly duplicate your research efforts. In developing a coordinated plan to do the work, consider these suggestions:

- Focus on the purpose of the project.
- Encourage all members to participate by positively reinforcing the contributions of others.
- Develop a strategy to share information (such as a common website) to avoid duplicating efforts.

Set Deadlines—While divvying up the work, establish a timeline of the due dates and periodically review how well you are adhering to that timeline.[29] Allow plenty of time for the group to discuss the information (rather than just compiling the facts and data) before you make final recommendations.[30] The more time allotted to solve a problem, the greater the chance that group members will share what they know. So, in addition to making assignments, indicate when the information should be shared with the group. Develop a concrete plan, including realistic deadlines, for structuring the workload.

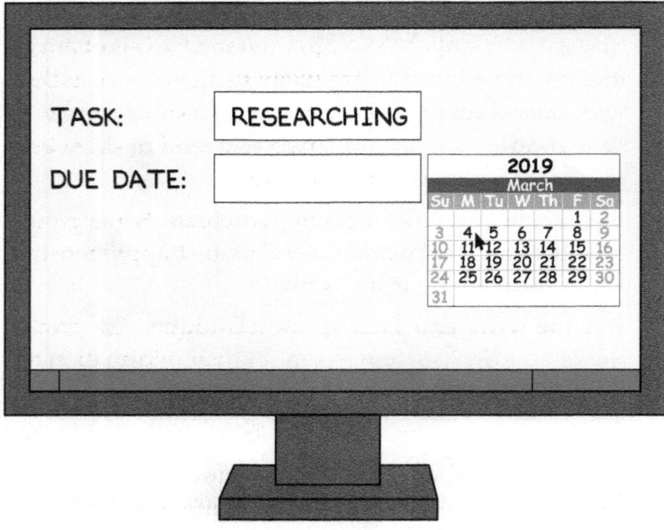

4.1.4: Follow a Structured Agenda to Accomplish the Task

OBJECTIVE: Write a group agenda

Here's a powerful principle for effective group communication: Groups and teams need a clear agenda to help them organize their discussion.

ALWAYS DISTRIBUTE A MEETING AGENDA BEFORE YOU MEET An **agenda** is a thoughtfully prepared list of the issues, topics, tasks, and questions that the group will discuss or accomplish. If your group doesn't have a designated group leader, either all of the group members could work together to develop an agenda or you could ask someone in the group to be responsible for preparing an agenda.

There is an art to preparing an agenda—it is not just a list of topics that come to mind. The most effective agenda items are phrased as a question, such as "How can we analyze the problem?" or "What information do we need?" Appendix A presents principles and practices for developing meeting agendas, as well as strategies for facilitating meeting discussion.

Examples of Agendas

Here are a few examples of agendas for meetings.

Agenda: Example 1

Agenda

Meeting Goal: By the end of the meeting the group should discuss the planning policy and approve the new personnel policy.

I. DISCUSSION ITEMS
   A. What is the history of the our department's planning policy?
   B. What are the advantages and disadvantages of the department's planning policy?

II. ACTION ITEMS
   A. Should we approve the new personnel policy?
   B. If approved, when should the personnel policy be implemented?

III. INFORMATION ITEMS
   A. Membership Report
   B. Update on changes to our calendar of events

Agenda: Example 2

Agenda

Meeting Goal: By the end of the meeting we will discuss how our group has raised funds in the past and make a decision about future fund-raising activities

I. DISCUSSION ITEMS
   A. What is our anticipated budget for this year?
   B. How have we developed new resources during the past two years?

II. ACTION ITEMS
   A. Should we develop new fund-raising strategies for the coming year?
   B. What are the examples of ways to raise new funds?
   C. What are the best ways to increase income for our group?

III. INFORMATION ITEMS
   A. Report from the Activity Committee
   B. Report from the Social Committee

USE A PROBLEM-SOLVING APPROACH If your group is solving a problem, then a straightforward problem-solving agenda should provide the necessary structure for your meeting agendas. The most basic problem-solving structure includes these steps:

1. Identify and define the problem.
2. Analyze the problem.
3. Generate several possible solutions.

4. Select the best solution or combination of solutions.
5. Test and implement the solution.

You may not need to include all of these steps at every meeting. Early meetings may focus on the problem; later meetings can seek solutions.

4.1.5: Share Information with Others

OBJECTIVE: Describe group information-sharing strategies

Groups typically make better decisions than individuals because typically more information is found among a group of people than in one person.[31] Researchers have consistently found that groups that have more information are more likely to arrive at a better solution or outcome.[32] But there's a problem: Group members sometimes don't share what they know.[33] Research has documented that we often talk about and think about ourselves rather than consider making the group goals our concern.[34]

SHARE WHAT YOU KNOW Which factors make group members more willing to share their knowledge? According to one study, you are more likely to share information in the following circumstances:

- Everyone in the group already knows the information—that is, there is a common core of information that group members talk about.
- At least one person knows the same information you know.
- You are perceived to be an expert on the topic at hand.[35]
- You want to enhance your position or influence in the group.

We tend to share information with people we like and withhold information from people we don't like.[36] As noted earlier, you might consider using virtual group strategies, such as social media, apps that facilitate collaboration, or a website to share and compile information.

TALK ABOUT THE INFORMATION SHARED WITH THE GROUP Sharing what you know and then talking about that information leads to more overall satisfaction with your participation in the group.[37] When groups don't share and discuss the information they have, they may forge ahead and make a decision or solve a problem based on incomplete information, so that their group's effectiveness diminishes.[38] In addition to giving groups more information on which to base their deliberations, shared information can help allay group conflict and tensions and sort through disagreements.[39]

When sharing information, be sure to identify how that information can help the group.[40] But don't let one person talk too much: Robert Bales found that some group members can dominate at least 40 percent of the talk time.[41] To maximize the benefits of information sharing and group deliberation, avoid letting one person run the show. Seek balanced participation and sharing of ideas and information. Researchers have also found that groups perform better when they share information with one another, as well as when they talk about how information should be shared.[42]

DEVELOP PRODUCTIVE STRATEGIES FOR SHARING INFORMATION So, what can group members do to ensure that they share information with one another? Consider these practical tips:

- **Develop a positive, conforming, and, cohesive group climate**[43]. Celebrate when your group achieves a short-term goal; find ways to catch group members doing things well and then offer a positive, reinforcing comment, such as "Good job of finding that key piece of information."[44]
- **Make each member feel valued.** Group members who feel positive about the group's goal, and who believe they are making important contributions, are more likely to share information with other group members.[45]
- **Assess the range of knowledge, education, and information among group members.** Research suggests that group members who have different levels of information and education are likely to share information with their team members only up to a certain point.[46] An educationally diverse group will tend to share less information among team members.
- **Encourage quiet members to participate.** Some group members are shy, while others are just apprehensive about speaking up in any situation.
- **Use the write-and-then-speak technique.** Ask group members to first jot down some of their information on a piece of paper and then take turns sharing what they have written. Having a written "script" may encourage quieter members to speak up.
- **Use online, e-mail, text, or instant messages to contribute information.** Consider asking group members to first provide a written report via e-mail or other electronic means to every group member. Using the structure provided by having information in written form may gently prod each group member to share what he or she knows.[47]
- **Explicitly talk about the problem of unshared information.** Also talk about the importance of being open to new information and new ideas.[48] Make it a group concern. Group members who receive training in the importance of sharing information do tend to share more information.[49]
- **Work together to find research and information.** Don't worry whether group members are finding similar information. One study found that if several group members found the same information, it was more likely to be shared with the entire group. So, if group

members discover the same information, it is likely that the information will be shared with the entire group.[50]

- **Share information with the entire group using inclusive pronouns such as "we," "us," and "our,"** rather than labeling the information as "my" information. This advice is especially important if you are new to the group.[51]

Skilled Collaboration

Group Members Who Don't Pull Their Weight

A common disadvantage of working in groups is that sometimes a member may not follow through on assignments, not actively contribute, or—even worse—not attend meetings. This behavior, known as **social loafing**, creates much discord and anguish, especially for group members who *are* following through on assignments and tasks. One of the biggest triggers of conflict is someone who thinks he or she is unfairly doing more work than others. Rather than ignore the problem (especially if a loafing group member is significantly hindering the work of the entire group), group members should confront the issue. But how can the problem be addressed without adding to the stress?

Understand the Problem

First, it helps to understand why someone may be loafing. Consider these possibilities:

- *Apathy:* The loafing group member may simply not care whether the group succeeds.
- *"Work-challenged":* The slacking group member may just not like to work very hard.
- *Too busy:* The loafer may have too much to do and has made working in the group a low priority.
- *No group accountability:* There may be no way tracking who does what; the loafer can skate through the process because there are no consequences from not doing the work.

Address the Problem

Understanding why someone may be goofing off may be interesting, but what you may really want to know is "How can we get someone to do his or her work?"

Develop Clear Ground Rules. Early in your group's history, establish an explicit rule that each group member is expected to complete his or her assignments. Talking together about how individual work should be accomplished makes the issue a group concern rather than a contentious issue between one or two group members.

Make Members Accountable. Build in greater accountability so that assignments and due dates are clear and each member must report to the entire group on the status of work accomplished. As a group, develop specific assignments for individual team members. Then provide deadlines for when the work should be completed. Group members could periodically provide a status update on this individual work, either as part of the group's regular agenda or by providing a status report via social media, collaboration apps, e-mail, texting, or a team webpage. Perhaps each meeting could begin with a status report from each group member.[52]

Make the Issue a Group Concern. One person should not attack the offending group member; that will just add to a climate of defensiveness and create more stress. Instead, the group as a whole should address the loafer, calmly describing how the lack of individual productivity is creating a problem for the group.[53]

Report the Problem

Rather than bearing the burden alone, if the problem seems to continue without any change, let your group leader or supervisor know that a problem exists. Also, when sharing the problem, let the leader or supervisor know what you have done to address the issue.

Although we've offered several suggestions, realize that ultimately you can't change another person's behavior. Despite what group members do (or don't do), there are no surefire strategies to spur a loafing member to action.[54] The rest of the group may simply have to pick up the slack.

4.1.6: Determine How to Present Your Information

OBJECTIVE: Compare presentation formats

Once you have shared information and developed recommendations or conclusions, you'll need to decide how best to present your information to others. Appendix B: Principles and Practices for Communicating to an Audience describes three common formats for doing this:

- Panel discussion
- Symposium presentation
- Forum presentation

In addition to presenting your conclusions orally, you may need to prepare a written report.

Consider organizing your written report around problem-solving steps: definition of the problem, analysis of the problem, possible solutions, and best solution or solutions. Most written reports are prepared for a specific individual or group, so keep that reader in mind as you develop the written report. Follow any specific guidelines or structure prescribed for you.

After you've developed your conclusions, you'll need to decide how best to present your information to others. Let's explore the options of a panel discussion, a symposium presentation, and a forum presentation.

Ways of Presenting Information

Panel Discussions—The most frequently used public group discussion format is a **panel discussion**—that is, a group discussion held before an audience with the purpose of (1) informing the audience about issues of interest, (2) solving a problem, or (3) encouraging the audience to evaluate the pros and cons of a controversial issue.

A panel discussion is usually facilitated by an appointed moderator or chairperson, who aims to keep the discussion on track. The moderator opens the discussion by announcing the discussion question. Most panel discussions include at least three panelists; if there are more than eight or nine, the panelists have difficulty participating equally. Because the panel is presented for the benefit of an audience, organizers should take care that the audience can see and hear the discussion clearly. Panelists usually sit in a semicircle or behind a table. Although they should be informed about the subject they will discuss, they should not rehearse their discussion; the conversation should be extemporaneous. Panelists may use notes to help them remember facts and statistics, but they should not use a prepared text.

After announcing the discussion question or topic, the moderator briefly introduces the panel members, perhaps noting each person's qualifications for being on the panel. To begin the discussion, the moderator may then direct a specific question to one or more panelists. An effective moderator encourages all panelists to participate. If one panelist seems reluctant, the moderator may direct a specific question to that person. If one panelist tends to dominate the discussion, the moderator may suggest politely that other panel members be given an opportunity to participate. Rather than let the discussion continue until the group has nothing more to say on the issue, the moderator usually sets a specific time limit. Most panel discussions last about an hour, but the time limit can be tailored to the needs of the audience and the topic. At the conclusion of the discussion, the moderator may either summarize the group members' comments or ask another group member to do so. Often the summary is followed by an invitation to the audience to ask questions of the panel.

Symposium Presentations—A **symposium presentation** consists of a series of short speeches that are usually unified by a central theme or issue. Unlike participants in a panel discussion, participants in a symposium either come with prepared speeches or speak extemporaneously from an outline. The speakers are usually experts who represent contrasting points of view. For example, imagine that your physics instructor has invited four experts in the field of nuclear energy to speak to your class. Each expert has selected a specific aspect of nuclear energy to present. Your instructor probably will briefly introduce the speakers, announce the central topic of discussion, and ask the speakers to address a discussion question. Each participant will then speak for eight to ten minutes. The speakers probably will not talk informally between speeches; they will likely know in advance which general areas the other speakers will discuss. After the speeches, your instructor may summarize the major ideas presented and allow the audience to participate in an open forum.

Technically, a symposium is not really a form of group discussion because there is little or no interaction among the participants. But a symposium often concludes with a more informal panel discussion or forum. There usually is a time limit for the audience forum following a symposium. A major advantage of the symposium is that it is easy to organize: Just line up three or four speakers to discuss a designated topic. In addition, when speakers with contrasting viewpoints present their ideas, a lively discussion often follows. The moderator of a symposium must make sure that the speakers know their time limits and address their assigned topics. An able moderator can prevent a symposium from digressing into a discussion of irrelevant issues.

Forum Presentations—When many people participate, improved decisions can result—a principle that the **forum presentation** capitalizes on. In ancient Rome, the forum was the public marketplace where citizens could assemble and voice their opinions about the issues of the day. After a panel discussion, symposium, or speaker's presentation, a forum permits an audience to get involved in the discussion. Rather than playing a passive role, as in a panel discussion, the audience directs questions and responses to a chairperson or to a group of individuals. For example, when holding a news conference, the president of the United States presents a prepared statement, which is then followed by questions and responses from reporters—a forum. Some talk radio stations have forum discussions on issues of the day. Many communities conduct town meetings or public hearings in which citizens can voice their opinions about issues affecting the community.

The audience in a forum has an opportunity to provide feedback, and sometimes their comments can indicate how successful a speaker or panel has been in enlightening the audience. The questions-and-responses exchanges also give the featured speakers an opportunity to clarify and elaborate their viewpoints.

Review

How to Develop a Discussion Plan

What to Do	How to Do It
Get acquainted with your group members	• Introduce yourself • Share your contact information • Discuss the experience you've had with the topic • Develop strategies for sharing information virtually (social media, e-mail, texting or other apps that facilitate collaboration)
Clarify the goals of the group	• Explicitly write down the purposes and goals of the group • Identify whether your key purpose is to (1) gather information, (2) make a choice or solve a problem, (3) put an idea into action, or (4) achieve two or more of these purposes • Describe what it will look like when your group is finished with its task. Answer this question: How will you know when you are done?
Develop a plan for gathering information and analyzing issues	• Identify and assess the information you already know • Develop a written plan that indicates what you already know and what you need to know • Give members assignments or request volunteers for gathering or analyzing information with a date for reporting back to the group
Follow a structured agenda to accomplish the task	• Identify the topics and issues you need to discuss at each meeting • Consider using the traditional problem-solving process to develop the overarching plan: Identify and define the problem, analyze, generate several solutions, select the best solution, test and implement the solution • Develop a written agenda for each meeting
Share information with others	• Develop a positive climate so group members feel comfortable sharing what they know • Explicitly ask other group members if they have information to share • If necessary ask group members to first write down the information they know and then share it orally • Explicitly talk about the problem of unshared information and then work together to make sure group members share what they know
Determine how to present your information	• Decide whether you will use a (1) panel discussion format, (2) symposium presentation, or (3) forum presentation (or some combination of all three) when presenting your information to an audience • Decide which written materials you need to develop and share with others • Consider using the traditional problem-solving structure (identify and define the problem, analyze the problem, generate several solutions, select the best solution, test and implement the solution) or organize both oral and written information using this structure

4.2: How to Formulate Discussion Questions

OBJECTIVE: Determine appropriate questions for group discussion

Questions are the primary way to focus a group discussion on the issues at hand. A good question is like a "mental can opener": It invites group members to share information. Well-worded discussion questions can serve as agenda items for group and team meetings.

A discussion question should be phrased with considerable care. The better a group crafts a well-worded discussion question, the more clearly articulated the group's goal will be, and the greater the chances for a productive and orderly discussion.

For some group discussions and conferences, the questions are predetermined. For example, that is the case with government committees and juries. Most groups, however, are faced with a problem or need and need to formulate a specific question to guide their deliberations. There are basically four types of discussion questions:

- Questions of fact
- Questions of prediction
- Questions of value
- Questions of policy[55]

By the end of this module, you will be able to:

4.2.1 Compose questions of fact
4.2.2 Compose questions of prediction
4.2.3 Compose questions of value
4.2.4 Compose questions of policy

4.2.1: Questions of Fact

OBJECTIVE: Compose questions of fact

Some **questions of fact** are phrased such that the answer to the question is either yes or no: Something either did or did not occur. (Of course, a yes or no response can also be qualified in terms of the probability of its accuracy.) The question "Did the Philadelphia Eagles win the Super Bowl in 2018?" is a question of fact—either the team did or it did not. Answers to these kinds of questions of fact can simply be looked up and probably don't require group deliberations. In contrast, a group may be asked to investigate a question of fact whose answer is not so easy to determine, such as "Did John Smith violate our company ethics policy last year?"

Dennis Gouran suggests that one way to investigate a question of fact is to construct a story or narrative to answer the discussion question.[56] To determine, for example, whether John Smith *did* violate an ethics policy, the group should reconstruct what John Smith did or did not do. Such a reconstruction involves developing a story with a beginning, a middle, and an end to answer the question.

In trying to answer a question of fact, make sure that all group members understand the key words and phrases in the discussion question. For example, when faced with the question "Have there been more hurricanes in the Atlantic Ocean in recent years due to climate change?" the group will need to clarify the specific factors that result in climate change before answering the question. By reducing the ambiguity of a question, a group can save considerable time in agreeing on a final answer.

Your group's objective will determine whether you should investigate a question of fact. If the group needs to discover what is true and what is false, then formulate a question of fact and define the key words in the question to give it greater focus and clarity. If the group needs to make a less objective value judgment or to suggest solutions to a problem, develop a question of prediction, value, or policy.

4.2.2: Questions of Prediction

OBJECTIVE: Compose questions of prediction

Will the levee withstand a Category 3 hurricane? Will the new airport security measures make air travel safer? A **question of prediction** asks whether something is likely to occur or may occur under a certain set of circumstances. In the question "Will a tuition increase result in the university having a balanced budget?", the set of circumstances is a tuition increase.

How does a group attempt to answer such a question? First, look for examples of what happened in similar situations. For instance, the university might survey other universities to see how their budgets were affected when tuition was increased. Also, simply use logic and reasoning based on the available evidence to determine what will or will not happen in the future. Will you use questions of prediction when communicating with others in small groups? That's a question of prediction that you'll answer based on your past experiences.

Group researcher Dennis Gouran suggests that, when investigating questions of prediction, an appropriate agenda for groups to follow would include four steps.[57]

How to Answer Questions of Prediction

Develop If-Then Statements—Identify one or more if-then statements to focus and clarify the issues. For example, "If tuition is increased, then the university will have a balanced budget," or "If tuition is increased, then the university can continue its expansion program."

Analyze the Problem—Spend time analyzing the likelihood that what is expected (a balanced budget) will actually occur. What are the causes, effects, and symptoms of the problem? What impact have previous tuition increases had on the budget in the past?

Use Evidence—Present evidence that documents the likelihood that X will lead to Y. In this example, X = a tuition increase and Y = a balanced budget.

Evaluate the Quality of the Evidence—Determine whether the evidence that attempts to document the likelihood that X will lead to Y is high-quality evidence. (Is the evidence recent? Is it from a credible source?)

Using this four-step agenda, groups can efficiently focus on determining whether the expected outcome will likely occur.

4.2.3: Questions of Value

OBJECTIVE: Compose questions of value

A **question of value** generally produces a lively discussion because it touches on related attitudes, beliefs, and values about what is good or bad or right or wrong. Answering a question of value is more complicated than simply determining whether an event did or did not occur. For example, "Which political party in the United States produced the best presidents?" is a question of value because individuals' responses to this question depend on their attitudes toward Democrats, Republicans, or other political parties.

An **attitude** is a learned predisposition to respond to a person, an object, or an idea in a favorable, neutral, or unfavorable way. In essence, the attitudes you hold about the world determine whether you like or dislike what you experience and observe. A favorable attitude toward Democrats will affect your response to the value question "Which political party in the United States produced the best presidents?"

A **belief** is what you hold to be true and false. Put another way, it is the way you structure reality. If you believe in God, you have structured your reality to assume that God exists. If you do not believe in God, you have structured your perception of what is true and false so that God is not part of your reality.

A **value** is often defined as an enduring conception of good and bad. Your values affect your perceptions of right and wrong. A value, such as the importance of being honest, is more resistant to change than an attitude or a belief.

What are your values? Which of your values have the most influence on your behavior? Because values are so central to how you respond in the world, you may have trouble coming up with a tidy list of your most important values. You may be able to list things you like and do not like (attitudes) or things that you classify as true and not true (beliefs), but your values—the guiding forces affecting your behavior—are sometimes difficult to identify.

In examining relationships between attitudes (likes and dislikes), beliefs (what is perceived as true or false), and values (what is perceived as good or bad), it is important to note that values tend to change infrequently, whereas attitudes are most susceptible to change. Figure 4-1 puts values in the center of the diagram because they are central to how you make sense out of what you experience: If you valued honesty yesterday, you will probably still value honesty today and in the future. Beliefs, the next ring, may change depending on your experiences and your perception of what is true and false. Attitudes are shown in the outer ring because they are likely to change more often; indeed, our attitudes may change daily. For example, one day you may like your small group communication class, and the next day you don't. Yet the underlying value you place on obtaining a good education probably will not vary.

Figure 4-1 Values, Beliefs, and Attitudes

Values are in the center because they are most resistant to change; values influence beliefs. Attitudes are on the outer circle because they are likely to change more frequently than values or beliefs.

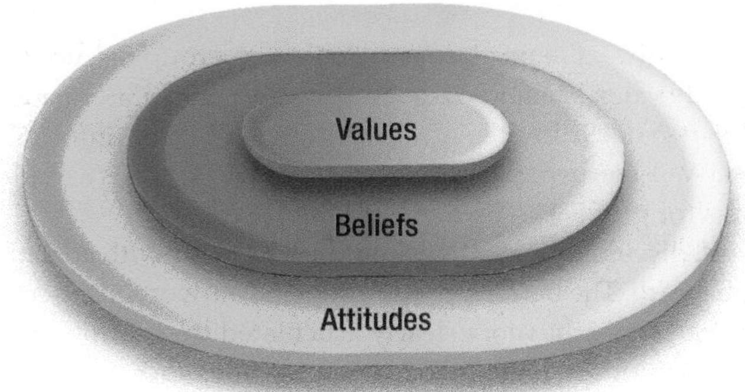

Understanding the differences among attitudes, beliefs, and values helps you better understand what happens when a group discusses a value question. You base your response to a value question on your own attitudes, beliefs, and values, as do other group members. If you can identify the underlying attitudes, beliefs, and values that influence the responses to a value question, you can examine and discuss them.

4.2.4: Questions of Policy

OBJECTIVE: Compose questions of policy

Most problem-solving discussions revolve around **questions of policy**—questions that help groups determine what course of action or policy change would enable them to solve a problem or reach a decision. For example, "What should be done to improve the quality of education in U.S. colleges and universities?" and "What can Congress do to reduce America's national debt?" are questions of policy. These questions can be identified easily because answers to them require changes of policy or procedure. Discussion questions including phrases such as "What should be done about . . . ?" or "What could be done to improve . . . ?" are policy questions. Most legislation in the U.S. Senate and House of Representatives is proposed in response to specific policy questions. A well-written policy question should adhere to three criteria.

Characteristics of a Well-Written Policy

A policy question should imply that a specific problem exists and must be solved.—The question "What should be done about UFOs?" is not an appropriate policy question because it does not provide enough direction to a specific problem. A discussion topic is not the same as a discussion question. If your group is going to discuss UFOs, it has a topic, but it is not trying to solve a problem. The group could rephrase the discussion question to make it more policy oriented: "What could be done to improve the way the government reports and investigates UFO sightings in the United States?" The rephrased question more clearly implies that there is a problem in the way the government investigates sightings of UFOs. The latter question provides clearer direction for research and analysis.

A policy question should be limited in scope.—Only tackle a complex problem if your group has the time and resources to solve it. For example, imagine yourself in a group with the task of formulating a policy question, discussing it, and then reporting the results of the discussion. Your group has three weeks to analyze and suggest possible solutions to the problem, which is "What should be done about health care?" Although the question clearly implies there is a specific problem, its lack of focus would frustrate the group. A more limited discussion question, such as "What should be done to improve access to affordable prescription drugs for older adults in our community?", would be more manageable. It's better to consider a simple, clearly worded question that can be analyzed in the time period allotted to your group than a question that would keep the U.S. Congress busy for months, if not years. Conversely, you should avoid phrasing a policy discussion question so that it requires only a yes or no answer or limits the group's options for solutions. So, "Should it be illegal to send text messages while driving in a school zone?" is a less-satisfactory policy discussion topic than "What can be done to ensure greater safety for children in a school zone?" The second question allows more options for consideration to achieve the goal of children's safety in a school zone.

A policy question should be controversial.—A policy question should focus on an important issue. An issue is a question about which individuals disagree. If group members disagree about how to solve a problem, they should not necessarily select another issue. Indeed, conflict, controversy, and disagreement should not always be viewed negatively. If group members agreed on how to solve a problem at the beginning of a discussion, they would have nothing to discuss. The purpose of a group discussion is to consider all alternatives and to agree on the best one. Therefore, do not reject a discussion question because other group members may hold contrasting points of view.

DEVELOP WELL-WRITTEN DISCUSSION QUESTIONS

The four types of discussion questions (of fact, of prediction, of value, and of policy) may not appear to overlap, but as one researcher observed, groups must concern themselves with questions of fact, prediction, and value when considering questions of policy:[58]

- They must judge evidence as true or false (questions of fact).
- They must ponder whether the proposed solution will be effective in the future (questions of prediction).
- Their attitudes, beliefs, and values (questions of value) will influence the decisions they make on policy changes (questions of policy).

A discussion question provides valuable direction to group deliberations. Such questions can also be modified as the group works through them. First, decide whether your group is considering a question of fact, of prediction, of value, or of policy. Identifying the type of question helps you understand the dynamics of the issue under discussion. Then, if you realize that the question "Should we legalize casino gambling in our community?" involves value judgments, you will be less likely to condemn group members who disagree with you.

Identifying Good Discussion Questions

Question Number	Policy Question	Analysis
1.	Did university officials violate the freshman-admission policy last year?	This is a good example of a question of fact, which asks whether something is true or false. It is not appropriate for discussion.
2.	Was Jimmy Carter elected president of the United States in 1978?	This is a question of fact and not appropriate for discussion, since the answer can easily be verified with an Internet search.
3.	Will the building renovations be completed by December?	This is a good example of a question of prediction, which asks whether something is likely to occur.
4.	Will the tariff restrictions be imposed during the next 10 years?	This is not a good question of prediction because there is no way to know the answer to this general question about the next decade. This question could be rephrased as a policy question asking if the tariff restrictions should be imposed during the next three to five years.
5.	What should be done to solve the drug problem?	This is not a good question of policy because it is too general and does not specify the location or type of drug being considered.
6.	What should be done to curtail gang violence in our community?	This is a good example of a question of policy, which considers whether a change in procedure should be made.
7.	What makes a movie good?	This is not a well-worded value question. It is too general and unfocused.
8.	What are the virtues of a democratic form of government?	This is a good example of a question of value, which considers something's worth or desirability.

CASE STUDY

Questioning the Cost of Textbooks

Imagine that your instructor has just announced a semester-long group project for your small group communication course. You are assigned to work with a group of five people to develop a solution to a problem and, in so doing, to answer a specific policy question. Your group has been assigned the following issue: What should be done to make college textbooks at our school bookstore more affordable for students at our school? You know that textbooks take quite a bite out of your budget, but you and other group members really don't understand how textbook prices are set or why used textbooks still have a high price tag. You also don't understand why popular books on best-seller lists at large bookstores cost less than $30 while most of your textbooks cost more than $60, with many having prices exceeding $100.

At the first group meeting, the members aren't quite sure how to begin addressing the question. You need to know more about how your local bookstore decides to set prices for both new and used books. Many students are buying their textbooks on the Internet and skipping the bookstore altogether. This sometimes results in students getting the wrong book or the wrong edition of the book. You've also heard that your school's bookstore generates a profit that is used to support other activities at your school, but you're not sure of the specific relationship between the bookstore and your school's budget.

Questions for Analysis: Questioning the Cost of Textbooks

1. Although the policy question is clear, what are related questions of fact, prediction, and policy that your group may need to investigate before answering the larger policy question?
2. What should the group do to develop a plan for gathering information and analyzing the issues that contribute to the problem under discussion?
3. What information do you think is available through electronic sources to help your group analyze the issues being investigated? What information probably will not be available on the Internet and will call for other research strategies? How would you go about dividing up the work to gather the information you need?
4. Based on the information in this chapter and the information about developing an agenda for a meeting included in Appendix A: Principles and Practices of Effective Meetings, prepare an agenda for your group's next meeting.
5. Develop a reasonable timeline for accomplishing your group's goal.
6. Your instructor has asked your group to present your analysis and recommendations to the class. Based on information included in Appendix B: Principles and Practices for Communicating to an Audience, what would be an appropriate format for your group's presentation?

Even though a discussion question may be clearly identified as one of fact, prediction, value, or policy, a group's discussion probably will include other types of questions. Once your group has a well-defined problem to discuss, members should begin researching and analyzing it.

4.3: How to Use Logic and Reasoning Effectively

OBJECTIVE: Support an argument using a logical reasoning method

In the search for truth, you will need to develop logical arguments and reach reasoned conclusions. Researchers have found that argument is at the heart of group deliberation.[59] During group discussion, the essence of what you do when you interact with others is advance arguments and listen and respond to the conclusions that others have reached.[60]

Reasoning is the process of drawing a conclusion from evidence. Your evidence will consist of the facts, examples, statistics, and opinions that you use to support the point you wish to make. For more than 2000 years, students have studied the principles of critical analysis that we now present in this section. Although you may be familiar with logic, reasoning, and evidence in another context (such as public speaking, argumentation, or philosophy), these important principles are also relevant to group and team deliberations. First, we will provide an overview of reasoning strategies and then we will describe how to use evidence effectively.

There are three major ways of structuring an argument to reach a logical conclusion:

- Inductive reasoning
- Deductive reasoning
- Causal reasoning

By the end of this module, you will be able to:

- 4.3.1 **Evaluate an inductive argument**
- 4.3.2 **Test the validity of a deductive argument**
- 4.3.3 **Assess a causal argument**

4.3.1: Inductive Reasoning

OBJECTIVE: Evaluate an inductive argument

Inductive reasoning is a method of arriving at a general, or "bottom-line," conclusion through the use of specific examples, facts, statistics, and opinions. For example, suppose you recently bought a used personal computer that didn't work the way it was supposed to when you got it home. You learn that one of your classmates also bought a used computer that didn't work well. Your uncle also bought a used computer from someone who ran an ad in the paper, and his computer didn't work properly either. Based on those three examples, you conclude that buying used computers will give you trouble. You've reached a general conclusion based on the specific examples you know about.

To help answer your group discussion question, make sure you reach a valid or logical conclusion. When you reason inductively (from specific examples to a general conclusion), keep the following questions in mind:

- **Are there enough specific examples to support the conclusion?** Are three examples of problems with used computers enough to prove your point that all used computers don't work well? There are millions of used computers; three is not a very large sample. If you coupled your examples with additional statistical evidence that more than 30 percent of people who purchased a used computer experienced computer problems, then your evidence would be more convincing.
- **Are the specific instances typical?** Were the three examples you cited representative of all used computers? How do you know? Perhaps you, your classmate, and your uncle bought computers that were not typical of most used computers. For example, maybe you all bought them from the same guy, who sells them out of the trunk of his car, whereas most people buy used computers from a reputable retail outlet. If the examples you use to develop your point aren't representative of the entire population, you run the risk of reaching a flawed conclusion.
- **Are the instances recent?** How long ago did you purchase your used computer? If you made your purchase three years ago, conditions may have changed. Perhaps used computers on the market today are more reliable.

WRITING PROMPT

Using Inductive Reasoning

You see an advertisement on TV promising that you will have more energy if you purchase these new supplement pills. The advertisement shows an example of two people who have taken the supplement and feel more energetic; it claims that if you buy the product you will too. Based on the questions we suggest you should ask when using inductive reasoning, how would you evaluate the effectiveness of the reasoning in the advertisement?

▶ The response entered here will appear in the performance dashboard and can be viewed by your instructor.

Submit

4.3.2: Deductive Reasoning

OBJECTIVE: **Test the validity of a deductive argument**

Deductive reasoning is the process of drawing a specific conclusion from a general statement or principle. It is the reverse of inductive reasoning. Deductive reasoning can be presented in the form of a **syllogism**—a way of organizing or structuring an argument in three parts:

1. **Major premise:** This is a generalization or an overall encompassing statement. For example, "All students who take a course in small group communication will have a successful career."
2. **Minor premise:** This is a more specific statement about an example that is linked to the major premise. For example, "Mark Stevens has taken a course in small group communication."
3. **Conclusion:** This is based on the major premise and the more specific minor premise. In reasoning deductively, ensure that the major and minor premises are true and can be supported with evidence. The conclusion to our example syllogism is "Mark Stevens will have a successful career."

To test the truth or validity of an argument organized deductively, consider the following questions:

- **Is the major premise (general statement) true?** Will all students who take a course in small group communication necessarily have successful careers? What evidence exists to support that generalization? The most important part of making a deductive argument hinges on whether your major premise is true. It takes evidence to document the soundness of your major premise. Obviously, just asserting that a statement or generalization is true and labeling it a major premise is not enough. You need facts, examples, statistics, or expert opinion to support your generalization.
- **Is the minor premise (the particular statement) also true?** If your minor premise is not true, your syllogism will fall apart. In our example, it is easy to confirm whether Mark Stevens has taken a course in small group communication. But not all minor premises can be verified as easily.

4.3.3: Causal Reasoning

OBJECTIVE: **Assess a causal argument**

Reaching a logical conclusion through **causal reasoning** involves relating two or more events and concluding that one event caused the other. For example, you might reason that in 2017, climate change was the contributing cause of Hurricane Harvey's tremendous power.

You can structure a causal argument in two ways:

- **Reason from cause to effect, moving from a known fact (cause) to predict a result (effect).** You know, for example, that the number of drug arrests in your community has increased; you know this is a fact because you have researched the police records. You reason that crime will decrease in your community if the drug offenders are locked up. Weather forecasters use the same method of reasoning when they predict the weather. They base a conclusion about what will happen tomorrow on what they know about today's weather.

- **Reason backward, from a known effect to an unknown cause.** You know, for example, that interest rates have decreased in the past six months. You hypothesize that the decrease has occurred because of a healthy economy. You can't be absolutely sure of your analysis, but you do know that interest rates have decreased (the effect). As with other forms of reasoning, you develop strong causal arguments by using evidence to link something known with something unknown.

If you understand how to use evidence effectively, you can enhance your use of inductive, deductive, and causal reasoning. For each of the following statements, identify whether it involves inductive, deductive, or causal reasoning. Compare your answers against the correct answers provided at the end of the chapter.

Identifying Forms of Reasoning

Statement Number	Example Statement
1.	All students who major in communication find good jobs in business and industry. Mary is majoring in communication, and she will likely find a good job in business.
2.	Andy majored in communication and found a good job. Jessica majored in communication and has just been promoted at her job. Zoe majored in communication and is making more than $100,000 per year. Majoring in communication will help you get a good job.
3.	People who have excellent communication skills are likely to make a lot of money because people who can communicate well are in high demand.
4.	I think we should recommend that our community ban plastic bags because this policy has worked well in the communities of Oak Grove, Blue Springs, and Grain Valley.
5.	The long-term forecast calls for more rain, which will create more potholes, so we need to invest more money in road repairs.
6.	My sister uses the same mobile phone company as my brother and my aunt. They like the service they get, so I'd recommend you use the same company.
7.	It's always dangerous to text and drive at the same time, so you should never text and drive at the same time.
8.	Jake had an accident when texting while driving; Angela and Kyle also had accidents while texting and driving. So, no one should be allowed to text while driving.
9.	Our university had the highest electric bill it's ever had; we also broke 10 records for having the hottest temperatures.

4.4: Using Evidence in Group Discussions

OBJECTIVE: Analyze the ways evidence is used in group discussions

The ancient rhetorician Aristotle said that the way to effectively persuade others is to do two things: State your case and then prove it. Evidence is how you prove what you are advocating. Using and evaluating evidence effectively is important when both presenting ideas during group discussion as well as when listening to the arguments of others.

By the end of this module, you will be able to:

4.4.1 **Evaluate evidence for its applicability to group discussion**

4.4.2 **Identify reasoning fallacies in group discussions**

4.4.1: Evaluating Evidence

OBJECTIVE: Evaluate evidence for its applicability to group discussion

After you formulate your discussion question, you need to define key terms and gather information on the issues implied by the question. Group members should also know something about the four kinds of evidence available: (1) facts, (2) examples, (3) opinions, and (4) statistics. Group members who use evidence effectively make better decisions. Indeed, a research study found that the key element in swaying a jury is the quality and quantity of the evidence presented.[61] Research also suggests that when reaching a final conclusion about the validity of an argument, most people find that an argument supported by multiple types of evidence is more persuasive than one backed up by only one source or one type of evidence.[62] Let's examine each of the four types of evidence in more detail.

Types of Evidence

Facts—A **fact** is any statement proven to be true. A fact cannot be a prediction about the future because such a statement cannot be verified; it must be a report of something that has already happened or that is happening. "It will rain tomorrow" is not a fact because it cannot be verified. "The weather forecaster predicts rain" may be a fact if the weather forecaster has made such a prediction; the accuracy of the forecast has nothing to do with whether the statement is a fact. Ask yourself these questions to determine whether a statement is a fact:

- Is it true?
- Is the source reliable?
- Are there any contrary facts?

Fact: Barack Obama was the 44th president of the United States.

Examples— An **example** is an illustration of a particular case or incident, and is most valuable when used to emphasize a fact. An example may be either real or hypothetical. A real example can also be called a fact because it actually exists or has happened. A hypothetical example is of little use in proving a point, but can add color and interest when used to illustrate an otherwise dry or boring factual presentation. Apply the following tests to examples:

- Is it typical?
- Is it significant?
- Are there any contrary examples?

Example: Students who pick up trash in their neighborhood is one example of community service.

Opinions—An **opinion** is a quoted comment. The fact-based opinions of unbiased authorities are most valuable as evidence. Like examples, opinions can dramatize a point and make it more interesting. Opinions are most effective when used in conjunction with facts or statistics. The following questions can help you determine the usefulness of opinions:

- Is the source reliable?
- Is the source an expert in the field?

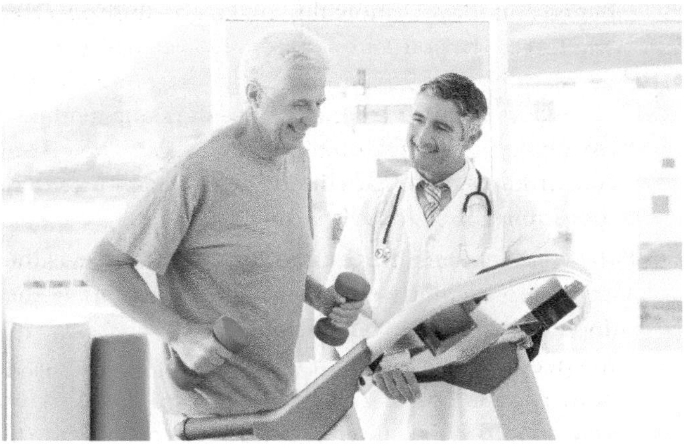

Opinion: In Dr. Richardson's opinion, you need to exercise regularly to stay healthy.
Wavebreak Media Ltd/123RF

- Is the source free from bias?
- Is the opinion consistent with other statements made by the same source?
- Is the opinion characteristic of opinions held by other experts in the field?

Statistics—Because they cannot present dozens of facts or examples in a given time limit, people often rely on statistics. A **statistic** is simply a number. Statistics provide firm support for important points. Unfortunately, statistics are often

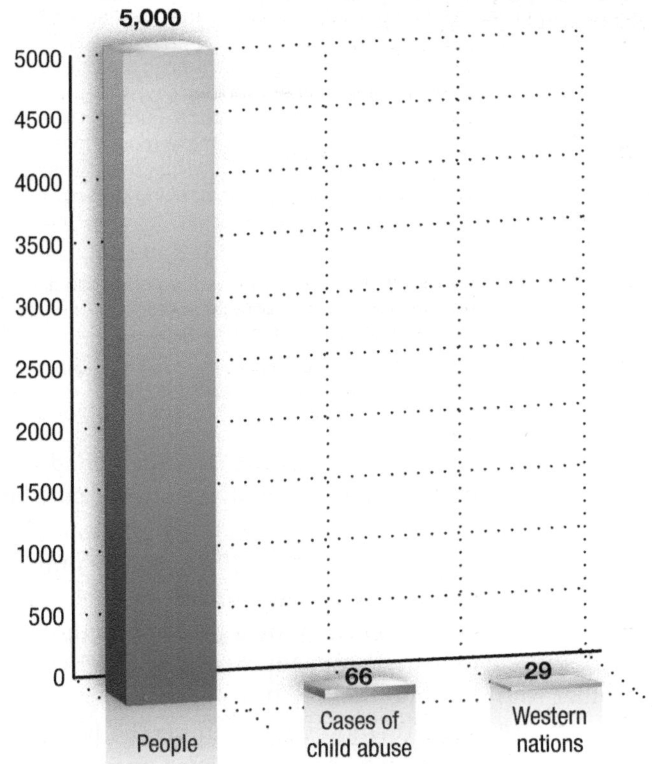

In a study of 5,000 people worldwide, 66 reported experiencing child abuse, 29 of whom were in Western nations.

misgathered and misinterpreted, so make sure they pass the following tests:

- Is the source reliable?
- Is the source unbiased?
- Are the figures recent? Do they apply to the time period in question?
- How were the statistics drawn? If from a sample, is the sample representative of the total population? Is the sample big enough to be reliable?
- Does the statistic actually measure what it is supposed to measure?
- Are there contrary statistics?

Once you have located and collected your evidence, keep in mind a couple of guidelines for applying it effectively. First, never take evidence out of context. Even if you find a statement that seems to be exactly the evidence you need, do not use it if the sentence following it says something like, "However, this idea has recently been proved false." Second, try to gather and use as much and as many types of evidence from as many sources as possible to support a point.

WRITING PROMPT

Practice Applying and Assessing Your Skills

Ricardo, one of the members of your work team, proposes that your company should lower the prices on the widget that it sells. Ricardo has found that another company in China lowered its prices and improved sales. He also found a newspaper column in the business section of the paper in which a customer admitted to making decisions about buying items based solely on the price. Further, Ricardo found a 2004 study indicating that companies make more money when they have the lowest-priced merchandise. What questions should be asked of Ricardo's evidence before agreeing with his conclusion?

The response entered here will appear in the performance dashboard and can be viewed by your instructor.

Submit

EVALUATING INTERNET RESEARCH When conducting research, your first strategy to gather evidence may be an Internet search. Newspapers, research journals, and a multitude of other resources are readily available online. Although your library has a large number of books and journals, the Internet is likely to be a primary method of gathering evidence to support your reasoning. Just as with any other source of information, it is important to evaluate the quality of information you obtain on the Internet. Information may be posted or self-published on this forum without a vetting or evaluation process.

INFORMATION TRIAGE: ASSESS THE QUALITY OF INFORMATION In the medical profession, *triage* is the process of making decisions about which patients need the most attention or medical care in an emergency room. **Information triage** is the process of sorting through information you have gathered from your search to determine what is most useful or needs the most critical attention. Because it is relatively easy to find a large amount of information via the Internet, the challenge is to decide which data are relevant to your discussion question, are accurate, and are credible. Although you can access hundreds of Internet sources and end up with a ream of documents, the volume of information is not nearly as important as your ability to actually use the information you gather.

As with any type of evidence, just because you find it on the Internet, that does not mean the evidence or information is accurate or reliable. Anyone with a computer and software can construct a website. Information on the Internet may not have gone through an extensive editorial process to be checked for accuracy. For example, information that you glean from the website of the *Wall Street Journal* is more credible than that from someone's personal website or the website of an organization with a particular political or profit-based agenda. When evaluating information you retrieve from the Web, consider the following criteria:[63]

- **Accountability.** Who is responsible for the website? What can you find out about the sponsor? To whom do the sponsors of the site owe allegiance? Knowing who is placing the information on the site can help you evaluate whether the information is biased or unbiased.
- **Objectivity.** Related to accountability of the website is the objectivity of the information presented. Consider the interests and philosophical or political biases of the organization or individual responsible for the site.
- **Accuracy.** Is the information accurate? Is it verifiable by other sources? Internet resources should also be relatively free of common grammar, spelling, and punctuation errors.
- **Recency.** How current is the information on the website? Look for clues that the site was recently posted or is kept current. Many sites indicate when they were posted and when they were last updated. As a general rule, the more recent the information (especially facts, statistics, and other data), the better.
- **Usability.** Is there information that you can actually use? Does it relate to the group's or team's goal? Also, consider the overall layout and design of the site, which should facilitate its use.

Ethical Collaboration

Proper Use of Evidence and Reasoning

When preparing for a group discussion or a team meeting, consider the following ethical obligations:

- **Use sound evidence and reasoning.** It is unethical to claim you have found "the truth" without adequately researching the issues you discuss. A discussion peppered with reasoning fallacies leads to inaccurate conclusions and an insensitivity to others' ideas and positions.
- **Give credit to your sources.** Avoid **plagiarism**—presenting the words and ideas of others as your own without giving proper credit to the source. Don't use quotes or paraphrase the ideas of others without acknowledging them. Give proper credit to ideas and information that are not your own, when speaking as well as writing. In group discussions, you can provide an oral footnote: Simply tell your listeners where you got the idea or information you are using. In your written work, use footnotes or references to document the original source of the ideas.
- **Follow through on commitments.** If you don't follow through on work you have promised to perform, you are not being an ethical group communicator. Don't promise to do more than you can accomplish, but accomplish all that you promise to do.

WRITING PROMPT

Handling Statistics Ethically

Imagine that you are watching television and see an interesting program that includes a wealth of statistics documenting the issues involved with immigration to the United States. Soon afterward, you are assigned to work on a group project that focuses on this policy question: Should the government take more aggressive steps to reduce the number of immigrants who enter the United States? You remember several of the statistics that were presented on TV, but you don't remember the precise program that included those statistics.

Is it acceptable to share your information with your group and make up a source for the statistics? You're fairly certain that your information is accurate and reliable; you just don't remember the exact source. No one will ever know that your figures aren't from the source you cite. Would you share the statistics with your group, even though you can't remember the correct source of the information?

The response entered here will appear in the performance dashboard and can be viewed by your instructor.

Submit

4.4.2: Developing Critical Analysis Skills

OBJECTIVE: Identify reasoning fallacies in group discussions

It's not enough just to have evidence or to be able to label the kind of reasoning that you're using to reach conclusions. If you want to critically analyze information and ideas, you must evaluate both the logic and the evidence used to reach a conclusion.

Critical thinkers who are members of groups and teams are able to use the following information identification, analysis, and evaluation skills.

Gather and Analyze Information

Discover new information	Find new relevant research
Organize information	Categorize and structure information
Analyze information	Break information down into pieces and interpret each piece
Synthesize information	Combine information, see new patterns, and put information together in new and meaningful ways
Clarify information	Focus on the important information and ensure that all group members understand what is shared.[64]

AVOID REASONING FALLACIES In addition to identifying and analyzing information, groups need to avoid committing reasoning **fallacies**—false or inaccurate reasoning that occurs when someone attempts to arrive at a conclusion without adequate evidence or with arguments that are irrelevant or inappropriate. Avoiding reasoning fallacies in your own arguments will enhance your critical-thinking skills. Being able to spot reasoning fallacies that others are using will make you a more discriminating and effective listener. Here are some of the most common fallacies.

Reasoning Fallacies

Causal Fallacy—Causal fallacy is the inappropriate assumption that one event causes another when actually little evidence connects the two. The Latin phrase used to summarize this fallacy is *post hoc, ergo propter hoc*, which translates as "after this, therefore because of this." Superstitions are prime examples of causal fallacies. Your assumption that your "lucky" rabbit's foot helps you perform better on math tests probably can't be demonstrated with facts and evidence. It's your ability to study and learn math that determines your test results, not whether you have a rabbit's foot. Be on the lookout for group members who try to connect one event to another without adequate cause and effective evidence.

Either/Or Fallacy—The either/or fallacy occurs when someone argues that there are only two approaches or solutions to a problem; it oversimplifies the options by suggesting we must do either X or Y. "It's either vote for new school taxes or we will have to send our kids to the next county to be educated," claims a parent at a school board meeting. Usually a range of options can be considered in any discussion. In fact, one hallmark of successful groups is the ability to identify several options to solving a problem.

Bandwagon Fallacy—"Everybody is in favor of expanding the city park, so you should favor it, too" is an example of the bandwagon fallacy. Someone using this fallacy tries to convince you that an idea is a good one simply because "everybody" else thinks it's good; hence, you should jump on the bandwagon and support the idea. Judge an idea on its merits, not just because it's popular. One disadvantage of group discussion is that the group may give in to pressure from others.

Hasty Generalization—A person reaching a conclusion on the basis of too little evidence or evidence that doesn't exist is making a hasty generalization. One or two examples do not prove your point. For example, because your friend got ripped off by a service station when vacationing in Texas doesn't mean that you should avoid all service stations in Texas. As another example, you might claim there's no need to spend more money on music education in our schools because your son listens to classical music at home, so you think other students can, too.

Attacking the Person—This fallacy—also known as *ad hominem,* Latin for "to the man"—involves attacking irrelevant personal characteristics about someone rather than examining the idea or proposal he or she advances. "We all know that Sue's idea won't work because she's been in local politics for years and we just can't trust her" does not really address the soundness of the idea, which may be a great one.

Red Herring—The red herring fallacy occurs when someone undermines an idea by using irrelevant facts or arguments as distractions. It gets its name from the old trick of dragging a red herring across a trail to divert the sniffing dogs who may be following. Someone uses a red herring fallacy to divert attention or distract listeners from the real issues. For example, someone who claims, "The real problem is not sexual harassment in the military, but the fact that we need to pay our military personnel more money," is trying to divert attention from the issue of sexual harassment and change the subject to the salary of military personnel. A group member who listens critically will recognize this distraction and return the discussion back to the issue at hand.

HOW TO DEAL WITH REASONING FALLACIES IN THE GROUP If in the course of your discussion you detect that someone reaches a conclusion using a reasoning fallacy, how do you bring it to his or her attention? We don't suggest that you use an accusatory voice and pounce on someone for having faulty logic. Making someone defensive doesn't foster a high-quality group climate. Instead, your first effort to draw attention to a reasoning fallacy should be to calmly and tactfully describe how the evidence offered does not support the point. Consider using an "I" statement: "I'm not sure I follow that argument. . . . " Describing how you don't see the logic of their point is a better way to challenge fellow group members than immediately labeling their logic as a "fallacious argument" and trying to belittle them. "You" statements ("You're wrong! Your evidence is terrible!") tend to raise the hackles of your listener and create a defensive, disconfirming climate.

Summary: Preparing to Collaborate

4.1: How to Develop a Discussion Plan

- Get to know each group member; exchange phone numbers, e-mail addresses, and other strategies to facilitate virtual collaboration.
- Develop a written description of the group goal.
- Develop a plan for gathering and analyzing information.
- Develop and follow a structured plan to accomplish the task.
- Share information you gather with other group members.
- Use critical-thinking and analysis skills to evaluate the information gathered and shared.
- Express verbal and nonverbal support for other group members.
- Decide how the information and recommendations will be presented to others.

4.2: How to Formulate Discussion Questions

- If your group is trying to decide whether something is true or false or whether something did or did not occur, formulate a question of fact.
- If your group is attempting to determine whether something will happen in the future, formulate a question of prediction.
- If your group is trying to decide whether one idea or approach to an issue is better than another, formulate a question of value.
- If your group is trying to develop a solution to a problem or determine whether action should be taken, formulate a question of policy.

4.3: How to Use Logic and Reasoning Effectively

- When using inductive reasoning, make sure you have enough examples that are typical or representative of other examples and that are recent.
- When using deductive reasoning, make sure that the general premise is true and that you have evidence to support it.
- When using causal reasoning, make sure that there is an actual cause-and-effect relationship between the events you link together; simply because two things happen at the same time (because they are correlated) does not mean one event causes the second event.

4.4: Using Evidence in Group Discussions

- When relying on facts to prove a point, ask yourself three questions: Are the facts true? Is the source of the facts reliable? Are there any contrary facts?
- When relying on examples, determine if the examples are typical and significant and whether there are any contrary examples.
- When quoting opinions of others, determine if the source of the opinion is reliable, if the person is an expert, if the source is free from bias, and if the opinion is consistent with other statements made by the source and other experts in the field.
- When using statistics, determine if the source is reliable and unbiased, the information is up to date, the sampling method used to gather the statistics was sound, and there are any contrary statistics.
- Develop the skill of information triage; sort out useful ideas and data from less important ones that you retrieve from your Internet searches or library research; evaluate Web information for accountability, objectivity, accuracy, recency, and usability.
- Use critical-thinking and analysis skills to evaluate reasoning.
- Don't assume a cause-and-effect relationship without adequate evidence (causal fallacy).
- Don't suggest that options boil down to either one solution or another (either/or fallacy).
- Don't accept an idea or a solution just because numerous people are in favor of it (bandwagon fallacy).
- Don't reach a conclusion without adequate evidence (hasty generalization).
- Don't criticize a person as part of attacking an idea; focus on evaluating the quality of the idea, not the person (attacking-the-person fallacy).
- Don't let the group get away with diverting attention from the key issue under discussion (red herring fallacy).

SHARED WRITING

Evaluating Your Values, Beliefs, and Attitudes

Think about an issue about which you have very strong feelings, such as protecting the environment, managing climate change, improving health care, or the importance of education. What attitudes (likes and dislikes) do you hold about this issue? What beliefs do you hold about this issue (what you think is true or not true)? What are your underlying values (enduring concepts of what is right and good compared with what is wrong and bad)? Note how with any issue there are related underlying values that influence what you may believe and the attitudes you hold. Write a short response that your classmates will read. Be sure to include specifics in your discussion.

A minimum number of characters is required to post and earn points. After posting, your response can be viewed by your class and instructor, and you can participate in the class discussion.

Post

Answers

Section 4.3.3: Identifying Forms of Reasoning

1. Deductive. 2. Inductive. 3. Causal. 4. Inductive. 5. Causal. 6. Inductive. 7. Deductive. 8. Inductive. 9. Causal.

Chapter 5

Relating to Others in Groups

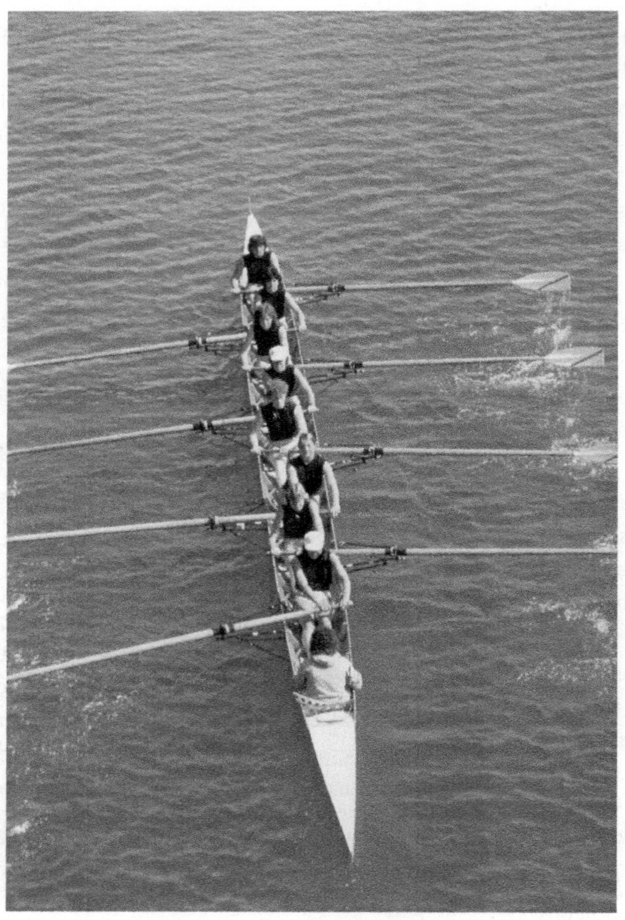

"In organizations, real power and energy is generated through relationships. The patterns of relationships and the capacities to form them are more important than the tasks, functions, roles and positions."

—Margaret Wheatley

Learning Objectives

5.1 Determine the impact of your roles and identities on your social interactions

5.2 Analyze the influence of norms on the actions of a group and its individual members

5.3 Predict group interactions based on status

5.4 Outline the path of power from its origin to its impact on a group

5.5 Evaluate the level of trust between group members

5.6 Analyze how group relationships change over time

Are you a leader or a follower in a small group? Do you talk a lot or very little? Your answers probably depend on the quality of your relationships with other group members. Communication scholar Joann Keyton defines *relational communication* in groups as the verbal and nonverbal messages that create the social fabric of a group by promoting relationships between and among group members. It is the affective (emotional) or expressive dimension of group communication as opposed to the instrumental, or task-oriented, dimension.[1]

Every message we communicate to someone else has both a content dimension and a relationship dimension. The content dimension of a message includes the specific information conveyed to that person. The relationship dimension involves message cues that provide hints about whether you like or dislike the person with whom you are communicating.

Several elements affect the quality of relationships you establish with other group members:

- The roles you assume
- The norms or standards the group develops
- The status differences that affect the group's productivity
- The power some members wield
- The trust that improves group performance
- Some additional effects of cultural differences

5.1: Roles

OBJECTIVE: Determine the impact of your roles and identities on your social interactions

Stop reading this chapter for just a moment, and reflect on the question, "Who are you?"

Who Are You?

I am ______

I am ______

I am ______

I am ______

I am ______

I am ______

I am ______

I am ______

I am ______

I am ______

Review your responses. They are part of your *self-concept*—who you think you are. This shapes your communication and relationships with others and affects how others relate to you.

In trying to reduce uncertainty when communicating in groups, we quickly assess the behaviors of others. We assign **roles**—sets of expectations—to others. In a small group, roles originate from sources:

- People's expectations about their own behavior—their **self-concepts**
- The perceptions others have about individuals' positions in the group
- People's actual behavior as they interact with others

Because self-concepts largely determine the roles people assume in small groups, it is important to understand how self-concepts develop.

By the end of this module, you will be able to:

5.1.1 **Relate self-concept to group interaction**

5.1.2 **Identify different roles that group members take**

5.1.1: Self-Concept and Group Roles

OBJECTIVE: Relate self-concept to group interaction

What are your responses to the question "Who are you?"

Beyond your natural genetic predispositions, many factors influence your self-concept.

OTHERS' PERCEPTIONS Significant other people influence who you think you are. Your parents gave you your name. Perhaps a teacher once told you that you were good in art. Maybe somebody once told you that you cannot sing very well. You listen to others, especially those whose opinions you respect, and internalize their perceptions to shape your self-concept.

GENDER One important part of everyone's self-concept is **gender**.[2] Your gender identity affects your communication with others. Research suggests that the psychological aspects of gender—how "feminine" or "masculine" a person is—may affect people's communication at least as much as biological sex does.[3] Some research supports small differences that "characterize women as using communication to connect with, support, and achieve closeness with others, and men as using communication to accomplish some task and to assert their individuality."[4] More recent studies reinforce the notion that gender still makes a difference. For example, Priya Raghubir and Ana Valenzuela's study of a television reality program showed how men and women both use sex in a strategic way to achieve a competitive advantage.[5] The same researchers also observed that, in a competitive setting, female players perform better when women constitute a majority on a team.[6]

SEXUAL ORIENTATION **Sexual orientation**[7] also affects our sense of self-concept, as well as how we relate to others. It is inappropriate to use derogatory terms or make jokes about a person's sexual orientation—or the person's gender identity. Being sensitive to attitudes about sexual orientation and gender identity is part of the role of an effective group communicator.

CULTURE OF ORIGIN Another important component of self-concept is culture of origin. For example, social life in Japan and North America flows from different premises. North Americans tend to prize the image of the rugged individualist; many Japanese, in contrast, view this image as suggestive of egotism and insensitivity. Studies show that in both types of cultures, strong cooperative relationships within a group or team enhance constructive conflict and lead to more innovative team outcomes.[8]

Culture influences self-concept and behaviors such as willingness to communicate in a group.[9] A wealth of evidence indicates that individuals from different cultures interpret situations and concepts very differently.[10] Therefore, understanding cultural differences is essential to effective group communication.

How might your self-concept determine the kinds of groups you prefer to work with?

AFFILIATIONS The various groups with which a person affiliates also help to define that individual's self-concept. If you attend college, you may describe yourself as a student. If you belong to a fraternity or sorority, you may think that group membership sets you apart from others. Your religious affiliation, political party, and membership in civic and social organizations all contribute to the way you perceive yourself.

SELF-OBSERVATION You also learn who you are by simply observing and interpreting your own behavior. Just as before leaving home, you check the mirror to see how you look, do you also try to see yourself through others' behavior toward you? Self-concept arises, in part, through the reflected appraisals of others.

5.1.2: Diversity of Roles in Small Groups

OBJECTIVE: Identify different roles that group members take

Your own perceptions and expectations provide the foundation for the roles you will assume. Yet your role is also worked out with the other group members.[11] As you interact, they form impressions of you and your abilities. As they react to your behavior in the group—reflected appraisals—you learn what abilities and behaviors they reinforce. These abilities and behaviors may, in turn, become part of your self-concept.

People assume roles because of their interests and abilities and because of the needs and expectations of the group. Some roles, especially in teams, are assigned formally. When police officers arrive on the scene of an accident, generally bystanders do not question their assumption of leadership. In a task-oriented small group, a member may be assigned the role of secretary, which includes specific duties and responsibilities. A chairperson may be elected to coordinate the meeting and delegate responsibilities. Assigning responsibilities and specific roles reduces uncertainty. A group can often get on with its task more efficiently when some roles are assigned. Of course, even if a person has been elected or assigned the role of chairperson, the group may reject his or her leadership in favor of another member. In other words, roles can be assigned formally or can evolve informally.[12] To be most successful, groups and teams require a balance of roles. When a balance of roles exists within a team, the team will likely be successful.[13]

The types of roles discussed so far are **task roles**, which are aimed at accomplishing the group's goal. Two other role categories are also distinguished: maintenance and individual. **Maintenance roles** define a group's social atmosphere. For example, a member who tries to maintain a peaceful, harmonious group climate by mediating disagreements and resolving conflicts performs a maintenance function. **Individual roles** call attention to individual group members and tend to be counterproductive to the overall group effort. Someone who is more interested in seeking personal recognition than in promoting the general benefit of the group is adopting an individual role.

Kenneth Benne and Paul Sheats have compiled a comprehensive list of possible informal roles that individual group members can assume; these roles are listed in Table 5-1.[14,15] Perhaps you can identify the various roles you have assumed while participating in small group discussions.

WHAT ROLES DO YOU FILL? In looking at the list of group roles in Table 5-1, you may recognize yourself—for instance, as a harmonizer or a follower—and say, "Yes, that's me." You may also try to classify others into these

Table 5-1 Comprehensive List of Group Roles[16]

Role Category	Type of Role	Description
Group Task Roles	Initiator-contributor	Proposes new ideas or approaches to group problem solving
	Information seeker	Asks for clarification of suggestions; also asks for facts or other information
	Opinion seeker	Asks for clarification of values and opinions
	Information giver	Provides facts, examples, statistics, and other evidence
	Opinion giver	Offers beliefs or opinions
	Elaborator	Provides examples based on his or her experience or the experience of others
	Coordinator	Clarifies relationships among the ideas and suggestions that have been provided by others
	Orienter (summarizer)	Summarizes what has occurred and keeps the group focused on the task
	Evaluator-critic	Makes an effort to judge the evidence and conclusions that the group suggests
	Energizer	Spurs the group to action; motivates and stimulates the group to greater productivity
	Procedural technician	Helps the group by performing tasks such as distributing papers, rearranging the seating, or running errands for the group
	Recorder	Writes down suggestions and ideas of others; keeps a record of the group's progress
Group-Building and Maintenance Roles	Encourager	Offers praise, understanding, and acceptance of others' ideas and suggestions
	Harmonizer	Mediates disagreements
	Compromiser	Attempts to resolve conflicts by trying to find acceptable solutions to disagreements
	Gatekeeper and expediter	Encourages less talkative group members to participate and tries to limit overly lengthy contributions of other group members
	Standard setter	Helps to set standards and goals for the group
	Group observer	Keeps records of the group's process and uses the gathered information to evaluate the group's procedures
	Follower	Goes along with suggestions and ideas of other group members; serves as an audience in group discussions
Individual Roles	Aggressor	Destroys or deflates the status of other group members; may try to take credit for someone else's contribution
	Blocker	Is generally negative, stubborn, and disagreeable without apparent reason
	Recognition seeker	Seeks the spotlight by boasting and reporting on personal achievements
	Self-confessor	Uses the group as an audience to report personal feelings, insights, and observations
	Joker	Tells stories and jokes that do not help the group
	Dominator	Asserts authority by manipulating group members; may use flattery or assertive behavior to dominate the discussion
	Help seeker	Tries to evoke a sympathetic response from others; often expresses insecurity or feelings of low self-worth
	Special-interest pleader	Works to serve an individual need; speaks for a special group or organization that best fits his or her own biases

categories. While identifying the characteristics of roles may help you understand their function in small group communication, stereotyping individuals can lock them into roles. When asked to analyze group roles, group members often categorize and label other members, based on the roles they are perceived to fill.[17] As you identify the roles adopted by group members, be flexible in your classifications. Realize that you and other members can assume several different roles during a group discussion. In fact, a group member rarely serves solely as an "encourager," "opinion seeker," or "follower." Roles are dynamic; they change with changing perceptions, experiences, and expectations. An individual can assume leadership responsibilities at one meeting and play a supporting role at the next.

DIFFERENT ROLES AT DIFFERENT TIMES Because a role is worked out jointly between you and the group, you will find yourself assuming different roles in different groups. Perhaps a committee needs someone to serve as a procedural leader or gatekeeper. Because you recognize this need and no one else keeps the group organized, you may find yourself steering the group back toward the topic, making sure all members have a chance to participate. In another committee, where others serve as procedural leaders, you may be the person who generates new ideas. Consciously or not, you develop a role unique to your talents and the needs of the group. In addition, your role changes from group to group.

EMERGENT TEAM ROLES Recent research on team roles has taken a communicative approach that reveals five emergent roles:

1. The solution seeker
2. The problem analyst
3. The procedural facilitator
4. The complainer
5. The indifferent

Compare these to the roles identified in Table 5-1. Where do they overlap? Some roles clearly facilitate the group's work, whereas others inhibit progress.[18]

INFORMAL AND FORMAL ROLES As discussed earlier, roles in groups and teams can be either informal or formal. In the case of teams, roles are likely to be more formally defined. For example, one team member may have primary responsibility for communicating with the supervisor or with other teams and departments. Another may head project planning. When roles within a team are established formally, it is important that these roles be clearly defined and coordinated with one another.[19] Lack of clarity can result in role stress and loss of team productivity.[20]

If you understand how group roles form and how various roles function, you will be better able to help a group achieve its purpose. Studies of asynchronous college discussion groups have found significant improvement in those groups' performance when roles such as moderator, starter, and summarizer are assigned to specific group members.[21] Groups also need members to perform both maintenance and task functions to help the group get the job done and help the group run smoothly. Although you cannot assume complete responsibility for distributing roles within your group, your insights can help solve some of the group's potential problems. Understanding group roles—and when to use them—is an important part of becoming a competent group communicator.

WRITING PROMPT

Your Role(s) in Groups

The most effective groups are those whose members perform positive roles when they are most needed. Review Table 5-1. Which of these roles are you most likely to perform? Why do you think that is? Can you identify situations where your natural abilities are most appropriate?

▶ The response entered here will appear in the performance dashboard and can be viewed by your instructor.

Submit

5.2: Norms

OBJECTIVE: Analyze the influence of norms on the actions of a group and its individual members

Have you noticed that in some classes it is okay to say something without raising your hand, but in others the instructor must call on you before you speak? Raising your hand is a norm. **Norms** are rules or standards that determine appropriate and inappropriate behavior in a group.

Why do different norms develop in two similar situations? There are at least two key reasons:

1. People develop norms in new groups based on the norms of previous groups to which they have belonged.
2. Norms develop based on what happens early in a group's existence.

By the end of this module, you will be able to:

- 5.2.1 **Explain the processes by which groups develop norms**
- 5.2.2 **Identify the norms of a group**
- 5.2.3 **Determine the factors that influence conformity to norms**
- 5.2.4 **Propose potential ground rules for a team based on its needs**

5.2.1: How Do Norms Develop?

OBJECTIVE: Explain the processes by which groups develop norms

Marshall Scott Poole suggests that a group organizes itself based, in part, on norms that members encountered in previous groups.[22] Giddens and Poole call this process *structuration*. Groups do things (become structured) based on the ways that things were done in other groups. If many of your classmates previously had classes in which they had to raise their hands before speaking, then they will probably introduce that behavior into other groups. If enough people accept it, a norm is born—or, more accurately, a norm is reborn.

In the long run, having a clear mutual understanding of a group's norms frees group members to focus their attention on the actual work of the group. Your own experience with group norms and your leadership in helping groups adopt norms that facilitate their work can be important resources that you provide to your groups.

Norms also develop from behaviors that occur early in a group's development. Because of our uncertainty about how to behave when our group first meets, we are eager to learn acceptable behavior. On the first day of class, if a student raises his or her hand to respond to the instructor, and another student does the same, that norm is likely to stick. In contrast, if several students respond without raising a hand, chances are that raising hands will not become a norm in the class.

Skilled Collaboration

Establishing Group Norms

Norms are the rules or standards that tell us what are acceptable versus unacceptable behaviors in a group. Structuration theory tells us that groups are structured by members' use of the rules and the various resources they bring with them into the group. So, a group's norms are established, in part, by members' previous experiences. Group members interact with one another to establish new group norms.

Real-Life Applications

You can leave the development of group norms to chance and relatively random group interaction, or you can approach the establishment of group norms intentionally—that is, you can develop norms for developing norms. Often, spending some time to establish norms when a group is first formed can save time and avoid conflict later. Just as establishing *mutuality of concern* among group members is important, so too is consciously setting some ground rules.

You might suggest discussing the ground rules for the group along with the usual discussions about how frequently and where you'll meet. What is acceptable and unacceptable behavior? Is it okay to show up late to a meeting or to miss one altogether? What will happen if you do? If you have to miss a meeting, how will you let the others know? What provisions will the group make for bringing a member who has missed a meeting up to date? If there is a virtual component to your group, how will you establish online norms?

5.2.2: Identifying Group Norms

OBJECTIVE: Identify the norms of a group

Norms reduce some of the uncertainty that occurs when people congregate. People's speech, the clothes they wear, and how and where they sit are all influenced group norms. Group norms also affect relationships among group members and the quality of group decisions.[23]

Norms are neither good nor bad. Indeed, it is possible for the same norm to be beneficial to one group but harmful to another. For example, a norm of permitting side conversations between two people within a group can be helpful in problem solving in groups where faction forming and debate are desirable. Conversely, the same behavior can impede a group's negotiation tasks where group unity is more desirable.[24]

How Can I Recognize Group Norms?

If you have recently joined a group, how do you recognize the group's norms?

One way to do so is to observe repeated behavior patterns, such as noting any consistencies in the way people talk or dress. In identifying normative behavior in a group, consider the following questions:

- How do group members dress?
- Does the group follow a prepared agenda?
- If your work will be conducted partly or entirely in a virtual environment, what are the expectations for how often and for how long you will meet in that way? Who will initiate virtual meetings?
- In a virtual group, is multitasking encouraged?
- What are group members' attitudes toward time? (Do group meetings begin and end on time? Are members often late to meetings?)
- What type of language is used by most group members? (Is swearing acceptable? Is the language formal?)
- In a virtual group, do members typically address the whole group or individual members in the group?
- Do group members use humor to relieve tension?
- Do group members address the group leader formally?
- Is it proper etiquette to address group members by their first names?

Noting when someone breaks a rule can also reveal group norms. If a member arrives late and other members scowl, they probably do not approve of tardiness. If, after a member uses obscene words, another member says, "I wish you wouldn't use words like that," you can be certain that for at least one person a norm has been broken. Punishment indicates violated norms. Often the severity of the punishment corresponds to the significance of the norm.[25] Punishment can range from subtle nonverbal expressions of disapproval (which may not even be noticed by the person expressing them) to exclusion from the group.

WRITING PROMPT

Group Norms

Reflect on a recent group meeting you attended. What group norms can you identify? (Time? Behavior? Language? Dress?) Can you identify any norms that were revealed when a group member did not conform to them?

The response entered here will appear in the performance dashboard and can be viewed by your instructor.

Submit

5.2.3: Conforming to Group Norms

OBJECTIVE: Determine the factors that influence conformity to norms

What influences how quickly and rigidly people conform to the rules and standards of a group? At least five factors affect conformity to group norms.[26]

1. **The individual characteristics of the group members.** Group members' past experiences and unique personality characteristics influence how they conform to established norms. In summarizing the research on conformity, Shaw makes the following observations:

   > More intelligent persons are less likely to conform than less intelligent persons; women usually conform more than men, at least on traditional tasks . . . and authoritarians conform more than nonauthoritarians.[27]

2. **The clarity of the norm and the certainty of punishment for breaking it.** The more ambiguous a group norm, the less likely it is that members will conform to it. The military spells out behavior rules so clearly that little, if any, ambiguity remains. Failure to abide by the rules results in swift and sure corrective sanctions. Thus, recruits quickly learn to conform. In small groups, as soon as rules become clear and norms are established, members will usually conform.

3. **The number of people who have already conformed to the norm.** Imagine walking into a room with five or six other people, as participants once did in a study by Solomon Asch. Three lines have been drawn on a blackboard, one of which is clearly shorter than the other two. One by one, each person is asked which line is the shortest, and each says that all the lines are the same length. Finally, it is your turn to judge which of the lines is the shortest. You are perplexed because your eyes tell you that one line is definitely shorter. But can all the other members of your group be wrong? You will probably answer that all of the lines are the same length—that is, you will conform. You do not want to appear odd to the other group members. Factors such as the size of a group, the number of people who agree with a certain policy, and the status of those who conform contribute to the pressure for conformity in a group.[28]

4. **The quality of the interpersonal relationships in the group.** A group whose members like one another and respect one another's opinions is more likely to support conformity than is a less cohesive group. Employees who like their jobs, bosses, and coworkers and take pride in their work are more likely to support group norms than those who have negative or frustrating relationships with their employers or colleagues. Workplace incivility is a norm violation that is a prevalent form of workplace deviance, characterized by rude or disrespectful behavior that violates workplace norms. Incivility can lead to extreme loss of productivity.[29]

5. **The sense of group identification.** If group members can readily identify with the goals of the group, and feel a sense of commitment to it, they are more likely to conform to standards of behavior. Fraternal and religious organizations often elicit a strong sense of commitment and, accordingly, conformity.

"Damn it, Hopkins, didn't you get yesterday's memo?"

GENERAL VERSUS OPERATIONAL NORMS Conforming to group norms requires participants to be aware of both general norms and operationalized norms, which are more specific. Groups often adopt general norms very quickly. For example, "We all need to communicate with one another frequently and log on promptly when meeting virtually" would be a common general group norm. But while a clear consensus might emerge around this general norm, it may mean different things to different people. "Frequently" might mean weekly to one person but daily to another. Thus, norms tend to evolve from the general to the operational (what the norms mean in terms of actual behaviors) over time as the specifics are negotiated. As always, communication about norms is key.[30]

NORMS AND CULTURE Culturally diverse groups often have difficulty establishing satisfactory roles and norms because of differences in cultural expectations. Such groups require extra effort in group building and maintenance.

When group members do not share a common native language, some additional tactics may be necessary:[31]

- *Slow down* communication.
- *Repeat* or paraphrase when nonverbal expressions suggest that listeners do not understand.
- *Verify* common understanding by having others restate the argument or idea.
- *Encourage restatement* in the listener's native language, if necessary (and possible).

Cultures vary widely in terms of their conversational style as well as the appropriateness assigned to topics of conversation. Be aware of such variations, and do not attribute such differences to impoliteness or insensitivity.

Ethical Collaboration

Prioritizing Loyalties

Relational communication is the process of building relationships between and among group members. But what happens when you see another group member behaving unethically?

Suppose that in the final semester of your senior year, you and a classmate are student interns for a not-for-profit organization that raises funds and develops programs to help children who have suffered abuse. Each of you receives a small stipend for your work on the organization's programming team, as well as three college credits (assuming successful completion of the internship and a favorable review by your supervisors).

It has come to your attention that your friend has been taking office supplies from the nonprofit organization for personal use. At first it was small packages of sticky notes, but now your friend has gone home with 500 sheets of printer paper, an ink cartridge, several rolls of tape, a tape dispenser, and a stapler.

WRITING PROMPT

Loyalty to the Group or to One Member?

Consider the preceding scenario. What would you do upon discovering that your friend has been taking office supplies for personal use? Weigh your obligations to your friend, to the nonprofit organization, and to yourself (to successfully complete the internship and earn course credits).

▶ The response entered here will appear in the performance dashboard and can be viewed by your instructor.

Submit

Although violating a group norm usually results in group disapproval and perhaps chastisement, such a violation can occasionally benefit a group. Just because members conform unanimously to a rule does not mean that the rule is beneficial. For example, in some situations the opinions of group members may matter more in the decision-making process than the facts they exchange.[32] When most group members, especially those of higher status, are in agreement, it is tempting for other group members to disregard contradictory evidence or facts and to go along with the majority. Such disregard for facts and evidence can lead to unfortunate consequences.

5.2.4: Establishing Ground Rules

OBJECTIVE: Propose potential ground rules for a team based on its needs

Norms often develop without anyone explicitly identifying what is or is not acceptable behavior. Sometimes, however, a group or team may decide to develop more precise rules to help accomplish its task. According to communication researcher Susan Shimanoff, a rule is "a followable prescription that indicates what behavior is obligated, preferred, or prohibited in certain contexts."[33] Group or team **ground rules** are explicit, agreed-on prescriptions for acceptable and appropriate behavior. Undoubtedly your school has rules about what constitutes appropriate behavior: Don't cheat on a test, plagiarize a paper, or consume alcohol in class—these are typical college and university rules. Rules help keep order so that meaningful work can be accomplished. Rules also state what the group or organization values. Honesty, fairness, freedom of speech, and personal safety are typical values embedded in rules.

GROUND RULES IN TEAMS Because teams are usually more structured and coordinated than a typical group discussion, most training sessions that teach people how to become an effective team stress that a high-performing team needs clear ground rules.[34]

How Does a Team Develop Ground Rules?

The team leader may facilitate a discussion to establish the ground rules. If a group has no designated leader, any team member can say, "To help us stay organized and get our work done, let's establish some ground rules." Groups and teams operate better if members develop their own ground rules rather than having them imposed from "on high" or from the leader.

To help your group or team develop ground rules, consider the following questions:

- How long should our meetings last?
- What part of our work (if any) will be conducted in a virtual environment?

- Should we have a standard meeting place and time?
- What should a member do if he or she can't attend a meeting?
- How will we follow up to ensure that each member is doing his or her assigned work?
- Who will organize the agenda for our meetings?
- How will we manage conflict?
- How will we make our decisions—by majority vote or by consensus?
- What kind of climate do we want in our meetings?
- What other kinds of guidelines do we need to develop?

Many teams establish at least the following ground rules:

- Everyone will attend all meetings.
- Meetings will start on time.
- Each team member will follow through on individual assignments.
- Each team member will be prepared for every meeting.
- We will make decisions by consensus rather than by majority vote.
- We will work together to manage conflict when it arises.

Often teams are given their assignments by someone from outside the group. Even when the team is given its goal, sometimes called a **charge** (a statement of the purpose of the team, group, or committee), the team should take some time to discuss its ground rules so that each person clearly understands and agrees to them.

Review

Conformity to Group Norms

Conformity to group norms depends on the following:

- The individual characteristics of group members
- The clarity of the norm and the certainty of punishment for breaking it
- The number of people who already conform to the norm
- The quality of interpersonal relationships in the group
- The sense of group identification that members have developed

5.3: Status

OBJECTIVE: Predict group interactions based on status

Awareness of status differences begins when we are children—who is better, brighter, more athletic, and attractive. **Status** is an individual's relative importance. People with higher social status generally have more prestige and command more respect than do people of lower status. People want to talk to and talk about, see and be seen with high-status individuals.

By the end of this module, you will be able to:

5.3.1 Relate status to group privilege

5.3.2 Explain how status affects group interactions

5.3.1: Privileges Accorded to High-Status Group Members

OBJECTIVE: Relate status to group privilege

Most people like to be perceived as enjoying some status within a group. Because occupying a position of status fulfills a need for attention, it also builds self-respect and self-esteem.

Communication scholar Ernest Bormann explains that:

> The group makes a high-status person feel important and influential . . . . Even in communication-class discussion groups, the high-status members receive considerable gratification of their social and esteem needs. One of the most powerful forces drawing people into groups is the attraction of high status.[35]

Perhaps you have participated in small groups in which the status of an individual afforded certain privileges that were not available to the rest of the group. Such privileges are motivation to seek higher status.

WRITING PROMPT

Status Levels in Groups

Think of groups from your own experience in which persons with varying levels of status have been present. How have you felt in these groups? If you had higher status, how did that affect your interactions with the group? Does it feel different to have lower status? How so? How does your relative status influence your interactions in groups?

The response entered here will appear in the performance dashboard and can be viewed by your instructor.

Submit

5.3.2: Effects of Status Differences

OBJECTIVE: Explain how status affects group interactions

Group members' status exerts a significant effect on their interpersonal relationships. Status affects who talks to whom and how often a member speaks. An individual's prior status or reputation certainly affects the role he or she assumes. In addition, norms about status differences develop quickly. Several researchers have observed how status differences affect the relationships among members of a small group. Consider the following research conclusions:

- High-status group members are more likely than low-status members to speak up with ideas and suggestions.[36]
- High-status group members communicate more with other high-status members than they do with members of lower status.[37]
- Low-status group members tend to direct their conversation to high-status group members rather than to members of lower or equal status.[38]
- Low-status group members communicate more positive messages to high-status members than they do to members of equal or lower status.[39]
- High-status members hold on to their individualistic tendencies more than do low-status members, who tend to conform.[40]
- High-status group members tend to talk to the entire group more than members of lower status do.[41]
- The leader of a small group is usually the member with the highest status. (An exception occurs when the leader emerges because of capability and competence and not necessarily because of popularity.)[42]
- What's your status level? Research shows that your perception of your own status in a group closely approximates others' views of you.[43]

Review

Effects of Status Differences in Groups

Group members with high status:

- Talk more
- Communicate more often with other high-status members
- Have more influence
- Generally abide by group norms
- Are less likely to be ignored
- Are less likely to complain about their responsibilities
- Talk to the entire group
- Are likely to serve in leadership roles
- Hold on to their individualistic views
- In online groups, are more likely to be instructive and use second-person pronouns

Group members with low status:

- Direct conversation to high-status members rather than to low-status members
- Tend to be more conforming
- Communicate more positive messages to high-status members
- Are more likely to have their comments ignored
- Communicate more irrelevant information
- Talk to high-status members as a substitute for climbing the social hierarchy in the group
- In online groups, are more likely than high-status members to use first-person pronouns and exclamation points

STATUS DIFFERENCES IN ONLINE GROUPS Research has found that lower-status members of online groups tend to be more conforming and agreeable in their messages. They also use more first-person singular voice (I, we) as well as more exclamation points. High-status members tend to be more instructive, with their messages including more complex words and second-person ("you") references.[44]

OBSERVING STATUS DIFFERENCES TO PREDICT GROUP DYNAMICS Knowing how status affects the relationships among group members helps you predict who will talk with whom. If you can perceive status differences, you can also predict the type of messages that will be communicated in a small group discussion. Research suggests that the social hierarchy of a group affects group cohesiveness, group satisfaction, and even the quality of a group's solution. One of the benefits of increased status within a group is the relative increase in that group member's influence or power.

WRITING PROMPT

How Much Does Status Matter?

Are you status-conscious? How impressed are you with titles such as "Doctor," "Captain," or "Professor"? Do you automatically respect persons who are in positions of authority? Why or why not? While status differences have a marked effect on group communication, your own sensitivity to those differences will affect your actions.

The response entered here will appear in the performance dashboard and can be viewed by your instructor.

Submit

5.4: Power

OBJECTIVE: Outline the path of power from its origin to its impact on a group

Although the concept is somewhat difficult to define, at its core **power** involves the ability of one person to control or influence some other person or decision.[45] Power in a small group is reflected in an individual's ability to get other members to conform to his or her wishes. Power is about influence.

Certain group members may have more power in the group than others. Sometimes the sources of their power are clear, such as in groups with large status differences. In other cases, the sources of power are more difficult to discern. To map out the territory of social power in small groups, we need to look at power bases and the effects of power on group processes.

By the end of this module, you will be able to:

5.4.1 **Differentiate between bases of group power**

5.4.2 **Summarize the impact of power on group interactions**

5.4.3 **Relate gender to group power**

5.4.4 **Interpret group status and power through a cultural lens**

5.4.1: Power Bases

OBJECTIVE: Differentiate between bases of group power

Your power base in a group is the sum of the resources that you can use to control or influence others. Because no two group members have exactly the same resources, each member operates from a different power base.

John French and Bertram Raven identified five power bases in their study of small groups[46]:

1. **Legitimate power** stems from a group member's ability to influence others because of being elected, appointed, or selected to exert control over a group. Legitimate power comes from occupying a position of responsibility. The principal of a school has the legitimate power to enforce school policy; the senators from your state have the legitimate power to represent their constituents. Many of the privileges enjoyed by high-status group members reflect this kind of power base. For example, a small group member who has been elected chairperson is given legitimate power to influence the group's procedures.
2. **Referent power** is the power of interpersonal attraction. People are attracted to others whom they admire and want to emulate. Put simply, people we like have more power over us than people we do not like.
3. **Expert power** stems from a group member's ability to influence others based on the knowledge and information the member possesses. As the saying goes, knowledge is power. Suppose you are a member of a group studying ways to improve the health of a river in your community. If one of your group members has a PhD in aquatic plant life, that person's knowledge and access to information give him or her expert power. More than likely, that person can influence the group. However, just because a group member has knowledge, that does not mean he or she will exert more influence in the group. The member's knowledge must be credible and useful to persuade others of its importance—and the member's power.
4. **Reward power** is based on a person's ability to reward behaviors. If you are in a position to help another member gain money, status, power, acceptance, or other rewards, you will have power over that person. Of course, group members are motivated by different needs and goals, so what is rewarding to one may not be seen as desirable by others. Reward power is effective only if a person finds the reward satisfying or

Virtual Collaboration

Democratic Values and Status Differences[48]

Technology development is not neutral, but rather reflects the values of the cultures in which it develops. A team of researchers at the University of California at Santa Barbara analyzed the structure of the Internet to determine the social impact of that technology. They found that the primary use (70 percent) of the Internet was information dissemination and gathering. Its decentralized structure makes government regulation of this medium extremely difficult and encourages open communication. According to the authors, the democratic values implicit in this technology reflect a North American cultural influence that will most certainly drive the future development of the Internet.

These democratic values may also reflect the fact that communication on a computer screen minimizes status differences that would be far more influential in face-to-face situations. Students and faculty members who use online chat rooms or threaded discussions in their classes report an interesting finding that supports this notion. The students who participate most actively in online discussions are often not the ones who participate most actively in face-to-face classroom discussions. Some students are simply more comfortable in an environment where they can choose their words more carefully and less publicly; it suits their personalities better.

As you use virtual group communication, keep these tips in mind:

- Online discussions may seem more democratic because of the factors noted previously. However, status differences don't disappear when we no longer can see the other person. Remember to adapt your messages to your audience—friend, peer, colleague, professor, supervisor, CEO—as appropriate.
- The disembodied messages of virtual communication can be easily misinterpreted if you do not attend to nonverbal signals. Be sure you understand the sender's meaning before you react.
- Resist the tendency to communicate solely online in lieu of face to face. Convenience and effectiveness are often competing values in communication.

Educators know that active engagement in the learning process and time on task are the best predictors of students' academic success. Thus, given the different personalities of group members and the democratic value of participation, a combination of face-to-face interaction and virtual communication may reduce the effects of status differences, maximize the contributions of each group member, and consequently maximize the effectiveness of your group.

valuable. Others must also believe that a person actually has the power and resources to bestow the reward.

5. **Coercive power**, the negative side of reward power, is based on the perception that you can be punished for acting or not acting in a certain way. The ability to demote others, reduce their salaries or benefits, force them to work overtime hours, or fire them is an example of the resources that can make up this power base.[47] Even though coercive power may achieve a desired effect, group members usually resent threats of punishment intended to make them conform to group norms.

5.4.2: Effects of Power on Group Process

OBJECTIVE: Summarize the impact of power on group interactions

Members who have power influence the group process. Whether their influence is positive or negative depends on how wisely the members use their power. The following principles summarize the impact of power on group deliberations:

- A struggle for power among group members can result in poor group decisions and less group cohesion.
- Members who overtly seek dominance and control over a group often focus attention on themselves rather than on achieving group goals.
- Group members with little power talk less frequently in a group.
- Charles Berger observed that "persons who talk most frequently and for the longest periods of time are assumed to be the most dominant group members. In addition, persons receiving the most communication are assumed to be most powerful."[49]
- Group members can lose power if other members think they use power for personal gain or to keep a group from achieving its goals.
- Group members usually expect individuals with greater power to have high-status privileges. But too many perks and privileges given to some members can sap a group's ability to do its job and trigger challenges to the influential group members.
- Too much power in one individual can lead to less group decision making and more autocratic decision making. Autocratic decision making occurs when one person with several power bases makes a decision alone rather than with the group as a whole. Group members may not speak their minds for fear of reprisals.
- Increasing your level of activity in a group can increase your power and influence. Individuals with high levels of dominance in their personalities attain high levels of influence in groups, not because of competence, but because their high level of activity makes them *appear* competent.[50]
- Groups with equal power distribution show higher-quality group communication than do groups with unequal power distribution.[51]
- In corporate work teams, individual power is related to the fact that group members must depend on one another.[52]

A person's power base in a group is the sum of the resources that the person can use to control or influence others. What types of power do you think Maine Senator Susan Collins uses when trying to persuade others?

If you participate in a group and sense that your influence is diminishing, try to participate more and to take an active role in helping the group achieve its goal. Volunteering to help with tasks and increasing your knowledge about group problems, issues, or decisions can also enhance your influence. If you see other group members losing influence, you can give them (or suggest that they take responsibility for) specific tasks that will bring them back into the group's mainstream.

Review

Power Bases and Sources of Influence

- Legitimate: Being elected, appointed, or selected to lead the group
- Reference: Being well liked
- Expert: Sharing relevant knowledge and information
- Reward: The ability to provide rewards for desired behavior
- Coercive: The ability to punish others

5.4.3: Power and Gender

OBJECTIVE: Relate gender to group power

Stereotypes portray women as being more easily influenced than men and as having less power over others than their male counterparts. Although results are mixed, research generally tends to dispel these illusions.[53] In one study, when women were placed in positions of power, they were just as likely as men to use strategies associated with power. Because men have historically held roles of higher power in society, the opportunity for them to use power strategies has been greater than that for women. This observation suggests that the unequal distribution of power results in the illusion of gender differences, which are really the result of women's and men's relative social status. Thus, apparent gender differences must be understood within a context of status and power.[54]

An interesting observation was offered in a *New York Times* essay by Thomas Page McBee, a 31-year-old transsexual man. He noted that when he began taking testosterone, people started listening as his voice deepened. As a woman, McBee was frequently interrupted and talked over, especially by men and especially at work; he had to fight harder to make a point. But when transitioning, it became clear to him that his more masculine presence brought a level of power he had not experienced before. Now he was developing the confidence to share a thought without rehearsing it first. Occasionally he would even catch himself and ask, "Am I mansplaining?"[55]

Clearly, inequities are present in the workplace. Nevertheless, social and organizational expectations for men and women have changed and will continue to do so. Evidence indicates that more firms are placing greater value on diversity in the ranks of management and believe that such diversity provides a competitive advantage. Indeed, evidence shows that having women at the top of management teams in firms making an initial public offering is associated with gains in both short-term and long-term financial performance.[56]

5.4.4: Status and Power across Cultures

OBJECTIVE: Interpret group status and power through a cultural lens

Status is primarily in the eye of the beholder. As a consequence, status in one culture may become meaningless when someone crosses a cultural boundary: A PhD will not be revered in a country dance hall. Communication scholar Marshall Singer offers this observation:

> The Ph.D. holder and the famous athlete have acquired high status and the ability to influence their respective "constituents." Because high status—whether ascribed or acquired—depends so much on its being perceived as such, it may be the least transferable, across cultural barriers, of all the components of power we are discussing.[57]
>
> Cultural differences in perceptions of status are revealed pointedly in the following letter. On June 17, 1744, commissioners from Maryland and Virginia negotiated a treaty with the Native American members of the Six Nations at Lancaster, Pennsylvania. The Native Americans were invited to send young men to William and Mary College. The next day they declined the offer, as the letter explains.
>
> We know that you highly esteem the kind of learning taught in those Colleges, and that the Maintenance of our young Men, while with you, would be very expensive to you. We are convinced, that you mean to do us Good by your Proposal; and we thank you heartily. But you, who are wise must know that different Nations have different Conceptions of things and you will therefore not take it amiss, if our ideas of this kind of Education happen not to be the same as yours. We have had some Experience of it. Several of our young People were formerly brought up at the Colleges of the Northern Provinces: They were instructed in all your Sciences; but, when they came back to us, they were bad Runners, ignorant of every means of living in the woods...neither fit for Hunters, Warriors, nor Counsellors, they were totally good for nothing.
>
> We are, however, not the less oblig'd by your kind Offer, tho' we decline accepting it; and, to show our grateful Sense of it, if the Gentlemen of Virginia will send us a Dozen of their Sons, we will take Care of their Education, instruct them in all we know, and make Men of them.[58]

WRITING PROMPT

Generational Markers and Status

Clothing, hair styles and colors, piercings, tattoos, footwear, facial hair, music, video games, literature, recreational activities—each generation seems to have its own cultural markers that are often disparaged by the generations that came before. These generational markers confer status within the peer group. What are the status symbols that mark your own generation? Are these symbols respected by your parents' or grandparents' generations? Why do you think that is? Why don't these symbols translate across generations?

The response entered here will appear in the performance dashboard and can be viewed by your instructor.

Submit

5.5: Trust

OBJECTIVE: Evaluate the level of trust between group members

Used-car salespeople and politicians are often stereotyped as people whose credibility is suspect. The untrustworthy images of such people are not always warranted, but when they want something—whether it is your money or a vote—you are often suspicious of the promises they make. When you trust people, you have faith that they will not try to take advantage of you and that they will be mindful of your best interests. In small groups, the degree of trust you have in others affects your developing interpersonal relationships with them. The following sections consider how trust in relationships affects group members and suggest how you can build more trust as you interact with others.

 **By the end of this module, you will be able to:**

5.5.1 **Explain how trusting relationships develop**

5.5.2 **Compare trust in physical and virtual teams**

5.5.1: Developing Trusting Relationships

OBJECTIVE: Explain how trusting relationships develop

Why do you trust some people more than others? What is it about your closest friend that enables you to confide your most private feelings? How can group members develop trusting relationships?

First, developing trust takes time. Just as assuming a role in a group discussion requires time, so does developing confidence in others. Second, you base trust on the previous experiences you have had with others. You probably would not give your bank account number to a stranger, but you would more than likely trust this number to your spouse or to a friend you have known for many years. As you communicate with other people, you gradually learn whether you can trust them. First you observe how they complete various tasks and responsibilities; then you decide whether you can rely on them to get things done.

TRUST DEFINED **Trust** in groups has been defined as "the extent to which a person is confident in, and willing to act on the basis of, the words, actions, and decisions of another."[59] As you participate in a group, you trust those who, because of their actions in the past, have given you reason to believe that they will behave predictably in the future. Group members establish trusting relationships as they develop mutual respect and as the group becomes more cohesive.

TRUST AND RISK However, even time and experience cannot guarantee trust. A certain amount of risk is always involved whenever you trust another person. As Richard Reichert suggests, "Trust is always a risk, a kind of leap in the dark. It is not based on any solid proof that the other person will not hurt you . . . trust is always a gamble."[60] Sometimes the gamble does not pay off. And if you have worked in a small group with several people who proved untrustworthy, you may be reluctant to trust others in future groups. Thus, your good and bad experiences in past groups affect the ways you relate to people in future groups.

WRITING PROMPT

Your Experience with Trust

Abraham Lincoln once observed that if you trust, you will be disappointed occasionally, but if you mistrust, you will be miserable all the time. What are your thoughts and feelings about trust? Do you trust others easily and quickly, or does it take time for you to develop trusting relationships? What is your experience with trust? Does it explain your current attitude? How so?

 The response entered here will appear in the performance dashboard and can be viewed by your instructor.

Submit

5.5.2: Trust in Face-to-Face and Virtual Teams

OBJECTIVE: Compare trust in physical and virtual teams

One interesting piece of research shows that in virtual teams, levels of trust among group members start at a lower point than in face-to-face groups. Over time, however, trust in virtual teams increases to a level comparable to that in face-to-face teams.[61] Groups and teams that have limited or no face-to-face interaction develop trust differently from those where face-to-face contact occurs on a frequent basis. Face-to-face teams develop trust mostly through social and emotional bonds that grow as they get to know one another. In virtual teams, trust is more likely to develop through frequent leader–member communications,[62] task-oriented responses such as timely information sharing, and appropriate, sound responses to electronic communications.[63] Trust will develop more rapidly in virtual teams when the participants first have an opportunity for face-to-face interaction. This is especially true when the context is competitive.[64]

A key to building trust in virtual groups is responsiveness. Everyone knows the frustration of sending a message that goes unheeded. A wise group leader will set standards for timely responses. Whether the standard is to set aside a certain time period where immediate responses are possible, or to expect responses within a certain time frame, setting and meeting expectations is a key to trust. When we can reasonably expect that our messages will receive timely and appropriate responses, a foundation for trust is established.

5.6: The Development of Group Relationships over Time

OBJECTIVE: Analyze how group relationships change over time

Groups are formed over time, and it takes time for trust to develop. You experience some tension and anxiety the first time you participate in a small group. You may be uncertain of your role, and the group may not have met long enough for norms to develop. Status differences can also create tension. Ernest Bormann has defined this initial uneasiness as **primary tension**, or "the social unease and stiffness that accompanies getting acquainted .... The earmarks of primary tensions are extreme politeness, apparent boredom or tiredness, and considerable sighing or yawning. When members show primary tension, they speak softly and tentatively. Frequently they can think of nothing to communication patterns."[65]

You can expect to find some primary tension during initial meetings, as it is a normal part of group development. A group leader can minimize this tension, however, by helping members get to know one another, perhaps through brief statements of introduction. While members of groups that meet only once might deem getting to know one another impractical, using a few minutes to break the ice and reduce some of the primary tension can help create more satisfying relationships among group members.

After a group resolves primary tension and its members become more comfortable with one another, secondary tension develops. According to Bormann, **secondary tension** occurs as conflicts arise and differences of opinion emerge. Whether recognized as a personality conflict or simply as a disagreement, secondary tension surfaces when members try to solve the problem or accomplish the task facing the group. This type of tension also results from power struggles, and it usually establishes group norms. Joking or laughing often helps manage secondary tension. But no matter how cohesive a group may be, some conflict over procedure will probably develop as relationships among members form.

Review

Group Tension

- *Primary tension:* Uneasiness and discomfort in getting acquainted and managing initial group uncertainty about the group task and group relationships
- *Secondary tension:* Tension that occurs as group members struggle for influence, develop roles and norms, and explore differences in approaching the group task.

CASE STUDY

Adjusting to Variable Status and Power

Your university has a Strategic Planning Committee composed of the following people:

- The Dean of the College
- The Vice President for Finance
- The Vice President for Development (fundraising)
- A representative from the Board of Trustees
- The Director of Admissions
- The Director of Planning and Institutional Research
- Three elected faculty members
- Two students selected by the Student Government Association
- An alumni representative

Some committee members (administrators) are appointed to the committee permanently. Others (faculty members and students) are appointed to one-year terms. The committee's charge is to make recommendations to the president about new goals and objectives for the university's strategic plan. To do this, the committee has been asked first to review the university's mission statement, as well as the institutional goals for graduates and how they relate to the mission. Then the committee is asked to evaluate progress made toward these goals since establishment of the previous strategic plan. The committee then must facilitate and coordinate the annual update of the plan before finally making its recommendations.

When responding to the following questions, you may find it helpful to refer to Table 5-1.

Questions for Analysis: Adjusting to Variable Status and Power

1. Consider the membership of the group in the scenario. What source(s) of power can you identify for each member based on their title or affiliation?
2. Review the list of group roles in Table 5-1. Can you predict which group members are most likely to enact certain group roles? Which members and which roles? Why do you think this?
3. Rank committee members by their status. What is the basis for your rankings?
4. This committee has relatively permanent members (dean, vice presidents, and directors) as well as members who serve for shorter terms (representatives from trustees, alumni, students, faculty). How will this affect the establishment of group norms from year to year?

By the end of this module, you will be able to:

5.6.1 **Describe how gender influences group relationships over time**

5.6.2 **Explain how culture influences conversational styles within groups**

5.6.3 **Determine how time influences the ways people interact within a group**

5.6.1: Communication and Gender

OBJECTIVE: Describe how gender influences group relationships over time

Both within a given culture and from one culture to another, men and women have different communication patterns.[66] Evidence indicates that men and women sometimes use language differently[67] and that they interpret nonverbal behavior differently, as summarized in Table 5-2.

Besides differing from men in their use of nonverbal behaviors, evidence indicates that women tend to receive and interpret nonverbal messages more accurately. Why do differences arise in the way males and females use and respond to nonverbal messages? Some theorize that the answer lies in physiological differences between men and women. The leading explanation, however, focuses on how men and women are socialized into society. Women typically are socialized to value interpersonal relationships and to respond to others' emotions, which are largely expressed nonverbally. Also, men typically are afforded higher status in North American culture and in many other cultures throughout the world. As we noted earlier, persons of higher status are typically talked to more; receiving verbal information from others may lessen men's need to interpret nonverbal messages.

The research conclusions reviewed here can help explain some of the differences in the way that men and women communicate in groups and teams. But note that these conclusions are generalizations: Not all men and all women will exhibit these differences. In your group deliberations, be cautious. Even so, recognizing that both verbal and nonverbal behaviors may differ by gender may help you become both more flexible and tolerant when communicating with others in groups.

Table 5-2 Gender Differences in Nonverbal Communication

Nonverbal Communication Categories	Women	Men
Move closer to women than to men[68]	Yes	Yes
Personal space[69]	Closer	Farther
Eye contact[70]	More	Less
Facial gestures[71]	More expressive	Less expressive
Hand gestures[72]	Fewer	More
Initiate touch[73]	Less	More
Vocal volume[74]	Softer	Louder

5.6.2: Conversational Style

OBJECTIVE: Explain how culture influences conversational styles within groups

Several cultural variables affect group formation, development, and relational styles—individualism/collectivism, high-context/low-context cultures, and high-contact/low-contact cultures. Another cultural difference is conversational style.

Consider the following statements:

"Jane is friendly."

"Jane brings cakes to my family on festival days."

These two statements reflect cultural differences in descriptions of the social world. People in North America, Europe, and Australia are more likely to describe a personality trait such as "friendly"; the more contextual Asian tendency is to describe a person's actions.[75]

Conversational norms vary by culture.[76] If not understood, these differences can cause misunderstanding, anxiety, and group conflict.

The white middle-class North American norm that leads one group member to quietly await a turn to speak may cause him or her to wait a very long time when those from other cultures do not share that norm. People from some cultures love a good argument, whereas others revere harmony and the ability to assimilate differences to build consensus.[77] Some cultures are put off by North Americans' frankness and relative lack of inhibition about sharing negative information. In Western cultures, control is exerted through speaking; in Eastern cultures, control is expressed through silence and in the outward show of reticence.[78]

The topics we address and our willingness to talk about personal matters vary by culture. Whereas Mexicans may talk about a person's soul or spirit, such talk may make residents of the United States and Canada uncomfortable. Persons from Hispanic cultures often begin conversations with inquiries about one's family, even with casual acquaintances or in a business meeting. Many from the United States and Canada view family matters as too personal to be discussed casually.[79]

Cultural differences and similarities influence nonverbal interaction when people communicate. How would you manage cultural differences in a group?

5.6.3: Perception of Time

OBJECTIVE: Determine how time influences the ways people interact within a group

Another cultural difference relates to the perception and use of time. While interviewing a group of Brazilian students, Thomas Fitzgerald asked them how they felt about a person who was consistently late. He was surprised to find that the students viewed such a person as probably more successful than those who were on time. A person of status, they reasoned, is *expected* to be late.[80]

Some people are **monochronic**: They are most comfortable doing only one thing at a time, like to concentrate on the job at hand, are more serious and sensitive to deadlines and schedules, like to plan how to use their time, and stress the importance of starting and ending meetings on time.[81] Other people are **polychronic**: They can do many things at once, are less influenced by deadlines and schedules, feel that relationships are more important than producing volumes of work, frequently change plans, and are less concerned about punctuality than are monochronic individuals.

TIME ORIENTATIONS Groups have different approaches to how they use time. Ballard and Seibold found that the groups they investigated had three general approaches to time: (1) flexible, (2) separation, and (3) concurrency.[82] Groups with a flexible approach to time set fewer deadlines and provided group members with more autonomy. Groups with a separation approach to time preferred to separate themselves physically from others when working on a group task; they were more likely to keep the door closed and get away from others. Concurrency groups were more likely to attempt to do several things at once (multitask); they would look for ways to combine projects and activities.

Being aware of how groups and teams use time can help you better understand why your group behaves as it does. If you're in a flexible group, you may need to monitor deadlines more closely. Separation groups may need to ensure they don't separate themselves so far from the organization that they lose sight of the overall organizational goal. Because concurrency groups have a tendency to do several things at once, such groups may need added structure and a system to keep track of the various projects undertaken.

TIME EXPECTATIONS The use of time and expectations about time can cause conflict and frustration if group members have widely differing perspectives. Time use and expectations vary from culture to culture.[83] People from the United States and Northern Europe tend to be more monochronic: They place great emphasis on deadlines and punctuality. Latin Americans, Southern Europeans, and Middle Easterners are more often polychronic: They give less attention to deadlines and schedules. Western cultures tend to approach problems in a linear, step-by-step fashion; how events are structured and sequenced is important to members of these cultures. Chinese and Japanese cultures approach time with a less-structured perspective. The observations of several researchers have been summarized in Table 5-3.

Even if your group does not have members from highly diverse cultures, you may notice that people have different approaches to time. Groups develop their own norms about time. It may be useful to explicitly discuss and clarify norms, such as the importance of deadlines, expectations for group productivity, and general attitudes about punctuality, so as to manage any uncertainty about time that may exist.

Whether a group is struggling with cultural differences or differences in role expectations, norms, status, perceived power, or trust, it's important to remember that through effective and appropriate communication, we can bridge differences and develop productive relationships with others.

Table 5-3 Cultural Differences in the Use of Time[84]

Western Cultures	Eastern Cultures
Time is something to be manipulated.	Time simply exists.
The present is a way-station between the past and the future.	The present is more important than the past or the future.
Time is a resource that can be saved, spent, or wasted.	Time is a limitless pool.
Time is an aspect of history rather than part of an immediate experience.	Events occur in time; they cause ripples, and the ripples subside.

Summary: Relating to Others in Groups

5.1: Roles

- Roles grow out of self-concept.
- Task roles that aim to get the job done and maintenance roles that nurture positive interpersonal relationships are both crucial to the long-term success of a group.
- Individual roles often interfere with a group's progress.
- If no one performs important group roles, point this out to the group or assume the responsibility for performing those roles yourself.

5.2: Norms

- Norms are rules that govern appropriate behavior in the group. They evolve based on previous group experiences and early behaviors in the new group.
- Identify group norms by noting repeated patterns of behavior and by observing what behaviors are rewarded and punished by the group.

5.3: Status

- Status derives from many sources. Identify the status of group members by the privileges that high-status group members receive.
- If you can spot status differences in small groups, you can predict who talks to whom. If you are aware of status differences, you can communicate more effectively and with greater influence.

5.4: Power

- The five power bases are legitimate power, reference power, expert power, reward power, and coercive power.

5.5: Trust

- Don't expect group members to form trusting relationships early—it takes time for trust to develop.
- Trusting involves risk. Taking these risks with others helps them to do the same with you.
- In virtual groups, frequent, timely, and appropriate responses help to build trust.

5.6: The Development of Group Relationships over Time

- Two types of tension may arise in groups: primary and secondary. Primary tension is felt in the early stages of group development, whereas secondary tension is related to the distribution of power in the group.

SHARED WRITING

Developing Ground Rules

Lenni has been assigned to a task force whose purpose is to make recommendations to management about how to improve employee morale. She is replacing another team member who has left the company. Lenni arrives at her first meeting a few minutes early, only to find that she is alone in the room. At 5:30, the appointed time, no one else has arrived. A few minutes later, two other members arrive, carrying food for their suppers. Others trickle in until 6:00 PM, when the chair finally arrives, mumbles something about being late, and calls the meeting to order. "Well," he says, "where were we last time?" For several minutes, the team discusses what was and was not accomplished at the last meeting. While Lenni vaguely knows some of the team members, she is lost in the conversation as a newcomer to the group. She has not been introduced. An hour after the meeting was to have started, the chair asks, "Does anyone have any new ideas?" Several ideas are offered and either ignored or rejected. No one takes notes. The meeting drags on until after 8:00 PM. Lenni is starving and grumpy. She thinks to herself: "I have some ideas about how to improve the morale of this task force!"

What might Lenni be thinking? This is a team in need of some new ground rules. What rules would you recommend? Write a short response that your classmates will read. Describe your recommendations specifically.

A minimum number of characters is required to post and earn points. After posting, your response can be viewed by your class and instructor, and you can participate in the class discussion.

Post

Chapter 6

Improving Group Climate

"All for one, one for all."

—Alexandre Dumas

Learning Objectives

6.1 Compare defensive and supportive group climates

6.2 Evaluate group climate for responsiveness

6.3 Analyze groups for factors that aid or limit cohesiveness

6.4 Analyze how size and distribution influence group climate

6.5 Relate group climate to productivity

What does the word "climate" call to mind? If you've taken a course in environmental science, physical geography, or meteorology, you might think of climate change, temperature gradients, barometric pressure, and how bodies of water, latitude, ocean currents, and mountains affect the weather of a particular region. Imagine traveling to Hawaii, Ireland, and the Himalayas. Consider the climate of each location, and envision the view from your window in each place. Does the weather make you want to curl up indoors with a book? Go to the beach? Go skiing? How do you feel about spending a cold, snowy night in front of a roaring fire in a cozy room? Would you say that climate affects your desire to engage in certain activities?

Group climate is roughly analogous to geographic climate. A variety of factors interact to create a group feeling or atmosphere. How group members communicate, with whom they communicate, and how often they communicate influence their satisfaction and productivity. How do people communicate in ways that help a group establish a positive climate in which it can be most productive?

6.1: Defensive versus Supportive Climates

OBJECTIVE: Compare defensive and supportive group climates

Think about two or three groups or teams you've participated in recently. How did you feel during meetings? Energized? Tense? Did you look forward to the meetings or did you hope they would be canceled? In other words, what was the group's climate?

How team members communicate with one another is a primary determinant of group climate. In some groups, we feel supported; in others, we may feel defensive. For several years, social psychologist Jack Gibb observed the communicative behavior of people in groups. Based on his observations, he identified categories of behaviors that contribute to defensive and supportive climates. Gibb suggests that a defensive climate is counterproductive in any group. People who are made to feel defensive try to protect themselves—worrying how they are perceived, how they can "win," and how they can generally defend themselves—instead of spending their energy building relationships and working toward the group's goal.

In contrast, when group members feel supported, they can focus on the group and its task, rather than on self-protection.[1] More recent research reinforces the relationship between a supportive climate and productivity.[2] Supportive communication in the workplace has been found to reduce stress and burnout for many employees. In addition, this type of communication provides links among employees or group members characterized by self-disclosure and a shared definition of the relationship. The key to building a supportive climate lies in what we communicate and how we communicate it.[3] A message can be delivered in ways that evoke either support or defense.

By the end of this module, you will be able to:

- **6.1.1** **Replace evaluative language with descriptive language**
- **6.1.2** **Identify controlling behavior**
- **6.1.3** **Explain how spontaneity improves group climate**
- **6.1.4** **Relate empathy to a supportive group climate**
- **6.1.5** **Describe how a preoccupation with superiority can create a defensive group climate**
- **6.1.6** **Explain how being open to new ideas can create a positive group climate**

6.1.1: Evaluation versus Description

OBJECTIVE: Replace evaluative language with descriptive language

When someone in your group puts forth a bad idea, you could respond by saying, "That's a ridiculous idea," or you could say, "As I think through that idea and apply it to our problem, I run up against some difficulties. Am I missing something?" Imagine yourself on the receiving end of the first comment. It is an example of evaluation. How would you feel? The second response, an example of description, is much more effective and supportive. It keeps the door open for further discussion of your idea. Further investigation into your bad idea may lead to a better one.

Evaluation is "you" language that directs itself to the worth of the other person or that person's ideas. It provokes defensiveness. Description, in contrast, is "I" language: It describes the speaker's thoughts about the person or idea. This type of response leads to more trust and cohesiveness in groups.

Some examples of evaluative statements are given in the following list. Rewrite these statements to make them descriptive statements.

Evaluative and Descriptive Statements

Statement 1	"You're wrong!"
Statement 2	"You can't get anything right today."
Statement 3	"That idea is ridiculous!"
Summary	Review your rewritten statements. Compare them with the ideal responses given here. "I disagree." "I see you're having trouble. Can I help?" "I'm not getting it. Help me understand what you're saying."

6.1.2: Control versus Problem Orientation

OBJECTIVE: Identify controlling behavior

Communicative behavior that aims to control others can make group members defensive. Various persuasive tactics aim to control behavior (as any student of television commercials or social media advertising can readily observe). The controller's assumption is "I know what's good for you." When we witness this attitude in another person, we frequently become defensive.

In a group, maintaining a "problem orientation" is a more effective approach. If others perceive you as a person

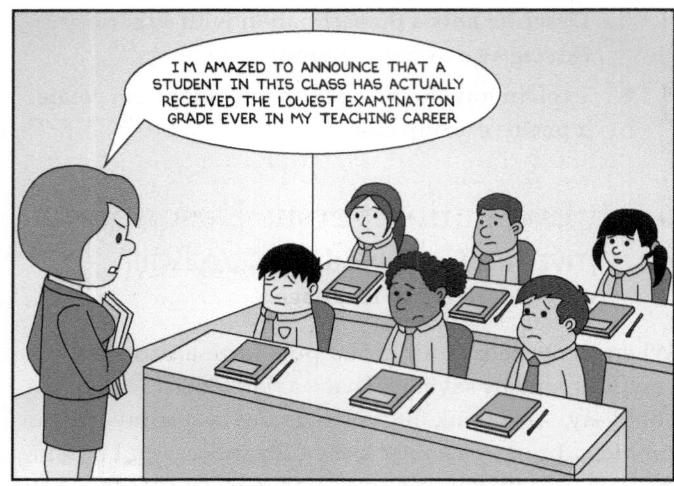

who genuinely strives for a solution that will benefit all concerned (rather than just yourself), this perception will contribute to a supportive climate, greater cohesiveness, and increased productivity.

Read the scenarios below and identify whether the character in the scenario is controlling, displaying a problem orientation or is ambiguous? Compare your answers against the correct answers provided at the end of the chapter.

Control or Problem Orientation?

No.	Scenario
1	A group member is pushing the group to "Just vote on it and be done!"
2	The group leader says, "Let's all write down what we see as the remaining issues we need to deal with. Then let's compare notes."
3	"Hey guys! You're going to love me. I went online and found the solution to our problem!"

6.1.3: Strategy versus Spontaneity

OBJECTIVE: Explain how spontaneity improves group climate

Like controlling behavior, **strategy**—staged, scripted communication—suggests manipulation because it implies preplanned communication. Such strategies range from "pitching a fit" and acting upset to withholding information or pouting. One often-used strategy is to compliment someone before criticizing the individual, leaving the person confused as to how to respond. This sort of behavior is self-serving and does not lead to the most effective solutions to group problems.

If others perceive you as a person who acts *spontaneously* (i.e., not from hidden motivations or agendas) and as a person who immediately and honestly responds to the present situation, you are likely to create a more supportive climate.

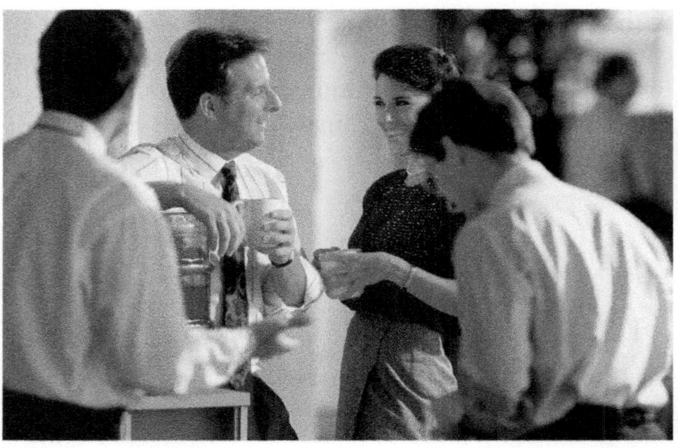

Communication that is spontaneous is perceived as more supportive than communication that appears planned. Why might these office workers appreciate spontaneous communication?

6.1.4: Neutrality versus Empathy

OBJECTIVE: Relate empathy to a supportive group climate

It is often said that the opposite of love is not hate—it's indifference. Neutrality carries implications about the other person's worth; it implies, "I don't care about you." If you behave in a detached, uncaring fashion, as if the people in your group and the outcome of the group's process do not concern you in the least, your behavior will probably arouse defensiveness. In contrast, caring, involvement, and genuine concern for the group task and for other group members are perceived as supportive. Empathy is usually conveyed nonverbally, through active listening and good eye contact.

6.1.5: Superiority versus Equality

OBJECTIVE: Describe how a preoccupation with superiority can create a defensive group climate

You probably know students who approach you in class after tests have been returned and ask, "What'd ya get?" Often they use this question merely as a pretext for showing you their superior grades. Most people think such superior behavior is obnoxious, and it makes them feel defensive. In groups, some people preface their remarks with words such as "obviously" or point out their greater knowledge, experience, or some other attribute that makes them superior to other members. Most likely, this behavior will meet with resistance. We create more supportive climates when we indicate a willingness to enter into participative planning as equal partners—with mutual trust and respect.

Why do you think some people need to feel superior to others?

6.1.6: Certainty versus Provisionalism

OBJECTIVE: Explain how being open to new ideas can create a positive group climate

Do you know people who always have all the answers, and who are intolerant toward people with "wrong" (i.e., different) attitudes? These highly dogmatic people are easily recognizable because of the defensiveness they produce in others. The usual response to such individuals is to want to prove them wrong. This behavior is counterproductive in groups. Individuals are likely to be more effective if their attitudes appear to be held provisionally—that is, if they appear flexible and genuinely committed to solving problems rather than focused on simply taking sides on issues. If we stay open to new information and can admit that, from time to time, we may be wrong about something, we'll be more effective group members and will help build more supportive group climates.

Review

Behaviors That Foster Defensive and Supportive Climates

Defensive Climate	Supportive Climate
Evaluation: Use of "you" language calls into question the worth of another person.	**Description:** "I" language describes your own feelings and ideas.
Control: Efforts to get others to do what you want them to do.	**Problem orientation:** Communication aimed at solving problems: "Let's find a solution that works for both of us."
Strategy: Planned communication—for example, saying something nice before criticizing someone.	**Spontaneity:** Here-and-now orientation; being honest rather than planning how to manipulate.
Neutrality: Emotional indifference—the unspoken attitude that "you'll get over it."	**Empathy:** Emotional involvement; nonverbal behavior is important.
Superiority: Attitude that you're better than the other person.	**Equality:** Communication based on mutual respect; "I'm okay, you're okay."
Certainty: Taking dogmatic, rigid positions; usually more interested in winning an argument than in solving a problem.	**Provisionalism:** Open to receiving new information; showing some flexibility in the positions you take.

As a communicator, you control your own actions. Your knowledge of both defensive and supportive behaviors will help you facilitate more effective group work. Another area of research and application related to group climate deals with interpersonal confirmation and disconfirmation. This area deals not with communicative behaviors that you initiate, but rather with the ways in which you respond to other group members.

Ethical Collaboration

Defensive Behaviors

Defensive behaviors and disconfirming responses are not effective communication, but might they also be unethical? What if you truly do not like another person in your group, or what if he or she has hurt you in some way? Is it unethical to ignore or be rude to that person?

Consider the following situation: Maria and Janell work together on a committee that frequently meets face to face to share vital information and to plan upcoming phases in the group's project. Meetings have been lively, efficient, and effective. Every member relies on every other person in the group. The group has developed great working relationships, high cohesiveness, and productive group norms.

Maria has just learned from someone outside the group that her boyfriend Tariq and Janell have been openly flirting. Janell has even been heard suggesting to Tariq that Maria may not be entirely faithful to him.

WRITING PROMPT

Honesty and Defensive Behaviors

You are a member of the group in the scenario. The group is meeting tonight, and important deadlines are approaching. Maria has just told you of her newfound source of conflict with Janell. There's no time for Maria and Janell to sort things out before the meeting. Janell does not know that Maria is aware of the situation. How would you advise Maria to behave toward Janell in tonight's meeting? Why would you advise this?

The response entered here will appear in the performance dashboard and can be viewed by your instructor.

Submit

6.2: Interpersonal Confirmation and Disconfirmation

OBJECTIVE: Evaluate group climate for responsiveness

Group process sometimes seems to stagnate, to "hit a wall." Questions are left unanswered and ideas remain ignored. One of group members' most frequent complaints is that communication in the group seems disconnected and disjointed, fostering vague feelings of uneasiness, as if the members were being disregarded.[4]

Our responses to others' communicative acts can often be classified as confirming or disconfirming. Simply stated, **confirming responses** are those that cause people to value themselves more, while **disconfirming responses** are those that cause people to value themselves less.[5]

By the end of this module, you will be able to:

- **6.2.1** Explain the impact of disconfirming group responses
- **6.2.2** Identify confirming group responses

6.2.1: Disconfirming Responses

OBJECTIVE: Explain the impact of disconfirming group responses

Some interpersonal responses are obvious examples of confirmation and disconfirmation, such as when a person responds to another with overt praise or sharp criticism. However, group members may disconfirm and confirm one another in much more subtle ways.[6]

- **Impervious response:** One speaker fails to acknowledge, even minimally, another speaker's communicative attempt.
- **Interrupting response:** One speaker cuts another speaker short or begins to talk while the other is still speaking.
- **Irrelevant response:** A speaker responds in a way that seems unrelated to what the other has been saying, or introduces a new topic without warning or returns to his or her earlier topic, apparently disregarding the intervening conversation.
- **Tangential response:** A speaker acknowledges another person's communication but immediately takes the conversation in another direction. Tangential responses are considered the most disconfirming responses because they first acknowledge the other's statement ("Yes, I heard you") but then change the subject ("but I'm going to talk about me now").
- **Impersonal response:** One speaker conducts a monologue, or exhibits speech behavior that appears intellectualized and impersonal, contains few first-person statements and many generalized "you" or "one" statements, or is heavily loaded with euphemisms or clichés.
- **Incoherent response:** A speaker responds with incomplete sentences; with rambling, difficult-to-follow statements; with sentences containing much retracing or rephrasing; or with interjections such as "you know" or "I mean."
- **Incongruous response:** A speaker engages in nonverbal behavior that contradicts the vocal content, which results in a response that may be called incongruous. Examples of such responses include "Who's angry? I'm not angry!" (said angrily) and "I already said that I love you!!!" (shouting and menacing).

WRITING PROMPT

Identifying Disconfirming Responses

What disconfirming responses can you identify in the following exchanges?

"I just had the most frustrating time with a car salesman."
"When one is shopping for a car, it's important to do plenty of research first."
"I have a rough day ahead of me."
"Would you like some more eggs?"
"I'm worried about . . . "
"Hey, are you going to eat that?"
"I had the worst day today."
"Oh yeah? Wait until you hear what happened to me!"

The response entered here will appear in the performance dashboard and can be viewed by your instructor.

Submit

6.2.2: Confirming Responses

OBJECTIVE: Identify confirming group responses

Just as disconfirming responses can be subtle, confirming responses can also be less than obvious. Consider the following responses, which signal approval without being explicit.

- **Direct acknowledgment:** A speaker acknowledges another person's communication and reacts to it directly and verbally.
- **Agreement about content:** A speaker reinforces information expressed by another.
- **Supportive response:** A speaker expresses understanding of another person or tries to reassure or make the other feel better.
- **Clarifying response:** A speaker tries to clarify another person's message or feelings. A clarifying response may involve requesting more information, encouraging the

other person to say more, or repeating what the other said and asking the person to confirm the speaker's understanding.

- **Expression of positive feeling:** One speaker describes his or her own positive feelings related to what another person has said—for example, "Okay, now I understand what you're saying."

When you perceive others' behavior as threatening to your emotional security or position in a group, your uncertainty about your role in the group increases. Individual needs are elevated to a place equal to or even greater than the group's task and process needs. If you respond defensively, you are likely to evoke further defensiveness from the rest of the group. People who find themselves in a defensive, disconfirming climate do not trust one another. The realization that you cannot trust another person suggests that this person's behavior is unpredictable—that you do not know for sure how he or she will respond. Such uncertainty is harmful to a problem-solving group. In contrast, in a supportive, confirming climate, where mutual respect and trust prevail, you are more certain of your own well-being. This security, in turn, allows you to increase your concentration on the task and the process needs of the group.

Confirming responses cause us to value ourselves more. What responses from others make you feel good during your group activities?

By using confirming rather than disconfirming responses when communicating with other group members, people contribute to the creation of a supportive, trustful climate, thereby promoting greater group effectiveness and individual satisfaction.

6.3: Group Cohesiveness

OBJECTIVE: Analyze groups for factors that aid or limit cohesiveness

Historically, cohesiveness has been considered one of the most important small group variables.[7] **Group cohesiveness** is the degree of attraction that members feel toward one another and toward the group. It is a feeling of deep loyalty, of "groupness" (often called by a French term, "esprit de corps"), and signals the degree to which each individual has made the group's goal his or her own. Group cohesiveness encompasses both a sense of belonging and a feeling of high morale.[8] Cohesiveness results from the interaction of a number of variables, including group composition, individual benefits derived from the group, task effectiveness, context,[9] and, first and foremost, communication.

The productivity of groups and teams is strongly related to their cohesiveness,[10] although there are some exceptions. In one study of a junior hockey team, high social cohesion was seen to be detrimental to team performance. The authors of the study hypothesized that in this case, high group cohesion and pressure to conform had led to a reduction in the need to evaluate one another's performance and, consequently, to deteriorating performance.[11] In other studies, the relationship of cohesiveness to team performance has been curvilinear, with team performance actually falling off when cohesion is too high.[12]

By the end of this module, you will be able to:

- 6.3.1 **Compare the impacts of similarity and diversity on group cohesiveness**
- 6.3.2 **Explain how meeting individual needs improves group cohesiveness**
- 6.3.3 **Relate a group's effectiveness to its cohesiveness**
- 6.3.4 **Explain how communication influences group cohesiveness**
- 6.3.5 **Describe cohesiveness challenges common to virtual teams**

6.3.1: Diversity and Building a Cohesive Team

OBJECTIVE: Compare the impacts of similarity and diversity on group cohesiveness

People often join groups because they feel an attraction toward the people in that group. Factors such as the similarity of group members, or the degree to which group members' needs and personalities[13] complement one another, are influential in the development of group cohesiveness.

To borrow a metaphor from the sports world, the best team has the right players at the right positions—and good coaching. Based on their size, speed, aggressiveness, reaction time, and so forth, different players are suited for different positions. The same is true of all groups and teams. For maximum effectiveness, they need participants with different talents that complement one another.

Which team is more likely to be the most cohesive and productive?

Cohesiveness develops around both the task and relationship dimensions of a group, such as roles, norms, status, power, and trust. Building a group solely on the basis of similarity in interpersonal attraction is likely to lead to strong cohesiveness based on relationships but mediocrity as a task group. This factor explains why self-selected groups are often more cohesive—but less productive—than groups in which membership has been assigned carefully, with the group's task in mind. After all, the characteristics we find most attractive in a friend may not be those best suited to help us do a job. Evidence from college classroom groups suggests strongly that self-selection is not usually the best policy. In one study, by a nearly two-to-one margin, students who formed their own groups reported that group as one of their worst group experiences.[14] Some research has suggested that when building a team, a blend of similarity and complementarity may be best—for example, similar personalities but complementary knowledge.[15] Other research shows that people like to affiliate with those who they perceive as superior in some way. However, a truly and vastly superior teammate can result not only in envy but also in defensiveness and physiological feelings of threat.[16]

Most work groups today are culturally and racially diverse, in addition to reflecting a range of talents and expertise. Such diversity can be a source of strength because of the multiple perspectives it brings to problem solving, as long as the group can work together to minimize misunderstandings that may stem from that diversity.[17] Notably, extreme diversity within a group brings stimulating perspectives to problem solving but may strain the relational aspects of group process. Contradictory findings on these effects have been called the "double-edged sword of diversity"[18]—recognizing that group diversity can be either positive or negative, or both. But the costs and benefits of diversity depend very much on context—the type of diversity, the nature of the task, the group's history, and its leadership.[19]

6.3.2: Individual Benefits and Cohesiveness

OBJECTIVE: Explain how meeting individual needs improves group cohesiveness

Cohesiveness is a combination of forces that hold people together in groups. Depending on the nature of the group, its members can derive benefits of affiliation, power, affection, and prestige. People like to be with groups in which these needs are satisfied. Group members who experience relational satisfaction also tend to perceive their groups as more cohesive and as reaching consensus.[20] The degree to which a particular group is capable of meeting members' needs can largely determine that group's cohesiveness. If people perceive that they derive benefits from a group that no other group could provide, they will be much more strongly attracted to that group. To some extent, this factor accounts for the intense attraction most of us feel toward our families or closest friends.

WRITING PROMPT

How Much Cohesiveness?

Think of your various group memberships. Which group best meets your needs? Which group is the least rewarding? Can you identify the reasons for your perceptions?

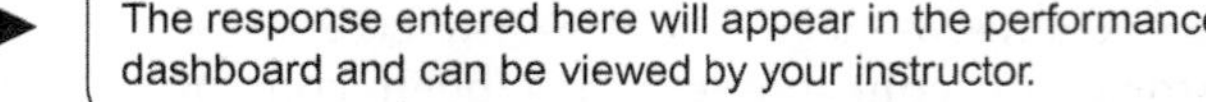

The response entered here will appear in the performance dashboard and can be viewed by your instructor.

Submit

6.3.3: Task Effectiveness and Cohesiveness

OBJECTIVE: Relate a group's effectiveness to its cohesiveness

Success breeds success. Winning teams develop confidence as a group. The performance of the group as a whole has considerable influence; success fosters cohesiveness.[21] In turn, cohesiveness fosters success. The mutuality of concern for the group's task, which provides the focal point for working toward that task, becomes socially rewarding when the task is completed successfully. In another example of the interrelatedness of the task and social dimensions, reaching a particular goal provides a common, rewarding experience for all group members. This commonality, or shared experience, then further sets that group apart from other groups.

A team's **confidence** builds as collective effort produces positive outcomes.

6.3.4: Communication and Cohesiveness

OBJECTIVE: Explain how communication influences group cohesiveness

Diversity, individual benefits, and efficacy alone are not enough to build a cohesive group. Rather, the interaction of these variables determines the degree of cohesiveness. Communication is the vehicle through which this interaction takes place. Through communication, individual needs are met and group tasks are accomplished. In other words, "the communication networks and the messages that flow through them ultimately determine the attractiveness of the group for its members."[22]

Communication creates symbolic convergence through which a cohesive group identity evolves. According to symbolic convergence theory, the group develops a unique identity through the sharing of fantasies or stories. The feeling of cohesiveness is likely to increase as group members share stories and other group members respond to those stories. A fantasy chain emerges when one story leads to another, thereby creating a bond among group members and the revelation of common fantasies.

An understanding of defensive and supportive communication suggests some ways in which people can adjust their communicative behavior to improve group cohesiveness. Research shows that an "agreeable" style is positively related to team members' willingness to share their own knowledge with their groups, which relates to job performance and to satisfaction with the group.[23] In addition to the quality of communication, the amount of communication in the group affects cohesiveness. According to George Homans, if "the frequency of interaction between two or more persons increases, the degree of their liking for one another will increase, and vice versa."[24] Free and open communication characterizes highly cohesive groups. The more people interact, the more they reveal themselves to each other. Through communication, people negotiate group roles, establish goals, reveal similarities and differences, resolve conflict, and express affection. Thus, as the frequency of communication within a group increases, so does the group's cohesiveness. Communication is also the foundation for interpersonal trust within the group, especially when the group is working in a virtual environment.

6.3.5: Cohesiveness in Virtual Teams

OBJECTIVE: Describe cohesiveness challenges common to virtual teams

As with face-to-face groups, the group's composition is important when building a virtual team. Such teams need the right blend of knowledge, experience, and skills, but

Virtual Collaboration

Building Trust in Virtual Groups[31]

When team members work in different locations, they can't rely on the usual face-to-face nonverbal cues to gauge sincerity or effort. This "behavioral invisibility" slows the development of trust and adds risk to virtual groups and teams.

Although virtual teams can and do reach levels of trust comparable to face-to-face groups, they often show lower *initial* levels of trust. Over time, however, virtual groups and teams can meet or exceed the trust levels in their face-to-face counterparts.

Indeed, time is the key to understanding this process. Groups pass through predictable stages in development, and virtual groups may take up to four times as long to exchange the same number of messages as face-to-face groups. That delay, coupled with the absence of visual cues, results in a much slower movement through the various developmental stages.

At the outset, members of virtual teams are more likely to use offensive or inflammatory language and to tease or antagonize one another. These behaviors are associated with lower levels of initial trust in such groups and teams. Eventually, virtual groups are able to achieve high levels of trust if given sufficient time.

The implications of research for working in virtual teams are clear:

- The long-term productivity of the group requires movement through developmental stages.
- Virtual teams can reach levels of trust and productivity comparable to their face-to-face counterparts, but doing so takes longer.
- Plan extra time for relationship- and trust-building in virtual teams.
- Recognize the absence of contextual cues and avoid communication that could be interpreted as inflammatory.

also a good blend of personality traits such as introversion and extroversion to facilitate good team communication.[25]

Compared to face-to-face teams, virtual teams often show lower levels of initial trust,[26, 27] cohesiveness, and satisfaction. This may be largely due to the difficulty of providing process feedback—information not only about tasks and goals but also about teamwork and interpersonal relationships—in virtual contexts. Regular contact and process feedback can lead to greater group performance, motivation, and satisfaction.[28] If possible, some initial face-to-face contact is recommended to build trust in virtual teams. If this is not possible, research suggests that virtual copresence—in which virtual group members are consistently available to one another—can help build trust.[29] In any virtual group, regular communication that seeks to clarify goals, role expectations, and norms is essential.[30]

6.4: Networks and Group Size

OBJECTIVE: Analyze how size and distribution influence group climate

Networks are the pattern of who talks to whom in a group. How many communications are directed to the group as a whole? Who are the more active participants, and to whom do they speak most often? As the size of a group expands, the complexity of the network increases.

By the end of this module, you will be able to:

6.4.1 **Describe the ways that group size affects group climate**

6.4.2 **Compare how networks influence group climate**

6.4.1: Group Size

OBJECTIVE: Describe the ways that group size affects group climate

Within a group, there is a positive relationship between the level of people's participation and the degree of their individual satisfaction. Also, there is a positive relationship between group cohesiveness and the opportunity for interaction between members—however, as group size increases, the opportunity for interaction decreases.[32] No one knows the precise number of people that will maximize the effectiveness of your group, but some observations may provide guidance. As a group's size increases, complexity increases and the principle of diminishing returns sets in. Moreover, individual group members' efforts tend to decrease.[33] What, then, is the optimal size?

Groups should be large enough to include people with the skills necessary to get the job done, but small enough to encourage maximum participation. As noted earlier, groups move through fairly orderly developmental stages. Smaller groups tend to move through these phases more quickly, so they become more productive sooner than larger groups. Groups containing three to six members tend to be more productive and developmentally advanced than groups with seven to ten members.[34] For face-to-face contact, a smaller group is often better in terms of cohesiveness and productivity. In virtual groups and teams, size appears to be less of a factor in this regard.[35]

Some research has found less clear effects of group size. One study of production work teams found group size to be unrelated to employees' perceptions of their work teams or their workplace commitment. Nevertheless, the same study showed that positive perceptions of their work teams were strongly related to members' commitment to their workplace and their productivity.[36] Although group size is a factor in group effectiveness, the opportunity to communicate may be more important than actual group size.[37]

WRITING PROMPT

Group Size and Individual Satisfaction

Think of the largest and smallest groups in which you participate. How satisfied are the individual group members in each? What effects do you see from the size of these groups?

The response entered here will appear in the performance dashboard and can be viewed by your instructor.

Submit

6.4.2: Communication Networks

OBJECTIVE: Compare how networks influence group climate

Along with group size, another influence on group climate is the **communication network**—the pattern of interaction within a group, or who talks to whom. Think about the group meetings in which you participate. It may seem that, although some people talk more than others, most of their communication is addressed to the group as a whole. Next time you are in a group, note who is talking to whom. You will find that most people address relatively few comments to the group as a whole and that they direct most of what they say in groups toward specific persons. These patterns are easily observable in both face-to-face and virtual groups.

Distribution of Communication within Groups[38]

Communication Addressed to the Leader—In some groups, members address most comments to one central person, perhaps the designated leader or chairperson. This type of network is more efficient, which enhances group cohesiveness.

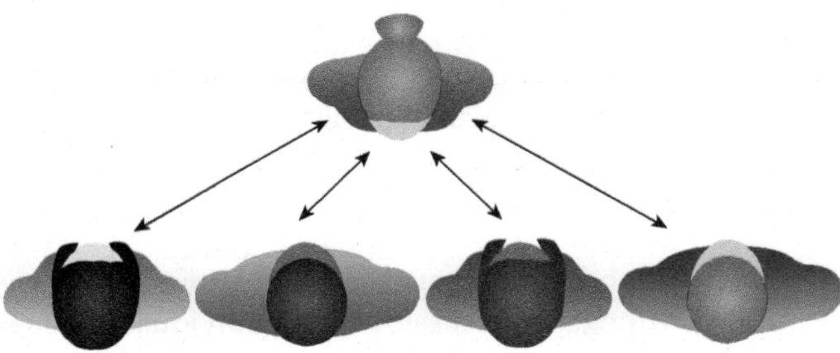

Equal Distribution of Communication—In other groups, communication tends to be distributed equally among group members. Free, open communication networks that include everyone in the group will more likely lead to accurate group judgments, better goal attainment, and better task performance.

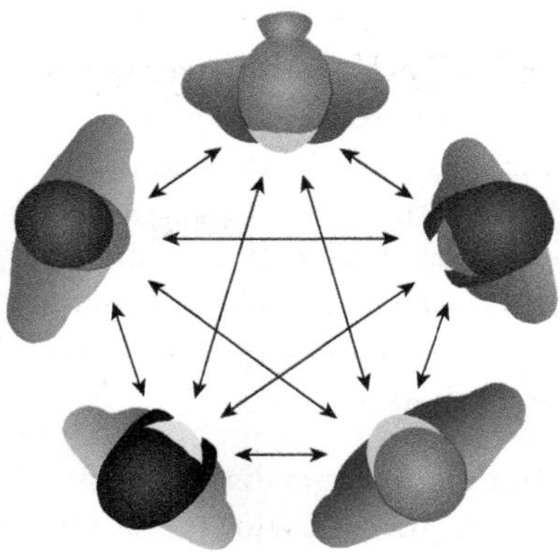

PATTERNS IN FACE-TO-FACE GROUPS Sometimes other patterns may emerge. These include circular patterns, in which people talk primarily to those individuals sitting next to them, or linear patterns, in which people communicate in a kind of chain reaction, with each group member chiming in successively to build on the previous comments. These patterns may be built into the group from the outset, or they may emerge spontaneously. Either way, networks tend to stabilize over time. Once people establish channels of communication, they continue to use the same channels. This network of channels influences group climate as well as group productivity.

CONCLUSIONS ABOUT NETWORKS A review of the research on groups suggests that "groups in which free communication is maximized are generally more accurate in their judgments, although they may take longer to reach a decision."[39] People also tend to feel more satisfied in groups in which they participate actively.[40] When interaction is stifled or discouraged, people have less opportunity to satisfy their needs through communication.

Skilled Collaboration

Cohesiveness and Productivity at Harley-Davidson

In the 1980s, the Harley-Davidson Motor Company experienced a widely celebrated turnaround that was achieved largely by replacing a "command-and-control" culture with a new culture in which assembly employees made important decisions in their work teams. At the Kansas City plant, there are no team leaders per se; instead, work teams—known at the plant as "natural work groups"—make consensus decisions.

Harley-Davidson's Kansas City plant provided a natural setting for researchers Phillip Chansler, Paul Swamidass, and Corlandt Cammann to study cohesiveness and productivity. Their studies found that much of the improvement in team cohesion that was evident after the reorganization at Harley-Davidson could be explained by two factors: employees' perception of the plant leadership's fairness and employees' influence on team staffing and training decisions. The researchers concluded that to improve cohesiveness within work teams, companies should do two things: (1) increase team members' influence over staffing and training and (2) treat employees with greater fairness and work to enhance perceptions of fairness.[41]

Real-Life Applications

In your own groups and teams, and especially those in which you serve as a leader, consider applying the lessons learned at Harley-Davidson:

- Encourage group members to take an active role in deciding who is responsible for performing specific tasks; don't dictate who should do what.
- Ask group members what training, information, and resources they need to accomplish their task.
- Be fair. One of the most corrosive behaviors of leaders and other members in groups and teams is treating other members unfairly.
- Don't let slackers get away with not doing their part; their low level of participation can hurt cohesiveness and productivity. How do you confront a slacker? At the very least, start with gentle questions and efforts to encourage the nonparticipant to do his or her share of the work.

6.5: Group Climate and Productivity

OBJECTIVE: Relate group climate to productivity

Many variables affect both group climate (e.g., defensive behavior, confirming and disconfirming responses, group cohesiveness, group size) and group productivity. When communication is free and open and when everyone participates, people tend to feel more attraction toward the group and consequently receive more personal satisfaction from belonging to that group. Another benefit of developing and maintaining a positive group climate is that climate affects productivity. Factors such as strong work norms and cohesiveness interact in groups and teams to increase productivity.[42]

In virtual groups, the members' familiarity with one another has a positive effect on the group's efficiency. As familiarity in these groups increases, the time it takes to reach a decision decreases. However, group members report lower satisfaction with virtual groups than with face-to-face groups. Furthermore, evidence suggests that decision accuracy is lower in virtual groups than in face-to-face groups.[43]

By the end of this module, you will be able to:

6.5.1 **Describe how trust between group members affects how groups manage conflict**

6.5.2 **Explain how adopting a group goal influences individuals and productivity**

6.5.1: Trust, Conflict, and Efficacy

OBJECTIVE: Describe how trust between group members affects how groups manage conflict

Trusting relationships are those in which we feel we can count on others to behave in certain ways and in which there is mutual respect. Trust is essential to achieve maximum group productivity. Communication scholars Judy Pearson and Paul Nelson note two kinds of trust that are relevant to small group communication:

> Having trust regarding the task means members can count on each other to get things done. A common source of conflict for many groups is having a member who doesn't contribute a fair share of the work, so others have to pick up the slack. That makes members angry and the climate tense. Having interpersonal trust means that members believe the others are operating with the best interests of the group in mind and not from hidden agendas.[44]

When a group has a trusting, open atmosphere and a high level of cohesiveness, members "do not fear the effects that disagreement and conflict in the task dimension can have on their social fabric. Cohesive groups have strong enough social bonds to tolerate conflict."[45] Through constructive conflict, groups deal with the difficult issues confronting them. When there is no conflict, it usually means that people do not trust one another enough to assert their individuality. But avoiding issues does not lead to clarity, and an absence of clarity prevents the group from reaching the most effective solutions.

A positive group climate and group cohesiveness don't mean everyone is necessarily nice all the time. Rather, in a highly cohesive group, members know that they will not be rejected for their views and, therefore, are more willing to express them—even though expressing them may provoke disagreement. Ernest Bormann notes:

> At a point where someone in a cohesive group would say "You're wrong!" or "I disagree!" an individual in a less cohesive group will say "I don't understand" or "I'm confused." Members of groups with little cohesion have yet to create much of a common social reality.[46]

This "common social reality," which includes group roles and group norms, gives people the freedom to assert their individuality within a predictable context. Cohesion and trust pave the way for constructive conflict within groups.

CASE STUDY

Avoiding Defensiveness

Not long ago I received a mysterious telephone call from a good friend. He said that he and his wife wanted to discuss a business proposition for us. Tuesday evening? They'd see us then.

Our curiosity piqued, we eagerly awaited the rendezvous. What could our friends possibly have up their sleeves? Right on time, the doorbell rang and we were surprised to find George and Margaret dressed in their best suits. They laughed nervously, marched past us, and set up a small demonstration board on our dining room table. Turning down our offer of wine, they asked if we could begin the meeting. This was strange. My wife and I began to feel as if we had invited insurance agents into our home—even though we had camped, hiked, canoed, and spent many an evening with George and Margaret. But our curiosity was aroused, so we played along.

It wasn't long before the experience became frustrating. George and Margaret asked us what we wanted out of life. We suggested that they probably should have some idea of that by now—we want to be good parents, and that most of our other goals were inward, state-of-being kinds of goals. They responded by suggesting that it might be nice if we never again had to worry about money. This was puzzling, but we agreed that it would, indeed, be pleasant. At this, they hauled out charts, graphs, and illustrations that, they claimed, proved that we could double our present income in a little over a year—in our spare time, of course.

After an hour, George and Margaret still refused to tell us what it was we would have to sell (we'd figured out that much) or to whom we'd have to sell it. Something was definitely wrong. I was in my own dining room with my wife and my friends, yet I felt as if I were back in middle school being told to please hold all my questions until the end. I've had similar experiences with aggressive salespeople. It was dehumanizing.

Finally, George and Margaret revealed the name of the company and its line of products and set about the task of showing how rapidly the company had grown as a result of its unique marketing concepts. But I had already decided not to accept their proposition. I felt insulted and abused by my friends. Why hadn't they simply told us that they were involved with the company (which we had heard of long before) and that they would like to explore the possibilities of our becoming involved as well? With friends, it would be a much more effective approach—certainly a more honest one.

Finally, they asked for our comments and questions. I was ready. I evaluated their entire presentation, emphasizing their failure to analyze their audience and to adapt their communication style accordingly. George and Margaret were shocked and hurt. They had not, they said, come into our home to be criticized. If they had offended us, they were sorry. No, they still did not care for a glass of wine. And they left abruptly.

Questions for Analysis: Avoiding Defensiveness

1. What previously existing group norms can you infer from this case study? How were the norms violated? What were the consequences?
2. Which of Gibb's "defensive communication" behaviors can you identify? Do you see any evidence that anyone tried to use supportive communication?
3. What evidence of group cohesiveness can you identify?
4. What kinds of confirming and disconfirming responses can you identify?
5. What recommendations would you give George and Margaret for avoiding such trouble in the future? What advice do you have for the case study's writer?

6.5.2: Adopting the Group's Goal Increases Productivity

OBJECTIVE: Explain how adopting a group goal influences individuals within a group and productivity

One aspect of a common social reality is the degree to which group members make the group's goal their own. Members of a highly cohesive group commit themselves to the group's well-being and to accomplishing the group's task. In part, this personal commitment can be attributed to the feeling that this particular group meets people's needs better than any other group. When this is the case, as it often is in a cohesive group, people have a degree of dependence on the group. This dependence increases the *power* the group has over individuals. To put this in a different way: "There can be little doubt that members of a more cohesive group more readily exert influence on one another and are more readily influenced by one another."[47]

These factors—personal commitment to the group, personal dependence on the group, and group power over individuals within the group—mesh in a positive group climate. The result is that cohesive groups work harder than groups with little cohesiveness, regardless of outside supervision.[48]

With few exceptions, building a group climate in which cohesiveness can grow leads not only to greater individual satisfaction but also to greater group productivity.[49]

WRITING PROMPT

Groups and Individual Satisfaction

Is there a group that you would truly miss if it disbanded? What makes this group special? Do you depend on this group to meet your needs? Is this group exceptionally productive? Reflect on what you would be missing personally without this group in your life.

The response entered here will appear in the performance dashboard and can be viewed by your instructor.

Submit

Summary: Improving Group Climate

6.1: Defensive versus Supportive Climates

- As a communicator, you control your own actions. To the extent that you engage in supportive—rather than defensive—communication, you will foster a positive group climate in which people are free to focus their attention on the group and its task.

6.2: Interpersonal Confirmation and Disconfirmation

- If you can develop a sensitivity to your own confirming and disconfirming behaviors, you can become more confirming in your group behavior, thereby contributing to a more positive group climate.

6.3: Group Cohesiveness

- Cohesiveness is the result of the interaction of a number of variables, including the group's composition, individual benefits derived from the group, task effectiveness, and communication. Cohesiveness is usually related positively to group productivity.

6.4: Networks and Group Size

- If you are forming a group, include just enough people to ensure the presence of all the relevant skills for problem solving—and no more.
- Free and open communication networks that include everyone in the group are more likely to lead to more accurate group judgments as well as to better goal attainment and task performance. More active participation in the group is associated with group members' satisfaction.

6.5: Group Climate and Productivity

- A positive group climate is essential if you are to reach your maximum potential as a working group. A trusting and open climate allows all members the freedom to be themselves: to agree or disagree, or to engage in conflict without fear of rejection.
- The ability of a group not just to withstand, but to benefit from, constructive conflict is crucial to a group's productivity. To build such a climate, learn to communicate more supportively and confirmingly, and avoid defensive, disconfirming behavior.

SHARED WRITING

Combating Neutrality

Glenda: I've got a great idea for our fundraiser!

(Group members continue staring into their devices)

Glenda: Hey everyone. Want to hear my idea?

Ramon: Go for it.

Lizzie: Do tell.

Glenda: I talked to the manager at Harley-Davidson. Let's raffle off a motorcycle!

Gregor: Whatever . . .

Imagine how Glenda is feeling during this exchange. If you were there, how would you respond if you agree that the raffle is a good idea? How would you respond if you don't? Write a short response that your classmates will read. Be sure to include specifics in your discussion. Keep in mind that empathy is an attempt to feel or to see things as another person sees them.

A minimum number of characters is required to post and earn points. After posting, your response can be viewed by your class and instructor, and you can participate in the class discussion.

Post

Answers

Section 6.1.2: Control or Problem Orientation?

1. Controlling. 2. Problem orientation. 3. Ambiguous, but probably controlling—not wanting to spend time working through the problem

Chapter 7
Enhancing Communication Skills in Groups

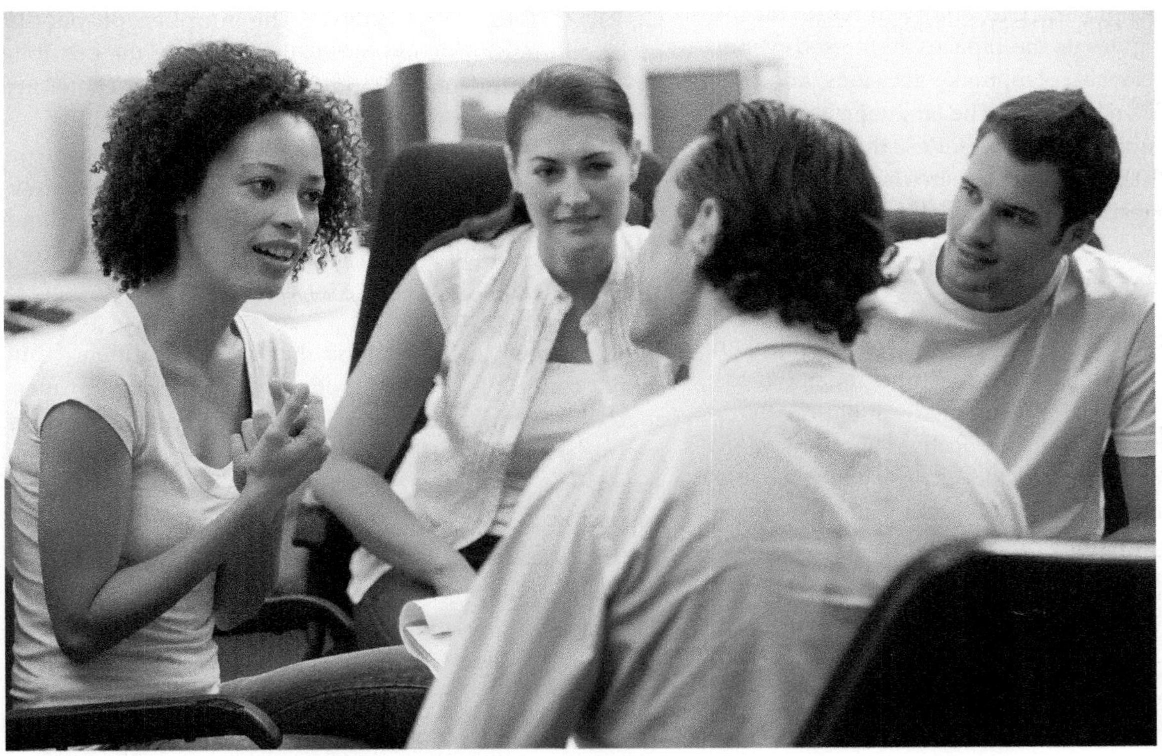

"As I grow older, I pay less attention to what people say; I just watch what they do."
—Andrew Carnegie

Learning Objectives

7.1 Analyze words for common barriers to communication

7.2 Evaluate listening behaviors in a small group environment

7.3 Apply research findings about nonverbal communication to groups

7.4 Interpret nonverbal communication in a group context

Good theory informs good practice. In the context of groups, theories and principles inform practices that can lead to more effective group and team communication. The core event in group communication is communication itself. In this chapter, we'll focus on three essential skills: using words accurately, listening, and communicating nonverbally.

7.1: Verbal Dynamics and Avoiding Communication Barriers

OBJECTIVE: Analyze words for common barriers to communication

The most obvious, yet elusive, component of small group communication is the spoken word. Words are at the heart of who and what people are. Our ability to represent the world symbolically gives us the capacity to foresee events, reflect on past experiences, plan, make decisions, and consciously direct our own behavior. The language we use can directly affect a group's effectiveness. Research has shown, for example, that a 10 percent increase in a leader's strategic language usage can result in a 2.5 percent increase in worker decision making.[1]

Words are the tools we use to make sense of the world and share that sense with others. Paradoxically, words can both facilitate and impede communication. Spoken language gives us access to the ideas and inner worlds of other group members, but it can also—intentionally or unintentionally—create barriers to effective communication.

If you grew up in the United States, you probably remember chanting defensively, "Sticks and stones can break my bones, but names can never hurt me." Despite your bravado, you knew that adage wasn't true. People often unwittingly use words in ways that threaten others and make them feel defensive. Some subtle but pervasive word barriers are:

- Bypassing
- Allness
- Fact–inference confusion

By the end of this module, you will be able to:

7.1.1 **Replace phrases that are open to bypassing**

7.1.2 **Identify untrue generalizations (allness statements)**

7.1.3 **Differentiate facts and inferences**

7.1.1: Bypassing

OBJECTIVE: Replace phrases that are open to bypassing

The meanings of your words seem so obvious to you that sometimes you may assume they elicit the same meanings from others. But it is not always so. **Bypassing** takes place when two people assign different meanings to the same word. Most words are open to almost limitless interpretations—consider, for example, the words "love," "respect," and "communication." Similarly, you may know precisely what you mean if you say that your bank account is "seriously overdrawn," but how are others to interpret that statement? How serious is "seriously"?

According to some estimates, the 500 most frequently used words in the English language have more than 14,000 dictionary definitions. Considering that a dictionary definition reflects only a tiny percentage of all possible meanings for a word, and that people from different cultures and with different experiences interpret words differently, it is amazing that people can understand one another at all.

CORRECTING BYPASSING The number of people involved in groups compounds the problem; the possibility of multiple misunderstandings always exists. Therefore, good feedback among group members is essential.

Feedback is any response by listeners that lets speakers know whether they have been understood accurately. To overcome word-related barriers, we must understand that words are subjective. For effective communication, you must ensure that what you understand from others is really what they intend.

Conversely, keep in mind that you can influence, but cannot control, the meaning others derive from your messages. Meaning is created in others.[2] Words do not have meaning in and of themselves. Consider the following statements, then rewrite them to eliminate the potential for bypassing.

Avoiding Bypassing

Statement 1	I'll see you later.
Statement 2	Meet me at the mall.
Statement 3	Would next Tuesday be a good day for you? (spoken on a Sunday)
Summary	Review your rewritten statements. Compare them with the ideal responses given here. Statement 1: I'll see you between 2:45 and 3:00 this afternoon. Statement 2: Meet me at the Northstar Mall, south entrance. Statement 3: Would this Tuesday—the day after tomorrow—be good for you?

7.1.2: Allness (Untrue Generalization)

OBJECTIVE: Identify untrue generalizations (allness statements)

Allness statements are simple but untrue generalizations. You have probably heard such allness statements as "Women are smarter than men," "Men can run faster than women," and "Football players aren't good students." These statements are convenient, but not accurate.

CORRECTING ALLNESS The danger of allness statements is that you may begin to believe them and to prejudge (stereotype) other people unfairly based on those broad characterizations. Be careful not to overgeneralize; remember that each individual is unique.

Read the following dialogue, then rewrite it to avoid making allness statements.

Avoiding Allness

Question	Bianca: "I can't believe how rude the other team's fans were!" Nick: "What else would you expect from a bunch of New Yorkers?" Bianca: "Especially the guys. They were rabid!" Nick: "No one has taught them to be gentlemen." Bianca: "I was proud of our side of the stadium, though. Good sportsmanship all around."
Summary	Review your rewritten statements. Compare them with the ideal responses given here. Bianca: "I can't believe how rude some of the other team's fans were!" Nick: "Yes, several of them were truly obnoxious!" Bianca: "Yes, some were. Apparently no one has taught them to be gentlemen." Nick: "I was proud of our side of the stadium, though. Mostly good sportsmanship."

7.1.3: Fact–Inference Confusion

OBJECTIVE: Differentiate facts and inferences

Fact–inference confusion occurs when people respond to something as if they have actually observed it, when in reality they have merely drawn a conclusion. The key distinction between a fact and an inference is that in statements of inference people can speculate about and interpret what they think occurred. As an example, suppose that you hear someone comment, "Men are better than women at math." If this statement were true, it would mean that all men and women had been tested and that the results indicated that men are better in math than women. The statement is an inference.

CORRECTING FACT–INFERENCE CONFUSION If the speaker is summarizing research that has investigated the issue, he or she should say, "Some studies have found that...." rather than "It's a fact that...." The first statement more accurately describes reality than does the second. Like bypassing and allness statements, fact–inference confusion can lead to inaccuracy and misunderstanding.

Fact or Inference?

No.	Statements	Answer
1.	It's going to rain tomorrow.	Inference
2.	I checked and sunrise is at 7:33 AM.	Fact
3.	Do you know Jimmy? He likes me.	Inference
4.	Amir is a liberal. I saw his Democratic Party bumper sticker.	Inference

Review

Word Barriers and How to Avoid Them

Barrier	Description	Approach
Bypassing	Occurs when the same word is used to mean different things	Use specific language; be aware of multiple interpretations of what you say; clarify.
Allness statements	Simple but untrue generalizations	Don't overgeneralize; remember that all individuals are unique.
Fact–inference confusion	Mistaking a conclusion you have drawn for an observation	Clarify and analyze; learn to recognize the difference between fact and inference, and communicate the difference clearly.

7.2: Listening

OBJECTIVE: Evaluate listening behaviors in a small group environment

Good listening skills are an essential component of being an effective group member or leader[3] and an effective team manager.[4] Conversely, poor listening habits are one of the most common sources of defensiveness and discord. It is easier to be a poor listener in groups than it is in interpersonal situations, because often in a group you needn't respond directly to the speaker. However, groups cannot reach their maximum effectiveness unless all members listen actively to one another.

Listening is a process of selecting, attending to, creating meaning from, remembering, and responding to verbal and nonverbal messages. It is a skill that can be improved with practice. To listen effectively, you must listen actively. This involves filtering out other stimuli that compete for your attention: hunger pangs, grocery lists, or curiosity about the attractive person nearby. Improving any skill takes knowledge and practice. This section will provide some knowledge; the practice is up to you. Are you listening?

By the end of this module, you will be able to:

- 7.2.1 **Compare listening styles**
- 7.2.2 **Describe common problems associated with poor listening skills**
- 7.2.3 **Outline the steps involved in active listening**

7.2.1: Listening Styles

OBJECTIVE: Compare listening styles

Do your ears perk up when you hear someone telling an interesting story, or would you be more interested in listening to data, facts, and details? Research suggests that different people have different listening styles.[5] Your **listening style** is your preferred way of making sense out of the spoken messages you hear.[6]

Types of Listening Styles

Listening researchers have identified four overarching listening styles: relational, analytical, critical, and task.[7] We'll discuss each of the four listening styles so that you can identify your most natural style and develop new strategies for listening.

Relational Listening Style—Relational listeners are most comfortable listening to other people's feelings and emotions; they are other-oriented.[8] In a small group, people-oriented, relational listeners focus on the stories others tell and are good at developing relationships by being empathic and fulfilling group maintenance roles. Relationally oriented listeners also have a personality that is both agreeable and open to the ideas of others.[9] Relationally oriented, interpersonally sensitive group leaders tend to have more satisfied subordinates.[10]

Analytical Listening Style—Analytically oriented listeners prefer to focus on facts and tend to withhold judgment before reaching a specific conclusion. They appreciate well-organized information. These listeners don't mind listening to an information-rich message. Analytically oriented listeners are more likely to assume task-oriented roles to achieve the group's goal.

Critical Listening Style—Critical listeners would make good judges. They are good at evaluating information and able to spot inconsistencies in what someone says. They are comfortable listening to detailed, complex information and zeroing in on the facts. They are also are skilled at catching errors in the overall logic and reasoning that are used to reach a conclusion. A critical listener would be a good person to review the overall conclusions and evidence used to reach a group or team conclusion.

Task Listening Style—Task-oriented listeners want to get things done. They prefer information that is well organized, brief, and error free. They listen for verbs—they want to know what to do with the information they hear. They also don't like to listen to long, rambling tangents from other group members. They appreciate efficient communicators who are aware of how much time is involved in getting things done. A task-oriented listener can help the group keep on schedule and stay focused on the agenda.

There is no single best listening style for communicating in groups and teams: Each style has its advantages and disadvantages. If you were focused only on distilling from the speaker's words a brief and concise message (analytically oriented listener), you would not be especially attuned to the relationships and feelings of others (relationally oriented listeners). And although it's good practice to focus on details (critically oriented listener) or on the proposed action steps (task-oriented listener), spending too much time on the task without being aware of relationships can be detrimental to a group. Just as it's a good thing for groups to have people play a variety of roles, it's also useful for groups to include people with differing listening styles. On the one hand, if most of the members are relationally oriented listeners, then the group will have to be more mindful of focusing on facts, data, and evidence. On the other hand, a team composed entirely of analytical- or task-oriented listeners may need to ensure that they are managing the relational aspects of the group.

Many people have more than one listening style.[11] Moreover, listening and other human communication processes appear to be changing to accommodate the media-saturated world of the twenty-first century.[12] Once you know your own preferred listening style(s), you can work to develop other styles, so you will be able to adapt your style to different situations.[13] To be an adaptive listener is to be a better listener.

WRITING PROMPT

Your Listening Style(s)

What is your listening style? How do you know? Do you have more than one listening style?

The response entered here will appear in the performance dashboard and can be viewed by your instructor.

Submit

7.2.2: Obstacles to Effective Listening

OBJECTIVE: Describe common problems associated with poor listening skills

Regardless of your listening style, you need to overcome the common obstacles to effective listening. Many such obstacles are possible—outside distractions, an uncomfortable chair, a headache—but the focus here will be on two prevalent and serious barriers: prejudging and rehearsing.

Serious Barriers to Effective Listening

Prejudging the Communicator or the Communication— Sometimes you simply dislike certain people or always disagree with them. You anticipate that what they will say will be wrong or offensive, and you begin to tune them out. An example of this behavior is many people's tendency to "tune out" the speeches of politicians who hold political beliefs different from their own. In a group, you must overcome the temptation to ignore those people you think are boring, pedantic, offensive, or wrong. Good ideas can come from anyone, even from people with whom you disagree. Likewise, you should not prejudge certain topics as being too complex, boring, or controversial. Maintaining this kind of neutrality can be difficult, especially when a cherished belief is criticized or when others say things about you that you might not want to hear. In fact, these are precisely the times when communication needs to be clear, open, honest, and confirming. To communicate effectively, you must *listen.*

It is especially important not to prejudge others on the basis of culture, ethnicity, sexual orientation, sexual identity, or race. Despite continuing social progress, such prejudices linger.[14] In one study, college students indicated that racial stereotypes are alive and well. African Americans said that Whites are "demanding" and "manipulative"; Whites reported that Blacks are "loud" and "ostentatious."[15] Such prejudices inhibit our ability to listen effectively and also foster defensiveness in groups.

Rehearsing a Response—Communication scholar John Shotter has observed that "in our talk with others, we listen for opportunities to express our own point of view, to add it to or contrast it with theirs."[16] While looking for such opportunities and planning what we will say, we are actually sacrificing an opportunity to fully understand and be understood. Rehearsing is perhaps the most difficult listening obstacle to overcome: It is the tendency of people to rehearse in their minds what they will say when the other person stops talking.

One reason why rehearsing occurs is the difference between speech rate and thought rate. Most people speak at a rate of about 100 to 125 words per minute, but they have the capacity to think or listen at a rate of 400 or more words per minute! This gives them the time to wander off mentally while keeping one ear on the speaker. The thought–speech differential is better used, though, to attend fully to what the speaker is saying—and not saying. When people learn to do this, their responses can be more spontaneous, accurate, appropriate, confirming, and supportive.[17]

7.2.3: A Guide to Active Listening

OBJECTIVE: Outline the steps involved in active listening

Supportive, confirming communication focuses not just on verbal messages, but also on the emotional content of the messages and on nonverbal behaviors. Learning to quiet one's own thoughts and to avoid prejudging others is a first step. Fully understanding others, though, involves considerable effort. Active listening is an attempt to clarify and understand another's thoughts and feelings.

To listen actively involves several steps. These steps may seem like common sense, but they are far from common practice.

Steps to Active Listening

1. Stop— Before you can effectively tune into what someone else may be feeling, you need to stop what you are doing, eliminate as many distractions as possible, and focus fully on the other person.[18] Two listening researchers conducted a study to identify the specific behaviors of good listeners.[19] What they discovered supports our admonition that the first thing you must do to be a better listener is to stop focusing on your own thoughts and instead be other-oriented. Specifically, you should take five actions during what the researchers called the "pre-interaction phase" of listening:

- Put your own thoughts aside.
- Be there mentally, not just physically.
- Make a conscious, mindful effort to listen.
- Take adequate time to listen—don't rush the speaker; be patient.
- Be open-minded.[20]

It boils down to this: When you listen, you are either on task or off task. When you're on task, you stop to focus on the message and make relevant mental observations about the message.[21]

2. Look—Now look for clues that help you identify how the other person is feeling. Most communication of emotion comes through nonverbal cues. The face provides important information about how a person is feeling, as do voice quality, pitch, rate, volume, and use of silence. Body movement and posture clearly indicate the intensity of a person's feelings. It is also important that you look at others when you are listening to them. Eye contact is how we signal that we are focused on what they are saying.

3. Listen—Listen for what the other person is telling you. Even though that person may not say exactly how he or she feels, look for cues. Match verbal with nonverbal cues to decipher both the content and the emotion of the person's message. In addition, ask yourself, "How would I feel if I were in his or her position?" Try to interpret the message according to the sender's code system rather than your own. Another key listening skill: Don't interrupt someone. In fact, there is power in simply pausing and letting someone finish his or her statement before you respond.

4. ***Ask Appropriate Questions***—As you try to understand another person, you may need to ask questions. Most of them will serve one of four purposes:
   1. To obtain additional information ("How soon will you be ready to give your part of our presentation?")
   2. To find out how someone feels ("Are you feeling overwhelmed by this assignment?")
   3. To ask for clarification of a word or phrase ("What do you mean when you say you didn't realize what you were getting into?")
   4. To verify your conclusion about your partner's meaning or feeling ("Are you saying that you can't complete the project without some additional staff assistance?")
5. ***Paraphrase Feelings***—Restate in your own words what you think the other person is saying. Paraphrasing is different from parroting back everything that person has said. After all, you can repeat something perfectly without understanding what it means. Rather, from time to time, summarize the message the other person has given you so far. Paraphrasing can help both the listener's and the speaker's understanding. Paraphrasing is also associated with increased liking for the listener.[22]

   Emily: I think this job is too much for me; I'm not qualified to do it.

   Malik: You think you lack the necessary skills.

At this point, Malik is dealing only with the content of Emily's message. The goal of active listening, though, is to understand both the feelings and the content of the other person's message.

In this example, Malik could follow his paraphrase of the content of the message with a question, such as "You're probably feeling pretty frustrated right now, aren't you?" Such a paraphrase would allow Emily either to agree with Malik's assessment or to clarify how she's feeling. For instance, she might respond, "No, I'm not frustrated. I'm just disappointed that the job's not working out."

To summarize active listening skills: *Act* like an active listener and *suspend judgment*. Effective listening skills can contribute a great deal to building a supportive, cohesive group.[23] Listening is the quintessential leadership skill.[24] Effective listening is also the cornerstone of critical thinking—the skill required to make decisions and solve problems effectively.

7.3: Applying Nonverbal Communication Research to Groups

OBJECTIVE: Apply research findings about nonverbal communication to groups

The second step of active listening is looking for nonverbal communication. **Nonverbal communication** is communication behavior that does not rely on written or spoken words. It includes body posture and movement, eye contact, facial expression, seating arrangement, spatial relationships, personal appearance, use of time, and even tone of voice. Although the words someone utters are not classified as nonverbal communication, the pitch, quality, and intonation of the voice, the rate of speaking, and the use of silence can speak volumes; thus, vocal tone is considered part of nonverbal communication.

Every message contains both content and information about relationships. Nonverbal messages, particularly facial expression and vocal cues, are often the primary source of information about interpersonal relationships. Thus, they play important functions in metacommunication—that is, communication about communication. The nonverbal aspects of a message communicate information about its verbal aspects.

Relatively few studies have investigated nonverbal behavior in groups, as researchers have found this aspect of communication difficult to observe and investigate. When group members simultaneously emit myriad nonverbal behaviors, it is difficult to systematically observe and interpret them. In addition, nonverbal messages are considerably more ambiguous than verbal messages. We suggest that you exercise caution, then, in attempting to interpret other group members' nonverbal behavior.

Fortunately, research has been conducted that can help you become more sensitive to your own nonverbal behavior and to the role nonverbal communication plays in group discussions. Specifically, researchers have investigated the following aspects of nonverbal group communication:

- Physical posture, movement, and gestures
- Eye contact
- Facial expressions
- Vocal cues
- Personal space
- Territoriality
- Seating arrangement
- Personal appearance
- The communication environment[25]

By the end of this module, you will be able to:

7.3.1 **Summarize the influence of nonverbal communication on group interactions**

7.3.2 **Describe the five major types of nonverbal behavior**

7.3.3 **Interpret eye contact in the context of group communication**

7.3.4 **Identify the facial expressions that communicate emotions**

7.3.5 **Relate vocal cues to group communication**

7.3.6 **Contextualize seating in a small group environment**

7.3.7 **Explain how the use of space reflects relationships in a group**

7.3.1: The Importance of Nonverbal Communication

OBJECTIVE: **Summarize the influence of nonverbal communication on group interactions**

You have undoubtedly participated in group and team meetings that were dull. Although poor or inappropriate nonverbal communication isn't always the reason for unexciting group discussion, group members' posture, facial expression, tone of voice, and unspoken enthusiasm (or lack of it) can dramatically affect a group's climate.

In a group or team discussion, usually only one person speaks at a time. The other members can, however, emit a host of nonverbal cues that influence the deliberations. (Some cues are controlled consciously, others are emitted less intentionally.) Eye contact, facial expression, body posture, and movement occur even when only one person is speaking. Because group members are usually within just a few feet of one another, they can easily observe most nonverbal cues. In other words, it is safe to say that "you cannot not communicate."

We'll examine three reasons why nonverbal communication is important to group discussion.

Why Is Nonverbal Communication Important?

Whether through sight, sound, smell, or touch, the majority of the social meaning in our interactions is elicited nonverbally. We enjoy "people watching" because even when people say nothing, their behavior is meaningful—their energy level, their attire, their hairstyles, and their physical characteristics. Human behavior communicates nonverbally.

More Time Is Spent Communicating Nonverbally Than Verbally

If a group member is dissatisfied with the group, you will probably detect those feelings by observing his or her nonverbal behavior—even before he or she verbalizes any frustration. If a member seems genuinely interested in the discussion and pleased with the group's progress, this, too, is observable through nonverbal behavior. Albert Mehrabian and some of his colleagues devised a formula that suggests how much of the emotional meaning of a message is based on verbal versus nonverbal components.[26] According to this research, only 7 percent of the emotional meaning of a message is communicated through its verbal content. About 38 percent of the emotional content is derived from the voice (its pitch, quality, and volume and the rate of speech). The largest source of emotional meaning, 55 percent, is a speaker's facial expression. Thus, approximately 93 percent of the emotional portion of a message is communicated nonverbally! Although these percentages cannot be applied to all situations, Mehrabian's research suggests that when inconsistencies exist between people's verbalized emotional states and their true emotions, expressed nonverbally, nonverbal cues carry more weight in determining how receivers interpret speakers' emotions.

Emotions and Feelings Are Typically Expressed Nonverbally

Nonverbal communication affects how others interpret our messages. Nonverbal cues are so important to communication that when a verbal message (either spoken or written) contradicts a nonverbal message, people are more inclined to believe the nonverbal message. The group member who sighs and, with a sarcastic edge, says, "Oh, what a great group this is going to be," communicates just the opposite meaning of that verbal message. One researcher suggests that as much as 65 percent of the way we convey meaning is through nonverbal channels.[27]

Nonverbal Messages Are Usually More Believable Than Verbal Messages

An understanding of nonverbal communication, then, is vital to even a superficial understanding of communication in general and of group communication in particular. As you become a more skillful observer of nonverbal behavior, you will understand with greater clarity the way people interact in small groups.

7.3.2: Posture, Movement, and Gestures

OBJECTIVE: Describe the five major types of nonverbal behavior

To observe and analyze posture, movement, and gestures, Paul Ekman and Wallace Friesen have identified five major types of nonverbal behavior[28]:

1. **Emblems** are nonverbal cues that have specific verbal counterparts and are shared by all group members. Emblems often take the place of spoken words, letters, or numbers. Group leaders who place index fingers vertically in front of their lips use a nonverbal emblem to take the place of the words "Shhhh, let's be quiet now." A hitchhiker's raised thumb and a soldier's salute are other examples of emblems. Group members who point to their watches to indicate that the group should get on with it because time is running out, or who use the thumbs-up signal to indicate that all is well, also depend on nonverbal emblems to communicate their messages.
2. **Illustrators** are nonverbal behaviors that add meaning to the accompanying verbal messages. For example, a group member who emphasizes a spoken message while jabbing a raised index finger in the air with each word illustrates conviction and determination. Several researchers have observed that people synchronize many of their body movements to their speech.[29] A blink of the eyes, a nod of the head, or a shift in body posture can accent spoken messages.
3. An **affect display** communicates emotion. The face is the primary source of emotional display, but the body indicates the intensity of the emotion being expressed. For example, the faces of group members may indicate that they are bored. If they are also slouched in their chairs, they are probably more than just moderately apathetic about the discussion.
4. **Regulators** are nonverbal behaviors that help control the flow of communication; people rely on them to know when they should talk and when they should listen. Eye contact, posture, gestures, facial expression, and body position all help regulate communication. Generally, large groups operate with a rather formal set of regulators; for example, participants may raise their hands so that the chairperson will recognize them. In a less formal discussion, group members rely on direct eye contact (to indicate that a communication channel is open), facial expression (raised eyebrows often signify a desire to talk), and gestures (such as a raised index finger) as cues to regulate the flow of communication. When nonverbal regulators are absent, such as during virtual collaboration when team members are not in the same physical location, team members have a more difficult time coordinating their conversation.
5. **Adaptors** are nonverbal acts that satisfy personal needs and help people adapt to their immediate environment, such as shifting in a chair for greater comfort. Generally, people are not aware of most of their adaptive nonverbal behavior. Self-adaptors, for example, are things people do to their own bodies, such as scratching, biting their nails, or twirling their hair. When people become nervous, anxious, or upset, they frequently display more self-adaptive behaviors.[30]

Can you identify some nonverbal communication elements here?

7.3.3: Eye Contact

OBJECTIVE: Interpret eye contact in the context of group communication

Have you ever felt uncomfortable because the person you were talking to seemed reluctant to establish eye contact? Maybe you've wondered, "Why doesn't she look at me when she's talking to me?" Perhaps you've had just the opposite experience—the person you were talking to would not stop staring at you. You become uneasy in these situations because they violate norms of eye contact. Although you may think that you do a relatively good job of establishing eye contact with others, researchers estimate that most people look at others only between 30 and 60 percent of the time.[31] Eye contact usually lasts less than 10 seconds.

Several factors determine when you look at another person:[32]

- You are listening rather than talking.
- You like the other person.
- You want to persuade or influence someone.
- You have a high need for approval or affiliation.
- You seek a response from someone.

Other circumstances will dictate when you are less likely to have eye contact:

- You are from a culture in which people tend not to look directly at others.
- You are embarrassed.
- You do not want to talk or participate in the discussion.
- You don't like someone.
- You are shy or introverted.
- You have a low need for approval.

Functions of Eye Contact[33]

When eye contact does occur in a small group setting, it may serve one or more important functions:

Cognitive Function—The cognitive function of eye contact (or lack of it) is to indicate thought processes. For example, some people look away when they are thinking of just the right word to say. Others look away before they speak so they won't be distracted by the person to whom they are talking.

Monitoring Function—Monitoring is the way you seek feedback from others when communicating with them. You make eye contact to determine how your message is being received. For example, if you say something that other group members disagree with, you may observe a change in their facial expressions, body posture, or restless movement. Because you've monitored their nonverbal expressions, you may then decide that you need to spend more time explaining your point.

Regulatory Function—Eye contact plays a vital role in regulating the back-and-forth flow of communication; it signals when the communication channel is open or closed. You can invite interaction simply by looking at others. If the chair of a committee asks for volunteers and you don't want to participate, you are unlikely to establish eye contact. Nonverbally this behavior says, "I don't want to talk; I don't want to participate."

Expressive Function—Although eyes generally do not provide clues about specific emotions, the areas of the face immediately around the eyes provide quite a bit of information about feelings, emotions, and attitudes.

Thus, eye contact—or lack of it—reveals information about thought processes, provides feedback, regulates communication channels, and expresses emotions. Eye contact also provides clues about status and leadership roles in small groups. Group members who talk more receive more eye contact.[34] In addition, eye contact is the predominant cue that regulates when you want to speak and when you want to stop speaking during group discussion.[35] When you engage in eye contact when speaking with others, you enhance your credibility.[36] In the next small group meeting you attend, determine who receives the most eye contact in the group. Where do group members look for information and guidance? They probably look at the group leader.

Review

Functions of Eye Contact

- Cognitive function: Provides cues about thought processes
- Monitoring function: Allows feedback from others
- Regulatory function: Signals when the communication channel is open and closed
- Expressive function: Provides information about feelings, emotions, and attitudes

7.3.4: Facial Expressions

OBJECTIVE: Identify the facial expressions that communicate emotions

The face is the most important revealer of emotions. Sometimes you can mask your emotional expressions, but the face is usually the first place you look to determine someone's emotional state. Facial expressions are particularly significant in face-to-face interpersonal and small group communication. Although the face can produce thousands of different expressions, researchers have identified six primary emotions: happiness, anger, surprise, sadness, disgust, and fear.[37]

Researchers have also developed a method of identifying which areas of the face play the most important roles in communicating emotion.[38] People communicate happiness with the area around their eyes and with smiles and raised cheeks. They reveal disgust with raised upper lips, wrinkled noses, lowered eyelids, and lowered brows; and fear with the area around their eyes, but with open mouths. When they are angry, people are likely to lower their eyebrows and stare intensely. They show surprise with raised eyebrows, wide-open eyes, and often open mouths; and sadness in the area around the eyes and mouth. Being able to recognize anger, contempt, disgust, fear, and sadness on someone's face has been shown to enhance the ability to manage conflict. Like an early warning system, noting that someone may be upset—before the person verbalizes his or her frustration—can be important in trying to defuse or manage conflict.[39]

Facial Expressions for the Six Primary Emotions

Expressions	Emotions
	Fear
	Anger
	Happiness
	Surprise

Expressions	Emotions
	Disgust
	Sadness
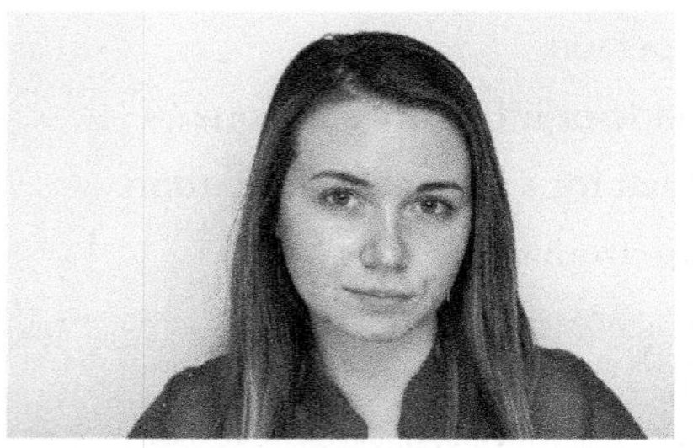	Ambiguous. Which emotion—or combination of emotions—could she be expressing?

Review

Categories of Nonverbal Communication

Category	Description	Example
Emblems	Movements and gestures that replace spoken messages	Group members shake their heads to communicate "no"
Illustrators	Nonverbal behaviors that add meaning to accompany verbal communication	A group member holds her hands 3 feet apart while saying, "We'll need about a yard of fabric"
Affect displays	Expressions of feeling	Frowning, smiling, grimacing, smirking
Regulators	Nonverbal behaviors that control the flow of communication within a group	Eye contact, raising a hand or a finger to signal you want to talk
Adaptors	Nonverbal acts that satisfy personal needs and help group members adapt to their environment	Scratching, yawning, adjusting your glasses

7.3.5: Vocal Cues

OBJECTIVE: Relate vocal cues to group communication

"Demetrius," remarked a group discussion member, obviously upset, "it's not that I object to what you said; it's just the way you said it." The pitch, rate, volume, and quality of your voice (also called **paralanguage**) are important in determining the meanings of messages. From a speaker's paralanguage cues, you can make inferences about how that person feels toward you. You can also base inferences about a person's competence and personality on vocal cues. A speaker who mispronounces words and uses "uhs" and "ums" will probably be judged as less credible than a speaker who is more articulate.[40]

Sometimes vocal cues contradict the verbal content. For example, if someone shouts "I'M NOT ANGRY!!!!!!!" or "I couldn't care less what she thinks!!!", the forceful vocal cue is much more believable than the verbal content. Vocal cues are powerful determinants of meaning.

WRITING PROMPT

Interpreting Vocal Cues

"Don't look at me in that tone of voice!"

This statement has its amusing elements, but it also acknowledges that tone of voice carries emotional meaning just as much as posture and gesture. When conflict arises in a group relationship, do you attend most to verbal, vocal, facial, or body language to read the emotions? When you're upset, what are the primary signals that you send to show your feelings? Would others know your feelings from vocal cues alone?

▶ The response entered here will appear in the performance dashboard and can be viewed by your instructor.

7.3.6: Seating Arrangement

OBJECTIVE: Contextualize seating in a small group environment

The area of study known as **small group ecology** examines the consistent way in which people arrange themselves in small, face-to-face groups. Understanding the effects of seating arrangement can give you insights into who is likely to talk to whom, who may emerge as a leader, and what will be the overall effects of seating arrangement on the communication climate in the group.

SEATING ARRANGEMENT AND INTERACTION PATTERNS Where you sit in a group can have an effect on who you are likely to talk to. When group members are seated in a circle, they are more likely to talk with those individuals across from them than to those persons on either side.[41] One research team observed groups of three people in snack bars, restaurants, and lounges and found that individuals who are more centrally located and most visible in a group usually receive more eye contact from others.[42] They also tend to initiate more communication than those who are less centrally located in the group. Furthermore, when other group members speak, they tend to direct their comments more to these centrally located members in the group. Group members in the center of the group tend to speak most often.[43]

Based on where people sit, their eye contact with others is an important factor in determining who speaks, who listens, and who has the greatest opportunity to dominate a conversation. Figure 7-1 illustrates some typical interaction patterns influenced by seating arrangement.

SEATING ARRANGEMENT AND LEADERSHIP EMERGENCE Where you sit in a group or team can influence

Figure 7-1 Group Interaction Patterns Are Influenced by Seating Arrangement

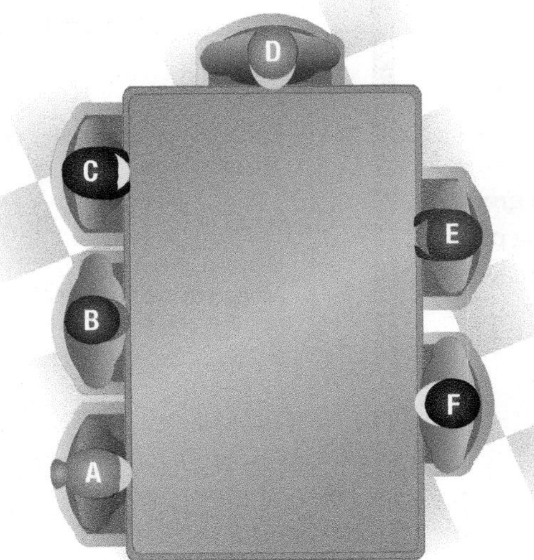

Person A:
A person sitting at a corner seat often contributes less to the group; the person is farther away from the "power seat" (person D).

Person D:
The person seated at the head of a rectangular table is often perceived as being seated in the "leadership seat."

Persons E and F:
The person who selects a seat that maximizes eye contact with others typically has greater control over the group's interaction; eye contact is a key variable that regulates who talks and who listens.

your chances of emerging as a leader. If you like to lead others, you may typically select a seat from which you can see other people in the group and maximize your eye contact with them. In one study, researchers had groups of five people seat themselves around a table: Three people sat on one side of the table, and the other two sat opposite them.[44] They discovered that participants had a greater probability of becoming leaders if they sat on the side of the table facing the three discussion members. The ability to make direct eye contact with more group members, which can subsequently result in greater control of verbal communication, may explain why the two individuals who faced the other three emerged as leaders.

There is also evidence that a person who aspires to leadership will select a seat to maximize his or her interaction with others. Dominant group members tend to select a seat at the head of a rectangular table or one that maximizes the opportunity to communicate with others.[45] In contrast, people who sit at the corners of tables generally contribute the least to a discussion and are less likely to emerge as leaders. Again, eye contact coupled with seating arrangement seems to be a major predictor of leadership emergence.

SEATING ARRANGEMENT AND STRESS Some people prefer greater personal space when they are under stress.[46] If, as a group or team leader, you know that an upcoming discussion will produce anxiety, hold the meeting in a room that permits members more freedom of movement. This will allow them to find their preferred personal distance from other group members. Or, if you know that an upcoming meeting may produce conflict, arrange the chairs so that there is more space around each participant. Crowding people together can amplify whatever emotions group members may feel.

SEATING ARRANGEMENT AND GENDER Evidence suggests that in North America, women tend to sit closer to others than men do (whether those others are men or women). Men generally prefer greater personal space when sitting next to other men.[47] We're not suggesting that you use this research conclusion to measure the distance between seats in an upcoming meeting; instead, simply realize that men and women may differ in terms of how much space they prefer to have around them. Where possible, let group members adjust their own seating distance from other members.

Collectively, the research on seating suggests that people do arrange themselves with some consistency in small group discussions. A discussion leader who understands seating preferences will be able to provide a comfortable group climate.

7.3.7: Personal Space

OBJECTIVE: Explain how the use of space reflects relationships in a group

The next time you are sitting in class, note the seat you select. Even though no one instructed you to do so, chances are that you tend to sit in the same general area, if not in the same seat, during each class. Perhaps in your family each person sits at a certain place at the dinner table. If someone sits in your chair, you may feel your territory has been invaded and try to reclaim your seat. Human behavior with respect to personal space and territoriality reflects competition between the need for affiliation with others and the need for privacy.[48]

Research pioneer Edward T. Hall investigated the silent language of how we use the personal space around us. His investigation of **proxemics**—the study of how close or far away we choose to be to other people and objects—helps us better understand how our use of personal space gives us clues about our relationships with others.[49]

Hall identified four spatial zones that people in Western cultures typically use, depending on the activity and nature of the relationship they have with those around them. Figure 7-2 illustrates each of these zones.

Of course, not every person you'll meet will interact with you using these zones; these are just estimates of typical interactions with others.

Review

Small Group Ecology

Interaction Patterns

- Whom you have eye contact with during group discussions usually affects whom you talk with.
- People who are more centrally located in a group often receive more oral messages from other group members than do people who are less central.
- You are more likely to talk with people seated directly across from you than with those next to you.

Leadership

- We often expect the person seated at the head of a rectangular table to be the leader.
- More outspoken, dominant individuals often choose to sit at the head of the table.
- People who sit at the corner of a rectangular table often contribute less to the discussion and consequently may have less influence in the group.
- People who are perceived to have high status are given more personal space around them.

Stress

- During times of stress or conflict, people prefer more space around them.

Gender

- Women generally sit a bit closer to others than men do.
- Men tend to prefer greater personal space when sitting next to other men.

TERRITORIALITY **Territoriality** is a term used in the study of animal behavior to refer to how animals stake out and defend given areas. Humans exhibit this behavior, too. Understanding territoriality may help you understand certain group behaviors. At the next meeting you attend, observe how people attempt to stake out territories. If the group is

Figure 7-2 Edward T. Hall's Four Zones of Space

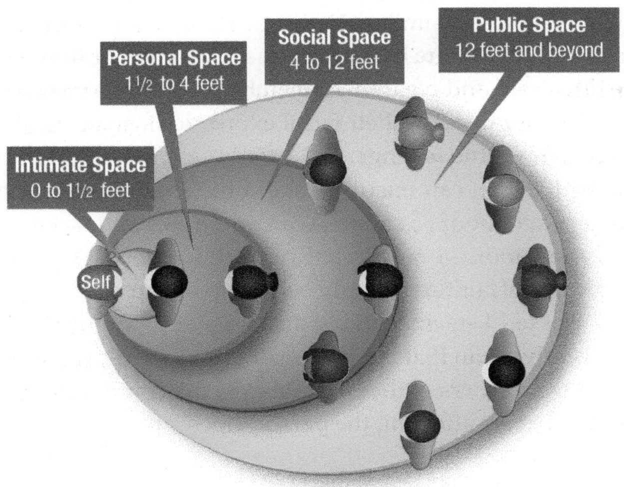

- **Intimate Zone:** Between 0 and 1½ feet. This is the zone in which our most personal and intimate conversation occurs. It would be unusual in a group to have someone this close to you unless you are whispering something confidential in his or her ear.
- **Personal Zone:** Between 1½ and 4 feet. Most conversations with family and friends occur in this zone. Group members may sit within this zone, but even at 4 feet we may feel that the other person is too close.
- **Social Zone:** Between 4 and 12 feet. Most group interaction happens within this zone. This is also the zone in which interaction with colleagues and other professionals occurs.
- **Public Zone:** 12 feet and beyond. Teachers and public speakers typically communicate with at least 12 feet between speaker and listener.

seated around a table, do members place objects in front of and around themselves to signify that they are claiming territory? Higher-status individuals generally attempt to claim more territory.[50] Notice how group members manipulate their posture and gestures if their space is invaded. Lower-status individuals generally permit greater territorial invasion. Also note how individuals claim their territory by leaving markers—such as books, papers, or a pencil—when they have to leave the group but expect to return shortly.

Skilled Collaboration

Improving Nonverbal Communication Skills

Body Posture, Movement, and Gestures

- You will be more effective when you use eye contact, maintain a direct body orientation, and remain physically close to others.
- You can often identify high-status group members (or at least those who perceive themselves as having high status) by such nonverbal cues as relaxed postures, loud voices, territorial dominance, expansive movements, and, sometimes, their tendency to keep themselves at a distance from others.

Eye Contact

- People sometimes interrupt eye contact with others because they are trying to think of the right words to say, not because they are uninterested.
- When talking with others in a small group, be sure to look at all members so that you can respond to the feedback they provide.
- You sometimes can draw a person into the conversation just by establishing direct eye contact, or quiet an overly talkative member by avoiding it.

Personal Space and Territoriality

- Members typically stake out their territory or personal space early in group gatherings.
- Because people prefer greater personal space when they are under stress, make sure group members have plenty of territory when you know that a meeting is going to be stressful.

Seating Arrangement

- If you want to increase your interaction with a group member, sit directly across from him or her.
- If you know that a group member generally monopolizes the conversation, try to get that person to select a corner seat rather than one at the head of a conference table.
- You are more likely to emerge as a group leader if you sit so that you can establish eye contact and a direct body orientation with shoulders squared toward most of the group members.

Review

Sources of Nonverbal Cues

Posture, movement, and gestures	Provide information regarding status, intensity of attitude, warmth, approval seeking, group climate, immediacy, deception.
Eye contact	Serves cognitive, monitoring, regulatory, and expressive functions.
Facial expression	Communicates emotion, especially happiness, anger, surprise, sadness, disgust, and fear.
Vocal cues	The pitch, rate, volume, and quality of the voice communicate emotion, credibility, and personality perceptions.
Personal space, territoriality, and seating arrangement	People in Western cultures use four zones of personal space, depending on their interpersonal relationships. They arrange themselves in consistent ways in groups and stake out space to reflect status, roles, stress levels, leadership, and personality traits.

7.4: Interpreting Nonverbal Communication

OBJECTIVE: Interpret nonverbal communication in a group context

Nonverbal cues do not create meaning independently of other communication cues (such as message content, language style, and message organization). Although there is much we still do not know about nonverbal communication, several principles apply when ascribing meaning to the posture and movement of others.

By the end of this module, you will be able to:

- **7.4.1 Contextualize cues seen in group communication**
- **7.4.2 Identify differences that influence communication**
- **7.4.3 Describe Mehrabian's model on how people interpret nonverbal behaviors**
- **7.4.4 Explain when to use perception checking**

7.4.1: Look for Cues in Context

OBJECTIVE: Contextualize cues seen in group communication

Look for a pattern of cues to help you interpret what a specific behavior means, rather than considering only one gesture, expression, or use of personal space. Seek corroborating cues can help you reach a more accurate conclusion about what a specific behavior means. For example, upon observing whether someone makes eye contact, also note whether vocal cues, posture, and gestures confirm your conclusion.

Facial expressions are important sources of information about a group's emotional climate, particularly if several members express similar emotions. Their expressions may suggest that they are bored with the discussion or that they are interested and pleased. Remember that group members may attempt to mask their facial expressions in an effort to conceal their true feelings.

Just as you can misunderstand the meaning of a sentence taken out of context, so can you make an inaccurate inference about a nonverbal behavior when it is interpreted out of context. Simply because a group member sits with crossed legs and folded arms, that posture does not necessarily mean that the person does not want to communicate with others. Other variables in the communication system may be affecting the person's posture and position.

7.4.2: Recognize Differences

OBJECTIVE: Identify differences that influence communication

Not all people express emotions in the same manner. Every individual is unique, and it may take considerable time before you can truly understand the underlying meaning of another person's specific nonverbal behaviors.

Keep the person's cultural background or gender in mind when you draw an inference from his or her nonverbal behavior. There is no nonverbal behavior that has a universal, generally accepted meaning. Even though some evidence indicates that facial expressions can be interpreted across several cultures, there are subtle as well as dramatic differences in the way nonverbal behaviors may be interpreted. In small group interactions, it is especially interesting to observe cultural differences in how people use space and territory.[52]

Virtual Collaboration

Nonverbal Virtual Communication

Technology can facilitate communication by eliminating the constraints of time and space, but it has drawbacks as well. One drawback is the difficulty of communicating emotion, since people rely so much on tone of voice and visual cues to ascertain others' feelings and reactions.

One study examined the performance of 64 virtual teams using four modes of technological collaboration: text only, audio only, text and video, and audio and video. The study found no significant difference in the quality of strategic decisions made by teams using text-only communication versus those using audio-only communication. When video was added to audio communication, however, team decisions improved significantly.[51]

The study leads to some recommendations about nonverbal communication in virtual groups. Consider the following:

- Whenever possible, groups and teams should meet face to face. There is no substitute for the "full picture" we get when in the presence of another human being.
- Especially in the formative stages of group interaction, meeting face to face is critical to help members get to know one another and to build predictability and trust. When face-to-face communication is not possible, video conferencing can improve the quality of a group's work.
- When face-to-face or video communication is not possible and you are limited to text or audio interactions, pay extra attention to emotional cues. Hearing a sigh, a yawn, or a nervous giggle—or seeing the word "sigh" or an emoticon :-) in the text on your screen—will help you interpret verbal messages.

WRITING PROMPT

Communication in Context

To know someone well is to be able to predict how that person will respond in different situations. Think about someone you know well. What are some specific things you know about this individual that help you predict his or her response in a given situation? Are cultural and gender factors involved? Is there a personal history or a personality quirk that come into play? Are there are things about this person that only you know? Can you see how other acquaintances might read this person differently, since they not have your deeper knowledge to help interpret the individual's responses?

▶ The response entered here will appear in the performance dashboard and can be viewed by your instructor.

Submit

7.4.3: Identify Cues That Communicate Liking, Power, and Responsiveness

OBJECTIVE: Describe Mehrabian's model on how people interpret nonverbal behaviors

Albert Mehrabian has developed a three-dimensional model that identifies how people respond to nonverbal messages. His research suggests that people derive meaning from nonverbal behavior based on the following:[53]

1. *Immediacy: behaviors that communicate liking and disliking.* Immediacy refers to whether people like or dislike others. The immediacy principle states that "people are drawn toward persons and things they like, evaluate highly, and prefer; and they avoid or move away from things they dislike, evaluate negatively, or do not prefer."[54] According to Mehrabian, such nonverbal behaviors as touching, leaning forward, reducing distance and personal space, and maintaining direct eye contact communicate liking or positive feelings. Based on the immediacy principle, group members who consistently sit closer to you, establish more eye contact with you, and, in general, are drawn to you probably like you more than group members who generally do not look at you and who regularly select seats away from you.
2. *Power: behaviors that communicate influence and status.* People of higher status generally determine the degree of closeness permitted in their interactions; a person of higher status and influence usually is surrounded by more space. A boss who sits at the head of the table is more likely to have empty chairs around him or her. A person of higher status generally has a more relaxed body posture when interacting with a person of lower status. High-status members also tend to have less eye contact with others, to use a louder voice, and to make more expansive movements and postures. In addition, the way they dress may reflect their elevated status.
3. *Responsiveness: behaviors that communicate interest and attention.* Body movements, facial expressions, and variation of vocal cues (such as pitch, rate, volume, and tone) all contribute to our perceptions of others as responsive or unresponsive. A group member who communicates energy and enthusiasm would be rated as highly responsive.

Ethical Collaboration

Advantages of Understanding Nonverbal Communication

An understanding of nonverbal communication and small group ecology can be used strategically to influence group interaction and group outcomes. For example, one of our friends has been seated twice on trial juries. In each case, when the jury moved to the jury room to deliberate, our friend walked confidently to the head of the table, put his hands on the table while intently surveying the faces of his fellow jurors, and said, "Well, the first thing we need to do is to elect a foreman." He was elected unanimously in both cases.

WRITING PROMPT

Strategically Using Nonverbal Communication

Imagine that you have been assigned to a task group with no designated leader. For a variety of reasons, you believe that you should be elected the leader. The information you've learned has given you insight into how you can manage the group's impression of you and of your competence through strategic use of nonverbal behaviors and small group ecology principles. Is it ethical for you to use what you know to get elected? Or does doing so amount to unfairly manipulating the group?

The response entered here will appear in the performance dashboard and can be viewed by your instructor.

Submit

Review

Dimensions of Nonverbal Meaning

Dimension	Definition	Nonverbal Cues
Immediacy	Behaviors that signal liking, attraction, and interest	Touching, forward leaning, close personal space, eye contact
Power	Behaviors that communicate power, status, and influence	Protected space, increased distance, relaxed posture
Responsiveness	Behaviors that communicate active interactions and attention	Eye contact, varied vocal cues, animated facial expression

7.4.4: Develop the Skill of Perception Checking

OBJECTIVE: Explain when to use perception checking

People judge you by your behavior, not by your intent. You judge others the same way—by what you see, not by what they are thinking. Unless you are a mind reader, the only way to check your perception of others' nonverbal behavior is to ask them. **Perception checking** is the skill of asking someone whether your interpretation of his or her unspoken message is accurate. It consists of three steps:

1. Observe the nonverbal cues (posture, movement, gestures, eye contact, facial expressions, vocal cues, personal space).
2. Mentally draw a conclusion about what the nonverbal behavior may mean.
3. Ask the other person if your inference was accurate.

Suppose you offer a solution to a problem your group has been discussing. After you announce your proposal, the group is silent, your colleagues break eye contact, and you see one person frown. To find out whether their nonverbal response means that your proposal has been rejected, you could ask, "Does your silence mean you don't like my idea?" We recommend that you not overuse perception checking. Stopping to seek confirmation of every facial expression or vocal tone would irritate others. However, do consider perception checking when you genuinely do not understand a group's or a group member's response.

These principles point to a key conclusion: Nonverbal messages are considerably more ambiguous than verbal messages. Always exercise caution when you attempt to interpret the nonverbal behavior of other people.

Review

Perception Checking

Steps	Factors to Consider
1. Observe someone's nonverbal behavior.	What is his or her facial expression? Does he or she make eye contact? What is his or her posture? What is his or her tone of voice?
2. Think about what the behavior may mean.	Does he or she appear to be angry, sad, depressed? Does the nonverbal message contradict the verbal message?
3. Check your perception by asking whether your interpretation is accurate.	"The expression on your face suggests you may be upset. Are you?"

CASE STUDY

Interpreting Indirect Communication

Scene One

Lourdes: Nice outfit. . . . Did you make it yourself?
Maria: No, my grandmother made it for me.
Lourdes: I was just wondering; it has such a "homespun" look.

Scene Two

She: Do these jeans make me look fat?
He: Uhhhhh. . . .

Scene Three

She: Dear, it's been a long time since we went out dancing on a Saturday night.
He: Sure has.

Scene Four

Boss: Thanks for coming in, Jean. I know it's short notice and you're pretty overloaded, but we have to get this contract done and back to the client first thing Monday morning. I'm looking for someone who can work over the weekend. Do you have any suggestions?
Jean: Let me check my calendar, Mr. Jefferson. Maybe I can do it.

Scene Five

She: Honey, I'm working on a guest list for our party. Did the Ronnings invite us to their open house last fall?
He: Beats me. . . .

Questions for Analysis: Interpreting Indirect Communication

1. These brief scenes are examples of indirect communication—the words convey a surface meaning that, with further analysis, may reveal deeper, unspoken meanings. Rewrite each scene using dialogue that is more direct.
2. If you were the recipient of the indirect communication in each case, what additional information would you need to verify whether your interpretation of the comment was correct? What nonverbal cues would you look for to help you interpret the comment in each case?
3. What emotions (if any) do you associate with these dialogues? Why? What nonverbal cues would you look for to identify these emotions?
4. What perception-checking responses might you use in similar situations?

Summary: Enhancing Communication Skills in Groups

7.1: Verbal Dynamics and Avoiding Communication Barriers

- Verbal barriers to communication include bypassing, allness statements, and fact–inference confusion.
- To avoid these barriers: Use specific language; be aware of multiple possible interpretations. Don't over generalize; remember that each individual is unique. Analyze. Learn to recognize the difference between a fact and an inference. Identify your own assumptions about conversational style. Work to adapt your style to the situation.

7.2: Listening

- The four listening styles are relational, analytical, critical, and task.
- Obstacles to listening include prejudging the communication and rehearsing a response.
- Be aware of your listening style. When listening, do so actively. Stop what you're doing; avoid doing anything that distracts you from listening. Look for nonverbal cues that can help you interpret what you're hearing. Listen with your eyes as well as with your ears. Listen for feelings; ask yourself how you would feel if you were in the other person's situation. Ask questions to clarify. Paraphrase content and feelings to confirm with the other person that you're understanding correctly. Act like an active listener and suspend judgment.

7.3: Applying Nonverbal Communication Research to Groups

- Emotions are typically expressed nonverbally, rather than verbally. More time is spent communicating nonverbally than verbally. Nonverbal messages are usually more believable than verbal messages.
- Areas of research related to nonverbal communication in groups include posture, movement, gestures, eye contact, facial expressions, personal space, territoriality, seating arrangement, personal appearance, and communication environments.

7.4: Interpreting Nonverbal Communication

- Interpret nonverbal communication in context. Look for clusters of cues. Consider your own past experience when interpreting nonverbal communication. Look for cues that communicate liking, power, and responsiveness. Develop the skill of perception checking.

SHARED WRITING

Functions of Nonverbal Cues

Describe how nonverbal behaviors may provide information about perceived honesty or dishonesty. Compare your answer to those of your classmates. Respond to their comments and invite them to respond to yours.

A minimum number of characters is required to post and earn points. After posting, your response can be viewed by your class and instructor, and you can participate in the class discussion.

Post

Chapter 8

Managing Conflict

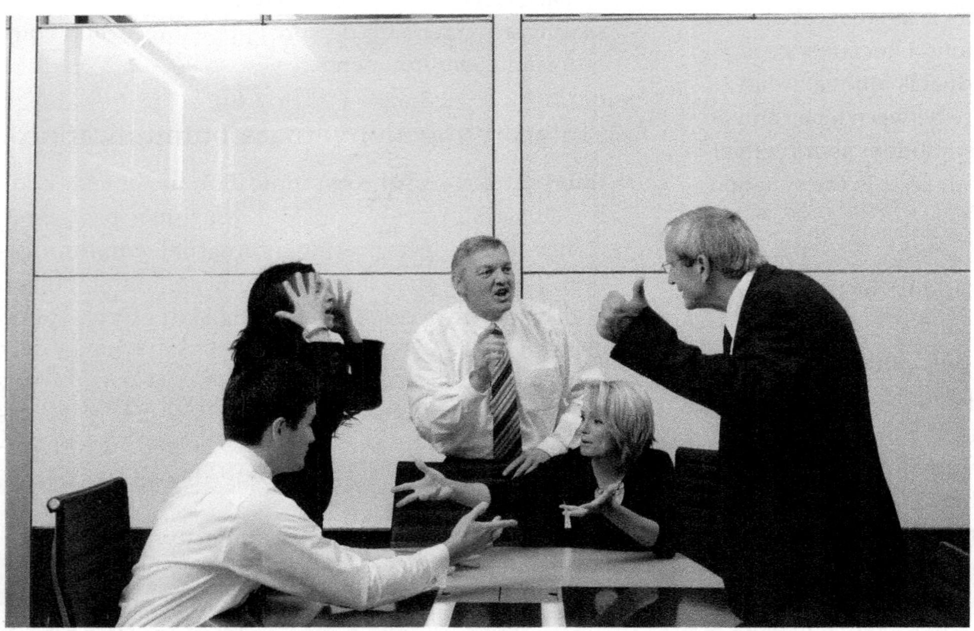

"When we all think alike, then no one is thinking."
—Walter Lippman

Learning Objectives

8.1 Analyze the ways in which conflicts are caused and maintained

8.2 Apply strategies for managing different kinds of conflict

8.3 Assess conflict management styles

8.4 Formulate solutions for groups that engage in groupthink

8.5 Use conflict management skills to address group problems

8.6 Apply strategies for reaching consensus

Adolph and his brother, Rudolph, lived in a small German town and had heard that the American sprinter Jesse Owens was coming to Germany to compete in the 1936 Berlin Olympics. The two brothers had a small cobbler shop and thought they would try making sports shoes for the famed runner. They approached Owens and asked if he would wear their shoes during the Olympic competition. Owens quickly accepted the offer of free shoes and proceeded to win four gold medals.

The two brothers parlayed that good fortune into subsequent success by making their small cobbler shop into a major producer of running shoes. There was just one problem: The two brothers didn't get along. In fact, they fought a lot. Eventually, because of the constant conflict, they decided to go their separate ways. Adolph, whose nickname was "Adi," took half of the shoemaking machines and started his own company on one side of the river in their town. You know it today as Adidas. Rudolph stayed on the other side of the river and called his new shoe company Puma. Their family conflict thus created two giant running-shoe corporations.[1]

Conflict is a fact of life. Throughout history, people have been involved in conflicts ranging from family feuds that spawned rival companies to nations that waged war against each other. Communication researchers and social psychologists conclude that when people interact with one another, they inevitably disagree.[2]

In this chapter, we will explore some ideas about the causes of conflict in groups and teams and propose strategies for managing it. Rather than aiming to eliminate group conflict, we'll discuss how to understand it and its importance in your group deliberations.

Despite the prevalence of conflict in group and team deliberations, much of what we know about group conflict has been generalized from research that has investigated interpersonal conflict.[3] It's important to understand how conflict in groups and teams can be both useful and detrimental to collaborative decision making.

8.1: Conflict Defined

OBJECTIVE: Analyze the ways in which conflicts are caused and maintained

Conflict happens when there is disagreement. Communication experts William Wilmot and Joyce Hocker[4] define *conflict* as:

1. **An expressed struggle:** A conflict becomes a concern to a group when the disagreement is expressed verbally or, more often, nonverbally. Early signs of conflict include furrowed brows, grimacing facial expressions, and flashes of frustration evident in the voice.[5] Research has found that the most dissenting group member is likely to receive more eye contact.[6] If the conflict persists, words are usually exchanged and unmanaged tempers may flare.
2. **Between at least two interdependent people:** From a systems theory perspective, people in a group are **interdependent**; what happens to one person influences others in the group. A conflict between even just two people in a group of five will undoubtedly affect the dynamics of the entire group.
3. **Incompatible goals, scarce resources, and interference:** Conflict often occurs because two or more people want the same thing, yet both can't have it. If resources are scarce or if something or someone is blocking what others want, conflict is likely to occur.
4. **Achieving a goal:** People involved in a conflict want something. Understanding this is an important step toward finding a way to manage the conflict.

Of course, if a group experienced no conflict, it would have little to discuss. One benefit of conflict is that it makes a group test and challenge ideas. However, conflict can be detrimental to group interaction and group decision making. Conflict has a negative impact on a group when it (1) keeps the group from completing its task, (2) interferes with the quality of the group's decision or productivity, or (3) threatens the existence of the group.[7]

By the end of this module, you will be able to:

- 8.1.1 **Identify origins of group conflict**
- 8.1.2 **Outline the stages of group conflict**
- 8.1.3 **Correct mistaken assumptions about conflict**

8.1.1: Causes of Conflict

OBJECTIVE: Identify origins of group conflict

Conflict doesn't just happen for no reason. Let's explore the causes of conflict so you can manage it when it does occur.

Sources of Conflict in Groups

Conflict results from differences between group members—differences in perception, personality, knowledge, culture, power, procedural expectations, and unequal resources.[8]

Perception—People literally see the world differently from one another; this difference in perspective results in differing attitudes, beliefs, and values that inevitably surface and cause conflict. No matter how much they try to empathize with others, people still have individual perspectives on the world.

Personality—Each person has a unique personality. Our personality differences that result in different group members' tolerance for taking risks also contribute to group conflict. By their very nature, some people are comfortable taking risks; others aren't.[9]

Knowledge—People also differ in the amount of knowledge they have about various topics. Group members soon realize that some of them are more experienced or more widely read than others. This difference in information contributes to different attitudes.

Culture—**Culture** is a learned system of knowledge, behavior, attitudes, beliefs, values, and norms that is shared by a group of people. The human tendency to tribalize and sort ourselves into groups according to our culture gives us identity with our cultural group and also contributes to the different ways humans experience life. Culturally diverse groups often experience more conflict than less culturally diverse groups.[10]

For example, **individualistic cultures** place emphasis on individual achievements, while **collectivistic cultures** emphasize group accomplishments.[11] Stella Ting-Toomey suggests that people in individualistic cultures are more likely to use direct, confrontational methods of managing disagreements than people who value a collective or team approach to group work. She also suggests that people from collectivistic cultures, especially cultures that place considerable stock in nonverbal messages, prefer nonconfrontational and indirect methods of resolving differences.[12]

Power and Status—People also have different levels of power, status, and influence over others—and all of these differences can increase conflict. People with power often try to use that power to influence others, but most people do not like to be told what to do or think.

Procedural Expectations—Conflict can also occur because of disagreement about procedures. Research suggests that entrenched disagreements about process issues (such as how decisions will be made) can be more disruptive over the long haul than a simple disagreement about a specific task issue.[13]

Perceived Resource Inequity—If we think someone has more resources or is getting more than his or her fair share, conflict often results.[14] Perceptions of fairness and inequity are especially powerful conflict triggers when resources are scarce and we think others have more than we have.

WRITING PROMPT

Identifying Sources of Conflict

Think about a recent group or team meeting in which you participated where conflict was present. What was the primary source of the conflict? Describe how the conflict began and how it affected the group's productivity.

The response entered here will appear in the performance dashboard and can be viewed by your instructor.

Submit

8.1.2: Stages of Conflict

OBJECTIVE: Outline the stages of group conflict

Conflict does not just happen; instead, it unfolds as a process influenced by conflict triggers. Communication scholar B. Aubrey Fisher found that group deliberations can be organized around four phases: orientation, conflict, emergence, and reinforcement.[15] Several researchers have discovered that the **conflict phase** in groups often emerges in predictable stages.[16]

1. **Persuasion:** We may first try to use logic and reasoning to convince others that we have not been treated fairly. Diplomats, for example, first try to appeal to equity differences based on the law and legal precedents.
2. **Seduction:** If logical and rational approaches to addressing the inequity don't work, we may try more seductive ways to "sweet talk" the other person or persons into being more equitable. We tend to use more emotional language when our logical, rational approaches don't work.
3. **Verbal aggression:** When both the logical appeals and emotional trying-to-catch-flies-with-honey methods aren't successful, we may threaten the other person or use appeals to fear. We may say, "If you don't give me X, then I will do Y to you." If the mild threats aren't successful, we may throttle up the intensity of the threat and become more aggressive.
4. **Physical action:** When all else fails, we may try to take the matter into our own hands and get what we want. Nations that feel they simply have no other choice resort to war. Physical aggression is usually preceded by persuasion, seduction, and verbal aggression.

Sequence of Conflict

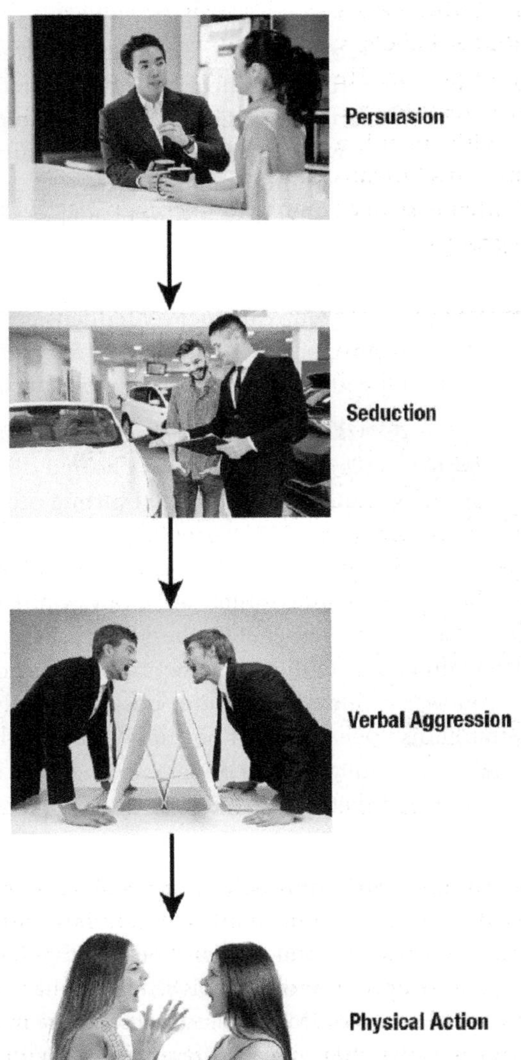

8.1.3: Misconceptions about Conflict

OBJECTIVE: Correct mistaken assumptions about conflict

People often make incorrect assumptions about the role of conflict in groups because they think that conflict is always bad and should be avoided. Considering the rates of divorce, crime, and international political tensions, it is understandable that we view conflict negatively.

Mistaken Assumptions about Conflict

The following misconceptions about conflict highlight some of the feelings you may have about conflict and point out how a different attitude might improve the quality of your group discussions.[17]

Misconception 1: Conflict Should Be Avoided at All Costs—Conflict is a natural by-product of communication. Unless participants in your group share the same attitudes, beliefs, and values (an unlikely situation), some conflict is apt to occur. Several studies have found that conflict is an important, even useful, part of group communication.[18] Members who believe that conflict is unhealthy may become frustrated when conflict erupts in a group. They should realize that conflict probably will occur and that it is a natural and healthy part of group communication.[19]

Group conflict can also spur group members to share more information with one another than they would if everyone simply agreed on the issues discussed. Research has found that dissent in a group can uncover hidden agendas—so the quality of group discussion can actually *increase* when people express different ideas, opinions, and perspectives.[20]

Misconception 2: All Conflict Occurs Due to Lack of Understanding—Have you ever been in a heated disagreement with someone and found yourself blurting out, "You just don't understand me!"? It's easy to assume that conflict occurs because another person does not understand your position, but not all conflicts arise out of misunderstandings. You may believe that if others really understood you, they would agree with you. Sometimes conflict occurs because you *have* communicated your position clearly, and others simply disagree with that position.[21] Although conflict can certainly result from not understanding what someone says, some conflicts actually intensify when a person clarifies his or her point.

Misconception 3: All Conflict Can Be Resolved—Perhaps you consider yourself an optimist, who likes to think that problems can be solved. You may also believe that if a conflict arises, a compromise will resolve it. In reality, not all conflicts can be resolved. Many disagreements are not simple. For example, fundamental differences between those who oppose abortion and those who support it can obviously not be resolved easily, if at all. Some ideologies are so far apart that resolving conflicts between them is unlikely. This does not mean that whenever a conflict arises in your group, you should despair and not even attempt to solve the disagreement: That would oversimplify the conflict management process. Because some conflicts cannot be resolved, group members may have to focus on those differences on which they *can* most likely reach agreement.

8.2: Conflict Types

OBJECTIVE: Apply strategies for managing different kinds of conflict

Communication scholars Gerald Miller and Mark Steinberg identify three classic types of interpersonal conflict that can occur in groups:

- Pseudo-conflict
- Simple conflict
- Ego conflict[22]

If you can identify the type of conflict, you'll be in a better position to manage it. In this section, we'll examine these three types of conflict in the context of small groups.

By the end of this module, you will be able to:

8.2.1 **Use strategies to manage pseudo-conflict**

8.2.2 **Practice skills that work to resolve simple conflict**

8.2.3 **Determine the best approaches for dealing with ego conflict**

8.2.4 **Analyze how diversity influences group collaboration**

8.2.1: Pseudo-Conflict

OBJECTIVE: Use strategies to manage pseudo-conflict

Pseudo-conflict occurs when individuals agree, but, because of poor communication, they misunderstand one another. "Pseudo" means fake or false. Thus, pseudo-conflict is conflict between people who really agree on issues but who don't realize that their differences are caused by misunderstandings or misinterpretations. "Oh, I see," said Tyrel after several minutes of heatedly defending a position he had suggested to the group. "I just misunderstood you. I guess we really agree."

To manage pseudo-conflict, consider these strategies:

- Ask others what they mean by terms or phrases they use.
- Establish a supportive rather than a defensive climate if misunderstandings occur.
- Become an active listener by using the following skills:

  Question: Ask appropriate questions about information or ideas that are unclear to you.

Paraphrase content: To test your understanding, summarize your conception of what your communication partner says.

Paraphrase feelings: When appropriate, check your perception of your partner's feelings.

Research clearly supports the importance of good listening skills in small groups and teams.[23]

Managing Pseudo-Conflicts

Review the following scenarios. What could you do to manage pseudo-conflict in each situation?

1. Hudson disagreed with Harper about the latest proposal from their boss. Hudson thought their boss was talking about the Borgmeyer Proposal, while Harper thought it was the Affolter Proposal.
2. Adeline, Curt, and Bryan were discussing when to start the meeting. Adeline thought 9 was much too late, thinking the time was 9 PM. Curt, who thought the start time was 9 AM, complained that 9 was much too early. Bryan didn't care when the meeting started.
3. Eric wanted to raise money for the group by selling Arnold bars, a low-fat, low-carbohydrate granola product. Maggie, who had never heard of Arnold bars, wanted to sell only healthy snacks.
4. Kory wanted the group to break for lunch, but kept saying, "Let's just stop now." The rest of the group thought Kory wanted to end the meeting rather than just break for lunch.

8.2.2: Simple Conflict

OBJECTIVE: Practice skills that work to resolve simple conflict

Simple conflict occurs when two people's goals or ideas are mutually exclusive or incompatible. "Simple conflict involves one person saying, 'I want to do X,' and another saying, 'I want to do Y,' when X and Y are incompatible forms of behavior."[24] Although the conflict may seem far from simple, it's called "simple conflict" because the issues are clear and each party understands the problem. For example, in a corporation with only a limited amount of money to invest, one board member may want to invest in real estate and another may want to make capital improvements. The issue is clear; the individuals simply believe the company should take different courses of action. Simple conflict tends to center on two general categories.

Task conflict occurs because of substantive differences about how to accomplish what the group is trying to achieve; that is, one or more members disagree about a specific idea, concept, or conclusion that the group has reached. For example, some members may feel strongly that a table of contents and bibliography should be included in the group's final report, whereas other members don't think those additions are necessary. In this case, the group members disagree about the task of how to prepare the final report. Groups that experience excessive, unresolved task conflict make poorer-quality decisions, are less productive, and have less creativity.[25] When addressing task conflict, we usually first try more integrative or collaborative approaches to managing the conflict by seeking solutions that are agreeable to all parties.[26]

Process conflict occurs when one or more group members disagree about how the task could or should be accomplished; there is a disagreement about group procedure or methods.[27] For example, one person may want the group to do an extensive Internet search to determine which organization should be hired to raise funds for a new hospital. Another member disagrees with that approach; she suggests simply interviewing previous clients of various fundraising firms to assess the organization's effectiveness. In this scenario, there is no disagreement about the overall goal or task of the group—to raise money for a new hospital; instead, the disagreement is about the process or procedures to achieve that task.

MANAGING SIMPLE CONFLICT Task conflict is a disagreement about *what* should be done; process conflict is a disagreement about *how* the task should be accomplished. When you understand what someone says but simply disagree with his or her point, consider using these skills:

- Clarify your perception and your communication partner's perception of the message.
- Keep the discussion focused on issues, not personalities.
- Use facts that support your point, rather than citing opinions or emotional arguments.
- Use a structured problem-solving approach to organize the discussion: Define, analyze, identify several solutions, evaluate the solutions, select the best one.
- When appropriate, look for ways to compromise.
- Make the conflict a group concern rather than a conflict between just two people; ask others for information and data.
- If there are several issues, decide which issues are the most important, and then tackle them one at a time.
- Find areas of agreement.
- If possible, postpone decisions until additional research can be conducted. Such a delay may also lessen tensions.

WRITING PROMPT

Resolving a Simple Conflict

Angela and Sam want their group to have more frequent meetings. Angela wants the group to meet virtually via Skype since she is very busy. Sam doesn't like virtual meetings and wants the group to meet in person. What strategies could Angela and Sam use to manage their disagreement?

The response entered here will appear in the performance dashboard and can be viewed by your instructor.

Submit

8.2.3: Ego Conflict

OBJECTIVE: Determine the best approaches for dealing with ego conflict

Ego conflict occurs when individuals become defensive about their positions because they think they are being personally attacked. The underlying cause of ego conflict is **relational conflict**, which makes personal the differences between people. Relational conflict occurs when one or more group members do not like, respect, or value another person.[28] Research has found that when either task or process conflict is present in the group, it can potentially result in relational conflict.[29] Of all the types of conflict we discuss, relational conflict is the most difficult to manage.[30]

Ego conflicts are charged with emotion; defensiveness in one individual often causes defensiveness in others. Power struggles underlie many ego conflicts.[31] For example, one person may say, "Just because you're the chair of the group, that doesn't give you the right to railroad decision making." Another might reply, "Well, you're just jealous. You think you should have been elected chairperson."

If you are trying to mediate an ego conflict, identify what the disagreeing parties can agree on. Emphasize the common ground between them, and encourage them to describe the sequence of events that created the conflict. Allow the disagreement to be verbalized without heightening the emotional tension. Simply venting anger and irritation won't lessen tensions, and ignoring the conflict won't make it go away. The emotional climate in a group shapes how effectively the conflict will be managed.

Here are additional strategies that may help manage the clash of egos:[32]

- Encourage active listening.
- Return the discussion to the key issues under discussion.
- Try to turn the discussion into a problem to be solved rather than a conflict someone must win.
- Seek new information and ideas to create a breakthrough.[33]

Which Type of Conflict?

For each strategy listed below, identify the type of conflict it can help resolve (pseudo-conflict, simple conflict, or ego conflict). Some strategies can help resolve multiple types of conflict, so choose the best match for each. Compare your answers against the correct answers at the end of the chapter.

1. Ask others to clarify what they mean by a specific term or phrase.
2. Use facts that support your point rather than opinions or emotional arguments when arguments become personal.
3. Clarify the issues and remained focused on the key areas of disagreement.
4. Turn the discussion into a problem to be solved rather than a conflict someone must win.
5. Cool the emotional climate by speaking calmly.
6. Sort out differences of opinion by using facts, examples, and statistics to support your position.

Review

Summary of the Three Types of Conflict

	Pseudo-Conflict	Simple Conflict	Ego Conflict
Source of Conflict	Individuals misunderstanding each other's perceptions of a problem.	Disagreement over a course of action, idea, policy, or procedure that may result in task conflict or process conflict.	Defense of ego: Individual believes he or she is being attacked personally, which may result in relational conflict.
Suggestions for Managing Conflict	1. Ask for clarification of perceptions. 2. Establish a supportive rather than a defensive climate. 3. Employ active listening: • Stop • Look • Listen • Question • Paraphrase content • Paraphrase feelings	1. Listen and clarify perceptions. 2. Make sure issues are clear to all group members. 3. Use a problem-solving approach to manage differences of opinion. 4. Keep the discussion focused on the issues. 5. Use facts rather than opinions as evidence. 6. Look for alternatives or compromise positions. 7. Make the conflict a group concern rather than an individual concern. 8. Determine which conflicts are the most important to resolve. 9. If appropriate, postpone the decision while additional research is conducted. This delay also helps relieve tensions.	1. Let members express their concerns, but do not permit personal attacks. 2. Employ active listening. 3. Call for a cooling-off period to manage emotions. 4. Try to keep the discussion focused on issues (simple conflict). 5. Encourage parties to be descriptive rather than evaluative and judgmental. 6. Use a problem-solving approach to manage differences of opinion. 7. Speak slowly and calmly. 8. Agree to disagree.

8.2.4: Conflict in Diverse Groups

OBJECTIVE: Analyze how diversity influences group collaboration

One of the most interesting questions that group communication researchers have explored is how diversity in group membership affects group performance. Although learning from diverse perspectives is one of the benefits of group work, do differences in race, ethnicity, culture, age, or gender enhance group quality? Is it only diversity that a person can physically see that influences the communication in groups and teams? And how does the diversity of group members, whether surface-level or deep-level, affect the conflict management process?

Surface-level diversity includes the social differences that are readily visible to us—such as differences in ethnicity, race, age, sex, and other social and observable categories. One research team found that ethnicity had an effect on group member satisfaction. Group members who were African American, Hispanic, Native American, or Asian American experienced overall more satisfaction with being in a group than did Whites. The researchers found that regardless of ethnicity, all group members said they valued having ethnically diverse members in the group.[34]

Deep-level diversity includes differences in attitudes, opinions, values, information, and other factors that take time to become evident in groups. These differences emerge only after conversation occurs and are not apparent just by looking at someone. As one research team noted, "People who look the same on the surface are expected to share the same task perspective, and people who look different are expected to have a different task perspective to share, even when the surface-level characteristic is not related to the task."[35] Researchers have found that we expect people who look like us and hold similar surface-level features to agree with us; thus, we are surprised when someone with our own surface-level characteristics disagrees with us.[36]

Another communication researcher also found that it's not differences in such demographic characteristics as race, gender, and other observable factors that affect group performance, but rather differences in underlying values or approaches to problems.[37]

Strategies for Managing Conflict in a Group

What are the best strategies for managing conflict stemming from differing cultural, racial, ethnic, or gender- or age-based points of view?

Suggestions for minority in a group—If you are in the minority in a group:

- Make sure that you tactfully, yet assertively, express your ideas, opinions, facts, and information to the group.
- Ask the group to consider an alternative point of view.

Suggestions for majority in a group—If you are in the majority in the group:

- Don't monopolize the conversation; be a gatekeeper by inviting those who have not spoken up to participate in the conversation.
- Encourage people, especially quiet members, to share ideas and information via e-mail.
- Be cautious about making sweeping generalizations; each person's opinions and ideas are unique and may not necessarily be shared by others in the same racial or ethnic group.
- Don't expect a person from a minority group to be a spokesperson for others in that group. For example, don't turn to an African American student and say, "So, what do blacks think about this topic?"

8.3: Conflict Management Styles

OBJECTIVE: Assess conflict management styles

Regardless of our cultural backgrounds or the types of conflict we experience, research suggests that each of us behaves in predictable ways to manage disagreements with others. What is your conflict management style? Do you tackle conflict head-on, or do you seek ways to remove yourself from the fray? Although these are not the only options available for managing conflict, when reduced to its essence, conflict management style often boils down to fight or flight.

Ralph Kilmann and Kenneth Thomas's classic approach to conflict suggests that your conflict management style is based on two factors:

- How concerned you are for other people
- How concerned you are for yourself[38]

These two factors, or dimensions, result in five conflict management styles, shown in Figure 8-1.

By the end of this module, you will be able to:

- 8.3.1 **Describe the impacts of conflict avoidance**
- 8.3.2 **Explain the functions of accommodation in a group conflict**
- 8.3.3 **Evaluate the pros and cons of group competition**
- 8.3.4 **Determine when compromise works and when it does not**
- 8.3.5 **Summarize how collaboration works for a group**

Figure 8-1 Five Conflict Management Styles

A style is a consistent pattern of communication you have when interacting with others. The five conflict management styles in relation to concern for others and concern for self are avoidance, accommodation, competition, compromise, and collaboration.

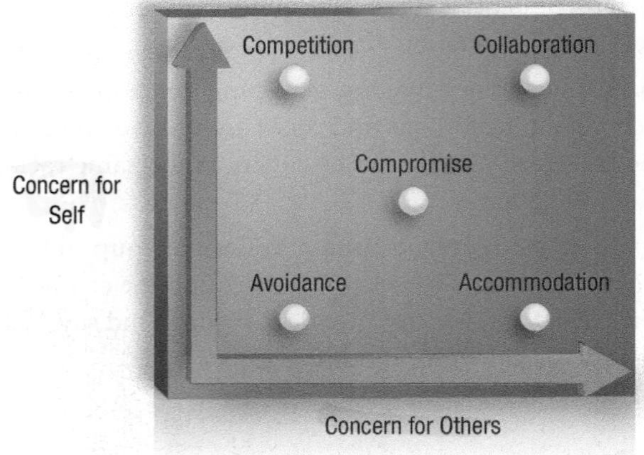

When a group has spent a long time working on a challenging issue that produces conflict, sometimes the best course of action is to take a break.

8.3.1: Avoidance

OBJECTIVE: Describe the impacts of conflict avoidance

Some people just don't like to deal with conflict, so they avoid it. The **avoidance** conflict management style is one in which a person attempts to ignore disagreements. Why do people sometimes avoid conflict? Individuals who sidestep conflict may dislike the hassle of dealing with a difficult, uncomfortable situation; they may be unassertive and afraid of standing up for their rights; or they may not want to hurt someone's feelings.

If you want to be the cause of conflict in a virtual group, research has found the best way to achieve that goal is to be a slacker or a deadbeat—or just don't do the work. Virtual group deadbeats tended to avoid conflict and withdraw from the group rather than actively try to manage conflict. Not surprisingly, in addition to being a source of conflict, deadbeats or those missing in action tended to create less trust in the group as well as less cohesion and satisfaction.[39]

Ignoring conflict has some significant disadvantages. If people avoid directly addressing the conflict, the cause of it may remain and emotions may escalate, making the conflict worse. Avoiding conflict may also signal to others that you simply don't care about the needs and interests of others in your group.

At other times, the wisest course is to avoid conflict. Taking a break from addressing a difficult, conflict-producing issue may be just what a group needs in some circumstances. Avoiding conflict could give the group time to cool off or to think about the issues that are causing the conflict. If the conflict focuses on something trivial or unimportant, it may not be worth the time and effort needed to manage the conflict.

8.3.2: Accommodation

OBJECTIVE: Explain the functions of accommodation in a group conflict

Some people simply give in when faced with conflict in an effort to avoid a major blow-up or controversy. The **accommodation** style attempts to make conflict go away by acceding to the wishes of others. This style is sometimes called a "lose–win" approach.

People may accommodate for several reasons. Perhaps they have a high need for approval, and they want others to like them. Or perhaps they want to reduce the threat to their sense of self-worth, so they decide to give in rather than defend their own views on an issue. Some people who accommodate appear to maintain their cool, doing what others want them to do, but in reality they are using accommodation to serve their own needs—to get other people to like them.

Sometimes accommodating others during conflict leads to an undesirable result. Giving in too quickly to what others want may cause the group to make a bad decision because the issues underlying the conflict have not been thoroughly examined. Since conflict is normal and expected, if several people quickly accommodate, then the group has lost a key advantage of using different points of view to hash out the best solution or decision.

Of course, there are also advantages in being accommodating. To agree with others can indicate that you are reasonable and that you want to help. If the issue is a trivial matter, it may be best to let it slide. If you realize that your position is wrong, then by all means go ahead and agree with others. If you admit your errors, then others may be more likely to admit their mistakes as well, which can help create a climate of trust. Stubbornly clinging to your position, even when you realize it's wrong, creates a defensive climate. Research suggests that one way to break an upward spiral of conflict is to find something about which members can agree.[40] So accommodating can help the group develop a supportive climate; just don't make a habit of *always* accommodating quickly to squelch *all* disagreement.

WRITING PROMPT

Giving in Gracefully

Think of a time when you were participating in a group and the group was deadlocked over how to solve a problem or make a decision. What could you or others in the group have done to facilitate agreement?

▶ The response entered here will appear in the performance dashboard and can be viewed by your instructor.

Submit

8.3.3: Competition

OBJECTIVE: Evaluate the pros and cons of group competition

People who have power or want more power often seek to compete with others. The **competition** conflict management style occurs when people stress winning a conflict at the expense of one or more other people. Think of it as an arm-wrestling match: One person tries to win so that the other person will lose. Winning is often about power, and power is about exerting control over others. Group members who seek power and position are frequently the ones who talk the most.[41] Research has found that if your group has a competitive, even contentious and cutthroat atmosphere, it's hard to break that cycle and evolve into a group with a more collaborative environment.[42] It takes both an awareness of the contentious climate and a willingness to talk about how to break out of the competitive environment to develop a more collaborative approach to managing conflict.

Creating a group climate built on competition can have several disadvantages. The competitive style may result in greater defensiveness, messages that blame others, and efforts to control other group members. We've continually stressed that it's important for group and team members to have a common goal and to work toward the common good. If some group members seek to promote their own interests over the group interests, then the undue competition diminishes the overall power of the group.

However, it isn't always wrong to compete: If you are certain that you have accurate information and that your insights and experiences can help the group achieve its goal, then stick to your position and seek to persuade others. Likewise, if some group members advocate a course of action that is immoral or illegal or that violates your personal instincts of what is right and wrong, it's appropriate to advocate a different course of action.

Be aware that competing with others can be a problem if you try to control without being sensitive to their needs or rights. Competition can also be detrimental if your method is simply to outlast or out-shout others, threaten them, or use unethical means of persuasion, such as knowingly using false information to win. When assertiveness crosses the line into aggression (trying to force others to support your point), most group members find that the competition style becomes tiresome over the course of several group meetings.

Sometimes a group can have a collaborative climate within a competitive context, such as when competing with other groups.

8.3.4: Compromise

OBJECTIVE: Determine when compromise works and when it does not

The **compromise** style of conflict management attempts to find a middle ground—a solution that somewhat meets the needs of all concerned. The word "somewhat" is important. Although on the surface a compromise can look like a win–win approach, it can also create a lose–lose result if nobody gets what they actually want or need. Often when people give up some of what they hope to achieve, no one gets precisely what they want. When trying to reach a compromise, you're really expected to lose something and win something simultaneously; you also expect others to lose and win. As the following illustration indicates, when you compromise, you have some concern for others as well as some concern for yourself.

Although compromise sounds good in principle, it may not always be best in practice. For example, if no one feels believes that the compromise solution is a good one, then it probably isn't the best solution. If group members try to reach a compromise quickly without hashing out why they disagree, the group may not discover the best solution or decision. Compromise can be tempting because it seemingly gives in to each position. An old joke says that a camel is a horse designed by a committee. When groups compromise, the final product may not quite be what anyone had in mind, and it may not really solve the problem.

Of course, there are also obvious advantages to crafting a compromise solution. If a decision is needed quickly and a compromise can be achieved that satisfies the time demands of the situation, then compromise may be best. Compromise may also help everyone save face, especially after a long, contentious conflict. In addition, it may maintain the balance of power in a group. Finally, a compromise on one issue can create a climate of cooperation that will serve the group well when it faces other challenges and disagreements.

8.3.5: Collaboration

OBJECTIVE: Summarize how collaboration works for a group

To **collaborate** is to have a high concern for both yourself and others. Group members who use a collaboration style of conflict management view conflict as a problem to be solved, rather than as a game in which some people win and others lose. In the long run, groups that take the time to collaborate have better results.[43] When group members work side by side, rather than jockeying for power and supremacy, the result may be a win–win outcome.[44] Several studies have found that when group members have cultural differences, a collaborative approach to conflict management works best.[45]

A collaborative style leaves personal grievances out of the discussion and focuses on describing problems without being judgmental or evaluating other people. To compromise is to realize that each person both loses something and wins something; to collaborate is to take the time to find a solution in which all parties are comfortable with the outcome rather than harboring a sense of loss and sacrifice.

The main disadvantage of a collaboration style is the time, effort, and skill it takes to collaborate. Collaboration requires patience. If your group needs a quick decision, group members may find that taking the time necessary to reach a truly "win–win" outcome is more trouble than the issue at hand is worth. Additionally, some people may use the appearance of collaboration as a pretense to compete: A person who is skilled in negotiation and who uses words well can manipulate a collaborative effort and ultimately "win."

The obvious advantage to investing time and energy in collaboration is the prospect of both a better solution to issues facing the group and more satisfied group members. Collaboration is also beneficial when the group needs fresh, new ideas because the old approaches of trying to hammer out a solution simply haven't worked. Working to develop a true consensus on a solution that all individuals support is a good goal for most groups to consider.

It may sound like the collaborative approach is always the best conflict management style to use. Certainly, it is worth pursuing in many, if not most, cases. But no specific conflict management style is effective in all circumstances. The "best conflict management style" varies from situation to situation.

WRITING PROMPT

Your Conflict Management Style

Which style(s) of conflict management do you tend to use? Why?

▶ The response entered here will appear in the performance dashboard and can be viewed by your instructor.

Submit

Virtual Collaboration

Managing Conflict in Virtual Groups

Whether you're interacting in person or using e-mail or other mediated messages, the same factors that contribute to conflict can arise. Virtual team members who are separated from each other geographically may experience an increase in conflict.[46] The limited amount of nonverbal cues in mediated settings appears to have an effect on how mediated teams manage conflict.

Virtual groups are more likely to avoid conflict. Research suggests that virtual groups tend to decrease the intensity of team conflict compared to face-to-face teams.[47] In addition, virtual groups tend to avoid conflict rather than addressing it head-on.[48] Yet, avoiding conflict has a negative effect on team performance. Confronting conflict directly typically results in a more positive team outcome. Researchers have also found that without the accompanying nonverbal cues, team members' attempts to negatively evaluate others have less of a sting.[49]

It's more difficult to manage relational conflict in virtual groups. Research has found that if a group has relational conflict, especially if the conflict is intensely personal, it may be best to sort the conflict out in person rather than using e-mail or other mediated methods.[50]

Virtual groups are more likely to use a collaborative conflict management style. Using a collaborative style is perceived as a positive conflict management approach in both virtual teams and face-to-face teams. Even so, virtual teams that attempt to reach a compromise, especially an early compromise before members have a chance to discuss the issues, are not as productive as face-to-face groups that do the same.

It's more challenging to address conflict in virtual groups. When attempting to brainstorm and generate ideas, members of virtual groups experience more negative conflict management behaviors than do members of face-to-face groups; virtual teams are less effective in managing conflict.[51]

Putting Principles into Practice

What are the best ways to manage conflict when it occurs in mediated or online groups?

- Cooperation and collaboration appear to be the best first approaches to use when conflict occurs in mediated settings.
- Don't sweep disagreements under the rug. Address differences of opinion, but do so thoughtfully and politely.
- When relational conflict erupts in a virtual team, especially intense conflict, meet face-to-face rather than try to manage the conflict online.
- The quality of virtual team decisions can be enhanced if group members contribute ideas by using e-mail or other software programs to help gather and evaluate ideas.[52]

8.4: Groupthink

OBJECTIVE: Formulate solutions for groups that engage in groupthin

Developing a pattern of avoiding conflict or quickly accommodating others creates another real problem—namely, **groupthink**. When a group reaches decisions too quickly, it may not properly consider all of the implications of its decisions. Groupthink occurs when too little conflict lowers the quality of group decisions. When a group does not take enough time to examine the positive and negative consequences of alternative decisions, the quality of its decision making is likely to suffer.[53]

Sociologist Irving Janis believes that many poor decisions and policies are the result of groupthink.[54] Here are two well-known tragedies that, in hindsight, illustrate the corrosive power of groupthink to result in poor decision making even among experts.

- ***Space Shuttle* Challenger:** The decision to launch the flawed space shuttle *Challenger* on that unforgettable January morning in 1986 is now believed to be a product of groupthink.[55] Corporate executives and others did not challenge assumptions in the construction and launch procedures, which resulted in the shuttle disintegrating soon after launch. There was also political pressure to launch on time. The rushed, ill-informed decision to launch the space shuttle ended in disaster.
- ***September 11 Terrorist Attacks:*** The Congressional 9/11 Commission investigated why U.S. intelligence organizations were not as vigilant as they should have been in anticipating the terrorists attacks on September 11, 2001, and concluded that groupthink was a contributing factor. The commission also found that leaders and analysts in intelligence organizations reached conclusions about the presence of weapons of mass destruction in Iraq that were based on unchallenged assumptions and unverified information.[56]

The *Challenger* disaster and the terrorist attacks of September 11 are dramatic examples of how groupthink has contributed to faulty decision making. The groups in which you participate are equally susceptible to this illusion of agreement.

The space shuttle *Challenger* broke apart shortly after lift-off on January 28, 1986, killing all seven crew members on board. The technical cause was O-ring failure. Some blame the disaster in part on groupthink at NASA.

Groupthink is most likely to occur when one or more of these factors exist:

- The group is apathetic about the task.
- Group members have low expectations about their ability to be successful.
- There is at least one highly qualified, credible group member.

- One group member is exceptionally persuasive.
- There is a norm that group members should conform rather than express negative opinions.[57]

You are more likely to think groupthink is a problem in your group after your group has struggled and gotten off track.[58] Indeed, teams are better able to diagnose groupthink as the culprit in making the group wobble *after* the wobbling is over rather than *during* a group's struggle. For this reason, it's important to recognize the symptoms of groupthink while your group is demonstrating those symptoms rather than after the damage has been done.

Although some small group communication scholars question the theoretical soundness of the theory of groupthink, it continues to serve as a useful and practical way of helping groups understand why they make poor decisions.[59]

By the end of this module, you will be able to:

8.4.1 **Identify evidence of groupthink**

8.4.2 **Explain how methods of reducing groupthink work**

8.4.1: Symptoms of Groupthink

OBJECTIVE: Identify evidence of groupthink

The first step in managing groupthink is being aware of the signs of groupthink. Knowing the signs can help you spot groupthink before it becomes a significant problem.

Identifying Signs of Groupthink

Can you identify groupthink when it occurs in your own groups? Here are some of the common symptoms of groupthink.

Critical Thinking Is Not Encouraged or Rewarded—If you are working in a group that considers disagreement or controversy to be counterproductive, chances are that groupthink is alive and well in your group. One advantage of working in groups is having an opportunity to evaluate ideas so that you can select the best possible solution. If group members seem overly proud that peace and harmony prevail at their meetings, they may suffer from groupthink.

Members Believe Their Group Can Do No Wrong—It can be a good thing for groups to have high confidence in their abilities—they tend to set more challenging goals and keep moving forward even in the face of significant obstacles. Yet being overconfident can have a negative effect if group members gloss over conflict, especially procedural conflict.[60] Groupthink is more likely to occur when the group thinks it has high power and is highly effective. In fact, groups that think they have low power actually do a better job of sorting through options and making decisions.[61] If your group is consistently overconfident in dealing with problems that may interfere with its goals, it may suffer from groupthink.[62]

Members Are Too Concerned about Justifying Their Actions—Members of highly cohesive groups like to feel that they are acting in their group's best interests. Therefore, groups that experience groupthink like to rationalize their positions on issues. A group susceptible to groupthink is too concerned about convincing itself that it has made proper decisions in the past and will make good decisions in the future.

Members Apply Pressure to Those Who Do Not Support the Group—Have you ever voiced an opinion contrary to the majority opinion, only to quickly realize that other members were trying to pressure you into going along with the rest of the group? Groups prone to groupthink have a low tolerance for members who do not "go along." They see controversy and conflict injected by a dissenting member as a threat to their *esprit de corps*. Therefore, a person voicing an idea different from the group's position is often punished.[63]

Sometimes the pressure is subtle, taking the form of frowns or grimaces, or failure to listen attentively to the dissident. Don't be too quick to label someone as a troublemaker simply because he or she has an opinion different from that of other group members.

Members Often Believe They Have Reached a True Consensus—A significant problem with groupthink is that members are not aware of the phenomenon, but rather think they have reached genuine consensus. For example, suppose you and your friends are trying to decide which movie to watch on Friday night. Someone suggests the new superhero movie. Even though you've already seen it, you don't want to be contentious, so you agree with the suggestion. Other group members also agree. Yet after your group has seen the movie, one your friends says, "I enjoyed it more when I saw it the first time." After a quick poll of the group, you discover that most of your friends had already seen the movie! They agreed to see it only because they did not want to hurt anyone's feelings. They thought everyone else agreed. As this example suggests, just because your group seems to have reached a consensus, that does not necessarily mean that all the members truly agree.

Members Are Too Concerned about Reinforcing the Leader's Beliefs—If group members place too much emphasis on the credibility or infallibility of their leader, groupthink may occur. Leaders who like to be surrounded by "yes people" (those who always agree with their ideas) lose the advantage of having their ideas tested. Leaders sensitive to the problem of groupthink will solicit and tolerate all viewpoints, because rigorously testing the quality of solutions requires different opinions.

Research has found that groups exhibiting groupthink tend to express more agreement without clarification and also use simpler and fewer substantiated agreements than groups that avoid groupthink.[64] In addition, groups that experience groupthink spend about 10 percent more of their discussion time making statements of agreement or disagreement than other groups. Groups that experience groupthink perpetuate the illusion of agreement by sprinkling in frequent affirming comments such as "Yeah, I see what you're saying," "That's right," or "Sure."

Assessing Groupthink in Your Group

Complete the following groupthink assessment scale to determine whether a group to which you belong avoids groupthink. For each statement, select a number between 1 (if your group never does what the statement describes) and 10 (if your group always does what the statement describes).

1. Members of our group encourage and reward other group members for evaluating evidence and using good reasoning skills.

1 2 3 4 5 6 7 8 9 10

2. Members of our group periodically ask whether we are making accurate, high-quality decisions.

1 2 3 4 5 6 7 8 9 10

3. Members of our group sometimes admit they made a mistake or acknowledge that they reached an inaccurate conclusion.

1 2 3 4 5 6 7 8 9 10

4. Members of our group let other group members make up their minds without pressuring them to agree with what others think.

1 2 3 4 5 6 7 8 9 10

5. Members of our group periodically check to make sure that decisions the group has made continue to be supported by other group members.

1 2 3 4 5 6 7 8 9 10

6. Members of our group voice their honest opinions and do not just agree with what the group leader or dominant or most vocal group members suggest.

1 2 3 4 5 6 7 8 9 10

Feedback: The higher your score, the better your group does in avoiding groupthink; a perfect score is 60.

Review

Symptoms of Groupthink

- Critical thinking is not encouraged or rewarded.
- Members think their group can do no wrong.
- Members are too concerned about justifying their actions.
- Members apply pressure to those who do not support the group.
- Members often believe that they have reached a true consensus.
- Members are too concerned about reinforcing the leader's beliefs.

8.4.2: Suggestions for Reducing Groupthink

OBJECTIVE: Explain how methods of reducing groupthink work

Ernest Borman's research suggests that some groups include a person who assumes the **central negative role**.[65] This person seems to routinely have negative things to say about the leader's ideas or other group members' suggestions. He or she may also offer negative comments to challenge the leader's power and position in the group. Although having someone play a strong central negative role in the group can be annoying, it can sometimes be useful. Rather than routinely trying to shut down the central negative role person, acknowledge the value that can come from having someone periodically challenge the ideas and opinions of the leader, other members, or the entire group. At the same time, it's important that the central negative person not make his or her critiques personal. If the criticism focuses on issues and not personalities, this person can fulfill a useful purpose in helping the group avoid groupthink.

So, don't shy away from voicing your opinion if it deviates from the general consensus of the group. In fact, research has found that groups ultimately appreciate someone who thoughtfully and tactfully brings up alternative points of view.[66] The key is to be respectful of others who may disagree with you.

Reducing Groupthink

How can you reduce the chance of groupthink occurring in your group? Consider the following specific suggestions, based on Janis's initial observations as well as on the theories and the research of several small group communication researchers.

Encourage Critical, Independent Thinking—The leader should clarify that he or she does not want the group to reach agreement until each member has critically evaluated the issues. Most leaders want to command the respect

of their groups, but a leader's insistence that the group members always agree with him or her does not encourage respect; instead, it may demonstrate a fear of disagreement. Thus, if you find yourself acting as the leader in a small group, encourage disagreement—not just for the sake of argument, but to eliminate groupthink. Even if you are not a leader, you can encourage a healthy discussion by voicing any objections you have to the ideas being discussed. Do not permit instant, uncritical agreement in your group.

Be Sensitive to Status Differences That May Affect Decision Making—Group members should not yield to status differences when evaluating ideas, issues, and solutions to problems. Instead, consider the merits of suggestions, weigh the evidence, and make decisions about the validity of ideas without being too concerned about the status of those making suggestions. Of course, this is easier said than done.

Numerous studies suggest that a person with more status will be more persuasive.[67] Cereal companies exploit this relationship when they hire famous athletes to sell breakfast food. The implied message is "Don't worry about the quality of the product. If this Olympic gold-medal winner eats it, you'll like it, too." The athlete's fame and status do not necessarily make the cereal good, but you may still buy the cereal—making your decision based on emotion, rather than fact. So, avoid agreeing with a decision just because of the status or credibility of the person making it. Evaluate the quality of the solution on its own merits.

Invite Someone from Outside the Group to Evaluate the Group's Decision-Making Process—Sometimes a person with an objective point of view from outside the group can identify unproductive group norms more readily than group members themselves, thereby helping prevent groupthink.[68] Many large companies hire consultants to evaluate organizational decision making, but you do not have to be part of a multinational corporation to ask someone to analyze your group's decision-making process. Ask someone from outside your group to sit in on one of your meetings. At the end of the meeting, ask the observer to summarize his or her observations and evaluations of the group. An outside observer may make some members uncomfortable, but if you explain why the visitor is there, the group will probably accept the visitor and eagerly await his or her objective observations.

Assign a Group Member to Play the Role of Devil's Advocate—If no disagreement develops in a group, members may enjoy getting along and never realize that their group suffers from groupthink. If you find yourself in a group with minimal or no conflict, play the role of devil's advocate by trying to raise objections and potential problems. Assign someone to consider the negative aspects of a suggestion before it is implemented. It could save the group from groupthink and enhance the quality of the decision.

Ask Group Members to Subdivide into Small Groups to Consider Potential Problems with the Suggested Solutions—In large groups, not all members will be able to voice their objections and reservations. That explains why the U.S. Congress does most of its work in committees. Members of Congress realize that to hear and thoroughly evaluate bills and resolutions, small groups of representatives must work together in committees. If you are working in a group that is too large for everyone to discuss the issues, suggest breaking into groups of two or three, with each group composing a list of objections to the proposals. Forward the lists to the group secretary, who could then weed out duplicate objections and identify common points of contention. Even in a group of seven or eight, two subcommittees could evaluate the group's recommendations. Members should be able to participate frequently and evaluate the issues carefully. Individuals could also write down their objections and then present them to the group.

Another technique to help reduce groupthink is to have groups divide into two teams to debate an issue. The underlying principle is simple: Develop a group structure that encourages critical thinking. Vigilant thinking fosters high-quality decisions.

Ethical Collaboration

Playing Devil's Advocate

Imagine that you are a member of your community's Planning and Zoning Board. A new apartment complex has been proposed that will be built on land near the beautiful and pristine San Stephen River, which runs through your city. The investors who want to build the new apartment complex have agreed to donate several acres of riverfront property to the city if their zoning request to build the apartments is approved. Most of the members of the Planning and Zoning Board think it is a good proposal; no one on the Board has raised any objections. You also think the proposal has merit. But to ensure that the Board avoids groupthink, you wonder if you should raise several possible concerns or objections that other community members may have.

WRITING PROMPT

Should You Rock the Boat?

Even if you approve of what a group or committee is doing, is it ethical to raise concerns and objections (which you don't really share) that could slow the group down, just to avoid groupthink? Is it ethical to play the "devil's advocate" role, which could stir up conflict and disagreement when the group seems to be reaching a quick consensus? What would you do?

The response entered here will appear in the performance dashboard and can be viewed by your instructor.

Submit

Identifying and correcting groupthink should help improve the quality of your group's decisions by capitalizing on opposing viewpoints. A textbook summary of suggestions for dealing with groupthink may lead you to think that this problem can be corrected easily: It cannot. Because many people think that conflict should be avoided, they need specific guidelines for identifying and avoiding groupthink. In essence, be critical of ideas, not people. Remember that some controversy is useful. A decision-making group uses conflict to seek the best decision everyone can agree on—it seeks consensus.

Review

Suggestions for Reducing Groupthink

- Encourage critical, independent thinking.
- Be sensitive to status differences that may affect decision making.
- Invite someone from outside the group to evaluate the group's decision-making process.
- Assign a group member to play the role of devil's advocate.
- Ask group members to subdivide into small groups (or to work individually) to consider potential problems with suggested solutions.
- Use a common website where people can contribute anonymously or other forms of technology that enable people to make anonymous contributions to reduce group member status differences.

8.5: Conflict Management Skills

OBJECTIVE: Use conflict management skills to address group problems

Evidence suggests that managers spend as much as 25 percent of their time dealing with conflict.[69] One author boldly claims that 98 percent of the problems we face are "people problems."[70] Scholars call people who overly stimulate conflict "group deviants"; you may call them a pain in the neck. Even though we hope that you will not have to deal with difficult or cantankerous group members, we are not naive.

It sometimes takes special "people skills" to deal with difficult group members who consistently instigate conflict. Which specific skills can help a group manage conflict collaboratively? No simple checklist of techniques will miraculously resolve or manage group differences. However, there are some helpful research-based strategies to keep in mind that can help you manage conflict.

By the end of this module, you will be able to:

8.5.1 **Analyze emotion management in a group setting**

8.5.2 **Practice emotional de-escalation**

8.5.3 **Analyze group arguments for their underlying issues**

8.5.4 **Remove the personal attack from a statement of disagreement**

8.5.5 **Identify the shared interests of a group in conflict**

8.5.6 **Determine alternative solutions to problems**

8.5.7 **Evaluate whether criteria are objective**

8.5.1: Address Emotions

OBJECTIVE: **Analyze emotion management in a group setting**

When you or other group members are emotionally charged during conflict, it can be difficult to keep a cool head and practice rational, logical methods of managing conflict.[71] One researcher offers this description of what happens within our bodies when we become upset:

> Our adrenaline flows faster and our strength increases by about 20 percent.... The veins become enlarged and the cortical centers where thinking takes place do not perform nearly as well.... the blood supply to the problem-solving part of the brain is severely decreased because, under stress, a greater portion of blood is diverted to the body's extremities.[72]

It's normal to feel angry when someone seems constantly to say or do things that make you feel judged or evaluated. In such situations, you may say or do something you later regret. Although expressing uncensored emotions can make matters worse, some people advocate expressing anger to "clear the air." Two communication researchers confirmed what most of us know intuitively: Unresolved conflict is a breeding ground for emotional upheaval in groups and organizations.[73] Although it's been said that "time heals all wounds," sometimes ignoring hurt feelings can exacerbate the conflict. Leaders and team members need to recognize when they should actively address emotional volatility.[74] Research has confirmed that teams composed of people with a well-developed sense of emotional intelligence (that is, they have empathy for others and are better able to manage their emotions) have less contentious and more productive meetings.[75]

EMOTION MANAGEMENT STRATEGIES Consider the following five strategies for managing emotions during conflict.

1. **Be aware of your anger level.** Candidates for anger management programs don't monitor their emotions well; before they know it, their emotions boil over. Uncensored emotional outbursts rarely enhance the quality of communication. An emotional purge may make you feel empowered momentarily, but it usually escalates conflict and tension.[76]
2. **Breathe.** It may sound trite and overly simple, but it really works. As you become aware of your increased emotional arousal, take a slow, deep breath. It can help calm you and manage the physiological changes that the rush of adrenaline produced by conflict creates. A slow, deep breath can help soothe your spirit and give you another focus besides lashing out at others.
3. **Use self-talk.** Your thoughts are linked to your feelings. You can manage your emotional state by first being aware that you are becoming upset, and then telling yourself to calm down and stay focused on the issues at hand. Eleanor Roosevelt's observation that "no one can make you feel inferior without your consent" acknowledges the power of self-talk to calibrate your emotional response to what others say and do.
4. **Monitor your nonverbal messages.** Emotions are usually communicated nonverbally rather than verbally. Monitoring your emotional signals can help de-escalate an emotionally charged situation before it erupts. For example, note whether your voice gets louder, your facial expression less friendly, and your gestures more dramatic or emphatic. Speaking more slowly and calmly, maintaining direct eye contact, and adopting a neutral facial expression can help ensure a climate of civility and decorum. We're not suggesting that you manipulate your nonverbal behavior so that you feel inauthentic or that you speak in a patronizing tone. However, being aware of how your nonverbal messages contribute to the emotional climate can help bring the emotional temperature down a degree or two.
5. **Avoid personal attacks.** When conflict gets personal (ego conflict), it becomes more difficult to manage. Calling people names and hurling negative personal messages at them usually worsens a deteriorating emotional group climate.
6. **Don't "gunny-sack." Gunny-sacking** is the unhappy practice of dredging up old problems and issues from the past, like pulling them out of an old bag (gunny sack) to use against your communication partner. Bringing up old problems that can't be changed now just makes matters worse, especially when emotions are raw. Focus on the present and what can be discussed now and changed in the future, rather than reliving past problems.
7. **Consider using the X-Y-Z formula.** [77] With the **X-Y-Z formula**, you say, "When you do X in situation Y, I feel Z." For example: "When you are 15 minutes late to our staff meetings, I feel like you don't care about us or our meetings." When you are the recipient of someone's

wrath, you could use the X-Y-Z formula to help manage your emotions by explaining how being yelled at makes it difficult for you to listen effectively: "When you are shouting at me during our conversation, I start to feel angry and I don't listen as effectively as I should."

Your Emotion Management Skills

On a scale of 1 (low) to 10 (high), rate yourself on the ability to use the emotion management skills discussed.

Emotion Management Skills	Your Rating
Be aware of your anger level	
Breathe	
Use self-talk	
Monitor your nonverbal messages	
Avoid personal attacks	
Don't "gunny-sack."	
Consider using the X-Y-Z formula	
Summary	*High score feedback* (43–70)—You have a solid grasp of emotion management skills. *Middle score feedback* (22–42)—You use some emotion management strategies effectively, but to maximize your efficacy you could start branching out and incorporating some additional strategies too. *Low score feedback* (7–21)—Consider reviewing the strategies for emotion management. Then look for opportunities to use these strategies the next time your group experiences conflict.

8.5.2: De-escalate by Describing What Is Upsetting You

OBJECTIVE: Practice emotional de-escalation

Be descriptive of your perception of the conflict rather than evaluative. Use a descriptive "I" message to explain to the other person how you are feeling; for example, "I find it difficult to listen to you when you raise your voice at me" or "I notice that is the fourth time you have interrupted me when I was trying to explain my point." To minimize defensiveness, avoid beginning sentences with the word "you." For example, "You shouldn't yell at me" or "You shouldn't interrupt me" are "you" statements. They are evaluative and are likely to increase resentment and anger.

However, two researchers have found that simply prefacing a statement with the word "I" may sometimes be too subtle to help defuse a conflict.[78] You may need to add a longer justification when you provide negative emotional information to another group member. We call this using "extended 'I' language," and it acts as a brief preface to a feedback statement. You might begin by saying something like "I don't want you to take this the wrong way. I really do care about you and I need to share something with you," or "I don't think this is completely your fault, but I find myself becoming more frustrated when I hear that you've talked to others about me." These extended comments may have a better chance of taking the sting out of a negative message than simply beginning a sentence with the word "I" instead of the word "you." There are no magic words that will de-escalate conflict. However, being sensitive and thoughtful about how others may respond to your messages can help you express your ideas in ways that are more likely to be heard and taken into consideration rather than immediately rejected.[79]

Although we recommend that you manage your emotions during the heat of conflict, we're not suggesting that you can't express your feelings. In fact, one study found that team members who constructively express how they feel can enhance the decision-making process.[80] Individuals who are aware of their own feelings and positively manage what one team of researchers called "affective influence" tend to develop better solutions and make better decisions.

Joyce Hocker and William Wilmot suggest that when you are the receiver of someone's emotional outburst, consider the following actions to help deescalate emotions:[81]

1. Acknowledge the person's feelings.
2. Determine which specific behavior is causing the intense feelings.
3. Assess the intensity and importance of the issue.
4. Invite the other person to join you in working toward solutions.
5. Make a positive relational statement.

Research also supports the value of using well-crafted arguments rather than emotion-laden opinions to help those in conflict sort through periods of contention.[82] Use good listening skills, acknowledge how others feel, and express your own feelings (without ranting and raving) to make a good start toward mediating challenging conflict situations.

WRITING PROMPT

Using "I" Statements

Think of the last conflict you had with someone. Write an "I" statement that appropriately discloses your feelings about the conflict issue or person you were in conflict with.

 The response entered here will appear in the performance dashboard and can be viewed by your instructor.

Submit

8.5.3: Return to the Issue of Contention

OBJECTIVE: Analyze group arguments for their underlying issues

The only way to return to a collaborative style of conflict management is to return to the issue that is fueling the disagreement: Avoiding the issue will not resolve it.[83] Sometimes one of the people in conflict has a hidden agenda that makes it difficult to confront the key issues. A wise person once said, "Often what we fight about is not what we fight about." Although an argument may seem on the surface to be about a substantive issue—such as which solution to adopt or whose research to use—the underlying issue may be about power and control. The conflict will be managed effectively only if this kind of underlying issue is exposed and addressed.

Sometimes you may need additional strategies for managing prickly people. Table 8-1 offers several specific ways to deal with group members who perform such self-focused roles as dominator and blocker or who are irresponsible or unethically aggressive. But remember: No one can change the behavior of another person.

Competent communicators have the knowledge, skill, and motivation to respond appropriately and effectively to others' behavior, even when that behavior is difficult, self-serving, or unethical.

8.5.4: Separate the People from the Problem

OBJECTIVE: Remove the personal attack from a statement of disagreement

Based on studies of what works and what doesn't work in conflict management, Roger Fisher and William Ury identified several strategies that can help feuding individuals come to an agreement and manage conflict effectively.[84] One of their suggestions that has resonated with others is the idea of separating the people from the problem. In other words, when you are having a conflict with someone, don't make the conflict personal; keep the

Table 8-1 How to Deal with Difficult Group Members

What the Group Member Does	Description	Options for Managing the Problem
Dominates	Tells people what to do without seeking permission from the group; tells rather than asks; monopolizes the conversation	1. Use gatekeeping skills to invite other group members to participate; explicitly state that you'd like to hear what others have to say. 2. Channel the dominator's energy by giving him or her a specific task to accomplish, such as recording the minutes of the meeting or periodically summarizing the group's progress. 3. In private, ask the dominating group member to be less domineering and to give others an opportunity to participate. 4. The group or team may collectively decide to confront the domineering member; clearly describe the behavior that the group perceives as inappropriate.
Blocks Progress	Has a negative attitude; is often stubborn and disagreeable without a clear reason; when the group is making progress, the blocker seems to keep the group from achieving its goal	1. Use humor to help defuse the tension that the blocker creates. 2. Assign the blocker the role of devil's advocate before the group makes a decision; giving the blocker permission to be negative at certain times can help the group avoid groupthink. 3. Ask for specific evidence as to why the blocker does not support the group's position. 4. Calmly confront the blocker and explain how consistently being negative creates a negative group climate.
Is Irresponsible	Does not carry through with assignments; is often absent from or late to meetings	1. Assign a mentor. Call the person or send an e-mail to remind him or her to attend the meeting. Ask for a progress report on the status of assigned work. Work one-on-one to help the irresponsible member see how his or her behavior hurts the group. Provide more structure. 2. Clarify who will get the credit. To minimize social loafing, tell the offending member that when the final product is complete, the group will clearly indicate her or his lack of participation. 3. Speak to the offending group member privately and convince him or her to pull his or her own weight. Explain how his or her irresponsibility is hurting other group members and the overall success of the group. 4. If confronting the offending group member first privately and then collectively does not get results, ask for help from a supervisor or instructor.
Is Unethically Aggressive	Is verbally abusive toward other group members or purposefully disconfirms others; tries to take credit for others' work	1. Become an advocate for other group members; support those who are attacked or singled out. 2. Do not accept unethical behavior in silence. Immediately describe the offensive behavior to the aggressor, and indicate its negative effect on individuals or the entire group. 3. Several group members may confront the offending group member collectively. The group as a whole should not tolerate mean-spirited actions toward others. 4. Seek help from an instructor or supervisor or from someone in authority outside the group to stop the unethical, offending behavior. Sometimes a bully only responds to a person of greater power.

conflict focused on the issue. Make it a simple conflict (a disagreement of an issue) rather than an ego conflict (a personal conflict).

Separating the person from the problem means valuing the other individual as a person, treating her or him as an equal, and empathizing with her or his feelings.[85] The keys to valuing others are using good listening skills, managing your emotions, and acknowledging the other person's feelings. Emotion is the fuel of conflict.[86]

Personal conflicts are usually best addressed in person rather than via e-mail, social media, or other mediated channels. Prior to meeting, ask individuals to identify facts and share information that can help de-escalate the emotional climate and keep the conflict focused on issues rather than personalities.[87]

Avoiding Ego Conflict

Read each scenario below. How would you rewrite each personal attack to remove the ego from the disagreement? Compare your answers against recommended answers at the end of the chapter.

1. "You always blame me for everything that goes wrong."
2. "You are doing a terrible job of leading this meeting."
3. "You are so arrogant. You talk too much. Stop trying to get all of the attention."
4. "Don't talk to me like that! You are not the boss of me or the leader of this group."

8.5.5: Focus on Shared Interests

OBJECTIVE: Identify the shared interests of a group in conflict

The words to an old song begin with the advice "Accentuate the positive; eliminate the negative." The collaborative style of conflict management focuses on areas of agreement and what all parties have in common.[88] If, for example, you are in a group debating whether public schools should distribute condoms, group members are more likely to have a productive discussion if they verbalize the goals and values they hold in common. A comment such as "We all agree that we want students in our school to be healthy" might be a good place to start such a discussion.

Conflict is goal-driven: The individuals embroiled in a conflict want something. Unless those goals are clear to everyone, it will be difficult to manage the conflict well. If you are involved in a conflict, first determine what your goals are, and then identify your partner's goals. Finally, identify where goals overlap and where they differ.

A goal is not the same as the strategy for achieving what you and a feuding group member want. For example, you might ask the group to make fewer copies on the copy machine. Your goal is to save money because you are in charge of managing the office. Asking that your colleagues make fewer copies is a strategy that you have suggested for achieving your goal. Clarifying the underlying goal (rather than just debating the merits of one strategy for achieving it) should help unravel clashes over issues or personalities.

WRITING PROMPT

Identifying Shared Interests

Think of a group experience you've had in which conflict arose between members. Did anyone in the group identify shared interests that helped unify the feuding members? If not, what points or questions could you have raised to the group that might have helped identify common ground?

The response entered here will appear in the performance dashboard and can be viewed by your instructor.

Submit

8.5.6: Generate Many Options to Solve Problems

OBJECTIVE: Determine alternative solutions to problems

When negotiation and conflict management degenerate into a verbal arm-wrestling match over only one or two options, where combatants perceive only one way to win, it creates a competitive climate in which the conflict

Virtual collaboration can encourage brainstorming and increase the number of options for consideration.

is less likely to be managed successfully. Collaborative conflict managers are more likely to use brainstorming or other strategies to identify a variety of options to manage the disagreement; they seek several solutions to overcome obstacles. Research suggests that using e-mail or other electronic support systems to generate and evaluate ideas can also be a productive way of increasing the number of options a group or team might consider.[89] If your group has a Facebook page or is using other social media applications, inviting members to share ideas in writing can increase group member participation. Sometimes feuding group members become fixated on only one solution.

8.5.7: Base Decisions on Objective Criteria

OBJECTIVE: Evaluate whether criteria are objective

Criteria are the standards for an acceptable solution to a problem. Typical criteria are such things as a limit to how much the solution can cost or a deadline by which a solution must be implemented. For example, suppose city council members want to increase city revenue, but they first decide that they do not want to raise taxes on anyone who earns less than $20,000 per year. In this case, they are using criteria to help identify an acceptable solution. Having a clear sense of the elements of an effective solution (criteria) will help the group make more rational decisions.

CASE STUDY

Applying Conflict Management Principles

You would think that board members of the Buckner Valley food bank would be, for the most part, pleasant, selfless people who were trying to give something back to the community by volunteering their time to help provide food for those who need a little assistance. Yet the board members often found themselves embroiled in conflict, partly due to some of their personalities.

Jeff meant well, but he seemed to have a need to dominate the board. He talked too much. Also, although he was not the current board chair, he wanted to insist that his ideas were the ones to be implemented. Jeff's dominance made other board members reactively reject his ideas, even when the ideas were good ones, such as purchasing a new van to make food deliveries. Tired of Jeff's overly bombastic style of trying to get his way, they usually disagreed with him regardless of the merit of his suggestions.

Aiden also meant well, but he missed about half of the twice-monthly meetings. He often didn't follow through on assignments. Yet he liked being on the board because it looked good on his résumé; he was planning on running for city council next year and wanted to demonstrate his concern for the community by being on the board. Even when Aiden was present, he seemed mentally absent; he didn't say much, even though as manager of the local grocery store he had much to offer.

Jessica was a hard worker—maybe too hard. She always followed through on her assignments and had little patience for people who didn't do what they were supposed to do. She did more than just raise her voice when expressing her concerns: She yelled and often screamed obscenities at members who made the smallest errors or mistakes. Because of her hard work, the board needed her—but members were a bit afraid of her wrath and just kept quiet when she shouted at them. They didn't want to upset Jessica further because they knew she would shout even more loudly.

Hudson always thought the food bank was running out of money (even when it wasn't). He longed for the good old days when just he and C. J. ran the food bank. Hudson was typically against any new idea, especially anything that would cost money. When strategies were suggested to raise more funds, Hudson was against it. He didn't agree with the philosophy, "It takes money to raise money," so he blocked most new ideas.

C. J., the current board chair, was the glue that held the board together. She was mild-mannered yet hard-working and talented at keeping the other board members moving forward (most of the time). Yet she was getting weary of the constant bickering, power struggles, and inactivity on the part of some.

It was time for the board to organize the annual holiday gift basket program for Buckner Valley, but the board simply wasn't making progress. The need was greater than ever this year because of the economic downturn. Many people had lost their jobs and would have no holiday if it weren't for the food bank. Jeff had a good idea for streamlining the operation so that more families could be fed, but other members rejected his idea because they didn't want Jeff to get credit for it. Since Aiden ran the grocery store, he could make a major difference in the community, but he didn't have time to attend many meetings and didn't seem to have real interest in the food bank. Hudson didn't want to spend a dime more than what was spent last year and was against any new plan that might cost more money. Jessica was at her prickly best, and, although she could do the work, she had nothing but critical comments for her fellow board members. C. J. knew the Buckner Valley community was depending on the board, so she was intent on doing whatever she could to feed even more people this year—families were depending on it.

Questions for Analysis: Applying Conflict Management Principles

1. What type or types of conflict do you see evident on the board?
2. What different styles of conflict management do you see among the board members? How do those different styles affect the level of conflict among board members?
3. Which collaborative conflict management principles and skills would be helpful for board members to implement to address the recurring conflicts they were experiencing?
4. Based on the strategies presented in Table 8-1, what suggestions would you make to help manage the array of personalities present on the board?

8.6: Conflict Management through Consensus

OBJECTIVE: Apply strategies for reaching consensus

Consensus occurs when all group members support and are committed to a decision. The tendency to seek agreement and work together for a collaborative goal is not unique to humans. Indeed, research has found that ants, honeybees, and some other species strive to achieve a common goal.[90] Even if a group does not reach consensus on key issues, it is not necessarily a failure. Good decisions can certainly emerge from groups whose members do not all completely agree on decisions. The U.S. Congress, for example, rarely achieves consensus, but that does not mean its legislative process is always ineffective.

Although conflict and controversy can improve the quality of group decision making, it is worthwhile to aim for consensus.[91] In this section, we will explore some strategies for managing conflict to help you achieve group consensus.

By the end of this module, you will be able to:

- 8.6.1 **Describe the impact of effective consensus**
- 8.6.2 **Explain how to keep a group in conflict focused on its goal**
- 8.6.3 **Correct behaviors that are not other-oriented**
- 8.6.4 **Summarize strategies for helping people engage with one another during a group conflict**

8.6.1: The Nature of Consensus

OBJECTIVE: Describe the impact of effective consensus

Consensus should not come too quickly or easily. If it does, your group is probably a victim of groupthink. In addition, quick consensus is a sign that the group may not be carefully considering all of the information it has.[92] Sometimes group agreement is built on agreements on minor points raised during the discussion. To achieve consensus, group members should try to emphasize these areas of agreement. This can be a time-consuming process, and some members may lose patience before they reach agreement. Regardless of how long a group takes to reach this outcome, consensus generally results from careful and thoughtful communication between members of the group.

Is taking the time to reach consensus worth the effort? Groups that reach consensus (not groupthink) and also effectively use good discussion methods, such as testing and challenging evidence and ideas, achieve better-quality decisions.[93] Evidence also suggests that groups that achieve consensus are likely to maintain agreement even after several weeks.[94]

Communication researchers agree that group members usually expend considerable effort before reaching consensus. Using specific communication strategies may help members more readily foster consensus in group and team meetings.[95]

8.6.2: Orient the Group Toward Its Goal

OBJECTIVE: Explain how to keep a group in conflict focused on its goal

Keep three key pieces of advice in mind when striving for group consensus:

- Help the group stay oriented toward the overall goal of the group.
- Be other-oriented and listen.
- Promote honest interaction and dialogue.

Here are some specific strategies to help the group stay focused on the overall goal:

- ***Use metadiscussional phrases.*** **Metadiscussion** is discussion about discussion. In other words, a metadiscussional statement focuses on the discussion process rather than on the topic under consideration.[96] For example, you might say, "Aren't we getting a little off the subject?" or "John, we haven't heard from you yet. What do you think?" or "Let's summarize our areas of agreement." These statements contain information and advice about the problem-solving process rather than about the issue at hand.
- ***Stay focused on the group's task.*** Metadiscussional phrases help to keep the group focused on the task or meeting agenda. Effective use of them is an exceptionally powerful and useful skill to learn, because you can offer metadiscussional statements even if you are not the designated leader of the group. Research clearly supports the importance of metadiscussion; simply having someone periodically reflect on where the group is on the agenda and review what has been accomplished can greatly help the group stay on track and reach consensus.[97]
- ***Keep the focus on the group's goal instead of on specific strategies to achieve the goal.*** Focusing on shared interests and reminding the group what the goals are can help the group move from debating only one or two strategies to achieving the goal. Group members sometimes fall in love with an idea or strategy and won't let go of it. To move forward, explicitly and frequently remind the group of the overarching goal you are trying to achieve.

Several studies show that groups perform better if group members make metadiscussional comments by helping orient the group toward its goal.[98] Questions such as "What is the goal of this conversation?" or "What is the purpose of having this discussion?" can help everyone stay focused on the group's goal.

- ***Display known facts for all group members to see.*** Consider using a whiteboard, PowerPoint, or a flipchart to display what is really known about the issues confronting the group. When group members cannot agree, they often retreat to restating opinions rather than advocating an idea based on hard evidence.[99] If all group members are reminded of what is known, consensus may be easier to reach.
- One way to display facts is to use the "is/is not" technique. Draw a line down the middle of the whiteboard or flipchart. On one side of the line, note what is known about the present issue. On the other side, identify what is unknown or is mere speculation. Separating facts from speculation can help group members focus on data rather than on unproven inferences.[100]
- ***Do not wait until the very end of the deliberations to suggest solutions.*** Research suggests that groups whose members delay identifying specific solutions until the very end of the discussion are less likely to reach consensus than groups whose members think about solutions earlier in the deliberations.[101] Of course, before jumping to solutions, groups need to analyze and assess the present situation.

WRITING PROMPT

Focusing the Group on the Goal

Think of a time you have been participating in a group that was off task or off the agenda. Which metadiscussional statements or questions could you use to refocus the group on the goal?

The response entered here will appear in the performance dashboard and can be viewed by your instructor.

Submit

8.6.3: Listen to the Ideas of Others

OBJECTIVE: Correct behaviors that are not other-oriented

Several other-oriented strategies can help bring groups closer to attaining their goal of consensus.

- ***Give your idea to the group.*** People often defend a solution or suggestion just because it is theirs. If you find yourself becoming defensive over an idea you suggest, so as to develop a more objective point of view, assume that your idea has become the property of the group; it no longer belongs to you.[102] Present your position as clearly as possible, then listen to other members' reactions and consider them carefully before you push for your point. Just because people disagree with your idea, that does not necessarily mean they respect you less.
- ***Do not assume that someone must win and someone must lose.*** When the discussion becomes deadlocked, try not to view it in terms of "us" versus "them," or "me" versus "the group." Try not to view communication as a game that someone wins and others lose. Instead, be willing to compromise and modify your original position. Of course, if compromising means finding a solution that is marginally acceptable to everyone but does not really solve a problem, then seek a better solution.
- ***Use group-oriented rather than self-oriented pronouns.*** Harry likes to talk about the problem as *he* sees it. He often begins sentences with phrases such as "I think this is a good idea" or "My suggestion is to. . . . " Studies suggest that groups that reach consensus generally use more pronouns like "we," "us," and "our," while groups that do not reach consensus use more pronouns like "I," "me," "my," and "mine."[103] Using group-oriented words can foster cohesiveness.
- ***Avoid opinionated statements that indicate a closed mind.*** Communication scholars consistently find that opinionated statements and low tolerance for dissenting points of view inhibit agreement. This is especially apparent when the opinionated person is the discussion leader. A group with a less opinionated leader is more likely to reach agreement. Using facts and relying on information obtained by direct observation may be the best ways to avoid making opinionated statements.
- ***Clarify misunderstandings.*** Although not all disagreements arise because conflicting parties fail to understand one another, misunderstanding another's meaning sometimes creates conflict and adversely affects group consensus. Handling misunderstanding is simple: Ask a group member to explain a particular word or statement that you do not understand. Constantly solicit feedback from your listeners. During periods of disagreement, consider repeating the previous speaker's point and ask if you've got it right before you state your position on an issue. This procedure can become time-consuming and stilted if overused, but it can help clarify matters when misunderstandings about meanings arise. It may also be helpful for you to remember that meanings are conveyed through people, not words. Stated another way, the meaning of a word comes from a person's unique perspective, perception, and experience.

- ***Emphasize areas of agreement.*** When the group gets bogged down in conflict and disagreement, it may prove useful to stop and identify the issues and information on which group members *do* agree. One study found that groups whose members were able to keep refocusing the group on areas of agreement, particularly following episodes of disagreement, were more likely to reach consensus than groups that continued to accentuate the negative.[104] Another study found that one of the most important ways of helping a group reach consensus is to be genuinely supportive of others.[105]

Other-Oriented Strategies

Consider the following situations. Which other-oriented strategy would you use to resolve each conflict? Compare your answers against recommended answers at the end of the chapter.

1. A group member suggests her idea is the only solution that will solve the problem.
2. A group member is advocating for a single, specific solution so that he can win the argument.
3. A group member says, "This is my idea" or "Here is what I think you should do."
4. A group member announces, "My mind is made up. This is the only solution."
5. A group member misunderstands when someone says, "We should keep the area around the circle drive clear," thinking it is the circle drive near campus, when the person actually is referring to the circle drive on the other side of town.
6. A group member says, "We are in constant turmoil and can't seem to agree on anything. This is hopeless!"

8.6.4: Promote Honest Interaction and Dialogue

OBJECTIVE: Summarize strategies for helping people engage with one another during a group conflict

There are several ways to encourage honest communication among group members, which can go a long way toward helping groups attain consensus.

- ***Do not change your mind too quickly just to avoid conflict.*** Although you may have to compromise to reach agreement, be wary of changing your mind too quickly just to reach consensus. Groupthink occurs when group members don't test and challenge each other's ideas. When agreement seems to come too quickly and easily, be suspicious. Reaching consensus takes time and often requires compromise. Be patient.
- ***Avoid easy techniques that reduce conflict.*** When you can't resolve a disagreement, you may be tempted to flip a coin or to take a simple majority vote. Resist that temptation, especially early in your deliberation. Of course, at times, a majority vote is the only way to resolve a conflict. When time permits, gaining consensus through communication is the best approach.
- ***Seek out differences of opinion.*** Disagreements may improve the quality of a group's decision. Armed with a variety of opinions and information, a group has a better chance of finding a good solution. Also, complex problems seldom have just one solution—perhaps more than one of the suggestions offered will work. Actively recruit opposing viewpoints if everyone seems to be agreeing without much discussion,[106] or appoint someone to play the role of devil's advocate. Of course, do not belabor the point if you think that group members genuinely agree after considerable discussion.
- ***Involve everyone in the discussion; frequently contribute to the group.*** Encourage less-talkative members to contribute. Several studies suggest that members will be more satisfied with a solution if they have had an opportunity to express their opinions and to offer suggestions.[107] Avoid dominating the discussion, and be a good listener.
- ***Use a variety of methods to reach agreement.*** Some research indicates that groups are more likely to reach agreement if members try several approaches to resolve a deadlocked situation, rather than using just one method of achieving consensus.[108] Consider (1) combining multiple ideas into one solution; (2) building, changing, or extending existing ideas; (3) using effective persuasion skills to convince others to agree; and (4) developing new ideas to move the discussion forward rather than just rehashing old ideas.
- ***Expand the number of ideas and alternatives.*** One reason a group may not agree is that none of the ideas or solutions being discussed are good ones. Each solution on the table may have flaws. If that is the case, the task should change from trying to reach agreement on the alternatives presented to generating more alternatives.[109] Switching from a debate to brainstorming may help pry group members away from foolishly adhering to existing solutions.

Assessing Group Consensus Procedures

Groups need individual members who are skilled in helping the group reach consensus. Even if you are not the official group leader, you can have an important effect on helping a group reach agreement. Take the following survey to take stock of how you apply group consensus skills.

1 = Almost never
2 = Not often
3 = Sometimes
4 = Usually
5 = Almost always

1. I use metadiscussional statements (discussion about discussion) to help a group be more aware of its process and procedures.	1	2	3	4	5
2. I remind the group what the goal or objective is when the group seems lost or off track.	1	2	3	4	5
3. I offer solutions, suggestions, and proposals to help the group develop options.	1	2	3	4	5
4. I consistently use group-oriented pronouns (we, us, our) rather than individual-oriented pronouns (I, me) to develop a sense of collaboration.	1	2	3	4	5
5. I summarize, paraphrase, or help to clarify when the group members don't seem to understand one another.	1	2	3	4	5
6. I look for areas of agreement among group members and verbalize the agreement to the entire group.	1	2	3	4	5
7. I look for ways in which all group members can win and be successful rather than assuming someone must win and someone must lose.	1	2	3	4	5
8. I try to involve all group members in the conversation, especially when the group seems bogged down and disagreement is high.	1	2	3	4	5
9. I don't change my mind quickly just to avoid conflict, but I try to resolve issues when the group seems stuck.	1	2	3	4	5
10. I help expand the number of ideas and options, especially when the group can't reach an agreement.	1	2	3	4	5

Feedback:

High score (35–40): You have a solid grasp of helping a group reach consensus.

Middle score (17–33): You effectively use some skills to help a group reach consensus, but to maximize your efficacy you could start branching out and incorporating some additional strategies too.

Low score (1–16): Consider reviewing the strategies for developing consensus. Then look for opportunities to use consensus-building statements the next time your group has difficulty reaching agreement.

Are there differences between the ways face-to-face groups and virtual groups reach consensus? One study found that virtual groups use more negative conflict management behaviors.[110] Such negative behaviors include taking a quick vote rather than discussing issues, suppressing differences of opinions, and assuming an "I must win/you must lose" approach to managing differences. Both online and in person, it's best to encourage honest conversation and dialogue and avoid squelching opposing viewpoints.

Conflict Management

Consider the following scenarios. In each, there is an obvious conflict among the group members, which could be addressed by using one of the communication strategies discussed in this module. Which strategy would you use to resolve each conflict? Compare your answers against the answers provided at the end of the chapter.

1. The group constantly gets off topic and wastes a lot of time in conversation that is unrelated to the group's goal.
2. The group is locked in conflict. Group members aren't listening. Voices are raised and emotions are hot.
3. Many group members are eager to make the meetings short and to get their job done quickly. The group has almost no conflict and reaches a quick agreement on the first issue that comes before it.
4. Two members of a group are trying to become the leader. They are verbally attacking each other, and the group is embroiled in conflict and tension.

In summary, research suggests that groups that search for areas of agreement while critically testing ideas and reducing ambiguity are more likely to reach consensus than groups that don't. Also, one study found that groups that strive for unanimous agreement ultimately are more likely to at least reach consensus than groups that seek only majority agreement.[111] As you work toward consensus, rather than just saying, "No, you're wrong," identify specific issues that need to be clarified. Groups that focus on disagreement about procedures rather than on substantive issues are less likely to reach consensus. Building consensus takes time and skill and is not necessarily the goal of the group, but if it can be achieved, consensus may result in a better-quality decision.

Review

Suggestions for Reaching Consensus

Strategy	Effective Group Members	Ineffective Group Members
Orient the group toward its goal	Talk about the discussion process using metadiscussional phrases.	Do little to help clarify the group's discussion.
	Help keep the group focused on the goal.	Go off on tangents and do not stay focused on the agenda.
	Display known facts for all members in the group to see.	Fail to provide summaries of issues or facts about which members agree, or rely only on oral summaries.
	Suggest possible solutions throughout the group's deliberation.	Wait until time is about to run out before suggesting solutions.
Be other-oriented; listen to the ideas of others	Give their ideas to the group.	Argue for an idea because it is their own.
	Approach conflict as a problem to be solved rather than a win–lose situation.	Assume that someone will win and someone will lose an argument.
	Use group-oriented pronouns to talk about the group.	Talk about individual accomplishments rather than group accomplishments.
	Avoid opinionated statements that are not based on facts or evidence.	Are closed-minded and inflexible.
	Clarify misunderstandings.	Do not clarify misunderstandings or check whether their message is understood.
	Emphasize areas of agreement.	Ignore areas of agreement.
Promote honest interaction and dialogue	Do not change their minds quickly just to avoid conflict.	Give in to the opinion of group members just to avoid conflict.
	Avoid easy conflict-reducing techniques.	Find easy ways to reduce the conflict, such as taking a quick vote without holding a discussion.
	SeWek out differences of opinion.	Do not recruit a variety of viewpoints.
	Try to involve everyone in the discussion and make frequent, meaningful contributions to the group.	Permit one person to monopolize the discussion or fail to draw out quiet group members.
	Use a variety of methods to reach agreement.	Use only one or two approaches to reach agreement.
	Expand the number of ideas and alternatives using various techniques.	Seek a limited number of options or solutions.

Summary: Managing Conflict

8.1: Conflict Defined

- Conflict is an expressed struggle between at least two interdependent people who perceive the existence of incompatible goals, scarce resources, and interference from others to achieve specific goals.
- Misconceptions about conflict include the following points:
  - Conflict should be avoided at all costs.
  - All conflict occurs because people do not understand one another.
  - All conflict can be resolved.

8.2: Conflict Types

- There are three types of conflict.
  - Pseudo-conflict occurs when individuals agree, but, because of poor communication, they believe that they disagree.
  - Simple conflict occurs when two people's goals or ideas are mutually exclusive or incompatible. Simple conflict can focus on task issues (task conflict) or process issues (process conflict).
  - Ego conflict occurs when individuals become defensive about their positions because they think they are being personally attacked; a contributing factor in ego conflict is relational conflict.

8.3: Conflict Management Styles

- There are five styles of managing conflict based on the two dimensions of (1) concern for self and (2) concern for others.
- The five conflict management styles are avoidance, accommodation, competition, compromise, and collaboration.

8.4: Groupthink

- The absence of conflict or a false sense of agreement is called groupthink. It occurs when group members are reluctant to voice their feelings and objections to issues.

- To help reduce the likelihood of groupthink, consider the following suggestions:
  - If you are the group leader, encourage critical, independent thinking.
  - Be sensitive to status differences that may affect decision making.
  - Invite someone from outside the group to evaluate the group's decision making.
  - Assign a group member to play the role of devil's advocate.
  - Ask members to subdivide into small groups to consider potential problems and suggested solutions.

8.5: Conflict Management Skills

- Collaborative conflict management skills include the following:
  - Manage your emotions.
  - Describe what is upsetting you.
  - Disclose your feelings.
  - Return to the issue of contention.
  - Separate the people from the problem.
  - Focus on shared interests.
  - Generate many options to solve problems.
  - Base decisions on objective criteria.

8.6: Conflict Management through Consensus

- Consider applying the following suggestions to help reach consensus and to help manage the conflicts and disagreements that arise in groups:
  - Keep the group oriented toward its goal.
  - Be other-oriented: Listen to the ideas of others.
  - Promote honest interaction and dialogue.

SHARED WRITING

Strategies that Facilitate Collaboration

What strategies would you apply when dealing with difficult group members? Examine the relevance of each strategy. Write a short response that your classmates will read.

A minimum number of characters is required to post and earn points. After posting, your response can be viewed by your class and instructor, and you can participate in the class discussion.

Answers

1. Section 8.2.3: Which Type of Conflict?

1. Pseudo-conflict. 2. Ego conflict. 3. Simple conflict. 4. Ego conflict. 5. Ego conflict. 6. Simple conflict.

2. Section 8.5.4: Avoiding Ego Conflict

1. "I understand that my actions may seem to be causing a problem. When I feel attacked, I tend not to listen very well."
2. "I'm not clear on where we are in our agenda. How I can contribute to the conversation?"
3. "I notice that some other people would like to contribute. Jake and Cally, would you like to add a comment?"
4. "I respond better to requests if I'm not yelled at."

3. Section 8.6.3: Other-Oriented Strategies

1. Rather than strongly advocating her own position, she should share it with the group and then give the idea to the group.
2. Don't assume someone must win and others lose. Look for compromise and ways to accommodate so that ideas from several people can be used to solve the problem or making the decision.
3. Use group-oriented pronouns: "Here is an idea we might consider" or "What should we do to help solve the problem?"
4. The group member should be open to the ideas of others and not insist that there is only one solution to a problem.
5. Clarify misunderstandings and potential misunderstandings. The speaker should clarify which circle drive he or she is referring to, or the listeners should ask, "Which circle drive are you thinking about?"
6. A group member should find some area of common concern, even if just noting that all group members agree that there is a problem to be solved.

4. Section 8.6.4: Conflict Management

1. Use metadiscussional phrases.
2. The group should take a break to cool off.
3. The group may be experiencing groupthink. Make sure issues are being discussed thoroughly and that the pros and cons of each idea are examined.
4. To manage the ego conflict, the group should keep conversations focused on issues.

Chapter 9
Leading Groups

"The first responsibility of a leader is to define reality. The last is to say thank you. In between, the leader is a servant."

—Max De Pree

Learning Objectives

9.1 Relate group leadership to group function

9.2 Anticipate how leadership style and situation will influence group conflict

9.3 Apply a transformational style to small group leadership

9.4 Determine how qualities of effective leadership work in small groups

Consider the following statements about leadership:

Leaders are born, not made.

An effective leader is always in control of the group process.

A leader is a person who gets others to do the work.

Leadership is a set of functions distributed throughout the group.

The leader should know more than other group members about the topic of discussion.

An authoritarian leader is better than one who allows the group to function without control.

It is best for a group to have only one leader.

A person who has been appointed leader is the leader.

Leaders are servants.

What do you think about these statements? Do you agree with some of them and disagree with others? Which ones? If it has not happened already, be assured that one day you will find yourself in a leadership position—on a committee, in an organization, or perhaps in the military. Whenever you participate in a decision-making group, your attitudes about leadership will affect your behavior, the behavior of others, and the effectiveness of the group.

When you think about "leadership," what comes to mind? A fearless commanding officer leading troops into battle? The chairperson of a committee? For our purposes, **leadership** is behavior or communication that influences, guides, directs, or controls a group. Leadership can be seen as a counteractive influence when groups get off track. It constitutes the behavior required when groups experience difficulty establishing the conditions necessary for making the best possible choices.[1]

In this chapter, we will explore the nature of leadership in groups according to three perspectives—trait, functional, and situational—and offer some specific suggestions to help you become a more effective group member and leader.

9.1: Functional Perspective of Leadership

OBJECTIVE: Relate group leadership to group function

Traditional studies of leadership have centered on traits of people who are successful leaders. Scores of trait studies have found that leaders have attributes such as intelligence, enthusiasm, dominance, self-confidence, social participation, and egalitarianism.[2] More recent studies have found leadership to be related to creativity and social–emotional competency in leaders.[3] Other researchers have found physical traits are related to leadership ability: Leaders seem to be larger, more active and energetic, and better looking than other group members.[4] Still other researchers have discovered that leaders possess tact, cheerfulness, a sense of justice, discipline, versatility, and self-control.

The **trait perspective**—a view of leadership as the personal attributes or qualities that leaders possess—seemed reasonable when it was first proposed, but it has actually yielded very little useful information. The traits beneficial in one situation, such as leading troops into battle, are not necessarily the traits required for other leadership positions, such as conducting a business meeting. For example, the trait of high dominance often found in leaders can actually be counterproductive in certain contexts. When there is instability in an organization's leadership hierarchy, such leaders may use their power to advance their self-interest rather than the group's goals.[5]

The trait approach emphasizes the physical and personality characteristics of leaders such as General George S. Patton.

Another problem with the trait approach is that it does not identify which traits are important to *becoming* a leader and which are important to *maintaining* the position. These studies also fail to distinguish adequately between leaders and followers who possess the same traits, and they are not useful to group participants who wish to improve their leadership skills. Therefore, although the trait approach is of interest from a historical perspective, we will move on to consider other, more useful approaches.

Rather than focusing on the characteristics of individual leaders, the **functional perspective** examines leadership as a series of behaviors that may be performed by any group member to maximize group effectiveness. Dean Barnlund and Franklyn Haiman identify leadership behaviors as those that guide, influence, direct, or control others in a group.[6] Identifying such behaviors is useful for anyone interested in improving his or her leadership abilities. Although the trait approach might help identify the sort of person who may be appointed to a leadership position, the functional approach describes the specific communicative behaviors that help a group function more effectively. By understanding these behaviors, people can participate more productively in group discussions.

According to the functional approach, leadership behaviors fall into two categories: (1) **task leadership** and (2) **process leadership** (also called "group building" or "maintenance"). Task-oriented behaviors are specifically aimed toward accomplishing a group goal, whereas process-oriented behaviors help maintain a satisfactory interpersonal climate within a group. Both types of leadership are essential.

By the end of this module, you will be able to:

9.1.1 **Identify behaviors associated with task leadership**

9.1.2 **Explain how process leadership works**

9.1.1: Task Leadership

OBJECTIVE: Identify behaviors associated with task leadership

When groups convene to solve problems, make decisions, plan activities, or determine policy, they are frequently hampered by group members' tendency to get off track. Even when they get down to business, the group process may stray. Sometimes one person monopolizes the conversation while others remain silent. Sometimes groups just can't seem to get started.

While a group's leader has a responsibility to keep the group moving, research has shown that *anyone* can perform the behaviors that keep a group on track. Just because a person has the title "leader," that does not necessarily mean that he or she is best equipped for the job. If leadership is a set of functions that are often distributed, a group is still quite capable of getting its job done regardless of who is designated as the leader. Thus, if you are a member of a disorganized group, you can provide the leadership the group needs even though you are not the formal "leader."

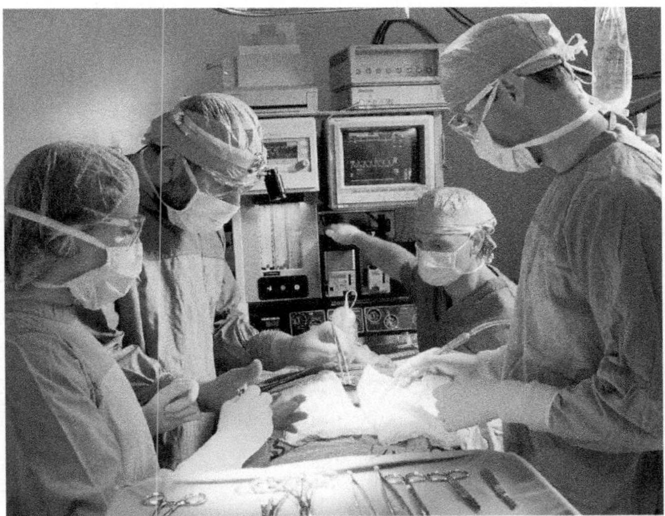

In an operating room, the role of each member of the surgical team is defined by the tasks required. What type of leader is best suited to lead such a team?

Task-Leadership Behaviors

The following list summarizes several key task-leadership behaviors.

Initiating—Task-oriented group discussions must generate ideas. Sometimes ideas are related to procedural matters; at other times a group must generate ideas to solve problems. If you say, "Let's get this meeting under way," you have initiated a change (assuming the group follows your suggestion). If, later in the meeting, you say, "Let's consider an alternative plan" or "Let's generate some more ideas before evaluating what we have here," you will again alter the course of the group's action. Without someone who initiates a discussion, a group has no direction. The ability to initiate is an essential group behavior that anyone can contribute.

Coordinating—People bring different expectations, beliefs, attitudes, values, and experiences to a group. Given the diversity in small groups, coordinating is often an important leadership function. Communicative behavior that helps a group explore the contributions of all members is valuable. For example, if you see a connection between the ideas that two members bring to the group, you should point it out to help focus the group. Coordinating members' efforts can help all group members see the "groupness" of their activities and reduce their uncertainty about the group, its problem, and its solutions.

Summarizing—Often, people in the middle of a discussion cannot tell exactly where the discussion began and where it is going. It doesn't take many tangential remarks to get the group off track. Summarizing reduces group uncertainty by showing how far the discussion has progressed and what it still needs to accomplish. By understanding when a group needs a summary—and then providing it—you can help move the group toward its goal.

Elaborating—Sometimes good ideas are ignored until they are expanded enough to be visualized. Suppose you attend a meeting of your organization, which is trying to determine ways of attracting new members. Someone in the group suggests that redecorating the meeting room might help. Several things might happen in the discussion: (1) Members might begin to evaluate the idea, with some being in favor of it and some not; (2) another idea might be suggested and recorded; or (3) you (or someone else) might elaborate on the idea by describing how the room might look with new carpeting, a pool table, soft lighting, free Wi-Fi, and a new sofa. Whereas the proposal for redecoration might have fallen flat on its own, your elaboration gives it a fighting chance.

Although initiating, coordinating, summarizing, and elaborating are some of the more important types of contributions you can make, this list is by no means complete. Task leadership includes any behavior that helps the group accomplish its goal. Making suggestions, offering new ideas, giving information or opinions, asking for more information, and making procedural observations or recommendations are all task-oriented leadership behaviors that can contribute to a group's effort. The functional approach reveals that leadership skill is associated with the ability to analyze a group's process and to choose appropriate behaviors to further that process.

9.1.2: Process Leadership

OBJECTIVE: Explain how process leadership works

If a group is to function effectively, it needs to address its internal issues. Groups are composed of people, and people have needs. Effective group communication must address both the group's task and the needs of its members. Failing to maintain a satisfying group climate can lead to a breakdown in a group's performance. In this respect, small groups resemble automobiles. Cars are great for getting you where you want to go, but they require regular tuning and maintenance if they are to run reliably and efficiently. If an owner does not maintain a car, eventually it will break down. The same is true of groups: They need tuning and maintenance.

Leadership research consistently indicates that groups have both task and process requirements. Process, leadership behaviors maintain interpersonal relations in a group and facilitate a climate satisfying to members and conducive to accomplishing the group's task. Group process leaders are communication facilitators.

Process-Leadership Behaviors

The following list presents some specific process-leadership behaviors that enhance group climate.

Releasing Tension—Think of times you have studied for exams. You cram more and more information into your head until you reach a saturation point. Everything runs together; ideas blur. You know it's time for a break. After a cup of coffee or an energy drink, a check-in on social media, and some relaxing conversation, you return to your books with renewed energy.

Sometimes the most effective leadership you can provide for a group is suggesting a break. When a group is tired, when its task is difficult, when the hour is late, and when tension and stress are high, a group needs relief. A joke, a bit of humor, a break, or even a motion to adjourn can often provide just what a group needs—tension release.

Gatekeeping—One advantage of working in small groups is summarized by the old adage, "Two (or several) heads are better than one." The diversity that makes group communication so complex also gives it strength. A group possesses more experience and intelligence than does any single individual, but experience and individual insights are useful to a group only when they are shared.

Some people like to talk more than others. Thus, in some groups, two or three people may monopolize the conversation while others remain relatively silent. This fairly common occurrence poses a problem for a group in two ways. First, quiet members are just as likely as more vocal group members to possess useful information and ideas, and their ideas may never surface unless they say something. Second, people who talk more tend to be more satisfied with a group. Thus, members who don't speak up can have a negative effect on a group in both the task and process dimensions.

Gatekeeping aims to coordinate discussion so that members can air their views. It may take the form of eliciting input ("Hilit, you must have given this a lot of thought. What are your views of the problem?") or even of limiting the contributions of more verbal group members ("Can we perhaps limit our comments to two or three minutes so that we can get everyone's ideas before we have to adjourn?"). Gatekeeping is an important leadership function because it ensures more input along the task dimension and higher member satisfaction along the process dimension.

Encouraging—People like praise; they feel good when someone recognizes them for their contributions. Encouragement is a leadership behavior aimed at increasing group members' self-esteem and raising their hopes, confidence, and aspirations. Improving the morale of a group can increase cohesiveness, member satisfaction, and productivity.

Mediating—Conflict is a normal, healthy part of group interaction. However, mismanaged conflict can lead to hurt feelings, physical or mental withdrawal from a group, reduced cohesiveness, and general disruption. Mediating aims to resolve conflict among group members and release any tension associated with the conflict. Whenever conflict becomes person-oriented rather than issue-oriented, it is a particularly appropriate time for mediation.

This list of behaviors that contribute to a group's process needs is not complete, but these behaviors are the most relevant to task and process leadership. A more complete list appears in Table 5-1. The behaviors just described are the most relevant to task and process leadership, and are highlighted here to emphasize their importance and to help you identify your own leadership behavior in groups.

Coaching is an activity that requires both task and process leadership skills. What might happen if this coach had poor leadership skills?

Both task and process leadership are essential to the success of a small group or team. When a group does not make progress on its task, members will feel frustrated and unsatisfied. In addition, if a group does not maintain a comfortable environment, members will tend to focus their attention and energy on their own dissatisfaction with the group rather than on their assigned task.

Resolving Conflict as a Leader

Read the following scenario and answer the questions below.

Janell: I think the plan I'm proposing has considerable merit and meets our needs.

Enrique: That's ridiculous. It'll never work.

Janell: Get off my case! I don't see you proposing any better solutions.

This potentially volatile situation could easily disrupt the group. You often have to work in groups with people you don't like. Obviously, Enrique and Janell do not get along well, but groups can function effectively in spite of personality clashes. Focus discussion on issues rather than on personalities. When interpersonal difficulties become so severe that they cannot be resolved by simply focusing on a group's task, they can seriously hinder a group. At this point it becomes necessary to deal with them either within or outside the group; ignoring problems will not make them go away.

1. As the leader, what do you do when two people in your group are in conflict?
2. How would you handle the situation between Janell and Enrique?
3. Have you dealt with similar situations in the past?

9.2: Situational Perspective of Leadership

OBJECTIVE: Anticipate how leadership style and situation will influence group conflict

The **situational perspective** on group leadership accommodates leadership behaviors, task needs, and process needs—and also takes into account leadership style and situation.

 **By the end of this module, you will be able to:**

9.2.1 Compare the three major leadership styles

9.2.2 Outline Hersey's model of situational leadership

9.2.3 Determine the impact of shared leadership on group performance

9.2.1: Leadership Style

OBJECTIVE: Compare the three major leadership styles

Leadership style is a relatively consistent pattern of behavior reflecting a leader's beliefs and attitudes. Although no two people lead in precisely the same way, people tend to use one of three basic styles:

- **Authoritarian (or autocratic):** Authoritarian leaders assume positions of intellectual and behavioral superiority in groups. They make the decisions, give the orders, and generally control all activities.
- **Democratic:** Democratic leaders have more faith in the group than authoritarian leaders do and consequently try to involve members in making decisions.
- **Laissez-faire:** Laissez-faire leaders see themselves as "first among equals," no better or no worse than other group members. They assume the group will direct itself. Laissez-faire leaders avoid dominating groups.

In one of the earliest studies of the effects of leadership style, researchers compared groups of schoolchildren led by graduate students who had been specifically trained in one of the three leadership styles.[7] Here is a brief summary of the results:

- Groups with democratic leaders generally were better satisfied and functioned in a more orderly and positive way.
- Groups with authoritarian leaders were more aggressive or more apathetic (depending on the group).
- Members of democratic groups were better satisfied than members of laissez-faire groups; a majority of group members preferred democratic to authoritarian leadership, although some members were better satisfied in authoritarian groups.
- Authoritarian groups spent more time engaged in productive work, but only when the leader was present.

It is tempting to conclude that participatory, democratic leadership will invariably lead to greater satisfaction and higher productivity. Unfortunately, the evidence does not warrant such a generalization. Several studies have shown that no single leadership style is effective in all situations. What works at General Motors may not work in a family business; an effective student body president may be a poor camp counselor. The expectations of one group differ from those of other groups.[8]

LEADER BEHAVIOR IN DIFFERENT SOCIAL CLIMATES Effective leadership is contingent on a variety of interrelated factors, such as culture, time constraints, group compatibility, and the nature of a group's task. Although the functional approach reveals the importance of fulfilling various leadership roles in a group, it does not explain which roles are most appropriate in which situation. It is essential to consider the setting in which leadership behavior occurs.

The situational approach views leadership as an interaction between leadership style and various situational factors. David Korten has suggested that under certain conditions groups are pressured to have centralized, authoritarian leadership, but that as these conditions change, groups often develop a more democratic, participative form of leadership.

Korten says that groups with highly structured goals and high stress move toward authoritarian leadership. Think of times when you were in a group with clear goals but whose members were uncertain of how to achieve them. Remember when a group felt stress because of an impending deadline or a group grade. At such times, group members will gladly follow any leader who can give direction and show them the means to reach their goal. When the situation changes—that is, when the group feels less uncertain, has less stress, and has less structured goals—it has less of a need for authoritarian leadership and instead needs more participative, democratic leadership. Contemporary studies continue to support this relationship: Under conditions of relative certainty, groups show a pro-democratic attitude.[9] As stress and goal structure increase, the tendency of a group to accept authoritarian leadership increases. As stress and goal structure decrease, groups need more democratic—or even laissez-faire—leadership. When the room is on fire, we want someone who will take charge and lead us to safety. But when the task is to discuss the book of the month, such take-charge leadership feels inappropriate.

9.2.2: Hersey's Situational Leadership Model

OBJECTIVE: Outline Hersey's model of situational leadership

Like other situational leadership theories, Paul Hersey's model uses various combinations of task- and relationship-oriented leadership behaviors to describe leadership style as it relates to different situations.[10] In this case, the readiness of the group is the situational variable.

Hersey's model describes the now-familiar task and relationship (process) dimensions of leadership behavior.

TELLING Leaders who strongly emphasize performance of the group task and pay little attention to relationship issues—that is, their orientation is high task and low relationship—are described as having a "telling" style.

Leader Behavior in Three "Social Climates"

Characteristic	Authoritarian	Democratic	Laissez-Faire
Policy development	Leader makes all determinations regarding policy.	Leader encourages and directs, but all policies are a matter of group discussion and decision.	Leader participates at a minimal level; complete freedom for group or individual decisions.
Distribution of information	Leader dictates techniques and activity steps one at a time, so group members are always largely uncertain of future steps.	Leader discusses activity steps with the group before the group begins work; general steps to the group goal are sketched, and when technical advice is needed, leader suggests alternative procedures.	Leader supplies various materials, making it clear he or she will supply information when asked, but taking no other part in discussion.
Division of tasks	Leader usually dictates work tasks and work companions for each member.	Leader leaves division of tasks to the group; members are free to work with anyone.	Leader does not participate in task or work companion assignments.
Feedback on work	Leader tends to be personal in praise and criticism of each member's work; remains aloof from active group participation except when demonstrating.	Leader tends to be objective or "fact-minded" in praise and criticism and tries to be a regular group member in spirit without doing too much of the work.	Leader makes only infrequent, spontaneous comments on member activities unless questioned; makes no attempt to appraise or regulate course of events.

SELLING Leaders whose style reflects a high task and high relationship approach are identified as having a "selling" leadership style. Thus, while both telling and selling styles are directive, leaders following a selling style are concerned that the group accept and internalize the orders given.

PARTICIPATING Leaders who focus less on task performance and place more emphasis on relationships exhibit a "participating" style.

DELEGATING A "delegating" style reflects low task performance emphasis coupled with low relationship emphasis. Leaders with a participating style are driven primarily by concern for relationships and a need for all group members to share in decision making. A leader with a delegating style takes a hands-off attitude and allows the group to direct itself.

According to Hersey, these four leadership styles may be more or less appropriate depending on a group's readiness—that is, the amount of willingness and ability the follower or group demonstrates while performing a specific task. When you view readiness in combination with the four leadership styles identified in Hersey's model, it becomes clear that a "telling" style is most appropriate with groups that are just starting out, perhaps in their orientation stage of development. As groups mature, effective leadership allows for more autonomy and the participating and delegating styles are more effective. "Just as parents should relinquish control as a function of the increasing maturity of their children, so too should leaders share more decision-making power as their subordinates acquire greater experience with and commitment to their tasks."[11]

Communication scholar Sarah Trenholm offers the following example of how Hersey's model might apply to a classroom:

> Consider teaching style as a form of leadership. Hersey would suggest that at the beginning of a course of study, with inexperienced students, a highly directive telling style is best. The teacher who tells a freshman class, "You decide what and how you want to learn. It's entirely up to you," is using a delegating style, which will fail because at this point students are not yet ready to take full responsibility for their own learning. As the course progresses, however, and as the students feel more comfortable with the course and each other, the teacher might use selling and participating styles and perhaps end up with a delegating approach. More mature students may be ready for autonomy and may even resent being told what to do.[12]

Hersey's model is widely used in training managers and executives, probably because it shows how managers can change styles according to their subordinates' readiness level. A delegating style can be used with one employee or group, and a telling style with another.[13]

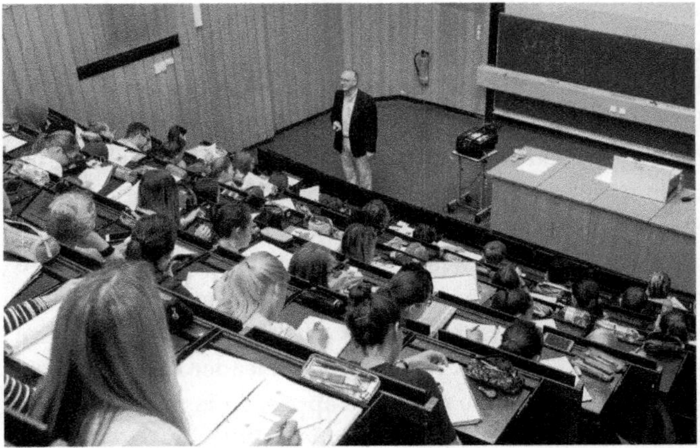

What leadership behavior would you expect from this professor in a lecture hall?

9.2.3: Shared Leadership in Teams

OBJECTIVE: Determine the impact of shared leadership on group performance

At first glance, the situational approach seems to cover all bases. It looks at the style of leadership, the group's task and process needs, and situational variables that influence groups. Unfortunately, most research using this approach has focused on the behavior of leaders rather than on leadership as a shared process of realizing group goals.[14] Thus, while the situational approach is useful, it is not as all-encompassing as the functional approach. Achieving a group goal involves everyone in the group, not just the leader.

Shared leadership (also called distributed leadership) is a relatively new area of study. This type of leadership occurs when two or more individuals within a team share leadership responsibilities. In contrast, focused leadership resides in a single individual, who is identified as the leader. Focused and distributed leadership can be considered endpoints on a continuum. Research has shown that when group or team members share leadership, their groups experience less conflict, greater consensus, and higher trust and cohesion than groups with focused leadership.[15]

Increasingly, organizations are relying on self-managing teams to perform much of their work.[16] Shared leadership can be viewed as "an emergent team property that results from the distribution of leadership influence across multiple team members."[17] Shared leadership originates when multiple group members exert influence over the team and other group members, resulting in a leadership network that shapes team and individual activities and outcomes. Research supports the hypothesis that the degree of shared leadership in a team is positively related to team performance.[18] Other research has identified traits of leaders and team members as situational variables that must be taken into account. The charisma of a leader and the group's self-efficacy (degree to which it can function on its own) are related to leadership style. A coaching (democratic) style of leadership appears to be more effective than the directive (autocratic) approach when the team leader is highly charismatic, whereas the directive approach is more effective when team members lack self-efficacy.[19]

Review

Perspectives on Leadership

Trait approach: Attempts to identify characteristics common to successful leaders

Functional approach: Views leadership as a set of behaviors that may be enacted by any group member

Situational approach: Relates effective leadership to the interaction between leadership style and the group situation

WRITING PROMPT

Which Type of Leadership?

Imagine yourself as leader of a scout troop on a weekend camping and canoeing expedition. Halfway through the weekend, you receive an alert on your cell phone that a storm upstream is likely to result in flash flooding at your location. What do you see as the group's leadership needs in this situation? Explain.

The response entered here will appear in the performance dashboard and can be viewed by your instructor.

Submit

9.3: Transformational Leadership

Objective: Apply a transformational style to small group leadership

A relatively new theory of leadership, which describes leadership in organizations, is **transformational leadership**. Transformational leaders "strive to change, elevate, and unify the goals of followers as well as inspire them to pursue challenging and shared objectives."[20] Transformational leadership has four defining characteristics, called the Four I's:[21]

1. *Idealized leadership* seeks to create within followers an inspiring vision of how things can be.
2. *Inspirational motivation* is the communicative ability of the leader to stir followers to action.
3. *Intellectual stimulation* is the leader's ability to engage followers in challenging the status quo and assumptions about processes.
4. *Individual consideration* is the leader's ability to be supportive and to nurture each individual's positive attributes, qualities, and strengths in support of the greater good.

Steve Jobs, Apple's CEO and co-founder, exemplified transformational leadership.

By the end of this module, you will be able to:

9.3.1 Summarize the skills associated with the transformational style of leadership

9.3.2 Explain how transformational culture affects small groups

9.3.1: Critical Skills of Transformational Leadership

OBJECTIVE: Summarize the skills associated with the transformational style of leadership

Research on shared leadership in virtual teams points to some common attributes of successful leadership behaviors. Especially important are the group members' technical, communication, and people (process) skills.[22] Whereas transactional leaders clarify expectations and reward followers or employees for meeting them, *transformational leaders* motivate others to move beyond self-interest and work for the greater collective good.[23] Transformational leaders have a sense of vision and purpose. Management consultant and author Peter Senge proposes that transformational leadership relies on three critical skills:[24]

1. *Building shared vision* is similar to establishing *mutuality of concern*. It involves encouraging individuals to express their visions of group or organizational goals while encouraging the development of a common, positive view.

Virtual Collaboration

Communication Modes and Leadership Styles

As a group or team leader, you may have considerable influence over how much group interaction takes place face to face (FTF) or through electronic media. But which modes (or combination of modes) will be most effective? How does leadership style interact with different types of communication media? Scholars Laura Hambley, Thomas O'Neill, and Theresa Kline tested different leadership styles against different media and outcomes.[26] They compared transactional and transformational leadership styles in three communication media settings: face to face, video conference, and text-based chat teams. In their study, these researchers defined transactional leadership as a process of exchange in which leaders tended to gain follower compliance through offering rewards or threatening punishment. They defined transformational leadership as being aimed at broadening followers' interests, motivating, and gaining commitment to goals and mission. Their research yielded the following findings:

- Mean constructive (supportive) interaction scores were higher in FTF teams than in video conference and chat teams.
- Teams working in richer (e.g., FTF) communication media did not achieve higher task performance than those working in less-rich media.
- Cohesiveness scores were higher in FTF and video conference teams than in chat teams.

While many studies have found that teams led by transformational leaders outperform those led by transactional leaders, some evidence also shows that the reward aspects of transactional leadership can be highly effective.[27] Both transactional and transformation leadership are related to performance in FTF teams, with the overall edge going to transformational leadership. Research on leadership styles in virtual teams suggests that transformational leadership is especially important in regard to building the trust necessary for team success.[28]

Communication media have important effects on team interaction and cohesiveness. Media with more richness (FTF, video conferencing) are generally more effective than less-rich text-based media.

2. *Surfacing and challenging mental models* is a process of identifying and challenging assumptions without creating defensiveness—a daunting task requiring supportive communication skills.
3. *Engaging in systems thinking* means understanding groups and organizations and the great complexity that characterizes them, which requires leaders to look beyond day-to-day operations to find underlying themes, forces of change, and interrelationships.[25]

Leadership that empowers and motivates others stimulates knowledge sharing, team efficacy, and greater performance. In the classic film *Star Wars*: *The Empire Strikes Back*, Luke Skywalker watches as Yoda levitates his spaceship out of the swamp.

LUKE: I don't believe it!

YODA: That is why you fail.

Often, the secret to reaching a goal (or vision) lies in the *belief* that it can be reached. Belief in the vision becomes more powerful than the followers' sense of lack, limitation, and doubt. This "belief-system shift" empowers followers to reach a higher level of commitment and achievement. It may even be so powerful as to convert followers into leaders and leaders into moral agents.

9.3.2: Transformational Cultures

OBJECTIVE: Explain how transformational culture affects small groups

Transformational leadership is not so much a set of behaviors that one can observe or emulate as it is a philosophy of leadership and change.[29] Small groups everywhere operate within the cultures of larger organizations and are influenced by those cultures. In innovative, transformational organizational cultures, we are likely to see assumptions that people can be trusted, that everyone has a contribution to make, and that complex problems should be handled at the lowest possible level. In a transformational culture, norms are flexible enough to adapt to changing external environments. Superiors serve as mentors, coaches, role models, and leaders.[30] Transformational leadership has the greatest capacity to motivate group members to debate ideas constructively.[31] Some evidence indicates that the most effective leaders in virtual teams are those who increase their transformational leadership.[32] Research also suggests that transformational leadership may lessen the negative aspects related to workgroup diversity, and strengthen a group's innovation climate and creativity.[33]

CASE STUDY

Adjusting the Leadership Style to the Situation

Division director Arthur has retired. Once an ambitious junior executive for the company, Arthur had, in recent years, taken a more laissez-faire attitude as team leader. As a result, his team showed the lowest productivity record in the company, and his employees did not receive minimal salary increments and other rewards from top management. Morale was very low.

Hoping to rejuvenate the group, management replaced Arthur with an extremely bright, dynamic, and aggressive young manager named Marilyn. Marilyn's instructions were: "Get your team's productivity up by 20 percent over the next 12 months, or we'll fire the whole group and start from scratch, with a new manager and new employees."

Marilyn began by studying the records of the employees in her group to determine each person's strengths and weaknesses. She then created goals and objectives for each employee and made assignments accordingly. She set a rigid timetable for each employee and made all employees directly accountable to her.

Employee response was overwhelmingly positive. Out of chaos came order. Each person knew what was expected and had tangible goals to achieve. Employees felt united behind their new leader as they all strove to achieve their objective of a one-year, 20 percent increase in productivity.

At the end of the year, productivity was up not 20 percent but 35 percent! Management was thrilled and awarded Marilyn a large raise and the company's certificate of achievement. Every team member received a handsome bonus.

Feeling that she had a viable formula for success, Marilyn moved into the second year as she had the first—setting goals for each employee, holding them accountable, and so forth. However, things went less smoothly the second year. Employees who had been quick to respond the first year were less responsive. Although the work Marilyn assigned was usually completed on time, its quality declined. Employees had a morale problem: Those who had once looked up to Marilyn as "Boss" were now sarcastically calling her "Queen Bee" and reminiscing about "the good old days" when Arthur was their manager.

Marilyn's behavior as a manager had not changed, yet her leadership was no longer effective.

Questions for Analysis: Adjusting the Leadership Style to the Situation

1. Evaluate Marilyn's leadership style over the course of two years. Do you see transactional and/or transformational elements?
2. Consider the situational variables that changed from the first year to the second year. What recommendations would you give Marilyn to help her succeed in this leadership role?

9.4: Emergent Leadership in Small Groups

OBJECTIVE: Determine how qualities of effective leadership work in small groups

Group leadership is often designated or appointed—but leadership also will emerge in groups with no identifiable leader at the outset. This emergent leadership often occurs through a process of elimination.

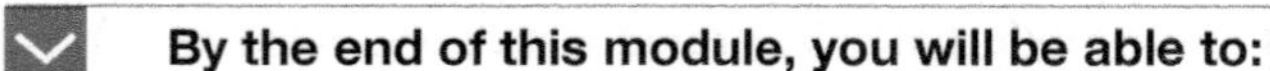

By the end of this module, you will be able to:

- **9.4.1** Characterize the kind of leader groups tend to choose for themselves
- **9.4.2** Compare the ways in which women and men serve and are perceived as leaders

9.4.1: The Minnesota Studies

OBJECTIVE: Characterize the kind of leader groups tend to choose for themselves

A fascinating series of leadership studies begun at the University of Minnesota (called the Minnesota Studies) sought the answer to the question, "Who is most likely to emerge as the perceived leader of a leaderless discussion group?" Led by Professor Ernest Bormann, the Minnesota Studies formed and observed "test-tube groups" that engaged in leaderless group discussions.

Most people think of a leader as someone who takes charge and organizes a discussion. Predictably, group members often perceive those who actively participate in the group and who direct communication toward procedural matters as leaders. Although studies show a clear correlation between perceived leadership and talkativeness, especially task-oriented talkativeness,[34] those persons who talk most are not the only ones who become leaders. In fact, most groups do not select leaders at all. Emergent leaders are those whose powers derive from their acceptance by other group members rather than from position, rank, or status.[35] The Minnesota Studies showed that such leaders emerge through a "method of residues," whereby group members are rejected for the role of leader until only one remains. The first members to be eliminated from consideration are the quiet ones who do not actively participate in the early stages of a group's discussion. The next to go are the talkative but overly aggressive or dogmatic group members, who are perceived as too inflexible for leadership positions.

The composition and needs of the group will determine, in part, which group member or members will emerge in leadership roles. When the needs are for task focus, evidence indicates that conscientious extroverts who are open to new experiences are likely to find support as leaders. Very agreeable individuals are likely to emerge when relationship needs are at the fore.[36] In the Minnesota Studies, members often rejected an authoritarian style on the grounds that the person was "too bossy" or "dictatorial." A separate study found that specific communication behaviors increase the likelihood of rejection as leader.[37] Group members who seem unable to contribute to either the group's tasks or the organization because they are quiet, vague, tentative, self-effacing, or always asking others for direction are usually rejected. Task-motivated group members often rejected a contender who was perceived as too process-oriented—that is, too concerned about everyone's feelings and moods to be decisive. Likewise, process-oriented members tended to reject those they saw as too concerned with the task. According to Bormann,

> In the final analysis, groups accepted the contender who provided the optimum blend of task efficiency and personal consideration. The leader who emerged was the one that others thought would be of most value to the entire group and whose orders and directions they trusted and could follow.[38]

Research is adding to our knowledge of emergent leadership in groups. Emergent leaders typically display more effective listening skills and may be more extroverted.[39] Individual task ability contributes to emergent leadership, as does commitment to the group's assigned goals.[40] Group goals are often strongly influenced by the emergent leader's personal goals for the group.[41] Under conditions of high uncertainty, a group will turn to emergent leaders who are seen as prototypical—those who embody the group's social identity.[42] Verbal aggressiveness is not associated with leadership emergence.[43] An individual's self-view as a leader affects the number of leadership nominations he or she receives, and the number of leadership nominations received affects the person's self-view as leader over time.[44]

Ethical Collaboration

The Leader as Gatekeeper

Some research indicates that the behavior of leaders or superiors in an organization is among the strongest influences on ethical behavior, playing a larger role than the actions of peers or, in some cases, people's individual ethical frameworks.[45] When you're a leader, you're a role model. As such, your power may extend far beyond your direct, immediate influence on your group's work.

Group and team leaders are often privy to information that other group members do not have. Organizations often communicate with groups only through their designated leaders. Thus, the leader acts as a gatekeeper for the group as a whole.

WRITING PROMPT

Making a Leadership Decision

Suppose that you are the leader of a team working on a project nearing completion. You are relieved because the holidays are approaching rapidly, your group has been working night and day, and the project must be completed so that the exhausted group members can take some time off with their families. You schedule the final meeting for tomorrow, when the team will put the finishing touches on the project and you will tell them they can have some time off.

Your boss has just brought you a report from another team, which he believes may have bearing on your project. You review the report, and while you understand your boss's view, you don't believe the other team's data are really relevant to your project. If you forward the report to your group, the members will have to take time to process it, which will cut into their much-needed vacation time. What would you do in this situation?

The response entered here will appear in the performance dashboard and can be viewed by your instructor.

Submit

9.4.2: Leadership and Gender

OBJECTIVE: Compare the ways in which women and men serve and are perceived as leaders

Leadership is often viewed by scholars as gendered because the concept traditionally is viewed in "masculine" terms—assertive, adversarial, goal-oriented, and competitive.[46] But when looking at leadership as something one does (functional approach) rather than as something that one is (trait approach), it becomes clear that "feminine" attributes—the ability to listen, speak openly about feelings, and create trust—are equally important for successful group leadership. The task and process dimensions, and the transactional and transformational styles, are all essential to group success, with some variability depending on the situation. Effective leaders need to *combine* the complementary styles of goal-oriented (transactional) and change-oriented (transformational) leadership.[47] Gendered expectations no doubt influence expectations for women and men as leaders. But expectations do not have to determine behaviors, and behaviors can reshape expectations.

Every time senior leaders speak, they are constructing and managing impressions of their profiles as a leaders.[48] Angela Merkel did not become chancellor of Germany by conforming to gender stereotypes. In this regard, strong role models can change expectations about how senior leaders should look, act, and speak. Such role models can change attitudes about leadership and empower women. Over time, these changes can help address the relative shortage of women in senior leadership positions.[49]

Skilled Collaboration

Servant Leadership

One of the most popular models of leadership today, which is significantly related to transformational leadership,[50] is servant leadership, a concept developed by Robert K. Greenleaf in 1970.[51]

> The servant-leader *is* servant first. . . . It begins with the natural feeling that one wants to serve, to serve *first*. Then conscious choice brings one to aspire to lead. That person is sharply different from one who is leader first, perhaps because of the need to assuage an unusual power drive or to acquire material possessions. For such it will be a later choice to serve—after leadership is established. The leader-first and the servant-first are two extreme types. Between them there are shadings and blends that are part of the infinite variety of human nature. . . . The difference manifests itself in the care taken by the servant-first to make sure that other people's highest priority needs are being served.[52]

Servant leaders are thought to be effective because their group members or followers are so well cared for by the leader that they can reach their full potential as team members and, therefore, perform at their best. Their leadership is the opposite of authoritarian, domineering leadership. This perspective asks leaders to think hard about how best to nurture, respect, value, and motivate their followers, employees, or team members.

Skills and Capacities of the Servant Leader

In his book about Greenleaf's work, Don M. Frick notes several characteristics of servant leaders.[53] All of these characteristics are components of effective group communication.

- Listening is the most important skill; servant leaders begin by being other-oriented, always responding to problems by listening first.
- Servant leaders use their power ethically; persuasion is always preferred over manipulation or coercion.
- Servant leaders seek **consensus**, when all group members support and are committed to a decision.
- While servant leaders may not always agree with others, they always approach others with acceptance and empathy.
- Servant leaders nurture community, understanding our interconnectedness with the broader communities in which we live.

Servant leaders are selfless, willing to do what is right even at the risk of their personal well-being or status. Servant leaders influence followers to emulate their behavior by prioritizing the needs of others above their own.[54] At its highest level, this is real leadership, like that of the Rev. Dr. Martin Luther King, Jr., who risked—and indeed gave—his life to stand up for what he believed.

As you work in your groups, consider the findings of researchers Susan Shimanoff and Mercilee Jenkins. Their extensive reviews of the research literature on gender and group leadership yielded the following conclusions:

- In problem-solving groups, both male and female leaders concentrate on task behaviors, but female leaders are slightly more responsive to the group's social–emotional needs.
- Males tend to talk more, which can increase their power, but women are equally effective in using evidence and making procedural suggestions, which are two critical leadership behaviors.

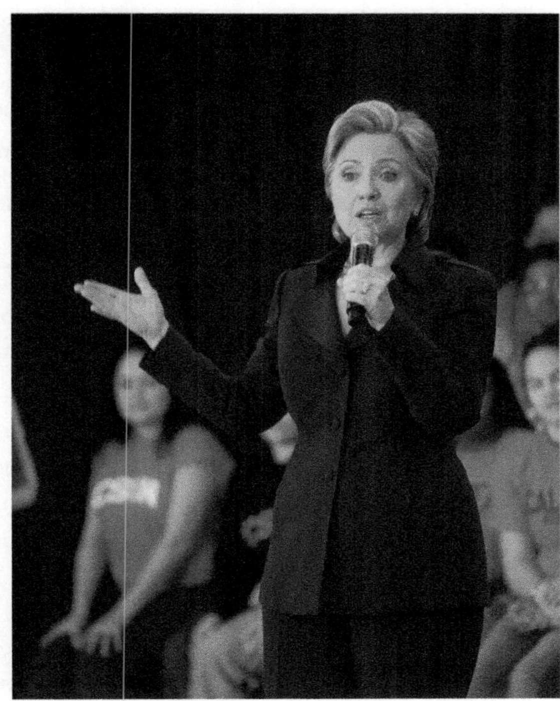

Despite persistent bias, women are increasingly rising to leadership positions such as secretary of State and Presidential candidate.

- Generally, men and women lead equally well. However, some evidence indicate that because of sex-role biases, female leaders may need to perform better than their male counterparts to be considered as good as men.[55]

Men and women appear to be equally suited to positions of leadership, yet men are still more likely to rise to positions of power. Shimanoff and Jenkins have offered the following suggestions for group members who wish to lower gender barriers and maximize effective leadership:

- Acknowledge and challenge sex-role biases; affirm egalitarian attitudes and remind group members of their importance.
- Celebrate the "traditional" strengths of women, but don't assume that women alone have these strengths.
- Increase the visibility and support of female role models.
- Designate leaders only after interacting, if at all.
- Listen attentively; support all members and treat them with respect.
- Learn from diverse groups and individuals.[56]

Even as women increasingly take their natural and proportional positions of leadership, gender bias may persist. One study found that subordinates' evaluations of group leaders were significantly less positive for female leaders with male subordinates than for female leaders with female subordinates. Male and female subordinates of male leaders rated their performance equally.[57]

We conclude this chapter as it began, with a quotation, this time from Lao Tsu, who wrote these words 2,500 years ago. They remain as true today as ever:

> The wicked leader is he whom the people despise,
> The good leader is he whom the people revere.
> The great leader is he of whom the people say,
> "We did it ourselves."

Summary: Leading Groups

9.1: Functional Perspective of Leadership

- Leadership is behavior or communication that influences, guides, directs, or controls a group. The most effective leadership behavior is the behavior that best meets the needs of the group.
- The trait perspective views leadership as a set of personal attributes—traits—that leaders possess. Its weakness is that traits useful in one situation may not be as helpful in another circumstance.
- The functional perspective views leadership as behaviors that may be performed by any group member to maximize group effectiveness.
- Task-leadership behaviors aim to accomplish a group goal. Process-leadership behaviors help maintain a satisfactory group climate.

9.2: Situational Perspective of Leadership

- The situational perspective takes into account the factors of leadership behaviors, task needs, and process needs, but also incorporates leadership style and situation.

9.3: Transformational Leadership

- Transformational leaders motivate others to move beyond self-interest and work for the greater collective good.[58] Transformational leaders have a sense of vision and purpose.
- Management consultant and author Peter Senge proposes that transformational leaders demonstrate three critical skills: (1) building shared vision, (2) surfacing and challenging mental models, and (3) engaging in systems thinking.[59]

9.4: Emergent Leadership in Small Groups

- In leaderless groups, leaders emerge through a "method of residues" in which the group eliminates contenders one by one. In the final analysis, groups are most likely to accept the leader who best blends a personal consideration for the group's members with a clear focus on the group's task.
- The leader who emerges is likely to be the one who others think will be most valuable to the entire group and whose orders and directions they trust and can follow.[60]

SHARED WRITING

Emerging Leadership in Groups

In a leaderless group, leaders emerge through a "method of residues."

Analyze this statement within the context of contemporary organizations. Is the emergent leadership theory applicable? If so, under what circumstances? Write a short response that your classmates will read. Be sure to include specifics in your discussion.

A minimum number of characters is required to post and earn points. After posting, your response can be viewed by your class and instructor, and you can participate in the class discussion.

Post

Chapter 10

Making Decisions and Solving Problems

"A sum can be put right: but only by going back till you find the error and working it afresh from that point, never by simply going on."[1]

—C. S. Lewis

Learning Objectives

10.1 Evaluate how a group makes a decision

10.2 Evaluate how a group solves a problem

10.3 Apply the descriptive approach to group problem solving and decision making

10.4 Compare effective and ineffective groups according to the functional approach to problem solving and decision making

10.5 Assess situations for cultural differences

John Stith Pemberton made his first batch in a brass kettle over an open fire. To mask the bitter taste of a wide array of ingredients, Pemberton decided to add sugar to his concoction to make it taste better. He sold a portion of the rights to Asa Candler, who worked with a team of people to make and distribute the tonic. Candler needed to solve the problem of how to sell the drink. After developing a system for making syrup and shipping it to local bottlers, Candler eventually sold the business to Ernest Woodruff, who helped make the company a household name by making good marketing decisions. You know the company as Coca-Cola. What started as a simple homemade tonic has become a multibillion-dollar business due to a little luck and a lot of good individual and collaborative problem solving and decision making.[2] As the case of Coca-Cola illustrates, the decisions you make and the problems you solve today can have significant consequences for the future.

In this chapter, we'll discuss the communication strategies that help groups make quality decisions. More research has been conducted on group problem solving and decision-making communication than about any other group objective. Groups discuss issues to accomplish a task—to search for truth, groups make decisions and solve problems.[3] Whether you work for a *Fortune* 500 company like Coca-Cola or are serving on your local school board, the quality of decisions and the approach to problem solving can have a major influence on others. To help you understand the nature of decision making and problem solving, we'll first discuss the elements, methods, and obstacles to quality decision making. Then we'll explore the nature of group problem solving, including three approaches to examining how groups solve problems: descriptive, functional, and prescriptive.

We end the chapter by identifying cultural assumptions about group problem solving and decision making. In Chapter 11, we continue our discussion of group problem solving while looking at techniques that can help groups do their work effectively and efficiently.

10.1: Group Decision Making

OBJECTIVE: Evaluate how a group makes a decision

One critical group task is **decision making**—the process of choosing from among several alternatives. For example, in deciding which college or university to attend, you probably considered several choices. Perhaps you started by gathering information about as many as 15 or 20 schools and then narrowed the alternatives as you considered the advantages and disadvantages of each institution. Eventually you narrowed your choice to two and made a final decision.[4] Groups make decisions in essentially the same way.

In this section, we'll consider the elements, methods, and characteristics of group decision making and examine some of the obstacles that keep groups from making high-quality decisions. Later, we contrast the decision-making (choice-making) process with the process of solving problems—a more comprehensive process that involves making choices to overcome an obstacle or barrier to achieve a goal.

By the end of this module, you will be able to:

10.1.1 Evaluate the effectiveness of a group decision-making process

10.1.2 Compare group decision-making methods

10.1.1: Effectiveness of Group Decision Making

OBJECTIVE: Evaluate the effectiveness of a group decision-making process

Group decision making usually follows a predictable pattern.[5] Groups tend to make better decisions if that pattern is clearly identified *and* then followed.[6] Research has identified factors that make group decision making effective and factors that make it ineffective.

Group Decision-Making Steps

The group decision-making process includes the following steps.[7]

Analyze the Decision to Be Made

Effective: The group assesses the present situation—A group should first analyze and assess a situation by breaking it down into smaller parts, and then make a decision.[8] As an example, suppose an airline's board of directors must decide whether to lower fares. Before making a decision, they first look at competitors' fares and the number of passengers those competitors transport each day.

Ineffective: The group fails to analyze the present situation accurately—How a group analyzes the information can dramatically affect its decision.[9] If a group improperly analyzes its current situation, it's likely to make a bad decision. Having too little evidence—or none—is one of the reasons groups sometimes fail to analyze the present situation accurately. Even if group members do have ample evidence, their decision-making process may be defective if they have not properly tested the evidence.

Also, merely having information does not necessarily mean the group will use it well. Reasoning is the process of drawing conclusions from information, and flawed reasoning can contribute to a bad decision. Whether the information a group has is good or bad, group members will tend to use the information if all members receive it, members discuss it, and at least one member champions the information.[10] Research suggests that groups perform better if they critically evaluate the information they have *and* consider the impact of their final decision on solving the problem.[11]

Involve All Members in Seeking Information

Effective: The group seeks input from each member—One primary advantage of working in groups is the opportunity to tap into the knowledge base of many people rather than that of just a few individuals. Research by John Oetzel documents that groups make better decisions when there is more equal participation in the discussion.[12]

Ineffective: Too few people are involved in the discussion—If several members dominate the conversation, decision quality suffers. Group members who believe they did not have an opportunity to voice their opinions and share information with others will not perceive the decision to have been reached fairly.[13]

Identify and Clarify the Goals of the Decision

Effective: The group identifies what it wants to accomplish—After assessing the current situation, the group should identify its objectives. A group whose members are uncertain about the task will have difficulty making a high-quality decision.[14] If its goal is clear, a group begins to identify alternatives or choices.

Ineffective: The group fails to establish clear and appropriate group goals—A group that has not clearly spelled out what it hopes to accomplish by making a decision has no means of assessing the effectiveness of the decision. Group members who focus on their own needs rather than the group's need are less likely to share information with others and may hinder the group's work.[15]

Group Members Identify Multiple Options

Effective: The group identifies several decision alternatives—The greater the number of alternatives a group generates, the greater the likelihood it will make a good decision. To identify good options, the group should review the information that it has gathered.

Ineffective: The group makes a decision based on only one or two options—Poor decision making occurs when groups pounce on the first or second option identified and fail to consider a wide range of possible options before making a decision.

Rationally Evaluate the Positive and Negative Consequences of Alternatives

Effective: Review the pros and cons of the options identified—After identifying alternatives, a group should rationally assess the positive and negative implications of each alternative before making a decision. An overly emotional group that does not review the facts and data is more likely to reach a flawed decision.[16] The pros and cons of each option should be based on the information the group has identified.

Ineffective: The group fails to identify both positive and negative effects of possible decisions—Bad decisions occur when groups are so eager to make a decision that they don't take enough time to consider the pros and cons of their actions. Ineffective groups fail to consider the consequences of their decision before they make it.[17] If you are in a competitive situation where you are trying to do a better job than other groups, research has found that you are more likely to evaluate both the pros and the cons when making a decision.[18]

After Analyzing the Data and Options, the Group Makes a Decision

Effective: The group selects the best alternative—The chosen option should potentially have a maximum positive outcome with minimal negative consequences. A group is more likely to select the best alternative if it has carefully assessed the situation, considered group goals, identified several choices, and noted the positive and negative implications of each.

Ineffective: The group makes a poor decision, an overly risky decision, or no decision—Groups make bad choices for a number of reasons. Perhaps they did not have adequate data or they incorrectly analyzed the information they had. Or perhaps members did not share the insights or information they had. One of the biggest reasons groups make bad choices is that they fail to consider the negative consequences of the option selected.[19] Sometimes, rather than making a decision, group members suggest no decision be made. But as the saying goes, not to decide is to decide.

One well-documented cause of ineffective decision making and problem solving is **risky shift**, in which people working in groups sometimes make risker decisions than individuals would.[20] Research has consistently found that group members may tend to make more polarizing decisions, or more extreme decisions, than they normally would when working individually.[21] Research suggests that very young and elderly group members tend to make *less* risky decisions for others.[22] Groups are especially prone to making a risky decision if the goal is either far away or very close to being accomplished.[23] "Let's go for it!" and "What do we have to lose?" are phrases group members may use when they are on the verge of making a risky decision.[24]

To avoid making decisions that may place others at risk, imagine how you would feel about the decision you are making for others if someone were imposing the same policy or procedure on you. Sometimes making a risky decision may be the best decision, but a group should be mindful of the proposal's chance of success or failure. Think about the consequences of the decision for others if the decision fails to achieve its goal.

WRITING PROMPT

Effective and Ineffective Group Decision Making

Reflect on an experience you've had in which your group made a good decision or successfully solved a problem. Then think about a group in which you participated that did *not* make a good decision or developed an ineffective solution to a problem. Describe the differences between the two group experiences. What made the effective group effective? Why was the ineffective group not effective?

▶ The response entered here will appear in the performance dashboard and can be viewed by your instructor.

Submit

10.1.2: Methods of Group Decision Making

OBJECTIVE: Compare group decision-making methods

Researchers who study artificial intelligence (AI) have found that computers with well-programmed AI software can make good decisions.[25] Experts suggest we will increasingly turn to computers to make decisions in the future.[26] Today, however, we still rely on groups of people to make the best-informed, highest-quality decisions. Understanding the methods of group decision making can give you and your group options to consider when a decision needs to be made.[27]

How Do Groups Make Decisions?

There are several common methods of group decision making.

Decision by Expert in Group—One person in a group may seem to be the best informed about the issue, and members can turn to this person to make the choice. This expert may or may not be a group's designated leader. Deferring to an expert from within a group may be an efficient way to make a decision, but if there is not adequate discussion, the group may not be satisfied with the outcome.

Decision by Expert Outside Group—A group may decide that none of its members has the credibility, knowledge, or wisdom to make a particular decision, and it may feel unable or unwilling to do so. In such a case, members may turn to someone outside the group who has authority to decide. Although an outside expert may make a fine decision, a group that gives up its decision-making power to one person loses the advantages of the greater input and variety of approaches that come from being a group in the first place.

Averaging Individual Rankings or Ratings—Group members can be asked to rank or rate possible alternatives. After the group averages the rankings or ratings, it selects the alternative with the highest average. This method of making choices can be a useful way to start discussions and to see where the group stands on an issue. However, it is not the best way to make a final decision because it does not take full advantage of the give-and-take of group discussion.

Random Choice—Sometimes groups become so frustrated that they do not make a well-considered decision, but instead resort to a coin toss or other random approach. These methods are not recommended for groups that take their decision making seriously.

Majority Rule—Majority rule is the most often-used method of group decision making. Although it can be swift and efficient, it can also leave an unsatisfied minority. Unless it allots enough time for discussing an issue, a group that makes a decision on the basis of majority rule may sacrifice decision quality and group cohesiveness for efficiency.

Decision by Minority—Sometimes a minority of group members makes a decision. These members may yell the loudest or threaten to create problems for the group unless they get their way. Members may ask, "Does anyone have any objections?" and, if no one answers immediately, consider the decision made. Minority members whose decision is adopted may temporarily rejoice, but over time, the group will have difficulty implementing a decision that is not widely accepted. In contrast, research suggests that when a majority of members support an idea and then the majority evaporates because several group members change their minds, the group is in a vulnerable position; a view that was previously held by a minority can swiftly become the majority view. So, in cases when you side with the minority, keep in mind that things change. Don't side with the majority simply because it's the majority. Groups work best when the members engage in honest dialogue in the search for truth.

Decision by Consensus—Consensus occurs when all group members can support a course of action. This decision-making method is time-consuming and difficult, but members are usually satisfied with the decision. If group members must also implement the solution, this method works well. To reach a decision by consensus, group members must listen and respond to individual viewpoints and manage conflicts that arise. Consensus is facilitated when group members are able to remain focused on the goal, emphasize areas of agreement, and combine or eliminate alternatives identified by the group. Although desirable, reaching consensus sometimes is not possible. A fallback approach is to seek a **supermajority decision**; a supermajority is two-thirds of the group or team.

Research suggests that our conclusions about group decision making apply to virtual groups as well as those that meet face-to-face. Even so, some evidence indicates that virtual groups may reach less effective decisions than groups that meet in person.[28] Additionally, virtual group members report less satisfaction with their computer-mediated group experience. Virtual group members say that it typically takes more time, rather than less time, to work with people online compared with face-to-face interaction. Also, when virtual groups make risky decisions, there is a need for more information that is sometimes challenging to obtain.[29]

What can group members do to make effective and efficient decisions? Research suggests that groups make the most efficient decisions (use their time wisely) and reach high-quality decisions when they do three things:[30]

1. They use clear criteria; they know what "good" looks like, and they make a decision based on clear standards for a good decision. They start the decision-making process with a vision of how the final outcome will look.
2. They focus on finding high-quality, useful information directly related to the issue at hand, rather than gathering a large amount of information just for the sake of gathering it.
3. They break up big issues into smaller, more manageable issues to discuss.

Making decisions takes time, energy, and effort. When he was U.S. president, Barack Obama had to make many important decisions every day. Reportedly, he often had others make some of the daily routine decisions for him (such as what he would eat, what he would wear, or other routine decisions); this kept his decision-making energy focused on major decisions rather than spending unnecessary effort on inconsequential issues.[31] While you may not be making decisions that have global or national significance, when you are working in a group or a team, it can still be helpful to make sure that you spend your decision-making energy on important tasks rather than waste them on insignificant issues.

Review

Methods of Group Decision Making

Method	Description	Advantages	Disadvantages
Decision by expert	Group defers to the member with the most expertise or experience or to someone outside the group with authority to make decisions	• Decision is made quickly • Uses the expertise of a knowledgeable source of information	• Group members may not be satisfied with the decision • The expert could be wrong
Averaging individual rankings or ratings	Group members rank or rate possible outcomes, and the alternative with the highest ranking or best rating is selected	• Uses a democratic process that taps all group members' thinking • Useful when the group needs to assess where it stands on an issue	• The average ranking or rating may be an alternative that no group member supports • Group loses the opportunity for give-and-take discussion
Random choice	Group members flip a coin or use a similar technique so they can move forward	• Easy • Fast	• More likely to result in an ineffective outcome because group members have not discussed the issues thoroughly • Suggests that the group does not care about making a high-quality decision
Majority rule	Decision is made by the majority of group members	• Often perceived as a fair way of making decisions • Can be an efficient way of making a decision	• Those who do not support the majority opinion may feel left out of the process • Group may lose cohesiveness
Decision by minority	Group decides to support a position advocated by a vocal minority of group members	• Decision is made by those who feel most passionate about the outcome • Helps to avoid groupthink by acknowledging opposing points of view	• The majority of group members may feel disenfranchised by the decision • Group decision may be difficult to implement because the majority of group members do not support the outcome
Decision by consensus	Through discussion, group members reach a decision that all members can support	• Group members are more likely to be satisfied with the outcome • Group members are more likely to participate in implementing a decision that all members support	• Takes time • Takes skill

10.2: Group Problem Solving

OBJECTIVE: Evaluate how a group solves a problem

The board of directors of a multinational corporation, a band-booster fundraising committee, and a group of students doing a project for a group communication class all have something in common—they have problems to solve. Have you ever been involved in group problem solving and thought to yourself, "If I weren't working in this silly group, I could be more productive"? Despite such frustrations, a small group of people has the potential of arriving at a better solution than do individuals working alone. Groups have more information and more creative approaches to surmounting obstacles available than individuals do, and these advantages contribute to a higher-quality decision.

By the end of this module, you will be able to:

10.2.1 **Explain the three elements of a problem**

10.2.2 **Describe group problems that influence problem solving**

10.2.1: Problem Solving Defined

OBJECTIVE: Explain the three elements of a problem

Problem solving is the process of overcoming obstacles to achieve a goal. Whereas decision making involves making a choice from among alternatives, problem solving usually requires a group to make *many* decisions or choices as it identifies a problem and determines how to solve it.

A problem consists of three elements:

- An undesirable existing situation
- A goal a group wishes to achieve
- Obstacles that keep a group from achieving its goal[32]

Three Elements of a Problem

Undesirable existing situation: The City Council has noted an increase in the amount of plastic trash bag litter in its parks and public places.

Goal: The City Council would like the city to be free of plastic bag litter.

Obstacle: Too many people are using plastic bags and not disposing of them properly. Those that are not recycled end up in landfills or as litter throughout the city. Plastic bags don't decompose as easily as paper bags do.

Problem solving allows a group to eliminate or manage the obstacles that keep it from achieving its objective.

Like decision making, problem solving begins with assessing the present situation. What's wrong with what is happening now? Almost every problem can be phrased in terms of something you want more or less of.[33] Problems often can be boiled down to such things as lack of time, money, information, or agreement. For example, a school board that decides a district needs a new high school, yet lacks the money to build a new school, has a problem: The district has too many students for the existing facilities. The board needs fewer students or more space. The goal the board wants to achieve is quality education for all students. The board cannot achieve this goal with the existing undesirable situation. The obstacles that keep the board from reaching its goal include lack of classroom space and lack of money to build more space. Every problem can be identified by noting its three elements: the undesirable present, the group goal, and the obstacles to achieving it.

Communication researchers Katherine Hawkins and Bryant Fillion surveyed personnel managers to find out what the managers considered the most important skills necessary for success in problem-solving groups.[34] Their results are reflected in the following scale. Rate each member of a group to which you belong on the following skills, using a scale from 1 to 5 (1 = not at all effective; 2 = generally not effective; 3 = uncertain; 4 = effective; 5 = very effective).

Problem-Solving Skills

Skill	Group Member A	Group Member B	Group Member C	Group Member D	Group Member E
1. Listens effectively	______	______	______	______	______
2. Understands roles and responsibilities	______	______	______	______	______
3. Actively contributes to the group	______	______	______	______	______
4. Asks clear questions	______	______	______	______	______
5. Establishes and maintains rapport with others	______	______	______	______	______
6. Is sensitive to people with different cultural backgrounds	______	______	______	______	______
7. Uses clear, concise, accurate, and professional language	______	______	______	______	______
8. Communicates well with people who have different professional backgrounds	______	______	______	______	______
9. Gives clear and accurate instructions	______	______	______	______	______
10. Presents a positive professional image nonverbally (through appropriate grooming and attire)	______	______	______	______	______

(continued)

Skill	Group Member A	Group Member B	Group Member C	Group Member D	Group Member E
11. Helps resolve conflicts	______	______	______	______	______
12. Accurately summarizes information to the group	______	______	______	______	______
13. Gives brief, clear, well-organized, and informative presentations to the group when appropriate	______	______	______	______	______
Total	______	______	______	______	______

Summary: Review your responses for each team member. Identifying the strengths and weakness of each member can inform the ways you interact with the other members, and inform your understanding of the group's overall dynamics. This has the potential to increase the effectiveness of your work together.

Review

Three Elements of a Problem

- Undesirable existing situation: Something is wrong with the way things are
- Goal: What the group wants to achieve
- Obstacle: Something that keeps a group from achieving its goal

10.2.2: Barriers to Group Problem Solving

OBJECTIVE: Describe group problems that influence problem solving

What prevents groups from working at their full capacity? Identifying these barriers can help you spot and eliminate them. One study found that lack of sleep is a major factor that explains poor problem solving: You will not communicate well if you are tired. One acronym to keep in mind is HALT, which stands for hungry, angry, lonely, or tired. When you or other group members experience these issues, you will not be functioning at your best, so it's a good idea to take a break to recharge and refresh before continuing.[35]

All decision making involves assessing a situation, identifying alternative solutions, and selecting the best alternatives. Which group decision-making methods have worked well in your group?

One research team spent more than six years asking people who participated in group discussions which barriers kept their group from operating at full capacity. The group members themselves reported these barriers; they are not just problems that an observer noted. Here's their list of the top 10 barriers:[36]

1. **Lack of structure:** Group members wanted specific methods to help their group function more efficiently.
2. **Lack of cultural sensitivity:** Some group members were put off by biases, prejudice, sexist comments, and the failure of some members to take cultural differences into account when interacting with others.
3. **Lack of planning:** Group members often weren't prepared or were unsure what the focus of the group was supposed to be.
4. **Lack of resources:** Sometimes groups had to meet in an inadequate physical space or just didn't have all the information and technical support needed to get the job done.
5. **Wrong people present:** The key people with the authority or information weren't involved in the discussion.
6. **Time pressure:** Groups felt pressured to achieve immediate results and to tell those in authority what they wanted to hear.
7. **Poor communication:** Misunderstandings, inattentiveness, and dominance by one group member or a small faction of members were cited as reasons for ineffective communication.
8. **Unsupportive social climate:** Group members sometimes did not feel they were cohesively working together, and perceived that they could not support or trust one another.
9. **Negative attitudes:** Some group members weren't flexible, were unwilling to compromise about procedures, or had unrealistic expectations about the group.
10. **Lack of problem-solving skill:** Group members tended to focus on the solution before defining the problem, or there was a lack of balanced participation.

WRITING PROMPT

Road Blocks to Success

Think about three different groups in which you've participated (or are currently a member). For each group, what barriers influenced the group's ability to solve problems?

The response entered here will appear in the performance dashboard and can be viewed by your instructor.

Submit

10.3: The Descriptive Approach to Problem Solving

OBJECTIVE: Apply the descriptive approach to group problem solving and decision making

Thus far we have defined group decision making and problem solving, noted the obstacles to and the characteristics of effective group decisions, and identified some barriers that keep groups from working well. We will examine three approaches to understanding group problem solving:

1. The **descriptive approach** to problem solving, which identifies the typical patterns of communication that occur when people interact to solve problems
2. The **functional approach** to problem solving, which identifies key task requirements and stresses the importance of effective communication as major factors that contribute to effective problem solving
3. The **prescriptive approach** to problem solving, which identifies specific agendas and techniques to improve group problem-solving performance.

In this chapter, we discuss the descriptive and functional approaches to group problem solving in detail; we introduce the prescriptive approach here but reserve a detailed discussion of it for Chapter 11.

A descriptive approach does not offer specific guidelines and techniques for solving problems in groups, but rather outlines how most groups go about solving problems. B. Aubrey Fisher makes two assumptions about the descriptive approach:[37] (1) There is a "natural," or normal, process of group problem solving, and (2) a group will follow a normal problem-solving approach unless some external authority interferes with its freedom to solve its problem (for example, a supervisor gives the group an agenda or a strong-willed group leader dictates how the group should approach its task).

By the end of this module, you will be able to:

10.3.1 Describe the phases of group discussion

10.3.2 Relate dialectical theory to group process

10.3.3 Describe the spiraling model of group process

10.3.4 Describe the punctuated equilibrium model of group discussion

10.3.5 Explain the multisequence model

10.3.1: Group Phases

OBJECTIVE: Describe the phases of group discussion

"Don't worry; he/she is just going through a phase." Does this sound like something an adult may have said about you as a child? Maybe that person was trying to alleviate your parents' concerns by assuring them that your behavior was not at all uncommon and that it surely would change over time. Implicit here is an assumption that individuals pass through several identifiable developmental stages, each of which leads to the next. Like individuals, problem-solving groups go through several stages. If you understand these stages, you can learn to communicate in ways that expedite a group's passage from one stage to the next.

Does every group neatly cycle through the same phases of group discussion? Of course not: Not all groups take the same path to solve a problem. Group discussion is often messy. Many groups do, however, go through phases. Knowing these phases can help you spot them if they occur in your group; it's like having a map that lets you know where you are in your group deliberations.

Several researchers have attempted to identify the phases of a problem-solving group. They have observed and recorded who speaks to whom and have categorized the comments group members exchange. Over the past 50 years, researchers have used various labels to describe these phases, and despite differing terminology, they have reached similar conclusions. (Of the research on developmental phases of groups, Fisher's is the most significant for small group communication, so we will use his terminology.) Although some researchers describe five phases, most scholars identify four, as illustrated in Figure 10-1.

ORIENTATION In the first phase of small group interaction, the **orientation phase**, "group members break the ice and begin to establish a common basis for functioning."[38] Communication during this phase tends to be oriented toward getting to know one another, sharing information about members' backgrounds, and tentatively approaching the group's task. You are not likely to say anything that might prompt the rest of the group to reject you. Fisher noted that "more ambiguous comments . . . are contained

Figure 10-1 Descriptive Phases of Group Discussion

Groups go through predictable phases (such as orientation, conflict, emergence, and reinforcement) when working on a task or solving a problem.

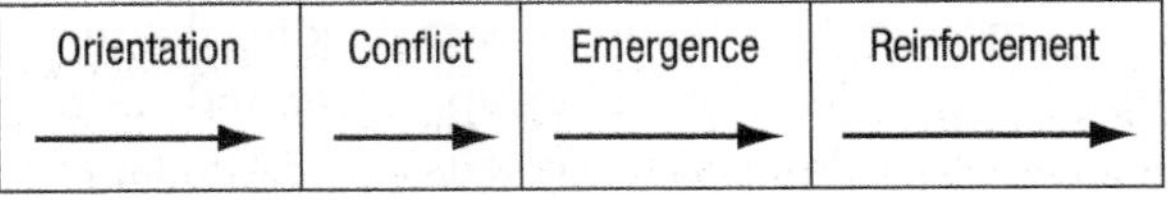

in Phase 1 than in any other phase except the third, which is also characterized by ambiguity."[39]

Research on the orientation phase suggests that group members' communication is directed at orienting themselves toward others as well as to the group's task, which can also be said about the other phases. What sets this phase apart from the others is the degree to which the social dimension is emphasized and the tentative, careful way in which the task dimension is approached.

Another characteristic of the orientation phase is **primary tension**. Primary tension occurs when group members are uncertain how to behave and feel somewhat awkward about what to do or say. Clear group role expectations have not emerged; clear social norms are not yet developed. Some group members may be quiet, others may be exceptionally polite, yet others may laugh nervously and smile—all of which are manifestations of the primary tension that occurs when groups first congregate.

Even the most efficient, task-motivated group will spend some time socializing and getting acquainted. Do not underestimate the importance of this type of interaction. Interpersonal trust—an essential ingredient for an effective working environment—does not happen all at once. You begin slowly, with small talk, to determine whether it is safe to move on to deeper levels of interaction. The orientation phase, then, develops trust and group cohesiveness, which are important for the group's survival in the second phase—conflict.

WRITING PROMPT

Productivity in the Orientation Phase

Imagine that you're leading a team that's about to make a final decision on the new salary review policy. You're running a meeting that is attended by Eric, Trish, and Fatima. You know that Trish tends to be worried about voicing her opinions in a group setting, that Daniel has an outgoing personality and tends to dominate the conversation, and that Fatima always does better when ample supporting research and data are available to support a policy change. Which specific questions can you include in your agenda to ensure that the orientation phase orients the group to the task at hand and also helps manage the group's relational needs?

The response entered here will appear in the performance dashboard and can be viewed by your instructor.

Submit

CONFLICT During the orientation phase, group members begin to form opinions about their own positions in the group and about the group's task. By the second phase of group discussion, they start asserting these opinions. They have tested the water in the first phase and now are ready to jump in. On the process (social) level, this is a period in which individuals compete for status in the group. Two or more potential leaders may emerge, with the support for each dividing the group into camps. This jockeying for leadership, power, and position in a group has been called **secondary tension**[40] Secondary tension arises after the initial, or primary, tension has diminished and the group settles down to focus on (1) the task at hand and (2) who will be influential in helping the group reach a conclusion. Secondary tension can occur abruptly. The group may be making progress when conflict suddenly erupts over an issue and the group gets off track from its agenda.

Communication during the **conflict phase** is characterized by persuasive attempts at changing others' opinions and reinforcing one's own position. Some participants relish the idea of a good argument, whereas others see conflict as something to avoid at all costs. Research has confirmed that a well-crafted argument, supported by evidence, can help a group manage conflict and make progress toward its goals.[41] Avoiding conflict means avoiding issues relevant and even crucial to the group's success. Just as individuals need to assert their own points of view, so do groups need to investigate all relevant alternatives to select the best solutions.

The conflict phase is necessary to both the task and the process dimensions of small group communication. Through conflict, you begin to identify the task issues that confront the group and clarify your own and others' roles. This clarification leads toward greater predictability, less uncertainty, and the establishment of group norms. Evidence shows that groups whose members spend a considerable amount of time together may have a shorter period of conflict, but they nonetheless do experience conflict.[42]

Ethical Collaboration

Are You Helping or Stepping on Toes?

Imagine that you're the vice president of the COMM Ambassadors Club, a group of students who are majoring or minoring in communication studies that meets once a month to learn about career opportunities for communication studies majors. Periodically you meet with the other officers of the club as an Executive Committee to make decisions about which guest speakers will be invited to speak to the entire club. The president of the club, Charise, is a likable and pleasant person, but she doesn't have the foggiest idea about how to structure a decision-making meeting. You dread the executive meetings because they often run over the planned time; they have no agenda, people get off topic, and Charise typically has to call another meeting because little was accomplished. You don't have the time for such wasteful meetings, yet you don't want to quit the group because being vice president of the COMM Ambassadors Club will look good on your résumé.

Because you've taken a course in small group communication, you have some ideas about how to make the meetings run more smoothly. You've gently suggested some of your ideas to Charise, but she just isn't picking up on the hints you're dropping. In fact, Charise seems to resent your suggestions and thinks you're really trying to take over the group. You don't want to be the leader; you just want to attend meetings that get something accomplished.

WRITING PROMPT

How Much Help Is Too Much?

Consider the preceding scenario. Is it appropriate or ethical to be more forceful in suggesting how to run the meetings? What could you do to help the meetings run more smoothly even though you're not the designated leader?

▶ The response entered here will appear in the performance dashboard and can be viewed by your instructor.

Submit

Orientation

Conflict

Emergence

EMERGENCE In Phase 3, new patterns of communication indicate a group's emergence from the conflict phase. If a group is going to function as a cohesive unit, it must resolve the conflict of Phase 2. Although conflict may persist in Phase 3, what sets the **emergence phase** apart from the preceding conflict phase is the way in which members deal with conflict. This shift is most apparent in the reappearance of ambiguity in task-related statements.

Task and process dimensions are interwoven at this stage. Although the group is divided, there is also clarity. Leadership patterns and roles have been established, the issues and problems confronting the group have been identified, and the need to settle differences and reach consensus has become apparent. One factor that helps decisions and solutions emerge is listening to group members who are perceived as experts.[43] As more people perceive someone as having high credibility and an expert point of view, groups will tend to agree with the expert as a way to manage conflict. Ambiguity appears to be the means by which individual group members can comfortably shift their positions toward group consensus. The group settles on norms and moves toward consensus via ambiguous statements that gradually modify dissenting positions. Such ambiguous statements might take the form of qualifiers or reservations to the previous position: "I still would like to see our company merge with the Elector Electronics Corporation, but maybe we could consider a merger later in the year. A merger may be more appropriate next fall." Such a statement allows a person to save face and still allows the group to reach consensus.

REINFORCEMENT A spirit of unity characterizes the fourth and final phase of group interaction. In the first three phases, group members struggle through the challenges of getting acquainted, building cohesiveness, expressing individuality, competing for status, and arguing over issues. The group eventually emerges from those struggles with a sense of direction, consensus, and a feeling of group identity. Not surprisingly, then, the **reinforcement phase** is characterized by positive feelings toward the group and its decisions. Finally, members feel a genuine sense of accomplishment.

Reinforcement predominates in communication:

Noah: I may have been against it at first, but I've finally seen the light. We're going in the right direction now.

Ayisha: Yes, but don't shortchange your contribution, Noah. If you hadn't opposed it so vehemently, we never would have developed the idea so fully.

Fisher noted that ambiguous and unfavorable comments all but disappear in the fourth phase, being replaced by uniformly favorable comments and reinforcement. At this time, all the hassle of group decision making and problem solving seems worthwhile.

In the reinforcement phase, the group is at its most cohesive, individual satisfaction and sense of achievement are high, and uncertainty is at a low level.

10.3.2: Dialectical Theory

OBJECTIVE: Relate dialectical theory to group process

Although it may appear that a group moves through four distinct phases of development in a predictable, easy-to-identify way, group deliberations are seldom that orderly. Communication does not typically operate in such a linear, step-by-step manner.[44]

One theory that helps to explain the messiness of group interaction is **dialectical theory**. Dialectical theory suggests that during communication there are often competing tensions pulling the conversation in multiple directions.[45] For example, groups like a sense of stability; they want to predict what will happen because many group members like familiar patterns.[46] Yet, because communication is dynamic, there is also an interest in developing new ideas and procedures—groups expect change. Another dialectical tension is being separate from others while also being connected. The team versus the individual and structure versus interaction are other dialectical tensions that occur when groups communicate.

Because of these tensions and because communication is not usually (or even often) orderly and neat, the four phases of orientation, conflict, emergence, and reinforcement have been observed in some, but not all, groups. In addition, group communication researchers have identified several other models that describe the patterns of communication within groups: the spiraling model, the punctuated equilibrium model, and the multisequence model.

10.3.3: Spiraling Model

OBJECTIVE: Describe the spiraling model of group process

Research conducted by group communication scholars Tom Scheidel and Laura Crowell suggests that groups may

Figure 10-2 The Repeating Phases of the Spiraling Model

Groups may go through several phases and then repeat the cycle again and again throughout the history of the group.

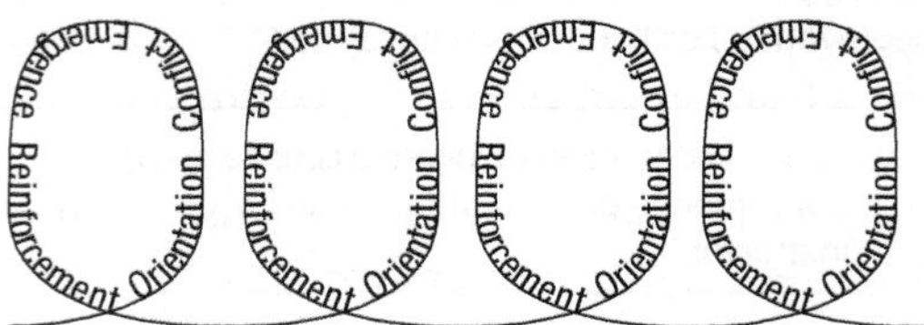

not march through the four phases described previously in linear fashion, but rather cycle, or spiral, through them throughout the group or team's development.[47] For example, the first issue confronting the group may be "What's the purpose of this group?" A group will probably spend some time getting oriented to this task, conflict may follow as members learn each person's objectives, and after discussion, a consensus may emerge about the group's purpose. Finally, members may assure one another that their purpose has been developed clearly. Perhaps the next issue to come before the group is "How will we organize our work—should we have a subcommittee?" Again, the members may go through orientation, conflict, emergence, and reinforcement about a specific issue. A pattern becomes apparent, as illustrated in Figure 10-2. Because group discussions tend to hop from topic to topic, a group may get bogged down in conflict, abandon the issue, and move to another issue. Thus, groups may spiral through phases for each issue, or group members may get sidetracked and abandon discussions about a particular topic.

Research has found that groups do seem to exhibit spiraling tendencies, but not all groups behave in quite the same way, thus confirming the challenge of formulating tidy descriptions of how groups do their work.[48] Researchers also suggests that the order in which groups discuss topics and issues may not be as important as *whether* the topics are discussed. Therefore, the content of what you say may be more important than the precise sequence in which the content is discussed.

10.3.4: Punctuated Equilibrium Model

OBJECTIVE: Describe the punctuated equilibrium model of group discussion

Connie Gersick describes what she calls a pattern of "punctuated equilibrium" in small group decision-making processes.[49] During the first half of a group's existence, group members may experience uncertainty and indecision about what to do or how to proceed; nothing seems to be happening. Then, about midway through the group's deliberation, a revolutionary transition, or **breakpoint**, shatters the seeming equilibrium, and "nothing happening" changes to "something happening." The equilibrium of inactivity is broken up by a burst of activity. Then there will be a second inertia phase—a phase in which the group seems to stop and again ponder which direction to go next before moving on to accomplishing the task, and so on, as illustrated in Figure 10-3. Gersick thinks this punctuated equilibrium model may occur only in groups that are working within a specific time limit; it may be less likely to occur in a group with an unstructured or open-ended time frame.

Additional research suggests that punctuated equilibrium can occur within the four phases of group discussion—orientation, conflict, emergence, and reinforcement.[50] During the conflict phase, for example, there will be bursts of progress in resolving the conflict, as well as periods of time when it appears that nothing much is happening.

Figure 10-3 Activity and Inactivity in the Punctuated Equilibrium Model

Groups go through a period of uncertainty and indecision punctuated by a breakthrough, followed by more uncertainty, until a pattern emerges.

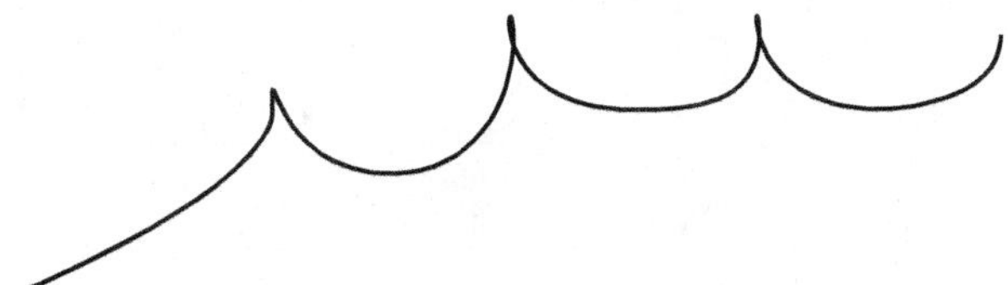

Virtual Collaboration

Technology and Group Problem Solving

Research continues to describe the impact of technology on group problem solving.[51] The use of technology does not inherently result in teams' creating better solutions and making better decisions; it's still people who make the decisions and solve the problems. Technology doesn't do the work, but rather is just another way of connecting to others. Yet group members who are trained to work in virtual groups usually do a better job than those who receive no training.[52] In addition, having a sense of cohesion among virtual group members enhances the quality of team decision making.[53]

Virtual group members may want to connect non-virtually. Although use of virtual team communication continues to grow, we apparently still like to connect at a face-to-face level if we're scattered in many locations trying to solve complex problems. One study found that the more different locations where virtual team members are found, the more likely it is that they will want to periodically connect face-to-face, if possible, rather than use only virtual communication channels.[54]

Virtual group members sometimes want to share private messages with other group members. Another study found that when working in virtual groups, some group members connect with others using text messages that aren't directed at all group members, but just another member or two—a practice that can help a group manage conflict.[55] The researchers suggested that these private instant messages are like "backstage" whispering. In face-to-face groups, some group members have side conversations. Apparently, the same thing happens in virtual groups, and these behind-the-scenes conversations can help groups move forward.

The advantages and disadvantages of making decisions and solving problems in virtual groups are as follows:

Advantages of Virtual Groups

- Such groups work best for more structured, linear tasks.
- The ideas of all members can more easily and accurately be captured and recorded.
- When brainstorming, usually more ideas are developed than in face-to-face groups.
- Group members are more likely to share information if they are periodically reminded to share what they know.[56]

Disadvantages of Virtual Groups

- There is sometimes less time for reflection and evaluation of ideas.
- Technology may sometimes help members make mistakes faster.
- Some virtual group members do a less thorough job of evaluating the pros and cons of assessing alternatives rather than when interacting in face-to-face settings.
- There is often more interpersonal conflict and less trust in virtual groups.[57]

10.3.5: Multisequence Model

OBJECTIVE: Explain the multisequence model

M. Scott Poole proposed the multisequence model to illustrate how groups typically function.[58] As the term "multisequence" implies, groups may be doing several things at once rather than cycling though predictable phases (Figure 10-4).

Poole builds on Fisher's phase research by suggesting that groups engage in three types of **activity tracks**, phases of problem solving that do not necessarily follow logical step-by-step patterns.

Figure 10-4 The Multisequence Model

Groups switch from one activity track to another as they engage in task-process activities, relational activities, or topical focus activities.

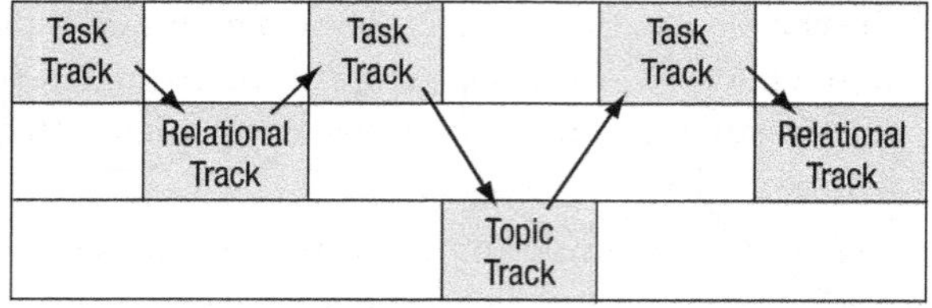

Activity Tracks in the Multisequence Model

Poole believes that three types of activities best describe group interaction.[59]

Task-Process Activities—These activities help the group accomplish its work, such as analyzing a problem, becoming oriented to the components of a problem, establishing criteria, and evaluating proposed solutions. Examples of task-process activities include answering such questions as "What's the problem here?", "How can we better understand the problem?", and "How effective will our solution be?" There are three types of task-process activities: (1) activities that focus on the problem, (2) activities that serve executive functions (such as keeping the discussion oriented and on task), and (3) solution activities.[60]

Relational Activities—These activities manage relationships and help maintain the group climate. For example, verbal or nonverbal communication that indicates who likes and dislikes whom can be categorized as relational activity. Communication has both a task dimension and a relationship dimension. Relational activities also include communication behaviors that sustain or damage interpersonal relationships among group members. Criticism, conflict, praise, and encouragement help group members understand their relationships with one another. Finally, relational activities affect a group's working climate. Relational activities include (1) discussion about work-focused relationships, (2) discussion that manages conflict, (3) integration talk (connecting one person's ideas to those of others), and (4) discussion about ambiguous relationships (expressing uncertainty about relationships).[61]

Topical Focus Activities—These activities deal with the "general themes, major issues, or arguments of concern to the group at a given point in the discussion."[62] Ernest Bormann and other researchers have noted that groups often focus their conversations on themes or topics that serve as the groups' actual agendas.[63] This third type of activity, then, deals with major topics that do not relate to a group's specific task or to member relationships.

Poole's three activity tracks do not all develop at the same rate or according to the same pattern. Some groups spend a large portion of their time developing relationships before discussing their tasks in great detail. In contrast, task-oriented groups often devote considerable energy to completing their tasks, letting relationships play minor roles in group deliberations. Groups may switch activity tracks at various breakpoints, as they switch topics, adjourn, or schedule planning periods. Another type of breakpoint, called a delay, occurs because of group conflict or inability to reach consensus. Whereas groups may expect and schedule some breakpoints, they usually do not schedule delays. As Poole notes, "depending on the nature of the delay and the mood of the group, [a] breakpoint can signal the start of a difficulty or a highly creative period."[64] A disruption, the third type of breakpoint, results from a major conflict or a realization that a group may not be able to complete its task. To manage disruption, a group must be flexible.[65]

Poole's analysis of group phases and group activity emphasizes the process nature of group communication and problem solving, rather than assuming that groups proceed through a linear, step-by-step approach.

A descriptive approach to group communication can help you better understand and explain why certain types of statements are made in groups and how a group develops over time. With an understanding of the process, you should be in a better position to evaluate and improve your participation in group meetings.

WRITING PROMPT

Description of Group Process

Attend a meeting of your school board or city council or another public meeting in which problems are discussed and solutions are recommended. Prepare a written analysis of the meeting in which you attempt to identify phases in the group's discussions. Also, try to identify examples of the three activity tracks (task process, relational, and topical focus). In addition, provide examples of breakpoints in the discussion of the group.

The response entered here will appear in the performance dashboard and can be viewed by your instructor.

Submit

10.4: The Functional Approach to Problem Solving

OBJECTIVE: **Compare effective and ineffective groups according to the functional approach to problem solving and decision making**

The descriptive approach to group problem solving does exactly what it implies: It describes what happens when groups communicate, whether the interaction involves going through phases, spirals, or sequences. The functional approach emphasizes that members of effective groups perform certain task requirements (functions) when they communicate with one another.[66] This approach includes some elements of description because the researchers who propose this approach have observed groups and described the task requirements of effective groups. There's also a hint of prescription in this approach, in that the task requirements are presumed to be useful strategies that will help groups make better-quality decisions and arrive at good solutions. Thus, the functional approach includes elements of the conceptual frameworks of both descriptive and prescriptive approaches.

The functional approach assumes that groups are goal oriented, and that to accomplish the group goal, certain activities or communication functions need to be performed. Groups become effective, argue the functional theorists, not just by applying communication techniques (the prescriptive approach), but also by communicating in ways that affect the fundamental processes of how the group achieves its goal.[67] It is through communication that group members perform key functions that enhance group problem solving and decision making.

The primary way researchers have identified the functions of effective problem solving is by examining the behaviors of both effective and ineffective groups. Certain types of communication and critical thinking distinguish effective groups from ineffective ones.[68]

By the end of this module, you will be able to:

10.4.1 Outline the key functions of effective problem solving

10.4.2 Describe communication functions of effective problem solvers

10.4.3 Summarize the bona fide group perspective

10.4.1: The Key Functions of Effective Problem Solving

OBJECTIVE: Outline the key functions of effective problem solving

What are the key functions of effective problem solving? According to Randy Hirokawa, groups must perform five key functions to develop a high-quality solution.[69]

Five Key Functions of Problem Solving

1. **Develop an accurate understanding of the problem.** Specify what the problem is. Identify the causes, symptoms, and history of the problem. Use data and information to help the group understand the problem.
2. **Develop requirements for an acceptable choice.** Establish criteria—explicit standards for an acceptable solution. Identify what a good solution will look like, so members will know one when they see it.
3. **Develop many alternatives to solve the problem.** The more high-quality alternatives generated, the greater the chance that the group will find a high-quality solution. Having just one or two ideas suggested early in the discussion will usually result in a less-effective solution.
4. **Assess the positive features of the alternatives or options for solving the problem.** Systematically identify the merits or benefits that will occur if the suggested solution or solutions are implemented.
5. **Assess the negative features of the alternatives or options for solving the problem.** Balance the positive benefits that have been identified with the negative features or disadvantages of the suggested solution or solutions.

Group communicators who incorporate these functions into their interactions with others are what Hirokawa and other researchers call **vigilant thinkers**. Vigilant thinkers are critical thinkers; they pay attention to the process of problem solving. Groups that believe they will be effective in using vigilant thinking skills will, in fact, do a better job of thinking critically and effectively.[70]

Of the key five functions of problem solving, is one more important than the others? Recent research points to the importance of all the functions, but the best predictors of quality group performance are functions 1, 2, and 5. So, for best results, (1) analyze the problem, being sure to use data and information rather than just sharing opinions when analyzing the current situation; (2) establish criteria—know what a good solution looks like; and (3) evaluate the potential negative consequences of possible solutions. Discuss the standards or expectations that group members have before hunting for a solution.[71]

Communication researcher Elizabeth Graham and her colleagues found that effective groups establish and use clear criteria and make positive comments about the alternative solutions that group members suggest; in essence, such groups have clear goals and say nice things about solutions.[72] The researchers suspected that the positive comments might help to establish a supportive group climate. In contrast, Kevin Barge suggests that the following functions are essential for an effective problem-solving group:

1. Network with others within and outside the group to gather effective information
2. Acquire the skill of data splitting—that is, analyzing information effectively
3. Generate and evaluate solutions
4. Manage their relationships effectively by means of listening, feedback, and negotiation skill[73]

The vigilant-thinking functions suggested by Hirokawa and his colleagues, as well as the functions identified by Barge, are similar to those suggested by Irving Janis: Gather accurate information, analyze the information, draw reasonable conclusions from the data, generate solutions, evaluate the costs and risks of the solutions, and select the best one.[74]

Although research does support the functional theory, not all research confirms that performing the functional task requirements *always* results in enhanced group decision making and problem solving.[75] In computer-mediated situations, for example, research has not found uniform support for functional theory. Although the research conclusions supporting functional theory have not been unanimous, the functional perspective of group problem solving continues to enjoy support and application among group communication researchers and educators.

10.4.2: Communication Functions

OBJECTIVE: Describe communication functions of effective problem solvers

The functional perspective assumes that a group will make a higher-quality decision if group members analyze information appropriately, generate an ample number of ideas, evaluate information and solutions, and remain sensitive to others.

Communication Functions of Effective Group Problem Solvers

Based on the work of several group communication researchers, the following specific communication functions are considered essential to effective problem solving.[76]

Analysis Function—Group members who effectively analyze information and ideas do several things:

- ***They establish clear criteria.*** Groups and teams have their goal clearly in mind as they analyze the issues.
- ***They see the problem from a variety of viewpoints.*** Individuals often look at a problem as it affects themselves. A skilled problem solver considers how the problem affects others, too, and is able to think about an issue from other people's vantage points.[77]
- ***They gather data and research issues.*** Good problem solvers do not rely solely on their own opinions. They spend time in the library or develop surveys to gather information and others' opinions about an issue.
- ***They use evidence effectively to reach a valid conclusion.*** Beyond just collecting evidence, a good problem solver needs to know how to use evidence to reach a conclusion.
- ***They ask appropriate questions.*** Groups often have difficulty keeping the discussion focused on the issues. Members often bounce from one idea or topic to the next. Good problem solvers know this and use questions to help keep the group moving toward its goal. Questions such as "Where are we now?" or "What's the next step in solving our problem?" or "Aren't we getting off the track here?" can help the group get back to the task.

Idea-Generation Function—An essential aspect of a well-functioning problem-solving group is having members who are creative and inventive, and who find ways to keep ideas flowing.

- ***They search for many alternatives or solutions to a problem.*** Effective groups are not content to have just one or two approaches to a problem. They identify many solutions that may help overcome the obstacles keeping the group from reaching its goal.
- ***They make high-quality statements to the group.*** High-quality statements are precise rather than rambling and abstract. They are consistent with previous evidence and relevant to the topic under discussion, and they positively reinforce the comments of other group members.[78]
- ***They take a vacation from a problem to revitalize the group.*** If the group gets bogged down and cannot reach agreement, postpone further discussion, if possible. Sometimes you may get a burst of creativity when you are not even thinking about a problem.[79] Have you ever had an idea come to you while you were jogging, driving somewhere, or taking a shower? Give your mind a chance to work on the problem by giving yourself a break from agonizing over a solution.

Evaluation Function—Being able to separate good ideas from bad ideas is a critical function of group members who are good problem solvers.

- ***They examine the pros and cons of potential solutions.*** Give special attention to considering what might go wrong before implementing a solution.
- ***They evaluate the opinions and assumptions of others.*** Do not accept another person's conclusion or opinion at face value. One study found that groups that reach better solutions include members who take the time to test the assumptions of others.[80] Although you should not attack another person's credibility, all opinions and assumptions need to be supported by evidence. A group that tactfully examines the basis for an opinion can determine whether the opinion is valid.
- ***They test solutions to see if they meet preestablished criteria.*** Criteria are standards for acceptable solutions. Such criteria as "It should be within the budget" and "It should be implemented within six months" are important considerations in problem solving. If a group has generated criteria for a solution, a good problem solver reminds the group what the criteria are and evaluates possible solutions according to these previously identified standards.

Personal-Sensitivity Function—Members of successfully functioning teams or groups are other-oriented, empathic, sensitive to the needs of others, and thoughtful listeners.[81]

- ***They are concerned for both the group task and the feelings of others.*** Being too task-oriented is not good for the overall group climate. Sensitivity to others' feelings can enhance the group climate and foster a supportive—rather than defensive—approach to achieving a group goal. One study found that group members who engage in storytelling, especially stories relevant to the task at hand, help the group balance the deliberative task talk with a more relationally focused story; the use of stories helps the group achieve a more effective outcome.[82]
- ***They listen to minority arguments and opinions.*** It is always tempting to disregard the voice of a lone dissenter. That individual may, however, have a brilliant idea or a legitimate complaint about the majority point of view. Assume that all ideas have merit; do not discount ideas because they come from members who are not supporting the majority at the moment.

Clearly, each approach has its own unique advantages. Ideally, you will draw on all three approaches as you work at becoming an effective problem-solving group participant.

According to the functional perspective, effective group members take breaks when they are having trouble solving a problem, instead of agonizing over a solution. Which activities help you generate ideas?

If the task is very simple, a group may not need a cumbersome, predetermined set of prescriptions. However, research suggests that if the task is complex (and many group tasks are), specific guidelines and procedures will help the group work more effectively. In Chapter 11, we describe in more detail prescriptive approaches, formats, and techniques to give you some options in structuring group problem solving.

CASE STUDY

Proposed Tuition Increase

The Association of Student Governance (ASG), the campus student governing board of The State University (TSU), had heard rumors that a major tuition increase might be implemented next year. TSU was trying to be nationally recognized as a top-ranked university, and to do that the university president had decided to hire more faculty so as to have a favorable student–faculty ratio. Hiring faculty was expensive, though. Students were concerned that hiring more faculty (a good thing) would increase the tuition so that many students wouldn't be able to afford attending TSU. To address those fears, the ASG president appointed a student task force to study the issue and make a recommendation as to whether the ASG group would support a tuition increase.

Five students were appointed to the task force: Celeste, Bart, Sarah, Alex, and Tisha. Celeste was appointed chair of the task force; she was a communication studies major who had recently completed a course in group communication and had an open mind about the tuition increase. Bart, a pre-med major, really didn't care how much tuition would cost; he anticipated that he would get a high-paying job after attending medical school and could easily pay back any loans. Sarah, who recently transferred from a community college, planned on being a teacher and wanted the tuition to remain as low as possible. Sarah's friends were hoping that she would also recommend no tuition increase. Alex, a music major, was planning on transferring to a music conservatory next year, so he didn't really care what TSU's new tuition would be. Tisha's grandparents paid for her tuition so she had no real concern about tuition increasing. But she also wanted TSU to be nationally recognized, so prior to the task force's discussion, she decided that tuition should increase—a high-quality education is expensive.

When Celeste called the first meeting, she quickly realized that the task force members already had their minds made up based upon their personal circumstances. Bart and Alex made it known, they didn't care whether tuition was increased. Sarah said if there was an increase, she'd have to drop out. Tisha was predisposed to no increase, but didn't really care since her tuition was fully paid by someone else. Celeste knew from her group communication course that the best decisions were made after thoroughly evaluating the information. She was determined to get the task force to make an informed decision rather than rely on preconceived personal opinions. Because TSU is a state-supported institution, all of the university's budget information was available to the group online.

Questions for Analysis: Proposed Tuition Increase

1. Is this group's primary task to make a decision or to solve a problem?
2. What barriers to group and team problem solving do you find evident in this group, and what should be done to overcome them?
3. How would you recommend Celeste organize the agenda of the meetings to achieve the key functions of problem solving and decision making?
4. Based on the analysis functions of communication, what could the group members do to make sure that they properly analyzed the issues before making a recommendation? What information would be helpful in analyzing the issues?

10.4.3: The Bona Fide Group Perspective

OBJECTIVE: Summarize the bona fide group perspective

The phrase "bona fide" simply means real, authentic, or genuine. The **bona fide perspective on groups** suggests that the context for and boundaries of the groups in which we participate move and change.[83] Thus, a bona fide perspective on groups is concerned with how actual groups function in the real world, given the tensions, pressures, and reality of being part of many groups simultaneously.

According to Linda Putnam, who has done extensive research and writing about bona fide groups, we need to be more sensitive to how groups really operate in natural settings. Most groups and teams do not exist in isolation from other groups and from the larger organization of which they are a part. Therefore, Putnam suggests focusing on two elements when considering bona fide groups:

- How the group is connected to other groups and the larger organization
- How the group operates in relationship to its external context

Real Groups in Real Organizations

You are likely to be a member of many groups at the same time—Most people do not belong to just one group and focus all of their energy and talent on one primary task. Right now, you are probably a member of many different kinds of groups.[84]

Most people belong to multiple groups simultaneously. For example, this woman may be a member of a parent group as well as a work group.

There are multiple influences on what happens in your group—Groups are connected to—and genuinely influenced by—what else is happening in an organization. If, for example, the organization is losing money and is operating on a tight budget, then the lack of money affects how a group works within the organization. A group does not do its work in isolation. Another aspect of a bona fide perspective involves the other people who work in the group.

You are likely to have group members who communicate virtually—You may be assigned to work with others who are not in the same physical location as you; they may work in another city, state, or country. And even if your group does meet on a face-to-face basis, you'll likely exchange information via text, e-mail, or social media.

What real-world applications does a bona fide perspective on groups have for the groups to which we belong?

- If you're a leader or a manager in an organization, be aware that the people who work under your supervision have multiple roles and multiple jobs. Just as your instructor needs to be aware that you're likely taking more than one class, so should a manager realize that her or his employees are likely to be working on multiple projects at the same time.

- Remember that the groups and teams you work with today may not be the same groups and teams you work with tomorrow. Group membership changes. The changing composition of the group may mean that the group goes through numerous periods of reorientation as members come and go.
- Group members may participate in the group via e-mail or phone and not face to face. Special effort must be made to integrate the long-distance group members into the fabric of the group.
- When people work on a group or a team task, they are constrained by the environment of the larger organization in which they work. Groups do not work in isolation—members are connected to others, even though all they may be aware of is the interaction in the group or team in which they work.

10.5: Cultural Assumptions

OBJECTIVE: Assess situations for cultural differences

Assumptions about the descriptions, functions, and prescriptions of group problem solving and decision making will be filtered through the cultural perspective(s) of the group members.[85] You need not travel abroad to experience different cultural perspectives. In the United States, you are likely to encounter individuals with a wide range of cultural and ethnic traditions.

By the end of this module, you will be able to:

10.5.1 Compare collectivist and individualist approaches to group decision making

10.5.2 Relate gender to how groups operate

In the United States, people of different genders, cultures, and ethnicities commonly work together.

10.5.3 Apply strategies to reduce discord in groups with cultural differences

10.5.1: Collectivism and Individualism

OBJECTIVE: Compare collectivist and individualist approaches to group decision making

The personal pronouns "I," "me," and "my" can be significant stumbling blocks to collaboration. A focus on individual concerns (me) can be a major challenge to collaborating with others (we). Most North Americans value individual achievement over collective group or team accomplishment. Researchers describe our tendency to focus on individual accomplishment as individualism. According to Geert Hofstede, individualism is the "emotional independence from groups, organizations, or other collectivities."[86] Some cultures (notably those of the United States, the United

Collectivism – Individualism World map

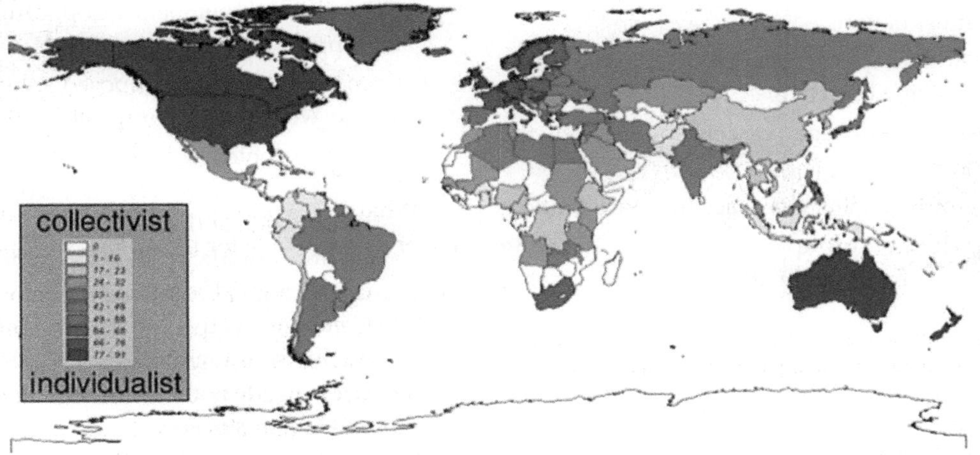

Map of Collectivist and Individualist Countries

Kingdom, and Northern Europe) assume an individualistic approach to accomplishing work, whereas other cultures (such as Asian cultures) assume a collaborative or collectivistic mind-set.[87]

10.5.2: Gender

OBJECTIVE: Relate gender to how groups operate

Gender also contributes to group differences that researchers suggest influence how group members interact to solve problems. For example, Katherine Hawkins and Christopher Power found that females tend to ask more probing questions during group deliberations than do males.[88] Competent group members are aware that others may have different assumptions and approaches to problem solving. They also don't stereotype others based on gender, culture, ethnicity, age, sexual orientation, sexual identity, or other differences.

10.5.3: Strategies to Bridge Cultural Differences

OBJECTIVE: Apply strategies to reduce discord in groups with cultural differences

What strategies can bridge cultural differences? Consider these suggestions.[89]

- **Develop mindfulness.** To be mindful is to be consciously aware of cultural differences and to note that there are differences between your assumptions and the assumptions of others.[90] Consciously say to yourself, "These group members may have a different assumption about how to accomplish this task. Before I impose my strategies on them, I'll listen and make sure I understand what they are saying."
- **Be flexible.** Realize that you may have to adapt and change according to the perceptions and assumptions others hold.
- **Tolerate uncertainty and ambiguity.** Working with others from a culture or cultures different from your own is bound to create a certain amount of uncertainty and confusion. Being patient and tolerant will help you manage cultural differences when collaborating with others.[91]
- **Resist stereotyping and making negative judgments about others.** Ethnocentrism is the assumption that your cultural heritage is superior. Assuming superiority when evaluating others typically produces defensiveness.[92]
- **Ask questions.** An essential element for any effective team is common ground rules. You can help create these guidelines by simply asking others how they work and solve problems, and about their preferences for establishing norms and ground rules.
- **Be other-oriented.** Empathy and sensitivity to others are keys to bridging cultural differences. Although simply considering an issue from someone else's point of view will not necessarily eliminate the difference, it will help enhance understanding.[93] One of the seven habits of highly effective people identified by Stephen Covey nicely summarizes this principle: Seek to understand before being understood.[94]

Summary: Making Decisions and Solving Problems

10.1: Group Decision Making

- Start the decision-making process by accurately assessing the present situation.
- Establish clear and appropriate group goals to frame the decision-making objective.
- Identify positive and negative consequences of the alternatives identified.
- Ensure that group members have accurate information.
- Determine whether group members are drawing reasonable conclusions from the information that is available.

10.2: Group Problem Solving

- When solving problems as a group or a team, answer the question, "What do we want more or less of?" Analyze the problem by identifying (1) the undesirable present, (2) the group's goal, and (3) obstacles that may keep you from achieving the goal.
- Give all group members the opportunity to help formulate appropriate group goals.
- Even when the first proposed solution seems reasonable or workable, examine other alternatives.
- Effective problem solvers:
  - Are vigilant thinkers; they appropriately analyze information and data.
  - Identify criteria; they define standards so they'll recognize a good solution when they see it.
  - Generate creative ideas; they search for many high-quality solutions.
  - Evaluate ideas and solutions; they examine the costs and benefits of solutions.
  - Are sensitive to others; they are concerned about both the task and the feelings of other group members.

- During group problem solving, interpret and evaluate the information you collect. Do not just accept the information at face value.
- Do not let yourself be satisfied after you generate a few potential solutions. Keep searching, unless the group needs a break.

10.3: The Descriptive Approach to Problem Solving

- Adopt a descriptive approach as a road map to help you determine where you are in the group problem-solving process.

10.4: The Functional Approach to Problem Solving

- Adopt a functional approach to group problem solving by performing the functions or tasks of effective problem solvers.
- Adopt a prescriptive approach to problem solving if your group needs strategies that provide the structure associated with a problem-solving agenda.

10.5: Cultural Assumptions

- Develop mindfulness: Become consciously aware of cultural differences.
- Be flexible: Be ready to adapt to the cultural expectations and traditions of others.
- Tolerate uncertainty and ambiguity: Be patient when working with individuals who have a cultural background different from your own.
- Avoid stereotyping and making negative judgments: Avoid an ethnocentric mind-set that assumes your cultural traditions are superior to those of others.
- Ask questions: Reduce your uncertainty by asking questions to help you, and your team members develop common ground rules and norms.
- Be other-oriented: Cultivate the skill of empathy and seek to understand others before expressing your ideas and opinions to others.

SHARED WRITING

Navigating Cultural Differences

What specific messages could you tell yourself to help you be mindful when communicating with someone from a culture different from your own? What could you tell yourself to help you tolerate uncertainty and be more comfortable with ambiguity when interacting with people from a different culture? Write a short response that your classmates will read.

A minimum number of characters is required to post and earn points. After posting, your response can be viewed by your class and instructor, and you can participate in the class discussion.

Post

Chapter 11
Using Problem-Solving Techniques

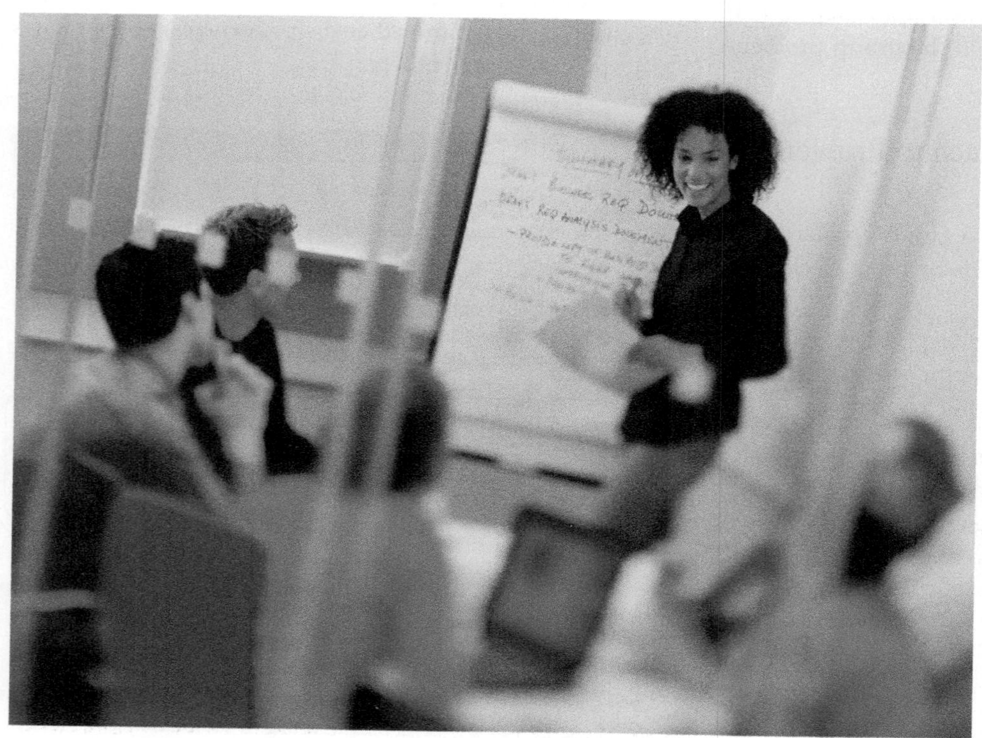

"All life is problem solving."

—Karl Popper

Learning Objectives

11.1 Create a basic agenda to address group problems using reflective thinking

11.2 Determine the structure and interactive methods needed to help groups work together

11.3 Formulate a solution using the reflective thinking process

11.4 Solve problems using question-oriented approaches

11.5 Evaluate your group decision-making skills

Whenever we present corporate communication training seminars for executives or business leaders on the topic of group or team problem solving, we begin our session by asking a simple question: What do you want to learn about group problem solving? The responses of the trainees are predictable. They want to know precisely what to do to make working in groups more effective. They ask questions like "How do I develop an agenda when the group has a problem to solve?", "What are the best techniques to help a group arrive at the best solution?", and "What should I do to ensure that my team operates at peak efficiency?" They want precise prescriptions for success.

Consider the three approaches to understanding problem solving: descriptive, functional, and prescriptive. If you're in a group, you could adopt a descriptive approach to problem solving and clue group members into some of the processes and phases that groups experience when trying to solve problems. You could, in essence, give them a road map to help them understand how groups operate. Alternatively, you could hand out a list of the group functions—that is, task requirements for groups: assess the problem, establish criteria, develop alternatives, and evaluate the pros and cons of the options identified, giving special attention to reviewing the negative consequences of options you may consider.

There's also a third approach—the prescriptive approach to problem solving. To prescribe is to offer specific and sometimes detailed do's or don'ts to help a group perform well. However, because there is no single best way to solve problems in groups, no list of prescriptive problem-solving techniques always works. Each group is unique, as is each group member.[1] Yet evidence indicates that guiding a group through a structured agenda can enhance its effectiveness.[2] In this chapter, we offer several suggestions for solving problems in groups.

11.1: Prescriptive Problem-Solving Strategies

OBJECTIVE: Create a basic agenda to address group problems using reflective thinking

A vast number of techniques are available that can help you facilitate group problem solving.[3] Most include references to five key elements:

1. Identify and define the problem.
2. Analyze the problem.
3. Identify possible solutions.
4. Select the best solution.
5. Implement the solution.

These steps outline the primary way most scientists in any discipline find answers to puzzling questions. We will examine the origin of these steps and consider why they continue to be used to structure group problem-solving discussion.

By the end of this module, you will be able to:

11.1.1 Summarize the prescriptive problem-solving strategy according to Dewey

11.1.1: The Origin of Prescriptive Problem-Solving Strategies

OBJECTIVE: Summarize the prescriptive problem-solving strategy according to Dewey

In 1910, philosopher and educator John Dewey, in his book *How We Think*, identified the steps most people follow to solve problems. According to Dewey, a reflective thinker considers these key questions:[4]

1. What is the "felt difficulty" or concern?
2. Where is it located, and how is it defined?
3. What are possible solutions to the felt difficulty?
4. What are logical reasons that support the solution?
5. What additional testing and observation need to be done to confirm the validity of the solution?

These five steps are very similar to the five key elements found in most problem-solving techniques. Although Dewey did not focus specifically on small groups, the steps he outlined, called **reflective thinking**—a series of logical, rational steps based on the scientific method of defining, analyzing, and solving a problem—have been used by many groups as a way to structure the problem-solving process. As new courses in group discussion were being designed in the 1920s and 1930s, teachers and authors adapted Dewey's framework as a standard agenda that could be used to tackle any problem-solving group discussion. One of the first communication texts to adapt these steps to group discussion was Alfred Dwight Sheffield's brief book *Creative Discussion: A Statement of Method for Leaders and Members of Discussion Groups and Conferences*, first published in 1926.[5] Soon other scholars began making similar references to this sequence, and it has become a **standard agenda** for structuring group problem solving.[6]

WRITING PROMPT

Felt Difficulties

The first step in Dewey's original steps of reflective thinking includes identifying a "felt difficulty." Think of several problems that you are experiencing in your life, or have experienced in the past. What is the "felt difficulty" of those problems? Once you've identified the "felt difficulty," phrase the difficulty as a problem statement.

The response entered here will appear in the performance dashboard and can be viewed by your instructor.

Submit

11.2: Balancing Group Structure and Group Interaction

OBJECTIVE: Determine the structure and interactive methods needed to help groups work together

Communicating with others in small groups to solve a problem is often a messy and disorganized process.[7] Some researchers have identified distinct phases in the course of a group's deliberation—for example, orientation, conflict, emergence, reinforcement is one sequence;[8] another is forming, storming, norming, and performing.[9] However, other researchers have found that group discussion often bounces from person to person and can be an inefficient, time-consuming process.[10] Also, groups may develop fantasy themes that can trigger a chain of stories—some that are related to the group's task and some that are not. Although these stories and group fantasies are important to forging a group's identity, extended off-task "storytelling" can have a negative effect on the group's productivity.

To help group members manage the messiness of discussion, a group needs a certain amount of structure to keep the discussion focused. Group **structure** consists of the agenda and other techniques and procedures used to help a group stay focused on the task at hand.

A group also needs the energy that comes from interaction. **Interaction** is simply the give-and-take conversation that occurs when people collaborate. We suggest that a group needs a balance of structure and interaction to be both efficient and effective.[11]

By the end of this module, you will be able to:

11.2.1 Explain how structure helps a group function

11.2.2 Describe the most beneficial group interactions

11.2.1: Groups Need Structure

OBJECTIVE: Explain how structure helps a group function

To counteract the messiness of group interaction, researchers investigating groups have suggested using an agenda to structure the discussion. The purpose of an agenda is to help keep the discussion on track—not to stifle group interaction or consciousness raising. Robert Bales found that most task-oriented groups spend a little more than 60 percent of their time talking about the task and almost 40 percent of their time talking about social, relational, or maintenance matters.[12] An agenda ensures that the time spent talking about the task helps the group accomplish its goal.

Groups that have no planned structure or agenda have many more procedural problems.[13] When researchers have observed "naturally occurring" or unhindered discussion, in which there is little or no structure, they have noticed the following points:

1. The group takes more time to deliberate; interaction is inefficient and often off task.
2. Group members prematurely focus on solutions rather than analyzing issues.
3. The group often jumps at the first solution mentioned.
4. Group members hop from one idea or proposal to the next without seeing the larger issues.
5. The group is more likely to be dominated by an outspoken group member.
6. Conflict is likely to go unmanaged.[14]

The conclusion to be drawn from these findings: Groups need help to keep them on track.

Of all the various ways used to organize or structure discussion, which method seems to work the best? Many sequences of techniques have not been tested empirically. Of those that have been compared in controlled studies, no single method seems to work best all of the time. One powerful conclusion, however, emerges from the research: Any method of structuring group problem solving is better than no method at all.[15]

Groups need structure because members have relatively short attention spans, and because uncertainty results both from the relationships among group members and from the group's definition of the task. In separate studies, researchers found that groups shift topics about once a minute.[16] Therefore, groups benefit from an agenda that keeps the discussion focused on their task. Another study found that some members need more structure than others. In particular, group members who prefer using more rigid procedures arrived at higher-quality decisions than those using a less-structured approach to organizing their discussion.[17] Yet another benefit of structuring conversation in a group is that group members are more likely to remember information presented during a more structured, focused discussion than that introduced in a less focused, freewheeling conversation.[18] Having members first write information down and then share their information with the group increases the likelihood that they will remember what they share. Your preference for whether you help contribute to the interaction or apply more structured approaches to help the group stay focused will reflect your personality and your experience in previous groups.[19]

Think of the various steps and tools we present here as a way to impose a common structure on a group's deliberation. Without that structure, a group is more likely to wobble, waste time, and be less productive.

11.2.2: Groups Need Interaction

OBJECTIVE: Describe the most beneficial group interactions

In addition to a structured agenda and procedures to help the group stay on task, groups need interaction—give-and-take conversation, talk, dialogue, and reaction to the messages of others. A group that has too much structure and not enough interaction is a group out of balance; participating in such a group would be like listening to someone give a speech rather than engaging in an interactive discussion. In trying to find the right balance between structure and interaction, researchers have found support for the following principles:

- High-quality contributions early in a group meeting improve group performance.
- The more individuals share their information with others early in the group's discussion, the more group performance improves.
- If group members not only share but also understand the value and importance of individual contributions, group performance will improve.[20]

To apply these principles in real-world groups, groups need someone to help balance structure and interaction so that all members participate. In other words, groups need a facilitator.

Not all group interactions are created equal. One team of researchers sought to identify the type of problem-solving group interaction that would result in the best solutions.[21] When they categorized the specific type of interactions that occurred during group discussions, they discovered that groups that did the following things made better decisions:

- Focused on analyzing the problem and then developing solutions
- Focused on procedures for making decisions
- Made supportive comments about other group members
- Made "action-oriented" comments focused on getting the work accomplished

Such groups not only had higher performance but also reported more satisfaction with the outcome of their interaction. What didn't help were group members who criticized one another and complained about a variety of issues; performance and satisfaction were lower when this type of interaction was present. The researchers also found that groups who criticized and complained less were perceived to have higher performance two and one-half years later.[22]

Figure 11-1 Finding the Right Balance

It is important to find a balance between structure and interaction in group discussion.

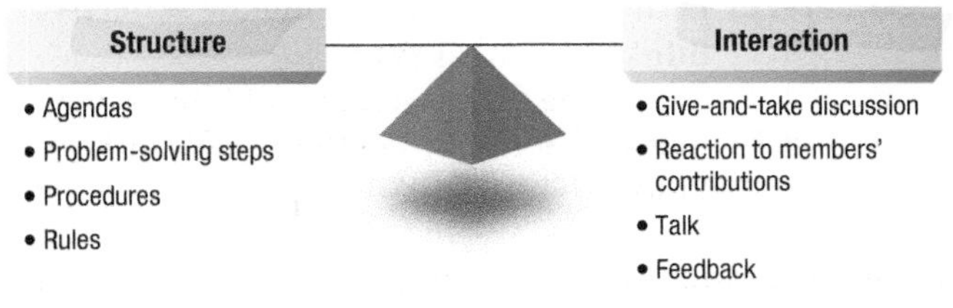

So it's not just interaction that makes a group effective, but the type of interaction that groups have.

In this chapter, we identify techniques that can not only help your group stay on track (structure) but also facilitate group conversation about the topic at hand (interaction). Ideally, a group should have balanced participation in which all members contribute.[23] A group member who talks too much can throw the group off balance.

As Figure 11-1 suggests, the goal is to find the right balance between structure and interaction. Based on his effective decision-making theory, John Oetzel has found that groups that have more equal participation enjoy better-quality results; this research supports the assumption that groups need balanced interaction to achieve their goals.[24] Interaction and collaboration have the advantage of enhancing cooperation in the group. One research team found that group members who first had a *collaborative* discussion about a decision, before making an *individual* decision about the issue, were more likely to make a decision that benefited the entire group.[25] The very act of group interaction facilitates group cooperation. Some studies suggest that groups that use networked computers to share information (a highly structured situation) generate lots of ideas but have difficulty reaching a decision.[26] A less-structured, interactive, face-to-face situation, they found, is better for discussing alternatives and reaching a final decision.

Here is a complete list of recommendations for group interactions that can enhance group problem solving:

- Make high-quality contributions early.
- Share information that you have with others.
- Value the individual contributions of others.
- Talk about analyzing the problem and then develop solutions.
- Discuss procedures for accomplishing the work.
- Make positive statements to support others.
- Make action-oriented comments that focus on results.
- Avoid criticizing others and complaining.

11.3: Reflective Thinking for Problem Solving

OBJECTIVE: Formulate a solution using the reflective thinking process

Some researchers and numerous group communication texts recommend reflective thinking (or one of its many variations) as the standard agenda for organizing or structuring group problem solving. Conversely, many group communication theorists today believe that reflective thinking is more useful as a description of the way some people solve problems than as an ideal pattern for all groups to solve problems. We describe the procedures and tools that can assist you and your groups in organizing the sometimes uncertain and fractious process of problem solving. The steps we present here are not intended to be a one-size-fits-all approach, but they do provide a logical, rational way of structuring group interaction.[27]

By the end of this module, you will be able to:

- **11.3.1 Use tools that help define a group problem**
- **11.3.2 Analyze a group problem using an appropriate analysis tool**
- **11.3.3 Identify criteria for a group solution**
- **11.3.4 Identify possible solutions for a problem**
- **11.3.5 Use an evaluation tool to consider different options**
- **11.3.6 Describe methods of testing proposed solutions**
- **11.3.7 Explain ways to apply reflective thinking to your group**

11.3.1: Step 1. Identify and Define the Problem

OBJECTIVE: Use tools that help define a group problem

Perhaps you have heard the saying, "A problem well stated is a problem half solved." A group first has to recognize that a problem exists. Indeed, this may be the group's biggest obstacle to solving that problem. The problem should be limited so that members know its scope and size. After identifying and limiting the problem, they should define key terms in light of the problem to establish a common understanding of the problem. For example, one student group recently decided to solve the problem of student apathy on campus. The students phrased their problem as a question: "What can be done to alleviate student apathy on campus?" They had identified a problem, but they soon discovered that they needed to decide what they meant by the word "apathy." Does it mean poor attendance at football games? Does it mean a sparse showing at the recent fund-raising activity "Hit Your Professor with a Pie"? After additional efforts to define the key word, they decided to limit their problem to low attendance at events sponsored by the student activities committee. With a clearer focus on their problem, they were ready to continue with the problem-solving process.

Researchers have consistently found that groups develop better solutions to their problems if they take the time to analyze the issues *before* jumping in and listing possible solutions. All too often, however, groups have a tendency to leap to a solution before they thoroughly examine and analyze the issues.[28]

Consider the following questions when attempting to identify and define a problem for group deliberations:

1. What is the specific problem the group is concerned about?
2. Which obstacles are keeping the group from its goal?
3. Is the question the group is trying to answer clear?
4. Which terms, concepts, or ideas need to be defined?
5. Who is harmed by the problem?
6. When do the harmful effects of the problem occur?

When trying to pin down precisely what the problem is, recognize that often a single factor is not causing the problem; systems theory suggests that a problem often has multiple sources. In addition to using the questions listed previously to identify and define the problem, four techniques that provide even more structure may help when your group needs "super" structure to clarify and define the problem.

Tools for Defining the Problem

Is/Is Not Analysis—This technique ensures that a group is, in fact, investigating a problem and not just a symptom of the problem.[29] Early in a group's deliberation, consider such questions as those shown in the chart. Group members can use the chart to focus on the specific problem under consideration. Members can first write down their answers and then share their responses one at a time. Having group members write before speaking is a way to help further structure their comments.

For example, one group was attempting to investigate the declining standardized test scores in one elementary school in their community. They thought the problem they were trying to solve was inadequate teaching that resulted in lowered scores. But when the group used the "is/is not" technique to identify when and where the problem was and was not observed, they discovered that the low test scores occurred in only three classrooms, which were in the same wing of the building and were all cooled by the same air-conditioning system. On further investigation, they realized that the air-conditioning units were not functioning, which

meant that classrooms in that wing were uncomfortably hot—which in turn affected student performance on the examinations. The problem changed from trying to eliminate bad teaching to repairing the air-conditioning system. The "is/is not" technique is a way to identify and define the problem rather than the symptoms of the problem.

Is/Is Not Analysis

	Is	Is Not
What	What is the area or object with the problem?	What is not the area or object with the problem?
Symptoms	What are the symptoms of the problem?	What are not the symptoms of the problem?
When	When is the problem observed?	When is the problem not observed?
Where	Where does the problem occur?	Where does the problem not occur?
Who	Who is affected by the problem?	Who is not affected by the problem?

Is/Is Not Chart

Journalist's Six Questions—Most news reporters are taught to quickly identify the key facts when writing a news story or broadcasting a news event. The key elements of almost any newsworthy story can be captured by addressing a **journalist's six questions**: Who? What? When? Where? Why? How? Answering these questions can help a group quickly structure how a problem is defined. Group members could be given a worksheet such as the one shown here and asked to answer these six questions before the next meeting.[30] The group could then pool their results and be well on the way to analyzing the problem. Alternatively, the group could brainstorm answers to these questions while the leader records the responses on a flip chart or chalkboard.

Journalist's Six Questions

Who
What?
When?
Where?
Why?
How?

Journalist's Six Questions Chart

Pareto Chart—A Pareto chart is a bar graph that shows data describing the cause, source, or frequency of a problem. The chart is arranged with the tallest bars on the left and the shortest bars on the right. A Pareto chart makes it easy to look at data and identify the source of the problem. The chart gets its name from the **Pareto principle**: The source of 80 percent of the problem comes from 20 percent of the incidents.[31] Here are some examples of the Pareto principle in action: 80 percent of the dirt on your carpet is on 20 percent of the

Pareto Charts

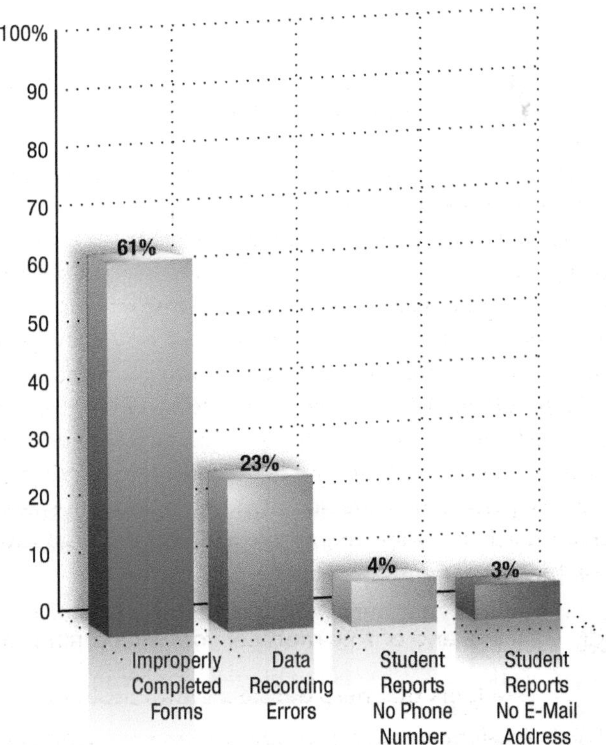

Pareto Chart: Causes of Errors on Financial Aid Statements

carpet's surface; 80 percent of the food you order comes from 20 percent of the menu; 80 percent of the conflict in a group is created by 20 percent of the group members; 80 percent of the clothes you wear come from 20 percent of the clothes in your closet. Most groups find that the primary source of the problem comes from only a few examples. When a group is struggling to figure out exactly what the problem is, a Pareto chart can help the group spot the issue easily.

For example, one group was interested in why so many errors occurred on the financial aid statements issued by their university; students weren't receiving their financial aid on time. They gathered data and displayed it on a Pareto chart, as shown in the figure, which clearly revealed the main source of the problem—the forms weren't being completed properly.

SWOT Analysis—SWOT is an acronym for strengths, weaknesses, opportunities, and threats. **SWOT analysis** is the technique used to help groups identify and analyze big issues that influence the group or organization; it can be helpful in both identifying and analyzing problems.

To conduct a SWOT analysis either individually or collectively as a group, you brainstorm a list of each of the strengths, weaknesses, opportunities, or threats for the group or organization, or use a template like the one shown here. Strengths and weakness are internal factors existing within the group or organization, whereas opportunities and threats are forces external to the group or organization

SWOT Analysis

	Strengths	Weaknesses
Internal		
	Opportunities	**Threats**
External		

Analyzing Organizational Strengths, Weaknesses, Opportunities, and Threats: SWOT

that serve as either an outside positive factor (opportunity) or something that may jeopardize (threaten) a current positive action.

After identifying the SWOTs, rank order the information in each box: What is the greatest strength? What is the greatest weakness? What is the biggest opportunity? What is the most significant threat?

After identifying and ranking each of the four categories, consider the following questions:

1. How can we build on or maximize our strengths?
2. How can we overcome or reduce our weaknesses?
3. How can we take advantage of the opportunities?
4. How can we address the threats and potential threats?

A SWOT analysis can help identify problems by noting weaknesses, or it could be a useful technique to analyze a problem.

11.3.2: Step 2. Analyze the Problem

OBJECTIVE: Analyze a group problem using an appropriate analysis tool

Ray Kroc, founder of McDonald's, was fond of saying that nothing is particularly hard if you divide it into small jobs. To analyze a problem is to break it into causes, effects, symptoms, and subproblems. During the analysis phase of group problem solving, members need to research and investigate the problem. In analyzing the problem, a group may wish to consider the following questions:

1. What is the history of the problem? How long has it existed?
2. How serious is the problem?
3. What are the causes of the problem?
4. What are the effects of the problem?
5. What are the symptoms of the problem?
6. Which methods does the group already have for dealing with the problem?
7. What are the limitations of those methods?
8. How much freedom does the group have in gathering information and attempting to solve the problem?
9. Which obstacles keep the group from achieving the goal?
10. Can the problem be divided into subproblems for definition and analysis?

How a group analyzes the information it gathers can make all the difference in how a group frames issues and, ultimately, solves problems. There's the story about a shoe factory manager who sends two marketing executives to another part of the world to scout out the possibility of selling shoes there. The first executive sends a telegram back to the home office saying, "Situation hopeless. No one wears shoes." The other marketing executive writes excitedly, "Glorious business opportunity. They have no shoes."[32] Both executives had the same information; they simply analyzed the situation differently.

TOOLS FOR ANALYZING A PROBLEM Groups may need help in breaking a problem down into its subcomponents. Two techniques can help sort out factors contributing to the problem: (1) force-field analysis and (2) cause-and-effect (fishbone) diagram. Each technique can help a group focus on data and facts rather than on vague impressions of what may be causing the problem.

FORCE-FIELD ANALYSIS This technique is based on the assumptions of Kurt Lewin, often called the father of group dynamics.[33] To use **force-field analysis**, a group needs to have a clear statement of its goal, which can be presented in terms of what the group wants more of or less of (e.g., "We need more money, more time, or less interference from others"). The group then analyzes the goal by noting which driving forces make it likely to be achieved and which restraining forces make it unlikely to be achieved.

Follow these steps to complete a force-field analysis chart such as the one in Figure 11-2:[34]

1. Identify the goal, objective, or target the group is trying to achieve (such as more money, fewer errors).
2. On the right side of the chart, list all the restraining forces—those that currently keep the group from achieving its goal.
3. On the left side of the chart, list all the driving forces—those that currently help the group achieve its goal.
4. The group can now decide whether to do one of three things: (a) increase the driving forces; (b) decrease the restraining forces; or (c) increase selected driving forces and decrease those restraining forces over which the group has control.

Figure 11-2 Force-Field Analysis Chart[35]

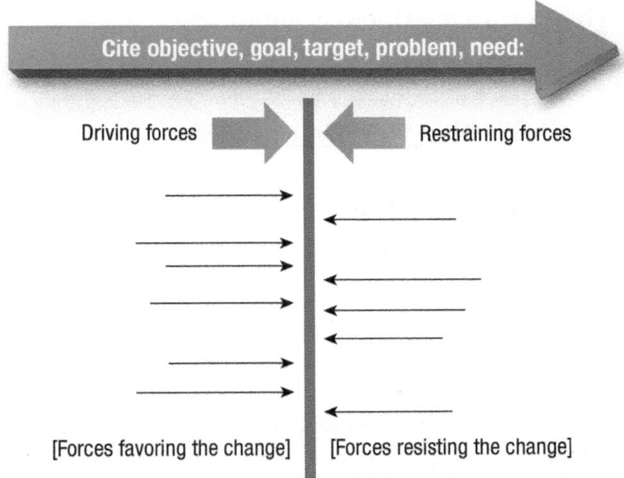

After the group has sorted through the facts and identified the driving and restraining forces, it will have an easier time focusing on the essential causes of a problem rather than on the problem's symptoms.

As an example, suppose you're working in a group whose goal is to increase teamwork and collaboration between faculty and students. Driving forces—forces that favor teamwork—include faculty members who are motivated to work with students, students who also want to work with faculty, and an existing training program that teaches teamwork and collaboration skills to both students and faculty. These and other driving forces could be included on the left-hand side of the force-field chart. Restraining forces—forces that work against increased collaboration—include current lack of knowledge of teamwork principles, the negative attitudes of a small but vocal group of faculty members who want to use more individual approaches to education, and the lack of a tradition of collaboration. These obstacles would be listed on the right side of the chart. Ideally, the group should work together on the force-field analysis diagram by using a flip chart or overhead projector. After generating ideas about additional driving and restraining forces, the group then turns its attention to the question, "What can be done to increase the driving forces and decrease the restraining forces?" The group's force-field analysis of the problem can provide new insights for overcoming the obstacles and achieving the goal.

CAUSE-AND-EFFECT (FISHBONE) DIAGRAM Another problem analysis tool often used in groups is the **cause-and-effect diagram**, also often called a "fishbone diagram" because the completed diagram looks like the skeleton of a fish. Developed by Kaoru Ishikawa, a Japanese specialist in quality management, this diagram helps groups visually examine the relationship between causes and their probable effects.[36]

To develop a cause-and-effect diagram, first think of the effect you want to analyze. For example, imagine your group is trying to identify possible causes for the drop in students' standardized test scores in your community high school. The drop in test scores is the effect, but you aren't sure what's causing it. To prepare a cause-and-effect diagram, draw a long horizontal line on a piece of paper, chalkboard, or flip chart. Then, angling out from the long line, draw lines to represent possible causes of the drop in scores. Here you must use your analytical skills. For example, as illustrated in Figure 11-3, the major causes could be that the test-administration instructions are unclear, that parents are not involved, that teachers may not have enough time to prepare students for the test, or that students may have too many competing activities to study for the test. Then, on each of the four angled lines, list possible contributing factors for each of the four main problem causes. For example, on the line suggesting that students have competing activities, you could draw lines to specify those competing activities. If you're stumped for a way to get started analyzing the problem, Ishikawa suggested that almost all problems boil down to issues related to the "four M's": Manpower (people), Machines, Materials, and Methods. You could begin your analysis by drawing a line angling off the horizontal line to represent each of these four categories.

The advantage of the cause-and-effect diagram is that all group members can work together to identify the relationships between causes and effects. A cause-and-effect diagram creates a shared space in which groups can collaborate. You don't need to make your diagram complicated; you don't always need four lines angling off the center line. Often, simpler is better.

PROMOD TECHNIQUE Erich Witte developed and tested a way of structuring interactions within a group to ensure that the problem is effectively analyzed and that information gleaned from the analysis is shared with the entire group.[37] PROMOD is designed to make sure group members have an opportunity to first individually analyze the problem or issue under consideration, and then systematically share that analysis with other group members. Results from his research studies have concluded that by first *individually* structuring the analysis of the problem and development of solutions, and then sharing the information more broadly, groups develop a better, high-quality solution than if the group had not used the PROMOD technique.

Witte suggests that group members first *individually* read a summary of the problem that includes a digest of all the information and data known about the issue. Having the problem summarized in writing ensures that all group members are aware of the problem and have a common foundation of information on which to base their analysis. The facilitation of the discussion is organized around four key steps that alternate between individual analysis and group sharing.

Figure 11-3 Cause-and-Effect (Fishbone) Diagram

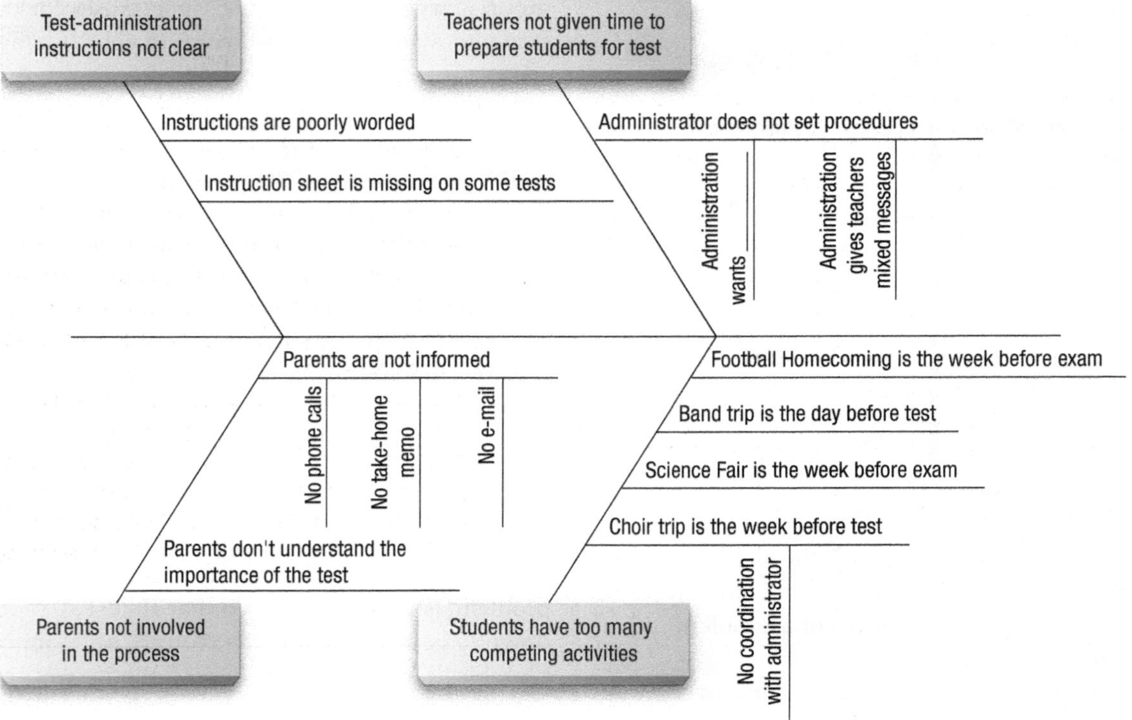

Step-by-Step Summary of the PROMOD Technique

PROMOD Step 1: Individual Problem Analysis

- Group members individually read the information and underline, mark, or highlight important information found in the written summary of the problem.
- Group members individually identify possible strategies that would influence the problem, as well as analyze problems and risks for the alternative strategies.
- Group members individually identify possible decisions/solutions to manage the issue or problem.
- Group members individually rank the decisions/solutions from best to worst.

PROMOD Step 2: Collaborative Group Information Exchange

- Group members share their written information and analysis with all of the group's members.
- Group members then review their analysis with other group members.
- Collaboratively, group members compare the rankings of how the issue could be managed.

PROMOD Step 3: Individual Problem Resolution

- Individually, group members revise their individual analysis and ranking of decisions.
- Group members privately make a final decision.
- Group members individually re-rank their list of solutions.

PROMOD Step 4: Collaborative Group Integration

- Group members collaboratively share their revised decisions.
- Group members discuss the results and seek a consensus on the outcome.
- Group members make a decision either by consensus, majority vote, or group ranking to reach a final decision.

The essence of PROMOD technique is to alternate individual analysis of the problem or issue with group sharing of the information. Writing down the analysis of the problem and then sharing that analysis ensures that all group members' ideas are considered. After a comprehensive analysis of the problem or issue, members make an individual recommendation, and then the group collectively seeks to reach a decision.

11.3.3: How to Establish Criteria

OBJECTIVE: Identify criteria for a group solution

Another task that is often part of the analysis step of the reflective thinking process is to formulate **criteria**—standards or goals for an acceptable solution. Articulating criteria helps the group know when it has developed a good solution because the criteria spell out what the final outcome should look like. Here are some questions that can help your group develop criteria:

1. What outcome are we trying to accomplish?
2. How will we know when we have completed our task?

Virtual Collaboration

Creating Group Structure

One of the ways a group can create structure is to do some of its work via e-mail, file sharing using Google Drive, or other apps that facilitate electronic collaboration. Rather than having people generate ideas during face-to-face meetings, assign group members some homework to be submitted online. Or consider inviting group members to share their ideas for defining and analyzing problems via e-mail or using another software application before meeting face-to-face. Here are some examples:

- If a group is attempting to define a problem, take time during a face-to-face meeting to teach the group how to conduct is/is not analysis. Then each group member should complete an is/is not analysis and submit the information to one individual via e-mail. The person to whom the information is sent can then cull out duplicated material and prepare a summary of the information that the group can discuss at its next meeting.
- According to research, virtual group members do a poorer job of sharing information compared to face-to-face groups. Where possible, use virtual group interaction to analyze and evaluate information rather than share information.[38]
- At a face-to-face meeting, the group could begin a general discussion about the nature of the problem it is attempting to solve. Then group members can submit e-mail responses to the journalist's six questions on a group website or Facebook page. One person can then collate and summarize the responses for the group to discuss.
- Conduct a force-field analysis via electronic collaboration. After clarifying the group goal, assign some group members to identify the driving forces that would increase the likelihood that the goal will be achieved. Others could submit a list of restraining forces. The information could be summarized and then discussed at the next meeting.
- Invite the group to do an analysis of the pros and cons of a particular solution virtually. Provide clear structure and directions as to precisely how group members should generate a list of pros and cons. Consider e-mailing each member a worksheet that includes specific directions for summarizing the advantages and disadvantages of a specific proposal.

3. Which criteria or standards are most important?
4. Which criteria are less important?

For example, criteria for a solution might include the following:

1. The solution should be inexpensive.
2. The solution should be implemented by a certain date and time.
3. The solution should address the causes of the problem, not just the symptoms.
4. All group members should agree to the solution.

WHEN TO APPLY CRITERIA IN SEARCH OF A SOLUTION Although we suggest setting criteria while analyzing the problem, research results are mixed as to when a group should explicitly identify criteria. One study found that the precise point during the problem-solving process when criteria were discussed did not seem to make a difference in the group's final outcome.[39] In fact, group members thought it made more sense to discuss criteria *after* they had identified several possible solutions.

Consider this principle: The more uncertain group members are about the goal of the discussion, the more important it is to explicitly talk about criteria. If the goal is fairly obvious (e.g., if a group has the task of cutting 10 percent of a budget), then it's probably not necessary to ask, "Okay, what are we looking for in a solution?" Everyone already knows what the standard for the solution is. But if the goal is less clear-cut, it may be helpful to confirm that the group knows what the outcome of its discussion should be. One of the most important behaviors of an effective team is to develop a clear, elevating goal.[40] Developing clear criteria is another way of ensuring that all group members know what the goal is, so that they know when they've identified a good solution.

11.3.4: Step 3. Generate Possible Solutions

OBJECTIVE: Identify possible solutions for a problem

After analyzing a problem and identifying criteria for a solution, the group should turn its attention to listing possible solutions in tentative, hypothetical terms. It was ancient Roman Emperor Marcus Aurelius who said, "Is your cucumber bitter? Throw it away. Are there briars in your path? Turn aside. That is enough. Do not go on and say, 'Why were things of this sort ever brought into the world?'"[41] His point: After defining and analyzing a problem, rather than just complaining that a problem exists, find a strategy to solve the problem.[42] It's important that the group not be tempted to start listing solutions too early in the discussion; better solutions occur when groups take time to thoroughly define and analyze the issues.

Creativity is needed at each step of the problem-solving process, but it is especially important when the group attempts to develop solutions. Creativity is such an important part of group deliberations that we devote the next chapter to discussing the principles and practices of group creativity.

Ethical Collaboration

Imbalanced Workload among Group Members

You have been assigned to work with four other students on a semester-long project that counts for 30 percent of your course grade. All members of your group will share the same grade. One member of your group, Enrique, has two small children to support and, in addition to attending your university, works a full-time job at a convenience store. You like and admire Enrique. He's a friendly person who is working hard to take care of his family. But he just isn't following through on his share of the work for your group. Enrique has missed almost half of the meetings, and although he e-mails everyone now and then with information and statistics to try to do his part, he has clearly contributed less to the group than the other members. Toward the end of the semester, his two-year-old child becomes ill and Enrique has to spend even more time away from the group.

Although your instructor in the course hasn't asked for information about how well other group members followed through on their work assignments, you're concerned that your entire group may get a lower grade due to Enrique's failure to do his fair share of the work. Some group members say, "Oh, cut him some slack. He's gotta do what he's gotta do." But others are upset about the imbalance of work. "It's just not fair for our grade to suffer because he isn't doing the work," say some group members.

WRITING PROMPT

Fairness to the Group or Compassion for One Member?

Consider the preceding scenario. Would you tell your instructor about the lopsided workload, especially if it would affect your grade, or just keep quiet? What are some solutions you might suggest for this problem?

The response entered here will appear in the performance dashboard and can be viewed by your instructor.

Submit

11.3.5: Step 4. Evaluate Options and Select Solutions

OBJECTIVE: Use an evaluation tool to consider different options

It's usually much easier for groups to generate options first, and then narrow the list down to one or two possible solutions. After a group has compiled a list of possible solutions to a problem, it should be ready to evaluate the various options and then select the best one. Teams who take time to systematically evaluate possible solutions tend to have better-quality solutions.[43]

How do you narrow down a long list of proposed solutions? One way is to refer to the criteria proposed during the analysis stage of the discussion (or to take time now to develop criteria) and consider each tentative solution in light of these criteria. The group should decide which proposed solution or combination of solutions best meets its criteria. The following questions may be helpful in analyzing the proposed solutions:

1. What are the advantages of each solution?
2. Are there any disadvantages to a solution? Do the disadvantages outweigh the advantages?
3. What would be the long-term and short-term effects of this solution if it were adopted?
4. Would the solution really solve the problem?
5. Does the solution conform to the criteria formulated by the group?
6. Should the group modify the criteria?

If group members agree, the criteria for a best solution may need to be changed or modified.[44]

Tools for Evaluating the Solutions

In addition to asking questions to guide discussion of the solutions or alternatives that the group has identified, here are some other ways of focusing or structuring discussion.[45]

Analyze the Pros and Cons—One of the most consistent research findings is that when groups weigh the positive and negative outcomes of solutions, they make better decisions.[46] One way to facilitate such a discussion is to make a **T-chart** (named for its shape), like the one here, to evaluate pros and cons of the proposed solution. If the group is large and you want to make sure everyone participates, you can have members first write their own lists of pros and cons (or risks and benefits) and then share their responses with the group. For example, if a group is trying to decide whether to purchase a new piece of property, one side of the center line might list positive aspects of the purchase. On the other side would be negative implications of the purchase. A thorough look at pros and cons can help a group consider alternatives before making a final decision. Evidence suggests that groups often find more positive benefits than negative implications when evaluating the pros and cons—so make sure the group identifies both positive and negative outcomes when reviewing various options.[47]

T-Chart

Pros	Cons
Good investment	Reduced cash flow
Property values increasing	Increased property taxes
Good location	Expensive lawyer fees

Average Rankings and Ratings—It's usually easier for a group to identify possible solutions than it is to narrow the list of alternatives and select the best solution. If a group has many solutions to evaluate, one way to narrow the list is to ask members to either rank or rate the solutions, and then average the rankings or ratings to see which solutions emerge as the most and least popular. Ranking or rating should be done after a group has discussed the pros and cons of the solutions. This technique works best if you have a maximum of five to seven solutions; people often have difficulty ranking more than seven items. If you have a very long list of solutions—a dozen or more—you might ask the group members to rank their top five choices, assigning a rank of 1 to their top choice, 2 to their next choice, and so on. One researcher has found that asking the group to rank order a list of possible alternatives is a better procedure than asking the group to pick the best solution. While ranking each option, members are forced to critically evaluate each alternative.[48]

Besides ranking solutions, group members could assign a rating score to each solution. Each solution could be rated on a five-point scale, with a rating of 1 being a very positive evaluation and 5 being a negative evaluation. Even a long list of 20 or more potential solutions could be rated. Group members' ratings for each solution could be averaged, and the most highly rated solutions could be discussed again by the entire group.

Ranking Chart

Which Property Should We Buy?

Each group member (Gabe, Olive, Brandon, and Lucinda) ranked each property from 1–5

	Gabe	Olive	Brandon	Lucinda	Total Score
The Oak Grove Property	1	4	5	5	10
The Buckner Property	2	1	1	3	7
The Grain Valley Property	5	3	3	2	13
The Blue Springs Property	4	2	2	1	9
The Sibley Property	3	5	4	4	16

The property with the lowest total score is ranked the highest.

Buckner	7
Blue Springs	9
Oak Grove	10
Grain Valley	13
Sibley	16

WRITING PROMPT

Making a T-Chart

Think of a decision that you are currently pondering. Make a pros/cons chart to identify the positive and negative aspects of each possible option you are considering. Then describe how a pros/cons analysis can be used in a small group setting.

The response entered here will appear in the performance dashboard and can be viewed by your instructor.

Submit

11.3.6: Step 5. Test and Implement the Solution

OBJECTIVE: **Describe methods of testing proposed solutions**

Perhaps you've heard this oft-quoted quip from an anonymous sage, "Failure to plan on your part does not constitute an emergency on my part." Groups that plan well are more likely to develop an effective solution that will solve the problem.

MAKE A PROTOTYPE A classic way to make sure the solution works is to develop a **prototype** of the solution. A prototype is a smaller version of the solution your team has developed, so you can test it before implementing the solution on a larger scale. For example, if your group has decided to design a new website for your organization to help promote events and communicate new policies, before making the website available to everyone, you should develop a sample or prototype webpage to see how it looks. You could then test it with a small group of people to see if the site is clear and does what you want it to do. When Thomas Edison and his team of researchers were developing the light bulb, they famously developed a prototype light bulb and tested it before deciding "This is it!" and announcing their discovery to the world.[49]

DEVELOP A PILOT PROGRAM If your group is developing a new procedure or process, you could plan a pilot program to test your process before implementing it. A pilot program allows for testing the solution on a limited basis, or testing on a small sample of people, before making a final decision. Software designers often first release what they call a beta version (test version) of the software before releasing the full version for widespread distribution.

After a group selects the best solution, it must determine how the solution can be put into effect. Consider the following questions:

1. How can the group get approval and support for its proposed solution?

2. Which specific steps are necessary to implement the solution?
3. How can the group evaluate the success of its problem-solving efforts?

In many groups, the people who choose a solution are not the same people who will implement it. If this is the case, group members who select the solution should clearly explain why they selected it to members who will put the solution into practice. If they can demonstrate that the group went through an orderly process to solve the problem, they usually can convince others that their solution is valid.

Tools for Implementing a Solution

There are two key tools for implementing a solution: action charts and flowcharts.

An **action chart** is a grid that lists the tasks that need to be done and identifies who will be responsible for each task. This chart is based on more elaborate diagrams and procedures, such as a PERT diagram. PERT (Program Evaluation and Review Technique) was originally developed by the U.S. Navy in the late 1950s to assist with the *Polaris* missile program.[50] The action chart here was developed by using the following steps:

1. Identify the project goal.
2. Identify the activities needed to complete the project.
3. Identify the sequence of activities (what should be done first, second, third, and so on).
4. Estimate the amount of time it should take to complete each task.
5. Determine which group members should be responsible for each task.
6. Develop a chart that shows the relationships among the tasks, times, people, and sequence of events that are needed to accomplish the project.

One reason solutions are sometimes not implemented is that people are uncertain about who should do what. An action chart provides needed structure to reduce this uncertainty. Everyone is aware of what needs to be done and everyone is accountable for their part.

A **flowchart** is a step-by-step diagram of a multistep process. For example, suppose a group was charged with choosing and carrying out a fundraising activity. The chart shown here displays how the group described the essential steps in holding a fundraiser. Flowcharts can help a group see whether the various procedures they have identified to solve a problem are practical and fit together. A flowchart can also help your group work through logistics and identify practical problems of moving from an idea's conception to its implementation. Like an action plan, a flowchart is a way to give structure to group thought. Flowcharts can be simple, as in our example, or very complex, like those used by computer programmers when writing sophisticated programs. The level of detail depends on the group's needs. However, don't to make the flowchart so detailed that your goal becomes developing a flowchart rather than describing and implementing a process. Use a flowchart as a tool to make sure all group members have a clear understanding of the critical parts of a more complex process.

11.3.7: How to Use Reflective Thinking in Your Group or Team

OBJECTIVE: Explain ways to apply reflective thinking to your group

Reflective thinking assumes that groups work best when their discussions are organized rather than disorganized or random. Use reflective thinking as a guide, not as an exact formula for solving every problem. Several researchers have discovered that groups do not necessarily solve problems in a linear, step-by-step process.[51] The process by which groups solve problems goes through several phases of growth and development as members interact.[52] Reflective thinking is most useful in helping groups understand the phases of problem solving. As Ernest Bormann has noted,

Action Chart

Names								
Ken	•	•			•	•		•
Mohan		•			•			
Steve			•		•			
Janice			•		•		•	
Carl				•	•	•	•	
Assignment	Conduct needs assessment	Write behavioral objectives	Develop training content outline	Write training facilitator guide	Develop audio-visual resources	Conduct training pilot test	Conduct training for client	Analyze evaluation data
Week	Week 1		Week 2		Week 3		Week 4	
Day	Monday	Friday	Monday	Friday	Monday	Friday	Monday	Friday

Flowchart

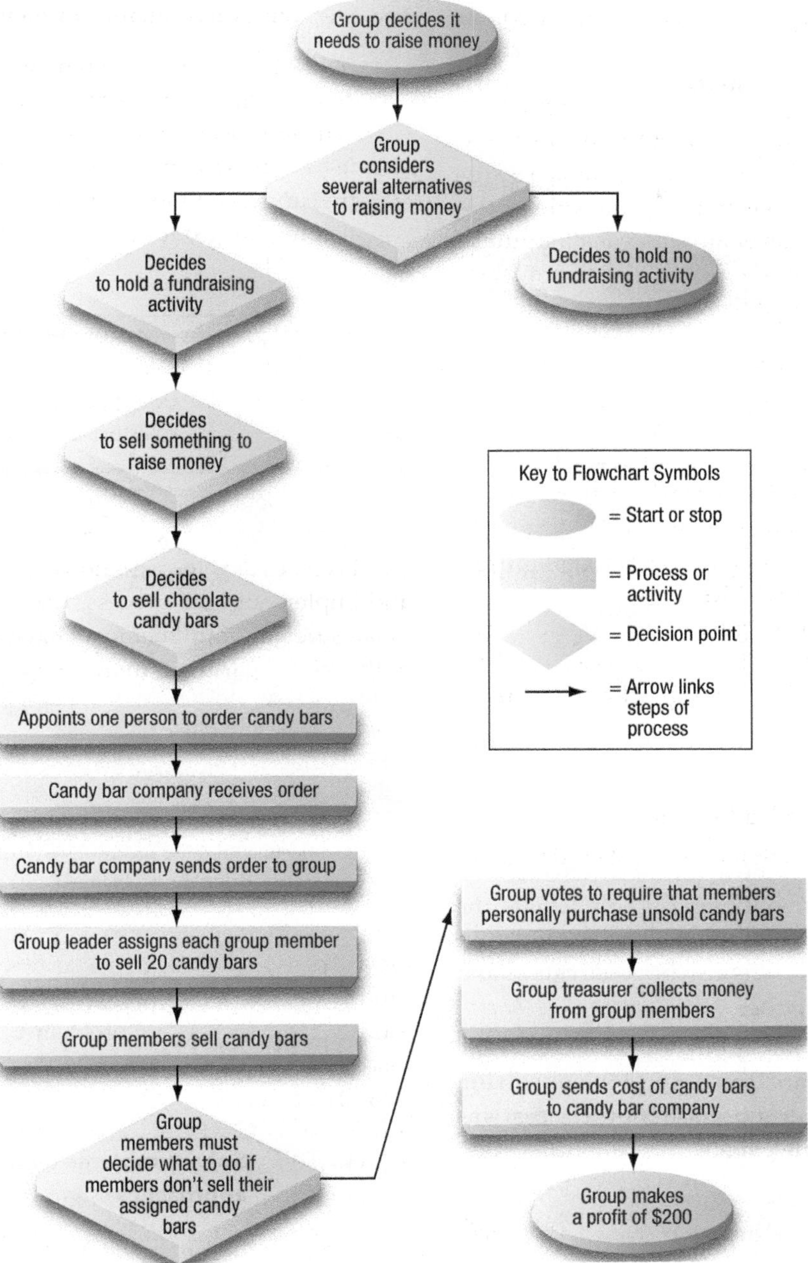

Flowchart of Group Decisions on Fundraising Activity

"Difficulties arise when [group] participants demand rationality from a group throughout its deliberations."[53]

In trying to apply reflective thinking to group problem solving, consider the following suggestions.

1. **Take time to reflect on the procedures the group is using and how group members are interacting.** To **reflect** is to consciously consider precisely how the group and individual group members are talking with one another.[54] Is the group following a structured plan? Are members first analyzing the problem before generating solutions? Is the group aware of how its members are communicating? Research supports the process of having at least one group member reflect and verbalize how the group is doing in following procedures and communicating effectively.[55] Groups that don't have someone helping them reflect perform less effectively. Reflecting helps both face-to-face and electronically mediated groups.

2. **Clearly identify the problem you are trying to solve.** Make sure that you're not merely discussing a topic. For example, a group decides to discuss the quality of the U.S. judicial system. The group selects a topic area, but it does not identify a problem. It should focus clearly on a specific problem, such as "How can we improve the quality of the judicial system in the United States?" or "What should be done to improve the education and training of lawyers in the United States?"
3. **Phrase the problem as a question to help guide group discussion.** Stating your group's problem as a question adds focus and direction to your deliberations.
4. **Do not suggest solutions until you have analyzed the problem.** Many researchers agree that until your group has researched the problem, you may not have enough information and specific facts to reach the best solution.[56]
5. **In the definition and analysis steps of reflective thinking, do not confuse the causes of the problem with its symptoms.** A fever and headache are symptoms, not necessarily causes, of a patient's ill health. The cause may be a cold or flu virus or a number of other things. A doctor tries to identify the cause of symptoms by running tests and analyzing a patient's medical history. In other words, a doctor needs to define, analyze, and solve a problem. In your own group work, you should try to clarify the differences between the causes and the symptoms (effects) of a problem. Perhaps your only goal is to alleviate the symptoms. However, you can better understand your group's goal if you can distinguish between causes and symptoms.
6. **Constantly evaluate your group's problem-solving method.** For many years, the only problem-solving method suggested to group-discussion classes was reflective thinking. However, some communication theorists suggest that for certain types of problems, alternative problem-solving methods work just as well, if not better, than reflective thinking.
7. **Appoint one or more group members to remind the group to use a structured method of solving problems.** One study found that groups in which one member is trained to help the group be mindful of the procedures it uses will make high-quality decisions.[57] Raters were trained to remind the group to use effective problem-solving and decision-making skills by asking the following questions at appropriate times:
   - Do we have enough evidence to support our choice of solution?
   - Have we looked at a sufficient number of alternatives?
   - Have we reexamined alternatives we rejected previously?
   - Have we avoided stereotypical thinking or premature judgments?

   Because you're taking a course in small group communication, you now know the importance of helping a group stay on track and be vigilant thinkers, so you can periodically ask these questions. Even if you're not the appointed leader of a group, you can have a positive impact on the quality of the group's discussion by helping the group examine its process.

Use the reflective thinking process as a flexible guide to help the group stay organized during the problem-solving process.

11.4: Question-Oriented Approaches to Problem Solving

OBJECTIVE: Solve problems using question-oriented approaches

The *reflective thinking* approach is one method of problem solving; another is the question-oriented approach. The latter requires groups to consider a series of questions to keep them focused on their goal. Two such approaches are (1) the ideal-solution format and (2) the single-question format. Both formats help groups identify the critical issues they need to resolve and organize their thinking about the best possible solutions.

By the end of this module, you will be able to:

11.4.1 **Describe the ideal-solution format**

11.4.2 **Explain how the single-question format works**

11.4.3 **Summarize tactics for using question-oriented approaches in a group**

11.4.1: Ideal-Solution Format

OBJECTIVE: Describe the ideal-solution format

Obviously, problem-solving groups want to identify the best solutions to problems. In the **ideal-solution format**, groups answer questions designed to help them identify ideal solutions. Alvin Goldberg and Carl Larson have devised the following agenda of questions:

1. Do all members agree on the nature of the problem?
2. What would be the ideal solution from the point of view of all parties involved in the problem?
3. Which conditions within the problem could be changed so that the ideal solution might be achieved?
4. Of the solutions available, which one best approximates the ideal solution?[58]

These questions help groups recognize the barriers that the problems under consideration have created. They also encourage groups to analyze a problem's cause and to evaluate proposed solutions. The advantage of the ideal-solution format over other problem-solving approaches is its simplicity. Group members simply consider each of the four questions one at a time. One expert recommends that the ideal-solution format be employed in discussions among people with varied interests; this format works best when acceptance of a solution is important.[59] In particular, it enables group members to see the problem from several viewpoints in their search for the best solution.

Although the ideal-solution format is similar to reflective thinking, it uses questions to help a group systematically identify and analyze a problem, pinpoint the best possible solution, and formulate specific methods for achieving a solution. Like other problem-solving formats, it helps a group—particularly one whose members have varying viewpoints and experiences—focus on a problem and devise ways to solve it in a rational, structured way.

Identifying an Ideal Solution

Imagine that you've joined a group of volunteers whose goal is to develop a new lifelong learning organization in your community. The group wants to identify and develop courses that older adults could take to continue their education or simply enrich their lives. It plans to develop several courses that older adults would find interesting and useful, find people to teach the courses, and develop an advertising program to promote the courses they develop. Use the four questions of the ideal-solution format to develop an agenda for the group's next meeting.

1. What would you say is the nature of the problem?
2. What would you identify as the ideal solution to the problem?
3. Which conditions could be changes so the ideal solution might be achieved?
4. What are available solutions, and which solution may be the ideal solution?

11.4.2: Single-Question Format

OBJECTIVE: Explain how the single-question format works

Like the ideal-solution format, the **single-question format** poses a series of questions designed to guide the group toward a best solution. Goldberg and Larson suggest that the answers to the following five questions can help a group achieve its goal:

1. What question does the group need to answer to accomplish its purpose?
2. Which subquestions must be answered before the group can answer the single question it has formulated?
3. Does the group have sufficient information to answer the subquestions confidently?
4. What are the most reasonable answers to the subquestions?
5. Assuming that the answers to the subquestions are correct, what is the best solution to the problem?[60]

Unlike the ideal-solution format, the single-question format requires a group to formulate a question to help obtain the information needed to solve a problem. The single-question format also helps a group identify and resolve issues that it must confront before it can reach a solution. As Goldberg and Larson note, "An assumption of the single-question form seems to be that issues must be resolved, however tentatively."[61] Thus, the single-question format probably works best for a group that is capable of reaching agreement on what the issues are, and how they can be resolved.

The success of this format depends on a group's agreeing on the subissues before trying to agree on the major issues. If you are working with a group that is characterized by conflict and has difficulty reaching agreement, the single-question format may not be the best approach. Such a group may become bogged down arguing about trivial matters while the major issues remain unexamined. Decide whether

WRITING PROMPT

Identifying Questions and Subquestions

Imagine that you are a member of your city councilperson's re-election campaign. You will be meeting with a group of volunteers who support the councilperson's reelection. You will lead the meeting, and you want to develop an agenda for it. Use the single-question format to:

1. Identify the single question that the group needs to answer to accomplish its purpose.
2. Identify subquestions that must be answered before the group can answer the single question that you have formulated.

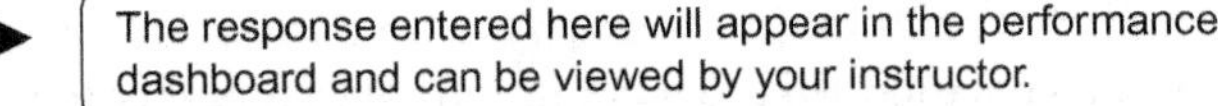

The response entered here will appear in the performance dashboard and can be viewed by your instructor.

Submit

your group will be able to agree on the minor issues before you decide to use the single-question format. If your group cannot reach agreement, either the ideal-solution format or the reflective thinking format may be a better method of organizing your group's deliberations.

11.4.3: How to Use Question-Oriented Approaches

OBJECTIVE: Summarize tactics for using question-oriented approaches in a group

You may notice some similarities among the single-question, ideal-solution, and reflective thinking formats. By guiding groups toward their goals with questions, the ideal-solution and single-question formats help groups agree on minor issues before they tackle solutions to problems. Carl Larson tried to find out whether an ideal-solution, single-question, or reflective thinking approach, or no format at all, would produce better solutions.[62] His study indicates that ideal-solution and single-question formats generated better solutions than did the reflective thinking approach. All three approaches fared better than no approach at all.

Of course, a single study does not prove that the single-question and ideal-solution formats are superior to the reflective thinking format, but it does suggest that under certain conditions, goal-oriented approaches may have certain advantages. In Larson's study, when groups were given alternatives and told to choose the best solution to a problem, their discussions lasted only about 20 minutes. That is, by considering specific questions, members were able to solve problems efficiently. Norman Maier also concluded that a problem-solving approach that has a group consider minor issues before major issues can improve group decisions.[63]

If you are going to lead a group discussion, the following suggestions may help you apply the ideal-solution and single-question approaches to problem solving:

1. **When using the ideal-solution or single-question approach, give group members copies of the questions that will guide their discussion.** You can reduce some of the uncertainty that occurs normally in groups by making sure that each person knows the procedure. Tell the group to use the questions as a guide.
2. **Explain why you are using the format you have selected.** Most groups are willing to go along with a particular discussion agenda, especially if you give them reasons for having selected it. Tell the group that considering specific questions in a developmental format can keep the discussion on track. If your group has a specified time period in which to meet, you can explain that using questions to guide the discussion can help make the discussion more efficient.
3. **Keep the discussion focused on the specific question under consideration.** Whether the group is using the ideal-solution or single-question format, some group members may be tempted to skip a question or may want to discuss an unrelated issue. In such a case, you may have to help the group focus on one question at a time. Several studies suggest that groups with members who try to keep participants aware of the pertinent issues by summarizing the discussion and requesting clarification have a good chance of agreeing on a solution and of being satisfied with their discussion.[64]
4. **Agree to use a collaborative approach to solving the problem.** Frank LaFasto and Carl Larson suggest that the effectiveness of the single-question format can be enhanced if group members explicitly consider the question, "What principles should we agree on to maintain a reasonable and collaborative approach through the [problem-solving] process?"[65] Consider this question early in the problem-solving process. Making collaboration a problem-solving value can enhance teamwork and cooperation.

Skilled Collaboration

When to Make a Decision Based on Careful Analysis and When to Trust Your "Gut Instincts"

Several structured group problem-solving methods provide step-by-step techniques for developing criteria and analyzing information when making decisions. But are there times when you should rely more on your intuition rather than on detailed data analysis?

Research by Erik Dane, Kevin Rockmann, and Michael Pratt suggests that in some instances, you can obtain better results if you rely on your "gut instincts" rather than your head to make decisions and solve problems.[66] These researchers had people evaluate how effectively a basketball player played basketball. In one condition, the subjects were told to just rely on their intuition and first impressions; in another condition, subjects developed and used an elaborate method of establishing criteria and then analyzing each basketball shot. The latter subjects were, in essence, told not to rely on their intuition. The researchers also wanted to know if the subjects' ability and experience in playing basketball was a factor in determining whether intuition or detailed analysis made a difference in how well they could evaluate the basketball players. The research discovered that subjects who had a lot of basketball experience and skill more accurately assessed the players' quality when relying on intuition rather than when using a detailed system of developing criteria and then carefully analyzing data.

Real-Life Applications

What are the implications of these findings and other research about intuition when making decisions and solving problems in small groups?[67]

- Relying on your intuition can be more effective if the task is to make an overall judgment or impression of quality.
- Carefully establishing criteria and using a detailed method of analysis is more effective if your group is solving a complex, highly structured problem.
- Don't ignore your "gut instincts" and intuition, especially if you are an expert or have considerable experience.
- If you and other group members have limited experience or expertise, then it's best to use a more structured technique that emphasizes a careful analysis of data and information.

11.5: Expanding Your Skills beyond Technique

OBJECTIVE: Evaluate your group decision-making skills

Although many skills, strategies, tips, and techniques for improving group process have been proposed, participating in groups involves more than simply applying "how to's." Communicating in groups is often a zipping, buzzing, humming, halting, and cacophonous process. **Systems theory** teaches that group communication is an interrelated, fragile process in which each person or element affects the entire group. Group and team research has not advanced to a state where we can guarantee that using the various techniques we discuss will *always* result in high-quality solutions and decisions. Working in a group is more complicated than that.[68]

By the end of this module, you will be able to:

11.5.1 Explain the role of adaptation in group process

11.5.2 Apply problem-solving principles to a difficult group decision

11.5.1: Adapt to the Group's Needs

OBJECTIVE: Explain the role of adaptation in group process

How do you know when to adopt a specific technique to help improve a group's process? We believe the key is to listen to your group, watch, observe, and identify what the group needs at a given time. In a word: adapt. Adapt to the needs of the group rather than assuming that a predetermined strategy or technique will somehow miraculously help the group or team achieve a breakthrough. If the group seems confused, disoriented, or stuck when defining or analyzing the task in front of it, then it may need to use a more structured technique such as the cause-and-effect diagram or force-field analysis. But if the group is making progress, we don't recommend that you haul out a group technique like is/is not analysis, a fishbone diagram, a T-chart, or some other structured technique. The power of a group does not reside in technique. In fact, group researchers have had some difficulty documenting precisely what makes a group successful—and we don't believe groups will *always* be successful. There is no *one* approach or technique that always works. Helping your group reflect on what it is doing and how it might perform better is an important and necessary role during group and team communication.[69]

WRITING PROMPT

Your Group Problem-Solving Skills

Considering what you've learned thus far, how do you feel about solving problems in groups now? What do you feel are your strengths? In what areas do you feel you need practice?

The response entered here will appear in the performance dashboard and can be viewed by your instructor.

Submit

11.5.2: A Case Study

OBJECTIVE: Apply problem-solving principles to a difficult group decision

Problem solving in groups is a multistage process that involves many considerations along the way. The following scenario is one example illustrating some of the complexities groups may encounter in the process.

CASE STUDY

Who Loses Their Job?

You are one of the managers of a department store in your community. You have just been informed by your supervisor that one of your employees must be laid off because of company cutbacks. You meet with your managerial colleagues to decide which employee will be chosen. All employees are full-time, and all work the same number of hours. There is one formal rule you have to follow: The reason for laying a person off must be job related. Which of the following employees would you and your colleagues choose? Make the best decision you can with the limited information you are given. Be prepared to discuss the reasoning behind your group's decision.[70]

Masha. Age 33, married, with two children, Masha has worked for the company for five years. She loves her job and requires little or no supervision. You have considered giving her a promotion when the opportunity arises. Other people go to Masha when they have questions because she is good at training others. She has been going to school on a part-time basis to get a management degree and will graduate in another year.

Bob. Age 49, divorced, with one child, Bob has worked with the company for 22 years. He keeps to himself but always gets work done. You never have to give Bob instructions because he knows his job so well. Others in the department call him "Pop" because he seems like a father figure to everyone and is well liked. He really adds a great deal of stability to your department. He does not want to change his job at all because he is happy. You put Bob in charge in your absence.

Trent. Age 19, single, a Native American, Trent just began working for your company 11 months ago. He went to an accelerated school as a child and started college when he was 15 years old. He has since graduated with a business degree and shows promise of going far in your company. He is already the best salesperson in your department. Most people get along with him well. Because he is new, Trent needs a lot of training, but his sales are worth your extra time.

Madeline. Age 25, married, and three months pregnant. She transferred to your store only last month but has more than three years' total experience in the company. You have not been very satisfied with her attendance because she is calling in sick a lot. However, she is the only person whom you feel you can give your most difficult tasks to because she is very thorough. She also has received more customer compliments than any other person in your department.

Catrina. Age 40, single, with three children, and is a recovering alcoholic. She fulfills a very necessary function in your department by doing maintenance work, which no one else really has time for. Catrina is efficient and is never late; however, she does not really associate with the others. She has worked with the company for more than 10 years but she cannot read or write; it is likely that this is one of the few places she could find work.

Antonio. Age 27, single, with no children. Antonio has worked for two years in your department, and in that time, he has won three awards for creating outstanding merchandise displays (the heart and soul of retail). He is your most conscientious worker and keeps your department looking great. You have wondered, though, whether he comes to work under the influence of drugs. Several customers have complained about his poor grooming habits and the language he uses. In the last month, however, he has made significant improvements.

Use your knowledge of group problem-solving techniques in combination with your understanding of group process to assess whether your group needs the structure of a specific technique or tool. Effective groups and members use techniques and strategies thoughtfully to help them make progress toward their goal depending on what is (or is not) happening in the group. Use techniques wisely.

Questions for Analysis: Who Loses Their Job?

1. What is the problem facing your group?
2. Which criteria did your group use to help develop a solution?
3. How would you assess the balance between structure and interaction in your group?
4. Before making a decision, how did your group assess the advantages and disadvantages of each option?
5. Did your group use any specific problem-solving or decision-making technique to help structure the discussion? If not, which structured technique could you have used to create a balance between structure and interaction and produce a good solution?

Summary: Using Problem-Solving Techniques

11.1: Prescriptive Problem-Solving Strategies

- In 1910, philosophy and educator John Dewey, in his book *How We Think*, identified the steps people use to solve problems.
- His original steps have been developed further into what is often called the standard agenda of group problem solving.

11.2: Balancing Group Structure and Group Interaction

- Groups are less productive if they have either too much structure (a rigid agenda or one person dominating the flow of discussion) or too much interaction (unstructured talk that does not focus on clear issues or topics).
- Achieving an appropriate balance between structure and interaction is a central goal of effective group discussion.

11.3: Reflective Thinking for Problem Solving

- To help your group or team define and limit a problem, phrase it as a question.
- Do not start suggesting solutions until your group has thoroughly analyzed a problem.
- Consider using tools such as is/is not analysis, force-field analysis, journalist's six questions, Pareto charts, and cause-and-effect (fishbone) diagrams to help your group analyze the problem.
- Formulate the criteria for a good solution before you begin suggesting solutions.
- If the other group members agree, you may need to change the criteria you have selected during the analysis phase of reflective thinking.
- Make sure that reflective thinking is the best method for your group; another problem-solving approach may work better.
- To help ensure that everyone knows and follows through on his or her assignment, consider using an action chart or a flowchart.

11.4: Question-Oriented Approaches to Problem Solving

- If you are the leader, tell the group why you have selected either the ideal-solution format or the single-question approach to problem solving.
- Use the ideal-solution format to help the group come to agreement on the nature of the problem.
- Use the single-question format if you are sure that your group is capable of agreeing on the issues and on how they can be resolved.
- Give members copies of the questions used in the ideal-solution format or the single-question format; this will help to keep your discussion on track.
- Remind group members to address only those questions and issues that are relevant to the discussion.

11.5: Expanding Your Skills beyond Technique

- Participating in a group involves more than just applying simple how to's.
- Use the prescriptive suggestions in this chapter as a menu of suggestions rather than as rigid rules to always follow in every situation.
- Adapt the strategies you use to your specific group rather than always using the same technique the same way in every group.

SHARED WRITING

Group Structure and Interaction

Analyze how significant it is to find a balance between group structure and interaction? Use real-life examples for this analysis. Compare your responses with that of your classmates.

▶ A minimum number of characters is required to post and earn points. After posting, your response can be viewed by your class and instructor, and you can participate in the class discussion.

Chapter 12
Enhancing Creativity in Groups

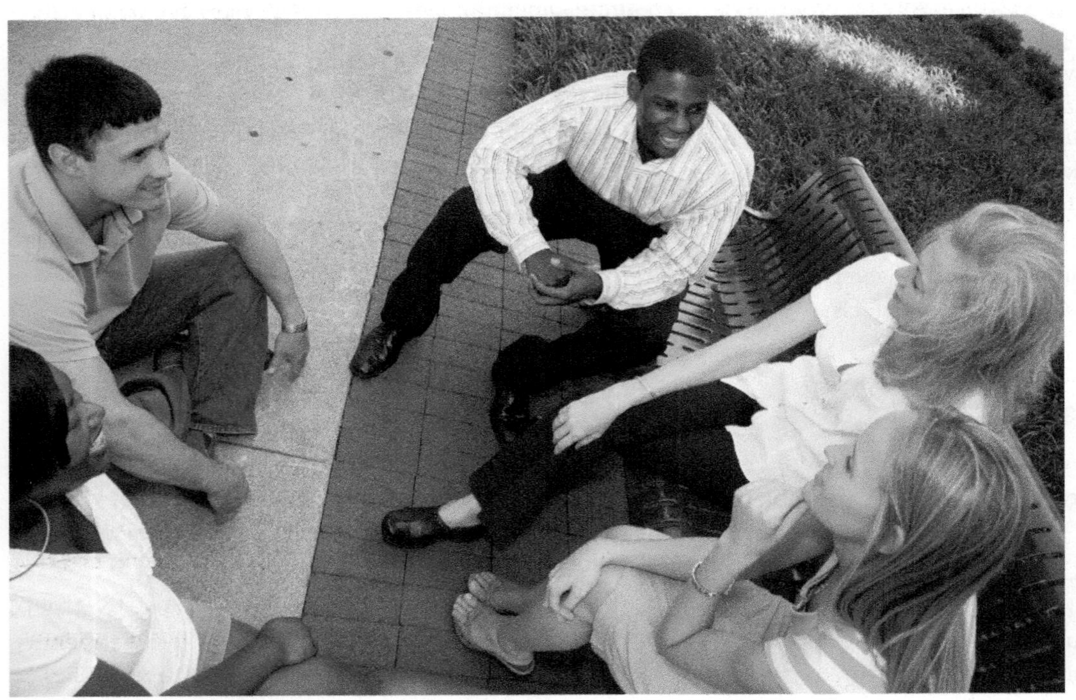

"If you act like an idea person, you will become one."
—Michael Michalko

Learning Objectives

12.1 Describe how creativity can be applied to the group process

12.2 Disprove common myths about creativity

12.3 Identify challenges to group creativity

12.4 Apply principles that enhance group creativity

12.5 Compare creativity techniques for groups

Kutol, the company that had made the product "Magic Wallpaper Cleaner" since the early 1900s, was in trouble. Because fewer people were heating their homes with coal, there was less of a need for the flour-based paste used to clean wallpaper. Sales were plummeting. By the mid-1950s, the company was barely making ends meet. But that's when Joe McVicker, son of the founder of the company, heard his sister-in-law complain that she couldn't find modeling clay for her young elementary school students. Joe wondered, "Could our Magic Wallpaper Cleaner be used as modeling clay?" He sent his sister-in-law some of his product, and history was made. The dough was perfect for the children to play with. You now know it as Play-Doh. Joe McVicker became a millionaire by the time he was 27.[1] Although it sometimes happens by chance, you never know where that great idea for the next creative breakthrough will come from.

Groups are tremendous incubators of creative ideas. It's been said that the best predictor of longevity in individuals or groups is the well-known principle of "survival of the fittest." However, rather than fitness or brute strength, it may be that the "survival of the most creative" is what truly predicts long-term success.[2]

One of the key prescriptive steps in solving problems is the ability to generate options and discover new approaches to problem solving. Now we turn our attention to the principles and practices of enhancing creativity in groups. Specifically, we define creativity, discuss why it's so important for group members, review commonly held myths about creativity, note barriers that inhibit creativity in groups, identify characteristics that nurture the creative split, and offer specific methods and prescriptive strategies for structuring creative interaction in groups.

12.1: Defining Creativity

OBJECTIVE: Describe how creativity can be applied to the group process

One research duo has counted more than 100 different definitions of creativity. The definition we like best has been distilled from several approaches to creativity: **Creativity** is the generation, application, combination, and extension of new ideas.[3] Essentially, to be creative is to invent something new that wasn't in existence before you invented it. In the context of groups, we're not necessarily talking about inventing a tangible object (although a group could very well create something real), but rather inventing or creating a new idea, strategy, principle, or approach to solving a problem. Some researchers make a distinction between creativity (thinking of new ideas) and **innovation** (putting new ideas into action). Communication scholar Phil Clampitt describes innovation as including four steps:

1. Idea generation
2. Feasibility analysis
3. Reality testing
4. Implementation[4]

Innovation extends the notion of creativity by transforming a creative idea into something that is put into practice.[5] Usually group members want to not only develop creative ideas but also implement them.

Another research team found that people who draw upon their intuition to make creative decisions ultimately make better decisions.[6] These researchers suggest that when we use our intuition to make decisions, we may not be completely conscious of what we're doing—intuition is a holistic, sometimes unconscious process of making a judgment.

Creativity researcher Jill Nemiro suggests that creativity and innovation are really intertwined. Both involve the generation of something, either an idea or a product, that didn't exist before.[7] So, whether you call that being creative or being innovative, it's essentially the same process—creating something new that wasn't there before and then using what you create.

By the end of this module, you will be able to:

12.1.1 Describe the phases of group creativity

12.1.2 Explain the six elements of creative problem solving

12.1.1: Phases in Group Creativity

OBJECTIVE: Describe the phases of group creativity

Just as problem solving has phases, so researchers have identified predictable phases in group creativity. Interestingly, Nemiro found parallel phases in face-to-face and virtual teams that are involved with developing creative ideas.[8]

1. *Idea generation phase:* Group members actively identify a range of new ideas, possibilities, and approaches to the issue at hand.
2. *Development phase:* Ideas are extended and additional information is gathered to support the initial nuggets of ideas.
3. *Finalization and closure phase:* The group agrees on the best ideas.
4. *Evaluation phase:* The team assesses the value and worth of the ideas selected.

Because we are discussing small group communication, we're more interested in creative messages than in the mental and psychological processes of creativity. In particular, communication researchers focus on such questions as "What should people say or do to enhance creativity?" and "How does a group or a team organize the agenda of a meeting to produce a creative solution or outcome?" Of course, the psychological or mental aspects of creativity are clearly linked to how we talk and what we do. But interaction and dialogue are what communication researchers typically explore, and those aspects are the focus of our study.

12.1.2: Why Study Creativity?

OBJECTIVE: Explain the six elements of creative problem solving

Long ago, the ancient Romans identified invention as one of the classical canons, or key elements, of the communication process. **Invention** is the process of developing new ideas as we communicate with others and attempt to persuade them to adopt our ideas and suggestions. Being inventive or creative is just as important today as it was in ancient times. In groups, it's especially vital to be able to generate and articulate ideas and suggestions. Research suggests that in addition to using our logical and analytical powers, our intuition can help us make high-quality decisions.[9]

Can people be trained to be more creative? The answer to this question is an unequivocal *yes;* people who are trained to be more creative are, in fact, more creative.[10] There are no surefire techniques that always enhance a person's skill, but several research studies suggest a clear link between being trained in creative skills and the resulting "creative competence" of the individuals taught. Whether it focuses on elementary school children or adults, research clearly suggests that creativity can be learned.[11]

Firestien's research found clear evidence that trained group members used humor to enhance the creative process and were more supportive and less critical of the ideas suggested by others (a very important element of being creative). Ultimately, groups that received training in creative problem-solving techniques produced many more ideas than did groups that had not. Being creative is an essential skill, and there is ample evidence that people who learn creativity do's and don'ts are more creative.

WRITING PROMPT

Applying the Six Elements of Creative Problem Solving

Imagine that the president of your university has appointed you to a task force to identify strategies to keep your campus community safe. Apply the six elements of creative problem solving to structure the conversation to identify solutions, along with ways to ensure the solution is accepted by faculty, students, and members of the community.

The response entered here will appear in the performance dashboard and can be viewed by your instructor.

Submit

Six Elements of Creative Problem Solving

Roger Firestien was particularly interested in the effects of creative problem-solving training on communication behaviors in small groups.[12] Members in the trained group were taught a six-stage model of the elements of creative problem solving.[13]

6 ACCEPTANCE FINDING: GENERATING WAYS TO IMPLEMENT THE SOLUTION AND DEVELOPING A PLAN FOR ACTION.

5 SOLUTION FINDING: USING CRITERIA TO SCREEN, SELECT, AND SUPPORT IDEAS SELECTED IN IDEA FINDING.

4 IDEA FINDING: GENERATING AND SELECTING THE BEST AVAILABLE ALTERNATIVE(S) FOR SOLVING THE PROBLEM.

3 PROBLEM FINDING: GENERATING AND SELECTING A STATEMENT THAT CAPTURES THE "ESSENCE" OF THE SITUATION.

2 DATA FINDING: GENERATING AND SELECTING THE MOST IMPORTANT DATA REGARDING THE MESS.

1 MESS FINDING: ISOLATING A CONCERN OR PROBLEM ON WHICH TO WORK.

12.2: Myths about Creativity

OBJECTIVE: Disprove common myths about creativity

Although you may recognize the value of learning creativity skills, you might still find the process shrouded in mystery. Many people harbor misconceptions about who can be creative and how creativity works. Let's consider three common misunderstandings or myths about the creative process.[14] Discrediting these myths can provide insight into how you can enhance your own creative powers.

CREATIVITY MYTH 1: CREATIVITY IS A MYSTERIOUS PROCESS THAT CAN'T BE LEARNED Research clearly documents that people *can* learn to be more creative.[15] And as for its being a mysterious process—yes, we're still learning more about how the brain works, both from a biological perspective and from a psychological perspective, but some well-documented principles and strategies have been demonstrated to enhance creativity. It's a mistake to think that you can't enhance your creative skill. Labeling yourself as "uncreative" can become a self-fulfilling prophecy: If you think you can't learn to be creative, you won't. So, don't buy into the myth that you can't improve your creative skills. There is clear evidence that you can.

CREATIVITY MYTH 2: ONLY A FEW GIFTED PEOPLE ARE CREATIVE Most of us have been around someone who has a special creative talent. Perhaps someone in your family is gifted in art, music, or drama, and you think that only certain people can be creative. While it's true that some people have special talents in the creative arts, or just seem to have a knack for coming up with new ideas, most people can be taught to enhance their creative skill. And if you're one of the talented people who have creative ability, evidence shows that you can further enhance your creative skills with both knowledge and practice.

CREATIVITY MYTH 3: CREATIVITY JUST HAPPENS Creativity is not a random process, a muse that periodically appears and disappears. Creativity can be cultivated, nurtured, and made to blossom.

WRITING PROMPT

Your Creativity

Do you feel you are creative? If so, how do you feel you got that way? If not, what do you think is the cause for your sense of a lack of creativity? How do creativity myths figure into your self-concept as a creative or uncreative person?

The response entered here will appear in the performance dashboard and can be viewed by your instructor.

Submit

12.3: Barriers to Group Creativity

OBJECTIVE: Identify challenges to group creativity

Research has identified several conditions and behaviors that inhibit creativity.[16] We'll identify them, so you can spot them and eliminate them from your group and team collaborations.

PREMATURE EVALUATION OF IDEAS Creativity is often inhibited by inappropriate evaluation of ideas as they are shared with the group. If members of the group believe that their ideas will be negatively evaluated, they will be less likely to share them. To enhance group creativity, it helps to establish that ideas won't be evaluated in any way when they are first offered to the group. Eventually, ideas and suggestions need to be sorted through, and the best ideas should be chosen from those offered. But when members first introduce ideas, avoid pouncing on them—you not only eliminate the idea you criticize but also stamp out other ideas that might have been forthcoming from your group or team members.

POOR PHYSICAL SURROUNDINGS Our creative abilities are affected by our physical space. It's hard to be creative if your group meets in a dingy, poorly lit, drafty, or too-warm location. If too many people are crowded around a cramped table or in a room that wasn't designed to accommodate that size of group, creative juices will be less likely to flow. Distractions such as outside noise can also inhibit creativity.

TOO MANY PEOPLE In a large group—say, more than 12 to 15 people—it's difficult to have equal participation when the group shares ideas orally. Research clearly documents that communication apprehension is very real.[17] Many people are fearful not just about giving a speech but also about speaking up in a group. Yet people who are anxious about speaking up may have just the creative idea your group needs. Asking people to be creative in a large group or conference setting may achieve some results, but many people will not generate as many creative ideas as they might in a smaller group.

POOR TIMING Sometimes it takes time for groups to be creative. Not giving group members enough time to let ideas bubble up can reduce the group's creativity.[18] On the other hand, some groups may be galvanized into action if given a tight deadline.[19] One study found that when a group was given a tight deadline, it kicked into high gear and became highly productive—but that productivity wasn't very creative. Yet later on, when the same group was given another tight deadline, creativity increased.[20] The members may have learned to deal with tight deadlines and, in turn, improved their creativity.

Another study found that when given longer periods in which to do their work, groups were more creative.[21]

The key to interpreting these studies may lie in looking at what the group does with the time it has. A group is either on task or off task. If a tight deadline can spur a group to focus on its task, then a short time period may be best. Depending on the nature of the creative task, however, group members may need more time to accomplish high-quality results. Group leaders and participants should monitor how time affects the group's level of creativity.

STINKING THINKING Motivational speaker Zig Ziglar often challenged his audience to get rid of what he called "stinking thinking." **Stinking thinking** consists of thoughts that limit the possibilities of an individual, a group, or an organization. Creativity is reduced when group or team members utter "sound bites" that discourage—rather than encourage—the group to think of new possibilities. Here are some examples:

- "We simply can't do this."
- "We've never done it this way before."
- "We tried that a few years ago, and it didn't work."
- "They won't let us do this."
- "You can't be serious."

You can probably identify other comments that bring creative conversation to an abrupt halt. For example, one study found that when we complain about "red tape" and overly restrictive policies, we become less creative and often give up trying to find a way through the bureaucracy rather than searching for a creative solution.[22] Instead of instantly silencing the person who offers such a comment, gently and tactfully invite the group to continue considering possibilities. Use an "I" message ("I think there are options that we have yet to consider") rather than a "you" message ("You always offer negative comments!") when attempting to change the tenor of thought in your group.

One technique for overcoming negative thinking, pioneered by Prescott Lecky, is called tick-tock. It's quite simple. You make an effort to flip a negative idea into a positive comment.[23] Here's how to do it. Make two headings on a sheet of paper: one called "tick" and the other called "tock." Whenever a negative thought or idea is presented, write it in the "tick" column. Now think of a substitute positive idea to counter the negative idea: The positive idea goes in the "tock" column. For example, you hear a group member say, "What a stupid idea. Everyone will laugh at us." That negative idea goes under the "tick" heading. Stop and think of a more positive response, such as "New ideas may not have popular appeal at first. Who cares if people laugh, if the idea works?" That positive response goes under the "tock" heading. Here's another example: "We did a terrible job with that last project"—tick. The "tock" response: "We've learned from our mistakes. We can do better now."

You can use this simple "tick-tock" technique to combat stinking thinking, whether it's just your own overly negative self-critique or a collaborative pity party. We're not suggesting that you or your group avoid honest evaluation of ideas and self-criticism. But if you or your group seem stuck in negative thinking, putting a positive spin on the critique can be empowering and spur the group to consider more options.

WRITING PROMPT

Using the Tick-Tock Technique

Think of the times when you get concerned or worried about something and find negative thoughts distracting you. Use the "tick-tock" method to identify positive responses to each of the negative thoughts you experience. How does considering rational responses to worries and concerns help you manage the problem that is confronting you?

The response entered here will appear in the performance dashboard and can be viewed by your instructor.

Submit

12.4: Principles of Group Creativity

OBJECTIVE: Apply principles that enhance group creativity

Understanding how creativity works and knowing the underlying principles that enhance the creative process can help you and your group members become more innovative. One researcher suggests that groups will be more creative if they are motivated; if they use creativity-fostering processes such as having everyone participate in the discussion; and if they communicate effectively by involving everyone, providing useful feedback, and addressing conflict when it arises.[24] Broadly speaking, group creativity research suggests that groups are more likely to be creative if they appropriately analyze and define the problem, intentionally foster a climate of freedom in which to be creative, listen to minority points of view, encourage members to assume new perspectives or roles, and find ways to structure the process.

Research suggests that sometimes an individual may hold the key to coming up with a creative solution. In contrast, a group that is too conforming or collectivistic may inadvertently put a damper on creativity.[25] Groups need to permit individuals to share their own ideas rather than emphasizing just going along with the majority opinion. In their book *Virtuoso Teams*, Andy Boynton and Bill Fischer advocate that teams that enable individuals to assert their creativity can enhance the team's overall skill in developing high-quality, creative solutions.[26]

By the end of this module, you will be able to:

- **12.4.1** Identify a group problem
- **12.4.2** Use strategies to develop a creative group climate
- **12.4.3** Listen to group members who voice opinions that are in the minority
- **12.4.4** Use strategies to help groups see things differently
- **12.4.5** Describe strategies to add structure to group discussion

12.4.1: Appropriately Define and Analyze the Problem

OBJECTIVE: Identify a group problem

It's difficult to come up with a creative solution to a problem if that problem has not been clearly defined and analyzed.[27] Groups that jump to solutions before thoroughly analyzing what is known and not known are less likely to develop high-quality solutions. Before attempting to come up with creative solutions to a problem, make sure the group knows what the problem is and has some information, data, or evidence to serve as a springboard for possible solutions.

Arthur VanGundy suggests that the group may need to reframe the problem or reanalyze the issues to come up with a creative slant on the challenge confronting the group.[28] For example, a group trying to develop a website where it could post answers to frequently asked questions decided that it already had a wealth of information; the group did not need to develop additional answers to questions, but rather needed to identify and highlight the information that already existed. By reframing the problem, the group made a subtle yet useful distinction that saved the members much time and energy.

WRITING PROMPT

Defining and Analyzing a Real-Life Problem

Are you experiencing a problem in your own life? Define the problem by noting what the problem is and what you want more or less of in its solution. Then analyze the problem by identifying the causes, symptoms, and effects the problem is having on your life. How does clearly defining and analyzing the problem help you develop creative options for managing the problem?

The response entered here will appear in the performance dashboard and can be viewed by your instructor.

Submit

12.4.2: Create a Climate of Freedom

OBJECTIVE: Use strategies to develop a creative group climate

For maximum creativity, group members need to have the freedom to express ideas—even partial ideas—without fear of being ridiculed. Research has found that group members who are motivated to be creative are more innovative. In turn, explicitly expressing an interest in creating a creative, free-wheeling climate can enhance creativity.[29] Consultants at one firm claim they can unlock creativity by encouraging group members to be playful and even somewhat silly. As part of the creativity training, group members are given toys such as modeling clay, rubber-band–powered airplanes, Nerf balls, and wooden blocks and are invited to play. Being playful encourages freedom of expression—a key ingredient of creativity. If, for example, your group is stymied by a problem, take time off to "play"; taking a walk, going for a snack, or doing something else the group members consider fun may be just what the group needs to boost its creativity.[30] Another study found that when team members had an attitude of being open to new experiences, they were more creative.[31]

One study found that groups in which members retain their individualism, rather than going along with a collectivistic group identity, generate more creative ideas. This finding suggests that it's a good thing when group members bring their individual points of view to a group.[32] Just make sure that each group member feels free to share his or her ideas with the others. Other researchers suggest that teams can best tap their creative resources if they approach problem solving as a collaborative fusion of ideas.[33] In keeping with the metaphor of "fusion cooking," in which culturally diverse cuisines are melded together to create a new flavor, groups (especially those that are culturally diverse) can see things differently if the members give up their own cultural approach to defining and analyzing a problem and truly fuse or join their ideas to create something brand new. Clinging to your own cultural comfort-zone thinking patterns can decrease creativity.[34]

Make sure you are not merely approaching problems and solutions the same way you've always done things in the past. Observe and listen for new ways of solving problems by being aware of the diverse cultural perspectives that are in your group or team.[35] Having a group composed of a wide variety of ages also seems to spur creativity, especially when interacting in online, virtual group situations.[36]

12.4.3: Listen to Minority Points of View

OBJECTIVE: Listen to group members who voice opinions that are in the minority

Creativity research suggests that groups with a diversity of opinions and ideas are more creative. Specifically, some researchers have concluded that groups with greater ethnic and racial diversity develop more creative solutions to problems.[37] Minority points of view challenge traditional thinking and ideas, and, if taken into consideration, can help group members see things in a new light.[38] Groups in which one or two people dominate the discussion, either because of extreme status differences or because of their lack of sensitivity to the need for balanced discussion, are less likely to develop creative ideas. Just as *groupthink* can quash ideas and limit logical decision making, so, too, can it smother creative minority points of view. Encourage quiet group members to contribute to the group. And when they do, listen thoughtfully to what they have to say.

In general, having more information available and listening to that information enhances group creativity.[39] However, when group members get too bogged down in details and don't keep the big picture in mind, creativity suffers.[40]

WRITING PROMPT

Identifying Minority Viewpoints

Imagine you are in a group with your class. Who might hold minority viewpoints? Who tends to be quiet or ignored? Who has interests different than those of the rest of the group? Whose identity might put them at odds with cultural assumptions made by the rest of the class? What could you say to encourage quiet members of the group to participate in the discussion?

The response entered here will appear in the performance dashboard and can be viewed by your instructor.

Submit

12.4.4: Encourage People to See Things and Themselves Differently

OBJECTIVE: Use strategies to help groups see things differently

It's become a cliché to say, "Let's think outside the box." Yet often phrases become clichés precisely because they express ideas succinctly. "Thinking outside the box" expresses the power of seeing facts, issues, and problems from a new vantage point. Instead of analyzing a problem from your own point of view, consider taking on a new role to gain a different point of view. For example, rather than thinking about a problem from the point of view of a student trying to identify solutions to the dramatic increases in the cost of tuition, or attempting to solve the vexing parking problem on your campus, imagine that you're the president of your university. How would she or he view the problem? Try to consider an alternative entry point into the problem.

Another specific way to help group members see familiar problems and issues in a fresh light is to bring new members into the group. Changing the membership in a group can spur group creativity because new people bring in new ideas.[41] In addition, having group members who have had direct experience with the problem you're trying to solve can enhance creativity.[42]

WRITING PROMPT

Getting a Fresh Perspective

Imagine you are in a group trying to start a new student leadership development program on your campus. What specific strategies could you use to encourage group members to bring a fresh, creative approach to developing this new program?

The response entered here will appear in the performance dashboard and can be viewed by your instructor.

Submit

12.4.5: Selectively Increase Group Structure

OBJECTIVE: Describe strategies to add structure to group discussion

Creative ideas may arise not only during periods of high stimulation but also during quiet periods, when the ideas silently creep into our consciousness. Invite group and team members to write and think individually before sharing ideas orally. Increasing group structure by alternating periods of personal reflection and writing with oral idea-sharing may help prime the group's creative pump.[43] Group members sometimes need enough space for ideas to emerge—not just physical space (groups do need a good work environment) but also psychological space so that ideas can percolate.

Research suggests that people who can live with some uncertainty and who don't need immediate closure are more likely to generate creative ideas than are people who need to find the right answer in a short period of time.[44] In other words, people who are patient and don't try to force an immediate answer to a question or a speedy solution to a problem are likely to be more creative.

Problem-solving procedures such as *reflective thinking* and techniques such as *journalist's six questions*, *force-field analysis*, and *fishbone analysis* are designed to give the problem-solving process additional structure. Structure helps channel a group's attention and energies to stay focused on the task at hand.[45] Several prescriptive techniques are designed to facilitate the generation of creative ideas.

Review

How to Enhance Creativity in Your Group

What to Do	How to Do It
Appropriately analyze and define the problem to be solved.	• Write the specific problem someplace where all group members can see it. • Have each group member write a statement of precisely what the group wants to achieve. • Separate the symptoms of the problem from the causes of the problem by using is/is not analysis.
Create a climate of individual freedom.	• Use structured methods of capturing ideas—for example, have group members first write ideas on paper or share ideas via e-mail or a website. • Encourage other group members by expressing positive reinforcement for ideas shared. • Encourage the group to play together; do something fun. • Take a break; take a walk; take time away from the problem.
Listen to minority points of view.	• When someone disagrees with a minority position, make sure that the minority position is not quickly dismissed. • Encourage quiet members to talk, and reinforce their ideas when they do contribute.
Encourage people to see things and themselves differently.	• Try "rolestorming": Ask group members to assume a role (e.g., president of the company, a customer) different from their actual role. • Try reverse-brainstorming: Ask the group to generate ideas that would make the problem worse. Then see if any of these ideas can be flipped to help solve the problem or generate fresh insights. • Use the tick-tock technique; turn a negative idea into a positive point. • Bring new members into the group.
Selectively increase group and team structure.	• Use techniques that help the group dissect the problem, such as force-field analysis, a fishbone diagram, or analyzing the pros and cons. • Use the affinity technique, brainstorming with sticky notes, to get people moving and on their feet.

12.5: Techniques for Enhancing Group Creativity

OBJECTIVE: Compare creativity techniques for groups

Group members often want to answer the question, "What techniques will enhance our creativity?" Beyond understanding general principles of creativity and promoting conditions to enhance creativity, which specific methods, approaches, or techniques can boost creativity? Sometimes, groups need the structure of a technique to achieve a creative breakthrough. Such techniques include brainstorming, the nominal-group technique, the Delphi technique, electronic brainstorming, and the affinity technique—each is a prescriptive technique for structuring the process of generating creative ideas. Research suggests that having standard procedures and some structure can enhance group member creativity.[46] In this module, we offer specific tips for incorporating these techniques into your group deliberations.

By the end of this module, you will be able to:

- 12.5.1 **Use brainstorming to develop creative options to solve a problem**
- 12.5.2 **Use the nominal-group technique in a group discussion**
- 12.5.3 **Apply the Delphi technique to a group problem**
- 12.5.4 **Describe how the affinity technique applies to a group discussion**

12.5.1: Brainstorming

OBJECTIVE: Use brainstorming to develop creative options to solve a problem

Imagine that your employer assigns you to a task force whose goal is to increase the productivity of your small manufacturing company. Phrased as a policy question, the problem is "What can be done to increase efficiency and productivity for our company?" Assume that your boss has clearly identified the problem for the group and has provided you with several documents analyzing the problem in some detail. Your group may decide that reflective thinking, which focuses on identifying and analyzing problems, is not the best process to follow. Your group needs innovative ideas and creative, original solutions. Perhaps your group could benefit from brainstorming.[47]

Brainstorming is a creative technique designed to help a group generate several solutions to a problem. It was first developed by Alex Osborn, an advertising executive who felt the need for a creative technique that did not emphasize evaluating and criticizing ideas, but instead would focus on developing imaginative and innovative solutions.[48] Brainstorming has been used by businesses, committees, and government agencies to improve the quality of group decision making. Although it can be used in several phases of group discussions, it may be most useful when a group needs original ideas or has trouble coming up with any ideas at all. Research suggests that a trained facilitator can improve the execution of group brainstorming.[49]

The general assumption underlying brainstorming is that the more ideas that are generated, the more likely it is that a creative solution will be found. In 1888, a fellow named Henry thought he could make a ton of money by investing in a 600-acre cucumber farm. He found out after his first year that cucumbers were not the road to riches: He went bankrupt. But instead of causing him to give up, his failure spurred him to develop more than one product—in fact, he came up with 57 different cucumber-based products. The multitude of options resulted in dramatic success: Today the Heinz company is a multimillion-dollar international corporation largely because Henry Heinz developed multiple solutions to his problem. Brainstorming is a classic way of generating multiple options.[50]

Research largely supports the brainstorming procedure, although some studies suggest that generating a few high-quality ideas is more useful to groups than merely identifying lots of bad ones.[51] Some research suggests that groups who use brainstorming earlier in their deliberations perceive it to be more valuable in helping them generate high-quality ideas.[52] Moreover, brainstorming is helpful when the group members must use evidence to help them find a specific, correct solution to a problem. Research also suggests that the most effective brainstorming groups keep at it; the more persistent group members are in generating ideas, even when idea generation slows, the better the result.[53] Other evidence indicates that women are more persistent than men in continuing to generate ideas during brainstorming.[54] Another factor that seems to enhance creativity during brainstorming is for group members to value group member diversity. Groups who have a higher appreciation for welcoming and even celebrating diverse approaches to solving problems appear to generate more creative approaches to finding a high-quality solution.[55]

TRADITIONAL BRAINSTORMING STEPS Traditional brainstorming is a process that follows certain specific guidelines.

1. *Select a specific problem that needs solving.* Be sure that all group members can identify and clearly define the problem.
2. *Set a clear time limit.*
3. *Ask group members to temporarily put aside all judgments and evaluations.* The key to fruitful brainstorming is to avoid criticism and evaluation during the process. Osborn makes these suggestions:
   - Acquire a "try anything" attitude.
   - Avoid criticism, which can stifle creativity.
   - Remember that all ideas are thought-starters.
   - Today's criticism may kill tomorrow's ideas.
4. *Ask group or team members to think of as many possible solutions to the problem as they can and share the ideas with the group.* Consider the following suggestions:
   - The wilder the ideas, the better.
   - It is easier to tame ideas down than to liven ideas up.
   - Think out loud and mention unusual ideas.
   - Someone's wild idea may trigger a good solution from another person in the group.
5. *Make sure the group understands that "piggybacking" off someone else's idea is useful.* Combine ideas; add to previous ideas. Adopt the philosophy that once an idea is presented to the group, no one owns it; instead, it belongs to the group, and anyone can modify it. Based upon Osborn's original suggestions, group facilitator Bob Eberle developed a list of ways to build on the ideas of others using the acronym SCAMPER.[56] Here are his suggestions:
   - **S**ubstitute something.
   - **C**ombine it with something else.
   - **A**dapt something to it.
   - **M**odify or magnify it.
   - **P**ut it to some other use.
   - **E**liminate something.
   - **R**everse or rearrange it.

   As you hear ideas and suggestions from others, use the SCAMPER list to transform other people's ideas into even more creative options.
6. *Have someone record all the ideas mentioned.* Ideas could be recorded on a flipchart, chalkboard, whiteboard, or overhead projector so that each group member can see them. You could also audio-record your discussions.
7. *Evaluate ideas when the time allotted for brainstorming has elapsed.* Consider these suggestions:
   - Approach each idea positively, and give it a fair trial.
   - Try to make ideas workable.
   - Encourage feedback about the success of a session. If even a few of the ideas generated by a group are useful, the session has been successful.

Assessing Group Brainstorming Skills

Group brainstorming is a tried-and-trusted method of generating creative options *if* (and it's a big *if*) group members appropriately use the principles and practices of effective brainstorming. Use the following assessment form to evaluate your group's application of brainstorming principles.

1 = Yes

2 = Sometimes Yes

3 = Uncertain

4 = Sometimes No

5 = No

1. The group reviews the rules of effective brainstorming.

1 2 3 4 5

2. Group members understand the specific problem they are trying to solve.

1 2 3 4 5

3. The group sets aside a specific time for brainstorming with a time limit made known to all group members.

1 2 3 4 5

4. Group members explicitly agree to not evaluate (verbally or nonverbally) suggestions offered to the group.

1 2 3 4 5

5. Group members who start to evaluate the ideas of others are politely reminded not to.

1 2 3 4 5

6. Group members are told to think of as many ideas as they can to solve a specific problem.

1 2 3 4 5

7. Group members are encouraged to develop wild and offbeat ideas.

1 2 3 4 5

8. Group members piggyback on the ideas of others; they use the ideas mentioned to stimulate new ideas.

1 2 3 4 5

9. All ideas shared by group members are recorded.

1 2 3 4 5

10. Ideas are evaluated after group members have had a time to share them.

1 2 3 4 5

Summary: Review your responses. In what areas did your group score the highest? The lowest? Identifying the areas with the most room for improvement can inform your approach to your group's next brainstorming session. How might you be able to help guide the group to improve the brainstorming process?

CASE STUDY

Clipping Negative Thinking

Business was terrible. The Paperclip Company, the primary supplier of paper clips to big-box discount stores, was having a sales slump. Because more people were using e-documents and e-files, fewer people were buying paper clips to fasten sheets of paper together. For the past three years, sales had dropped by 15 percent each year. The company had already been forced to reduce the size of its manufacturing plant and lay off several employees.

The vice president of marketing decided to increase sales by identifying new, creative uses for paper clips other than holding sheets of paper together. She had assembled her brightest, most creative managers to develop possible new ways paper clips could be used. The vice president decided to use the brainstorming method. She announced the rules of brainstorming and set a 15-minute time frame. She turned on a digital audio recorder to capture the verbal comments and the ideas suggested; her administrative assistant would type the list later and share it with the group.

It didn't go well. Several team members couldn't resist critiquing the ideas of others. The senior managers did more talking than the junior managers. One of the junior managers tried to share some ideas but received a glowering frown from a senior manager, and all of the junior managers realized that they would risk being criticized if they shared their ideas. After about eight minutes of brainstorming, the senior managers had offered a few ideas, the junior managers had not spoken, and the vice president was becoming increasingly frustrated. She finally blurted out, "Oh, this isn't working!"

Questions for Analysis: Clipping Negative Thinking

1. What are the key problems with the brainstorming done by the Paperclip Company's managers?
2. Why did those problems occur? What should the vice president have done differently to set up the brainstorming session? What were the managers doing wrong?
3. Other than oral brainstorming, which alternative techniques could be used to generate ideas?
4. Based on the principles of group creativity, what could be done to develop a creative group climate, regardless of the specific technique used?

12.5.2: The Nominal-Group Technique

OBJECTIVE: Use the nominal-group technique in a group discussion

In her book *Quiet: The Power of Introverts in a World That Can't Stop Talking*, author Susan Cain suggests that some people just don't perform well in an environment filled with lots of talk and interaction—the environment of oral brainstorming.[57] If you gain energy by retreating to a quiet place of solitude rather than being around other people, you are likely more introvert than extrovert. An introvert is someone who is not necessarily shy but simply prefers thinking and listening rather than speaking and interacting with others.

The **nominal-group technique** is a creativity-enhancing procedure that uses some of the principles and methods of active brainstorming but has members write their ideas while being quiet and thinking before sharing them with the group.[58] Introverts will prefer using this technique because it gives them time to think and reflect. Specifically, research has found that having group members alternate between individual, silent brainstorming and group conversation can enhance the quality of ideas generated.[59] The nominal-group technique gets its name from the principle that the group is nominal (it is a group in name only), in the sense that members work on problems individually rather than during sustained group interaction. This technique uses **silent brainstorming** to overcome some of the disadvantages researchers have discovered in exclusively oral brainstorming.

Why does silent brainstorming often produce better results than oral brainstorming? During traditional brainstorming, group and team members blurt out their ideas. But if someone laughs at an idea or says, "That's cool" or "That won't work," then the idea has been evaluated. *The key to make brainstorming work is to separate the generation of ideas from the evaluation of ideas.* In oral brainstorming, it's hard not to evaluate ideas. During traditional brainstorming, despite their best intentions, group members often evaluate ideas as soon as they are verbalized, so group members may be less likely to share ideas. Criticism and evaluation diminish creativity.[60] Even if group members don't verbalize their evaluation, their nonverbal expressions often convey positive or negative evaluation of ideas. In addition, some people are apprehensive or nervous about speaking up in a group, and traditional oral brainstorming makes it less likely that those communication-apprehensive members will participate and share their ideas. Silent brainstorming overcomes those problems by encouraging even apprehensive group and team members to participate by first writing their ideas.[61] Once they have a written "script," they will be more comfortable sharing their ideas.

Researchers have also found that people work more diligently if they have an individual assignment than if they have a group assignment.[62] Moreover, with traditional brainstorming, the creative talents of some members sometimes seem to be restricted just by the very presence of others.[63] Group and team members may generate more ideas if members first work alone and then regroup. After they reconvene, group members can modify, elaborate on, and evaluate ideas. So, the generation of ideas (writing them down) has been effectively separated from the evaluation of ideas.

Silent brainstorming can be done even before a group meets for the first time. For example, you could describe a problem and ask group members to brainstorm individually before assembling. E-mail makes this easier; one communication researcher found that electronic brainstorming worked just as well as face-to-face brainstorming.[64]

APPLYING THE NOMINAL-GROUP TECHNIQUE The nominal-group technique adds structure to the brainstorming process. The following steps summarize how to use the nominal-group technique:

1. All group members should be able to define and analyze the problem under consideration.
2. Working individually, group members write down possible solutions to the problem.
3. Group members report the solutions they have identified to the entire group one at a time. Each idea is noted on a chart, chalkboard, whiteboard, or overhead projector for all group members to see.
4. Group members discuss the ideas gathered—not to advocate for one idea over another, but rather to make sure that all the ideas are clear.
5. After discussing all proposed solutions, each group member ranks the solutions. If the list of solutions is long, the group members can rank the five solutions they like best. The results are tabulated.
6. The entire group discusses the results of the rankings. If the first round of ranking is inconclusive, or if the group is not comfortable with the results, the options can be ranked again after additional discussion. Research suggests that using this organized method of gathering and evaluating information results in better solutions than if the group attacks a problem in a disorganized fashion.[65] One researcher has found that the nominal-group technique works better than other prescriptive approaches such as *reflective thinking*.[66]

This individual method of idea generation and evaluation has the advantage of involving all group members in deliberations. It can be useful if some group members are uncomfortable making contributions because of status differences in the group. Also, alternating group discussion with individual deliberation can be useful in groups plagued by conflict and tension. Research has also found that participants using the nominal-group technique are likely to remember more of what they discuss, perhaps because they do not just talk about their ideas in the group but also write their ideas before they share the information with others.[67]

To achieve the maximum benefits from using the nominal-group technique, consider investing a short period of time to make sure each group member understands the technique. Research has found that group and team members who receive training in the nominal-group technique are more effective than those who don't receive such training.[68] So, groups and teams can improve their skill level if they have an opportunity to learn structured ways of developing and organizing their contributions.

Both traditional brainstorming and the nominal-group technique can be used in any phase of the problem-solving process. For example, you could combine the nominal-group technique with *force-field analysis* by asking group members to silently brainstorm about the forces driving and restraining attainment of a group goal. Or, you could ask members to brainstorm possible causes or symptoms of the problem during problem analysis. Or, you could use brainstorming or the nominal-group technique to generate possible strategies for implementing a solution the group has settled on.

WRITING PROMPT

Using the Nominal-Group Technique

Think of a group experience you've had when the traditional brainstorming method was not effective because group members began evaluating each other's ideas. How could the nominal-group technique have been used to provide more structured discussion and separate the generation of ideas from the evaluation of ideas?

▶ The response entered here will appear in the performance dashboard and can be viewed by your instructor.

Submit

Skilled Collaboration

Using Your Whole Mind

Daniel Pink, in his book *A Whole New Mind: Why Right-Brainers Will Rule the Future,* argues that as we become awash in data, numbers, and statistics, it is increasingly important that we use what he calls "The Whole Mind" to make sense out of the bits of information that bombard us.[69] Using the whole mind draws upon what has been dubbed both left-brain logical thinking and right-brain creativity. Applying this kind of whole-mind thinking to groups can help those groups develop more creative solutions to problems. Pink draws upon contemporary brain research to identify what he calls the "six senses for a conceptual age." Applying Pink's six senses to group deliberations can help groups and teams make more creative decisions.

- *Focus on design, not just function.* To be functional is to describe what something does—to identify its purpose. To focus on design is to understand how something was created. To use the whole mind, group members should be designers, which means they should have the freedom to create new solutions—not just think in old patterns about what something does (function), but explore how something new can be created and design something that hasn't existed yet.
- *Find the big story.* Instead of looking only at the logical argument underlying why a process or a procedure exists, try to find the overall story. Stories are narratives that give meaning to the pieces of information we see. When trying to solve a problem, look for the story by considering these questions: Who are the characters involved? Are there good characters, bad characters, or both good and bad? Do some obstacles keep the people in the story from achieving what they want? What are the sources of conflict? Seeing the underlying story in a situation can help a team think in new ways.
- *Listen to the entire symphony, not just to one note or one instrument.* Pink thinks that the skill of synthesis—seeing how things work together in harmony, rather than picking out one melody—can help develop new insights. Analyzing individual elements in a problem is useful, but supplement your detailed analysis with holistic thinking that looks at how all the parts of the process fit together.
- *Be empathic.* Rather than being coldly rational and logical like Mr. Spock from *Star Trek,* make sure to empathize with others and feel what others are feeling. Empathy is the ability to connect to the emotions of others, to sense what others are emotionally experiencing. Empathy doesn't *replace* logic, but rather *connects to* logic so that we can better understand the thoughts of others. When solving problems, consider what others may feel when you are identifying a problem (how they feel about the problem), analyzing the problem (consider their emotions), or suggesting a solution to the problem (how they might feel if the solution were implemented).
- *Make time to play.* As the saying goes, all work and no play makes Jack a dull boy and Jill a dull girl. Groups should be encouraged to play with ideas, experiment, and have fun, and be given permission to creatively explore ideas and options. Children play by pretending to be someone else for a while; they eagerly try new things, or simply enjoy the spontaneity of creating a new game or adventure. Sometimes a *fantasy theme* may be just what the group needs to energize it. Groups need to periodically bring a sense of play to the process of creating new options. Balancing the serious with play and fantasy can help a group get unstuck.
- *Find the meaning.* It's not just about accumulating more "stuff," says Pink; it's about finding the meaning in what we already have, or what we think we want that we don't yet have. Our quest to get more (money, power, and fame) than others should be replaced by reflecting on what truly gives meaning to our lives. Simply having more should not be the goal; rather, attaining a greater sense of individual and collective purpose should underlie our striving.

Connecting the dots between what we think we want and how that accumulation brings true satisfaction should be something that groups talk about occasionally. Groups should ask such questions as "How will achieving this goal be meaningful to the group, to other individuals, or to the community?"

Design, story, symphony, empathy, play, and meaning are ways of balancing our logical talents with creative skills. These six senses provide an underlying perspective of how groups can be creative, as well as give specific behaviors that can stimulate creativity.

Real-Life Applications

When you are in a group that is stuck, bogged down, and not making progress, consider asking one or more of the following questions to help the group get unstuck and develop a broader, more creative perspective:

- How can we redesign the procedure or process we are focusing on?
- What is the underlying story we are discussing?
- How are all of the pieces fitting together to work together as a "symphonic" whole?
- What would others feel about what we're recommending? What would be their emotional response?
- How can we bring a sense of play and experimentation to the discussion?
- What is the meaning behind what we really want to achieve?

12.5.3: The Delphi Technique

OBJECTIVE: Apply the Delphi technique to a group problem

Whereas the nominal-group technique invites participants to contribute ideas by first writing them down and then sharing them with the group, the **Delphi technique** takes this idea one step further. This method, named after the ancient oracle at Delphi, has been called "absentee brainstorming" because individuals share ideas in writing or via e-mail, without meeting face-to-face. One person coordinates the information and shares it with the rest of the group. This approach is especially useful when conflict within the group inhibits effective group interaction, or when time and distance constraints make it difficult for group members to meet. Here is a step-by-step description of the Delphi technique.[70]

1. The group leader selects a problem, issue, policy, or decision that needs to be reviewed.
2. The leader corresponds with group members in writing, informing them of the task and inviting their suggestions and input. A specific questionnaire may be developed, or members may be asked to individually brainstorm suggestions or reactions to the issue confronting the group.
3. The respondents complete the questionnaire or generate a list of their brainstormed responses and send it to the leader.
4. The leader summarizes all the responses from the group and shares the summary with all group members, asking for additional ideas, suggestions, and reactions. Team members are asked to rate or rank the ideas and return their comments to the leader.
5. The leader continues the process of summarizing the group feedback and asking for more input until general consensus emerges and decisions are made. It may take several rounds of soliciting ideas and evaluating ideas before consensus is achieved.

This method often produces many good ideas. All participants are treated equally because no one is aware of who submitted which idea. It is, however, a time-consuming process. Also, because of the lack of face-to-face interaction, some ideas worthy of elaboration and exploration may get lost in the shuffle. Using the Delphi technique in combination with face-to-face meetings can help eliminate some disadvantages of the procedure.

ELECTRONIC BRAINSTORMING **Electronic brainstorming** is a technique that makes it possible for a group to generate solutions or strategies by typing ideas on an electronic device and having them be displayed to the entire group. This high-tech method resembles the nominal-group technique in that group members write ideas before sharing them with the group. Because they can see ideas in written form, group members can piggyback off the ideas of others. Electronic brainstorming can be performed with all group members in the same room or computer lab or with members at their own home or office computers.

Research suggests that groups using electronic brainstorming generate more ideas than traditional face-to-face brainstorming groups.[71] One research team found that when some members of a group meet face-to-face and are supported with ideas from group members who are not physically present but rather use electronic means to share information, more ideas, of higher quality, are generated than if all members meet face-to-face.[72] Some researchers theorize that this happens because the ideas are generated anonymously.[73] Members may feel less fear or anxiety about being criticized for unconventional ideas because no one knows who suggested them. Thus, when group members move to the phase of evaluating ideas, they are not sure whether they are evaluating an idea that came from a

Virtual Collaboration

Pros and Cons of Electronic Brainstorming

Using electronic brainstorming has several advantages. It allows groups to generate ideas quickly and from remote locations. It may also be less expensive to invite team members to turn on their home or office computers to brainstorm ideas than to have all members travel to the same geographic location to hold a meeting. Nonetheless, several challenges and barriers should be considered when using electronic brainstorming. In their book *Virtual Teaming*, Deborah York, Lauren Davis, and Susan Wise note some of the following challenges in collaborating virtually:[75]

- Fear of working with technology (technophobia)
- Lack of needed technical skills
- Incompatibility of hardware and software
- Uneven writing skills due to differences in cultural background, language use, and education
- Technical difficulties (the power goes out, the computers are down)
- E-mail overload—people have too much e-mail to process

To overcome these obstacles, make sure group members understand how to use the hardware and software programs. In case technical glitches occur, have a backup plan—such as a phone number to call or an alternative e-mail address to use. Have someone who is knowledgeable about technology available to help group members or, at the very least, give each group member a number to call or a website to use if technical problems arise.

boss or a group leader or a new intern. All ideas are considered on their own merit and quality. Another reason more ideas may be generated is due to the piggyback effect, as group members are inspired to build on the ideas of other members.

One obvious disadvantage of electronic brainstorming is the need to have access to a computer network and appropriate software. Nevertheless, recent evidence strongly supports the value of this variation of the brainstorming method, in which computers add structure to the process.

Another disadvantage of anonymous, electronic brainstorming is that, because the idea-sharing is supposed to be anonymous, it is difficult to publicly recognize outstanding contributions. Research has found that when someone is praised for contributing good ideas, creativity is enhanced—both for the individual praised and for the entire group. Yet when group members privately and anonymously brainstorm ideas, it might seem like a breach of anonymity to publicly praise a good idea.[74]

12.5.4: The Affinity Technique

OBJECTIVE: Describe how the affinity technique applies to a group discussion

Have you ever sat down at a desk cluttered with papers from a variety of projects and realized that you needed to sort the papers into piles to help you organize your desk? The **affinity technique** is a method for sorting through and organizing the ideas that a group generates.[76] It is similar to the nominal-group technique, but instead of listing ideas on paper, group members write ideas on Post-it notes. Like the other variations of brainstorming that we've discussed, the group is assigned an issue or a problem about which to generate ideas. The entire group (or a smaller subcommittee) then organizes the ideas that have an "affinity," or are similar to each other, into categories.

The affinity technique is a way to make brainstorming sessions more fun and let people move around during a meeting. You can ask group members to post their notes on a wall (or another smooth surface, such as a chalkboard or whiteboard) and then to move around the room, review the ideas, and group them into categories. If your group sticks the notes on a chalkboard or whiteboard, you could draw a circle around the notes and label the category using a word or terms that capture the theme of the suggestions. This technique will allow your group to quickly identify how many people have generated the same idea. The group will be able to see that one affinity category may have six or seven ideas, whereas another category may have only one or two. After creating the categories, the group may decide to combine them. Someone should be assigned to record the ideas that have been developed. The affinity technique may take a bit longer than the nominal-group technique, but for certain groups it may be the best way to develop a sense of collaboration in generating ideas.

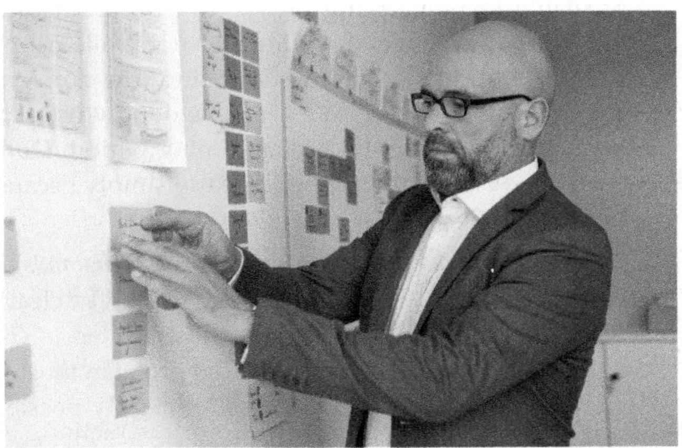

The affinity technique can make brainstorming less intimidating for group members, thus encouraging more participation and contribution from all members. It is also an effective means of organizing ideas.

Comparing Creative Techniques[77]

Creative Technique	Advantages	Disadvantages
Nominal-group technique	• Can build on ideas of others • Provides a written record of ideas suggested • Controls more talkative, dominating group members	• Requires a good leader to organize the process • Less time for free flow of ideas • Difficult to implement with a large group
Delphi technique	• Group does not have to meet face-to-face • Provides a written record of ideas suggested • Helps group members prepare for the upcoming meeting	• No synergy is created by hearing the ideas of others • Minimizes opportunities for elaborating on ideas • Group members may be suspicious that someone has manipulated the results
Affinity technique	• Builds acceptance • Provides for interaction and acceptance of ideas • Preserves a written record of ideas presented	• Need Post-it notes • Takes more time than other techniques • A skilled facilitator must orchestrate the technique
Brainstorming	• Easy to use • No special materials needed • Group members can piggyback on each other's ideas	• High potential for group members to evaluate ideas as they are being generated • Takes more time than highly structured methods • Quiet members are less likely to participate
Electronic brainstorming	• Very efficient • Anonymity increases the number of ideas generated	• Need special equipment • Need training in using computer software • Time is needed to describe the procedures of electronic brainstorming

HOW TO USE BRAINSTORMING IN YOUR GROUP You may still have some questions about how you can apply brainstorming methods of creative problem solving to your group discussions. Consider the following suggestions:[78]

- *Set aside a definite amount of time for brainstorming.* Decide as a group how much time you want to devote to brainstorming. You may want to set a goal for a certain number of ideas that should be recorded: "We'll stop brainstorming when we get 60 ideas."
- *Do not make the time limit for brainstorming too short.* Research suggests that groups given only a short time (four minutes) to brainstorm can be very productive, but not as creative as groups that have a longer time available for generating ideas.[79] If you brainstorm orally, don't worry about a little silence while people think. If you use silent brainstorming (the nominal-group technique), it's okay if people don't write furiously during the entire brainstorming period. Don't cut off the brainstorming period early simply because people are silent or not writing.
- *Be certain that each group or team member understands the specific problem to be solved.* The problem must be clearly defined and understood, and must be limited in size and scope. A broad, vaguely worded problem must be clarified before a group attempts to identify possible solutions.
- *Make sure that each group member follows the brainstorming rules.* Brainstorming will be most effective if group members stop criticizing and evaluating ideas. Group members can criticize ideas both verbally and nonverbally—that is, through tone of voice, facial expression, or posture. Everyone in the group must feel completely free to communicate ideas that may solve the problem. What should you do if a few members just cannot stop evaluating the ideas that are suggested? You may have to remind them courteously to follow the rules, ask them to be quiet, ask them to record the ideas of others, or ask them to leave the group. You may also consider using another technique (nominal-group, affinity, or electronic brainstorming) as an alternative to oral brainstorming.
- *If you serve as the group's leader, try to draw less-talkative group members into the discussion.* Call people by name: "Curt, you look like you've got some good ideas. What do you suggest?" You can also compliment the entire group when members do a good job of generating ideas: "Good job, people! We've got 30 ideas so far. Let's see if we can come up with 30 more."
- *Consider reverse-brainstorming.*[80] *With* ***reverse-brainstorming***, group members brainstorm ideas or solutions that would make the problem *worse.* After generating such a list, the group can consider the implications of doing the opposite of what was identified.
- *Consider rolestorming.*[81] **Rolestorming** is one way of "thinking outside the box." With this method, group members assume the roles of someone else to help unlock ideas and increase group creativity. If you focus on a problem in your community, ask group members to assume the role of the mayor, the school superintendent, or the city manager. If it is a government problem, have them imagine that they are the governor, a

member of the legislature, or even the president of the United States.

- *Tell the group what will happen with the ideas and suggestions generated.*[82] Don't finish the brainstorming session with a long list of ideas that may be shelved. Perhaps a subcommittee can be formed to combine ideas and eliminate obvious overlapping suggestions. The subgroup might also be asked to evaluate the ideas or determine which ideas need further exploration or more information.
- *Try the random-word technique.* One strategy to enhance the power of brainstorming that seems to work for some groups is the **random-word technique**. As described by Edward de Bono, while a group is brainstorming or pondering a problem, one person is assigned the task of saying a random word so others can hear it. The word is selected from a list of random words.[83] The spoken word is supposed to act as a trigger for new or creative ideas. This technique is another way to stimulate "thinking outside the box."
- *Establish a brainstorming bulletin board.* Write the specific problem to be solved on a bulletin board or whiteboard. Encourage group members to brainstorm ideas by periodically writing creative solutions that could solve the problem. Consider posting the problem and inviting creative responses for a week or more, and encourage people to build on the ideas of others.[84]
- *Try brainsketching.* The **brainsketching** technique asks people to come up with creative ideas by drawing something, rather than using words to describe a proposal. Some ideas may flow better if people are encouraged to use images rather than text to develop creative ideas.[85]

Review

Overview of Problem-Solving Steps and Techniques

Steps	Techniques
Identify and define the problem	• Is/is not analysis • Journalist's six questions • Gather data • Pareto charts • SWOT
Analyze the problem	• Is/is not analysis • Cause-and-effect (fishbone) diagram • Journalist's six questions • Force-field analysis • Develop criteria • Identify history, causes, effects, symptoms, goals, and obstacles • PROMOD technique
Generate solutions	• Brainstorming • Rolestorming • Reverse-brainstorming • Nominal-group technique • Delphi technique • Affinity technique • Electronic brainstorming
Evaluate solutions and select the best solution or combination of solutions	• Compare pros and cons • Apply solutions to criteria • Appoint a subgroup • Combine alternatives • Average rankings and ratings
Test and implement the solution	• Identify implementation steps • Develop a group action plan • Develop a flowchart • Develop a prototype

Summary: Enhancing Creativity in Groups

12.1: Defining Creativity

- Creativity is the generation, application, combination, and extension of new ideas.
- Creative groups are more effective groups.
- Creativity is a skill that can be taught.
- A six-stage model of creative problem solving includes the following steps: mess finding, data finding, problem finding, idea finding, solution finding, and acceptance finding.

12.2: Myths about Creativity

- Creativity is a mysterious process that can't be learned.
- Only a few gifted people are creative.
- Creativity just happens.

12.3: Barriers to Group Creativity

- Don't seek creative solutions to problems prematurely; wait until the problems have been clearly defined and analyzed.

- Find a suitable place to meet and work. Groups will be more creative in a comfortable physical space.
- Make sure the group isn't too large; creative thinking is less likely in groups much larger than 12 or 15 people.
- Give groups enough time to be creative.
- Be positive; don't cut off creative efforts with negative and discouraging comments.

12.4: Principles of Group Creativity

- Appropriately analyze and define the problem.
- Create a climate of freedom.
- Listen to minority points of view.
- Encourage people to see things and themselves differently.
- Selectively increase group structure.

12.5: Techniques for Enhancing Group Creativity

- Follow the rules of brainstorming and encourage others to follow the rules, especially the rule about not evaluating ideas until the proper time.
- Consider using a silent or more structured brainstorming technique, such as the nominal-group technique, the Delphi technique, or the affinity technique, to encourage all group and team members to contribute.
- Use electronic brainstorming to eliminate status differences and to permit anonymous contributions by group members who may otherwise feel too inhibited to contribute creative ideas.
- Try to draw less-talkative group members into the discussion; compliment members when they come up with good ideas during the period of evaluating ideas.

SHARED WRITING

Improving Collaboration and Creativity in Groups

Dave has great ideas and likes to take the lead during group discussions. During traditional brainstorming sessions, he often suggests more ideas than anyone else. But he also just can't seem to avoid evaluating and criticizing other people's ideas. Dave's presence in a group sometimes intimidates others, so they don't contribute. Group members have asked him to resist evaluating other people's suggestions, but he just can't seem to stop doing it. Should the group ask Dave to leave? He makes a considerable contribution to the group but also limits the contributions of others. Do group members have an ethical responsibility to balance concern for an individual member of the group against the needs of the entire group?

In this situation, what would you do and why? Write a short response that your classmates will read. Be sure to include specifics in your discussion.

▶ A minimum number of characters is required to post and earn points. After posting, your response can be viewed by your class and instructor, and you can participate in the class discussion.

Post

Appendix A
Principles and Practices for Effective Meetings

A meeting is a collection of the unfit chosen from the unwilling by the incompetent to do the unnecessary.

> If you want to get a job done, give it to an individual; if you want to have it studied, give it to a committee.
>
> Sign on conference wall: "A meeting is no substitute for progress."
>
> Business meetings are important. They demonstrate how many people the company can do without.
>
> President John F. Kennedy said, "Most committee meetings consist of twelve people to do the work of one."
>
> Humorist Dave Barry said, "If you had to identify, in one word, the reason why the human race has not achieved, and never will achieve, its full potential, that word would be 'meetings'."[1] He also compared business meetings with funerals, in the sense that "you have a gathering of people who are wearing uncomfortable clothing and would rather be somewhere else. The major difference is that most funerals have a definite purpose. Also, nothing is ever really buried in a meeting."[2]

Frankly, most people do not like meetings. Although this generalization has exceptions, it is safe to say that few individuals relish the thought of a weekly appointment calendar peppered with frequent meetings. An estimated 25 million meetings are held each day in the United States, and with the prevalence of technology and virtual meetings, the number of meetings is increasing.[3] MCI Worldcom Conferencing research found that most professionals spend nearly three hours a day in business meetings, and more than one-third of those surveyed reported that the meetings are a waste of time. Why are meetings held in such low esteem? Probably because many meetings are not well managed, either by the meeting leader or by the participants. One study found that more than 40 percent of people who attend meetings say that the quality of these meetings is poor.[4] Another study estimated that $37 billion is wasted each year because of unproductive business meetings.[5] What bothers meeting attendees the most? Listed here are the results of studies that ranked meeting "sins":[6]

1. Getting off the subject
2. No goals or agenda
3. Too lengthy
4. Poor or inadequate preparation
5. Inconclusive
6. Disorganized
7. Ineffective leadership/lack of control
8. Irrelevance of information discussed
9. Time wasted during meetings
10. Starting late
11. Not effective for making decisions
12. Interruptions
13. Individuals who dominate discussion
14. Rambling, redundant, or digressive discussion
15. No published results or follow-up actions
16. No premeeting orientation
17. Canceled or postponed meetings

Here's another meeting mistake: Don't take calls while you are in a meeting with others. That's the conclusion of a research team who found that using a phone during meetings is perceived as rude.[7] Although you may think no one will know if you sneak a peek at your phone during a meeting, realize that others may see you and take offense. It may appear that you are not focused on what the group is doing but prefer to be elsewhere.

A team of researchers found that men and women reacted in different ways to someone using a phone in a meeting, whether when talking on the phone or checking for messages. Men were almost twice as likely to think it is acceptable to use a phone during a meeting compared to women.[8] Here is a rank ordering of the worst phone meeting "sins," with at least 50 percent of the respondents reporting these behaviors as offensive:

- Writing and sending text or e-mail messages
- Making or taking phone calls
- Browsing on the Internet
- Checking whether if you have received a message

About one-third of the respondents found the following behaviors rude:

- Leaving the meeting to take a call
- Checking for incoming calls
- Glancing at the time[9]

In light of the research that suggests just the presence of a phone during a conversation can be distracting, it's wise to keep your phone out of sight during a face-to-face meeting and focus on what's happening in the meeting.

To be effective, a meeting needs to balance two things: structure and interaction. Throughout this text, we talk about the importance of helping a group stay on task by structuring the interaction; following the steps of reflective thinking when solving a problem is one way of helping a group stay on task. As you examine the preceding lists, note how many of the problems associated with meetings stem from a lack of clear structure or agenda. But while structure is important, group members also need to have the freedom to express ideas and react to the comments of others. If there is too much structure, the meeting is not really a meeting; it is a lecture—one person talks and others listen. In contrast, with too much unstructured interaction, a group meeting bounces along with no clear focus. In unstructured meetings, minimal attention is given to the time it takes to get the job done.[10] In this appendix, we will offer suggestions for providing both structure and interaction in group meetings. In particular, an agenda is the primary tool for structuring a group meeting. Facilitation skills and an understanding of how to plan interaction can ensure that meeting participants will then be free to interact and that their contributions will be relevant and on target.

Effective groups and teams consider the cultural expectations and backgrounds of the people involved in the task. Being culturally sensitive is especially important when participating in a meeting. Two researchers made this astute observation about cultural differences when holding a meeting:

> In the United States, a team meeting is held to make decisions. . . . In Japan, a team meeting is held to publicly confirm decisions that were discussed among members in smaller groups as they developed their analyses. . . . In Mexico, a meeting is a time to build relationships and trust with each other. . . . In the Netherlands, a meeting may be a time to identify all the weaknesses and criticisms of a particular approach or plan.[11]

Giving Meetings Structure

Getting off the subject and having no goals or agenda are the two most often mentioned complaints about meetings. The principal tool that ensures meetings are appropriately structured and the deliberation achieves the intended goal is a meeting agenda—a list of key issues, ideas, and information that will be presented, in the order in which they will be discussed. Uncertainty and lack of an agenda can be major barriers to accomplishing a task as a group. Consider the following steps in drafting your meeting agenda.

Determine the Meeting Goals

Meet only when there is a specific purpose and when it is advantageous or desirable to discuss issues, solve problems, or make decisions as a group. Before beginning to draft an agenda, you need to know the meeting goal. Most meetings have one or more of three goals: (1) information needs to be shared, (2) issues need to be discussed, and (3) action needs to be taken.

As you prepare for a meeting, identify what you would like to have happen as a result of the meeting.[12] A typical goal might be "At the end of this meeting, we will have selected the firm that will produce our new advertising campaign" or "At the end of this meeting, we will have reviewed the applicants for the management position and identified our top three choices." Without a specific goal that the meeting leader and participants are all aware of, little is likely to be accomplished.

Identify Items That Need to Be Discussed to Achieve the Goal

With the goal in mind, you next need to determine how to structure the meeting to achieve the goal. Consider generating a list of topics that are essential to accomplishing the goal: Which information needs to be shared, which issues need to be discussed, and which action needs to be taken? In the brainstorming phase, do not worry about the order of the items; you can rearrange the items in the agenda later.

Organize the Agenda Items to Achieve the Goal

After you have a list of items to be addressed, organize them in some logical way. A key constraint in organizing items and determining what to include in a meeting agenda is the amount of time budgeted for the meeting. Many meeting planners underestimate the amount of time discussion will take.

When you have identified potential agenda items, review your meeting goal and eliminate any items that will not help you achieve your goal. Armed with your meeting goal and your list of agenda items, begin drafting the meeting agenda.[13] Consider organizing it around the three meeting goals: information items, discussion items, and action items.

Most meeting experts suggest that your first agenda item should be to ask the group to approve or modify the agenda you have prepared. If meeting participants make no modifications, then you know that your agenda was on target. Before making final decisions about which items you should cover and the order in which you should cover them, estimate how long it will take to deal with each item. You may want to address several small issues first before tackling major ones. Or you may decide to arrange your agenda items in terms of priority: Discuss the most important items first and less important ones later.

One additional tip: Phrase each agenda item as a question. A question provides a direction for discussion. When you have answered the question, you can move on to the next agenda item. Questions help keep the discussion focused and pointed in the right direction. In addition, making writing notes as to how the question was answered become the meeting minutes.

Review

How to Prepare a Goal-Centered Meeting Agenda

1. Determine your meeting goals.
2. Identify what needs to be discussed to achieve the goals.
3. Organize the agenda items to achieve the goals.

John Tropman and Gershom Morningstar recommend using the "bell-curve agenda."[14] As indicated in Figure A-1, the middle of the meeting is reserved for the most challenging or controversial issues. The opening and closing of the meeting include more routine or less vital issues.

In contrast to Tropman and Morningstar's recommendations, others suggest that you avoid putting routine announcements and reports at the beginning of a meeting. The rationale is that meeting members are less sensitive to the time constraints of a meeting at its beginning and, therefore, may spend too much time and energy on routine matters. To take advantage of the early energy in a group, you may want to start with a discussion or an action item that will involve all meeting participants.

Often issues are discussed during meetings but nothing happens afterward. As the following sample meeting agenda shows, one of your last agenda items should be to summarize the actions that are to be taken following the meeting.

Sample Agenda

Meeting goals: To identify problems with the new work reporting system, identify at least three advantages and three disadvantages of the new-product team proposal, revise the personnel hiring proposal, and make a decision about donating to the school-volunteer program.

I. Finalize meeting agenda

II. Discussion items

- **A.** What are the problems with our new work report system?
- **B.** What are the advantages and disadvantages of the new-product team proposal (distributed by e-mail)?

III. Action items

- **A.** Which policies should be revised in our personnel hiring procedures? (distributed by e-mail)
- **B.** Should we donate $5000 to the school-volunteer program?

IV. Information items

- **A.** New employee orientation report
- **B.** Planning committee report

Figure A-1 Bell-Curve Agenda[15]

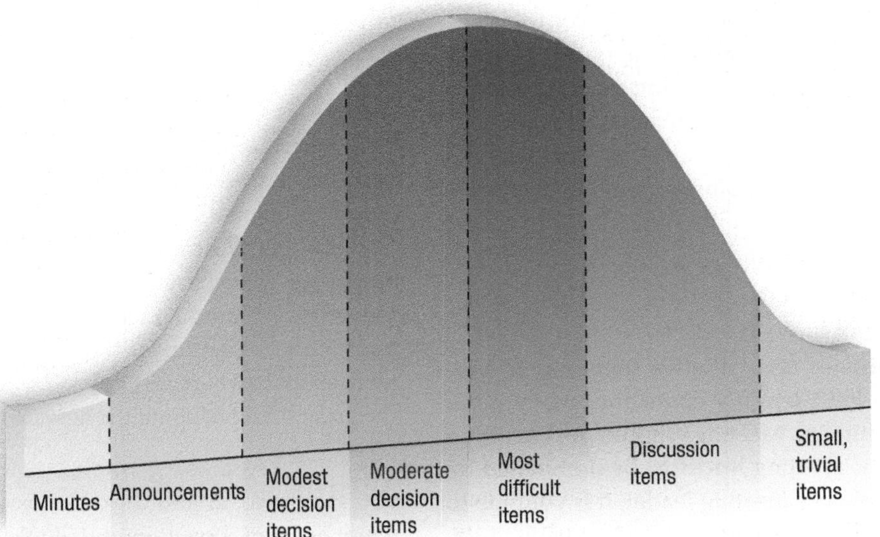

C. Finance committee report

D. Announcements

V. Summarize action that needs to be taken after today's meeting

Distribute your agenda to the meeting participants well before the meeting. Participants should come prepared to discuss the issues on the agenda. Obviously, if they do not have an agenda before the meeting, they cannot come prepared for a meaningful discussion.

Becoming a Meeting Facilitator: Managing Group and Team Interactions

The essential task of a meeting facilitator is to manage the interaction so as to achieve the goals of the group. Without interaction—the give-and-take dialogue and contributions that participants make during meetings—meetings become monologues.[16] Conversely, with too much interaction, meetings can become disorganized, with rambling, redundant, or digressive discussions that waste time and are inconclusive. Meeting leaders and participants can help ensure a balance of structure and interaction by using the facilitation skills of gatekeeping, reminding the group of meeting goals, helping the group be sensitive to the time that elapses during discussion, and using strategies that structure group interaction.

When managing the interaction in a meeting, it's important to keep attitudes positive; overly negative comments or comments that detract from the meeting climate decrease meeting effectiveness. One study found that meeting members who had positive attitudes about the meeting and its goals were more effective.[17] Another study found that meeting participants were more likely to contribute to a meeting if they had a positive attitude about themselves and the entire group.[18] Clearly, managing meeting interaction is more than just serving as a conversation traffic cop to try to keep messages flowing; it also involves keeping a positive attitude and helping others maintain a positive climate.

Be a Gatekeeper

A gatekeeper encourages less-talkative members to participate and tries to limit lengthy contributions by more loquacious group members. Meetings should not consist of a monologue from the meeting leader or be dominated by just a few participants. As a meeting leader, it is your job to make sure that you involve all meeting participants in the discussion.

Review

Meeting Agenda Pitfalls and Strategies

Potential Pitfall	Suggested Strategy
Participants tend to spend too much time on early agenda items.	Make the first agenda item something worthy of discussion rather than beginning with a trivial report or announcement.
Participants will find a way to talk even if you don't want them to talk.	Invite input and discussion early in the meeting rather than having participants try to interrupt.
Participants aren't prepared to have a meeting; they have not read what they were supposed to read.	Take a few minutes to have participants read information or have them prepare by writing ideas or suggestions using the silent-brainstorming technique.
Participants won't stick to the agenda.	Remind the group what the meeting goals are, or, with input from the group, change the agenda item.
A meeting is scheduled late in the day or participants are tired.	Schedule an early agenda item that involves all meeting participants rather than having participants sit silently.
The agenda includes a controversial item that will create conflict and disagreement.	Put one or more items on the agenda ahead of the conflict-producing item. Addressing easier agenda items first will establish a feeling of accomplishment and agreement before the group tackles the more conflict-producing item.

Focus on the Goal

Members need to understand a group's goals. Once they do, the group's agenda for each meeting should provide a road map for moving toward those goals. A leader often has to keep the group on course, and one of the most effective tools for doing so is summarizing. Periodically, use *metadiscussion* skills and review your understanding of the group's progress with brief comments: "Okay. Dennis agrees with John that we need to determine how much our project will cost. Are we ready for the next issue?" Such summaries help a group take stock of what it has done and what it has yet to accomplish. Communication researchers Fred Niederman and Roger Volkema, in studying the effects of meeting facilitators on group productivity, found that the most experienced facilitators helped orient the group toward the goal, helped them adapt to what was happening in the group, and involved the group in developing the agenda for the meeting.[19]

Monitor Time

Another job of a meeting leader is to keep track of how much time has been spent on the planned agenda items and how much time remains. Think of your agenda as a map, helping you plan where you want to go. Think of the clock as your gas gauge, telling you the amount of fuel you have to get where you want to go. In a meeting, just as on any car trip, you need to know where you are going and how much fuel you need to reach your destination. If you are running out of fuel (time), you will need to either fill up the tank (budget more time) or recognize that you will not get where you want to go. Begin each meeting by asking how long members can meet. If you face two or three crucial agenda items, and one-third of your group has to leave in an hour, you will want to make certain to schedule important items early in the meeting.

Structure Interaction

To ensure that all members participate in the discussion, you may need to use some prescriptive decision-making and problem-solving tools and techniques. For example, if your meeting goal is to identify new ideas to solve a particular problem, consider using brainstorming or the nominal-group technique as a way to generate ideas. The is/is not analysis technique, the journalist's six questions, and the Pareto chart are other tools you can use to invite people to contribute ideas, while still structuring the interaction so that meeting members do not lose sight of their goals. A key task of the meeting facilitator is to orchestrate meaningful interactions during the meeting so that all participants have the opportunity to give input. Structured methods of inviting involvement are effective in garnering contributions from all group members.

As noted earlier, another strategy that can help encourage interaction is to phrase each discussion item on the printed agenda as a question. Questions are a useful tool to help encourage focused and productive discussion.

How to Lead Meetings

As mentioned, a meeting leader needs to be especially sensitive to balancing meeting structure with interactions. An effective meeting leader should facilitate—rather than dictate how—the group conducts the meeting. One study found that groups generated more and better ideas when team leaders simply listened and waited for team members to contribute ideas before stating their own ideas than they did when the leader spoke first.[20] Different groups accept (or tolerate) different levels of direction from their designated leaders. One simple rule of thumb is this: A group will generally allow a leader who emerges naturally from the group or who leads a one-time-only ad hoc group to be more directive.

Certain tasks are generally expected of leaders. One of the most important of those leader tasks is to keep the group focused on its agenda during the meeting. In addition, the leader should clarify the procedures and keep the group focused on the issues at hand.[21] Of course, that means the leader needs to have an agenda. We strongly urge that agendas be distributed well in advance of a meeting. As we have stressed, the leader should give participants a chance to shape the agenda both before the meeting and as the meeting opens.

Review

How to Facilitate Meeting Interaction

Facilitation Skill	Description	Examples
Use gatekeeping skills.	Listen to the discussion to encourage less-talkative members to participate and limit the contributions of oververbalizers.	"Dale, we've not heard from you. Do you have some thoughts on this idea?" "Heather, I know you have some strong opinions about this project, but I'd like to hear from others who have not spoken on the issue."
Focus the group's attention on the agenda or goal of the discussion.	Especially when discussion seems to be off target, remind the group of the purpose of the meeting or state the goal of the group.	"Although we seem to be interested in talking about some of the recent hassles we've had at the university, I'd like to bring us back to the purpose of today's meeting. Let's return to our second agenda item, to help us solve the problem we're addressing."
Monitor the group's use of time.	Remind the group how much time is left for discussion if the group gets unnecessarily bogged down on one issue; suggest a strategy to help the group move on to another issue.	"I note that we've been talking about this issue for more than 20 minutes, and we have only 15 minutes left in our discussion. Would you like to continue talking about this issue, or would you prefer to appoint a subcommittee to tackle this problem and get back to us with a recommendation?"
Provide appropriate structure to channel the discussion, and keep it focused on the issues at hand.	Consider inviting all group members to write their ideas on paper before verbalizing; consider using silent brainstorming, the nominal-group technique, the affinity technique, the is/is not analysis technique, a T-chart, or force-field analysis. Also, phrase issues for discussion as a question on the printed agenda rather than just listing a topic to talk about.	"We have a couple of options to consider. Why don't we first each write down the advantages and disadvantages of each option and then share our ideas with the entire group."

In general, meeting leaders are expected to do the following:

- Call the group together, which may involve finding out when participants can meet.
- Call the meeting to order.
- If it is a formal meeting, determine if there is a **quorum**—the minimum number of people who must be present to conduct business.
- Keep the meeting moving; go on to the next agenda item when a point has been thoroughly covered. Use effective facilitation and gatekeeping skills.
- Use a dry-erase board or other visual means to summarize meeting progress; the written notes of a meeting become the "group mind" and help keep the group on track.
- If the meeting is a formal one, decide when to take a vote. Make sure the issues are clear before a vote is taken.
- Prepare a committee report (or delegate someone to prepare a report) after one or many meetings. Groups need a record of their progress. Many groups designate someone to act as secretary and prepare the minutes or summary of what occurred at the meeting. As noted earlier, if the meeting agenda is organized around key questions, then the meeting minutes simply answer the questions on the agenda.

One of the time-tested strategies for leading a large group is **parliamentary procedure**—a comprehensive set of rules that prescribe how to take action on specific issues that come before the group. This procedure provides an orderly way for large groups (of 20 or more people) to conduct business, although it is less useful for small groups (in which it leads to win/lose patterns of decision making rather than consensus).

All groups need structure—and the larger the group, the greater the need for structure. In effect, parliamentary procedure provides the needed structure to help large groups stay focused on the business at hand. Research suggests that parliamentary procedure can be an effective method of adding structure and rules to coordinate quality discussion in a large group.[22] For a complete guide to parliamentary procedure, consult *Robert's Rules of Order* online.

How to Participate in Meetings

So far, we have stressed the meeting leader's responsibility to give the meeting structure and ensure interactions. But meeting participants also have similar obligations. In many respects, each meeting participant has leadership responsibilities. Leadership means "to influence," and as a meeting participant, you will have many opportunities to influence the group process. Be sensitive to both the level of structure and the interactions taking place in the meeting.

Your key obligation as a meeting participant is to come to the meeting prepared to work. If the leader has distributed an agenda before the meeting (as leaders should), then you will have a clear sense of how to prepare and which information you should bring to the meeting. Even if no agenda has been provided, try to anticipate what will be discussed.

Roger Mosvick and Robert Nelson, in their book *We've Got to Start Meeting Like This!*, identify six guidelines of competent meeting participants.[23]

1. **Organize your contributions.** Just as a well-organized speech makes a better presentation, well-organized contributions make better meetings. Rambling, disorganized, disjointed ideas increase the likelihood that the meeting will become sidetracked.
2. **Speak when your contribution is relevant.** Before you make a comment, listen to the person who is speaking. Is your comment useful and helpful? Groups are easily distracted by irrelevant contributions.
3. **Make one point at a time.** Even though you may be bursting with good ideas and suggestions, your colleagues will be more likely to listen to your ideas if you present them one at a time rather than as a string of unrelated points.
4. **Speak clearly and forcefully.** No, we are not advocating that you aggressively try to dominate the conversation. Unassertive mumbling, however, will probably get lost in the verbal shuffle of most meetings.
5. **Support your ideas with evidence.** One of the key determinants of good decisions and effective solutions is the use of evidence to support your ideas and opinions. Opinions are ubiquitous—everyone has them. Facts, statistics, and well-selected examples help keep the group focused on the task.
6. **Listen actively to all aspects of the discussion.** Group meetings provide one of the most challenging listening contexts. When several people are attempting to make points and counterarguments, you will have to gear up your powers of concentration and listening. Checking your understanding by summarizing or paraphrasing can dramatically improve communication and decrease misunderstanding.[24]

Review

Providing Meeting Structure and Interaction

How to Give a Meeting Structure

- Prepare an effective agenda by determining your meeting goals.
- Identify what needs to be discussed to achieve the goals.
- Organize the agenda to achieve the goals.

How to Ensure Managed Interaction

- Use effective gatekeeping skills.
- Use metadiscussion to help the group focus on the goals.
- Help the group be sensitive to time that has elapsed and time that remains for deliberation.
- Use strategies to structure interaction (e.g., write before speaking, nominal-group technique, or silent brainstorming).

Skilled Collaboration

How to Make a Meeting Better When You're Not the Meeting Leader

Throughout this text, we've cited theories and principles about how groups and teams work to help you be a better leader. If you're the meeting leader, you can obviously have a major impact on how the meeting is run; you're in charge of setting the agenda and facilitating the discussion. But if you're not in charge, can you still improve the meeting? The answer is a definite "yes." Here's how:

1. **If there is no agenda:** If the meeting leader has not provided an agenda before the meeting, politely ask the leader for one. Here's a way to phrase your request: "To help me prepare for the upcoming meeting, may I please see an agenda?" or "Can you tell me what are the key issues and questions we'll be considering at our meeting?" Asking "What are our key goals today?" at the start of a no-agenda meeting can give the meeting some structure. Politely asking for an agenda might spur the leader into developing one. And even if there is no agenda forthcoming, you have at least done your part by asking for one.
2. **If the conversation is unstructured and unconnected:** Use metadiscussional phrases to help keep the meeting on track. A metadiscussion phrase focuses on the discussion process (discussion about discussion). "I'm not sure where we are on the agenda" and "I'm not sure how this discussion relates to the topic at hand" are statements that focus on the discussion process. These comments help make the entire group more aware of whether they are on task or off task.
3. **If the group is not on task and is off the agenda:** Summarize what the meeting has accomplished. By periodically summarizing what has been accomplished in a meeting, you help the group become more aware of where it is on the agenda. Summarizing the progress of the meeting can also energize the group by reminding the meeting participants of what has been accomplished.
4. **If some people are dominating or some people are not participating:** Serve as a gatekeeper. You don't have to be the meeting leader to invite quieter members to participate in the meeting. If you notice that some meeting members are not participating or seem disengaged in the meeting, simply ask for their ideas and opinions. Don't make them uncomfortable by saying, "Well, Carmaleta, you've not said much. Why don't you participate?" Just politely and simply ask, "Carmaleta, I'd like to hear your ideas." Or you could say, "You've been listening to our discussion and we seem to be stuck on one idea. What do you think about our ideas?"
5. **If there are meeting tangents between just a few people:** Suggest a private meeting between two people who are monopolizing the conversation. If a meeting is getting bogged down because of a long, drawn-out conversation between a couple of people, or two people are in conflict and are doing all of the talking, suggest that they discuss the issue outside the meeting. Note that we are not suggesting that the feuding participants *not* try to work out the disagreement; instead, we recommend inviting them to do so "offline" on their own time rather than using the meeting to hash out an issue that may not be relevant to the entire group.
6. **If the group is wasting time:** Monitor the time. By making the entire group aware of the time left to talk about an issue, you can gently prod individuals to use time wisely rather than going on and on about something. Sometimes groups simply aren't aware of the resource of time. Making meeting members aware of the time left to spend on a topic is like pointing out the balance in the "time bank": If people are aware that they don't have much time left to spend, then they may spend it more wisely.
7. **If the group doesn't follow through on tasks and assignments:** Volunteer to take notes or record the minutes. Being the note taker gives you additional authority to ask questions, summarize, and make sure that the group is staying on track. The person who takes the minutes has the power to shape the meeting results. It's your ethical responsibility to record what happened at the meeting accurately. You can also influence what happens after the meeting by ensuring that the action steps are recorded and that it's clear who is supposed to do what to achieve the meeting goals.

Appendix B
Principles and Practices for Communicating to an Audience

Throughout this book, we have featured principles and skills that can help you communicate with others in groups, meetings, and teams. Most of your group communication will be private discussions among members of your group. Some group discussions, however, are intended to be heard by others. Public-communication formats help an audience understand all sides of an issue, particularly if individuals with diverse viewpoints are involved in the discussion. In this appendix, we offer some general guidelines for speaking to an audience.

Planning What to Say to an Audience

Speaking to an audience involves skills in planning what you are going to say and presenting your information to your listeners. Your school probably offers a course in public speaking. The discussion that follows highlights some of the essential skills that public presenters should master when speaking to an audience, whether in a panel, symposium, or forum-group presentation.[1] The more formal the presentation (a symposium presentation, for example), the more planning it requires. We will offer some general tips for both planning a presentation and presenting your ideas to others.

Every speaker needs a plan. Speakers who are part of a group effort to communicate with an audience need to coordinate their plans with those of other group members. Central to all these planning elements is a consideration of your audience. Indeed, Figure B-1 presents an overview of the public speaking process, and in the center of the model is the suggestion to "Consider the audience." Throughout every step of the process of presenting a message to others, your first and foremost priority is to make sure you consider their needs and backgrounds. A speaking plan also typically involves clarifying, narrowing, and coordinating your topic with other group members, and then deciding on your specific purpose or objective, identifying your central ideas, and supporting and organizing your ideas.

Consider Your Audience

To consider your audience means finding out as much as you can about your listeners and then analyzing the information you have discovered. Why will they be listening to you? What are their expectations? What are their attitudes toward you, your group, and your topic? Answers to these questions can help you make choices throughout the planning process. If you are speaking to a captive audience—people who have little choice about listening to you, such as your classmates in small-group communication class—you need to be especially sensitive to their needs. If class members have to show up, your group needs to work extra hard to immediately make the information interesting and relevant to the listeners.

Select and Narrow Your Topic

Your topic for your presentation is likely to share the results of your group deliberations with your audience. As you ponder how to narrow your topic, in addition to the time

Figure B-1 The Audience-Centered Model of Presentations

Consider the audience at each step of the process when preparing a message for others.[2]

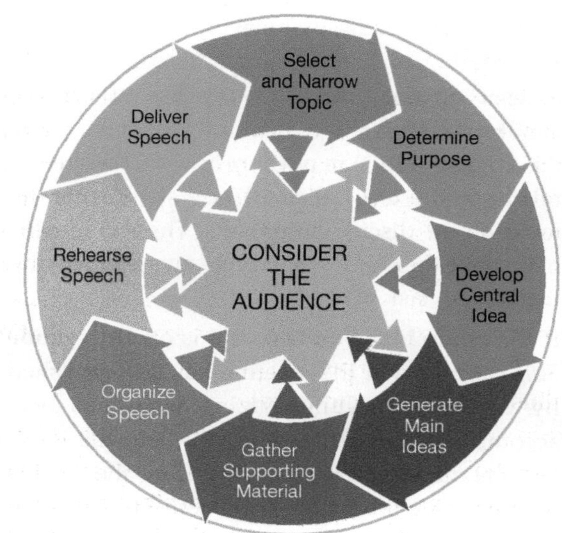

limits of your presentation, keep the needs and interests of your audience foremost in mind.

Determine Your Purpose

After selecting and narrowing your topic, determine your purpose. Keep your specific presentation objective clearly in mind as you prepare for your public presentation. Is your goal primarily to inform the audience about decisions your group has already made? Or is your goal to persuade your listeners to adopt a solution you are proposing? You might give a public presentation to let the audience eavesdrop on your conversation as you debate issues and share information. If an audience is present, though, you should be keenly aware of the audience's needs and not become lost in a conversation that ignores those who came to hear what you have to say. It is a good idea for all group members involved in the presentation to talk explicitly about the overall goal of sharing information and ideas with the audience.

Develop Your Central Idea

Your specific purpose indicates what you want the audience to be able to do when you have finished your speech. Your central idea summarizes the essence of your message—think of it as a one-sentence summary of your presentation.

Identify Your Major Ideas

With your central idea in mind, identify the key points you will make. When you speak in public, do not just start sharing unrelated pieces of information; instead, think about major ideas you want to share. If you were to boil your information down to one, two, or three ideas, what would they be? The major points you want to address flow from the information you have gathered and the discussion that may have taken place in your group.

Support Your Major Ideas

A presentation to an audience does not consist of just asserting points or drawing a conclusion and sharing that conclusion with your listeners. Support your major points with evidence or examples. In addition to using facts, examples, opinions, and statistics, you could support a point you are making with a hypothetical example or a personal story. Realize, however, that although hypothetical examples and personal experiences can add interest to your presentation, they are not sufficient to prove a point; instead, their value lies in illustrating ideas and issues.

Again, we urge you to keep your audience in mind as you make choices about how you will support your major points. It is also a good idea to check with other group members to make sure that you are not duplicating information your colleagues plan to share.

Organize Your Ideas

The last step in developing a presentation plan is to arrange your major ideas and supporting material in a logical way. If you are relating a sequence of steps or discussing the history of an issue, you probably will use chronological order, which means arranging your ideas by telling your listeners what happened first, second, third, and so forth.

Another classic method of organizing ideas is the topical method. With this approach, you simply organize your presentation by topics or natural divisions in your presentation. If you were informing an audience about the functions of your local government, for example, you could arrange your presentation topically by saying, "Our government provides for our safety through the police and fire departments, our education through schools and libraries, and our transportation through funding public transportation and maintaining our roads."

Spatial arrangement, in which you organize information according to location or position, is another approach. In describing your campus to your listeners, you might first talk about the west campus, then the central campus, and finally the east campus, rather than hopping around a map depicting the layout of your school.

There are other ways to organize information:

- **Problem/solution:** First talk about the problem and then the solution.
- **Pro versus con:** Compare advantages and disadvantages.
- **Complexity:** Move from simple ideas to more complex ones.

Regardless of the specific method you select, make sure your overall organizational strategy makes sense both to you and to your listeners. Most public-speaking teachers strongly urge speakers to develop an outline of their presentation. The introduction to the presentation should, at a minimum, provide an overview of the key ideas and catch and hold the listeners' attention. The body of the presentation covers the key ideas and supporting material. The conclusion's prime function is to summarize and, if appropriate, call for listeners to take specific action.

Rehearse Your Presentation

With your objective in mind, key ideas thoughtfully prepared, and a logical organization of your points at hand, you are ready to consider how to deliver your information to your listeners. Your unspoken messages play a major role in communicating your ideas and feelings to your listeners.

The first time you or other group members hear your presentation should not be when you are giving your presentation to your audience. Instead, you should rehearse your presentation beforehand. Make your rehearsal realistic.

Imagine that your audience is present when you practice what you will say and how you will share information with your listeners.

As you rehearse, consider the four primary delivery methods: (1) manuscript (reading), (2) memorized, (3) impromptu, and (4) extemporaneous style. Most communication teachers have definite biases about which methods are most and least effective. We do not recommend that you read from a manuscript: Such an approach is stilted and does not permit you to adapt to your listeners. Giving a presentation totally from memory also has its pitfalls, especially if you have many statistics or other forms of evidence that you want to share. In particular, you run the risk of forgetting key points.

Speaking impromptu means that you speak with minimal preparation or none at all—you just try to wing it. This has some obvious disadvantages as well. Impromptu speaking negates all the suggestions we made for planning your presentation.

The style of delivery that seems to work best is extemporaneous delivery. With this approach, you know the major ideas you want to present and you may have an outline, but you do not memorize the exact wording of your presentation. This approach has the advantage of encouraging you to plan your message, but gives you the flexibility to adapt to the specific audience to which you are speaking. Your delivery also sounds more natural and interesting when you speak extemporaneously than when you read or memorize your remarks.

Deliver Your Message Effectively

When speaking to an audience, there are several fundamental principles to keep in mind. First and foremost, have eye contact with your audience. Research suggests this behavior is the single most important nonverbal delivery variable.[3]

When you are giving your portion of a group presentation, it is not unusual to deliver your message while remaining seated at a table. If your group remains seated, you can still use gestures to emphasize key points and add interest and animation to your talk. Effective gestures should be natural, not overly dramatic, and coordinated with your verbal message. Usually speakers use fewer gestures when seated than when standing to give a speech.

If you are participating in a symposium presentation, you will likely be expected to stand when you speak. When standing, ensure that your posture communicates your interest in your listeners.

Besides having eye contact and monitoring your physical delivery, you have a fundamental obligation to speak so that others can hear you and to convey interest and enthusiasm in your voice. Speaking with adequate volume and varying your vocal pitch, rate, and quality are essential to effective speech delivery.

Consider Using Visual Aids

Many groups find that visual aids help communicate statistical information and survey results and can help dramatize the problem the group is attempting to solve. One group, wanting to illustrate the parking problem on campus, made a video to show exactly how overcrowded the parking lots were. Audio and video interviews can also add interest and credibility to a group's effort to document problems and solutions. However, we caution you against overusing visual aids. The purpose of most group presentations is to present information, not to entertain. Resist the temptation to spend so much time and energy on visuals, video, and audio material that your overall objective takes a back seat to your method of presentation.

In addition to video and audio tapes, visual aids can include objects, models, people, drawings, photographs, slides, maps, charts, and graphs. Bar, pie, and line graphs are especially effective in presenting statistical information to an audience. Most audiences today expect to see high-quality, computer-generated visual aids.

When using any type of visual aid, follow these guidelines:

- Make sure all audience members can see the visual aid easily.
- Give yourself plenty of time to prepare your visual aid before you speak.
- Rehearse with your visual aid.
- Have eye contact with your audience, not with your visual aid.
- Talk about your visual aid, do not just show it.
- Do not pass objects among your audience while you are speaking; it distracts from your oral presentation.
- Use handouts during the presentation only if your listeners need to have the information in front of them while you speak.
- Keep your visual aids simple.

The last suggestion we offer for using visual aids is to have a backup plan if your visual aid is crucial to your presentation. Taking an extra extension cord, making another copy of your homemade video, and making sure the overhead projector has a spare bulb are examples of backup plans to ensure that your presentation goes smoothly.

Ask other group members to help you manage the visual aids. For example, ask someone to change the transparencies on the overhead projector or to help display charts or graphs. Since you are part of a team, involve other group members to help you present information clearly and effectively.

Use Computer-Generated Graphics Effectively

Many contemporary audiences expect a presentation to be supported with computer-generated graphics such as PowerPoint, Prezi, Keynote, or other presentation software. Visual support can help enhance your message if you use computer graphics effectively.[4] But don't overdo it. Perhaps you have been in the audience when you have experienced an overuse of computer images, also known as "Death by PowerPoint."

When using a computer to develop your visuals, keep the following suggestions in mind:

- Use more images than words. Avoid text-heavy visuals; include no more than seven lines of text on one slide. Use computer graphics to convey messages that can't be presented with words.
- Allow plenty of time to design the graphics. If you are familiar with the software, it may not take you long to draft quality visuals, but you should still not wait until the last minute to develop them.
- Don't get carried away with the technology. Your goal is to communicate ideas, not to dazzle your listeners with glitzy graphics.
- Use a common background or template for your presentation to give your information a unified look. As with other types of visual aids, simple ideas are best.
- Consider the effects of room lighting on your presentation. Fluorescent light, in particular, washes out the images projected by video projectors. Make sure you have the proper equipment to project clear images to your audience.
- Your group should practice using computer graphics. Consider making the presentation a team effort by having group members assist with presenting computer-generated slides.

Appendix C
Assessing Competencies of Problem-Solving Groups

Competencies are specific behaviors that group and team members perform. The assessment form provided here lists nine competencies organized into four general categories. Use the evaluation form here to assess small-group communication competencies in a group or team discussion.[1]

Here's how to use the form:

1. Observe a group or team that is attempting to solve a problem. Write the names of the group members at the top of the form. (If the group includes more than six group members, photocopy the form so that each group member can be evaluated.)
2. When using the form, first decide whether each group member has performed each competency. Circle NO if the group member was not observed performing the competency. Circle YES if you did observe the group member performing the competency (defining the problem, analyzing the problem, identifying criteria, and so on).
3. For each competency for which you circled YES, determine how effectively the competency was performed. Use the scale, which ranges from 0 to 3.
   - **0** This competency was performed, but it was performed inappropriately or inadequately. For example, the person observed tried to define a problem but did so poorly.
   - **1** Overall, performance of this competency was adequate.
   - **2** Overall, performance of this competency was good.
   - **3** Overall, performance of this competency was excellent.
4. Total the score for each group member in each of the four categories. If the competency was performed, the total number of points will range from 0 to 6 or 0 to 9. The higher the number of points, the better the individual performed on this competency.
   - **Problem-Oriented Competencies** consist of items 1 and 2. These behaviors help the group or team member define and analyze the problem.
   - **Solution-Oriented Competencies** include items 3, 4, and 5, with a point range from 0 to 9. These competencies focus on how well the team member helped develop and evaluate a solution to the problem.
   - **Discussion-Management Competencies,** items 6 and 7, help the group or team remain focused or manage interaction. The points for this category range from 0 to 6.
   - **Relational Competencies** are behaviors that focus on dealing with conflict and developing a positive, supportive group climate. Items 8 and 9 reflect this competency; points range from 0 to 6.
5. You can also assess the group's or team's ability to perform these competencies. The column marked "Group Assessment" can be used to record your overall impression of how effectively the group or team behaved. Circle NO if no one in the group performed a particular competency. Circle YES if at least one person in the group or team performed a competency. Then evaluate how well the entire group performed each competency, using the 0 to 3 scale.

Sometimes it is difficult to make judgments about group competencies by just viewing a group discussion once. Many people find that it's easier to videotape a group discussion so that you can observe the group discussion more than once.

The Competent Group Communicator Assessment Form

Problem-Solving Competencies	Group Member ______	Group Member ______	Group Member ______	Group Member ______	Group Member ______	Group Member ______	Group Member ______	Group Member ______
Problem-Oriented Competencies								
1. Defined the problem by identifying the obstacle(s) that prevent the group from achieving its goal; identified what the group wants more or less of to achieve the goal.	NO YES 0 1 2 3	NO YES 0 1 2 3	NO YES 0 1 2 3	NO YES 0 1 2 3	NO YES 0 1 2 3	NO YES 0 1 2 3	NO YES 0 1 2 3	NO YES 0 1 2 3
2. Analyzed the problem that the group attempted to solve: Used relevant information, data, or evidence; discussed the causes, history, symptoms, or significance of the problem.	NO YES 0 1 2 3	NO YES 0 1 2 3	NO YES 0 1 2 3	NO YES 0 1 2 3	NO YES 0 1 2 3	NO YES 0 1 2 3	NO YES 0 1 2 3	NO YES 0 1 2 3
Solution-Oriented Competencies								
3. Identified criteria for an appropriate solution to the problem; developed standards for an acceptable solution; identified ideal outcomes of the solution.	NO YES 0 1 2 3	NO YES 0 1 2 3	NO YES 0 1 2 3	NO YES 0 1 2 3	NO YES 0 1 2 3	NO YES 0 1 2 3	NO YES 0 1 2 3	NO YES 0 1 2 3
4. Generated solutions or strategies that would solve the problem that the group identified.	NO YES 0 1 2 3	NO YES 0 1 2 3	NO YES 0 1 2 3	NO YES 0 1 2 3	NO YES 0 1 2 3	NO YES 0 1 2 3	NO YES 0 1 2 3	NO YES 0 1 2 3
5. Evaluated solution(s): Identified positive and/or negative consequences of the proposed solutions; considered the pros and cons of suggested solutions.	NO YES 0 1 2 3	NO YES 0 1 2 3	NO YES 0 1 2 3	NO YES 0 1 2 3	NO YES 0 1 2 3	NO YES 0 1 2 3	NO YES 0 1 2 3	NO YES 0 1 2 3
Discussion-Management Competencies								
6. Maintained task focus: Helped the group stay on or return to the task, issue, or topic the group was discussing.	NO YES 0 1 2 3	NO YES 0 1 2 3	NO YES 0 1 2 3	NO YES 0 1 2 3	NO YES 0 1 2 3	NO YES 0 1 2 3	NO YES 0 1 2 3	NO YES 0 1 2 3
7. Managed group interaction: Appropriately initiated and terminated discussion, contributed to the discussion, or invited others to contribute to the discussion.	NO YES 0 1 2 3	NO YES 0 1 2 3	NO YES 0 1 2 3	NO YES 0 1 2 3	NO YES 0 1 2 3	NO YES 0 1 2 3	NO YES 0 1 2 3	NO YES 0 1 2 3
Relational Competencies								
8. Managed conflict: Appropriately and constructively helped the group stay focused on issues rather than on personalities when conflict occurred.	NO YES 0 1 2 3	NO YES 0 1 2 3	NO YES 0 1 2 3	NO YES 0 1 2 3	NO YES 0 1 2 3	NO YES 0 1 2 3	NO YES 0 1 2 3	NO YES 0 1 2 3
9. Maintained climate: Offered positive comments or nonverbal expressions that helped maintain a positive group climate.	NO YES 0 1 2 3	NO YES 0 1 2 3	NO YES 0 1 2 3	NO YES 0 1 2 3	NO YES 0 1 2 3	NO YES 0 1 2 3	NO YES 0 1 2 3	NO YES 0 1 2 3

Scoring: NO = Not observed   YES   0 = Inappropriate or inadequate performance of competency overall   1 = Adequate performance of competency overall   2 = Good performance of competency overall   3 = Excellent performance of competency overall

Problem-Oriented Competencies (0–6)

Solution-Oriented Competencies (0–9)

Discussion-Management Competencies (0–6)

Relational Competencies (0–6)

Glossary

Accommodation. Conflict-management style that involves giving in to the demands of others.

Action chart. A grid that lists tasks that need to be done and identifies who will be responsible for each task.

Activity tracks. Phases of problem solving that do not follow linear, step-by-step patterns.

Ad hoc committee. A committee that disbands when it completes its task.

Adaptor. A nonverbal act that helps people adapt to their immediate environment.

Affect display. A nonverbal behavior that communicates emotion.

Affection. Human warmth and closeness.

Affinity technique. A method of generating and organizing ideas by using Post-it notes; group members write each idea on a note and then sort the ideas into common categories.

Agenda. A list of issues, topics, tasks, and questions to be discussed or accomplished in a meeting.

Allness statement. A simple but untrue generalization.

Asynchronous message. Interaction in which e-mail messages are responded to after a time delay; the communication thus does not occur in real time.

Attitude. A learned predisposition to respond to a person, object, or idea in a favorable, neutral, or unfavorable way.

Avoidance. Conflict-management style that involves ignoring disagreements in an effort to sidestep conflict.

Belief. What someone considers to be true or false.

Bona fide perspective on groups. The view that the context and boundaries of groups change.

Brainsketching. A brainstorming technique in which people come up with creative ideas by drawing something rather than using words to describe a proposal.

Brainstorming. A problem-solving technique that helps a group generate creative options.

Breakpoint. A point in a group discussion at which members shift to a different activity.

Bypassing. A barrier to communication that occurs when two people interpret the same word differently.

Causal reasoning. Relating two or more events in such a way as to conclude that one event caused the other.

Cause-and-effect diagram. An analysis tool that charts the causes and effects of a problem or outcome; also called a fishbone diagram.

Central negative role. An individual role that is characterized by consistently challenging the leader's power and position and often offering negative comments about the group's progress.

Channel. The means or pathway by which a communication message is sent to a receiver.

Charge. The purpose of a team, group, or committee.

Coercive power. Power derived from the ability to punish people for acting or not acting in a certain way.

Cohesiveness. The degree of attraction group members feel toward one another and toward the group.

Collaborate. To use positive communication strategies in conflict management in an attempt to achieve a positive solution for all involved.

Collectivistic cultures. Cultures that emphasize group accomplishment.

Committee. A small group given a specific task by an individual or a larger group.

Communication. The process of acting on information; the process that allows a group to move toward its goals.

Communication network. A pattern of interaction within a group; who talks to whom.

Competent group communicator. A person who is able to interact appropriately and effectively with others in small groups.

Competition. Conflict-management style that stresses winning at the expense of others involved.

Complementarity. The tendency of individuals to be attracted to others who have knowledge, skills, or other attributes that they themselves lack but that they admire.

Compromise. Conflict-management style that attempts to find the middle ground in the conflict.

Confirming response. A communication response that causes a person to value himself or herself more.

Conflict. An expressed struggle between at least two interdependent people who perceive incompatible goals, scarce resources, and interference from others in an attempt to achieve a specific goal.

Conflict phase. Fisher's second phase of group interaction, in which disagreement and individual differences arise.

Consensus. Support for and commitment to a decision on the part of all group members.

Context. The physical and psychological environment for communication.

Control. The use of status and power to achieve a goal.

Creativity. The generation, application, combination, and extension of new ideas.

Criteria. Standards for an acceptable solution to a problem.

Cross-functional team-role training. Training that prepares members of a team to perform several roles or duties of other team members.

Cues-filtered-out theory. A theory that suggests that there are minimal relational messages expressed when communicating via e-mail or text-only messages because of fewer nonverbal cues.

Culture. A learned system of knowledge, behavior, attitudes, beliefs, values, and norms that is shared by a group of people.

Decision making. Making a choice from among several alternatives.

Decision-making group. A group whose purpose is to make a choice from among several alternatives.

Deductive reasoning. The process of reasoning from a general statement or principle to a specific conclusion.

Deep-level diversity. Human differences that are less readily visible, such as attitudes, opinions, values, information, and other factors, and that take time to detect.

Delphi technique. A technique whereby people share ideas in writing, without meeting face to face; also known as absentee brainstorming.

Descriptive approach. An approach to problem solving that helps people understand how a group solves a problem.

Dialectical theory. A descriptive model of group problem solving which suggests that during communication, competing tensions can pull the conversation in multiple directions; group members may feel simultaneously separate from the group and connected to the group.

Disconfirming response. A response that causes another person to value himself or herself less.

Dyad. Two people.

Ego conflict. Conflict that occurs when individuals become defensive because they feel they are being attacked.

Electronic brainstorming. A method of generating creative ideas using electronic devices; group members write out their own ideas, which are then displayed to all other members.

Emblem. A nonverbal cue with a specific verbal counterpart, such as a word, letter, or number.

Emergence phase. Fisher's third phase of group interaction, in which a group begins to manage disagreement and conflict.

Entropy. The measure of the randomness and chaos in a system.

Equifinality. A systems-theory principle that a final state may be reached by multiple paths and from different initial states.

Ethics. Beliefs, values, and moral principles by which people determine what is right and wrong.

Example. An illustration of a particular case or incident.

Expert power. The influence someone has over others because of greater knowledge and information.

Explanatory function. The power of a theory to explain things.

Fact. Any statement proven to be true.

Fact–inference confusion. Reaching a conclusion as if something had been actually observed (as if it was a fact), when in reality the conclusion was reached based on an inference (something not directly observed).

Fallacy. False reasoning that occurs when someone attempts to persuade without adequate evidence or with irrelevant or inappropriate arguments.

Fantasy. In symbolic convergence theory, a group's creative and imaginative shared interpretation of events that fulfills a group psychological or rhetorical need.

Fantasy chain. A string of connected stories that revolve around a common theme and that is created when a group is sharing a group fantasy.

Fantasy theme. The common or related content of the stories that a group is sharing during a group fantasy.

Feedback. Any response by listeners that lets speakers know whether they have been understood accurately.

Flowchart. A step-by-step diagram of a multistep process.

Focus group. A small group selected to discuss a particular topic so that others can better understand the group's responses to that topic.

Force-field analysis. A method of structuring the analysis of a problem to assess the driving and restraining forces that may affect the attainment of a goal.

Forum presentation. A discussion that directly follows a panel discussion or symposium and allows audience members to respond to ideas.

Function. The effect or consequence of a given behavior within a group system.

Functional approach. An approach to problem solving that emphasizes the performance of certain activities and effective communication to accomplish a group goal.

Functional perspective. A view of leadership that assumes all group members can initiate leadership behaviors.

Gender. Socially learned and reinforced characteristics that include one's biological sex and psychological (feminine, masculine, androgynous) characteristics.

Goal. An end that a group is working to achieve.

Ground rules. Explicit, agreed-on prescriptions for acceptable and appropriate behavior in a group or team.

Group climate. The emotional environment of a group, which affects and is affected by interaction among members.

Group cohesiveness. The degree of attraction members feel toward one another and their group.

Grouphate. The dread and repulsion people sometimes feel about working in groups and teams or participating in meetings.

Groupthink. The illusion of agreement exhibited by group members who try to minimize conflict and reach consensus without critically testing, analyzing, and evaluating ideas.

Gunny-sacking. A poor communication technique of dredging up old problems and issues from the past to use against your communication partner, like pulling them out of an old gunny sack.

High-contact culture. A culture in which people tend to touch others and to require less personal space.

Human communication. The process of making sense out of the world and sharing that sense with others by creating meaning through the use of verbal and nonverbal messages.

Ideal-solution format. A problem-solving method that helps a group define a problem, speculate about an ideal solution, and identify the obstacles that may keep it from achieving its goal.

Illustrator. A nonverbal behavior that accompanies and embellishes verbal communication.

Inclusion. The human need for affiliation with others.

Individual roles. Roles characterized by behavior that calls attention to the individual contributions of group members.

Individualistic cultures. Cultures that emphasize individual achievement.

Inductive reasoning. The method of arriving at a general conclusion through the use of specific instances or examples.

Information triage. The process of sorting through information to assess its importance, value, or relevance.

Innovation. A creative process of putting new ideas into action; innovation includes idea generation, feasibility analysis, reality testing, and implementation of the idea.

Interaction. The give-and-take conversation, talk, dialogue, and reaction to the messages of others that occur during a group discussion.

Interdependence. A relationship among components in a system such that a change in one component affects all other components.

Interpersonal level. Dyadic, between two people.

Intrapersonal level. Within one's self.

Invention. The process of developing new ideas.

Is/is not analysis. A method of separating the causes from the symptoms of a problem by considering such questions as the following: What is or is not the problem? What are or are not symptoms of the problem? When and where does the problem occur or not occur?

Journalist's six questions. The six questions news reporters use to analyze an event: Who? What? When? Where? Why? and How?

Knowledge. Cognitive understanding or accurate information about a subject—one of the elements essential to being a competent communicator.

Leadership. Behavior or communication that influences, guides, directs, or controls a group.

Leadership style. A relatively consistent behavior pattern that reflects a leader's beliefs and attitudes; classified as authoritarian, laissez-faire, or democratic.

Legitimate power. Power derived from being elected or appointed to control a group.

Listening. The active process of selecting, attending, understanding, and remembering.

Listening style. An individual's preferred way of making sense out of spoken messages.

Low-contact culture. A culture in which people are uncomfortable being touched and require more personal space.

Maintenance roles. Roles that influence a group's social atmosphere.

Media richness theory. The theory that a communication medium is rich if it has (1) potential for instant feedback, (2) verbal and nonverbal cues that can be processed by senders and receivers, (3) natural language, and (4) a focus on individuals.

Mediated setting. A context for communication that is not face to face but instead occurs through a phone line, fiber-optic cable, TV signal, or other means.

Message. Written, spoken, and unspoken elements of communication to which people assign meaning.

Metadiscussion. A statement about the process of discussion itself rather than about the discussion's topic; discussion about discussion.

Method theories. Theories that offer prescriptions for behavior.

Monochronic. A typically Western view of time as linear and segmented; also, a person who is more comfortable doing one thing at a time.

Motivation. An internal drive to achieve a goal.

Mutuality of concern. The degree to which members share the same level of commitment to a group or team.

Noise. Anything that interferes with a message being interpreted by the receiver as intended by the source.

Nominal-group technique. A problem-solving brainstorming method in which members work individually on ideas, rank the suggested solutions, and then report their findings for group discussion.

Nonverbal communication. Communication behavior that does not rely on written or spoken words.

Norms. Rules or standards that determine appropriate and inappropriate behaviors in a group.

Opinion. A quoted comment.

Orientation phase. Fisher's first phase of small group interaction, in which members try to understand one another and the task before their group.

Panel discussion. A group discussion intended to inform an audience about a problem or to encourage the audience to evaluate the pros and cons of an issue.

Paralanguage. Vocal cues such as pitch, volume, speaking rate, and voice quality that provide information about the meaning of a message.

Pareto principle. The principle that the source of 80 percent of a problem comes from 20 percent of the incidents.

Perception checking. The skill of asking someone whether your interpretation of his or her message is accurate; the skill requires observing behavior, thinking about what the behavior may mean, and asking whether your interpretation is accurate.

Plagiarism. Presenting someone else's words and ideas as one's own.

Polychronic. A view of time that places less emphasis on punctuality; also, a person who is able to do many things simultaneously.

Power. The ability to influence or exert control over others.

Predictive function. The ability of a theory to predict events.

Prescriptive approach. An approach to solving problems that identifies specific agendas and techniques to improve problem solving.

Primary group. A group (such as a family) that fulfills people's needs to associate with others.

Primary tension. Anxiety and tension that occur when a group first meets and members feel awkward and uncertain about how to behave.

Problem solving. A process that attempts to overcome or manage an obstacle so as to reach a goal.

Problem-solving group. A group that exists to resolve an issue or overcome an obstacle.

Process conflict. Conflict that occurs when one or more group members disagree about how a task could or should be accomplished; there is a difference of opinion about group procedures to accomplish the task.

Process leadership. Communication directed toward maintaining interpersonal relations and a positive group climate; also called group building or maintenance.

Process theories. Theories that explain human behaviors in a variety of contexts, including group and team phenomena.

Prototype. A model or smaller version of a solution to a problem that is developed to test the solution, product, or process before implementing the solution on a larger scale.

Proxemics. The study of how close to or far away from other people and objects we choose to be.

Pseudo-conflict. Conflict that occurs when individuals disagree because of poor communication.

Question of fact. A question that asks whether something is true or false or did or did not occur.

Question of policy. A question that asks about a course of action or a change in a procedure or behavior.

Question of prediction. A question that asks whether something is likely to occur under certain circumstances.

Question of value. A question that asks whether something is good or bad or right or wrong.

Random-word technique. A method used to enhance creative brainstorming in which one person says a random word to stimulate the development of new ideas.

Reasoning. The process of drawing conclusions from evidence.

Receiver. The person who interprets a communication message.

Referent power. Power based on interpersonal attraction.

Reflect. Having one or more group members consciously observing and verbalizing how the group and individual group members are following procedures and rules and interacting with one another.

Reflective thinking. John Dewey's problem-solving method, which includes the steps of defining a problem, analyzing it, suggesting possible solutions for it, selecting the best solution for it, and testing and implementing that solution.

Regulator. A nonverbal behavior that helps a group control the flow of communication.

Reinforcement phase. The fourth and final phase of group development in which group members express positive regard for the group and its members and offer comments that build cohesiveness.

Relational conflict. Conflict that occurs when one or more group members do not like, respect, or value another person.

Reverse-brainstorming. Brainstorming ideas or solutions that would make the problem *worse*, and then considering the implications of doing the opposite.

Reward power. Power based on the ability to reward desired behavior.

Risky shift. The tendency for groups to take more risks and make more extreme, riskier decisions than individuals do.

Roles. Sets of expectations people hold for themselves and for others in a given context.

Rolestorming. A brainstorming technique that involves assuming the role of someone else to help unlock ideas and increase creativity.

Rule. A prescription for acceptable behavior. Rules identify the appropriate or expected behavior of team or group members.

Secondary group. A group that exists to accomplish a task or achieve a goal.

Secondary tension. Conflict and stress that occur in a group as members vie for positions of leadership and influence or when group members begin to openly express disagreement about the task at hand.

Self-concept. The characteristics and attributes an individual believes himself or herself to have; one's theory about oneself.

Sexual orientation. The tendency of a person to develop a sexual, emotional, and intimate connection with another person of either the same sex or gender, different sex or gender, both male and female genders, or other gender variations.

Silent brainstorming. A period of individual brainstorming that occurs before group members share their ideas with the group; integral to the nominal-group technique; also may be used as part of traditional brainstorming.

Similarity. The tendency of individuals with like experiences, beliefs, attitudes, and values to be attracted to one another.

Simple conflict. Conflict that occurs when two people's goals or ideas are mutually exclusive or incompatible.

Single-question format. A problem-solving agenda that helps a group identify key issues and subissues of a problem.

Situation. The context in which group communication occurs.

Situational perspective. A perspective that views leadership as the interaction of group needs and goals, leadership style, and the situation.

Skill. An effective behavior that can be repeated when appropriate.

Small group. At least three people interacting with one another.

Small group communication. Interaction among a small group of people who share a common purpose, who feel a sense of belonging to the group, and who exert influence on one another.

Small-group ecology. The consistent way in which people in small groups arrange themselves physically.

Social exchange theory. A description of human relationships in terms of costs and rewards or profits and losses.

Social facilitation. The tendency for the presence of others to affect human behavior, specifically, to cause people to work harder.

Social information-processing theory. A theory that suggests that relationships do develop via mediated channels but that expressing and interpreting relational cues takes longer than during face-to-face interaction.

Social loafing. The tendency for people to hold back from contributing (to loaf) in a group because they assume someone else will do the work.

Social presence. The feeling of acting or thinking as if a person is involved in face-to-face communication via electronically mediated communication.

Source. Originator of a thought or emotion, who puts it into a code that can be understood by a receiver.

Standard agenda. A prescriptive agenda for solving a group or team problem that includes (1) identifying and defining the problem, (2) analyzing the problem, (3) identifying possible solutions, (4) selecting the best solution, and (5) implementing the solution.

Standing committee. A committee that remains active for an extended period of time.

Statistic. A numerical summary or quantitative summary of data.

Status. An individual's importance.

Stinking thinking. Thoughts that limit a person's, group's, or organization's possibilities.

Strategy. Staged, scripted communication.

Structuration theory. A general framework that explains how people use rules and resources to interact in a social system.

Structure. Methods used to keep a group discussion focused and on task, which include using an agenda, rules, procedures, and problem-solving steps.

Study group. A group whose primary purpose is to gather information and learn new ideas.

Supermajority decision. A decision based on agreement on a solution, action, or decision by at least two-thirds of a group.

Surface-level diversity. Social differences that are more readily visible, such as differences in ethnicity, skin color, age, sex, and other observable categories.

SWOT analysis. The process of identifying the multiple strengths, weaknesses, opportunities, and threats that a group or an organization has.

Syllogism. A way of structuring an argument in three parts: (1) a major premise, (2) a minor premise, and (3) a conclusion.

Symbol. Word, sound, or visual image that represents something else, such as a thought, concept, or object.

Symbolic convergence theory. The theory that a group develops a shared consciousness and identity through the sharing of fantasies or stories, which are often chained together and have a common theme.

Symposium presentation. A series of short speeches unified by a central issue or theme.

Synchronous message. Virtual interaction that takes place in real time.

Synergy. A condition in which the whole is greater than the sum of its parts.

System. An organic whole composed of interdependent elements.

Systems theory. A theory that describes group behavior in terms of input, processes, and output.

Task conflict. Conflict that occurs because of substantive differences about how to accomplish what the group is trying to achieve.

Task leadership. Communication directed toward accomplishing a group's task or goal.

Task roles. Roles that members assume to help accomplish the group's mission.

T-chart. A diagram (in the shape of a large T) on which the pros and cons of a particular proposition are listed on either side of the middle line.

Team. A group of individuals organized to work together to achieve a common goal.

Territoriality. Use of space to claim or defend a given area.

Theory. A set of interrelated facts, observations, and ideas that explains or predicts something.

Therapy group. A group led by a trained professional whose purpose is to help individuals with personal problems.

Trait perspective. A view of leadership as the personal attributes or qualities that leaders possess.

Transactional. Involving both sending and receiving simultaneously.

Transformational leadership. Leadership that aims to change an organization by realigning its culture around a new vision.

Trust. The extent to which a person is confident in, and willing to act on the basis of, the words, actions, and decisions of another.

Value. A person's perception of what is right or wrong, good or bad.

Vigilant thinkers. People who use logic, reasoning, evidence, and data to analyze issues and problems; they also establish clear decision criteria and evaluate the positive and negative consequences of a decision.

Virtual small group communication. Communication among group members who are not together in the same physical location.

X-Y-Z formula. A way to describe feelings by saying, "When you do X, in situation Y, I feel Z."

Notes

CHAPTER 1

1. E. E. Lawler, S. A. Mohrman, and G. Benson, *Organizing for High Performance: Employee Involvement, TQM, Reengineering, and Knowledge Management in the Fortune 1000.* (San Francisco: Jossey-Bass, 2001); also see F. A. Kennedy, M. L. Loughry, T. P. Klammer, and M. M. Beyerlein, "Effects of Organizational Support on Potency in Work Teams: The Mediating Role of Team Processes," *Small Group Research* 40, no. 1 (2009): 72–93.
2. Lawler, Mohrman, and Benson, *Organizing for High Performance.*
3. R. K. Mosvick and R. B. Nelson, *We've Got to Start Meeting Like This*! (Glenview, IL: Scott, Foresman, 1987); R. Y. Hirokawa, "Communication and Group Decision-Making Efficacy," in R. Y. Hirokawa, R. S. Cathcart, L. A. Samovar, and L. D. Henman, eds., *Small Group Communication Theory and Practice: An Anthology* (Los Angeles, CA: Roxbury Publishing Company, 2002), 125.
4. P. D. Hart Research Associates, *How Should Colleges Prepare Students to Succeed in Today's Global Economy?* (Washington, DC: Peter D. Hart Research Associates, December 2006); also see Quora, "Why and Where Is Teamwork Important?" *Forbes* (January 23, 2013), https://www.forbes.com/sites/quora/2013/01/23/why-and-where-is-teamwork-important/#5d161d37287a. Accessed September 20, 2017.
5. Thomas Friedman has written about our hyperconnected age. Our description of hyperconnectivity comes from: T. L. Friedman, "It's P.Q. and C.Q. as much as I.Q." *The New York Times*, January 30, 2013: A25; also see T. L. Friedman, *Thank You for Being Late: An Optimist's Guide to Thriving in the Age of Accelerations* (New York: Farrar, Straus and Giroux, 2016).
6. A. Anders, "Team Communication Platforms and Emergent Social Collaboration Practices," *International Journal of Business Communication* 53, no. 2 (2016): 224–61.
7. M. Stein and J. Pinto, "The Dark Side of Groups: A 'Gang at Work' in Enron," *Group and Organization Management* 36, no. 6 (2011): 692–721.
8. S. Herrera, "Firms Looking to Chatbots to Advance AI Capabilities," *Austin American Statesman* (Austin, TX), September 24, 2017: F3.
9. C. N. DeWall, D. S. Chester, and D. S. White, "Can Acetaminophen Reduce the Pain of Decision-Making?," *Journal of Experimental Social Psychology* 56 (2015): 117–20.
10. S. Sorenson, "Grouphate," paper presented at the annual meeting of the International Communication Association, Minneapolis, MN, May 1981.
11. F. E. X. Dance and C. Larson, *Speech Communication: Concepts and Behavior* (New York: Holt, Rinehart & Winston, 1972).
12. Our definition of human communication is based on a discussion in S. A. Beebe, S. J. Beebe, and M. V. Redmond, *Interpersonal Communication: Relating to Others*, 8th ed. (Boston: Pearson, 2017).
13. J. F. Yates and S. D. Olvera, "Culture and Decision Making," *Organizational Behavior and Human Decision Processes* 136 (2016): 106–18.
14. M. S. Weber and H. Kim, "Virtuality, Technology Use, and Engagement within Organizations," *Journal of Applied Communication Research* 43, no. 4 (2015): 358–407.
15. A. K. Offner, T. J. Kramer, and J. P. Winter, "The Effects of Facilitation, Recording, and Pauses on Group Brainstorming," *Small Group Research* 27 (1996): 283–98; V. Brown and P. B. Paulus, "A Simple Dynamic Model of Social Factors in Group Brainstorming," *Small Group Research* 27 (1996): 91–114; M. W. Kramer, C. L. Kuo, and J. C. Dailey, "The Impact of Brainstorming Techniques on Subsequent Group Processes," *Small Group Research* 28 (1997): 218–42; V. Brown, M. Tumeo, T. S. Larey, and P. B. Paulus, "Modeling Cognitive Interactions during Group Brainstorming," *Small Group Research* 29 (1997): 495–526.
16. S. G. Straus, "Getting a Clue: The Effects of Communication Media and Information Distribution on Participation and Performance in Computer-Mediated and Face-to-Face Groups," *Small Group Research* 27 (February 1996): 115–42; S. G. Straus, "Technology, Group Process, and Group Outcomes: Testing the Connections in Computer-Mediated and Face-to-Face Groups," *Human–Computer Interaction* 12 (1997): 227–66; S. P. Weisband, "Group Discussion and First Advocacy Effects in Computer-Mediated and Face-to-Face Decision Making Groups," *Organizational Behavior and Human Decision Processes* 53 (1992): 352–80.
17. S. Trzcielinski and M. Wypych-Zottowska, "Toward the Measure of Virtual Teams' Effectiveness," *Human Factors and Ergonomics in Manufacturing* 18 (2008): 501–14.
18. C. Pavitt, "Does Communication Matter in Social Influence during Small Group Discussion? Five Positions,"

Communication Studies 44 (Fall 1993): 216–27; D. E. Hewes, "Small Group Communication May Not Influence Decision Making: An Amplification of Socio-egocentric Theory," in R. Y. Hirokawa and M. S. Poole, eds., *Communication and Group Decision Making* (Thousand Oaks, CA: Sage, 1996), 179–212; R. A. Meyers and D. R. Seibold, "Making Foundational Assumptions Transparent: Framing the Discussion about Group Communication and Influence," *Human Communication Research* 35 (2009): 286–95; J. A. Bonito and R. E. Sanders, "The Existential Center of Small Groups: Members' Conduct and Interaction," *Small Group Research* 42, no. 3 (2011): 343–58.

19. A. J. Salazar, "Ambiguity and Communication Effects on Small Group Decision-Making Performance," *Human Communication Research* 23 (1996): 155–92; R. Y. Hirokawa, D. DeGooyer, and K. Valde, "Using Narratives to Study Task Group Effectiveness," *Small Group Research* 31 (2000): 573–91; S. Jarboe, "Procedures for Enhancing Group Decision Making," in R. Y. Hirokawa and M. S. Poole, eds., *Communication and Group Decision Making* (Thousand Oaks, CA: Sage, 1996); G. R. de Moura, T. Leader, J. Pelletier, and D. Abrams, "Prospects for Group Processes and Intergroup Relations Research: A Review of 70 Years' Progress," *Group Processes & Intergroup Relations* 11 (2008): 575–96.

20. J. S. Mueller, "Why Individuals in Larger Teams Perform Worse," *Organizational Behavior and Human Decision Processes* 117 (2012): 111–24; B. R. Staats, K. L. Milkman, and C. R. Fox, "The Team Scaling Fallacy: Underestimating the Declining Efficiency of Larger Teams," *Organizational Behavior and Human Decision Processes* 118 (2012): 132–42; B. M. Waller, L. Hope, N. Burrowes, and E. R. Morrison, "Twelve (Not So) Angry Men: Managing Conversational Group Size Increases Perceived Contribution by Decision Makers," *Group Processes & Intergroup Relations* 14, no. 6 (2011): 835–43.

21. A. B. Henley and K. H. Price, "Want a Better Team? Foster a Climate of Fairness," *Academy of Management Executive* 16 (August 2002): 153–54.

22. Evidence suggests that groups do experience emotions, and these collaboratively felt emotions help unite a group. See E. R. Smith, C. R. Seger, and D. M. Mackie, "Can Emotions Be Truly Group Level? Evidence Regarding Four Conceptual Criteria," *Journal of Personality and Social Psychology* 93 (2007): 431–46.

23. N. Li, "Toward a Model of Work Team Altruism," *Academy of Management Review* 39, no. 4 (2014): 541–65.

24. D. Romig, *Side by Side Leadership: Achieving Outstanding Results Together* (Austin, TX: Bard Press, 2001).

25. J. W. Bishop, K. D. Scott, and S. M. Burroughs, "Support, Commitment, and Employee Outcomes in a Team Environment," *Journal of Management* 26 (2000): 1113–32; L. G. Snyder, "Teaching Teams about Teamwork: Preparation, Practice, and Performance Review," *Business Communication Quarterly* (March 2009): 74–79.

26. J. L. Wildman and W. L. Bedwell, "Practicing What We Preach: Teaching Teams Using Validated Team Science," *Small Group Research* 44 (2013): 381–94; M. L. Miller Henningsen, D. D. Henningsen, M. G. Cruz, and J. Morrill, "Social Influence in Groups: A Comparative Application of Relational Framing Theory and the Elaboration Likelihood Model of Persuasion," *Communication Monographs* 70, no. 3 (September 2003): 175–97. For an excellent review of teamwork principles and strategies, see D. A. Romig, *Breakthrough Teamwork: Outstanding Results Using Structured Teamwork* (New York: Irwin, 1996); V. Rousseau, C. Aube, and A. Savoie, "Teamwork Behaviors: A Review and an Integration of Frameworks," *Small Group Research* 37 (2006): 540–70; P. J. Sullivan and S. Short, "Further Operationalization of Intra-team Communication in Sports: An Updated Version of the Scale of Effective Communication in Team Sports (SECTS-2)," *Journal of Applied Social Psychology* 41, no. 2 (2011): 471–87; J. R. Hollenbeck, B. Beersma, and M. E. Schouten, "Beyond Team Types and Taxonomies: A Dimensional Scaling Conceptualization for Team Description," *Academy of Management Review* 37, no. 1 (2012): 82–106.

27. J. A. Kliegl and K. D. Weaver, "Teaching Teamwork through Coteaching in the Business Classroom," *Business and Professional Communication Quarterly* 77, no. (2 (2014): 204–16; J. K. Ellington, and E. C. Dierdorff, "Individual Learning in Team Training: Self-Regulation and Team Context Effects," *Small Group Research* 45 (2014): 37–67; J. R. Katzenback and D. K. Smith, *The Wisdom of Teams: Creating the High-Performance Organization* (New York: Harper Business, 1993); M. Schrage, *No More Teams! Mastering the Dynamics of Creative Collaboration* (New York: Currency Doubleday, 1995); Romig, *Breakthrough Teamwork*; D. C. Strubler and K.M. York, "An Exploratory Study of the Team Characteristics Model Using Organizational Teams," *Small Group Research* 38 (2007): 670–95.

28. Y. Gong, T.-Y. Kim, D.-R. Lee, and J. Zhu, "A Multilevel Model of Team Goal Orientation, Information Exchange, and Creativity," *Academy of Management Journal* 56 (June 2013): 827–51; D. F. Crown, "The Use of Group and Groupcentric Individual Goals for Culturally Heterogeneous and Homogeneous Task Groups," *Small Group Research* 38 (2007): 489–508; A. N. Pieterse, D. van Knippenberg, and W. P. van Ginkel, "Diversity in Goal Orientation, Team Reflexivity, and Team Performance," *Organizational Behavior and Human Decision Processes* 114 (2011): 153–64.

29. N. Katz and G. Koenig, "Sports Teams as a Model for Workplace Teams: Lessons and Liabilities," *Academy of Management Executive* 15 (August 2001): 56–67.

30. D. J. Devine, L. D. Clayton, J. L. Philips, B. B. Dunford, and S. B. Melner, "Teams in Organizations: Prevalence, Characteristics, and Effectiveness," *Small Group Research* 30 (1999): 678–711.

31. M. L. Shuffler, M. Jimenez-Rodriguez, and W. S. Kramer, "The Science of Multiteam Systems: A Review and Future Research Agenda," *Small Group Research* 46, no. 6 (2015): 659–99.

32. J. S. Christian, M. S. Christian, M. J. Pearsall, and E. C. Long, "Team Adaptation in Context: An Integrated Conceptual Model and Meta-Analytic Review," *Organizational Behavior and Human Decision Processes* 140 (2017): 62–89.

33. E. Salas, D. R. Nichols, and J. E. Driskell, "Testing Three Team Training Strategies in Intact Teams: A Meta-Analysis," *Small Group Research* 38 (2007): 471–88; also see R. S. Tindale and T. Kameda, "Group Decision-Making from an Evolutionary/Adaptationist Perspective," *Group Processes & Intergroup Relations* 20, no. 5 (2017): 669–80.

34. See P. R. Scholtes, B. L. Joiner, and B. J. Streibel, *The Team Handbook*, 2nd ed. (Madison, WI: Joiner Associates, 1996); Romig, *Breakthrough Teamwork*; Schrage, *No More Teams!*

35. C. Klein, D. DiazGranados, E. Salas, H. Le, C. S. Burke, R. Lyons, and G. F. Goodwin, "Does Team Building Work?," *Small Group Research* 40, no. 2 (2009): 181–222.

36. J. Staggers, S. Garcia, and E. Nagelhout, "Teamwork through Team Building: Face-to-Face to Online," *Business Communication Quarterly* 71 (2008): 472–87.

37. R. Y. Hirokawa and J. Keyton, "Perceived Facilitators and Inhibitors of Effectiveness in Organizational Work Teams," *Management Communication Quarterly* 8 (1995): 424–46; E. Salas, D. E. Sims, and C. S. Burke, "Is There a 'Big Five' in Teamwork?" *Small Group Research* 36 (2005): 555–99.

38. D. J. Devine and J. L. Philips, "Do Smarter Teams Do Better? A Meta-Analysis of Cognitive Ability and Team Performance," *Small Group Research* 32 (2001): 507–35.

39. J. R. Mesmer-Magnus, D. R. Carter, R. Asencio, and L. A. DeChurch, "Space Exploration Illuminates the Next Frontier for Teams Research," *Group & Organization Management* 41, no. 5 (2016): 595–628.

40. C. E. Larson and F. M. J. LaFasto, *Teamwork: What Must Go Right/What Can Go Wrong* (Beverly Hills, CA: Sage, 1989); also see L. A. Erbert, G. M. Mearns, and S. Dena, "Perceptions of Turning Points and Dialectical Interpretations in Organizational Team Development," *Small Group Research* 36 (2005): 21–58.

41. M. Hoegl and K. Parboteeah, "Goal Setting and Team Performance in Innovative Projects: On the Moderating Role of Teamwork Quality," *Small Group Research* 34 (2003): 3–19.

42. K. T. Goh, P. S. Goodman, and L. R. Weingart, "Team Innovation Processes: An Examination of Activity Cycles in Creative Project Teams," *Small Group Research* 44, no. 2 (2013): 159–94.

43. M. A. Marks, J. E. Mathieu, and S. J. Zaccaro, "A Temporally Based Framework and Taxonomy of Team Processes," *Academy of Management Review* 26 (2001): 356–76.

44. C. G. Endacott, R. T. Hartwig, and C. H. Yu, "An Explanatory Study of Communication Practices Affecting Church Leadership Team Performance," *Southern Communication Journal* 82, no. 3 (2017): 129–39.

45. E. Minei, and R. Bisel, "Negotiating the Meaning of Team Expertise: A Firefighter Team's Epistemic Denial," *Small Group Research* 44 (2014): 7–32.

46. Devine et al., "Teams in Organizations"; M. H. Jordan, H. S. Field, and A. A. Armenakis, "The Relationship of Group Process Variables and Team Performance: A Team-Level Analysis in a Field Setting," *Small Group Research* 33 (2002); 121–50; S. Sonnentag and J. Volmer, "Individual-Level Predictors of Task-Related Teamwork Processes: The Role of Expertise and Self-Efficacy in Team Meetings," *Group & Organization Management* 34 (2009): 37–66.

47. N. Lehmann-Willenbrock, M. M. Chiu, Z. Lei, and S. Kauffeld, "Understanding Positivity within Dynamic Team Interactions: A Statistical Discourse Analysis," *Group & Organizational Management* 42 (2017): 39–78.

48. A. M. Hardin, M. A. Fuller, and J. S. Valacich, "Measuring Group Efficacy in Virtual Teams: New Questions in an Old Debate," *Small Group Research* 37 (2006): 65–85.

49. Emily Ross and Angus Holland, *100 Great Businesses and the Minds behind Them* (Naperville, IL: Sourcebooks, Inc., 2006), 358–61.

50. P. Balkundi and D. A. Harrison, "Ties, Leaders, and Time in Teams: Strong Inference about Network Structure's Effects on Team Viability and Performance," *Academy of Management Journal* 49 (2006): 49–68.

51. F. A. Kennedy, M. L. Loughry, T. P. Klammer, and M. M. Beyerlein, "Effects of Organizational Support on Potency in Work Teams: The Mediating Role of Team Processes," *Small Group Research* 40 (2009): 72–93.

52. J. R. Hackman and R. Wageman, "A Theory of Team Coaching," *Academy of Management Review* 30 (2005): 269–87.

53. M. S. Limon and F. J. Boster, "The Effects of Performance Feedback on Group Members' Perceptions of Prestige, Task Competencies, Group Belonging, and

Loafing," *Communication Research Reports* 20 (Winter 2003): 13–23; J. N. Choi, "External Activities and Team Effectiveness: Review and Theoretical Development," *Small Group Research* 33 (2002): 181–208.

54. F. LaFasto and C. Larson, *When Teams Work Best* (Thousand Oaks, CA: Sage, 2001). Our discussion of the six characteristics of effective team members is based on information presented in Chapter 1, pp. 4–25.

55. S. A. Rains and V. Young, "A Meta-analysis of Research on Formal Computer-Mediated Support Groups: Examining Group Characteristics and Health Outcomes," *Human Communication Research* 35 (2009): 309–36.

56. J. L. Thompson, "Building Collective Communication Competence in Interdisciplinary Research Teams," *Journal of Applied Communication Research* 37 (2009): 278–97.

57. N. Lehmann-Willenbrock, M. M. Chiu, Z. Lei, and S. Kauffeld, "Understanding Positivity within Dynamic Team Interactions: A Statistical Discourse Analysis," *Group & Organization Management* 42 (2017): 39–78.

58. A. T. Pescosolido, "Group Efficacy and Group Effectiveness: The Effects of Group Efficacy over Time on Group Performance and Development," *Small Group Research* 34 (2003): 20–43.

59. B. Beersma, J. R. Hollenbeck, S. E. Humphrey, H. Moon, D. E. Conlon, and D. R. Ilgen, "Cooperation, Competition, and Team Performance: Toward a Contingency Approach," *Academy of Management Journal* 46 (2002): 572–90.

60. M. A. G. Peeters, C. G. Rutte, H. F. J. M. van Tuijl, and I. M. M. J. Reymen, "The Big Five Personality Traits and Individual Satisfaction with the Team," *Small Group Research* 37 (2006): 187–211.

61. A. English, R. L. Griffith, and L. A. Steelman, "Team Performance: The Effect of Team Conscientiousness and Task Type," *Small Group Research* 35 (2004): 643–65.

62. A. Edmondson, "Psychological Safety and Learning Behavior in Work Teams," *Administrative Science Quarterly* 44 (199): 350–83. Also see C. M. J. H. Savelsbergh, B. I. J. M. van der Heijden, and R. F. Poell, "The Development and Empirical Validation of a Multidimensional Measurement Instrument for Team Learning Behaviors," *Small Group Research* 40 (2009): 578–607.

63. J. S. Christian, M. S. Christian, M. J. Pearsall, and E. C. Long, "Team Adaptation in Context: An Integrated Conceptual Model and Meta-Analytic Review," *Organizational Behavior and Human Decision Processes* 140 (2017): 62–89.

64. J. S. Prichard and M. J. Ashleigh, "The Effects of Team-Skills Training on Transactive Memory and Performance," *Small Group Research* 38 (2007): 696–726; T. L. Rapp and J. E. Mathieu, "Evaluating an Individually Self-Administered Genetic Teamwork Skills Training Program across Time and Levels," *Small Group Research* 38 (2007): 532–55.

65. Prichard and Ashleigh, "The Effects of Team-Skills Training"; Rapp and Mathieu, "Evaluating an Individually Self-Administered Genetic Teamwork Skills Training Program."

66. The discussion of the advantages and disadvantages of working in small groups is based in part on N. R. F. Maier, "Assets and Liabilities in Group Problem Solving: The Need for an Integrative Function," *Psychological Review* 74 (1967): 239–49. Also see Michael Argyle, *Cooperation: The Basis of Sociability* (London: Routledge, 1991); R. S. Tindale, C. M. Smith, A. Dykema-Engblade, and K. Kluwe, "Good and Bad Group Performance: Same Process—Different Outcomes," *Group Processes Intergroup Relations* 15, no. 5 (2012): 603–18.

67. J. Surowiecki, *The Wisdom of Crowds* (New York: Anchor Books, 2005).

68. A. L. Mellow and J. R. Rentsch, "Cognitive Diversity in Teams: A Multidisciplinary Review," *Small Group Research* 46(6) (2015): 623–58.

69. C. R. Chartier and S. Abele, "Groups Outperform Individuals in Tacit Coordination by Using Consensual and Disjunctive Salience," *Organizational Behavior and Human Decision Processes* 141 (2017): 74–81.

70. See F. C. Broadbeck and T. Breitemeyer, "Effects of Individual versus Mixed Individual and Group Experience in Rule Induction on Group Member Learning and Group Performance," *Journal of Experimental Social Psychology* 36 (October 2002): 621–48; G. S. Van Der Vegt and J. S. Bunderson, "Learning and Performance in Multidisciplinary Teams: The Importance of Collective Team Identification," *Academy of Management Journal* 48 (2005): 532–47; J. R. Larson, "Deep Diversity and Strong Synergy Modeling the Impact of Variability in Members' Problem-Solving Strategies on Group Problem-Solving Performance," *Small Group Research* 38 (2007): 413–36.

71. R. A. Cooke and J. A. Kernaghan, "Estimating the Difference between Group Versus Individual Performance on Problem-Solving Tasks," *Group & Organizational Studies* 12, no. 3 (September 1987): 319–42; P. R. Laughlin, E. C. Hatch, J. Silver, and L. Boh, "Groups Perform Better Than the Best Individuals on Letters-to-Numbers Problems: Effects of Group Size," *Journal of Personality and Social Psychology* 90 (2006): 644–51.

72. F. C. Brodbeck, R. Kerschreiter, A. Mojzisch, and S. Schulz-hardt, "Group Decision Making under Conditions of Distributed Knowledge: The Information Asymmetries Model," *Academy of Management Review* 32 (2007): 459–79.

73. Cooke and Kernaghan, "Estimating the Difference."

74. D. D. Stewart, "Stereotypes, Negativity Bias, and the Discussion of Unshared Information in Decision-Making Groups," *Small Group Research* 29 (1998): 643–68; J. R. Larson, "Modeling the Entry of Shared and Unshared Information into Group Discussion: A Review and BASIC Language Computer Program," *Small Group Research* 28 (1997): 454–79.

75. J. N. Ervin, J. A. Bonito, and J. Keyton, "Convergence of Intrapersonal and Interpersonal Processes across Group Meetings," *Communication Monographs* 84, no. 2 (2017): 200–20.

76. J. Platania and G. P. Moran, "Social Facilitation as a Function of the Mere Presence of Others," *Journal of Social Psychology* 141 (Spring 2001): 190–97.

77. R. Zajonc, "Social Facilitation," *Science* 149 (1965): 269–74; M. Gagne and M. Zuckerman, "Performance and Learning Goal Orientations as Moderators of Social Loafing and Social Facilitation," *Small Group Research* 30 (1999): 524–41; R. G. Geen, "Social *Motivation,*" *Annual Review of Psychology* 42 (1991): 377–99.

78. I. L. Janis, "Groupthink," *Psychology Today* 5 (November 1971): 43–46, 74–76.

79. G. Yilmaz and R. Youngreen, "The Application of Minority Influence Theory in Computer-Mediated Communication Groups," *Small Group Research* 47, no. 6 (2016): 692–719.

80. V. Penarroja, V. Orengo, and A. Zornoza, "Reducing Perceived Social Loafing in Virtual Teams: The Effect of Team Feedback with Guided Reflexivity," *Journal of Applied Social Psychology* 47 (2017): 424–35.

81. Gagne and Zuckerman, "Performance and Learning Goal Orientations."

82. A. BarNir, "Can Group and Issue-Related Factors Predict Choice Shift? A Meta Analysis of Group Decisions on Life Dilemmas," *Small Group Research* 29 (1998): 308–38.

83. E. M. Stark, J. D. Shaw, and M. K. Duffy, "Preference for Group Work, Winning Orientation, and Social Loafing Behavior in Groups," *Group and Organization Management* 32 (2007): 699–723.

84. D. R. Forsyth, *An Introduction to Group Dynamics* (Monterey, CA: Brooks/Cole, 1983), 424.

85. S. N. Fraidin, "When Is One Head Better Than Two? Interdependent Information in Group Decision Making," *Organizational Behavior and Human Decision Processes* 93 (2004): 102–13.

86. G. Hofstede, *Culture's Consequences: International Differences in Work-Related Values* (Beverly Hills, CA: Sage, 1980), 221.

87. In addition to the work of Hofstede, see J. A. Wagner III and M. K. Moch, "Individualism–Collectivism: Concept and Measure," *Group and Organizational Studies* 11 (September 1986): 280–304; H. C. Triandis, C. McCusker, and C. H. Hui, "Multimethod Probes of Individualism and Collectivism," *Journal of Personality and Social Psychology* 59 (1990): 1006–20; C. H. Hui, "Measurement of Individualism–Collectivism," *Journal of Research in Personality* 22 (1988): 17–36; C. R. Bantz, "Cultural Diversity and Group Cross-Cultural Team Research," *Journal of Applied Communication Research* (February 1993): 1–20; M. R. Hammer and J. N. Martin, "The Effects of Cross-Cultural Training on American Managers in a Japanese–American Joint Venture," *Journal of Applied Communication Research* (May 1992): 161–82; T. H. Cox, S. A. Lobel, and P. L. McLeod, "Effects of Ethnic Group Cultural Differences on Cooperative and Competitive Behavior on a Group Task," *Academy of Management Journal* 34, no. 4 (1991): 827–47; B. L. Kirkman and D. L. Shapiro, "Understanding Why Team Members Won't Share: An Examination of Factors Related to Employee Receptivity to Team-Based Rewards," *Small Group Research* 31 (2000): 175–209.

88. Adapted from John Mole, *Mind Your Manners: Managing Business Cultures in Europe* (London: Nicholas Brealey, 1995).

89. For an excellent discussion of small group communication in naturalistic settings, see L. R. Frey, "The Naturalistic Paradigm: Studying Small Groups in the Postmodern Era," *Small Group Research* 25 (1994): 551–77; L. R. Frey, "Applied Communication Research on Group Facilitation in Natural Settings," in L. R. Fey, ed., *Innovations in Group Facilitation: Applications in Natural Settings* (Cresskill, NJ: Hampton, 1995), 1–23.

90. For a comprehensive review of the history of group decision-making research, see L. R. Frey, "Remember and 'Remembering': A History of Theory and Research on Communication and Group Decision-Making," in R. Y. Hirokawa and M. S. Poole, eds., *Communication and Group Decision Making*, 2nd ed. (Thousand Oaks, CA: Sage, 1996), 19–51.

91. C. E. Timmerman and C. R. Scott, "Virtually Working: Communicative and Structural Predictors of Media Use and Key Outcomes in Virtual Work Teams," *Communication Monographs* 73 (2006): 108–36.

92. S. G. Cohen and C. B. Gibson, "Putting the Team Back in Virtual Teams," paper presented at the Society for

Industrial/Organizational Psychology, Orlando, FL, April, 2003; also see D. S. Staples and J. Webster, "Exploring Traditional and Virtual Team Members' 'Best Practices': A Social Cognitive Theory Perspective," *Small Group Research* 38 (2007): 60–97.

93. K. Parry, M. Cohen, and S. Bhattacharya, "Rise of the Machines: A Critical Consideration of Automated Leadership Decision Making in Organizations," *Group & Organizational Management* 41, no. 5 (2016): 571–94; C. R. Scott, "A Whole-Hearted Effort to Get It Half Right: Predicting the Future of Communication Technology Scholarship," *Journal of Computer-Mediated Communication* 14 (2009): 753–57; also see M. S. Poole, "Collaboration, Integration, and Transformation: Directions for Research on Communication and Information Technologies," *Journal of Computer-Mediated Communication* 14 (2009): 758–63.

94. S. K. Johnson, K. Bettenhausen, and E. Gibbons, "Realities of Working in Virtual Teams: Affective and Attitudinal Outcomes of Using Computer-Mediated Communication," *Small Group Research* 40, no. 6 (2009): 623–49; S. Green-Hamann, K. C. Eichhorn, and J. C. Sherblom, "An Exploration of Why People Participate in Second Life Social Support Groups," *Journal of Computer-Mediated Communication* 16 (2011): 465–91.

95. S. P. Nicholls and R. E. Rice, "A Dual-Identity Model of Responses to Deviance in Online Groups: Integrating Social Identity Theory and Expectancy Violations Theory," *Communication Theory* 27 (2017): 243–68; M. S. Poole, "Collaboration, Integration, and Transformation: Directions for Research on Communication and Information Technologies," *Journal of Computer-Mediated Communication* 14 (2009): 758–63.

96. D. Jude-York, L. D. Davis, and S. L. Wise, *Virtual Teaming: Breaking the Boundaries of Time and Place* (Menlo Park, CA: Crisp Learning, 2000), 71.

97. D. Knox, V. Daniels, L. Sturdisvant, and M. E. Zusman, "College Student Use of the Internet for Mate Selection," *College Student Journal* 35 (March 2001): 15.

98. D. Misner, "Everyone Lies on the Internet, According to New Research," http://www.cbc.ca/news/technology/misenere-internet-lies-1.3732328. Accessed September 25, 2017.

99. N. Bos, J. Olson, D. Gergle, G. Olson, and Z. Wright, "Effects of Four Computer-Mediated Communications Channels on Trust Development," *Proceedings of ACM CHI Conference on Human Factors in Computing Systems: Changing Our World, Changing Ourselves* (New York: ACM Press, 2002): 135–40; also see J. B. Walther and R. U. Bunz, "The Rules of Virtual Groups Trust, Liking, and Performance in Computer-Mediated Communication," *International Communication Association* (2005): 828–46.

100. R. R. Provine, R. J. Spencer, and D. L. Mandell, "Emotional Expression Online: Emoticons Punctuate Website Text Messages," *Journal of Language and Social Psychology* 26, no. 3 (September 2007): 299–307.

101. B. Parkinson, A. H. Fisher, and A. S. R. Manstead, *Emotion in Social Relations: Cultural, Group, and Interpersonal Processes* (New York: Psychology Press, 2004).

102. I. Sproull and S. Kiesler, "Reducing Social Context Cues: Electronic Mail in Organizational Communication," *Management Science* 32 (1986): 1492–513.

103. L. K. Trevino, R. L. Draft, and R. H. Lengel, "Understanding Managers' Media Choices: A Symbolic Interactionist Perspective," in J. Fulk and C. Steinfield, eds., *Organizations and Communication Technology* (Newbury Park, CA: Sage, 1990), 71–94.

104. Based on Trevino, Daft, and Lengel, "Understanding Managers' Media Choices."

105. L. C. Tidwell and J. B. Walther, "Computer-Mediated Communication Effects on Disclosure, Impressions, and Interpersonal Evaluations: Getting to Know One Another a Bit at a Time," *Human Communication Research* 28 (July 2002): 317–48.

106. Tidwell and Walther, "Computer-Mediated Communication Effects on Disclosure, Impressions, and Interpersonal Evaluations." For an excellent discussion of the effects of computer-mediated communication and interpersonal communication, see J. B. Walther, "Interpersonal Effects in Computer-Mediated Interaction: A Relational Perspective," *Communication Research* 19 (1992): 52–90; J. B. Walther, "Relational Aspects of Computer-Mediated Communication: Experimental and Longitudinal Observations," *Organization Science* 6 (1995): 186–203; J. B. Walther, J. F. Anderson, and D. Park, "Interpersonal Effects in Computer-Mediated Interaction: A Meta-Analysis of Social and Anti-Social Communication," *Communication Research* 21 (1994): 460–87; N. Negroponte, *Being Digital* (New York: Knopf, 1995); J. B. Walther and L. Tidwell, "When Is Mediated Communication Not Interpersonal?" in K. Galvin and P. Cooper, *Making Connections* (Los Angeles, CA: Roxbury Press, 1996): 300–07; P. Wallace, *The Psychology of the Internet* (Cambridge, UK: Cambridge University Press, 1999).

107. J. B. Walther and J. K. Burgoon, "Relational Communication in Computer-Mediated Interaction," *Human Communication Research* 19 (1992): 50–88.

108. J. B. Walther and R. U. Bunz, "The Rules of Virtual Groups Trust, Liking, and Performance in Computer-Mediated Communication," *International Communication Association* (2005): 828–46.

109. Trzcielinski and Wypych-Zottowska, "Toward the Measure of Virtual Teams Effectiveness."

110. R. L. Clark, "Leadership Trust in Virtual Teams Using Communication Tools: A Qualitative Correlational Study," Unpublished doctoral dissertation, University of Phoenix, 2014.

111. A. Anders, "Team Communication Platforms and Emergent Social Collaboration Practices"; H. C. Xie, "The Role of Computer Mediated Communication Competence on Unique Information Pooling and Decision Quality in Virtual Teams," unpublished M.A. thesis, Michigan State University, Department of Psychology, 2015.

112. D. S. Staples and J. Webster, "Exploring Traditional and Virtual Team Members' 'Best Practices': A Social Cognitive Theory Perspective," *Small Group Research* 38 (2007): 60–97.

113. S. Trzcielinski and M. Wypych-Zottowska, "Toward the Measure of Virtual Teams Effectiveness," *Human Factors and Ergonomics in Manufacturing* 18 (2008): 501–14; R. L. Clark, "Leadership Trust in Virtual Teams Using Communication Tools: A Qualitative Correlational Study," Unpublished doctoral dissertation, University of Phoenix, 2014.

114. M. E. Mayer, "Behaviors Leading to More Effective Decisions in Small Groups Embedded in Organizations," *Communication Reports* 11 (1998): 123–32.

115. B. H. Spitzberg, "Communication Competence as Knowledge, Skill, and Impression," *Communication Education* 32 (1983): 323–29.

116. B. Hollingshead, "Group and Individual Training: The Impact of Practice on Performance," *Small Group Research* 29 (1998): 254–80.

117. S. A. Beebe and J. K. Barge, "Assessing Small Group Problem Solving Communication Competencies," in R. Cathcart and L. Samovar, eds., *A Reader in Small Group Communication* (New York: Roxbury, 2004): 275–88; S. A. Beebe, J. K. Barge, P. Mottet, and C. Tustl, "The Competent Group Communicator," presented at the National Communication Association Annual Conference, San Antonio, TX, November 2006.

118. K. W. Hawkins and B. P. Fillion, "Perceived Communication Skill Needs for Work Groups," *Communication Research Reports* 16 (1999): 167–74.

CHAPTER 2

1. The notion of theorizing as an everyday activity was advanced by F. E. X. Dance and C. E. Larson, *The Functions of Human Communication: A Theoretical Approach* (New York: Holt, Rinehart & Winston, 1976), 4.

2. G. A. Kelly, *A Theory of Personality: The Psychology of Personal Constructs* (New York: Norton, 1963), 18.

3. R. Buehler, D. Messervey, and D. Griffin, "Collaborative Planning and Prediction: Does Group Discussion Affect Optimistic Biases in Time Estimation?" *Organizational Behavior and Human Decision Processes* 97 (2005): 47–63.

4. D. Barnlund, "Toward a Meaning-Centered Philosophy of Communication," in K. G. Johnson et al., eds., *Nothing Never Happens* (Beverly Hills, CA: Glencoe Press, 1974), 213.

5. L. Dithurbide, P. Sullivan, and G. Chow, "Examining the Influence of Team-Referent Causal Attributions and Team Performance on Collective Efficacy: A Multilevel Analysis," *Small Group Research* 40 (2009): 491–507.

6. Sunwolf, "Decisional Regret Theory: Reducing the Anxiety about Uncertain Outcomes During Group Decision Making through Shared Counterfactual Storytelling," *Communication Studies* 57 (2006): 107–34.

7. T. Halfhill, E. Sundstrom, J. Lahner, W. Calderone, and T. M. Nielsen, "Group Personality Composition and Group Effectiveness: An Integrative Review of Empirical Research," *Small Group Research* 36 (2005): 83–105.

8. J. A. Bonito, "The Analysis of Participation in Small Groups: Methodological and Conceptual Issues Related to Interdependence," *Small Group Research* 33 (2002): 412–38.

9. J. K. Brilhart, *Effective Group Discussion*, 8th ed. (Dubuque, IA: Brown, 1995), 26.

10. P. R. Laughlin, E. C. Hatch, J. Silver, and L. Boh, "Groups Perform Better Than the Best Individuals on Letters-to-Numbers Problems: Effects of Group Size," *Journal of Personality and Social Psychology* 90 (2006): 644–51.

11. S. W. Littlejohn, *Theories of Human Communication*, 7th ed. (Belmont, CA: Wadsworth, 1996).

12. M. W. Kramer, "Communication and Social Exchange Processes in Community Theatre Groups," *Journal of Applied Communication Research* 33 (2005): 159–82.

13. M. M. Miller and J. M. Bermudez, "Intersecting Gender and Social Exchange Theory in Family Therapy," *Journal of Feminist Family Therapy* 16 (2004): 25–42.

14. E. Bormann, *Small Group Communication: Theory and Practice*, 3rd ed. (New York: HarperCollins, 1990).

15. E. Bormann, "Symbolic Convergence Theory," in R. Y. Hirokawa, R. S. Cathcart, L. A. Samovar, and L. D. Henman, eds., *Small Group Communication Theory and Practice* (Los Angeles: Roxbury, 2003), 41.

16. K. M. Propp and G. Kreps, "A Rose by Any Other Name: The Vitality of Group Communication Research," *Communication Studies* 45 (1994): 7–19.

17. See A. Giddens, *New Rules of Sociological Method*, 2nd ed. (Palo Alto, CA: Stanford University Press, 1993); and A. Giddens, *Studies in Social and Political Theory* (New York: Basic Books, 1979).

18. M. S. Poole, D. R. Seibold, and R. D. McPhee, "A Structurational Approach to Theory Building in Group Decision-Making Research," in R. Y. Hirokawa and M. S. Poole, eds., *Communication and Group Decision Making*, 2nd ed. (Thousand Oaks, CA: Sage, 1996).

19. F. Den Hond, F. Kees Boersma, L. Heres, E. H. J. Kroes, and E. van Oirschof, "Giddens a la Carte? Appraising Empirical Applications of Structuration Theory in Management and Organization Studies," *Journal of Political Power* 5 (2012): 239–64.

20. D. F. Witmer, "Communication and Recovery: Structuration as an Ontological Approach to Organizational Culture," *Communication Monographs* 64 (1997): 324–49.

21. S. Siebold and D. R. Seibold, "Jurors' Intuitive Rules for Deliberation: A Structurational Approach to Communication in Jury Decision Making," *Communication Monographs* 65 (1998): 282–307.

22. J. B. Walther and N. N. Bazarova, "Misattribution in Virtual Groups: The Effects of Member Distribution on Self-Serving Bias and Partner Blame," *Human Communication Research* 33 (2007): 1–26.

23. M. S. Poole, "Group Communication Theory," in L. R. Frey, ed., *The Handbook of Small Group Research* (Thousand Oaks, CA: Sage, 1996).

24. D. S. Gouran and R. Y. Hirokawa, "Effective Decision Making and Problem Solving in Groups: A Functional Perspective," in R. Y. Hirokawa, R. S. Cathcart, L. A. Samovar, and L. D. Henman, eds., *Small Group Communication Theory and Practice* (Los Angeles: Roxbury, 2003): 29.

25. D. Gouran and R. Y. Hirokawa, "Functional Theory and Communication in Decision-Making Groups: An Expanded View," in R. Y. Hirokawa and M. S. Poole, eds., *Communication and Group Decision Making*, 2nd ed. (Thousand Oaks, CA: Sage, 1996).

26. D. E. Hewes, "The Influence of Communication Processes on Group Outcomes: Antithesis and Thesis," *Human Communication Research* 35 (2009): 249–71.

27. D. F. Crown, "The Use of Group and Groupcentric Individual Goals for Culturally Heterogeneous and Homogenous Task Groups," *Small Group Research* 38 (2007): 489–508.

28. M. A. Hogg and S. A. Reid, "Social Identity, Self-Categorization, and the Communication of Group Norms," *Communication Theory* 16 (2006): 7–30.

29. A. A. G. Walvoord, E. R. Redden, L. R. Elliott, and M. D. Coovert, "Empowering Followers in Virtual Teams: Guiding Principles from Theory and Practice," *Computers in Human Behavior* 24 (2008): 1884–906.

CHAPTER 3

1. For an illuminating discussion of this topic, see S. Pinker, *How the Mind Works* (New York: Norton, 1997).

2. A. Maslow, *Toward a Psychology of Being*, 3rd ed. (Princeton, NJ: Van Nostrand, 1999).

3. A. Maslow, *Motivation and Personality* (New York: HarperCollins, 1954).

4. D. Stacks, M. Hickson III, and S. R. Hill, Jr., *Introduction to Communication Theory* (Chicago: Holt, Rinehart & Winston, 1991).

5. W. Schutz, *The Interpersonal Underworld* (Palo Alto, CA: Science & Behavior Books, 1958).

6. F. E. X. Dance, "A Helical Model of Communication," in F. E. X. Dance, ed., *Human Communication Theory* (New York: Holt, Rinehart & Winston, 1967), 294–98.

7. D. F. Crown, "The Use of Group and Groupcentric Individual Goals for Culturally Heterogeneous and Homogeneous Task Groups: An Assessment of European Work Teams," *Small Group Research* 38 (2007): 489–508.

8. C. M. Mason and M. A. Griffin, "Group Task Satisfaction: Applying the Construct of Job Satisfaction to Groups," *Small Group Research* 33 (2002): 271–312.

9. For a full discussion of mutuality of concern, see R. Patton and T. M. Downs, *Decision-Making Group Interaction: Achieving Quality*, 4th ed. (Boston: Allyn & Bacon, 2002).

10. M. A. G. Peeters, C. G. Rutte, H. F. J. M. van Tuijl, and I. M. M. J. Reyman, "The Big Five Personality Traits and Individual Satisfaction with the Team," *Small Group Research* 37 (2006): 187–211.

11. S. T. Bell, "Deep-Level Composition Variables as Predictors of Team Performance: A Meta-Analysis," *Journal of Applied Psychology* 92 (2007): 595–615.

12. M. W. Kramer, "Communication in a Community Theatre Group: Managing Multiple Group Roles," *Communication Studies* 53 (2002): 151–70.

13. O. Alnuaimi, L. P. Robert, Jr., and L. M. Maruping, "Team Size, Dispersion, and Social Loafing in Technology-Supported Teams," *Journal of Management Information Systems* 27 (2010): 203–30.

14. C. S. Palazzo, "The Social Group: Definitions," in R. S. Cathcart and L. A. Samovar, eds., *Small Group Communication: A Reader*, 6th ed. (Dubuque, IA: Brown, 1991), 11–12.
15. F. G. Chen and D. T. Kenrick, "Repulsion or Attraction? Group Membership and Assumed Attitude Similarity," *Journal of Personality and Social Psychology* 83 (2002): 111–25.
16. S. B. Feichtner and E. A. Davis, "Why Some Groups Fail: A Survey of Students' Experiences with Learning Groups," in A. Goodsell, M. Maher, and V. Tinto, eds., *Collaborative Learning: A Sourcebook for Higher Education* (University Park, PA: National Center on Postsecondary Teaching, Learning, and Assessment, 1997), 59–67.
17. J. Thibaut and H. Kelley, The Social Psychology of Groups (New Brunswick, NJ: Transaction Publishing, 1986).
18. J. C. Jackson, E. P. Lemay, Jr., D. Bilkey, and J. Halberstadt, "Beyond 'Birds of a Feather': A Social Inference Approach to Attachment-Dependent Grouping," *Journal of Experimental Social Psychology* 73 (2017): 216–21.
19. D. M. Buss, "Sex Differences in Mate Preferences: Evolutionary Hypotheses Tested in 37 Different Cultures," *Behavioral and Brain Sciences* 12 (1989): 1–49.
20. E. Hehman, J. B. Leitner, M. P. Deegan, and S. L. Gaertner, "Picking Teams: When Dominant Facial Structure Is Preferred," Journal of Experimental Social Psychology 59 (2015): 51–9.
21. R. Zajonc, "Attitudinal Effects of Mere Exposure," Journal of Personality and Social Psychology 9 (1968): 1–29.
22. M. Shaw, *Group Dynamics: The Psychology of Small Group Behavior* (New York: McGraw-Hill, 1981), 93.
23. Shaw, *Group Dynamics*, 85.
24. A. L. Johnson, M. T. Crawford, S. J. Sherman, A. M. Rutchick, D. L. Hamilton, M. B. Ferreira, and J. V. Petrocelli, "A Functional Perspective on Group Memberships: Differential Need Fulfillment in a Group Typology," Journal of Experimental and Social Psychology 42 (2006): 707–19.
25. D. Trafimow and K. A. Finlay, "The Accessibility of Group Memberships," Journal of Social Psychology 141 (2001): 509–22.
26. Definition based on one by A. G. Smith, ed., Communications and Culture (New York; Holt, Rinehart & Winston, 1966).
27. J. K. Barge and L. R. Frey, "Life in a Task Group," in L. R. Frey and J. K. Barge, eds., *Managing Group Life: Communicating in Decision-Making Groups* (Boston: Houghton Mifflin, 1997) 39.
28. Barge and Frey, "Life in a Task Group."
29. R. Shuter, "A Field Study of Nonverbal Communication in Germany, Italy, and the United States," *Communication Monographs* 44 (1977): 298–305.
30. Dodd, *Dynamics of Intercultural Communication.*
31. B. J. McCauliffe, J. Jetten, M. J. Hornsey, and M. A. Hogg, "Individualist and Collectivist Norms: When It's OK to Go Your Own Way," European Journal of Social Psychology 33 (2003): 57–70.
32. H. S. Park and T. R. Levine, "The Theory of Reasoned Action and Self-Construal: Evidence from Three Cultures," Communication Monographs 66 (1999): 199–218; M.-S. Kim, J. E. Hunter, A. Miyahara, A.-M. Horvath, M. Bresnahan, and H. Yoon, "Individual- vs. Culture-Level Dimensions of Individualism and Collectivism: Effects on Preferred Conversational Styles," Communication Monographs 63 (1996): 29–49.
33. E. T. Hall, Beyond Culture (Garden City, NY: Doubleday, 1976).
34. Hall, Beyond Culture.
35. Hall, Beyond Culture.
36. C. H. Dodd, Dynamics of Intercultural Communication (Dubuque, IA: Brown, 1997).
37. F. Yousef and N. Briggs, "The Multinational Business Organization: A Schema for the Training of Overseas Personnel in Communication," International and Intercultural Communication Annual 2 (1975): 74–85.
38. E. T. Hall, Beyond Culture (Garden City, NY: Doubleday, 1976).
39. *2012 Household Data* Annual Averages, p. 1. Bureau of Labor Statistics, Department of Labor. Washington, DC.
40. D. van Knippenberg, W.P. van Ginkel, and A.C. Homan, "Diversity Mindsets and the Performance of Diverse Teams," organizational Behavior and Human Decision Processes 121 (2013): 183–93.
41. E. Kearney, D. Gebert, and S. Voelpel, "When and How Diversity Benefits Teams: The Importance of Team Members' Need for Cognition," Academy of Management Journal 52 (2009): 581–98.
42. M. Bayazit and E. A. Mannix, "Should I Stay or Should I Go? Predicting Team Members' Intent to Remain in the Team," Small Group Research 34 (2003): 290–321.
43. A. Hajro, C.B.Gibson, and M. Pudelko, "Knowledge Exchange Processes in Multicultural Teams: Linking Organizational Diversity Climates to Teams' Effectiveness," Academy of Management Journal 60 (2017): 345–72.
44. See, for example, the cases of extreme international and expertise diversity presented in L. Gratton,

A. Voigt and T.J. Erickson, "Bridging Faultlines in Diverse Teams," MIT Sloan Management Review 48 (2007): 22–29.

45. K. Fritz, "The Diversity Dilemma: Dealing with Difference," paper presented at the Vocation of a Lutheran Institution Conference, Selinsgrove, Pennsylvania, 1999.

46. K. Van Oudenhoven-van der Zee, P. Paulus, M. Vos, and N. Parthasarathy, "The Impact of Group Composition and Attitudes Towards Diversity on Anticipated Outcomes of Diversity in Groups," Group Processes & Intergroup Relations 12 (2009): 257–80.

47. D. L. Duarte and N. Tennant Snyder, *Mastering Virtual Teams* (San Francisco, CA: Jossey-Bass, 2001) 60. Based on research by Geert Hofstede.

48. A. Sivunen, "Strengthening Identification with the Team in Virtual Teams: The Leaders' Perspective," Group Decision and Negotiation 15 (2006): 345–66.

49. R. Meneses, R. Ortega, J. Navarro, and S. D. Quijano, "Criteria for Assessing the Level of Group Development (LGD) of Work Groups," Small Group Research 39 (2008): 492–514.

50. B. W. Tuckman, "Developmental Sequence in Small Groups," Psychological Bulletin 63 (1965): 384–99.

51. R. L. Moreland and J. M. Levine, "Socialization and Trust in Work Groups," Group Processes and Intergroup Relations 5 (2002): 185–201.

52. N. Anderson and H. D. C. Thomas, "Work Group Socialization," in M. S. West, ed., Handbook of Work Group Psychology (Chichester, England: Wiley, 1996).

53. G. Chen and R. J. Klimoski, "The Impact of Expectations on Newcomer Performance in Teams as Mediated by Work Characteristics, Social Exchanges, and Empowerment," Academy of Management Journal 46 (2003): 581–607.

CHAPTER 4

1. M. Schittekatte and A. Van Hiel, "Effects of Partially Shared Information and Awareness of Unshared Information on Information Sampling," *Small Group Research* 27 (1996): 431–49.

2. D. A. Romig, *Breakthrough Teamwork: Outstanding Results Using Structured Teamwork* (Chicago: Irwin, 1996); P. R. Scholtes, B. L. Joiner, and B. J. Streibel, *The Team Handbook*, 2nd ed. (Madison, WI: Joiner Associates, 1996).

3. S. Burkhalter, J. Gastil, and T. Kelshaw, "A Conceptual Definition and Theoretical Model of Public Deliberation in Small Face-to-Face Groups," *Communication Theory* (November 2002): 398–422; C. Pavitt, "Does Communication Matter in Social Influence during Small Group Discussion? Five Positions," *Communication Studies* 44 (1993): 216–27.

4. Burkhalter, Gastil, and Kelshaw, "A Conceptual Definition and Theoretical Model."

5. For an excellent review of the importance of preparing for group discussion, see H. K. Gardner, F. Gino, and B. R. Staats, "Dynamically Integrating Knowledge in Teams: Transforming Resources into Performance," *Academy of Management Journal* 55, no. 4 (2012): 998–1022.

6. F. Rink, and N. Ellemers, "The Pernicious Effects of Unstable Work Group Membership: How Work Group Changes Undermine Unique Task Contributions and Newcomer Acceptance," *Group Processes & Intergroup Relations* 18 (2015): 6–23.

7. D. D. Chrislip and C. E. Larson, *Collaborative Leadership* (San Francisco: Jossey-Bass, 1994); J. R. Katzenback and D. K. Smith, *The Wisdom of Teams: Creating the High-Performance Organization* (New York: HarperBusiness, 1993); Romig, *Breakthrough Teamwork.*

8. W. P. van Ginkel and D. van Knippenberg, "Knowledge about the Distribution of Information and Group Decision Making: When and Why Does it Work?", *Organizational Behavior and Human Decision Processes* 108 (2009): 218–29.

9. K. J. Emich, "How Expectancy Motivation Influences Information Exchange in Small Groups," *Small Group Research* 43, no. 3 (2012): 275–94.

10. D. Cooper, "Dissimilarity and Learning in Teams: The Role of Relational Identification and Value Dissimilarity," *International Journal of Intercultural Relations* 37 (2013): 628–42.

11. V. Rousseau and C. Aubé, "Team Self-Managing Behaviors and Team Effectiveness: The Moderating Effect of Task Routineness," *Group & Organization Management* 35, no. 6 (2010): 751–81.

12. M. R. Baumann, and B. L. Bonner, "Member Awareness of Expertise, Information Sharing, Information Weighting, and Group Decision Making," *Small Group Research* 44, no. 5 (2013): 532–62.

13. J. A. Bonito, "A Longitudinal Social Relations Analysis of Participation in Small Groups," *Human Communication Research* 32 (2006): 302–21.

14. L. A. Perlow, G. A. Okhuysen, and N. P. Repenning, "The Speed Trap: Exploring the Relationship between Decision Making and Temporal Context," *Academy of Management Journal* 45 (October 2002): 931–35.

15. C. Saunders and S. Miranda, "Information Acquisition in Group Decision Making," *Information and Management* 34 (1998): 55–74.

16. M. J. Burtscher, and B. Meyer, "Promoting Good Decisions: How Regulatory Focus Affects Group Information Processing and Decision-Making," *Group Processes & Intergroup Relations* 17, no. 5 (2014): 663–81.

17. S. Covey, *The Seven Habits of Highly Effective People* (New York: Simon and Schuster, 1989).

18. M. J. Burtscher and B. Meyer, "Promoting Good Decisions."

19. D. R. Seibold and P. Kang, "Using Critical Praxis to Understand and Teach Teamwork," *Business Communication Quarterly* 71 (2008): 421–38.

20. R. Mitchell, B. Boyle, and S. Nicholas, "The Impact of Goal Structure in Team Knowledge Creation," *Group Processes & Intergroup Relations* 12, no. 5 (2009): 639–51.

21. J. Kruger and M. Evans, "If You Don't Want to Be Late, Enumerate: Unpacking Reduces the Planning Fallacy," Journal of Experimental Social Psychology 40 (2004): 586–98.

22. R. Buehler, D. Messervey, and D. Griffin, "Collaborative Planning and Prediction: Does Group Discussion Affect Optimistic Biases in Time Estimation?" *Organizational Behavior and Human Decision Processes* 97 (2005): 47–63.

23. A. W. Woolley, M. E. Gerbasi, C. F. Chabris, S. M. Kosslyn, and J. R. Hackman, "Bringing in the Experts: How Team Composition and Collaborative Planning Jointly Shape Analytic Effectiveness," *Small Group Research* 39 (2008): 352–71.

24. L. A. DeChurch and C. D. Haas, "Examining Team Planning through an Episodic Lens: Effects of Deliberate, Contingency, and Reactive Planning on Team Effectiveness," *Small Group Research* 39 (2008): 542–68.

25. J. Kotlarsky, B. V. D. Hooff, and L. Houtman, "Are We on the Same Page? Knowledge Boundaries and Transactive Memory System Development in Cross-Functional Teams," *Communication Research* 42, no. 3 (2015): 319–44.

26. S. N. Fraidin, "When Is One Head Better Than Two? Interdependent Information in Group Decision Making," *Organizational Behavior and Human Decision Processes* 9 (2004): 102–13.

27. S. Huang and H. N. Cummings, "When Critical Knowledge Is Most Critical: Centralization in Knowledge-Intensive Teams," *Small Group Research* 42, no. 6 (2011): 669–99.

28. K. C. Kostopoulos and N. Bozionelos, "Team Exploratory and Exploitative Learning: Psychological Safety, Task Conflict, and Team Performance," *Group & Organization Management* 36, no. 3 (2011): 385–415.

29. L. G. Snyder, "Teaching Teams about Teamwork: Preparation, Practice, and Performance Review," *Business Communication Quarterly* (2009): 74–79.

30. J. Campbell and G. Stasser, "The Influence of Time and Task Demonstrability on Decision-Making in Computer-Mediated and Face-to-Face Groups," *Small Group Research* 37 (2006): 271–94.

31. J. A. Bonito, "A Local Model of Information Sharing in Small Groups," *Communication Theory* 17 (2007): 252–80; J. A. Bonito, M. H. DeCamp, and E. K. Ruppel, "The Process of Information Sharing in Small Groups: Application of a Local Model," *Communication Monographs* 75 (2008): 136–57; T. Reimer, S. Kuendig, U. Hoffrage, E. Park, and V. Hinsz, "Effects of the Information Environment on Group Discussions and Decisions in the Hidden-Profile Paradigm," *Communication Monographs* 74 (2007): 1–28; M. J. Burtscher and B. Meyer, "Promoting Good Decisions."

32. D. D. Stewart and G. Stasser, "Expert Role Assignment and Information Sampling during Collective Recall and Decision Making," *Journal of Personality and Social Psychology* 69 (1995): 619–28; also see D. D. Stewart, "Stereotypes, Negativity Bias, and the Discussion of Unshared Information in Decision-Making Groups," *Small Group Research* 29 (1998): 643–68; J. R. Larson, Jr., "Modeling the Entry of Shared and Unshared Information into Group Discussion: A Review and BASIC Language Computer Program," *Small Group Research* 28 (1997): 454–79; G. Stasser, "Pooling of Unshared Information during Group Discussion," in S. Worchei, W. Wood, and J. A. Simpson, eds., *Group Process and Productivity* (Newbury Park, CA: Sage, 1992), 48–67; D. D. Henningsen and M. L. M. Henningsen, "The Effect of Individual Difference Variables on Information Sharing in Decision-Making Groups," *Human Communication Research* 30 (2004): 540–55.

33. T. A. Grice, C. Gallois, E. Jones, N. Paulsen, and V. J. Callan, "We Do It, But They Don't: Multiple Categorizations and Work Team Communication," *Journal of Applied Communication Research* 34 (2006): 331–48; T. Reimer, A. Reimer, and U. Czienskowski, "Decision-Making Groups Attenuate the Discussion Bias in Favor of Shared Information: A Meta-Analysis," *Communication Monographs* 77, no. 1 (2010): 121–42.

34. J. A. Bonito and R. A. Meyers, "Examining Functional Communication as Egocentric or Group-Centric: Application of a Latent Group Model," *Communication Monographs* 78, no. 4 (2011): 463–85.

35. G. M. Wittenbaum, A. B. Hollingshead, and I. C. Botero, "From Cooperative to Motivated Information Sharing

in Groups: Moving beyond the Hidden Profile Paradigm," *Communication Monographs* 71 (2004): 286–310; A. O. Galinsky and L. J. Kray, "From Thinking about What Might Have Been to Sharing What We Know: The Effects of Counterfactual Mind-Sets on Information Sharing in Groups," *Journal of Experimental Social Psychology* 40 (2004): 606–18.

36. M. Huang, "A Conceptual Framework of the Effects of Positive Affect and Affective Relationships on Group Knowledge Networks," *Small Group Research* 40 (2009): 323–46.

37. M. W. Kramer, P. J. Benoit, M. A. Dixon, and J. Benoit-Bryan, "Group Processes in a Teaching Renewal Retreat: Communication Functions and Dialectical Tensions," *Southern Communication Journal* 72 (2007): 145–68; S. S. K. Lam and J. Schaubroeck, "Information Sharing and Group Efficacy Influences on Communication and Decision Quality," *Asian Pacific Journal of Management* 28, (2011): 509–28.

38. D. D. Henningsen and M. L. M. Henningsen, "Do Groups Know What They Don't Know? Dealing with Missing Information in Decision-Making Groups," *Communication Research* 34 (2007): 507–25.

39. T. M. Franz and J. R. Larson, "The Impact of Experts on Information Sharing during Group Discussion," *Small Group Research* 33 (2002): 383–411.

40. C. J. Resick, T. Murase, K. R. Randall, and L. A. DeChurch, "Information Elaboration and Team Performance: Examining the Psychological Origins and Environmental Contingencies," *Organizational Behavior and Human Decision Processes* 124 (2014): 165–76.

41. R. F. Bales, *Personality and Interpersonal Behavior* (New York: Holt, Rinehart and Winston, 1970).

42. Van Ginkel and D. van Knippenberg, "Knowledge about the Distribution of Information and Group Decision Making"; W. P. van Ginkel and D. van Knippenberg, "Group Information Elaboration and Group Decision Making: The Role of Shared Task Representations," *Organizational Behavior and Human Decision Processes* 105 (2008): 82–97.

43. F. C. Brodbeck, R. Kerschreiter, A. Mojzisch, and S. Schulz-Hardt, "Group Decision Making under Conditions of Distributed Knowledge: The Information Asymmetries Model," *Academy of Management Review* 32 (2007): 459–79; K. Mehlhorn, N. Ben-Asher, V. Dutt, and C. Gonzalez, "Observed Variability and Values Matter: Toward a Better Understanding of Information Search and Decisions from Experience," *Journal of Behavioral Decision Making* 27 (2014): 328–39.

44. A. W. Woolley, J. B. Bear, J. W. Chang, and A. H. DeCostanza, "The Effects of Team Strategic Orientation on Team Process and Information Search," *Organizational Behavior and Human Decision Processes* 122 (2013): 114–26.

45. J. R. Spoor and J. R. Kelly, "The Evolutionary Significance of Effect in Groups: Communication and Group Bonding," *Group Processes & Intergroup Relations* 7 (2004): 398–412.

46. K. B. Dahlin, L. R. Weingart, and P. J. Hinds, "Team Diversity and Information Use," *Academy of Management Journal* 48 (2005): 1107–23.

47. J. R. Mesmer-Magnus, L. A. DeChurch, M. Jimenez-Rodriguez, J. Wildman, and M. Shuffler, "A Meta-analytic Investigation of Virtuality and Information Sharing in Teams," *Organizational Behavior and Human Decision Processes* 115 (2011): 214–25.

48. R. Mitchell, B. Boyle, and S. Nicholas, "The Impact of Goal Structure in Team Knowledge Creation," *Group Processes & Intergroup Relations* 12, no. 5 (2009): 639–51.

49. J. R. Rentsch, L. A. Delise, E. Salas, and M. P. Letsky, "Facilitating Knowledge Building in Teams: Can a New Team Training Strategy Help?," *Small Group Research* 41, no. 5 (2010): 505–23.

50. G. Stasser, S. Abele, and S. V. Parsons, "Information Flow and Influence in Collective Choice," *Group Processes & Intergroup Relations* 15, no. 5 (2012): 619–35.

51. A. A. Kane and F. Rink, "When and How Groups Utilize Dissenting Newcomer Knowledge: Newcomers' Future Prospects Condition the Effect of Language-Based Identity Strategies," *Group Processes & Intergroup Relations* (2016): 1–17.

52. H. Ding and X. Ding, "Project Management, Critical Praxis, and Process-Oriented Approach to Teamwork," *Business Communication Quarterly* 71 (2008): 456–71.

53. C. Brooks and J. Ammons, "Free Riding in Group Projects and the Effects of Timing, Frequency, and Specificity of Criteria in Peer Assessments," *Journal of Education for Business* 78 (2003): 268–72.

54. E. M. Stark, J. D. Shaw, and M. K. Duffy, "Preference for Group Work, Winning Orientation, and Social Loafing Behavior in Groups," *Group and Organization Management* 32 (2007): 699–723.

55. E. G. Bormann, *Discussion and Group Methods: Theory and Practice* (New York: Harper & Row, 1969). For an excellent discussion of each of the four types of discussion questions, see D. S. Gouran, "Reflections on the Type of Question as a Determinant of the Form of Interaction in Decision-Making and Problem-Solving Discussions," *Communication Quarterly* 51 (2003): 111–25.

56. Gouran, "Reflections on the Type of Question."

57. Gouran, "Reflections on the Type of Question."

58. D. S. Gouran, *Discussion: The Process of Group Decision-Making* (New York: Harper & Row, 1974), 72.
59. D. R. Seibold and R. A. Meyers, "Group Argument: A Structuration Perspective and Research Program," *Small Group Research* 38 (2007): 312–36.
60. For a discussion of the importance of arguments in helping a group achieve its goals, see M. B. Fornoff and D. D. Henningsen, "Testing the Linear Discrepancy Model in Perceptions of Group Decision-Making," *Western Journal of Communication* 81, no. 4 (2017): 507–21.
61. A. B. Pettus, "The Verdict Is In: A Study of Jury Decision-Making Factors, Moment of Personal Decision, and Jury Deliberations from the Jurors' Point of View," *Communication Quarterly* 38 (Winter 1990): 83–97.
62. N. Karelaia, "Thirst for Confirmation in Multi-attribute Choice: Does Search for Consistency Impair Decision Performance?", *Organizational Behavior and Human Decision Processes* 100 (2006): 128–43.
63. For additional information about evaluating websites, see Elizabeth Kirk, "Practical Steps in Evaluating Internet Resources," http://Milton.mse.jhu.edu:8001/research/education/practical.html.
64. E. K. Aranda, L. Aranda, and K. Conlon, *Teams: Structure, Process, Culture, and Politics* (Englewood Cliffs, NJ: Prentice Hall, 1998).

CHAPTER 5

1. J. Keyton, "Relational Communication in Groups," in L. Frey, D. S. Gouran, and M. S. Poole, eds., *The Handbook of Group Communication and Research* (Thousand Oaks, CA: Sage, 1999), 192.
2. For a full discussion of gender and communication, see J. T. Wood, *Gendered Lives: Communication, Gender and Culture*, 3rd ed. (Belmont, CA: Wadsworth, 1999); and D. K. Ivy and P. Backlund, "Exploring Gender Speak: Personal Effectiveness," in J. C. Pearson, L. H. Turner, and W. Todd-Mancillas, eds., *Gender and Communication* (New York: McGraw-Hill, 1994).
3. L. Stafford, M. Dainton, and S. Haas, "Measuring Routine and Strategic Relational Maintenance: Scale Revision, Sex versus Gender Roles, and Prediction of Relational Characteristics," *Communication Monographs* 67 (2000): 306–23; E. A. Seeley, W. L. Gardner, G. Pennington, and S. Gabriel, "Circle of Friends or Members of a Group? Sex Differences in Relational and Collective Attachments to Groups," *Group Process and Intergroup Relations* 6 (2003): 251–63.
4. M. S. Woodward, L. B. Rosenfeld, and S. K. May, "Sex Differences in Social Support in Sororities and Fraternities," *Journal of Applied Communication Research* 24 (1996): 260.
5. A. Valenzuela and P. Raghubir, "The Role of Strategy in Mixed-Gender Group Interactions: A Study of the Television Show *The Weakest Link*," *Sex Roles: A Journal of Research* 57 (2007): 293–303.
6. P. Raghubir and A. Valenzuela, "Male–Female Dynamics in Groups: A Field Study of *The Weakest Link*," *Small Group Research* 41 (2010): 41–70.
7. Definition of sexual orientation adapted from "Definitions and Common Language," Office of Student Diversity and Inclusion, Texas State University, San Marcos, TX. http://www.sdi.txstate.edu/Support-and-Empowerment/LGBTQIA-and-Allies/educationalinfo.html. Accessed September 10, 2018.
8. J.-F. Lu, D. Tjosvold, and K. Shi, "Team Training in China: Testing and Applying the Theory of Cooperation and Competition," *Journal of Applied Social Psychology* 40 (2010): 101–34.
9. J. C. McCroskey and V. P. Richmond, "Willingness to Communicate: Differing Cultural Perspectives," *Southern Communication Journal* 56 (1990): 72–77.
10. M. L. Hecht, S. Ribeau, and J. K. Alberts, "An Afro-American Perspective on Interethnic Communication," *Communication Monographs* 56 (1989): 385–410.
11. For a good review of role development in groups, see A. P. Hare, "Types of Roles in Small Groups: A Bit of History and a Current Perspective," *Small Group Research* 25 (1994): 433–48; and A. J. Salazar, "An Analysis of the Development and Evolution of Roles in the Small Group," *Small Group Research* 27 (1996): 475–503.
12. S. R. Bray and L. R. Brawley, "Role Efficacy, Role Clarity, and Role Performance Effectiveness," *Small Group Research* 33 (2002): 233–53.
13. A. Aritzeta, B. Senior, and S. Swailes, "Team Role Preference and Cognitive Styles: A Convergent Validity Study," *Small Group Research* 36 (2005): 404–36.
14. K. D. Benne and P. Sheats, "Functional Roles of Group Members," *Journal of Social Issues* 4 (Spring 1948): 41–49.
15. See also T. Driskell, J. E. Driskell, C. S. Burke, and E. Salas, "Team Roles: A Review and Integration," *Small Group Research* 48 (2017): 482–511.
16. K. D. Benne and P. Sheats, "Functional Roles of Group Members," *Journal of Social Issues* 4 (Spring 1948): 41–49.

17. E. G. Bormann, *Discussion and Group Methods: Theory and Practice*, 3rd ed. (New York: Harper & Row, 1989), 209.

18. N. Lehmann-Willenbrock, S. L. Beck, and S. Kauffield, "Emergent Team Roles in Organizational Meetings: Identifying Communication Patterns via Cluster Analysis," *Communication Studies* 67 (2016): 37–57.

19. J. W. Strijbos, R. L. Martens, W. M. G. Jochems, and N. J. Broder, "The Effect of Functional Roles on Group Efficiency: Using Multilevel Modeling and Content Analysis to Investigate Computer-Supported Collaboration in Groups," *Small Group Research* 35 (2004): 195–229.

20. C. Savelsbergh, J. M. P. Gevers, B. I. J. M. van der Heijden, and R. F. Poell, "Team Role Stress: Relationships with Team Learning and performance in Project Teams," *Group and Organization Management* 37 (2012): 67–100.

21. B. De Wever, T. Schellens, H. Van Keer, and M. Valcke, "Structuring Asynchronous Discussion Groups by Introducing Roles: Do Students Act in Line with Assigned Roles?" *Small Group Research* 39 (2008): 770–94.

22. M. S. Poole, "Group Communication and the Structuring Process," in R. S. Cathcart and L. A. Samovar, eds., *Small Group Communication: A Reader*, 6th ed. (Dubuque, IA: Brown, 1992), 275–87.

23. T. Postmes, R. Spears, and S. Cihangir, "Quality of Decision Making and Group Norms," *Journal of Personality and Social Psychology* 80 (2001): 918–30.

24. R. Swaab, K. Phillips, D. Diermeier, and V. Husted Medvec, "The Pros and Cons of Dyadic Side Conversations in Small Groups: The Impact of Group Norms and Task Type," *Small Group Research* 39 (2008): 372–90.

25. S. Schacter, "Deviation, Rejection, and Communication," *Journal of Abnormal and Social Psychology* 46 (1951): 190–207.

26. H. T. Reitan and M. E. Shaw, "Group Membership, Sex-Composition of the Group, and Conformity Behavior," *Journal of Social Psychology* 64 (1964): 45–51.

27. M. Shaw, *Group Dynamics: The Psychology of Small Group Behavior* (New York: McGraw-Hill, 1981), 281.

28. S. Asch, "Studies of Independence and Submission to Group Pressures," *Psychological Monographs* 70 (1956) (whole issue).

29. D. Paulin and B. Griffin, "Team Incivility Climate Scale: Development and Validation of the Team-Level Incivility Climate Construct," *Group and Organization Management* 42 (Sage, 2015): 315–45.

30. C. R. Graham, "A Model of Norm Development for Computer-Mediated Teamwork," *Small Group Research* 34 (2003): 322–52.

31. Adapted from C. R. Bontz, "Cultural Diversity and Group Cross-Cultural Team Research," *Journal of Applied Communication Research* 21 (1993): 12.

32. M. G. Cruz, D. Henningsen, and M. L. M. Williams, "The Presence of Norms in the Absence of Groups? The Impact of Normative Influence under Hidden-Profile Conditions," *Human Communication Research* 26 (2000): 104–24.

33. S. B. Shimanoff, "Group Interaction via Communication Rules," in R. S. Cathcart and L. A. Samovar, eds., *Small Group Communication: A Reader*, 6th ed. (Dubuque, IA: Brown, 1992).

34. P. R. Scholtes, B. L. Joiner, and B. J. Streibel, *The Team Handbook*, 2nd ed. (Madison, WI: Joiner, 1996); J. R. Katzenbach and D. K. Smith, *The Wisdom of Teams: Creating the High-Performance Organization* (New York: HarperCollins, 1993); D. A. Romig, *Breakthrough Teamwork: Outstanding Results Using Structured Teamwork®* (Chicago: Irwin, 1996).

35. Bormann, *Discussion and Group Methods*, 215.

36. V. Venkataramani, L. Zhou, M. Wang, H. Liao, and J. Shi, "Social Networks and Employee Voice: The Influence of Team Members' and Team Leaders' Social Network Positions on Employee Voice," *Organizational Behavior and Human Decision Processes* 132 (2016): 37–48.

37. J.J. Hurwitz, A.F. Zander, and B. Hymovitch, "Some Effects of Power on the Relations among Group Members," in D. Cartwright and A. Zander, eds., *Group Dynamics: Research and Theory* (New York: Harper and Row, 1953) 483–92.

38. Hurwitz, Zander, and Hymovitch, "Some Effects of Power."

39. D. C. Barnlund and C. Harland, "Propinquity and Prestige as Determinants of Communication Networks," *Sociometry* 26 (1963): 467–79.

40. V. Iacoviello and F. Lorenzi-Cioldo, "Individualistic Tendencies: When Group Status Makes the Difference," *Group Processes and Intergroup Relations* 18 (2015): 540–56.

41. Bormann, *Discussion and Group Methods*, 215.

42. Bormann, *Discussion and Group Methods*, 215.

43. C. Anderson, J. Beer, S. Srivastava, S. Spataro, and J. Chatman, "Knowing Your Place: Self-Perceptions of Status in Face-to-Face Groups," *Journal of Personality and Social Psychology* 91 (2006): 1094–110.

44. A. Dino, S. Reyson, and N. R. Branscombe, "Online Interactions between Group Members Who Differ in Status," *Journal of Language and Social Psychology* 28 (2009): 85–93.

45. R. S. Franz, "Task Interdependence and Personal Power in Teams," *Small Group Research* 29 (1998): 226–53.

46. J. R. P. French and B. H. Raven, "The Bases of Social Power," in D. Cartwright and A. Zander, eds., *Group Dynamics* (Evanston, IL: Row, Peterson, 1962) 607–23.

47. M. Mooijman, W. W. van Dijk, N. Ellemers, and E. van Dijk, "Why Leaders Punish: A Power Perspective," *Journal of Personality and Social Psychology* 109 (2015): 75–89.

48. For more information, see Andrew Flanigan and Wendy Jo Mayard Farinola, "The Technical Code of the Internet/World Wide Web," *Critical Studies in Media Communication* 17 (2000): 409–28. Also see Merlyna Lim and Mark E. Kann, "Democratic Deliberation and Mobilization on the Internet," Networked Publics–Annenberg Center for Communication (2005–2006). http://netpublics.annenberg.edu/about_netpublics/democratic_deliberation_and_mobilization_on_the_internet.

49. C. R. Berger, "Power in the Family," in M. Roloff and G. Miller, eds., *Persuasion: New Direction in Theory and Research* (Beverly Hills, CA: Sage, 1980), 217.

50. C. Anderson and G. J. Kilduff, "Why Do Dominant Personalities Attain Influence in Face-to-Face Groups? The Competence-Signaling Effects of Trait Dominance," *Journal of Personality and Social Psychology* 96 (2009): 491–503.

51. M. R. Singer, *Intercultural Communication: A Perceptual Approach* (Englewood Cliffs, NJ: Prentice Hall, 1987), 118.

52. R. S. Franz, "Task Interdependence and Personal Power in Teams."

53. K. M. Propp, "An Experimental Examination of Biological Sex as a Status Cue in Decision-Making Groups and Its Influence on Information Use," *Small Group Research* 26 (1995): 451–74; L. M. Grob, R. Meyers, and R. Schuh, "Powerful/Powerless Language Use in Group Interactions: Sex Differences or Similarities?" *Communication Quarterly* 45 (1997): 282–303.

54. L. M. Sagrestano, "Power Strategies in Interpersonal Relationships: The Effects of Expertise and Gender," *Psychology of Women Quarterly* 16 (1992): 481–95.

55. Thomas Page McBee, "My Voice Got Deeper. Suddenly, People Listened." *New York Times*, August 9, 2018. https://www.nytimes.com/2018/08/09/style/transgender-men-voice-change.html.

56. T. Welbourne, C. S. Cycyota, and C. J. Ferrante, "Wall Street Reaction to Women in IPOs," *Group and Organization Management* 32 (2007): 524–47.

57. S. S. Li, "Power and Its Relationship with Group Communication," Ph.D. dissertation, University of Iowa, 1993.

58. V. I. Armstrong, *I Have Spoken: American History through Voices of the Indians* (Chicago: Swallow Press, 1971).

59. D. McAllister, "Affect and Cognition-Based Trust as Foundations for Interpersonal Cooperation in Organizations," *Academy of Management Journal* 38 (1995): 24.

60. R. Reichert, *Self-Awareness through Group Dynamics* (Dayton, OH: Pflaum/Standard, 1970), 21.

61. J. M. Wilson, S. G. Straus, and B. McEvily, "All in Due Time: The Development of Trust in Computer-Mediated and Face-to-Face Teams," *Organizational Behavior and Human Decision Processes* 99 (2006): 16–33.

62. O. O. Oyeleye, "Trust and Virtual Teams: The Influence of Leadership Behavior, Communication, and Gender Behavior of Virtual Team Leaders on the Development of Trust in Virtual Teams," Ph.D. Dissertation, University of Maryland, 2013.

63. L. Peters and R. J. Karren, "An Examination of the Roles of Trust and Functional Diversity on Virtual Team Performance Ratings," *Group and Organizational Management* 34 (2009): 479–504.

64. N. S. Hill, K. M. Bartol, P. E. Tesluk, and G. A. Langa, "Organizational Context and Face-to-Face Interaction: Influences on the Development of Trust and Collaborative Behaviors in Computer-Mediated Groups," *Organizational Behavior and Human Decision Processes* 108 (2009): 187–201.

65. Bormann, *Discussion and Group Methods*, 181–82.

66. C. Mayo and N. Henley, *Gender and Nonverbal Behavior* (New York: Springer, 1981).

67. D. K. Ivy and P. Backlund, *Exploring Gender Speak: Personal Effectiveness in Gender Communications*, 2nd ed. (New York: McGraw-Hill, 2000).

68. G. Leventhal and M. Matturro, "Differential Effects of Spatial Crowding and Sex on Behavior," *Perceptual Motor Skills* 50 (1980): 111–19.

69. R. Sommer, "Studies in Personal Space," *Sociometry* 22 (1959): 247–60.

70. P. C. Ellsworth and L. M. Ludwig, "Visual Behavior in Social Interaction," *Journal of Communication* 22 (1972): 375–403.

71. A. Mehrabian, *Nonverbal Communication* (Chicago: Aldine Atherton, 1972).

72. N. M. Henley, *Body Politics: Power, Sex and Nonverbal Communication* (Englewood Cliffs, NJ: Prentice-Hall, 1977).

73. Henley, *Body Politics*.

74. N. N. Markel, J. Long, and T. J. Saine, "Sex Effects in Conversational Interaction: Another Look at Male

Dominance," *Human Communication Research* 2 (1976): 35–64.

75. Y. Kashima, E. S. Kashima, U. Kim, and M. Gelfand, "Describing the Social World: How Is a Person, a Group, and a Relationship Described in the East and the West?", *Journal of Experimental Social Psychology* 42 (2006): 388–96.

76. T. Katriel, "Communicative Style in Cross-Cultural Perspective: Arabs and Jews in Israel." Paper presented at the annual meeting of the Western Speech Communication Association, Sacramento, CA, 1990.

77. D. Barnlund, *Communicative Styles of Japanese and Americans: Images and Realities* (Belmont, CA: Wadsworth, 1989).

78. S. Ishii and T. Bruneau, "Silence and Silences in Cross-Cultural Perspective: Japan and the United States," in L. A. Samovar and R. E. Porter, eds., *Intercultural Communication: A Reader*, 6th ed. (Belmont, CA: Wadsworth, 1991).

79. J. Condon, " . . . So Near the United States: Notes on Communication between Mexicans and North Americans," in L. A. Samovar and R. E. Porter, eds., *Intercultural Communication: A Reader*, 6th ed. (Belmont, CA: Wadsworth, 1991).

80. T. K. Fitzgerald, *Metaphors of Identity: A Culture-Communication Dialogue* (Albany: SUNY Press, 1993).

81. E. T. Hall and M. R. Hall, *Understanding Cultural Differences* (Yarmouth, ME: Intercultural Press, 1989).

82. D. I. Ballard and D. R. Seibold, "Time Orientation and Temporary Variation across Work Groups: Implications for Group and Organizational Communication," *Western Journal of Communication* 64 (Spring 2000): 218–42.

83. Ballard and Seibold, "Time Orientation and Temporary Variations across Work Groups."

84. Donald W. Klopf and James McCroskey, *International Encounters: An Introduction to Intercultural Communication* (Boston: Allyn & Bacon, 2006).

CHAPTER 6

1. J. R. Gibb, "Defensive Communication," *Journal of Communication* 11 (September 1961): 141.

2. C. H. Tandy, "Assessing the Functions of Supportive Messages," *Communication Research* 19 (1992): 175–92.

3. E. B. Ray, "The Relationship among Communication Netwoles, Job Stress, and Burnout in Educational Organizations," *Communication Quarterly* 39 (1991): 91–100.

4. A. Goldberg and C. Larson, *Group Communication: Discussion Processes and Applications* (Englewood Cliffs, NJ: Prentice Hall, 1975), 105.

5. E. Sieburg and C. Larson, "Dimensions of Interpersonal Response," paper delivered at the annual conference of the International Communication Association, Phoenix, April 1971, 1.

6. Goldberg and Larson, *Group Communication*, 103–4.

7. A. V. Carron and L. R. Brawley, "Cohesion: Conceptual and Measurement Issues," *Small Group Research* 31 (2000): 89–106.

8. K. A. Bollen and R. H. Hoyle, "Perceived Cohesion: A Conceptual and Empirical Examination," *Social Forces* 69 (1990): 479.

9. F. Chiocchio and H. Essiembre, "Cohesion and Performance: A Meta-Analytic Review of Disparities between Project Teams, Production Teams, and Service Teams," *Small Group Research* 40 (2009): 382–420.

10. P. G. Bain, L. Mann, and A. Pirola-Merlo, "The Innovation Imperative: The Relationships between Team Climate, Innovation, and Performance in Research and Development Teams," *Small Group Research* 32 (2001): 55–73; A. Chang and P. Bordia, "A Multidimensional Approach to the Group Cohesion–Group Performance Relationship," *Small Group Research* 32 (2001): 379–405.

11. E. Rovio, J. Eskola, S. A. Kozub, J. L. Duda, and T. Lintunen, "Can High Group Cohesion Be Harmful?: A Case Study of a Junior Ice-Hockey Team," *Small Group Research* 40 (2009): 421–35.

12. W.-W. Park, M. S. Kim, and S. M. Gully, "Effect of Cohesion on the Curvilinear Relationship Between Team Efficacy and Performance," *Small Group Research* 48 (2017): 455–81.

13. J.L. Morgan, "Effects of Personality, Communication, and Cross-Training on Virtual Team Performance," Master's Thesis, University of Alabama in Huntsville, 2014.

14. S. B. Fiechtner and E. A. Davis, "Why Some Groups Fail: A Survey of Students' Experiences with Learning Groups," in A. Goodsell, M. Maher, and V. Tinto, eds., *Collaborative Learning: A Sourcebook for Higher Education* (University Park, PA: National Center on Postsecondary Teaching, Learning, and Assessment, 1992). 59–67.

15. R. DeCooman, T. Vantilborgh, M. Bal, and X. Lub, "Creating Inclusive Teams through Perceptions of Supplementary and Complementary Person–Team Fit: Examining the Relationship between Person–Team Fit and Team Effectiveness," *Group and Organization Management*41 (2016): 310–42.

16. C. Cleveland, J. Blascovich, C. Gangi, and L. Finez, "When Good Teammates Are Bad: Physiological Threat on Recently Formed Teams," *Small Group Research* 42 (2011): 3–31.
17. C. A. Bowers, J. A. Pharmer, and E. Salas, "When Member Homogeneity Is Needed in Work Teams," *Small Group Research* 31 (2000): 305–27.
18. S. S. Weber and L. M. Donahue, "Impact of Highly and Less Job-Related Diversity on Work Group Cohesion and performance: A Meta-Analysis," *Journal of Management* 27 (2001): 141–62.
19. A. Joshi and H. Roh, "The Role of Context in Work Team Diversity Research: A Meta-Analytic Review," *Academy of Management Journal* 52 (2009): 599–627.
20. C. M. Anderson, M. M. Martin, and B. L. Riddle, "Small Group Relational Satisfaction Scale: Development, Reliability and Validity," *Communication Studies* 52 (2001): 220–23.
21. C. M. Mason and M. A. Griffin, "Identifying Group Task Satisfaction at Work," *Small Group Research* 34 (2003): 413–42.
22. E. G. Bormann, *Discussion and Group Methods: Theory and Practice*, 2nd ed. (New York: Harper & Row, 1975) 162–63.
23. R. E. de Vries, B. van den Hoof, and J. A. de Ridder, "Explaining Knowledge Sharing: The Role of Communication Styles, Job Satisfaction, and Performance Beliefs," *Communication Research* 33 (2006): 115–35.
24. G. C. Homans, *The Human Group* (New York: Harcourt Brace, 1992).
25. E. C. Bartone, "The Relationship between the Perceived Level of Contribution of Virtual Team Members and Their Energization Source as Described in Jung's Typology," Ph.D. Dissertation, Eastern Michigan University, 2013.
26. F. Kuo and C. Yu, "An Exploratory Study of Trust Dynamics in Work-Oriented Virtual Teams," *Journal of Computer-Mediated Communication* 14 (2009): 823–54.
27. J. M. Wilson, S. G. Straus, and B. McEvily, "All in Due Time: The Development of Trust in Computer-Mediated and Face-to-Face Teams," *Organizational Behavior and Human Decision Processes* 99 (2006): 16–33.
28. S. Geister, U. Konradt, and G. Hertel, "Effects of Process Feedback on Motivation, Satisfaction, and Performance in Virtual Teams," *Small Group Research* 37 (2006): 459–89.
29. S. Altschuller, "Trust, Performance, and the Communication Process in Ad Hoc Decision-Making Virtual Teams," *Journal of Computer-Mediated Communication* 16 (2010): 27–47.
30. A.E. Wilson, "The Electronic Progress Log (EPL): Collaborative Development of a Tool to Improve Communication between Leaders and Staff in a Virtual Team Environment," Ph.D. Dissertation, Capella University, 2013.
31. Wilson, Straus, and McEvily, "All in Due Time."
32. B. Mullen, T. Anthony, E. Salas, and J. E. Driskell, "Group Cohesiveness and Quality of Decision Making," *Small Group Research* 25 (1994): 189–204.
33. M. G. Cruz, F. W. Boster, and J. I. Rodriguez, "The Impact of Group Size and Proportion of Shared Information on the Exchange and Integration of Information in Groups," *Communication Research* 24 (1997): 291–313.
34. S. A. Wheelan, "Group Size, Group Development, and Group Productivity," *Small Group Research* 40 (2009): 247–62.
35. P. B. Lowry, T. L. Roberts, N. C. Romano, Jr., and P. D. Cheney, "The Impact of Group Size and Social Presence on Small-Group Communication: Does Computer Mediated Communication Make a Difference?" *Small Group Research* 37 (2006): 631–61.
36. B. Ogungbamila, A. Ogungbamila, and G. A. Adetula, "Effects of Team Size and Work Team Perception on Workplace Commitment: Evidence from 23 Production Teams," *Small Group Research* 41 (2010): 725–45.
37. C. Pavitt and L. Broomwell, "Group Communication During Resource Dilemmas: 4: The Effect of Group Size," *Human Communication Research* 42 (2016): 1–20.
38. B. Prasad and D. A. Harrison, "Ties, Leaders, and Time in Teams: Strong Inference about Network Structure's Effects on Team Viability and Performance," *Academy of Management Journal* 49 (2006): 49–68.
39. A. P. Hare, *Handbook of Small Group Research*, 2nd ed. (New York: Free Press, 1976), 345.
40. J. A. Bonito, "The Effect of Contributing Substantively on Perceptions of Participation," *Small Group Research* 31 (2000): 528–53.
41. P. Chansler, P. Swamidass, and C. Cammann, "Self-Managing Work Teams: An Empirical Study of Group Cohesiveness in 'Natural Work Teams' at a Harley-Davidson Motor Company Plant," *Small Group Research* 34 (2003): 101–20.
42. C. W. Langfred, "Is Group Cohesiveness a Double-Edged Sword? An Investigation of the Effects of Cohesiveness on Performance," *Small Group Research* 29 (1998): 124–43.
43. S. J. Adams, S. G. Roch, and R. Ayman, "Communication Medium and Member Familiarity: The Effects on Decision Time, Accuracy, and Satisfaction," *Small Group Research* 36 (2005): 321–53.

44. J. C. Pearson and P. E. Nelson, *An Introduction to Human Communication* (Madison, WI: Brown and Benchmark, 1997).
45. Bormann, *Discussion and Group Methods*, 144–45.
46. D. Cartwright and A. Zander, *Group Dynamics: Research and Theory*, 3rd ed. (New York: Harper & Row, 1968), 104.
47. Hare, *Handbook of Small Group Research* 340.
48. C. Burningham and M. A. West, "Individual, Climate, and Group Interaction Processes as Predictors of Work Team Innovation," *Small Group Research* 26 (1995): 106–17.

CHAPTER 7

1. M. Mayfield and J Mayfield, "The Effects of Motivating Leader Language Use on Employee Decision Making," *International Journal of Business Communication* 53 (2016): 465–84.
2. J. Coupland, "Small Talk: Social Function," *Research on Language and Social Interaction* 36 (2003): 1–6; M. M. Step and M. O. Finucane, "Interpersonal Communication Motives in Everyday Interactions," *Communication Quarterly* 50 (2002): 93–100.
3. R. W. Young and C. M. Cates, "Emotional and Directive Listening in Peer Mentoring," *International Journal of Listening* 18 (2004): 21–33; also see A. N. Kluger and K. Zaidel, "Are Listeners Perceived as Leaders?" *International Journal of Listening* 27(2) (2013): 73–84; D. A. Romig, *Side by Side Leadership* (Marietta, GA: Bard, 2001).
4. K. J. Lloyd and S. C. Voelpel, "From Listening to Leading: Toward an Understanding of Supervisor Listening within the Framework of Leader–Member Exchange Theory," *International Journal of Business Communication* 54 (2017): 431–51.
5. G. D. Bodie and D. L. Worthington, "Revisiting the Listening Styles Profile (LSP-16): A Confirmatory Factor Analytic Approach to Scale Validation and Reliability Estimation," *International Journal of Listening* 24, no. 2 (2010): 69–88; L. Rehling, "Improving Teamwork through Awareness of Conversational Styles," *Business Communication Quarterly* 67 (2004): 475–82.
6. Rehling, "Improving Teamwork through Awareness of Conversational Styles."
7. G. D. Bodie and D. L. Worthington, "Revisiting the Listening Styles Profile (LSP-16): A Confirmatory Factor Analytic Approach to Scale Validation and Reliability Estimation," *International Journal of Listening* 24.2 (2010): 69–88.
8. G. D. Bodie and D. L. Worthington, "Revisiting the Listening Styles Profile (LSP-16)"; G. D. Bodie, C. C. Gearhart, and D. L. Worthington, "The Listening Styles Profile—Revised (LSP-R): A Scale of Revision and Evidence for Validity," *Communication Quarterly* 61, no. 1 (2013): 72–90; G. D. Bodie, J. P. Denham, and C. C. Gearhart, "Listening as a Goal-Directed Activity," *Western Journal of Communication* 78, no. 5 (2014): 668–84.
9. C. M. Sims, "Do the Big-Five Personality Traits Predict Empathic Listening and Assertive Communication?" *International Journal of Listening* 31 (2017): 163–88.
10. L. A. Janusik, "Building Listening Theory: The Validation of the Conversational Listening Span," *Communication Studies* 58, no. 2 (June 2007): 139; R. W. Young and C. M. Cates, "Emotional and Directive Listening in Peer Mentoring," *International Journal of Listening* 18 (2004): 21–33; also see Romig, *Side by Side Leadership.*
11. L. L. Barker and K. W. Watson, *Listen Up* (New York: St. Martin's Press, 2000); also see M. Imhof, "Who Are We as We Listen? Individual Listening Profiles in Varying Contexts," *International Journal of Listening* 18 (2004): 36–45.
12. For support of the validity and reliability of the Listening Styles Profile, see D. L. Worthington, "Exploring the Relationship between Listening Style Preference and Personality," *International Journal of Listening* 17 (2003): 68–87; also see J. B. Weaver, K. W. Watson, and L. L. Barker, "Individual Differences in Listening Styles: Do You Hear What I Hear?" *Personality and Individual Differences* 20 (1996): 381–87; S. Sargent, J. B. Weaver, and C. Kiewitz, "Correlates between Communication Apprehension and Listening Style Preferences," *Communication Research Reports* 14 (1997): 74–78; M. K. Johnston, J. B. Weaver, K. W. Watson, and L. B. Barker, "Listening Styles: Biological or Psychological Differences?" *International Journal of Listening* 14 (2000): 32–46.
13. Bodie, Denham, and Gearhart, "Listening as a Goal-Directed Activity."
14. L. L. Barker and K. W. Watson, *Listen Up*; also see M. Imhof, "Who Are We as We Listen? Individual Listening Profiles in Varying Contexts," *International Journal of Listening* 18 (2004): 36–45.
15. M. S. Mast, K. Jonas, C. K. Cronauer, and A. Darioly, "On the Importance of Interpersonal Sensitivity for Good Leadership," *Journal of Applied Social Psychology* 42 (2012): 1043–68.
16. L. A. Janusik and A. D. Wolvin, "24 Hours in a Day: A Listening Update to the Time Studies," *International Journal of Listening* 23 (2009): 104–20.

17. B. J. Allen, "Diversity and Organizational Communication," *Journal of Applied Communication Research* 23 (1995): 143–55.
18. R. Leonard and D. C. Locke, "Communication Stereotypes: Is Interracial Communication Possible?" *Journal of Black Studies* 23 (1993): 332–43.
19. J. Shotter, "Listening in a Way that Recognizes/Realizes the World of 'the Other'," *The International Journal of Listening* 23 (2009): 21.
20. K. K. Halone and L. L. Pecchioni, "Relational Listening: A Grounded Theoretical Model," *Communication Reports* 14 (2001): 59–71.
21. L. A. Janusik and S. A. Keaton, "Toward Developing a Cross-Cultural Metacognition Instrument for Listening in First Language Contexts: The (Janusik-Keaton) Metacognitive Listening Instrument," *Journal of Intercultural Communication Research* 44, no. 4 (2015): 288–306.
22. D. F. Barone, P. S. Hutchings, H. J. Kimmel, H. L. Traub, J. T. Cooper, and C. M. Marshall, "Increasing Empathic Accuracy Through Practice and Feedback in a Clinical Interviewing Course," *Journal of Social and Clinical Psychology* 24 (2005): 156–71.
23. M. Imhof, "How to Listen More Efficiently: Self-Monitoring Strategies in Listening," *International Journal of Listening* 17 (2003): 2–19.
24. Kluger and Zaidel, "Are Listeners Perceived as Leaders?"
25. A. Mehrabian, *Nonverbal Communication* (Chicago: Aldine Atherton, 1972), 108.
26. K. K. Halone and L. L. Pecchioni, "Relational Listening: A Grounded Theoretical Model," *Communication Reports* 14 (2001): 59–71.
27. For a review of the role of empathy in enhancing the quality of interpersonal relationships, as well as in addressing social and political problems, see J. D. Trout, The Empathy Gap: Building Bridges to the Good Life and the Good Society (New York: Viking, 2009).
28. V. Brown, M. Tumeo, T. S. Larey, and P. B. Paulus, "Modeling Cognitive Interactions During Group Brainstorming," *Small Group Research* 4 (1998): 495–536.
29. R. L. Birdwhistell, *Kinesics and Context* (Philadelphia: University of Pennsylvania, 1970). For a comprehensive review of nonverbal communication in small groups, see S. M. Ketrow, "Missing Link: Nonverbal Messages in Group Communication Research," paper presented at the annual meeting of the Speech Communication Association, November 1994.
30. For an excellent literature review of nonverbal communication and groups, see S. M. Ketrow, "Nonverbal Aspects of Group Communication," in L. Frey, ed., *The Handbook of Group Communication Theory and Research* (Thousand Oaks, CA: Sage, 1999), 251–87.
31. P. Ekman and W. V. Friesen, "The Repertoire of Nonverbal Behavior: Categories, Origins, Usage, and Coding," *Semiotica* 1 (1969): 49–98.
32. W. S. Condon and W. D. Ogston, "Soundfilm Analysis of Normal and Pathological Behavior Patterns," *Journal of Nervous and Mental Disease* 143 (1966): 338–47.
33. P. Ekman and W. V. Friesen, "Hand Movements," *Journal of Communication* 22 (1972): 353–74; also see P. E. R. Bitti and I. Poggi, "Symbolic Nonverbal Behavior: Talking through Gestures," in R. S. Feldman and B. Rime, eds., *Fundamentals of Nonverbal Behavior* (Cambridge, UK: Cambridge University Press, 1991).
34. M. Argyle and A. Kendon, "The Experimental Analysis of Social Performance," in L. Berkowitz, ed., *Advances in Experimental Social Psychology*, vol. 3 (New York: Academic Press, 1967), 55–98.
35. M. L. Knapp and J. A Hall, *Nonverbal Communication in Human Interaction* (Boston: Wadsworth/Cengage, 2014), 297.
36. S. A. Beebe, "Eye Contact: A Nonverbal Determinant of Speaker Credibility," *Speech Teacher* 23 (1974): 21–25; S. A. Beebe, "Effects of Eye Contact, Posture and Vocal Inflection upon Credibility and Comprehension," *Australian Scan Journal of Nonverbal Communication* 7–8 (1979–1980): 57–70; Martin Cobin, "Response to Eye Contact," *Quarterly Journal of Speech* 48 (1963): 415–19; T. R. Wagner, "The Effects of Speaker Eye Contact and Gender on Receiver's Assessments of the Speaker and Speech," *Ohio Communication Journal* 51 (2013): 217–36.
37. A. Kendon, "Some Functions of Gaze-Direction in Social Interaction," *Acta Psychologica* 26 (1967): 22–63.
38. A. Kalma, "Hierarchisation and Dominance Assessment at First Glance," *European Journal of Social Psychology* 21 (1991): 165–81.
39. S. H. Yoo and S. E. Noyes, "Recognition of Facial Expressions of Negative Emotions in Romantic Relationships," *Journal of Nonverbal Behavior* 40 (2016): 1–12.
40. A. Kalma, "Gazing in Triads: A Powerful Signal in Floor Apportionment," *British Journal of Social Psychology* 31 (1992): 21–39.
41. J. K. Burgoon, "Spatial Relationships in Small Groups," in R. Y. Hirokawa, R. S. Cathcart, L. A. Samovar, and L. D. Henman, eds., *Small Group Communication: Theory and Practice* (Los Angeles: Roxbury, 2003), 85–96.

42. E. T. Hall, *The Hidden Dimension* (Garden City, NY: Doubleday, 1966); also see R. Sommer, "Studies in Personal Space," *Sociometry* 22 (1959): 247–60; N. M. Henley, *Body Politics: Power, Sex and Nonverbal Communication* (Englewood Cliffs, NJ: Prentice Hall, 1977).

43. A. Mehrabian, "Significance of Posture and Position in the Communication of Attitude and Status Relationships," *Psychological Bulletin* 71 (1960): 363.

44. B. Steinzor, "The Spatial Factors in Face-to-Face Discussion Groups," *Journal of Abnormal and Social Psychology* 45 (1950): 552–55.

45. R. L. Michelini, R. Passalacqua, and J. Cusimano, "Effects of Seating Arrangements on Group Participation," *Journal of Social Psychology* 99 (1976): 179–86.

46. C. H. Silverstein and D. J. Stang, "Seating Position and Interaction in Triads: A Field Study," *Sociometry* 39(1976): 166–70.

47. L. T. Howells and S. W. Becker, "Seating Arrangements and Leadership Emergence," *Journal of Abnormal and Social Psychology* 64 (1962): 148–50.

48. K. K. Sereno and G. J. Hawkins, "The Effect of Variations in Speakers' Nonfluency upon Audience Ratings of Attitude toward the Speech Topic and Speakers' Credibility," *Speech Monographs* 34 (1967): 58–64; G. R. Miller and M. A. Hewgill, "The Effect of Variations in Nonfluency on Audience Ratings of Source Credibility," *Quarterly Journal of Speech* 50 (1964): 36–44.

49. J. R. Davitz, *The Communication of Emotional Meaning* (New York: McGraw-Hill, 1964); P. Ekman and W.V. Friesen, "Hand Movements," *Journal of Communication* 22 (1972): 353–74.

50. G. Baker, "The Effects of Synchronous Collaborative Technologies on Decision Making: A Study of Virtual Teams," *Information Resources Management Journal* 15 (2002): 79–93.

51. Baker, "The Effects of Synchronous Collaborative Technologies on Decision Making."

52. D. Morris, *People Watching* (London: Vantage Press, 2002) 104. For a review of eye contact and facial expression research in intercultural settings, see M. Yuki, W. M. Maddux, and T. Masuda, "Are the Windows to the Soul the Same in the East and West? Cultural Differences in Using Eyes and Mouths as Cues to Recognize Emotions in Japan and the United States," *Journal of Experimental Social Psychology* 43 (2007): 303–11.

53. A. Mehrabian, *Silent Messages* (Belmont, CA: Wadsworth, 1981), 108.

54. Mehrabian, *Silent Messages*, 108.

CHAPTER 8

1. E. Ross and A. Holland, *100 Great Businesses and the Minds behind Them* (Naperville, IL: Sourcebooks, 2006), 105.

2. G. Kraus, "The Psychodynamics of Constructive Aggression in Small Groups," *Small Group Research* 28 (1997): 122–45.

3. S. M. Farmer and J. Roth, "Conflict-Handling Behavior in Work Groups: Effects of Group Structure, Decision Processes, and Time," *Small Group Research* 29 (1998): 669–713.

4. W. W. Wilmot and J. L. Hocker, *Interpersonal Conflict* (New York: McGraw-Hill, 2007), 8.

5. D. Paulin and B. Griffin, "Team Incivility Climate Scale: Development and Validation of the Team-Level Incivility Climate Construct," *Group & Organizational Management* 42, no. 3 (2017): 315–45.

6. J. T. Garner and D. L. Iba, "Why Are You Saying That? Increases in Gaze Duration as Responses to Group Member Dissent," *Communication Studies* 68, no. 3 (2017): 353–67.

7. M. Burgoon, J. K. Heston, and J. McCroskey, *Small Group Communication: A Functional Approach* (New York: Holt, Rinehart & Winston, 1974), 76.

8. J. Wombacher and J. Felfe, "The Interplay of Team and Organizational Commitment in Motivating Employees' Interteam Conflict Handling," *Academy of Management Journal* 60, no. 4 (2017): 1554–81

9. O. Dahlback, "A Conflict Theory of Group Risk Taking," *Small Group Research* 34 (2003): 251–89.

10. T. Hentschel, M. Schemla, J. Wegge, and E. Kearney, "Perceived Diversity and Team Functioning: The Role of Diversity Beliefs and Affect," *Small Group Research* 44, no. 1 (2013): 33–61.

11. V. Schei and J. K. Rognes, "Small Group Negotiation: When Members Differ in Motivational Orientation," *Small Group Research* 36 (2005): 289–320.

12. S. Ting-Toomey, "Toward a Theory of Conflict and Culture," in W. Gudykunst, L. Stewart, and S. Ting-Toomey, eds., *Communication, Culture, and Organizational Processes* (Beverly Hills, CA: Sage, 1985).

13. L. L. Greer, K. A. Jehn, and E. A. Mannix, "Conflict Transformation: A Longitudinal Investigation of the Relationships between Different Types of Intragroup Conflict and the Moderating Role of Conflict Resolution," *Small Group Research* 39 (2008): 278–302.

14. V. D. Wall and J. L. Nolan, "Small Group Conflict: A Look at Equity, Satisfaction, and Styles of Conflict-Management," *Small Group Behavior* 18 (May 1987): 188–211.

15. B. A. Fisher, "Decision Emergence: Phases in Group Decision Making," *Speech Monographs* 37 (1970): 60.
16. K. A. Jehn and E. A. Mannix, "The Dynamic Nature of Conflict: A Longitudinal Study of Intragroup Conflict and Group Performance," *Academy of Management Journal* 44 (April 2001): 238–52.
17. Portions of the following discussion of misconceptions about conflict were adapted from R. J. Doolittle, *Orientations to Communication and Conflict* (Chicago: Science Research Associates, 1976), 7–9.
18. F. E. Jandt, ed., *Conflict Resolution through Communication* (New York: Harper & Row, 1973).
19. C. R. Franz and K. G. Jin, "The Structure of Group Conflict in a Collaborative Work Group during Information Systems Development," *Journal of Applied Communication Research* 23 (1995): 108–27.
20. U. Klocke, "How to Improve Decision Making in Small Groups: Effects of Dissent and Training Interventions," *Small Group Research* 38 (2007): 437–68; S. Schulz-Hardt, A. Mojzisch, F. C. Brodbeck, R. Kerschreiter, and D. Frey, "Group Decision Making in Hidden Profile Situations: Dissent as a Facilitator for Decision Quality," *Journal of Personality and Social Psychology* 91 (2006): 1080–93.
21. Doolittle, *Orientations to Communication*, 8.
22. G. R. Miller and M. Steinberg, *Between People: New Analysis of Interpersonal Communication* (Chicago: Science Research Associates, 1975), 264.
23. S. D. Johnson and C. Bechler, "Examining the Relationship between Listening Effectiveness and Leadership Emergence: Perceptions, Behaviors, and Recall," *Small Group Research* 29 (1998): 452–71.
24. Miller and Steinberg, *Between People*.
25. F. R. C. D. Wit, K. A. Jehn, and D. Scheepers, "Task Conflict, Information Processing, and Decision-Making: The Damaging Effect of Relationship Conflict," *Organizational Behavior and Human Decision Processes* 122 (2013): 177–89; K. Yong, S. J. Sauer, and E. A. Mannix, "Conflict and Creativity in Interdisciplinary Teams," *Small Group Research* 45, no. 3 (2014): 266–89; S. E. Humphrey, F. Aime, L. Cushenbery, A. D. Hill, and J. Fairchild, "Team Conflict Dynamics: Implications of a Dyadic View of Conflict for Team Performance," *Organizational Behavior and Human Decision Processes* 142 (2017): 58–70.
26. Wit, Jehn, and Scheepers, "Task Conflict"; Yong, Sauer, and Mannix, "Conflict and Creativity in Interdisciplinary Teams"; Humphrey, Aime, Cushenbery, Hill, and Fairchild, "Team Conflict Dynamics."
27. For a discussion of the origin, function, and significance of process conflict, see K. J. Behfar, E. A. Mannix, Randall S. Peterson, and W. M. Trochim, "Conflict in Small Groups: The Meaning and Consequences of Process Conflict," *Small Group Research* 42, no. 2 (2011): 127–76.
28. D. J. Devine, "Effects of Cognitive Ability, Task Knowledge, Information Sharing, and Conflict on Group Decision-Making Effectiveness," *Small Group Research* 30 (1999): 608–34.
29. S. Kerwin, A. Doherty, and A. Harman, "'It's Not Conflict, It's Differences of Opinion': An In-Depth Examination of Conflict in Nonprofit Boards," *Small Group Research* 42, no. 5 (2011): 562–94.
30. H. Guenter, H. V. Emmerik, B. Schreurs, T. Kuypers, A. V. Iterson, and G. Notelaers, "When Task Conflict Becomes Personal: The Impact of Perceived Team Performance," *Small Group Research* 47, no. 5 (2016): 569–604.
31. J. Sell, M. J. Lovaglia, E. A. Mannix, C. D. Samuelson, and R. K. Wilson, "Investigating Conflict, Power, and Status within and among Groups," *Small Group Research* 35 (2004): 44–72.
32. B. M. Gayle and R. W. Preiss, "Assessing Emotionality in Organizational Conflicts," *Management Communication Quarterly* 12 (1998): 280–302; A. Ostell, "Managing Dysfunctional Emotions in Organizations," *Journal of Management Studies* 33 (1996): 525–57.
33. J. Meng, J. Fulk, and Y. C. Yuan, "The Roles and Interplay of Intragroup Conflict and Team Emotion Management on Information Seeking Behaviors in Team Contexts," *Communication Research* 42, no. 5 (2015): 675–700.
34. T. Abdel-Monem, S. Bingham, J. Marincic, and A. Tomkins, "Deliberation and Diversity: Perceptions of Small Group Discussions by Race and Ethnicity," *Small Group Research* 41, no. 6 (2010): 746–76.
35. K. W. Phillips and D. L. Loyd, "When Surface and Deep-Level Diversity Collide: The Effects on Dissenting Group Members," *Organizational Behavior and Human Decision Processes* 99 (2006): 143–60.
36. K. W. Phillips, G. B. Northcraft, and M. A. Neale, "Surface-Level Diversity and Decision-Making in Groups: When Does Deep-Level Similarity Help?" *Group Processes and Intergroup Relations* 9 (2006): 467–82.
37. R. Rodriguez, "Challenging Demographic Reductionism: A Pilot Study Investigating Diversity in Group Composition," *Small Group Research* 26 (1998): 744–59.

38. R. Kilmann and K. Thomas, "Interpersonal Conflict-Handling Behavior as Reflections of Jungian Personality Dimensions," *Psychological Reports* 37 (1975): 971–80.

39. K. Furumo, "The Impact of Conflict and Conflict Management Style on Deadbeats and Deserters in Virtual Teams," *Journal of Computer Information Systems* (Summer 2009): 66–73.

40. U. Becker-Beck, "Methods for Diagnosing Interaction Strategies: An Application to Group Interaction in Conflict Situations," *Small Group Research* 32 (2001): 259–82.

41. T. M. Brown and C. E. Miller, "Communication Networks in Task-Performing Groups: Effects of Task Complexity, Time Pressure, and Interpersonal Dominance," *Small Group Research* 31 (2000): 131–57.

42. B. Beersma, J. R. Hollenbeck, D. E. Conlon, S. E. Humphrey, H. Moon, and D. R. Ilgen, "Cutthroat Cooperation: The Effects of Team Role Decisions on Adaptation to Alternative Reward Structures," *Organizational Behavior and Human Decision Processes* 108 (2009): 131–42.

43. A. Sinclair, "The Effects of Justice and Cooperation on Team Effectiveness," *Small Group Research* 34 (2003): 74–100.

44. D. Romig, *Side-by-Side Leadership: Achieving Outstanding Results Together* (Austin, TX: Bard Press, 2001).

45. C. Kirchmeyer and A. Cohen, "Multicultural Groups," *Group & Organization Management* 17 (June 1992): 153–70; C. L. Wong, D. Tjosvold, and F. Lee, "Managing Conflict in a Diverse Work Force: A Chinese Perspective in North America," *Small Group Research* 23 (August 1992): 302–21.

46. J. T. Polzer, C. B. Crisp, S. L. Jarvenpaa, and J. W. Kim, "Extending the Faultline Model to Geographically Dispersed Teams: How Colocated Subgroups Can Impair Group Functioning," *Academy of Management Journal* 49 (2006): 659–92.

47. M. A. Dorado, F. J. Medina, L. Munduate, I. F. J. Cisneros, and M. Euwema, "Computer-Mediated Negotiation of an Escalated Conflict," *Small Group Research* 33 (2002): 509–24.

48. J. B. Walther, "In Point of Practice, Computer-Mediated Communication and Virtual Groups: Applications to Interethnic Conflict," *Journal Applied Communication Research* 37, no. 3 (August 2009): 225–38.

49. M. Montoya-Weiss, A. P. Massey, and M. Song, "Getting It Together: Temporal Coordination and Conflict Management in Global Virtual Teams," *Academy of Management Journal* 44 (December 2001): 1251–62.

50. J. P. Walsh and N. G. Maloney, "Collaboration Structure, Communication Media, and Problems in Scientific Work Teams," *Journal of Computer-Mediated Communication* 12 (2007): 712–32. Also see P. Bosch-Sijtsema, "The Impact of Individual Expectations and Expectation Conflicts on Virtual Teams," *Group Organization Management* 32 (2007): 358–88; S. B. Nicholls and R. E. Rice, "A Dual-Identity Model of Responses to Deviance in Online Groups: Integrating Social Identity Theory an Expectancy Violations Theory," *Communication Theory* 27 (2017): 243–68.

51. A. Zornoza, P. Ripoll, and J. M. Peiro, "Conflict Management in Groups That Work in Two Different Communication Contexts: Face-to-Face and Computer-Mediated Communication," *Small Group Research* 33 (2002): 481–508.

52. S. M. Miranda, "Avoidance of Groupthink: Meeting Management Using Group Support Systems," *Small Group Communication Research* 25 (February 1994): 105–36.

53. D. D. Henningsen, M. L. M. Henningsen, J. Eden, and M. G. Cruz, "Examining the Symptoms of Groupthink and Retrospective Sensemaking," Small Group Research 37 (2006): 36–64.

54. I. L. Janis, *Victims of Groupthink* (Boston: Houghton Mifflin, 1973); D. C. Matz and W. Wood, "Cognitive Dissonance in Groups: The Consequences of Disagreement," *Journal of Personality and Social Psychology* 88 (2005): 22–37.

55. R. Y. Hirokawa, D. S. Gouran, and A. Martz, "Understanding the Sources of Faulty Group Decision Making: A Lesson from the *Challenger* Disaster," *Small Group Behavior* 19 (November 1988): 411–33.

56. D. Jehl, "Panel Unanimous: 'Group Think' Backed Prewar Assumptions, Report Concludes," *New York Times* (July 10, 2004), p. I; also see *The 9/11 Commission Report: Final Report of the National Commission on Terrorist Attacks upon the United States* (Washington, DC: National Commission on Terrorist Attacks, 2004).

57. J. F. Veiga, "The Frequency of Self-Limiting Behavior in Groups: A Measure and an Explanation," *Human Relations* 44 (1991): 877–95.

58. Adapted from I. L. Janis, "Groupthink," *Psychology Today* 5 (November 1971): 43–46, 74–76.

59. M. D. Street, "Groupthink: An Examination of Theoretical Issues, Implications, and Future Research Suggestions," *Small Group Research* 28 (1997): 72–93; M. D. Street and W. P. Anthony, "A Conceptual Framework Establishing the Relationship between Groupthink and Escalating Commitment Behavior," *Small Group Research* 28 (1997): 267–93; A. A. Mohaned and

F. A. Wiebe, "Toward a Process Theory of Groupthink," *Small Group Research* 27 (1996): 416–30; K. Granstrom and D. Stiwne, "A Bipolar Model of Groupthink: An Expansion of Janis's Concept," *Small Group Research* 29 (1998): 32–56; W. Park, "A Comprehensive Empirical Investigation of the Relationships among Variables in the Groupthink Model," *Journal of Organizational Behavior* 21 (2000): 873–87.

60. J. A. Goncalo, E. Polman, and C. Maslach, "Can Confidence Come Too Soon? Collective Efficacy, Conflict and Group Performance Over Time," *Organizational Behavior and Human Decision Process* 113 (2010): 13–24.

61. L. L. Greer, H. M. Caruso, and K. A. Jehn, "The Bigger They Are, the Harder They Fall: Linking Team Power, Team Conflict, and Performance," *Organizational Behavior and Human Decision Process* 116 (2011): 116–28.

62. W. Park, "A Review of Research on Groupthink," *Journal of Behavioral Decision Making* 3 (1990): 229–45; Street, "Groupthink"; Street and Anthony, "A Conceptual Framework Establishing the Relationship between Groupthink and Escalating Commitment Behavior."

63. R. Hotz and N. Miller, "Intergroup Competition, Attitudinal Projection, and Opinion Certainty: Capitalizing on Conflict," *Group Processes and Intergroup Relations* 41 (2001): 61–73.

64. R. J. W. Cline, "Detecting Groupthink: Methods for Observing the Illusion of Unanimity," Communication Quarterly38 (Spring 1990): 112–26.

65. For a discussion of the role of the central negative, see E. G. Bormann, *Discussion and Group Methods: Theory and Practice* (New York: Harper & Row, 1969).

66. P. Hutchison, J. Jetten, and R. Gutierrez, "Deviant But Desirable: Group Variability and Evaluation of Atypical Group Members," *Journal of Experimental Social Psychology* 47 (2011): 1155–61.

67. K. Andersen and T. Clevenger, Jr., "A Summary of Experimental Research in Ethos," *Speech Monographs* 30 (1963): 59–78.

68. C. B. Gibson and T. Saxton, "Thinking Outside the Black Box: Outcomes of Team Decisions with Third-Party Intervention," *Small Group Research* 36 (2005): 208–36.

69. K. Thomas and W. Schmidt, "A Survey of Managerial Interests with Respect to Conflict," *Academy of Management Journal* 19 (1976): 315–18.

70. J. M. Juran, *Juran on Planning for Quality* (New York: Free Press, 1988).

71. J. M. George and E. Dane, "Affect, Emotion, and Decision Making," *Organizational Behavior and Human Decision Processes* 136 (2016): 47–55.

72. Robert Bolton, *People Skills: How to Assert Yourself, Listen to Others, and Resolve Conflicts* (New York: Touchstone, 1986), 217.

73. Gayle and Preiss, "Assessing Emotionality in Organizational Conflicts."

74. A. Ostell, "Managing Dysfunctional Emotionality in Organizations," *Journal of Management Studies* 33 (1996): 523–57.

75. O. B. Ayoko, V. J. Callan, and C. E. J Härtel, "The Influence of Team Emotional Intelligence Climate on Conflict and Team Members' Reactions to Conflict," *Small Group Research* 39 (2008): 121–49.

76. For an excellent review of causes of anger during conflict, see R. J. Turner, D. Russell, R. Glover, and P. Hutto, "The Social Antecedents of Anger Proneness in Young Adulthood," *Journal of Health and Social Behavior* 45 (2007): 68–83; W. R. Cupach, D. J. Canary, and B. H. Spitzberg, *Competence in Interpersonal Conflict* (Long Grove, IL: Waveland Press, 2010), 91–106.

77. J. Gottman, C. Notarius, J. Godso, and H. Markman, *A Couple's Guide to Communication* (Champaign, IL: Research Press, 1976).

78. A. M. Bippus and S. L. Young, "Owning Your Emotions: Reactions to Expressions of Self- versus Other-Attributed Positive and Negative Emotions," *Journal of Applied Communication Research* 33 (2005): 26–45.

79. Bippus and Young, "Owning Your Emotions."

80. M. Seo and L. F. Barrett, "Being Emotional during Decision Making—Good or Bad? An Empirical Investigation," *Academy of Management Journal* 50 (2007): 923–40.

81. J. L. Hocker and W. W. Wilmot, *Interpersonal Conflict Management* (New York: McGraw-Hill, 2007).

82. R. A. Meyers and D. E. Brashers, "Argument in Group Decision Making: Explicating a Process Model and Investigating the Argument–Outcome Link," *Communication Monographs* 65 (1998): 261–81.

83. Becker-Beck, "Methods for Diagnosing Interaction Strategies."

84. R. Fisher and W. Ury, *Getting to Yes: Negotiating Agreement without Giving In* (Boston: Houghton Mifflin, 1991).

85. R. Fisher and W. Ury, *Getting to Yes.*"

86. Hocker and Wilmot, *Interpersonal Conflict Management*; Fisher and Ury, *Getting to Yes*; R. Bolton, *People Skills: How to Assert Yourself, Listen to Others and Resolve Conflict* (New York: Simon & Schuster, 1979) 217; D. A. Romig and L. J. Romig, *Structured Teamwork Guide* (Austin, TX: Performance Resource, 1990); D. A. Romig, *Breakthrough Teamwork: Outstanding Results Using Structured Teamwork* (New York: Irwin, 1996).

87. J. B. Walther, "In Point of Practice, Computer-Mediated Communication and Virtual Groups: Applications to Interethnic Conflict," *Journal of Applied Communication Research* 37 (2009): 225–38; also see J. W. Chesebro, D. T. McMahan, and P. C. Russett, *Internet Communication* (New York: Peter Lang, 2014).

88. Becker-Beck, "Methods for Diagnosing Interaction Strategies."

89. Miranda, "Avoidance of Groupthink."

90. T. Kameda, T. Wisdom, W. Toyokawa, and K. Inukai, "Is Consensus-Seeking Unique to Humans? A Selective Review of Animal Group Decision-Making and its Implications for (Human) Social Psychology," *Group Processes & Intergroup Relations* 15, no. 5 (2012): 673–89.

91. For an excellent discussion of the definition of consensus, see M. A. Renz, "The Meaning of Consensus and Blocking for Cohousing Groups," *Small Group Research* 37 (2006): 351–76.

92. P. J. Boyle, D. Hanlon, and J. E. Russo, "The Value of Task Conflict to Group Decision," *Journal of Behavioral Decision Making* 25 (2012): 217–27.

93. R. Y. Hirokawa, "Consensus Group Decision-Making, Quality of Decision and Group Satisfaction: An Attempt to Sort 'Fact' from 'Fiction,'" *Central States Speech Journal* 33 (Summer 1982): 407–15.

94. R. S. DeStephen and R. Y. Hirokawa, "Small Group Consensus: Stability of Group Support of the Decision, Task Process, and Group Relationships," *Small Group Behavior* 19 (May 1988): 227–39.

95. Portions of the following section on consensus were adapted from J. A. Kline, "Ten Techniques for Reaching Consensus in Small Groups," *Air Force Reserve Officer Training Corps Education Journal* 19 (Spring 1977): 19–21.

96. D. S. Gouran, "Variables Related to Consensus in Group Discussions of Questions of Policy," *Speech Monographs* 36 (August 1969): 385–91; T. J. Knutson, "An Experimental Study of the Effects of Orientation Behavior on Small Group Consensus," *Speech Monographs* 39 (August 1972): 159–65; J. A. Kline, "Orientation and Group Consensus," *Central States Speech Journal* 23 (Spring 1972): 44–47.

97. A. Gurtner, F. Tschan, N. K. Semmer, and C. Nagele, "Getting Groups to Develop God Strategies: Effects of Reflexivity Interventions on Team Process, Team Performance, and Shared Mental Models," *Organizational Behavior and Human Decision Processes* 102 (2007): 127–42.

98. Gouran, "Variables Related to Consensus in Group Discussions of Questions of Policy"; Knutson, "Experimental Study of the Effects of Orientation Behavior on Small Group Consensus"; Kline, "Orientation and Group Consensus."

99. E. Paulson, "Group Communication and Critical Thinking Competence Development Using a Reality-Based Project," *Business Communication Quarterly* 74, no. 4 (December 2011): 399–411.

100. Hirokawa, "Consensus Group Decision-Making, Quality of Decision and Group Satisfaction"; R. Y. Hirokawa, "Discussion Procedures and Decision-Making Performance: A Test of the Functional Perspective," *Human Communication Research* 12 (Winter 1985): 203–24; R. Y. Hirokawa and D. R. Scheerhorn, "Communication in Faulty Group Decision-Making," in R. Y. Hirokawa and M. S. Poole, eds., *Communication and Group Decision-Making* (Beverly Hills, CA: Sage, 1986), 63–80.

101. Hirokawa, "Consensus Group Decision-Making, Quality of Decision and Group Satisfaction."

102. D.-W. Choi and E. Menghrajani, "Can Group Discussion Promote Cooperative Ultimatum Bargaining?," *Group Processes & Intergroup Relations* 14, no. 3 (2011): 381–98.

103. J. A. Kline and J. L. Hullinger, "Redundancy, Self-Orientation, and Group Consensus," *Speech Monographs* 40 (March 1973): 72–74. Also see G. Yilmaz, "The Tale of We, You and I: Interpersonal Effects on Pronoun Use in Virtual Teams, *Florida Communication Journal* 42, no. 2 (Fall 2014): 27–38.

104. C. A. VanLear and E. A. Mabry, "Testing Contrasting Interaction Models for Discriminating between Consensual and Dissentient Decision-Making Groups," *Small Group Research* 30 (1999): 29–58.

105. K. L. Sager and J. Gastill, "The Origins and Consequences of Consensus Decision Making: A Test of the Social Consensus Model," *Southern Communication Journal* 73 (March 2006): 1–24.

106. A. Van Hiel and V. Franssen, "Information Acquisition Bias during the Preparing of Group Discussion: A Comparison of Prospective Minority and Majority Members," *Small Group Research* 34 (2003): 557–74; A. S. Martin, R. I Swaab, M. Sinaceur, and D. Vasiljevic, "The Double-Edged Impact of Future Expectations in Groups: Minority Influence Depends on Minorities' and Majorities' Expectations to Interact Again," *Organizational Behavior and Human Decision Processes* 128 (2015): 49–60.

107. H. W. Riecken, "The Effect of Talkativeness on Ability to Influence Group Solutions of Problems," *Sociometry* 21 (1958): 309–21.

108. R. C. Pace, "Communication Patterns in High and Low Consensus Discussion: A Descriptive Analysis,"

Southern Speech Communication Journal 53 (Winter 1988): 184–202.

109. VanLear and Mabry, "Testing Contrasting Interaction Models."

110. A. Zornoza, P. Ripoll, and J. M. Peiro, "Conflict Management in Groups That Work in Two Different Communication Contexts: Face-to-Face and Computer-Mediated Communication," *Small Group Research* 33 (2002): 481–508.

111. S. Mohammed and E. Ringseis, "Cognitive Diversity and Consensus in Group Decision Making: The Role of Inputs, Processes, and Outcomes," *Organizational Behavior and Human Decision Processes* 85 (July 2001): 31–35.

CHAPTER 9

1. D. S. Gouran, "Leadership as the Art of Counteractive Influence in Decision-Making and Problem-Solving Groups," in R. Y. Hirokawa, R. S. Cathcart, L. A. Samovar, and L. D. Henman, eds., *Small Group Communication: Theory and Practice* (Los Angeles: Roxbury, 2003), 172–83.

2. A. P. Hare, *Handbook of Small Group Research*, 2nd ed. (New York: Free Press, 1976).

3. C. T. Matthew, "Leader Creativity as a Predictor of Leading Change in Organizations," *Journal of Applied Social Psychology* 39 (2009): 1–41.

4. D. Archer, "The Face of Power: Physical Attractiveness as a Non-verbal Predictor of Small Group Stratification," *Proceedings of the 81st Annual Convention of the American Psychological Association* 8, Part I (1973): 177–78.

5. J. K. Maner and N. L. Mead, "The Essential Tension Between Leadership and Power: When Leaders Sacrifice Group Goals for the Sake of Self-Interest," *Journal of Personality and Social Psychology* 99 (2010): 482–497.

6. D. Barnlund and F. Haiman, *The Dynamics of Discussion* (Boston: Houghton Mifflin, 1960), 275–79.

7. R. White and R. Lippitt, "Leader Behavior and Member Reaction in Three 'Social Climates'," in D. Cartwright and A. Zander, eds., *Group Dynamics*, 3rd ed. (New York: Harper & Row, 1968), 319.

8. J. Gastil, "A Meta-analytic Review of the Productivity and Satisfaction of Democratic and Autocratic Leadership," *Small Group Research* 25, no. 3 (1994): 384–410.

9. C. Schoel, M. Bluemke, P. Mueller, and D. Stahlberg, "When Autocratic Leaders Become an Option: Uncertainty and Self-Esteem Predict Implicit Leadership Preference," *Journal of Personality and Social Psychology* 100 (2011): 1–20.

10. P. Hersey and K. Blanchard, *Management of Organizational Behavior: Utilizing Human Resources*, 6th ed. (Englewood Cliffs, NJ: Prentice Hall, 1992).

11. V. H. Vroom and A. G. Jago, *The New Leadership: Managing Participation in Organizations* (Englewood Cliffs, NJ: Prentice Hall, 1988), 52.

12. S. Trenholm, *Human Communication Theory* (Englewood Cliffs, NJ: Prentice Hall, 1990).

13. D. J. York, L. D. Davis, and S. L. Wise, *Virtual Teaming* (Menlo Park, CA: Crisp Publications, 2000), 48–49.

14. D. Gorman, "Conceptual and Methodological Approaches to the Study of Leadership," *Central States Speech Journal* 21 (Winter 1970): 217–23.

15. J. Z. Bergman, J. R. Rentsch, E. E. Small, S. W. Davenport, and S. M. Bergman, "The Shared Leadership Process in Decision-Making Teams," *Journal of Social Psychology* 152 (2012): 17–42.

16. L. Wang, J. Han, C.M. Fisher, and Y. Pan, "Learning to Share: Exploring Temporality in Shared Leadership and Team Learning," *Small Group Research* 48 (2017): 165–89.

17. J. B. Carson, P. E. Tesluk, and J. A. Marrone, "Shared Leadership in Teams: An Investigation of Antecedent Conditions and Performance," *Academy of Management Journal* 50, no. 5 (2007): 1217–34.

18. H. H. McIntyre and R. J. Foti, "The Impact of Shared Leadership on Teamwork Mental Models and Performance in Self-Directed Teams," *Group Process and Intergroup Relations*16 (2013): 46–57.

19. D. D. DeRue, C. M. Barnes, and F. P. Morgeson, "Understanding the Motivational Contingencies of Team Leadership," *Small Group Research* 41, no. 5 (2010): 621–51.

20. T. Whitford and S. A. Moss, "Transformational Leadership in Distributed Work Groups: The Moderating Role of Follower Regulatory Focus and Goal Orientation," *Communication Research* 26 (2009): 811.

21. J.-W. Huang, "The Effects of Transformational Leadership on the Distinct Aspects Development of Social Identity," *Group Processes and Intergroup Relations* 16 (2013): 87–104.

22. E. Musil, "Leadership Attributes for the Virtual Environment: A Qualitative Study," Ph.D. Dissertation, University of Phoenix, 2014.

23. G. Wang, I. Oh, S. H. Courtright, and A. E. Colbert, "Transformational Leadership and Performance Across Criteria and Levels: A Meta-analytic Review of

25 Years of Research," *Group and Organization Management* 36, no. 2 (2011): 223–70.

24. P. M. Senge, "Leading Learning Organizations," in R. Beckhard et al., eds., *The Leader of the Future* (San Francisco: Jossey-Bass, 1996).

25. P. M. Senge, "The Leader's New Work: Building Learning Organizations," *Sloan Management Review* 32, no. 1 (Fall 1990): whole issue.

26. A. Srivastava, K. M. Bartol, and E. A. Locke, "Empowering Leadership in Management Teams: Effects of Knowledge Sharing, Efficacy, and Performance," *Academy of Management Journal* 49, no. 6 (2006): 1239–51.

27. L. Little, "Transformational Leadership," *Academic Leadership* 15 (November 1999): 4–5.

28. O. O. Oyeleye, "Trust and Virtual Teams: The Influence of Leadership Behavior, Communication, and Gender Behavior of Virtual Team Leaders on the Development of Trust in Virtual Teams," Doctor of management issertation, University of Maryland University College, 2013.

29. F. J. Yammarino and A. J. Dubinsky, "Transformational Leadership Theory: Using Levels of Analysis to Determine Boundary Conditions," *Personnel Psychology* 47, no. 4 (1994): 787–809.

30. B. M. Bass and M. J. Avolio, "Transformational Leadership and Organizational Culture," *International Journal of Public Administration* 17, no. 3/4 (1994): 541–54.

31. I. Kotlyar and L. Karakowsky, "Leading Conflict? Linkages Between Leader Behaviors and Group Conflict," *Small Group Research* 37, no. 4 (2006): 377–403.

32. R. K. Purvanova and J. E. Bono, "Transformational Leadership in Context: Face-to-Face and Virtual Teams," *Leadership Quarterly* 20 (2009): 343–57.

33. P. Wang, J. C. Rode, K. Shi, Z. Luo, and W. Chen, "A Workgroup Climate Perspective on the Relationships Among Transformational Leadership, Workgroup Diversity, and Employee Creativity," *Group and Organization Management* 38 (2013): 334–60.

34. J. K. Barge et al., "Relational Competence and Leadership Emergence: An Exploratory Study," paper presented at the annual meeting of the Central States Speech Association, Schaumberg, Illinois, April 14–16, 1988.

35. McIntyre and Foti, "The Impact of Shared Leadership on Teamwork Mental Models and Performance in Self-Directed Teams."

36. C. Emery, T. S. Calvard, and M. E. Pierce, "Leadership as an Emergent Group Process: A Social Network Study of Personality and Leadership," *Group Processes and Intergroup Relations* 16 (2013): 28–45.

37. D. C. Baker, "A Qualitative and Quantitative Analysis of Verbal Style and the Elimination of Potential Leaders in Small Groups," *Communication Quarterly* 38 (1990): 13–26.

38. E. Bormann, *Discussion and Group Methods*, 2nd ed. (New York: Harper & Row, 1975), 256.

39. S. D. Johnson and C. Bechler, "Examining the Relationship Between Listening Effectiveness and Leadership Emergence," *Small Group Research* 29, no. 4 (1998): 452–71.

40. B. L. Bonner, "The Effects of Extroversion on Influence in Ambiguous Group Tasks," *Small Group Research* 31 (2000): 225–44.

41. G. De Souza and H. J. Klein, "Emergent Leadership in the Group Goal-Setting Process," *Small Group Research* 26 (1995): 475–96.

42. D. E. Rast III, A. M. Gaffney, M. A. Hogg, and R. J. Crisp, "Leadership Under Uncertainty: When Leaders Who Are Non-prototypical Group Members Can Gain Support," *Journal of Experimental Social Psychology* 48, no. 3 (2012): 646–53.

43. M. S. Limon and B. H. La France, "Communication Traits and Leadership Emergence: Examining the Impact of Argumentativeness, Communication Apprehension, and Verbal Aggressiveness in Work Groups," *Southern Communication Journal* 70 (2005): 123–33.

44. C. Emery, K. Daniloski, and A. Hamby, "The Reciprocal Effects of Self-View and Leader Emergence," *Small Group Research* 42 (2011): 199–224.

45. M. Schminke, D. Wells, J. Peyrefitte, and T. C. Sebora, "Leadership and Ethics in Work Groups," *Group & Organizational Management* 27 (2002): 272–93.

46. J. Baxter, "Who Wants to Be the Leader? The Linguistic Construction of Emerging Leadership in Differently Gendered Teams," *International Journal of Business Communication* 52 (2015): 427–51.

47. Ibid. p. 430.

48. J. Clifton, "A Discursive Approach to Leadership: Doing Assessments and Managing Organizational Meanings," *Journal of Business Communication* 49 (2012): 148–68.

49. I. M. Latu, M. S. Mast, J. Lammers, and D. Bombari, "Successful Female Leaders Empower Women's Behavior in Leadership Tasks," *Journal of Experimental Social Psychology* 49 (2013): 444–48.

50. J. E. Barbuto, Jr., and D. W. Wheeler, "Scale Development and Construct Clarification of Servant Leadership," *Group and Organizational Management* 31 (2006): 300–26.

51. R. K. Greenleaf, *The Servant as Leader* (Indianapolis: Greenleaf Center for Servant Leadership, 1970, 1991), 8.

52. Greenleaf, *The Servant as Leader*, 7.
53. Excerpted by permission from D. M. Frick, *Robert M. Greenleaf: A Life of Servant Leadership* (San Francisco: Berrett-Koehler, 2004).
54. R. C. Liden, S. J. Wayne, C. Liao, and J. D. Meuser, "Servant Leadership and Serving Culture: Influence on Individual and Unit Performance," *Academy of Management Journal* 57 (2014): 1434–52.
55. S. B. Shimanoff and M. M. Jenkins, "Leadership and Gender," in R. Y. Hirokawa, R. S. Cathcart, L. A. Samovar, and L. D. Henman, eds., *Small Group Communication: Theory and Practice* (Los Angeles: Roxbury, 2003).
56. Shimanoff and Jenkins, "Leadership and Gender," 194.
57. R. Ayman, K. Korabik, and S. Morris, "Is Transformational Leadership Always Perceived as Effective? Male Subordinates' Devaluation of Female Transformational Leaders," *Journal of Applied Social Psychology* 39, no. 4 (2009): 852–79.
58. Wang, Oh, Courtright, and Colbert, "Transformational Leadership and Performance Across Criteria and Levels."
59. Senge, "Leading Learning Organizations."
60. Bormann, *Discussion and Group Methods*.

CHAPTER 10

1. C. S. Lewis, *The Great Divorce: A Dream* (London: Geoffrey Bless, Centenary Press, 1945), 8.
2. E. Ross and A. Holland, *100 Great Businesses and the Minds Behind Them* (Naperville, IL: Sourcebooks, 2006), 74.
3. For a discussion of the importance of focusing on the group task, see N. L. Kerr, "The Most Neglected Moderator in Group Research," *Group Processes & Intergroup Relations* 20, no. 5 (2017): 681–92.
4. Researchers have found that some people are more competent than others in making individual decisions. See A. M. Parker and B. Fischhoff, "Decision-Making Competence: External Validation through an Individual-Differences Approach," *Journal of Behavioral Decision Making* 18 (2005): 1–27.
5. D. S. Gouran and R. Y. Hirokawa, "Functional Theory and Communication in Decision-Making and Problem-Solving Groups: An Expanded View," in R. Y. Hirokawa and M. S. Poole, eds., *Communication and Group Decision Making* (Thousand Oaks, CA: Sage, 1996), 55–80; D. S. Gouran, R. Y. Hirokawa, K. M. Julian, and G. B. Leatham, "The Evolution and Current Status of the Functional Perspective on Communication in Decision-Making and Problem-Solving Groups," in S. A. Deetz, ed., *Communication Yearbook* 16 (Newbury Park, CA: Sage, 1993), 573–600; E. E. Graham, M. J. Papa, and M. B. McPherson, "An Applied Test of the Functional Communication Perspective of Small Group Decision Making," *Southern Communication Journal* 62 (1997): 169–279.
6. B. R. Newell, T. Rakow, N. J. Weston, and D. R. Shanks, "Search Strategies in Decision Making: The Success of 'Success'," *Journal of Behavioral Decision Making* 17 (2004): 117–37.
7. Gouran and Hirokawa, "Functional Theory and Communication in Decision-Making and Problem-Solving Groups," 69; also see K. Halvorsen, "Team Decision Making in the Workplace: A Systematic Review of Discourse Analytic Studies," *Journal of Applied Linguistics and Professional Practice* 7, no. 3 (2010): 273–96; M. Schaeffner, H. Huettermann, D. Gerbert, S. Boerner, E. Kearney, and L. J. Song, "Swim or Sink Together: The Potential of Collective Team Identification and Team Member Alignment for Separating Task and Relationship Conflicts," *Group & Organization Management* 40, no. 4 (2015): 467–99.
8. L. Zhou, Y. Y. Zhang, Z. J. Wang, L. L. Rao, W. Wang, S. Li, X. Li, and Z. Y. Liang, "A Scanpath Analysis of the Risky Decision-Making Process," *Journal of Behavioral Decision Making* 29 (2016): 169–82.
9. D. A. Rettinger and R. Hastie, "Content Effects on Decision Making," Organizational Behavior and Human Decision Processes 85 (July 2001): 336–59; M. S. Eastin, L. A. Kahlor, M. C. Liang, and N. A. Ghannam, "Information-Seeking as a Precaution Behavior: Exploring the Role of Decision-Making Stages," Human Communication Research 41 (2015): 603–21.
10. O. S. Chernyshenko, A. G. Miner, M. R. Baumann, and J. A. Sniezek, "The Impact of Information Distribution, Ownership, and Discussion on Group Member Judgment: The Differential Cue Weighting Model," *Organizational Behavior and Human Decision Processes* 91 (2003): 12–25.
11. A. R. Dennis, "Information Exchange and Use in Small Group Decision Making," *Small Group Research* 27 (1996): 532–50; see also G. M. Wittenbaum, "Information Sampling in Decision-Making Groups: The Impact of Members' Task-Relevant Status," *Small Group Research* 29 (1998): 57–84; K. M. Propp, "Information Utilization in Small Group Decision Making: A Study of the Evaluation Interaction Model," *Small Group Research* 28 (1997): 424–53; C. Gonzalez, "Decision Support for Real-Time, Dynamic Decision-Making Tasks," *Organizational Behavior and Human Decision Processes* 96 (2005): 142–54.

12. J. G. Oetzel, "Explaining Individual Communication Processes in Homogeneous and Heterogeneous Groups through Individual–Collectivism and Self-Construal," *Human Communication Research* 25 (1998): 202–24.
13. K. H. Price, J. J. Lavelle, A. B. Henley, F. K. Cocchiara, and F. R. Buchanan, "Judging the Fairness of Voice-Based Participation across Multiple and Interrelated Stages of Decision Making," *Organizational Behavior and Human Decision Processes* 99 (2006): 212–26.
14. M. P. Healy, T. Vuori, and G. P. Hodgkinson, "When Teams Agree while Disagreeing: Reflexion and Reflection in Shared Cognition," *Academy of Management Review* 40, no. 3 (2015): 399–422.
15. K. Sassenberg, F. Landkammer, and J. Jacoby, "The Influence of Regulatory Focus and Group vs. Individual Goals on the Evaluation Bias in the Context of Group Decision Making," *Journal of Experimental Social Psychology* 54 (2014): 153–64.
16. J. M. George and E. Dane, "Affect, Emotion, and Decision Making," *Organizational Behavior and Human Decision Processes* 136 (2016): 47–55.
17. R. Y. Hirokawa and D. R. Scheerhorn, "Communication in Faulty Group Decision-Making," in R. Y. Hirokawa and M. S. Poole, *Communication and Group Decision Making* (Beverly Hills, CA: Sage, 1986), 67.
18. P. Lofstrand and I. Zakrisson, "Competitive versus Non-Competitive Goals in Group Decision-Making," *Small Group Research* 45, no. 4 (2014): 451–64.
19. J. Gonzales, S. Mishra, and R. D. Camp II, "For the Win: Risk-Sensitive Decision-Making in Teams," *Journal of Behavioral Decision Making* 30 (2017): 462–72.
20. N. Kogan, "Risky-Shift Phenomenon in Small Group Decision-Making: A Test of the Information-Exchange Hypothesis," *Journal of Experimental Social Psychology* 3 (1967): 75–84; L. M. Van Swol, "Extreme Members and Group Polarization," *Social Influence* 4 (2009): 185–99: E. Y. Chou and L. F. Nordgren, "Safety in Numbers: Why the Mere Physical Presence of Others Affects Risk-Taking Behaviors," *Journal of Behavioral Decision Making* 30 (2017): 671–82.
21. Chou and Norgren, "Safety in Numbers"; S. Mishra, "Decision-Making under Risk: Integrating Perspectives from Biology, Economics, and Psychology," *Personality and Social Psychology Review* 18 (2014): 280–307; J. Gonzales, S. Mishra, and R. D. Camp II, "For the Win: Risk-Sensitive Decision-Making in Teams," *Journal of Behavioral Decision Making* 30 (2017): 462–72.
22. R. Prislin, W. M. Limbert, and E. Bauer, "From Majority to Minority and Vice Versa: The Asymmetrical Effects of Losing and Gaining Majority Position within a Group," *Journal of Personality and Social Psychology* 79, no. 3 (2000): 385–97; J. A. Weller, I. P. Levin, and N. L. Denburg, "Trajectory of Risky Decision Making for Potential Gains and Losses from Ages 5 to 85," *Journal of Behavioral Decision Making* 24 (2011): 331–44.
23. Mishra, "Decision-Making under Risk."
24. Gonzales, Mishra, and Camp, "For the Win."
25. K. Parry, M. Cohen, and S. Bhattacharya, "Rise of the Machines: A Critical Considerations of Automated Leadership in Decision Making in Organizations," *Group & Organization Management* (2016): 1–24.
26. Parry, Cohen, and Bhattacharya, "Rise of the Machines."
27. See J. K. Brilhart and G. Galanes, *Communicating in Groups* (Madison, WI: Brown & Benchmark, 1997) 256; D. W. Johnson and F. P. Johnson, *Joining Together: Group Theory and Group Skills* (Englewood Cliffs, NJ: Prentice Hall, 1987) 99–104; K. Adams and G. Galanes, *Communicating in Groups: Applications and Skills*, 9th ed. (New York: McGraw-Hill, 2015), 211.
28. B. B. Baltes, M. W. Dickson, M. P. Sherman, C. C. Bauer, and J. S. LaGanke, "Computer-Mediated Communication and Group Decision Making: A Meta-Analysis," *Organizational Behavior and Human Decision Processes* 87 (2002): 156–79.
29. V. Dutt, H. Arlo-Costa, J. Helzner, and C. Gonzalez, "The Description–Experience Gap in Risky and Ambiguous Gambles," *Journal of Behavioral Decision Making* 27 (2014): 316–27.
30. M. A. Roberto, "Strategic Decision-Making Processes: Beyond the Efficiency–Consensus Trade-Off," *Group & Organization Management* 29 (2004): 626–58.
31. M. Lewis, "Obama's Way," *Vanity Fair* (October 2012): 211.
32. C. H. Kepner and B. B. Treogoe, *The Rational Manager* (New York: McGraw-Hill, 1965); see also J. K. Brilhart and G. Galanes, *Effective Group Discussion* (Dubuque, IA: Brown, 1992), 232.
33. We thank Dennis Romig for this observation. For additional information about structuring problem solving in teams, see D. A. Romig, *Breakthrough Teamwork: Outstanding Results Using Structured Teamwork* (New York: Irwin, 1996).
34. K. W. Hawkins and B. P. Fillion, "Perceived Communication Skill Needs for Work Groups," *Communication Research Reports* 16 (1999): 167–74.
35. C. M. Barnes and J. R. Hollenbeck, "Sleep Deprivation and Decision-Making Teams: Burning the Midnight Oil or Playing with Fire?," *Academy of Management Review* 34, no. 1 (2009): 56–66.

36. B. J. Broome and L. Fulbright, "A Multistage Influence Model of Barriers to Group Problem Solving: A Participant-Generated Agenda for Small Group Research," *Small Group Research* 26 (February 1995): 24–55.
37. Fisher, Small Group Decision Making, 130.
38. B. Aubrey Fisher, "Decision Emergence: Phases in Group Decision Making," *Speech Monographs* 37 (1970): 60.
39. Fisher, "Decision Emergence," 130–31.
40. E. G. Bormann, *Discussion and Group Methods: Theory and Practice* (New York: Harper & Row, 1969).
41. M. B. Fornoff and D. D. Henningsen, "Testing the Linear Discrepancy Model in Perceptions of Group Decision-Making," *Western Journal of Communication* 81, no. 4 (2017): 507–21.
42. S. Wheelan, B. Davidson, and T. Felice, "Group Development across Time: Reality or Illusion?" *Small Group Research* 34 (2003): 223–45.
43. G. Tajeddin, F. Safayeni, C. E. Connelly, and K. Tasa, "The Influence of Emergent Expertise on Group Decision Processes," *Small Group Research* 43, no. 1 (2012): 50–74.
44. J. A. Bonito, "The Analysis of Participation in Small Groups: Methodological and Conceptual Issues Related to Interdependence," *Small Group Research* 33 (2002): 412–38. For an excellent review of description group problem solving, see A. Chang, J. Duck, and P. Bordia, "Understanding the Multidimensionality of Group Development," *Small Group Research* 37 (2006): 327–49.
45. For an excellent discussion of dialectical theory, see L. A. Baxter and B. M. Montgomery, *Relating: Dialogues and Dialectics* (New York: Guilford, 1996).
46. L. A. Erbert, G. M. Mearns, and S. Dena, "Perceptions of Turning Points and Dialectical Interpretations in Organizational Team Development," *Small Group Research* 36 (2005): 21–58.
47. T. M. Scheidel and L. Crowell, "Idea Development in Small Discussion Groups," *Quarterly Journal of Speech* 50 (1994): 140–45.
48. C. Pavitt and K. K. Johnson, "The Association between Group Procedural MOPs and Group Discussion Procedure," *Small Group Research* 32 (2001): 595–624; C. Pavitt and K. K. Johnson, "Scheidel and Crowell Revisited: A Descriptive Study of Group Proposal Sequencing," *Communication Monographs* 69 (March 2002): 19–32.
49. C. J. Gersick, "Time and Transition in Work Teams: Toward a New Model of Group Development," *Academy of Management Journal* 32 (1989): 274–309; C. J. Gersick and J. R. Hackman, "Habitual Routines in Task-Performing Groups," *Organizational Behavior and Human Decision Processes* 47 (1990): 65–97.
50. A. Chang, P. Bordia, and J. Duck, "Punctuated Equilibrium and Linear Progression: Toward a New Understanding of Group Development," *Academy of Management Journal* 46 (2003): 106–17.
51. For example, see P. L. McLeod, "Distributed People and Distributed Information: Vigilant Decision-Making in Virtual Teams," *Small Group Research* 44, no. 6 (2013): 627–57.
52. S. L. Wright, *Examining the Impact of Collaboration Technology Training Support on Virtual Team Collaboration Effectiveness*, unpublished doctoral dissertation, Nova Southeastern University, 2013.
53. O. Saafein and G. A. Shaykhian, "Factors Affecting Virtual Team Performance in Telecommunication Support Environment," *Telematics and Informatics* 31 (2014): 459–62; also see S. Hazari, and S. Thompson, "Investigation Factors Affecting Group Processes in Virtual Learning Environments," *Business and Professional Communication Quarterly* 78 (2015): 33–54.
54. C. E. Timmerman and C. R. Scott, "Virtually Working: Communicative and Structural Predictors of Media Use and Key Outcomes in Virtual Work Teams," *Communication Monographs* 73 (2006): 108–36.
55. A. R. Dennis, J. A. Rennecker, and S. Hansen, "Invisible Whispering: Restructuring Collaborative Decision Making with Instant Messaging," *Decision Sciences* 41, no. 4 (2010): 845–86.
56. McLeod, "Distributed People and Distributed Information."
57. J. Olson and L. Olson, "Virtual Team Trust: Task, Communication and Sequence," *Team Performance Management* 18 (2012): 256–76; M. K. Alsharo, *Knowledge Sharing in Virtual Teams: The Impact on Turst, Collaboration, and Team Effectiveness*, unpublished doctoral dissertation, University of Colorado–Boulder, 2013.
58. M. S. Poole, "Decision Development in Small Groups, III: A Multiple Sequence Model of Group Decision Development," *Communication Monographs* 50 (December 1983): 321–41.
59. Poole, "Decision Development in Small Groups, III"
60. M. S. Poole, "A Multisequence Model of Group Decision Development," in R. Y. Hirokawa, R. S. Cathcart, L. A. Samovar, and L. D. Henman, eds., Small Group Communication Theory and Practice: An Anthology (Los Angeles, CA: Roxbury Publishing, 2003).
61. Poole, "A Multisequence Model of Group Decision Development."

62. Poole, "Decision Development in Small Groups, III."

63. See E. G. Bormann, *Discussion and Group Methods* (New York: Harper & Row, 1975).

64. Poole, "Decision Development in Small Groups," 330.

65. For a description of turning points in group deliberations, see L. A. Erbert, G. M. Mearns, and S. Dena, "Perceptions of Turning Points and Dialectical Interpretations in Organizational Team Development," *Small Group Research* 36 (2005): 21–58.

66. G. M. Wittenbaum, A. B. Hollingshead, P. B. Paulus, R. Y. Hirokawa, D. G. Ancona, R. S. Peterson, K. A. Jehn, and K. Yoon, "The Functional Perspective as a Lens for Understanding Groups," *Small Group Research* 35 (2004): 17–43.

67. D. S. Gouran and R. Y. Hirokawa, "Effective Decision Making and Problem Solving in Groups: A Functional Perspective," in R. Y. Hirokawa, R. S. Cathcart, L. A. Samovar, and L. D. Henman, eds., *Small Group Communication Theory and Practice: An Anthology* (Los Angeles, CA: Roxbury Publishing, 2003): 27–38.

68. For a discussion and critique of functional group communication theory, see L. VanderVoort, "Functional and Causal Explanations in Group Communication Research," *Communication Theory* (November 2002): 469–86.

69. R. Y. Hirokawa, "Discussion Procedures and Decision-Making Performance: A Test of a Functional Perspective," *Human Communication Research* 12, no. 2 (Winter 1985): 203–24; R. Y. Hirokawa and K. Rost, "Effective Group Decision-Making in Organizations: Field Test of the Vigilant Interaction Theory," *Management Communication Quarterly* 5 (1992): 267–88; R. Y. Hirokawa, "Why Informed Groups Make Faulty Decisions: An Investigation of Possible Interaction-Based Explanations," *Small Group Behavior* 18 (1987): 3–29; R. Y. Hirokawa, "Group Communication and Decision-Making Performance: A Continued Test of the Functional Perspective," *Human Communication Research* 14 (Summer 1988): 487–515; M. O. Orlitzky and R. Y. Hirokawa, "To Err Is Human, to Correct for It Divine: A Meta-Analysis of Research Testing the Functional Theory of Group Decision-Making Effectiveness," *Small Group Behavior* 32 (2001): 313–41; R. Y. Hirokawa and A. J. Salazar, "Task-Group Communication and Decision-Making Performance," in L. Frey, ed., *The Handbook of Group Communication Theory and Research* (Thousand Oaks, CA: Sage, 1999), 167–91; Gouran and Hirokawa, "Functional Theory and Communication in Decision-Making and Problem-Solving Groups."

70. K. Tas and G. Whyte, "Collective Efficacy and Vigilant Problem Solving in Group Decision Making: A Non-Linear Model," *Organizational Behavior and Human Decision Processes* 96 (2005): 119–29.

71. Orlitzky and Hirokawa, "To Err Is Human."

72. Graham, Papa, and McPherson, "An Applied Test."

73. K. Barge, *Leadership: Communication Skills for Organizations and Groups* (New York: St. Martin's, 1994).

74. I. L. Janis, *Victims of Groupthink* (Boston: Houghton Mifflin, 1973); I. L. Janis, *Critical Decision: Leadership in Policymaking and Crisis Management* (New York: Free Press, 1989).

75. S. S. Li, "Computer-Mediated Communication and Group Decision Making: A Functional Perspective," *Small Group Research* 38 (2007): 593–614.

76. See R. Y. Hirokawa and R. Pace, "A Descriptive Investigation of the Possible Communication-Based Reasons for Effective and Ineffective Group Decision Making," *Communication Monographs* 50 (December 1983): 363–79. The authors also wish to acknowledge D. A. Romig, Performance Resources, Inc., Austin, Texas, for his contribution to the discussion.

77. K. A. Liljenquist, A. D. Galinsky, and L. J. Kray, "Exploring the Rabbit Hole of Possibilities by Myself or with My Group: The Benefits and Liabilities of Activating Counterfactual Mind-Sets for Information Sharing and Group Coordination," *Journal of Behavioral Decision Making* 17 (2004): 263–79.

78. D. G. Leathers, "Quality of Group Communication as a Determinant of Group Product," *Speech Monographs* 39 (1972): 166–73; R. Y. Hirokawa and D. S. Gouran, "Facilitation of Group Communication: A Critique of Prior Research and an Agenda for Future Research," *Management Communication Quarterly* 3 (August 1989): 71–92.

79. See F. J. Sabatine, "Rediscovering Creativity: Unlearning Old Habits," *Mid-American Journal of Business* 4 (1989): 11–13.

80. Graham, Papa, and McPherson, "An Applied Test of the Functional Communication Perspective of Small Group Decision Making."

81. J. R. Spoor and J. R. Kelly, "The Evolutionary Significance of Affect in Groups: Communication and Group Bonding," *Group Processes & Intergroup Relations* 7 (2004): 398–412; K. L. Sager and J. Gastill, "The Origins and Consequences of Consensus Decision Making: A Test of the Social Consensus Model," *Southern Communication Journal* 73 (March 2006): 1–24.

82. D. Ryfe, "Narrative and Deliberation in Small Groups," *Journal of Applied Communication Research* 34 (2006): 72–93; also see Sunwolf, "Decisional Regret Theory: Reducing the Anxiety about Uncertain Outcomes

during Group Decision Making through Shared Counterfactual Storytelling," *Communication Studies* 57 (2006): 107–34.

83. For a comprehensive discussion of bona fide groups, see L. L. Putnam, "Rethinking the Nature of Groups: A Bona Fide Group Perspective," in R. Y. Hirokawa, R. S. Cathcart, L. A. Samovar, and L. D. Henman, eds., *Small Group Communication Theory and Practice: An Anthology* (Los Angeles, CA: Roxbury Publishing, 2003): 8–16.
84. M. B. O'Leary, M. Mortensen, and A. W. Woolley, "Multiple Team Membership: A Theoretical Model of Its Effects on Productivity and Learning for Individuals and Teams," *Academy of Management Review* 26, no. 3 (2011): 461–78.
85. See K. Y. Ng and L. Van Dyne, "Individualism–Collectivism as a Boundary Condition for Effectiveness of Minority Influence in Decision Making," *Organizational Behavior and Human Decision Processes* 84, no. 2 (March 2001): 198–225.
86. Geert Hofstede, *Culture's Consequences: International Differences in Work-Related Values* (Beverly Hills, CA: Sage, 1984), 40.
87. For an excellent review of literature exploring the role of culture on decision making and problem solving, see J. F. Yates and S. de Oliveira, "Culture and Decision Making," *Organizational Behavior and Human Decision Processes* 136 (2016): 106–18; also see Ng and Van Dyne, "Individualism–Collectivism as a Boundary Condition."
88. K. Hawkins and C. B. Power, "Gender Differences in Questions Asked during Small Decision-Making Group Discussions," *Small Group Research* 30 (1990): 235–56.
89. This discussion of bridging cultural differences is based on a discussion in S. A. Beebe, S. J. Beebe, and M. V. Redmond, *Interpersonal Communication: Relating to Others* (Boston: Allyn & Bacon, 2011).
90. See W. B. Gudykunst, *Bridging Differences: Effective Intergroup Communication* (Newbury Park, CA: Sage, 1998).
91. Oetzel, "Explaining Individual Communication Processes in Homogeneous and Heterogeneous Groups."
92. N. Zaidman, and A. Malach-Pines, "Stereotypes in Bicultural Global Teams," *International Journal of Intercultural Relations* 40 (2014): 99–112.
93. T. Reimer, "Attributions for Poor Group Performance as a Predictor of Perspective-Taking and Subsequent Group Achievement: A Process Model," *Group Processes and Intergroup Relations* 4, no. 1 (2001): 31–47.
94. S. R. Covey, *The 7 Habits of Highly Effective People* (New York: Simon & Schuster, 1989).

CHAPTER 11

1. R. S. Tindale and T. Kameda, "Group Decision-Making from an Evolutionary/Adaptationist Perspective," *Group Processes & Intergroup Relations* 20, no. 5 (2017): 669–80.
2. J. K. Brilhart and L. M. Jochem, "Effects of Different Patterns on Outcomes of Problem-Solving Discussion," *Journal of Applied Psychology* 48 (1964): 174–79; W. E. Jurma, "Effects of Leader Structuring Style and Task Orientation Characteristics of Group Members," *Communication Monographs* 49 (1979): 282–95; S. Jarboe, "A Comparison of Input–Output, Process–Output, and Input–Process–Output Models of Small Group Problem-Solving Effectiveness," *Communication Monographs* 55 (June 1988): 121–42; A. B. VanGundy, *Techniques of Structured Problem Solving* (New York: Van Nostrand Reinhold, 1981).
3. J. K. Brilhart and G. J. Galanes, *Effective Group Discussion* (Dubuque, IA: Brown, 1992); J. F. Cragan and D. W. Wright, *Communication in Small Group Discussions* (St. Paul, MN: West, 1986); Brilhart and Jochem, "Effects of Different Patterns on Outcomes of Problem-Solving Discussion"; J. Dewey, *How We Think* (Boston: Heath, 1910); R. C. Huseman, "The Role of the Nominal Group in Small Group Communication," in R. C. Huseman, C. M. Logue, and D. L. Freshley, eds., *Readings in Interpersonal and Organizational Communication*, 3rd ed. (Boston: Holbrook, 1977) 493–507; C. E. Larson, "Forms of Analysis and Small Group Problem Solving," *Speech Monographs* 36 (1969): 452–55; N. R. F. Maier, *Problem Solving and Creativity in Individuals and Groups* (Belmont, CA: Brooks/Cole, 1970); J. H. McBuirney and K. G. Hance, *The Principles and Methods of Discussion* (New York: Harper, 1939); R. S. Ross, *Speech Communication: Fundamentals and Practice* (New York: McGraw-Hill, 1974); D. W. Wright, *Small Group Communication: An Introduction* (Dubuque, IA: Kendall/Hunt, 1975); C. H. Kepner and B. B. Tregoe, *The Rational Manager* (New York: McGraw-Hill, 1965); P. B. Crosby, *The Quality Is Free: The Art of Making Quality Certain* (New York: New American Library, 1979); S. Ingle, *Quality Circles Master Guide: Increasing Productivity with People Power* (Englewood Cliffs, NJ: Prentice Hall, 1982); K. J. Albert, *How to Solve Business Problems* (New York: McGraw-Hill, 1978); D. L. Dewar, *Quality Circle Leader Manual and Instructional Guide* (Red Bluff, CA: Quality Circle Institute, 1980); D. S. Gouran, *Discussion: The Process of Group Decision-Making* (New York: Harper & Row, 1974); VanGundy, *Techniques of Structured Problem Solving*; F. LaFasto and C. Larson, *When Teams Work Best* (Thousand Oaks, CA: Sage, 2001); J. N. Kim and J. E. Grunig, "Problem Solving and

Communicative Action: A Situational Theory of Problem Solving," *Journal of Communication* 61 (2011): 120–49.

4. Dewey, *How We Think*; see also R. V. Harnack, "John Dewey and Discussion," *Western Speech* 32 (Spring 1969): 137–49.
5. For a complete discussion of the history of teaching group discussion, see H. Cohen, *The History of Speech Communication: The Emergence of a Discipline, 1914–1945* (Annandale, VA: Speech Communication Association, 1994): 274–322.
6. For an excellent discussion of the history of teaching group discussion, see D. S. Gouran, "Communication in Groups: The Emergence and Evolution of a Field of Study," in L. R. Frey, ed., *The Handbook of Group Communication Theory and Research* (Thousand Oaks, CA: Sage, 1999), 3–36.
7. K. Atuahene-Gima, "The Effects of Centrifugal and Centripetal Forces on Product Development Speed and Quality: How Does Problem Solving Matter?", *Academy of Management Journal* 46 (2003): 359–73; also see J. N. Ervin, J. A. Bonito, and J. Keyton, "Convergence of Intrapersonal and Interpersonal Processes across Group Meetings," *Communication Monographs* 84, no. 2 (2107): 200–20.
8. B. A. Fisher, "Decision Emergence: Phases in Group Decision Making," *Speech Monographs* 37 (1970): 60.
9. B. W. Tuckman, "Developmental Sequence in Small Groups," *Psychological Bulletin* 63 (1965): 384–99.
10. J. A. Bonito, "The Analysis of Participation in Small Groups: Methodological and Conceptual Issues Related to Interdependence," *Small Group Research* 33 (2002): 412–38.
11. S. A. Beebe, "Structure–Interaction Theory: Conceptual, Contextual and Strategic Influences on Human Communication," *Russian Journal of Linguistics Vestnik Rudn: Special Issue: Intercultural Communication Theory and Practice* 19, no. 4 (2015), 7–24.
12. R. F. Bales, *Interaction Process Analysis* (Chicago: University of Chicago Press, 1976).
13. N. L. Kerr and R. S. Tindale, "Group Performance and Decision Making," *Annual Review of Psychology* 55 (2004): 623–55; C. G. Endacott, R. T. Hartwig, and C. H. Yu, "An Exploratory Study of Communication Practices Affecting Church Leadership Team Performance," *Southern Communication Journal* 82, no. 3 (2017): 129–39.
14. For an excellent summary of the literature documenting these problems, see Sunwolf and D. R. Seibold, "The Impact of Formal Procedures on Group Processes, Members, and Task Outcomes," in L. Frey, ed., *The Handbook of Group Communication Theory and Research* (Thousand Oaks, CA: Sage, 1999), 395–431.
15. D. S. Gouran, C. Brown, and D. R. Henry, "Behavioral Correlates of Perceptions of Quality in Decision-Making Discussion," *Communication Monographs* 45 (1978): 60–65; L. L. Putnam, "Preference for Procedural Order in Task-Oriented Small Groups," *Communication Monographs* 46 (1979): 193–218; see also VanGundy, *Techniques of Structured Problem Solving*; B. J. Broome and L. Fulbright, "A Multistage Influence Model of Barriers to Group Problem Solving: Participant Generated Agenda for Small Group Research," *Small Group Research* 26 (1995): 25–55; J. P. Klubuilt and P. F. Green, *The Team-Based Problem Solver* (Burr Ridge, IL: Irwin, 1994). E. H. Witte, "Toward a Group Facilitation Technique for Project Teams," *Group Processes and Intergroup Relations* 10 (2007): 299–309; Y. C. Liu, and P. L. McLeod, "Individual Preference for Procedural Order and Process Accountability in Group Problem-Solving," *Small Group Research* 45, no. 2 (2014): 154–75.
16. D. M. Berg, "A Descriptive Analysis of the Distribution and Duration of Themes Discussed by Task-Oriented Small Groups," *Speech Monographs* 34 (1967): 172–75; see also E. G. Bormann and N. C. Bormann, *Effective Small Group Communication*, 2nd ed. (Minneapolis: Burgess, 1976) 132; M. S. Poole, "Decision Development in Small Groups III: A Multiple Sequence Model of Group Decision Development," *Communication Monographs* 50 (1983): 321–41.
17. R. Y. Hirokawa, R. Ice, and J. Cook, "Preference for Procedural Order, Discussion Structure and Group Decision Performance," *Communication Quarterly* 36 (Summer 1988): 217–26.
18. D. D. Stewart, C. B. Stewart, and J. Walden, "Self-Reference Effect and the Group-Reference Effect in the Recall of Shared and Unshared Information in Nominal Groups and Interacting Groups," *Group Processes and Intergroup Relations* 10 (2007): 323–39.
19. J. E. Mathieu, S. I. Tannenbaum, M. R. Kukenberger, J. S. Donsbach, and G. M. Alliger, "Team Role Experience and Orientation: A Measure and Tests of Construct Validity," *Group & Organization Management* 40 (2015): 6–34.
20. Witte, "Toward a Group Facilitation Technique for Project Teams."
21. S. Kauffeld and N. Lehmann-Willenbrock, "Meetings Matter: Effects of Team Meetings on Team and Organizational Success," *Small Group Research* 43 (2012): 130–158.
22. Kauffeld and Lehmann-Willenbrock, "Meetings Matter."
23. C. Pavitt, M. Philipp, and K. K. Johnson, "Who Owns a Group's Proposals: The Initiator or the Group as a Whole?" *Communication Research Reports* 21 (2004): 221–30.

24. J. G. Oetzel, "Explaining Individual Communication Processes in Homogeneous and Heterogeneous Groups through Individualism, Collectivism, and Self-Construal," *Human Communication Research* 25 (1998): 202–24.

25. T. Hopthrow and L. G. Hulbert, "The Effect of Group Decision Making on Cooperation in Social Dilemmas," *Group Processes and Intergroup Relations* 8 (2005): 89–100.

26. S. R. Hiltz, K. Johnson, and M. Turoff, "Experiments in Group Decision Making: Communication Process and Outcome in Face-to-Face versus Computerized Conferences," *Human Communication Research* 13 (Winter 1986): 225–52.

27. C. A. Van Lear and E. A. Mabry, "Testing Contrasting Interaction Models for Discriminating between Consensual and Dissent Decision-Making Groups," *Small Group Research* 30 (1999): 29–58; R. Y. Hirokawa, "Group Communication and Decision-Making Performance: A Continued Test of the Functional Perspective," *Human Communication Research* 14 (1985): 487–515.

28. For an excellent review of the literature about various rational and nonrational problem-solving methods, see S. Jarboe, "Procedures for Enhancing Group Decision Making," in R. Y. Hirokawa and M. S. Poole, eds., *Communication and Group Decision Making* (Thousand Oaks, CA: Sage, 1996): 345–83.

29. See Kepner and Tregoe, *The Rational Manager*; our application of is/is not analysis is based on D. A. Romig and L. J. Romig, *Structured Teamwork® Guide* (Austin, TX: Performance Resources, 1990); see also D. A. Romig, *Breakthrough Teamwork: Outstanding Results Using Structured Teamwork®* (Chicago: Irwin, 1996).

30. This discussion of the journalist's six questions is based on a discussion by J. E. Eitington, *The Winning Trainer* (Houston, TX: Gulf Publishing, 1989) 157.

31. P. R. Scholtes, B. L. Joiner, and B. J. Streibel, *The Team Handbook* (Madison, WI: Joiner and Associates, 1996) 2–20.

32. R. S. Zander and B. Zander, *The Art of Possibility: Transforming Professional and Personal Life* (New York: Penguin, 2002).

33. K. Lewin, "Frontiers in Group Dynamics," *Human Relations* 1 (1947): 5–42.

34. Eitington, *The Winning Trainer*, 158.

35. Eitington, *The Winning Trainer*. Used with permission. All rights reserved.

36. K. Ishikawa, *Guide to Quality Control* (Tokyo: Asian Productivity Organization, 1982).

37. Witte, "Toward a Group Facilitation Technique for Project Teams," 309.

38. A. Chiravuri, D. Nazareth, and K. R. Murthy, "Cognitive Conflict and Consensus Generation in Virtual Teams during Knowledge Capture: Comparative Effectiveness of Techniques," *Journal of Management Information Systems* 28, no. 1 (Summer 2011): 311–50.

39. Brilhart and Jochem, "Effects of Different Patterns on Outcomes of Problem-Solving Discussion."

40. C. E. Larson and F. M. J. LaFasto, *Teamwork: What Must Go Right/What Can Go Wrong* (Beverly Hills, CA: Sage, 1989).

41. https://www.leadershipnow.com/probsolvingquotes.html, accessed September 20, 2017.

42. Kauffeld and Lehmann-Willenbrock, "Meetings Matter."

43. M. C. Schippers, A. C. Edmondson, and M. A. West, "Team Reflexivity as Antidote to Team Information-Processing Failures," *Small Group Research* 45, no. 6 (2014): 731–69.

44. For evidence to support this modification of the reflective thinking pattern, see J. K. Brilhart, "An Experimental Comparison of Three Techniques for Communicating a Problem-Solving Pattern to Members of a Discussion Group," *Speech Monographs* 33 (1966): 168–77.

45. Both social choice theory and social decision scheme theory provide explanations as to how group members take a large amount of information, sift through the data, and then sort the information or options. For additional information, see P. R. Laughlin, "Social Choice Theory, Social Decision Scheme Theory, and Group Decision-Making," *Group Processes & Intergroup Relations* 14, no. 1 (2011): 63–79.

46. R. Y. Hirokawa, "Why Informed Groups Make Faulty Decisions: An Investigation of Possible Interaction-Based Explanations," *Small Group Behavior* 18 (1987): 3–29; R. Y. Hirokawa, "Group-Communication and Decision-Making Performance: A Continued Test of the Functional Perspective," *Human Communication Research* 14 (1985): 487–515; R. Y. Hirokawa and K. Rost, "Effective Group Decision-Making in Organizations: Field Test of the Vigilant Interaction Theory," *Management Communication Quarterly* 5 (1992): 267–88; R. Y. Hirokawa, "Consensus Group Decision-Making, Quality of Decision and Group Satisfaction: An Attempt to Sort 'Fact' from 'Fiction'," *Central States Speech Journal* 33 (1982): 407–15.

47. O. Huber, O. W. Huber, and A. S. Bär, "Information Search and Mental Representation in Risky Decision Making: The Advantages First Principle," *Journal of Behavioral Decision Making* 24 (2011): 223–248.

48. A. B. Hollingshead, "The Rank-Order Effect in Group Decision Making," *Organizational Behavior and Human Decision Process* 68 (1996): 181–93.

49. For a description of Thomas Edison's use of prototypes, see A. Boynton and B. Fischer, *Virtuoso Teams: Lessons from Teams That Changed Their World* (Harlow, UK: Prentice Hall Financial Times), 76.

50. Federal Electric Corporation, *A Programmed Introduction to PERT* (New York: Wiley, 1963).

51. For example, see R. F. Bales and F. L. Strodtbeck, "Phases in Group Problem-Solving," *Journal of Abnormal and Social Psychology* 46 (1951): 485–95; T. M. Schiedel and L. Crowell, "Idea Development in Small Groups," *Quarterly Journal of Speech* 50 (1964): 140–45; B. A. Fisher, "Decision Emergence: Phases in Group Decision-Making," *Speech Monographs* (1970): 53–66; and Poole, "Decision Development."

52. Chapter 10 discusses in detail the phases of a group's growth and development.

53. E. G. Bormann, *Discussion and Group Methods: Theory and Practice*, 2nd ed. (New York: Harper & Row, 1975) 282.

54. A. Wiedow and U. Konradt, "Two-Dimensional Structure of Team Process Improvement: Team Reflection and Team Adaptation," *Small Group Research* 42, no. 1 (2011): 32–54.

55. Gurtner, A., F. Tschan, N. K. Semmer, and C. Nägele, "Getting Groups to Develop Good Strategies: Effects of Reflexivity Interventions on Team Process, Team Performance, and Shared Mental Models," *Organizational Behavior and Human Decision Processes* 102 (2007): 127–42.

56. N. R. F. Maier, *Problem-Solving and Discussions and Conferences* (New York: McGraw-Hill, 1963), 123.

57. B. Schultz, S. M. Ketrow, and D. M. Urban, "Improving Decision Quality in the Small Group: The Role of the Reminder," *Small Group Research* 26 (1995): 521–41.

58. A. A. Goldberg and C. E. Larson, *Group Communication: Discussion Processes and Applications* (Englewood Cliffs, NJ: Prentice Hall, 1975) 149.

59. Goldberg and Larson, *Group Communication*, 150.

60. Goldberg and Larson, *Group Communication*, 150.

61. Goldberg and Larson, *Group Communication*, 150.

62. Larson, "Forms of Analysis and Small Group Problem Solving."

63. E. Dane, K. W. Rockmann, and M. G. Pratt, "When Should I Trust My Gut? Linking Domain Expertise to Intuitive Decision Making Effectiveness," *Organizational and Behaviour and Human Decision Processes* 119 (2012): 187–94.

64. D. G. Gouran, "Variables Related to Consensus in Group Discussions of Questions of Policy," *Speech Monographs* 36 (1969): 385–91; T. J. Knutson, "An Experimental Study of the Effects of Orientation Behavior on Small Group Consensus," *Speech Monographs* 39 (1972): 159–65; J. A. Kline, "Orientation and Group Consensus," *Central States Speech Journal* 23 (1972): 44–47; S. A. Beebe, "Orientation as a Determinant of Group Consensus and Satisfaction," *Resources in Education* 13 (October 1978): 19–25.

65. LaFasto and Larson, *When Teams Work Best*.

66. N. R. F. Maier, "An Experimental Test of the Effect of Training on Discussion Leadership," *Human Relations* 6 (1953): 166–73.

67. Also see M. Sinclair, "Misconceptions about Intuition," *Psychological Inquiry*, 21 (2010): 378–86.

68. This activity was developed by Russ Wittrup, Department of Speech Communication, Texas State University—San Marcos.

69. E. Hedman-Phillips and J. K. Barge, "Facilitating Team Reflexivity about Communication," *Small Group Research* 48, no. 3 (2017): 255–87.

70. See R. Y. Hirokawa and A. J. Salazar, "Task Group Communication and Decision-Making Performance," in L. Frey, ed., *The Handbook of Group Communication Theory and Research* (Thousand Oaks, CA: Sage, 1999), 167–91; Sunwolf and Seibold, "The Impact of Formal Procedure."

CHAPTER 12

1. E. Ross and A. Holland, *100 Great Businesses and the Minds behind Them* (Naperville, IL: Sourcebooks, 2006), 402.

2. M. Csikszentmihalyi, *Creativity: Flow and the Psychology of Discovery and Invention* (New York: HarperCollins, 1996); for an excellent discussion and review of the literature about creativity in small groups that informs this chapter, see "Getting to Group 'Aha!'" in L. R. Frey, ed., *New Directions in Small Group Communication* (Thousand Oaks, CA: Sage, 2002): 203–17.

3. C. E. Johnson and M. Z. Hackman, *Creative Communication: Principles and Applications* (Prospect Heights, IL: Waveland Press, 1995).

4. P. G. Clampitt, *Communicating for Managerial Effectiveness* (Thousand Oaks, CA: Sage, 2005).

5. C. C. Miller and R. D. Ireland, "Intuition in Strategic Decision Making: Friend or Foe in the Fast-Paced 21st Century?" *Academy of Management Executive* 19 (2005): 19–30.
6. E. Dane and M. G. Pratt, "Exploring Intuition and Its Role in Managerial Decision Making," *Academy of Management Review* 32 (2007): 33–54.
7. J. E. Nemiro, "The Creative Processes in Virtual Teams," *Creativity Research Journal* 14, no. 1 (2002): 69–83.
8. J. E. Nemiro, "The Creative Processes in Virtual Teams," *Creativity Research Journal* 14, no. 1 (2002): 69–83.
9. E. Dane, K. W. Rockmann and M. G. Pratt, "When Should I Trust My Gut? Linking Domain Expertise to Intuitive Decision-Making Effectiveness," *Organizational Behavior and Human Decision Processes* 119 (2012): 187–94.
10. S. J. Parnes and R. B. Noller, "Applied Creativity: The Creative Studies Project: Part II. Results of the Two-Year Program," *Journal of Creative Behavior* 6 (1972): 164–86; R. L. Firestien, "Effects of Creative Problem-Solving Training on Communication Behaviors in Small Groups," *Small Group Research* 21 (1990): 507–22.
11. J. Baer, *Creativity and Divergent Thinking: A Task-Specific Approach* (Hillsdale, NJ: Lawrence Erlbaum, 1993).
12. Firestien, "Effects of Creative Problem Solving Training."
13. Firestien, "Effects of Creative Problem Solving Training."
14. Johnson and Hackman, *Creative Communication.*
15. Johnson and Hackman, *Creative Communication.*
16. S. Jarboe, "Group Communication and Creativity Processes," in L. R. Frey, D. S. Gouran, and M. S. Poole, eds., *The Handbook of Group Communication Theory and Research* (Thousand Oaks, CA: Sage, 1999), 335–68.
17. J. Ayres and T. S. Hopf, "The Long-Term Effect of Visualization in the Classroom: A Brief Research Report," *Communication Education* 39 (1990): 75–78.
18. D. D. Henningsen, and M. L. M. Henningsen, "Generating Ideas About the Uses of Brainstorming: Reconsidering the Losses and Gains of Brainstorming Groups Relative to Nominal Groups," *Southern Communication Journal* 78 (2013): 42–55.
19. J. R. Kelly and T. J. Loving, "Time Pressure and Group Performance: Exploring Underlying Processes in the Attentional Focus Model," *Journal of Experimental Social Psychology* 40 (2004): 185–98.
20. J. R. Kelly and S. J. Karau, "Entrainment of Creativity in Small Groups," *Small Group Research* 24 (1993): 179–98.
21. J. R. Kelly and J. E. McGrath, "Effects of Time Limits and Task Types on Task Performance and Interaction of Four-Person Groups," *Journal of Personality and Social Psychology* 49 (1985): 395–407.
22. G. Hirst, D. van Knippenberg, and J. Zhou, "A Cross-Level Perspective on Employee Creativity: Goal Orientation, Team Learning Behavior, and Individual Creativity," *Academy of Management Journal* 52, no. 2 (2009): 280–93.
23. See M. Michalko, *Thinkertoys: A Book of Creative-Thinking Techniques* (Berkeley, CA: Ten Speed Press), 5.
24. S. Taggar, "Individual Creativity and Group Ability to Utilize Individual Creative Resources: A Multi-Level Model," *Academy of Management Journal* 45 (April 2002): 315–30.
25. J. A. Goncalo and B. M. Staw, "Individualism: Collectivism and Group Creativity," *Organizational Behavior and Human Decision Processes* 100 (2006): 96–109.
26. A. Boynton and B. Fischer, *Virtuoso Teams: Lessons from Teams That Changed Their Worlds* (Harlow, UK: Prentice Hall Financial Times, 2005).
27. L. Alexander, and D. V. Knippenberg, "Teams in Pursuit of Radical Innovation: A Goal Orientation Perspectdive," *Academy of Management Review* 39, no. 4 (2014): 423–38.
28. A. B. VanGundy, *Managing Group Creativity: A Modular Approach to Problem Solving* (New York: AMA-COM, 1984).
29. M. N. Bechtoldt, C. K. W. De Dreu, and H.-S. Choi, "Motivated Information Processing, Social Training, and Group Creativity," *Journal of Personality and Social Psychology* 99, no. 4 (2010): 622–37.
30. Taggar, "Individual Creativity and Group Ability to Utilize Individual Creative Resources."
31. M. C. Schilpzand, D. M. Herold, and C. E. Shalley, "Members' Openness to Experiences and Teams' Creativity Performance," *Small Group Research* 42, no. 1 (2011): 55–76.
32. Goncalo and Staw, "Individualism."
33. M. Janssens and J. M. Brett, "Cultural Intelligence in Global Teams: A Fusion Model of Collaboration," *Group Organization Management* 31 (2006): 124–53.
34. L. L. Martins and C. E. Shalley, "Creativity in Virtual Work: Effects of Demographic Differences," *Small Group Research* 42, no. 5 (2011): 536–61.
35. S. J. Shin, T.-Y. Kim, J.-Y. Lee, and L. Bain, "Cognitive Team Diversity and Individual Team Member Creativity: A Cross-Level Interaction," *Academy of Management Journal* 55, no. 1 (2012): 197–212.

36. Martins and Shalley, "Creativity in Virtual Work."
37. P. L. McLeod, S. A. Lobel, and T. H. Cox, Jr., "Ethnic Diversity and Creativity in Small Groups," *Small Group Research* 27 (1996): 248–64; A. Miura and M. Hida, "Synergy between Diversity and Similarity in Group-Idea Generation," *Small Group Research* 35 (2004): 540–64.
38. For additional information about the role of conforming to group norms and expectations, see J. A. Goncalo and M. M. Duguid, "Follow the Crowd in a New Direction: When Conformity Pressure Facilitates Group Creativity (and When It Does Not)," *Organizational Behavior and Human Decision Processes* 118 (2012): 14–23.
39. S. Y. Sung and J. N. Choi, "Effects of Team Knowledge Management on the Creativity and Financial Performance of Organizational Teams," *Organizational Behavior and Human Decision Processes* 118 (2012): 4–13.
40. E. Miron-Spektor, M. Erez, and E. Naveh, "The Effect of Conformist and Attentive-to-Detail Members on Team Innovation: Reconciling the Innovation Paradox," *Academy of Management Journal* 54, no. 4 (2011): 740–60.
41. H. S. Choi and L. Thompson, "Old Wine in a New Bottle: Impact of Membership Change on Group Creativity," *Organizational Behavior and Human Decision Processes* 98 (2005): 121–32.
42. F. Gino, L. Argote, E. Miron-Spektor, and G. Todorova, "First, Get Your Feet Wet: The Effects of Learning from Direct and Indirect Experience on Team Creativity," *Organizational Behavior and Human Decision Processes* 111 (2010): 102–115.
43. O. Goldenberg, J. R. Larson Jr., and J. Wiley, "Goal Instructions, Response Format, and Idea Generation in Groups," *Small Group Research* 44, no. 3 (2013): 227–56.
44. A. Chirumbolo, L. Mannetti, A. Pierro, A. Areni, and A. W. Kruglanski, "Motivated Closed-Mindedness and Creativity in Small Groups," *Small Group Research* 36 (2005): 59–82.
45. For a description and application of using structured problem-solving techniques to enhance creativity, see D. A. Jameson, "What's *the* Right Answer? Team Problem-Solving in Environments of Uncertainty," *Business Communication Quarterly* (2009): 215–21.
46. L. L. Gilson, J. E. Mathieu, C. E. Shalley, and T. M. Ruddy, "Creativity and Standardization: Complementary or Conflicting Driver of Team Effectiveness?" *Academy of Management Journal* 48 (2005): 521–31.
47. Taggar, "Individual Creativity"; P. B. Paulus and H. Yang, "Idea Generation in Groups: A Basis for Creativity in Organizations," *Organizational Behavior and Human Decision Processes* 82 (2000): 76–87.
48. A. F. Osborn, *Applied Imagination* (New York: Scribner's, 1962).
49. T. J. Kramer, G. P. Fleming, and S. M. Mannis, "Improving Face-to-Face Brainstorming Through Modeling and Facilitation," *Small Group Research* 32 (2001): 533–57.
50. This example is described in Michalko, *Thinkertoys: A Book of Creative-Thinking Techniques*, 154.
51. E. F. Rietzschel, B. A. Nijstad, and W. Stroebe, "Productivity Is Not Enough: A Comparison of Interactive and Nominal Brainstorming Groups on Idea Generation and Selection," *Journal of Experimental Social Psychology* 42 (2006): 244–51; also see P. B. Paulus and M. T. Dzindolet, "Social Influence Processes in Group Brainstorming," *Journal of Personality and Social Psychology* 64 (1993): 575–86; P. B. Paulus, K. L. Dugosh, M. T. Dzindolet, H. Coskun, and V. K. Putman, "Social and Cognitive Influences in Group Brainstorming: Predicting Production Gains and Losses," *European Review of Social Psychology* 12 (2002): 299–326.
52. R. P. McGlynn, D. McGurk, V. S. Effland, N. L. Johll, and D. J. Harding, "Brainstorming and Task Performance in Groups Constrained by Evidence," *Organizational Behavior and Human Decision Processes* 93 (2004): 75–87.
53. B. A. Nijstad, A. E. M. van Vianen, W. Stroebe, and H. F. M. Lodewijkx, "Persistence in Brainstorming: Exploring Stop Rules in Same-Sex Groups," *Group Processes & Intergroup Relations* 7 (2004): 195–206.
54. Nijstad, van Vianen, Stroebe, and Lodewijkx, "Persistence in Brainstorming."
55. T. Nakui, P. B. Paulus, and K. I. van der Zee, "The Role of Attitudes in Reactions Towards Diversity in Workgroups," *Journal of Applied Social Psychology* 41, no. 10 (2011): 2327–51; also see: R. C. Giambatista and A. D. Bhappu, "Diversity's Harvest: Interactions of Diversity Sources and Communication Technology on Creativity Group Performance," *Organizational Behavior and Human Decision Processes* 111 (2010): 116–126.
56. As described in Michalko, *Thinkertoys: A Book of Creative-Thinking Techniques*, 74.
57. S. Cain, *Quiet: The Power of Introverts in a World That Can't Stop Talking* (New York: Crown Publishers, 2012).
58. A. L. Delbecq, A. H. Van de Ven, and D. H. Gustafson, *Group Techniques for Program Planning: A Guide to Nominal-Group and Delphi Processes* (Glenview, IL: Scott, Foresman, 1975), 7–16.
59. P. B. Paulus, D. S. Levine, V. Brown, A. A. Minai, and S. Doboli, "Modeling Ideational Creativity in Groups: Connecting Cognitive, Neural, and Computational Approaches," *Small Group Research* 41, no. 6 (2010):

688–724; also see T. M. Hess, T. L. Queen, and T. R. Patterson, "To Deliberate or Not to Deliberate: Interactions between Age, Task Characteristics, and Cognitive Activity on Decision Making," *Journal of Behavioral Decision Making* 25 (2012): 29–40.

60. B. L. Smith, "Interpersonal Behaviors That Damage the Productivity of Creative Problem-Solving Groups," *Journal of Creative Behavior* 27, no. 3 (1993): 171–87.

61. D. D. Stewart, C. B. Stewart, and J. Walden, "Self-Reference Effect and the Group-Reference Effect in the Recall of Shared and Unshared Information in Nominal Groups and Interacting Groups," *Group Processes and Intergroup Relations* 10 (2007): 323–39.

62. G. Philipsen, A. Mulac, and D. Dietrich, "The Effects of Social Interaction on Group Generation of Ideas," *Communication Monographs* 46 (June 1979): 119–25; F. M. Jablin, "Cultivating Imagination: Factors That Enhance and Inhibit Creativity in Brainstorming Groups," *Human Communication Research* 7, no. 3 (Spring 1981): 245–58; S. Jarboe, "A Comparison of Input–Output, Process–Output, and Input–Process–Output Models of Small Group Problem-Solving Effectiveness," *Communication Monographs* 55 (June 1988): 121–42. The idea of incorporating individual or silent brainstorming into the traditional brainstorming approach emerges from the nominal-group technique suggested by Delbecq, Van de Ven, and Gustafson, *Group Techniques for Program Planning*, 7–16; see also S. Jarboe, "Enhancing Creativity in Groups: Theoretical Boundaries and Pragmatic Limitations," a paper presented at the annual meeting of the Speech Communication Association, Atlanta, GA, November 1, 1991; F. M. Jablin and D. R. Seibold, "Implications for Problem-Solving Groups of Empirical Research on 'Brainstorming': A Critical Review of the Literature," *Southern Speech Communication Journal* 43 (1978): 327–56. See also A. B. VanGundy, *Techniques of Structured Problem Solving* (New York: Van Nostrand Reinhold, 1981).

63. J. J. Sosik, B. J. Avolio, and S. S. Kahai, "Inspiring Group Creativity: Comparing Anonymous and Identified Electronic Brainstorming," *Small Group Research* 29 (1998): 3–31.

64. H. Barki, "Small Group Brainstorming and Idea Quality: Is Electronic Brainstorming the Most Effective Approach?" *Small Group Research* 32 (2001): 158–205.

65. D. H. Gustafson, R. K. Shukla, A. Delbecq, and G. W. Walster, "A Comparative Study of Differences in Subjective Likelihood Estimates Made by Individuals, Interacting Groups, Delphi Groups and Nominal-Groups," *Organizational Behavior and Human Performance* 9 (1973): 280–91; VanGundy, *Techniques of Structured Problem Solving*.

66. Jarboe, "A Comparison of Input-Output, Process-Output, and Input-Process-Output Models."

67. Stewart, Stewart, and Walden, "Self-Reference Effect and the Group-Reference Effect in the Recall of Shared and Unshared Information in Nominal Groups and Interacting Groups."

68. J. Baruah and P. B. Paulus, "Effects of Training on Idea Generation in Groups," *Small Group Research* 39 (2008): 523–41. For an excellent review of brainstorming and the nominal-group technique, see P. B. Paulus, T. Nakui, L. V. Putman, and V. R. Brown, "Effects of Task Instructions and Brief Breaks on Brainstorming," *Group Dynamics: Theory, Research, and Practice* 10 (2006): 206–19.

69. These ideas are developed in D. H. Pink, *A Whole New Mind: Why Right-Brainers Will Rule the Future* (New York: Riverhead Books, 2006), 65–67.

70. Delbecq, Van de Ven, and Gustafson, *Group Techniques for Program Planning*.

71. M. C. Roy, S. Gauvin, and M. Limayem, "Electronic Group Brainstorming: The Role of Feedback on Productivity," *Small Group Research* 27 (1996): 215–47.

72. Sosik, Avolio, and Kahai, "Inspiring Group Creativity"; W. H. Cooper, R. B. Gallupe, S. Pollard, and J. Cadsby, "Some Liberating Effects of Anonymous Electronic Brainstorming," *Small Group Research* 29 (1998): 147–77.

73. Sosik, Avolio, and Kahai, "Inspiring Group Creativity."

74. P. L. McLeod, "Effects of Anonymity and Social Comparison of Rewards on Computer-Mediated Group Brainstorming," *Small Group Research* 42, no. 2 (2011): 475–503.

75. D. J. York, L. D. Davis, and S. L. Wise, *Virtual Teaming* (Menlo Park, CA: Crisp Publications, 2000), 77.

76. E. K. Aranda, L. Aranda, and K. Conlon, *Teams: Structure, Process, Culture, and Politics* (Englewood Cliffs, NJ: Prentice Hall, 1998).

77. Adapted from Aranda, Aranda, and Conlon, *Teams: Structure, Process, Culture, and Politics*, 89.

78. A. K. Offner, T. J. Kramer, and J. P. Winter, "The Effects of Facilitation, Recording, and Pauses on Group Brainstorming," *Small Group Research* 27 (1996): 283–98; V. Brown and P. B. Paulus, "A Simple Dynamic Model of Social Factors in Group Brainstorming," *Small Group Research* 27 (1996): 91–114; M. W. Kramer, C. L. Kuo, and J. C. Dailey, "The Impact of Brainstorming Techniques on Subsequent Group Processes," *Small Group Research* 28 (1997): 218–42; V. Brown, M. Tumeo, T. S. Larey, and P. B. Paulus, "Modeling Cognitive Interactions

during Group Brainstorming," *Small Group Research* 29 (1997): 495–526. For an excellent review of group communication and creativity, see Jarboe, "Group Communication and Creativity Processes."

79. Kelly and Karau, "Entrainment of Creativity in Small Groups."
80. J. E. Eitington, *The Winning Trainer* (Houston, TX: Gulf Publishing, 1989).
81. Eitington, *The Winning Trainer*.
82. D. A. Romig and L. J. Romig, *Structured Teamwork Guide* (Austin, TX: Performance Resources, 1990).
83. E. de Bono, *Sur/petition: Creating Value Monopolies When Everyone Is Merely Competing* (New York: HarperBusiness, 1992).
84. Michalko, *Thinkertoys*, 319.
85. Michalko, *Thinkertoys*, 321.

APPENDIX A

1. D. Barry, *Dave Barry's Guide to Life* (New York: Wings Books, 1991), 311.
2. D. Barry, *Dave Barry's Guide to Life*, 311.
3. S. Dockweiler, "How Much Time Do We Spend In Meetings? (Hint: It's Scary), *The Muse* https://www.themuse.com/advice/how-much-time-do-we-spend-in-meetings-hint-its-scary. Accessed September 25, 2017. Also see N. C. Sauer and S. Kauffeld, "Meetings as Networks: Applying Social Network Analysis to Team Interaction," *Communication Methods and Measures* 7 (2013): 26–47; S. Kauffeld and N. Lehmann-Willenbrock, "Meetings Matter: Effects of Team Meetings on Team and Organizational Success," *Small Group Research* 43 (2012): 130–58.
4. A. Schell, *European Business Meeting Culture: An Ad-Hoc Survey of Employees and Managers Who Regularly Participate in Business Meetings* (Munich: Schell Marketing Consulting, 2010). Also see Kauffeld and Lehmann-Willenbrock, "Meetings Matter."
5. Dockweiler, "How Much Time Do We Spend In Meetings?"
6. R. K. Mosvick and R. B. Nelson, *We've Got to Start Meeting Like This*! (Glenview, IL: Scott, Foresman, 1987).
7. M. Washington, E. Okoro, and P. Cardon, "Perceptions of Civility for Mobile Phone Use in Formal and Informal Meetings," *Business and Professional Communication*, 77 (2013): 52–64.
8. Washington, Okoro, and Cardon, "Perceptions of Civility for Mobile Phone Use."
9. Washington, Okoro, and Cardon, "Perceptions of Civility for Mobile Phone Use."
10. S. A. Beebe and J. T. Masterson, "Toward a Model of Small Group Communication: Application for Teaching and Research," *Florida Speech Communication Journal* 8, no. 2 (1980): 9–15.
11. J. J. DiStefan and M. L. Maznevski. "Creating Value with Diverse Teams in Global Management," *Organizational Dynamics* 29 (2000): 45–63. Also see T. Köhler, C. D. Cramton, and P. J. Hinds, "The Meeting Genre Across Cultures: Insights from Three German–American Collaborations," *Small Group Research* 43, no. 2 (2012): 159–85.
12. See D. A. Romig and L. J. Romig, *Breakthrough Teamwork* (Chicago: Irwin, 1996); T. A. Kayser, *Mining Group Gold* (El Segundo, CA: Serif Publishing, 1990).
13. H. L. Ewbank, Jr., *Meeting Management* (Dubuque, IA: Brown, 1968).
14. J. E. Tropman and G. C. Morningstar, *Meetings: How to Make Them Work for You* (New York: Van Nostrand Reinhold, 1985) 56; J. E. Tropman, *Making Meetings Work* (Thousand Oaks, CA: Sage, 1996). Also see M. Doyle and D. Straus, *How to Make Meetings Work* (New York: Playboy Press, 1976); Mosvick and Nelson, *We've Got to Start Meeting Like This*!; G. Lumsden and D. Lumsden, *Communicating in Groups and Teams: Sharing Leadership* (Belmont, CA: Wadsworth, 1993); D. B. Curtis, J. J. Floyd, and J. L. Winsor, *Business and Professional Communication* (New York: HarperCollins, 1992); Romig and Romig, *Breakthrough Teamwork*; D. A. Romig and L. Romig, *Structured Teamwork Guide* (Austin, TX: Performances Resources, 1990); Kayser, *Mining Group Gold*.
15. J. E. Tropman and G. C. Morningstar, *Meetings: How to Make Them Work for You* (New York: Van Nostrand Reinhold, 1985), 56. Reprinted by permission.
16. Kauffeld and Lehmann-Willenbrock, "Meetings Matter."
17. T. A. O'Neill and N. J. Allen, "Team Meeting Attitudes: Conceptualization and Investigation of a New Construct," *Small Group Research* 43, no. 2 (2012): 186–210.
18. S. Sonnentag and J. Volmer, "Individual-Level Predictors of Task-Related Teamwork Processes: The Role of Expertise and Self-Efficacy in Team Meetings," *Group & Organization Management* 34, no. 1 (2009): 37–66.
19. F. Niederman and R. J. Volkema, "The Effects of Facilitator Characteristics on Meeting Preparation, Set Up,

and Implementation," *Small Group Research* 30 (1999): 330–60.

20. T. Ludwig and E. S. Geller, "Assigned versus Participatory Goal Setting and Response Generalization: Managing Injury Control Among Professional Pizza Deliveries," *Journal of Applied Psychology* 82 (1997): 253–61. For an excellent review of facilitation and collaborative leadership in teams and organizations, see D. A. Romig, *Side by Side Leadership* (Austin, TX: Bard, 2001), 9, 103–10.
21. Kauffeld and Lehmann-Willenbrock, "Meetings Matter."
22. A. Weitzel and P. Geist, "Parliamentary Procedure in a Community Group: Communication and Vigilant Decision Making," *Communication Monographs* 65 (1998): 244–59.
23. Mosvick and Nelson, *We've Got to Start Meeting Like This!*
24. M. E. Haynes, *Effective Meeting Skills* (Los Altos, CA: Crisp Publications, 1988).

APPENDIX B

1. Our suggestions for helping you plan and present your speech are adapted from S. A. Beebe and S. J. Beebe, *Public Speaking: An Audience-Centered Approach*, 10th ed. (Boston: Pearson, 2018).
2. Beebe and Beebe, *Public Speaking*, 20.
3. S. A. Beebe, "Eye Contact: A Nonverbal Determinant of Speaker Credibility," *Speech Teacher* 23 (January 1974): 21–25; S. A. Beebe, "Effects of Eye Contact, Posture, and Vocal Inflection upon Credibility and Comprehension," *Australian Scan Journal of Nonverbal Communication* 7–8 (1979–1980): 57–80.
4. E. Bohn and D. Jabush, "The Effects of Four Methods of Instruction on the Use of Visual Aids in Speeches," *Western Journal of Speech Communication* 46 (Summer 1982): 253–65; A. Buchko, K. Buchko, and J. Meyer, "Perceived Efficacy and the Actual Effectiveness of PowerPoint on the Retention and Recall of Religious Messages in the Weekly Sermon: An Empirical Field Study," *Journal of Communication & Religion* 36 (2013): 292–313; M. T. Thielsch and I Perabo, "Use and Evaluation of Presentation Software," *Technical Communication* 59 (2012): 112–23; H. J. Bucher and P. Niemann, "Visualizing Science: The Reception of PowerPoint Presentation," *Visual Communication* 22 (2015): 283–306.

APPENDIX C

1. S. A. Beebe and K. Barge, "Evaluating Group Discussion," in R. Hirokawa, R. S. Cathcart, L. A. Samovar, and L. A. Henman, eds., Small Group Communication Theory and Practice: An Anthology (Los Angeles, CA: Roxbury, 2003), 275–88.

Credits

Text Credits

Chapter 1 P. 1: Rob Gilbert (June 1, 2009). http://gilbertsuccesshotline.blogspot.com/2009/05/message-785-working-together-works.html.; P. 14: Adapted from John Mole, Mind Your Manners: Managing Business Cultures in Europe (London: Nicholas Brealey, 1995).; P. 15: Frost, Robert. (1917). North of Boston. Henry Holt & Company.; P. 19: Based on L. K. Trevino, R. L. Daft, and R. H. Lengel, "Understanding Managers' Media Choices: A Symbolic Interactionist Perspective," in J. Fulk and C. Steinfield, eds., Organizations and Communication Technology (Newbury Park, CA: Sage, 1990) 71–94.; P. 23: B. H. Spitzberg, "Communication Competence as Knowledge, Skill, and Impression," Communication Education 32 (1983): 323–29.

Chapter 2 P. 27: Ballou, M.M., Treasury of Thought: Forming an Encyclopedia of Quotations from Ancient and Modern Authors (Houghton, Mifflin, 1884).; P. 28: G. A. Kelly, A Theory of Personality: The Psychology of Personal Constructs (New York: Norton, 1963), 18.; P. 30: D. Barnlund, "Toward a Meaning-Centered Philosophy of Communication," in K. G. Johnson et al., eds., Nothing Never Happens (Beverly Hills, CA: Glencoe Press, 1974), 213.; P. 37: D. S. Gouran and R. Y. Hirokawa, "Effective Decision Making and Problem Solving in Groups: A Functional Perspective," in R. Y. Hirokawa, R. S. Cathcart, L. A. Samovar, and L. D. Henman, eds., Small Group Communication Theory and Practice (Los Angeles: Roxbury, 2003).

Chapter 3 P. 41: Henry Ford quoted from Larry R. Collins, Disaster Management and Preparedness (CRC Press, 2000), 39.; P. 42: Maslow, Abraham, Motivation and Personality (New York: HarperCollins, 1954).; P. 50–51: J. K. Barge and L. R. Frey, "Life in a Task Group," in L. R. Frey and J. K. Barge, eds., Managing Group Life: Communicating in Decision-Making Groups (Boston: Houghton Mifflin, 1997) 39.; P. 52: Shwom, Business Communication: Polishing Your Professional Presence, 4e (Pearson Education, 2018), Fig. 2.7, p. 53.; P. 54: Based on B. W. Tuckman, "Developmental Sequence in Small Groups," Psychological Bulletin 63 (1965): 384–99.; P. 54: Jeanne M. Wilson, Susan G. Straus, and Bill McEvily, "All in Due Time: The Development of Trust in Computer-Mediated and Face-to-Face Teams," Organizational Behavior and Human Decision Processes 99 (2006): 16–33.

Chapter 4 P. 58: Albert Einstein quoted in Stephen M. Kosslyn and Bob Kerrey, Building the Intentional University: Minerva and the Future of Higher Education (MIT Press, 2017).; P. 60: S. Covey, The Seven Habits of Highly Effective People (New York: Simon and Schuster, 1989).; P. 63: A. W. Woolley, J. B. Bear, J. W. Chang, and A. H. DeCostanza, "The Effects of Team Strategic Orientation on Team Process and Information Search," Organizational Behavior and Human Decision Processes 122 (2013): 114–26.

Chapter 5 P. 78: Margaret Wheatley.; P. 79: M. S. Woodward, L. B. Rosenfeld, and S. K. May, "Sex Differences in Social Support in Sororities and Fraternities," Journal of Applied Communication Research 24 (1996): 260.; P. 81: K. D. Benne and P. Sheats, "Functional Roles of Group Members," Journal of Social Issues 4 (Spring 1948): 41–49.; P. 84: M. Shaw, Group Dynamics: The Psychology of Small Group Behavior (New York: McGraw-Hill, 1981) 281.; P. 85: Susan Shimanoff, S. B. Shimanoff, "Group Interaction via Communication Rules," in R. S. Cathcart and L. A. Samovar, eds., Small Group Communication: A Reader, 6th ed. (Dubuque, IA: Brown, 1992).; P. 86: Bormann, Discussion and Group Method, 2nd Ed. (Upper Saddle River, NJ: Pearson Education, 1975).; P. 89: Charles Berger, C. R. Berger, "Power in the Family," in M. Roloff and G. Miller, eds., Persuasion: New Direction in Theory and Research (Beverly Hills, CA: Sage, 1980) 217.; P. 90: V. I. Armstrong, I Have Spoken: American History Through Voices of the Indians (Chicago: The Swallow Press, 197.; P. 90: V. I. Armstrong, I Have Spoken: American History Through Voices of the Indians (Chicago: The Swallow Press, 1971).; P. 91: D. McAllister, "Affect- and Cognition-Based Trust as foundations for Interpersonal Cooperation in Organizations," Academy of Management Journal 38 (1995): 24.; P. 91: R. Reichert, Self-Awareness Through Group Dynamics (Dayton, OH: Pflaum/Standard, 1970) 21.; P. 92: Bormann, Discussion and Group Method, 2nd Ed. (Upper Saddle River, NJ: Pearson Education, 1975).; P. 94: From Donald W. Klopf and James McCroskey, International Encounters: An Introduction to Intercultural Communication (Boston: Allyn & Bacon, 2006).

Chapter 6 P. 96: Alexandre Dumas; P. 102: S. S. Weber and L. M. Donahue, "Impact of Highly and Less job-Related Diversity on Work Group Cohesion and performance: A Meta-Analysis," Journal of Management 27 (2001): 141–62; P. 103: Bormann, Discussion and Group

Method, 2nd Ed. (Upper Saddle River, NJ: Pearson Education, 1975).; P. 103: George Homans, G. C. Homans, The Human Group (New York: Harcourt Brace, 1992).; P. 104: Jeanne M. Wilson, Susan G. Straus, and Bill McEvily, "All in Due Time: The Development of Trust in Computer-Mediated and Face-to-Face Teams," Organizational Behavior and Human Decision Processes 99 (2006): 16–33.; P. 105: A. P. Hare, Handbook of Small Group Research, 2nd ed. (New York: Free Press, 1976) 345.; P. 105: B. Prasad and D. A. Harrison, "Ties, Leaders, and Time in Teams: Strong Inference about Network Structure's Effects on Team Viability and Performance," Academy of Management Journal 49 (2006): 49–68.; P. 106: J. C. Pearson and P. E. Nelson.; P. 106: Bormann, Discussion and Group Methods (New York: Harper & Row, 1969).; P. 106: Bormann, Discussion and Group Method, 2nd Ed. (Upper Saddle River, NJ: Pearson Education, 1975).; P. 107: D. Cartwright and A. Zander, Group Dynamics: Research and Theory, 3rd ed. (New York: Harper & Row, 1968) 104.

Chapter 7 P. 109: Andrew Carnegie.; P. 113: J. Shotter, "Listening in a Way that Recognizes/Realizes the World of 'the Other'." The International Journal of Listening 23 (2009): 21.; P. 117: W. S. Condon and W. D. Ogston, "Soundfilm Analysis of Normal and Pathological Behavior Patterns," Journal of Nervous and Mental Disease 143 (1966): 338–47.; P. 117: P. Ekman and W. V. Friesen, "Hand Movements," Journal of Communication 22 (1972): 353–74. See also P. E. R. Bitti and I. Poggi, "Symbolic Nonverbal Behavior: Talking Through Gestures," in R. S. Feldman and B. Rime, eds., Fundamentals of Nonverbal Behavior (Cambridge, England: Cambridge, 1991).; P. 123: Mehrabian, Silent Messages (Belmont, CA: Wadsworth, 1981) 108.

Chapter 8 P. 126: Walter Lippman quoted in Martin F. Sturman, Effective Medical Imaging: A Signs and Symptoms Approach (William & Wilkins, 1993).; P. 131: Miller and Steinberg, Between People: A New Analysis of Interpersonal Communication (Science Research Associates, 1975), p. 264.; P. 133: K. W. Phillips and D. L. Loyd, "When Surface and Deep-Level Diversity Collide: The Effects on Dissenting Group Members," Organizational Behavior and Human Decision Processes 99 (2006): 143–60.; P. 141: J. M. Juran, Juran on Planning for Quality (New York: Free Press, 1988).; P. 142: Robert Bolton, People Skills: How to Assert Yourself, Listen to Others, and Resolve Conflicts (New York: Touchstone, 1986), 217.; P. 142: Eleanor Roosevelt, This is My Story (Harper Row, 1937).; P. 145: George Baker, Accentuate the Positive; Eliminate the Negative (1921).; P. 148: J. A. Kline and J. L. Hullinger, "Redundancy, Self-Orientation, and Group Consensus," Speech Monographs 40 (March 1973): 72–74.

Chapter 9 P. 153: Max De Pree, Leadership is an Art (Currency, 2004).; P. 158: R. White and R. Lippitt, "Leader Behavior and Member Reaction in Three 'Social Climates' in D. Cartwright and A. Zander, eds., Group Dynamics, 3rd ed. (New York: Harper & Row, 1968) 319.; P. 159: V. H. Vroom and A. G. Jago, The New Leadership: Managing Participation in Organizations (Englewood Cliffs, NJ: Prentice Hall, 1988) 52.; P. 159: J. B. Carson, P. E. Tesluk, and J. A. Marrone, "Shared Leadership in Teams: An Investigation of Antecedent Conditions and Performance," Academy of Management Journal 50, no. 5 (2007): 1217–34.; P. 160: T. Whitford and S. A. Moss, "Transformational Leadership in Distributed Work Groups: the Moderating Role of Follower Regulatory Focus and Goal Orientation," Communication Research 26 (2009): 811.; P. 163: E. Bormann, Discussion and Group Methods, 2nd ed. (New York: Harper & Row, 1975) 256.; P. 164: Greenleaf, The Servant as Leader, 7.

Chapter 10 P. 167: C.S. Lewis, The Great Divorce: A Dream (London: Geoffrey Bless: The Centenary Press, 1945). 8.; P. 175: B. Aubrey Fisher, "Decision Emergence: Phases in Group Decision Making," Speech Monographs 37 (1970): 60.; P. 175: Fisher, B. A. (1970a). Decision emergence: Phases in group decision-making. Speech Monographs, 37, 53–66.; P. 180: Poole, "Decision Development in Small Groups, III: A Multiple Sequence Model of Group Decision Development, III" Communication Monographs, December 1983, 330.; P. 180: Marshall Scott Poole, "Decision Development in Small Groups, III: A Multiple Sequence Model of Group Decision Development," Communication Monographs, December 1983, 50 (4): 321–341.; P. 185: Geert Hofstede, Culture's Consequences: International Differences in Work-Related Values (Beverly Hills, CA: Sage, 1984), p. 40.; P. 185: Geert Hofstede, Gert Jan Hofstede, and Michael Minkov, Cultures and Organizations: Software of the Mind: Intercultural Cooperation and Its Importance for Survival, 3rd ed. (New York: McGraw-Hill, 2010) pp 95–97. Copyright (c) 2010. Reprinted by permission of the author.

Chapter 11 P. 188: Kalr Popper, All Life is Problem Solving (Routledge, 1999), p. 100; P. 194: R. S. Zander and B. Zander, The Art of Possibility: Transforming Professional and Personal Life (New York: Penguin, 2002).; P. 195: Julius E. Eitington, The Winning Trainer (Houston, TX: Gulf Publishing, 1989).; P. 197: The Thoughts of the Emperor M. Aurelius Antoninus (George Bell & Sons, 1897); P. 201: E. G. Bormann, Discussion and Group Methods: Theory and Practice, 2nd ed. (New York: Harper & Row, 1975) 282.; P. 203: Goldberg and Larson, Group Communication: Discussion Processes and Applications (Prentice Hall, 1975), 150.; P. 204: LaFasto and Larson, When Teams Work Best: 6,000 Team

Members and Leaders Tell What it Takes to Succeed (Sage, 2001), p. 85.

Chapter 12 P. 208: Michael Michalko, Thinkertoys: A Handbook of Creative-Thinking Techniques (Potter/Ten Speed/Harmony/Rodale, 2010); P. 208: Emily Ross, Angus Holland, 100 Great Businesses and the Minds Behind Them (Naperville, IL: Sourcebooks, 2006) 402.; P. 210: R. L. Firestien, "Effects of Creative Problem-Solving Training on Communication Behaviors in Small Groups," Small Group Research 21 (1990): 507–22.; P. 219: D. H. Pink, A Whole New Mind: Why Right-Brainers Will Rule the Future (New York: Riverhead Books, 2006) 65–67.; P. 219: D. H. Pink, A Whole New Mind: Why Right-Brainers Will Rule the Future (New York: Riverhead Books, 2006) 65–67.; P. 222: Eileen K. Aranda, Luis Aranda, Kristi Conlon, Teams: Structure, Process, Culture, and Politics (Prentice Hall, 1998), p. 89.

Appendix A P. 225: Seymour M. Hersh, The Dark Side of Camelot (Little, Brown, 1 Sep 1998); P. 225: Dave Barry, Dave Barry's Guide to Life (Wings Books: 1991) p. 311; P. 226: Joseph J. Distefano and Martha L. Maznevski, "Creating Value with Diverse Teams in Global Management," Organizational Dynamics (2000), Vol. 29, No. 1, pp. 45–63; P. 227: John Tropman and Gershom Morningstar, Meetings: How to Make Them Work for You (New York: Van Nostrand Reinhold, 1985), 56.

Photo Credits

Chapter 1 P. 1: Photo 01-01 Hannah Foslien/Getty Images; P. 14: Photo 01-02 Harry Bliss/The Cartoon Bank; P. 15: Photo 01-03 szefei/123RF; P. 15: Photo 01-04 Wavebreak Media Ltd/123RF; P. 16: Photo 01-05A Dmitriy Shironosov/123RF; P. 16: Photo 01-05B Andriy Popov/123RF; P. 16: Photo 01-05C Wavebreak Media Ltd/123RF; P. 17: Photo 01-05D Wavebreak Media Ltd/123RF; P. 17: Photo 01-05E goodluz/123RF; P. 17: Photo 01-05E lightfieldstudios/123RF; P. 24: Photo 01-06 Jim Sizemore/CartoonStock Ltd.

Chapter 2 P. 27: Photo 02-01 Robert Voets/ CBS Photo Archive/Getty Images; P. 29: Photo 02-02 Ismiza binti Ishak/Shutterstock; P. 30: Photo 02-03 Nick Downes/Conde Nast Publications/The Cartoon Bank; P. 31: Photo 02-04 Cathy Yeulet/123RF; P. 33: Photo 02-05 Huntstock/Getty Images; P. 35: Photo 02-06A Cathy Yeulet/123RF; P. 35: Photo 02-06B Cathy Yeulet/123RF; P. 36: Photo 02-07A rawpixel/123RF; P. 36: Photo 02-07B moodboard/123RF; P. 37: Photo 02-07C rawpixel/123RF.

Chapter 3 P. 41: Photo 03-01 Robert Brenner/PhotoEdit; P. 45: Photo 03-02 Nick Downes /The New Yorker Collection/The Cartoon Bank; P. 46: Photo 03-03A BFG Images/Getty Images; P. 46: Photo 03-03B NPS/Alamy Stock Photo; P. 46: Photo 03-03C GaudiLab/Shutterstock; P. 46: Photo 03-03D Jacob Lund/Shutterstock; P. 47: Photo 03-04 Julian Maldonado/Shutterstock; P. 52: Photo 03-05A nito/Shutterstock; P. 53: Photo 03-05B Lipik Stock Media/Shutterstock; P. 53: Photo 03-05C Edhar Yuralaits/123RF.

Chapter 4 P. 58: Photo 04-01 YAKOBCHUK VIACHESLAV/Shutterstock; P. 65: Photo 04-02A ID1974/Shutterstock; P. 65: Photo 04-02B Tetra Images/LLC/Alamy Stock Photo; P. 66: Photo 04-02C Alf Ribeiro/Shutterstock; P. 73: Photo 04-03A Ralf-Finn Hestoft/Contributor/Getty Images; P. 73: Photo 04-03B Vietnam Stock Images/Shutterstock; P. 73: Photo 04-03C Wavebreak Media Ltd/123RF.

Chapter 5 P. 78: Photo 05-01 Jose Carrillo/PhotoEdit; P. 80: Photo 05-02 MarcusPhoto1/Getty Images; P. 84: Photo 05-03 Jack Ziegler/Cartoon Bank; P. 89: Photo 05-04 JOHN G. MABANGLO/epa european pressphoto agency b.v./Alamy Stock Photo; P. 94: Photo 05-05 Gino Santa Maria/Shutterstock.

Chapter 6 P. 96: Photo 06-01 Barry Diomede/Alamy Stock Photo; P. 98: Photo 06-02 Bruce Ayres/Getty Images; P. 99: Photo 06-03 Iakov Filimonov/123RF; P. 101: Photo 06-04 Aleksandr Davydov/123RF; P. 102: Photo 06-05A Pavel Shchegolev/Shutterstock; P. 102: Photo 06-05B Eric Dubost_Photographer/Shutterstock; P. 103: Photo 06-06A Christian Bertrand/Alamy Stock Photo; P. 103: Photo 06-06B Nippon News/Aflo Co. Ltd./Alamy Stock Photo.

Chapter 7 P. 109: Photo 07-01 Shutterstock; P. 115: Photo 07-02A Anton Gvozdikov/123RF; P. 115: Photo 07-02B wang Tom/123RF; P. 116: Photo 07-02C Leslie Banks/123RF; P. 116: Photo 07-03 iStock/Getty Images Plus; P. 118: Photo 07-04A Benoit Daoust/123RF; P. 118: Photo 07-04B bowie15/123RF; P. 118: Photo 07-04C Michael Simons/123RF; P. 118: Photo 07-04D Ion Chiosea/123RF; P. 118: Photo 07-04E Ion Chiosea/123RF; P. 118: Photo 07-04F atic12/123RF; P. 118: Photo 07-04G olgaosa/123RF.

Chapter 8 P. 126: Photo 08-01 ImagesbyTrista/Getty Images; P. 129: Photo 08-02A mentatdgt/Shutterstock; P. 129: Photo 08-02B Olha Povozniuk/Shutterstock; P. 129: Photo 08-02C blueskyimage/123RF; P. 129: Photo 08-02D Antonio Guillem/123RF; P. 134: Photo 08-03 jesterpop/Shutterstock; P. 135: Photo 08-04 David Pimborough; P. 137: Photo 08-05 NASA Archive/Alamy Stock Photo; P. 145: Photo 08-06 Rawpixel.com/Shutterstock.

Chapter 9 P. 153: Photo 09-01 David De Lossy/Getty Images; P. 154: Photo 09-02 ScreenProd/Photononstop/

Alamy Stock Photo; P. 155: Photo 09-03 Stockbyte/Getty Images; P. 156: Photo 09-04 Shutterstock/Shutterstock; P. 157: Photo 09-05 Charles Barsotti/The Cartoon Bank; P. 159: Photo 09-06 Olaf Doering/Alamy Stock Photo; P. 160: Photo 09-07 dpa picture alliance archive/Alamy Stock Photo; P. 162: Photo 09-08 Ruslan Grechka/Shutterstock; P. 165: Photo 09-09 Jose Gil/Shutterstock.

Chapter 10 P. 167: Photo 10-01 Bruce Ayres/Getty Images; P. 174: Photo 10-02 Aleksandr Davydov/123RF; P. 178: Photo 10-03 Wavebreak Media Ltd./123RF; P. 183: Photo 10-04 Aleksandr Davydov/123RF; P. 184: Photo 10-05A Katarzyna Białasiewicz/123RF; P. 184: Photo 10-05B rawpixel/123RF; P. 184: Photo 10-05C Andrey_Popov/Shutterstock; P. 185: Photo 10-06 rawpixel/123RF.

Chapter 11 P. 188: Photo 11-01 Ryanstock/Getty Images.

Chapter 12 P. 208: Photo 12-01 Steve Debenport/E+/Getty Images; P. 221: Photo 12-02 Westend61 GmbH/Alamy Stock Photo.

Index

D

E